ENGLAND AND WALES.

COUNTY AND BOROUGH REPRESENTATION BEFORE THE REFORM ACT.

† Grampound was the sole borough disfranchised before 1832. Its members were given to the West Riding of York.

§ Enfranchised in lieu of a shire town in Merioneth.

Boroughs underlined disappeared at the Reform of 1832.
Boroughs marked [1] retained one member.
Welsh boroughs marked in each county were grouped to elect one member.

1 Long. W. of Greenw.   O Long. E. of Greenw.   1

REPRINTS OF ECONOMIC CLASSICS

The Unreformed House Of Commons

THE
UNREFORMED
HOUSE OF COMMONS

PARLIAMENTARY REPRESENTATION
BEFORE 1832

BY EDWARD PORRITT

Vol. I.

REPRINTS OF ECONOMIC CLASSICS

Augustus M. Kelley, Bookseller
New York 1963

First edition 1903. Second printing 1909. Reprinted 1963.

Library of Congress Catalogue Card Number:
63-21104

Manufactured in the United States of America
by SENTRY PRESS, New York 19, N. Y.

THE

UNREFORMED
HOUSE OF COMMONS

THE
UNREFORMED
HOUSE OF COMMONS

PARLIAMENTARY REPRESENTATION BEFORE 1832

BY

EDWARD PORRITT

ASSISTED BY

ANNIE G. PORRITT

VOLUME I

ENGLAND AND WALES

Cambridge :
at the University Press
1903

PREFACE.

THESE volumes are concerned with Parliamentary representation in England and Wales, in Scotland, and in Ireland
before 1832. My aim has been to trace the changes that representation in all four countries underwent from the time that the
House of Commons in England began to have a continuous
existence until the Reform Act of 1832.

With the Houses of Lords in England and in Ireland I have
had no concern, except in so far as touches the relations which
in both countries existed between the House of Commons and
the House of Lords. In treating of the Parliament of Scotland
I have described the place of the First Estate. This has been
necessary to an adequate presentation of the organisation and
working of the Parliament of Scotland, as the peers and the
representatives of the shires and burghs sat in one chamber. But
in regard to the Parliaments of England and Ireland I have
concerned myself only with the elected members. My care has
been exclusively with the Houses of Commons and the representative system on which the Commons were chosen. In regard
to all four countries my purpose has been to trace the changes
which came about in the representative systems from the thirteenth
century to the nineteenth, and to show how these changes affected
both the House of Commons and municipal life. In a word,
I have attempted such a history of Parliamentary representation
as would enable a student of constitutional developement to realise
what the representative system actually was when, in 1831, Grey,
Russell, Althorp, and Brougham undertook the great work of
Parliamentary Reform.

Further, it has been my purpose to trace the changing relations which from the thirteenth century to the nineteenth existed between electors and elected; the incoming of the system under which so many members were at least for a century and a half prior to 1832 chosen to the House of Commons by patrons; to show the relations which existed between members so chosen and the men who sent them into the House of Commons; and how it was that in 1832 the representative systems of England and Wales, Scotland, and Ireland were so greatly in need of a touch of the supreme authority to set them right, to restore the representation to something like the basis on which it had stood in the early centuries of Parliament.

In respect to all three Parliaments I have also tried to show the changing character of the representative assemblies chosen on the various franchises of the five centuries preceding reform, and the way in which each of these assemblies became gradually organised for its legislative work; and in particular, in the House of Commons at Westminster, the developement of the organisation and procedure which exist to-day. I have gone into this part of the subject with some detail, because in the three centuries in which the House of Commons met in the old Chapel of S. Stephen's there was slowly developed an organisation and a code of written and unwritten laws which have been duplicated almost to the last detail in the popularly elected chambers of all the self-governing British colonies, and which have also to a great degree shaped the organisation and procedure of Congress at Washington, and of the forty-five American State Legislatures.

Still further it has been my aim to show the relations towards the outside world of the representative assemblies of England, Scotland, and Ireland, and of the House of Commons subsequent to the Unions, and also to trace how the representative system of Scotland in 1707 and that of Ireland in 1800 were merged into the nondescript system on which, between 1800 and 1832, the 658 members from England and Wales, Scotland, and Ireland were chosen. Another aim has been to bring out the relations of the Crown to the representative system; to show how the Crown concerned itself with Parliamentary elections in order to influence or control the House of Commons, first during the long era of personal government which came to an end at the Revolution, and next during the shorter period after government by Cabinet had become established.

These have been my aims. Now as to what I have not sought to do. Into the changes made by the Reform Act of 1832, and again by the Reform Acts of 1867 and 1884–85, I have not gone with any pretence at completeness. In the few instances in which the changes have been indicated, the object has been to make the story self-contained. I have not treated of these nineteenth-century reforms in detail for the same reason that only allusively have I mentioned the short-lived reform of the representative system made during the Commonwealth. Cromwell's reform, as I have come to view it, is really a part of the movement three centuries long for the reforms which began with the Reform Act of 1832. This movement is traceable back as far as the reign of Elizabeth; and Cromwell's reform seems more properly to belong to its history than to that of the old representative system, of which it was not more than an incident, and on which it left no traceable permanent impression.

At some future time I may write the history of the movement for Parliamentary reform from the time of Queen Elizabeth to the Acts of 1884–85, extending the franchise in the counties and finally breaking up the old system under which knights of the shire were so long chosen to Westminster. Then I hope to trace the varying phases of the movement; how at one time it was sporadic, represented only by isolated movements for wider franchises in individual boroughs; how at other times, as during the Commonwealth, it was general; how it was aided by the American Revolution; how partial success came in 1832, and how in later years the movement was revived, and resulted in the Reform Acts of 1867 and 1884.

The research for the history of the movement has already been done. At the outset it was my purpose to include in one work the history of the movement for Reform and to bring the history down to 1832. But the wealth of material regarding the old systems of representation, and the desire to present an adequate history of the representation in Scotland and Ireland, and of the Unions of 1707 and 1800, so far as representation is concerned, seemed to make it expedient to defer to a later volume the history of the long contest which ended in 1885.

The actual writing of these volumes is the work of one pen; but in the research, in the shaping of the plan, in the final form of the volumes, and in reading them for the press, I have had the constant collaboration and suggestive help of my wife, without whom indeed the work would not have been undertaken.

This book has been written during a nine years' residence in the United States; and the standpoint has been affected by a close and continuous observation of the political systems of the United States and Canada. While engaged on it, I have been much in attendance on the sessions of Congress at Washington, of the Dominion Parliament at Ottawa, and of several of the State and Provincial Legislatures. At least five-sevenths of the research have been done in the libraries of Congress, of the Dominion Parliament, and of the State and Provincial capitols; in the libraries of the Universities of Yale and Columbia; of Trinity College, Hartford; in the Watkinson Library, and in that of the Connecticut Historical Society, both also at Hartford; in the public libraries of Hartford, Boston, and New York; in the library of the New York Bar Association; and in numerous other libraries in America, public and private, of which the use has been kindly and helpfully extended to me. Some of the research has of necessity been done in England; but the bulk of the work in the Journals of Parliament, Statute books, official returns and reports, Parliamentary histories, Hansards, calendars of State papers, State trials and Election Committee and Law reports, reports of the Historical Manuscripts Commission, municipal council books and municipal histories, and the publications of the numerous English and Scotch printing societies, as well as the greater part of the reading of memoirs, letters and diaries, has been done in American libraries, whose well-ordered and easily accessible wealth in all these departments of history must come as a pleasant surprise to an English student in the United States.

FARMINGTON, CONNECTICUT.
June, 1903.

CONTENTS.

PREFACE v

PART I.

THE REPRESENTATION OF ENGLAND AND WALES.

CHAPTER I.

PARLIAMENTARY REPRESENTATION IN 1832. 1–19.

The purpose of the Reform Act, 1.   Early recognitions of the need of reform, 1.   Changes in the representative system between 1604 and 1832, 2. Several descriptions of borough franchises, 4.   Boroughs begin to prize Parliamentary representation, 5.   Controverted election cases and the narrowing of borough franchises, 7.   Last determinations, 8.   Boroughs as property, 9.   Local movements for wider franchises, 10.   National movement for reform, 12.   Reform needed in boroughs more than in counties, 14. Membership of the House in 1832, 15.   Few changes between 1677 and 1832, 15.   Treatment of delinquent boroughs, 15.   Distribution of representation in England, 17.   Cities and boroughs of counties, 17.

CHAPTER II.

THE COUNTY FRANCHISE. 20–28.

The early county franchise, 20.   The Act of 1430, 20.   County seats in demand, 21.   Multiplication of freehold qualifications, 22.   Disappearance of residential qualification, 24.   Statutory qualifications, 24.   Registration of voters, 25.   The abortive registration Act of 1788, 26.

CHAPTER III.

THE BOROUGH FRANCHISES. 29–84.

Four groups of boroughs, 29.

(1) Scot and Lot and Potwalloper Boroughs. 30–33.

Diversity in scot and lot boroughs, 30.   The potwalloper franchise, 31. Parliamentary and municipal boroughs not coterminous, 32.   Boroughs of restricted area easy of control, 32.

(2) Burgage Boroughs. 33–41.

Usually of small electorates, 33.   Intrinsic and extrinsic value of burgages, 34.   Residential qualification, 34.   Snatch-paper burgages, 35. Droitwich salt springs, 36.   Downton burgages, 36.   Opposition to establishment of a residential qualification, 37.   Burgage franchises and election committees, 38.   Local qualifications in burgage boroughs, 39.   Women burgage owners and the franchise, 40.

(3) Corporation Boroughs. 41–57.

Origin of the right of corporations to elect, 41.   Early elections by corporations, 42.   Corporations begin to value the right, 42.   Elections by corporations general, 43.   Awakening of popular interest in elections, 44. Efforts to exclude the commonalty, 45.   Outside influence on corporations, 45. Developement of the patron, 46.   Right of corporations to elect confirmed by charter, 46.   Contests with corporations over Parliamentary franchise, 47. Attacks on corporations at the Restoration, 48.   Peculiar result of contest at Preston, 49.   Charles II and James II favour corporation control, 50.   Corporations assailed in 1688, 50.   Appreciating value of seats in the Pensioner Parliament, 51.   Effect of increased value on constituencies, 52.   Corporations defeated in local contests, 52.   Indirect corporation control, 52. Complete corporation control, 53.   Non-resident mayors and members of corporations, 53.   Neglect of municipal government, 54.   Dissenters in corporation boroughs, 55.   Degradation and end of the corporations, 55.

(4) Freeman Boroughs. 58–84.

The freeman franchise, 57.   Extensions and restrictions, 58.   Use of the word "freeman," 58.   Non-residents representing boroughs made freemen, 59. Patrons and their adherents made honorary freemen, 60.   Freemen who had ceased to be resident allowed to vote, 63.   Swamping of electorates by honorary freemen, 63.   A slight check to the making of freemen, 65. Further attempts at reform, 67.   No real check until 1832, 67.   Residential and rate-paying qualifications in some freeman boroughs, 68.   Prisoners allowed to vote, 69.   Corporation control by increasing or restricting the number of freemen, 70.   Pressure by corporations on individual voters, 73. The use of patronage, 74.   Attempts at reform by disfranchising officeholders, 74.   The value of his vote to a freeman, 75.   Cost of elections in freeman constituencies, 76.   Corruption before and after the Restoration, 77.

The freeman franchise transmitted through women, **78**. Women share in the bribes to voters, **79**. Parliamentary electioneering and aristocratic patrons, **80**. Compensation for patrons suggested in 1832, **81**. The degradation of municipal life due to the system, **82**. A modern revival with a difference, **84**.

CHAPTER IV.

THE ELECTORAL MAP IN 1832. 85–98.

Distribution of electoral power unrelated to population, **85**. No legislative redistribution until 1821, **85**. The transfer of Grampound's franchise, **86**. Principle of reform involved in Grampound Act, **87**. No other change in the map between 1677 and 1832, **89**. Disproportionate number of boroughs in maritime counties due to early economic conditions, **90**. The Cornish boroughs, **92**. Twin boroughs of Dorset, Sussex and Yorkshire, **93**. Landmarks on the electoral map, **96**.

CHAPTER V.

UNIVERSITY REPRESENTATION. 99–103.

Universities petition for enfranchisement, **99**. Charters of James I, **99**. The first election, **100**. Crown influence, **101**. Mode of election, **102**. University qualifications, **103**.

CHAPTER VI.

THE REPRESENTATION OF WALES. 104–118.

Distribution of representation in Wales, **104**. Enfranchising Acts of 1535–36 and 1543–44, **104**. Borough franchise based on the payment of wages, **105**. Shire towns and contributory towns, **106**. Forty-shilling freehold franchise in the counties, **106**. An inhabitant householder franchise in the towns, **107**. One corporation borough, **108**. Contests between shire towns and contributory towns, **108**. Incoming of honorary burgesses, **108**. Boroughs freed from contributory towns, **109**. The contest between Beaumaris and Newborough, **111**. Patrons and Welsh boroughs, **115**. Wales free from much of the electoral rottenness of the English system, **117**.

PART II.

RELATIONS BETWEEN MEMBERS AND CONSTITUENTS.

CHAPTER VII.

RESTRICTIONS ON THE CHOICE OF CONSTITUENCIES. 121–144.

The residential qualification, 122.   A short-lived social qualification for knights of the shire, 122.   Eldest sons of peers excluded and admitted, 123. Sheriffs and mayors excluded, 123.   When electors had the freest choice, 124. Clergymen excluded by law of Parliament and by statute, 125.   Roman Catholic clergy excluded, 127.   Religious oaths imposed after the Reformation, 127.   The Act of 1563, 127.   Roman Catholics excluded from the House of Commons, not from the House of Lords, 128.   Prayers and attendance at service, 129.   The Act of 1606 imposing Oaths of Allegiance and Abjuration, 130.   The test of the taking of Communion, 130.   Vigilance in the exclusion of Papists, 131.   Attitude of the House after the Restoration, 132. Bills to exclude Dissenters, 133.   The Test Act and the electoral franchise, 134.   Quakers and the oaths, 134.   The struggle for the relief of Quakers, 135.   The first Quaker returned to the House, 137.   New barriers against Roman Catholics, 137.   The declaration against transubstantiation, 137. The Relief Act of 1829, 138.   The first Roman Catholic member, 139. O'Connell and the Relief Act, 140.   Scotch Roman Catholics disqualified by enactment, 140.   Civil disabilities of Jews, 140.   The movement for the removal of Jewish disabilities, 141.   Jews admitted in 1858, 144.

CHAPTER VIII.

RESTRICTIONS ON CHOICE FOR THE PROTECTION OF THE CROWN. 145–150.

Oaths to protect the Crown against the Papacy, 145.   Safeguarding the Revolution settlement, 146.   Protection against the exiled Stuarts, 147. Remodelling of the oaths in 1866 and 1868, 148.   The Scotch Episcopal Church and the Jacobites, 149.

CHAPTER IX.

MEN WITHOUT MEANS EXCLUDED FROM THE HOUSE OF COMMONS. 151–203.

Usages and laws excluding men without means, 151.   Election expenses thrown on candidates, 152.   Wages cease to be paid, 153.   Candidates offer

inducements to constituencies, **154.** Members accept reduced allowances, **155.**
Candidates agree to serve without pay, **157.** Members make gifts to constituencies, **157.** Constituencies become more demanding, **159.** Municipal
patriotism at the expense of candidates, **163.** Modern survivals of the practice
of bribing constituencies, **165.**

PROPERTY QUALIFICATIONS FOR MEMBERS. **166–181.**

Qualification imposed by Act of 1710, **166.** The agitation for the Act, **166.**
The bill in Parliament, **168.** Provisions of the Act, **169.** The operation of
the Act, **170.** The creation of fictitious qualifications, **171.** The Act
amended in 1760, **171.** Few cases of exclusion under the Act, **172.** Quali-
fications bestowed by friends, **173.** The business of making qualifications, **174.**
Sir William Molesworth's retrospect of the working of the Act, **174.** The
Act amended in 1838, **176.** Personal property made a qualification, **176.**
The Act repealed in 1858, **179.** Uselessness of the Acts, **179.**

ELECTION EXPENSES THROWN ON CANDIDATES. **181–203.**

Abiding importance of the custom of throwing election expenses on candidates, **181.** Election expenses originally small and not authorised by
statute, **182.** Fees and charges made proportional to eagerness of candidates
for election, **183.** Election charges regarded as an abuse before the Revolution, **184.** The first Act throwing charges on candidates, **185.** The
developement of election machinery, **186.** Cost of elections borne by candidates previous to statutory requirement, **186.** The Act of 1712, **187.** The
first Act special and trivial, **187.** The Act of 1745 makes certain charges
general, **188.** Acts of 1781 and 1794 add to expenses of candidates, **189.**
Act of 1794 the first to apply to boroughs, **191.** Dispute about payment of
election charges at Coventry, **192.** Litigation concerning Westminster
election charges in 1807, **193.** Westminster Act of 1811, **195.** Act of
1828, **195.** Proposals to relieve candidates of election charges, **196.**
Parliamentary Return of Election Charges in 1833, **197.** Legislation since
the Reform Act, **201.**

CHAPTER X.

OFFICE-HOLDERS, PENSIONERS, AND CONTRACTORS EXCLUDED. 204–222.

Agitation for the exclusion of office-holders begun in 1675, **204.** The
movement for general exclusion and for excluding holders of specified
places, **206.** Exclusion bills between 1693 and 1705, **206.** The clause in
the Act of Settlement, **210.** Its abrogation in 1705, **210.** The principle of
re-election after taking office in the Act of 1705, **211.** The working and
interpretation of the Act, **211.** Inefficacy of exclusion laws against pensioners, **214.** Later place bills, **215.** The Act of 1742, **215.** The Act of
1733 excluding Scotch judges, **215.** Act of 1782 excluding government
contractors, **217.** Great need for this Act, **217.** The Act a concession to
public opinion, **218.** The last exclusion Act before 1832, **220.** The laws
with regard to placemen and contractors at the present time, **220.** The
effect of the exclusion Acts, **222.**

CHAPTER XI.

MINORS AND ALIENS ON THE EXCLUSION LIST. 223–236.

Minors excluded first by law of Parliament and later by enactment, 223. Law of Parliament unheeded, 223.   Minors of the House from the sixteenth century, 223.   Protests against their presence in the reign of James I, 224. Boys of fifteen in the Pensioner Parliament, 224.   Minors excluded by Act of 1695–96, 226.   Act not at once effective, 227.   Minors still of the House but do not vote, 227.   Minors elected but do not take their seats until of age, 230.   Fox the last minor to address the House, 230.   Public opinion causes the law to become effective, 230.   Election of locum tenens until minors come of age, 231.   Gradual reform of the representative system due to public opinion, 234.

ALIENS AND NATURALISED SUBJECTS.   235–236.

Aliens excluded by common law, 235.   Exclusion of naturalised subjects until 1870, 236.

CHAPTER XII.

THE TIE BETWEEN ELECTORS AND ELECTED. 237–255.

Nature of the tie in the early years of Parliament, 237.   Power of the House over the attendance of members, 238.   Members liberated by issue of new writs, 238.   Writs sometimes refused by the House, 240.   Hold of the House on its members, 241.   Stewardship of the Chiltern Hundreds, 242. Stewardships conferred by Government, and the House loses its hold on members, 244.   Partisan use of the Stewardships, 245.   Bills to place members on an equality in respect to resignation, 246.   Break-down of the partisan method of granting Stewardships, 248.   Constituencies never able to rid themselves of their representatives, 250.   Constituencies long indifferent to conduct of members, 251.   Protest from Canterbury against an absentee member, 252.   Still no law enforcing attendance, 253.   Modern relation of members to constituencies due to public opinion, 254.

CHAPTER XIII.

POLITICAL RELATIONS BETWEEN MEMBERS AND CONSTITUENTS.   256–282.

Relations close in early days of House of Commons, 256.   Members account to constituents on receiving their wages, 257.   Relations close while legislation was based on petitions, 258.   Extra-Parliamentary duties, 258. Members carry weights and measures, 259.   Report recusants, 259.   Keep order in counties, 260.   Aid in collection of poll tax, 260.   Members and local legislation, 261.   Heavy claims on members from large cities, 262. Members receive instructions from constituents, 263.   Members show deference to opinion of constituents, 267.   Loyal addresses to offset instructions, 268.   Government instigates loyal addresses, 269.   Passing of instructions, 270.   Members cease to consider themselves as representing only their constituencies, 271.   Pledges demanded of candidates, 271. Infrequent before 1832, 272.   Public opinion never entirely ignored by House of Commons, 273.   Efforts of Government to influence public opinion, 273.   Government uses House of Lords to defeat bills demanded by public opinion, 275.   Not possible for members from large constituencies to ignore public opinion, 276.   Influence of an approaching election on the House, 279.   Public opinion and eighteenth century legislation, 281.

CHAPTER XIV.

LETTERS BETWEEN MEMBERS AND CONSTITUENTS.   283–291.

Franking established to facilitate intercourse between members and constituents, 283.   Franking authorised by the Commonwealth Parliament, and continued after the Restoration, 284.   Correspondence of members with constituents, 284.   Abuses of the franking privilege, 286.   Eagerness for franks, 287.   Use of franks in social and business correspondence, 288. First real check to abuses in 1802, 289.   Franking of newspapers, 289. Franking entirely abolished, 290.   Franking in the United States and Canada, 290.

CHAPTER XV.

MEMBERS, ELECTORS, AND THE CIVIL SERVICE.   292–308.

Government patronage passes into the hands of members of the House of Commons, 292.   Early instances of the use of patronage in elections, 293. Increase in amount of patronage in eighteenth century, 294.   Share of the corporation and freeman boroughs, 294.   Church patronage as political spoils, 296.   Bishops and clergy busy in elections, 296.   Evil effect on the Church, 298.   Borough masters and Crown livings, 299.   Multiplication of offices in admiralty boroughs, 299.   Disfranchisement of revenue officers no check on use of patronage, 300.   Work thrown on members of the House of Commons by patronage system, 301.   The scramble for patronage at the treasury, 302.   Creation of office of Patronage Secretary, 303.   Effect of spoils system on the civil service, 303.   On Parliament, 306.   On members personally, 306.   On the Church, 307.   Effect of reform of civil service on electorate, 308.

CHAPTER XVI.

RELATIONS BETWEEN MEMBERS AND PATRONS. 309–364.

Period at which patronage began, 309. Number of members returned by patrons in 1793 and 1827, 310. Fox's characterisation of the system, 311. Seats for counties and large towns preferred to nomination boroughs, 312. Gladstone's eulogy of patronage system ill-founded, 313. Nomination boroughs serviceable to office-holders or after defeat elsewhere, 314. Nominated members expected to act with their patrons, 315. Pitt's relation to Lowther, 316. Lowther as a patron, 316. Conduct expected from nominees, 318. Nominees who opposed their patrons, 318. Family seats and their holders, 323. How far patrons dictated the conduct of their members, 326. When the system reached its height, 326. Peerages earned by use of House of Commons patronage, 327. Official patronage distributed among borough owners, 329. An instance of a bargain for a peerage, 331. Horne Tooke's proposal to buy out borough masters with peerages, 331. Borough masters and their demands on the treasury, 332. No public spirit in politics of borough masters and nominated members, 333. Deference of nominated members to patrons, 335. Little evidence to sustain a favourable view of the patronage system, 337. Evidence to the contrary from Abbot, Denman, and Staunton, 337.

TREASURY BOROUGHS. 340–348.

Boroughs controlled from the treasury, 340. Seats purchased from borough masters by the treasury, 340. Members nominated by the treasury, 341. Relations of the treasury to borough patrons, 342. The treasury as a patron, 342. Relation of nominated members to the treasury, 344. The Whigs and the management of treasury boroughs, 345. Steady allegiance of treasury nominees, 347.

MEMBERS NOMINATED ON EASY CONDITIONS. 348–353.

Borough owners in opposition usually easy patrons, 348. Nominees expected to be in political sympathy with patrons, 349. Some instances of nominees left politically free, 350. Nominated members insecure in the tenure of seats, owing to family claims on patrons or changes of fortune, 351. Absolute independence of patrons impossible for nominated members, 352.

SEATS ACQUIRED BY PURCHASE. 353–364.

Boroughs sold in Tudor times, 353. Purchase of seats common from beginning of eighteenth century, 354. Price of seats advancing throughout eighteenth century, 355. Open traffic in seats, 357. Their value in 1832, 358. Sale of seats unconditional or with conditions attached, 358. Use of the purchase system by its adversaries to secure reform, 359. Borough masters without political conscience, 360. A way into the House for independent members, 361. Patronage system and the encouragement of genius, 363.

PART III.

THE CROWN AND THE FRANCHISE.

CHAPTER XVII.

THE CROWN AND THE FRANCHISE—TO THE END OF THE SIXTEENTH CENTURY. 367–378.

The Crown and the value of seats in the House, 367.   Early interference of the king in elections, 367.   Richard II and the sheriffs, 368.   The Lancastrian kings, 369.   Henry VI's charters of enfranchisement, 369. The dominance of Henry VII, 371.   Henry VIII's interest in elections, 371. Cromwell as election manager for Henry VIII, 372.   The subserviency of his Parliaments, 372.   Additions to the House in his reign, 373.   Edward VI recommends men for election, 373.   Twenty-two boroughs added, 373. Mary's fourteen new charters, 374.   Maidstone forfeits its charter, 375. Elizabeth's thirty-one charters, 375.   Newly enfranchised boroughs at once under control, 376.   Elizabeth's Council and the boroughs, 376.   Directions from the Court to the sheriffs, 377.

CHAPTER XVIII.

THE CROWN AND THE FRANCHISE—FROM JAMES I TO THE REVOLUTION. 379–405.

James I's proclamation on calling his first Parliament, 379.   A protest against undertaking in 1614, 380.   Another royal proclamation in 1620, 381. Recommending candidates to boroughs, 381.   The charters of James I, 382. Charles I and elections, 382.   His scheme for excluding obnoxious members, 383.   The making of sheriffs, 383.   Charles dissolves his second Parliament, 384.   His efforts in county elections in 1628, 385.   The magistrates of Cornwall and the county election, 385.   James Bagg as an election manager, 386.   His efforts and his care for his partisans, 387. Surly response of the country to Charles I's efforts, 388.   He dissolves his third Parliament, 389.   The elections for the fourth and fifth Parliaments, 389.   Charles I's personal part in elections, 390.   Buckingham's share in Crown electioneering, 390.   Additions to the House of Commons from the reign of Henry VI, 391.   Charles II and the attack on the corporations, 393.   *Quo Warranto* proceedings against the City of London, 393. Other cities and boroughs surrender or forfeit their charters, 394.   Charles II and James II's electioneering activity, 395.   James II's commands and recommendations, 397.   Unexpected opposition from his Parliament, 398. The King's electioneering tour in 1687, 399.   Resumption of *Quo Warranto* proceedings, 399.   Repeated remodelling of charters, 400.   An instance at Bury St Edmunds, 400. At York, 401. The King's failure in the boroughs, 402. His efforts to control county elections, 403. Their non-success, 404. The failure cf the Stuarts, 405.

CHAPTER XIX.

THE CROWN AND THE FRANCHISE—FROM THE REVOLUTION TO THE REFORM ACT. 406-420.

William III, 406. The dissolution of 1695, 406. His electioneering tour, 407. No Crown interference in elections between William III and George III, 407. The state of the representative system in the reign of George III, 408. George III's activity in electioneering, 409. His watchfulness of by-elections, 411. He chooses a time for dissolving Parliament, 411. Westminster and Middlesex elections in 1774, 412. The general election of 1780, 414. George III's contributions to the election fund, 414. His help at Windsor, 415. The King's expenditures on elections, 415. His attitude towards reform, 419. The elimination of Crown interference in elections, 420.

PART IV.

THE HOUSE AND ITS USAGES.

CHAPTER XX.

THE PLACE OF MEETING. 423-431.

S. Stephen's Chapel part of a royal palace, 424. Meeting places previous to the use of S. Stephen's, 425. Edward VI assigns S. Stephen's Chapel to the Commons, 425. Relations of the Crown to S. Stephen's, 425. Description of the Chamber of the Commons in Elizabeth's reign, 425. Seating accommodation in the House always inadequate, 427. The galleries, 429. Proposals for new chambers, 429. The old and the new era at S. Stephen's, 430.

CHAPTER XXI.

THE SPEAKER. 432-444.

Hungerford the first recorded Speaker, 432. Speakers chosen by the Crown, 433. Speakers attached to party, 433. Speakers as a link between the Crown and the House, 433. Nominated by the Crown, 434. Dependent on the Crown, 435. Charles I and his Speakers, 437. Contest over the election of Seymour, 437. Ceremonial excuses by the Speaker, 438. Seymour omits them, 439. Seymour not approved by the King, 439. Resentment of the Commons, 439. Compromise effected, 442. Advantage with the Commons, 443. Later attempts of the Crown to influence election of Speaker, 444.

CHAPTER XXII.

THE EVOLUTION OF THE NON-PARTISAN SPEAKER. 445–481.

The Speakership ceases to be a courtier office, **445**. The Speaker's rights in committee, **445**. Foley, **446**. His successors until 1715, **446**. Compton becomes minister, **447**. Ex-Speakers in the House, **447**. Speakers and legislation, **448**. Arthur Onslow, **448**. His ideal, **449**. His conduct in the Chair, **450**. Changes he effected, **451**. Pensions and peerage for the Speaker, **453**. Onslow's impress on the Speakership, **454**. Political life in his time, **454**. Changes after the accession of George III, **455**. Cust, **458**. Sir Fletcher Norton, **458**. George III's hostility to Norton, **459**. Cornewall, **460**. Grenville, **461**. Addington, **461**. His connection with party and legislation, **461**. Influence of the Speaker on the House, **462**. Objections to Ex-Speakers in the House, **462**. Abbot, **463**. His opposition to the Catholic Relief bill of 1813, **463**. His address to the Prince Regent, **464**. His conduct challenged in the House of Commons, **465**. Public opinion on his action, **469**. Increased interest in Parliamentary proceedings, **470**. Growing importance and dignity of the Speakership, **471**. Rewards and social duties of the Speaker, **471**. His salary, **473**. His rank, **473**. His *ex-officio* positions, **474**. Popular conception of the Speakership, **474**. Manners-Sutton, **474**. His interventions in committee, **475**. His impartiality in the House, **476**. His connection with party, **477**. His failure of re-election in 1835, **478**. Abercrombie, **479**. Shaw Lefevre, **480**. The first of the modern' Speakers, **480**. The modern ideal, **480**. The Speaker's constituency, **481**.

CHAPTER XXIII.

THE ATTITUDE OF THE HOUSE TOWARDS THE CHAIR. 482–488.

Deportment of members towards the Chair, **482**. Rules concerning the Speaker's control, **483**. Concerning order in debate, **484**. Phraseology used in the House, **485**. The Speaker empowered to reconcile disputes, **486**. The Speaker subject to the House, **486**. Spokesman to the Crown, **487**.

CHAPTER XXIV.

THE OFFICERS OF THE HOUSE. 489–501.

The Clerk, **489**. His emoluments and duties, **490**. His table, **491**. The Sergeant-at-Arms, **491**. His appointment, **491**. His duties, **492**. The Mace, **493**. The Sergeant's dress and pay, **495**. Prayers in the House, **496**. A Chaplain appointed, **498**. Preferment for the Chaplain, **499**. His duties, **500**. The Prayer for Parliament, **500**.

CHAPTER XXV.

THE SEATING OF THE HOUSE. 502–510.

Feudal distinctions, 502. Knights and burgesses, 503. Difference in the fees paid by knights and burgesses, 503. Privileges of knights, 503. No distinction in seating, 504. Places accorded to peers' sons, 505. Front benches for privy councillors, 505. Courtesy places, 505. Party lines in seating, 506. Opposition benches, 508. Party whips, 509. His Majesty's Opposition, 510.

CHAPTER XXVI.

THE PERSONNEL OF THE HOUSE. 511–527.

Knights of the shire chosen from the landed classes, 511. Change in the class of men chosen from the boroughs, 512. Lawyers as non-resident members from the boroughs, 512. An attempt to exclude them, 513. They seek advantages from their membership, 513. Objections to their presence in the House, 514. They claim pre-audience in the courts, 516. Their neglect of Parliamentary duties, 516. The distrust of them in the eighteenth century, 517. Lawyers in the modern House, 518. Merchants as members of Parliament, 519. The new men of wealth, 520. Their purchase of seats, 520. Returned East Indians, 521. Manufacturers in the House, 522. The iron-masters, clothiers, and cottoners, 522. George III and men in trade, 524. Cabinet rank for the newly rich, 525. Scotchmen and English constituencies, 525. Irishmen before the Union, 526.

CHAPTER XXVII.

PROCEDURE OF THE HOUSE. 528–544.

Little change in procedure since 1547, 528. Legislation by petition and by bill, 528. Stages of a bill in 1572, 529. Debate at second reading stage, 530. Committees, 531. The Chairman of Committees, 532. Deputy Speaker, 533. Instructions to committee, 534. Private bill committees, 535. Divisions in the House, 535. An experiment in voting by ballot, 537. Determination of election petitions by committees, 538. Petitions heard at the bar, 538. The Grenville Act, 540. Grenville committees, 541. The working of the Act, 541. The reading of a bill *pro formâ*, 542. Obstruction in the seventeenth century, 543. Conservatism of the House, 544.

CHAPTER XXVIII.

RELATIONS OF THE HOUSE OF COMMONS TO THE HOUSE
OF LORDS. 545–564.

Interference of the Lords, direct and indirect, in elections to the House
of Commons, 545. Efforts to exclude it, 546. The contest as to the voting
and appropriating of money, 548. The stand made by the Commons in
1661, 1671, and 1678, 548. The victory of the Commons, 554. Their
vigilance in guarding their right, 555. The constitutional result of the
struggle, 556. Relations between the two Houses in regard to legislation, 557. Conferences, 557. Jealousies between the two Houses, 559.
Messages between the two Houses, 560. Bills affecting the Lords originate
in the Upper House, 562. Attendance of Commons at the bar of the
Lords, 562. The peers' gallery, 563. Lawyer members of the Commons
pleading before the Lords, 563.

CHAPTER XXIX.

RELATIONS OF THE HOUSE TO THE OUTSIDE WORLD.
565–583.

The House insists on order outside its meeting place, 565. Westminster,
the Parliament City, 566. Privilege of Members of Parliament—for
their persons, 567 ; for their actions and speeches in the House, 568.
Hooker's account of privilege, 569. Stretching privilege, 569. Legislation
restricting privilege, 570. Bankrupts and privilege, 572. Petitions, 573.
Their regulation by Act of Parliament and orders of the House, 573.
London and Dublin privileged to present petitions, 574. Debates on Petitions, 575. Strangers in the House, 575. Their exclusion, 576. Efforts
to relax the exclusion orders, 577. The orders evaded, 578. Privileged
visitors, 579. Women as visitors, 580. Excluded from the gallery, 581.
Admitted to the ventilator, 581. The strangers' gallery, 582.

CHAPTER XXX.

THE HOUSE OF COMMONS AND THE PRESS. 584–596.

Proceedings of the House kept secret until the seventeenth century, 584.
Acts and processes made public, 585. Journals kept by members, 585. The
House orders publication of proceedings in 1641, 585. Official publications
on sale, 587. Efforts to check unofficial publications, 588. News-letter
writers, 588. Their conflict with the House, 589. The newspapers, 590.
Fear of misrepresentation in the newspapers, 591. Newspaper reports prohibited in 1762, 592. The contest with the Press in 1771, 592. Defeat of
the House, 594. Reporters gain a footing, 595. Still in the House on
sufferance, 595.

MAP

Showing the English and Welsh Constituencies on the
Eve of the Reform Act .   .   .   *Frontispiece*

PART I

THE REPRESENTATION OF ENGLAND AND WALES.

CHAPTER I.

PARLIAMENTARY REPRESENTATION IN 1832.

On the 7th of June, 1832, in the second year of the reign of The Reform Act of 1832. William IV, after an agitation which can be traced back to the days of Queen Elizabeth[1], the royal assent was given to an Act of Parliament reforming the constitution of the House of Commons. The preamble declares that "it is expedient to take effectual measures for correcting divers abuses that have long prevailed in the choice of members to serve in the Commons' House of Parliament; to deprive many inconsiderable places of the right of returning members; to grant such privilege to large, populous and wealthy towns; to increase the number of knights of the shire; to extend the elective franchise to many of his Majesty's subjects who have not hitherto enjoyed the same; and to diminish the expense of elections[2]."

Sovereigns as far back as Elizabeth and James I had admitted the existence of these divers abuses in the electoral system. Early Recognition of Electoral Abuses. Each of these sovereigns had urged their correction. A partial and temporary correction was made during the Commonwealth by Cromwell; a reform which even so strong a royalist as Clarendon described as "a warrantable alteration and fit to be made in better times." A permanent correction was urged at the Restoration; again at the Revolution of 1688; again at the union of Scotland with England in 1707; and once more in 1800, at the union of Ireland with Great Britain. From the time of Elizabeth, when Wylson, Her Majesty's Secretary of State, in refusing the request of the Earl of Rutland for the Parliamentary enfranchise-

---

[1] Cf. *Hist. MSS. Comm. 12th Rep.*, App., pt. IV. p. 117.
[2] 2 W. IV. c. 25.

ment of Newark, wrote " it is thought that there are overmany (burgesses) already, and there will be a device hereafter to lessen the number for the decayed towns [1]," and from the time of James I, who in calling the Parliament of 1604 charged the sheriffs not to direct "a writ to any ancient town, being so ruined that there were not residents sufficient" to make choice of burgesses [2]; and in 1624 refused the royal assent to a bill "for the County Palatine of Durham to send knights to Parliament, on the ground that the House was already too large, and that some decayed towns, as Old Salisbury, must be deprived of their members before this desire could be granted [3]," the question of the reform of the House of Commons had never long been at rest.

Every sovereign from Elizabeth to William IV knew of these divers abuses, and of the ruined and decayed towns referred to by Wylson and James I. Six of the sovereigns, James I, Charles I, Charles II, James II, William III, and George III, can be shown to have turned these divers abuses to their advantage, when seeking control of the House of Commons; and it remained for William IV, two and a half centuries after Queen Elizabeth's Secretary of State had foreshadowed a measure of Parliamentary reform, to fulfil, in respect to the representative system, that part of the coronation oath which binds the sovereign to "restore the things that are gone into decay; maintain that which is restored; purify and reform what is amiss; confirm that which is in good order."

Changes after 1604.
In the two centuries and a quarter which had intervened between the proclamation of 1604, in which James I charged sheriffs not to direct writs to decayed boroughs for elections of members of the House of Commons, and the drafting of the preamble of the Parliamentary Reform Act of 1832, the electoral system in England had undergone but little organic change. In this period the payment of wages by constituencies to members of the House had come to an end. The residential qualification for members, which existed in the early days of the House of Commons, when the franchise was uniform and when every householder who did watch and ward could vote at a Parliamentary election, had been

---

[1] Thomas Wylson, Secretary of State, to Earl of Rutland, June 17th, 1579, *Hist. MSS. Comm. 12th Rep.*, App., pt. IV. p. 117.

[2] *Parl. Hist.* I. 967.

[3] *Cal. State Papers*, 1623–25, pp. 265, 266.

allowed to fall into desuetude[1], and had been finally abrogated by Act of Parliament[2]. The clergy of the Church of England had also become of the electorate. After the Restoration, the Church "secured nearly as many votes at the election of knights of the shire as there were beneficed clergy in each county[3]." The clergy came in gradually. Many of them voted at the first election after the Restoration[4]; and by an Act passed in the session of 1664–65, which taxed the clergy in common with the laity, their new status as Parliamentary electors was confirmed[5]. Further than this, fifty-one additional English members had been added to the House of Commons, twenty-seven from fourteen boroughs enfranchised in the reign of James I, eighteen from boroughs enfranchised in the reign of Charles I, and six by the enfranchisement of the County and City of Durham and the borough of Newark in the reign of Charles II. The union with Scotland in 1707 had added forty-five members; and in 1801 there had been another addition of one hundred members, consequent upon the union of Ireland with Great Britain.

These additions to the House of Commons between 1604 and 1832 had brought no marked organic changes in the electoral system in England. There had been increases in the number of county electors. The throwing of corrupt boroughs into the hundreds as a punishment for corruption had wrought some local changes, and had added to the electoral power of forty-shilling freeholders in the rapes or hundreds into which the corrupt boroughs of Shoreham, Cricklade, Aylesbury, and Retford had been thrown. One ancient borough also, that of Grampound, for reasons similar to those which had led to the enlargement of the electorates in the four boroughs which have been named, had been deprived of its franchise entirely, and its two members had been transferred to Yorkshire, the largest county in England, which heretofore had been represented by only two members. Apart from these changes the new enfranchisements during the Stuart period, the coming of the clergy into the electorate after the

No Organic Reform.

---

[1] There is authoritative evidence that the laws of Henry V and Henry VI had not been enforced since 1620; cf. *H. of C. Journals*, xxxiv. 706. In 1659 they were adjudged obsolete ; cf. Parry, 528.

[2] 14 Geo. III, c. 58.

[3] Heywood, *County Election Law Digest*, 75.

[4] *Hist. MSS. Comm. 11th Rep.*, App., pt. vi. p. 152.

[5] 16 and 17 Car. II, c. 1.

Restoration, the additions to the House at the union of England
and Scotland and of Great Britain and Ireland, and the throwing
of corrupt boroughs into the hundreds, the general system on
which the House of Commons was elected was much the same in
the opening years of the seventeenth century, when James I was
urging reform, as it was immediately before the Act of 1832
totally disfranchised sixty boroughs; deprived forty-six other small
boroughs each of one member; gave the franchise to twenty-one
large towns and cities, which had hitherto not been directly represented in the House of Commons; made uniform the franchise
in the English and Scotch boroughs, and wrought other minor
changes in the system of representation.

No Uni-
formity in
Borough
Franchises.
    There was no uniformity in the electoral system of the boroughs
when James I ineffectually sought to bring about a reform by
his proclamation to the sheriffs, and there was none when Parliament approached the work of reform in 1832. In the reign of
James I, there were scot and lot boroughs, where the right to
vote went with the payment of local taxation; and there were
inhabitant householder boroughs and potwalloper boroughs, in all
of which the electoral system had retained its early democratic
characteristics. There were also, in the days of James I, burgage
boroughs where the right to vote was in the owners or occupiers
of ancient tenements[1], "holden of the superior lord of a borough
by an immemorial certain rent distinctly reserved[2]"; freeman
boroughs, in which the right to vote was in the freemen, and in
which already the change was making from the medieval freemen
to the freemen who figured so largely in municipal life until the
reform of the corporations in 1835; and boroughs in which
elections to the House of Commons were made by the municipal
corporations, or the bodies which in the days of the Tudor and
Stuart dynasties corresponded to the more modern but still unreformed municipal corporations. Many boroughs, whether the
elections were by the householders, by the burgage voters, by the
freemen, or by the municipal corporations, were, in the reign of
James I, and even at an earlier period, under the control of
the landed aristocracy who nominated members to the House of

[1] Burgage—"A tenure of lands in England by the performance of certain
determinate services, distinguished both from knight service, in which the
render was uncertain, and from villenage where the service was of the meanest
kind."—F. Pollock.

[2] Heywood, *Borough Election Laws*, 276.

Commons. They did this usually in agreement with the electorates, or with the men whom the electors allowed to act for them; but with little regard either to the resolutions of the House condemning this mode of electing members, or to the enactments still on the Statute books, which declared that citizens and burgesses sent to Parliament must be of the constituencies they represented.

In 1832, when the decayed boroughs, of which Wylson wrote in 1579, and of which James I contemplated the disfranchisement in 1604 and 1624, were finally legislated out of the representative system, or their representation in the House of Commons was reduced from two members to one, the same types of boroughs were in existence. Parliament in 1832 had to deal with inhabitant householder boroughs, in which to quote the proclamation of James I " there were not residents sufficient " to make choice of burgesses; with burgage boroughs; with freeman boroughs; and with boroughs in which the municipal councils had for centuries arrogated to themselves the right to choose members of the House, to the exclusion of the inhabitant householders with whom the choice had rested in the early days of the representative system. The chief difference between 1604 and 1832 was that in scores of these boroughs the curious and varying franchises had been confirmed by determinations of the House of Commons or of its election committees, and had been stamped and still more securely fastened on the boroughs by Act of Parliament, whereas up to the end of the Tudor period these borough franchises had only tradition, usage, and in some instances charters to support them.

From the time when seats in the House of Commons became generally in demand, which may be dated from the early years of the sixteenth century; from the time when the landed aristocracy was fastening itself on the boroughs, and obtaining the hold which it gained increasingly as time went on, and only partially lost in 1832; from the time when outsiders, nominated by the aristocracy or working independently in their own behalf, were willing without pay to represent boroughs with which they had no local connection, and were willing to confer favours and advantages on towns and townspeople who would thus elect them, the right to return members to the House began to be of value. From the time when this right to elect began to be prized, from the days when boroughs had no longer to compel their own burgesses to accept Parliamentary service, when manucaptors who were pledged to see that the burgesses elected to the House of Commons started

Borough Franchises in 1832.

Borough Franchises prized.

on their journey to attend the meeting of Parliament had disappeared, and when, instead of manucaptors whose duties were to
see that the elected rendered service, there came on the scene men
of aristocratic rank who were anxious to nominate members, and
lawyers, courtiers and political adventurers who were equally anxious
to be chosen of the Parliament, the right of a borough to be
represented rapidly appreciated. Cities and boroughs now no longer
sought to evade the precept from the sheriff when a Parliament
was called. Instead of constituencies ignoring the sheriff's precept,
or pleading poverty as an excuse for making no return to it, the
sheriff was now pressed for the delivery of his precepts; and bribes
and other underhand means were used by men eager to secure the
precepts from the county sheriffs as the first step towards their
election.

Petitions for Enfranchisement.
Minehead, a small borough in Somerset, was the last that
failed to respond to a precept from the sheriff for the election
of members to the House of Commons. This was in 1614[1]. It
never afterwards failed to elect; and, long before the failure of
Minehead in the reign of James I, boroughs which in the early
days of the House of Commons had similarly failed and permitted
their right to lapse, had sought and secured a revival of it; and
many boroughs which had not had representatives, had by this
time possessed themselves of the right; while others, such as
Newark in the reign of Elizabeth, and Durham in the reign of
James I, had sought it unsuccessfully. The county and city of
Durham[2] and the borough of Newark[3] subsequently came in; but
other towns, in respect of which petitions for enfranchisement were
presented between the reign of Charles II and the end of the
seventeenth century, were not so successful. There were unavailing
petitions in behalf of Wirksworth in the reign of Charles II[4]; in
behalf of Torrington at the Restoration[5]; and in behalf of Basingstoke in 1693[6]. Torrington and Basingstoke had sent members
to the House in its early days, and the petitions from these
boroughs were for a revival of their ancient rights. The petition
from Basingstoke in 1693 was the last for representation until
Birmingham and Manchester petitioned at the time the movement

---

[1] Parry, 273.
[2] 25 Car. II, c. 9.   [3] 29 Car. II.
[4] *Hist. MSS. Comm.*, *9th Rep.*, App., pt. II. p. 398.
[5] *Cal. State Papers*, 1661–62, 579.
[6] *H. of C. Journals*, XI. 85.

for Parliamentary reform became general after the revolt of the American colonies.

In the early days of the House of Commons, when contro- Controverted Election Cases. verted elections were exceedingly few, because as yet men were not desirous of being of the House, these cases were tried in Chancery. From 1428 to 1586, they were tried locally before judges of assize. From 1586 until 1868, controverted election cases were determined by the House or by its select committees; and the House of Elizabeth's day was no sooner in possession of this power than the Commons " began to seclude one another upon the pretence of undue elections and returns; and that rather to strengthen or weaken a party in the House than to rectify undue elections and returns[1]." This removal of disputed election cases from the courts to the House of Commons had much to do with the narrowing of the franchise in the boroughs which went on between the reign of Elizabeth and the Revolution. Then began the usurpations which can be ascribed to no legal origin; but which moulded the borough representation for two centuries to come.

From the time seats in the House began to be coveted, there Restrictions of the Franchise. had obviously been interests within and without the boroughs, municipal and aristocratic, which could be served by these usur- pations, by these restrictions of the franchise. When the heads of local territorial families were pressing their nominations on the electorates, and candidates were outbidding each other to secure election, and were willing not only to serve without pay but to bestow their largess on boroughs as a whole and on electors individually, to build bridges and quays, to restore guildhalls, or to deepen harbours and rivers, and also to pay individual electors in kind or in money for their votes, the municipal corporations which had arrogated to themselves the right of election became more tenacious of this power, and increasingly on their guard against those of their fellow-townsmen who were disposed to question or assail it, and to demand a more democratic franchise. When those who exercised the franchise, instead of having, as in the early period of the House of Commons, to meet the charges of members sent there, could obtain a bribe or an advantage whenever they were called upon to vote at Parliamentary elections, burgages began to have a market value determined by other

---

[1] Prynne, *Plea for the Lords*, 413.

considerations than the intrinsic worth of the holdings. In the freeman boroughs also, when the medieval freemen had given place to the new freemen, freedoms became more prized and the freemen more anxious to restrict the right of election to freemen as distinct from inhabitant householders. Even in the inhabitant house-holder boroughs, when Parliamentary votes became of value, there were efforts, sometimes successful, to restrict the area of the borough so far as the Parliamentary electorate was concerned, and thus keep down the number of electors.

Borough Franchises in 1688.

All these various and continuously active local interests and influences, together with party feeling and party interests in the House of Commons, were at work between 1586, when the House obtained the control over disputed elections, and the Revolution ; and they were largely though not entirely responsible for the absence of uniformity in the electoral system of the boroughs, and for the narrow franchise in many of them, on which Shaftesbury commented at the Revolution when some measure of Parliamentary reform, affecting in particular the smaller boroughs, was expected from the Convention Parliament. "I conceive," wrote Shaftes-bury[1], "it may become the prudence of this Parliament to look into the constitutions and customs of such boroughs which have right to elect, and which in several particulars seem to require a touch of the supreme authority to set them right. The first incon-venience they labour under is the variety of their respective titles, some claiming to elect by prescription ; others by grant ; some again by a select number ; others by the populacy ; some by the magistrates, burgesses and freemen and commonality ; and some also in respect of their ancient borough houses only, the rest of the town which is the much more considerable part, being excluded."

Last Deter-minations.

The touch of the supreme authority to set the boroughs right was not forthcoming from the Convention Parliament. The move-ment for reform or for wider borough franchises, which had been going on in individual boroughs with narrow franchises for a century prior to the Revolution, soon received a set-back from which it did not recover until after the American Revolution. This set-back came through the Last Determinations Act, passed in 1696[2], which was made more positive and definite by a second

[1] "Observations concerning the Regulating of Elections for Parlia-ment," Somers, *Tracts*, viii. 396.

[2] 7 and 8 W. III, c. 7.

Act passed in 1729[1]. The first of these Acts declared illegal any return from a city or borough which was made contrary to the last determination of the right of election by the House of Commons. Almost immediately after the Act of 1696, the House decided that it did not bind it, or regulate its decisions in controverted elections; but established only a rule for returning officers in making their returns; and in pursuance of this decision an election committee heard a petition from Tavistock, which called in question a determination of the right which had been made before the Act of 1696[2]. But in 1729, when the House passed a Bill for the more effectual preventing of bribery and corruption at Parliamentary elections, the House of Lords availed itself of this opportunity to remove all doubt as to the intention of the Act of 1696. When the bribery Bill was before the House of Lords, a clause was added which set out that "such votes shall be deemed to be legal which have been so declared by the last determination in the House of Commons, which last determination concerning any county, shire, city, borough, cinque port or place, shall be final to all intents and purposes whatsoever, any usage to the contrary notwithstanding[3]." The Bill with this amendment was accepted by the Commons; and stands out as a landmark in eighteenth century legislation affecting the English electoral system.

In 1735, when the question of last determinations was again under discussion in the House of Commons, it was stated that the amendment to the Act of 1729 was introduced in the Lords with a view to bringing about the rejection of the Bill; that it was put there from a feeling that the Commons would not accept the interference of the Lords in a matter affecting the determination of controverted elections; and that the House of Commons would rather see the Bill fail than that it should pass with the last determination clause[4]. There is little ground for accepting this theory of the introduction of the clause. There were, in 1729, nearly as many borough owners in Parliament as there were in 1832. Boroughs were as much property in the reign of George II as they were in that of George III, or in that of William IV, when it was expected that Parliament would compensate borough owners for the disfranchisement of their boroughs by the Reform Act.

(marginal note: Boroughs as Property.*)*

---

[1] 2 Geo. II, c. 24.
[2] *H. of C. Journals*, II. 510.
[3] *Lords' Journals*, XXIII. 363–4.
[4] Chandler, *Debates*, IX. 97.

Enhanced
Value of
Boroughs.

Nomination boroughs were certainly not so valuable in 1729 as they became during the long reign of George III, because the value of boroughs was greatly enhanced by the larger payments from nominees to borough owners and borough patrons, and by the increased money value of votes in boroughs during the last three-quarters of a century of the unreformed House of Commons. But in 1729 every man who had a borough in his possession or control, and enjoyed the right of nominating members to the House, realized that his electoral influence was safeguarded ; that opposition inside the borough from the unenfranchised inhabitants, and opposition from outside by men desirous of breaking down his domination, were effectually warned off by the second of the Last Determinations Acts. This Act had almost as much effect in enhancing the value of Parliamentary boroughs as property as the Septennial Act; for it reduced the expense and worry of borough holding; and in the House of Commons, and alike in the House of Lords, there must have been many members who hailed with satisfaction and relief the royal assent to the Act of the reign of George II. What practically amounted to a Parliamentary title was given by this Act of 1729 to many of the borough owners; and it had an effect in delaying the reform, finally brought about by the Act of 1832, which it is hardly possible to overestimate.

The First
Movements
for Reform.

From the time when the corporations, the burgage owners, and the freemen began to claim and to exercise exclusive rights in the electoral franchise their unenfranchised neighbours in the cities and boroughs had contended for a wider suffrage. The Journals of the House of Commons, all through the Stuart period, are full of the records of these disturbing local contests, as waged before the House or the committees on controverted elections. These records show that the popular movement for a wider franchise was never at rest in the constituencies from the time of James I to the coming of William III. These records of controverted elections, of isolated but still numerous local struggles for political equality, which bulk so largely in the Journals, and which afford the fullest, the most authentic, and the most picturesque descriptions extant of social and political life in provincial England from the reign of Elizabeth to the Reform Act of 1832, establish another fact of significance in the history of the English electoral franchise. They make it clear that the popular movement for Parliamentary reform, for the sweeping away of the little oligarchies, aristocratic, or municipal, or a combination of both, which for two centuries and a half prior to 1832 controlled borough representation in the House of Commons, began not with the inhabitants of great towns, such as Manchester, Leeds, Birmingham and Sheffield, which did not send members to Parliament; but in those towns and cities which were directly represented in the House. The movement began in these places, because the electorate was confined in many to the municipal corporations; in others to the burgage holders; and in others to freemen who might be resident or non-resident as the usage of the borough determined; and because, when a Parliament was called, oftentimes the larger body of the inhabitants in these places had to act merely as spectators while a handful of electors exercised the franchise.

After the Act of 1729, which for the sake of distinction has been described here not by its title, but as the Last Determinations Act, these local contests were at an end in more than a hundred boroughs; and it was not possible to contest last determinations with the least hope of success until within about forty years of the great reform of 1832. The avenue which had been partly closed in 1696, and completely closed on the initiative of the House of Lords in 1729, was partially reopened in 1788[1], when in an Act amending the law governing controverted elections, and proceedings before House of Commons' committees trying these cases, a clause was inserted making it "lawful for any person or persons" within twelve months after the determination of the right of election "to petition the House to be admitted as a party or parties to oppose that right of election." But by this time the movement for Parliamentary reform had become general. Pitt, while Prime Minister, had associated himself with it, and as yet in 1788 had not openly and finally abandoned the cause. The American Revolution had stirred the country to the need of reform. Reform had frequently been discussed in Parliament. The large unenfranchised towns were now agitating for direct representation, and the movement had got beyond the stage at which it stood between Queen Elizabeth's reign and the Revolution. Then outside Parliament it was sporadic; and except during the Commonwealth, when the army demanded biennial Parliaments, and a redistribution of seats by which burgesses were to be taken from "poor and inconsiderable towns, and additions made to counties[2],"

The Movement renewed.

---

[1] 28 Geo. III, c. 52.   [2] Parry, 478.

it was confined to the Parliamentary boroughs in which the inhabitants were contending for a less restricted suffrage.

The
Movement
National.

When these seventeenth and eighteenth century contests were being waged there was no newspaper press. People in one borough could have little knowledge of political movement in other boroughs. The reformers in each borough were making independent fights against the electoral system as it presented itself to them; in one place against the corporation; in another against the freemen, resident and non-resident. With better means of communication and with a newspaper press, these sporadic movements for reform must soon have become general, and they could not long have been withstood. In scores of boroughs they were crushed out by the Last Determinations Act; and when, after 1788, it was possible to contest last determinations of the right of election which narrowed the franchise, or confirmed an existing narrow franchise, the movement for Parliamentary reform was on much broader lines. It was now national instead of local, and although it had still tremendous obstacles to overcome, and was to be delayed for one generation by the French Revolution, the end was in sight.

Controverted Elections and Franchises.

The spirit in which the House of Commons determined controverted elections in Queen Elizabeth's reign is manifest in Prynne's statement that these determinations were "rather to strengthen or weaken a party in the House than to rectify undue elections and returns." Prynne's is not contemporary evidence. He was, however, near enough to the time when the House first obtained jurisdiction over controverted elections, to be familiar with its mode of dealing with the borough contests; and there is abundant contemporary evidence as to how controverted elections were determined during the seventeenth century, and from the Revolution to 1770, when the Grenville Act[1] was passed, and the determination of these cases was transferred to select committees, so chosen as to guarantee fair treatment for all parties concerned, whether candidates or electors, and to increase the likelihood of equitable decisions. The rights of electors were little considered during the hundred and eighty years which intervened between the time the House obtained jurisdiction over controverted elections and the first of the Grenville Acts. The interests, municipal and territorial, which were to be served by the narrowing of the borough franchise, were oftentimes powerful when controverted elections

[1] 10 Geo. III, c. 16.

were before the House; and scores of the exclusive borough franchises which obtained until 1832, derived Parliamentary title between the time election cases ceased to be tried before the judges of assize, and 1770, when the Grenville Committees came into being.

Controverted election cases from the boroughs had been dealt Closing with by the House of Commons, usually with an utter disregard of the Door to Reform. every principle founded upon equity, law, or common sense, for a century and a half when the Act of 1729 perpetuated the deter- minations as to the right of election made in the contests which had been carried to the House during this long period, and the Act further gave the House the exclusive power of finally deter- mining the right in all cases which should henceforward come before it. In 1729, there were two hundred and eighteen English and Welsh boroughs electing members to Parliament. As far as I have been able to trace, determinations had then been made in respect to the right of election in one hundred and twenty-seven English boroughs; so that in these one hundred and twenty-seven boroughs, and in others, in respect of which there were determinations be- tween 1729 and 1788, when determinations became no longer final, it was useless for the unenfranchised at the recurring elections to attempt to widen the borough franchise. The local contests which had been waged to this end all through the seventeenth century and particularly at the Restoration, and again at the Revolution, were now necessarily at an end in most boroughs; and as the last determinations clause in the enactment of 1729 was read by the returning officer in boroughs before he began to take the poll, the unenfranchised inhabitants had due notice that it would be of no avail for them to enter on a contest.

In most of the boroughs affected by the Act of 1729, whether The Door the determinations were before or subsequent to that enactment, reopening. exclusive groups, in some cases municipal corporations, in others the burgage-holders or the freemen, were by these last deter- minations put in undisputed possession of the right of election, and continued in possession until the Reform Act of 1832 swept sixty small boroughs out of existence, and for the first time made the franchise uniform in all boroughs which thereafter sent members to the House of Commons. The local contests for a wider franchise, which had gone on throughout the seventeenth century, and which had been begun even before that century, were resumed in a few boroughs in the closing decades of the eighteenth, and the early decades of the nineteenth century. Local reformers had now better ground for hope when they entered on these contests. These contests were hopeful, because the Grenville Committees were fair tribunals, and because the general question of Parliamentary reform was now being urged on Parliament, and this general movement made its influence felt on the local contests. In a few boroughs, notably at Scarborough and Steyning[1], less exclusive franchises than those previously existing were established as a result of these contests in the half century which preceded the Reform Act. But these wider franchises in isolated places, made possible by the Act of 1788, were not sufficient to work any marked changes in the system of borough representation as it stood when the Grey Administration took the general question of reform in hand and created a uniform franchise in all the Parliamentary boroughs.

Where Reform was most needed.

The Act of 1729 was applicable to last determinations in controverted election cases from counties. All through the history of the unreformed House of Commons, however, controverted election cases from counties were very much fewer than from boroughs, and the actual right of election in counties could seldom be in dispute, because there was a statutory franchise, the forty-shilling freeholder Act of 1430[2], which could be appealed to; while as concerns the boroughs, there was no such statute, and there was no statutory uniformity of franchise in boroughs from the time boroughs first sent representatives to Parliament in 1265 until the Act of 1832. It was the controverted elections from the boroughs which kept the House, or the committees on privileges, or the select committees under the Grenville Acts, busy in the early days of each new Parliament. It was on the borough representation that the partisan method of determining controverted elections, which usually prevailed from Queen Elizabeth's reign until the end of the first decade of that of George III, buttressed as this method was by the Act of 1729, had its most lasting and pregnant consequences; for nearly all the abuses of the unreformed House of Commons, and especially the unconstitutional influence which the Crown was so long able to exert on Parliament, grew out of centuries of manipulation of the borough representation. It was

---

[1] At Scarborough in 1791 "the ancient right of inhabitant householders resiants" was recovered. At Steyning the burgage-holders, who had been in possession since 1715, had in 1792 to give place to the householders, inhabitants paying scot and lot and not receiving alms. Oldfield, *Representative Hist.*, v. 319 and v. 41.

[2] 8 Hy. VI, c. 7.

the working of the seventeenth and early eighteenth century methods of dealing with the controverted elections, preceded as these methods were in the seventeenth century by local endeavours to narrow the borough franchises, which had so large a part in the creation and perpetuation of the nondescript, undemocratic and illogical system of borough representation which survived until 1832. Of this system the last vestiges, the control of boroughs by landed families, and the electoral corruption of the smaller boroughs, did not disappear until after the Parliamentary Reform and Redistribution of Seats Acts of 1884 and 1885, enactments which after nearly three centuries of agitation, at some periods local and at others general, put the electoral system back on the democratic basis on which it originated, alike in the boroughs and in the counties, in the thirteenth century.

Prior to the Reform Act of 1832, there were 658 members The Commons. of the House of Commons of the Parliament of Great Britain and Ireland. Of these, 513 were from England and Wales; 45 from Scotland ; and 100 from Ireland. The members from each country were elected on franchises peculiar to each, the one condition uniform throughout was that all members of the House of Commons served without pay.

The number of members representing England and Wales at Changes this time had been stationary at 513 for one hundred and fifty- in Repre- sentation. five years. In this period there had been some slight redistribution of electoral power, due to the mode in which Parliament from 1770 had dealt with boroughs of proved delinquency. Long before 1770, the House of Commons had sought, but had never obtained, the support of the other branch of the Legislature in dealing with boroughs in which corruption had become so deep-seated, so general and so notorious as to call for measures of partial disfranchisement. From the Revolution, writs had been frequently withheld from such delinquent boroughs, and Bills for their partial disfranchisement had been introduced in the House of Commons. In 1701, for instance, the House passed a Bill throwing the borough of Hindon into the Hundred of Downton. It was sent to the House of Lords, where it failed[1]; and until 1770, the House of Lords had never given its assent to any of these Bills, and no statutory measures had been carried for penalising delinquent boroughs. But by 1832, as the result of Acts passed with this

---

[1] *H. of C. Journals,* xiv. 184; Burnet, *Hist. of His Own Times,* iii. 427.

intent, there were five fewer self-contained Parliamentary boroughs than in 1677, after the enfranchisement of Newark, the last English constituency to come into the representative system.

Grampound.   Up to 1832, only one of these delinquent boroughs, for generations previously the plague-spots of the electoral system, had completely lost its franchise.   This was the long notorious Grampound, a name which even to-day, after an interval of eighty years from its disfranchisement, always recalls the unreformed House of Commons, and is yet a synonym of electoral squalor and corruption. Grampound lost its franchise in 1821[1] when its right to elect two members was transferred to Yorkshire, and there was thereby made the first addition to the number of English county representatives subsequent to the admission of the county of Durham into the representative system in 1674.

Other Delinquent Boroughs.   The other four delinquent boroughs which had been dealt with by Act of Parliament prior to 1832, New Shoreham in 1770[2], Cricklade in 1782[3], Aylesbury in 1804[4], and East Retford in 1828[5], unlike Grampound did not entirely lose their franchise.   At New Shoreham the old scot and lot franchise survived.   At Cricklade the right, determined in 1685 as being in the freeholders, copyholders and leaseholders, was retained; and until the Reform Act, Cricklade had the distinction of being the only constituency, borough or county, in which copyholders were of the electorate. At Aylesbury the householders' franchise, which had been settled by determination in 1695, was retained; and at East Retford the freeman franchise was continued.   But by these Acts of 1770, 1782, 1804 and 1828, while the old rights of election of these corrupt boroughs were thus continued, to quote the words of the New Shoreham enactment, "in the persons who by the custom and usage of the said borough have or shall hereafter have a right to vote," the electorate in each was enlarged, and the Parliamentary area greatly extended by the addition of the forty-shilling freeholder voters of the rape of Bramber in the case of Shoreham, and of the hundreds in which the other three delinquent boroughs were situated.   The result of these reforms was that these freeholders had votes at the elections for their counties, as well as at the elections for the boroughs whose electoral areas had been thus enlarged.

[1] 1 and 2 Geo. IV, c. 47.   [2] 10 Geo. III, c. 55.
[3] 22 Geo. III, c. 31.   [4] 44 Geo. III, c. 60.
[5] 1 W. IV, c. 74.

These were the only changes in the distribution of political power between the enfranchisement of Newark and the general and sweeping but still incomplete reform which was made by the Act of 1832.

Between the disfranchisement of Grampound in 1821 and the end of the unreformed Parliament, the 513 members representing England and Wales in the House of Commons were thus apportioned:— *Distribution of Representation.*

40 Counties in England	82	Members.
12 Counties in Wales	12	,,
24 Cities[1]	50	,,
166 Boroughs	332	,,
2 Universities	4	,,
5 Single-Member boroughs[2]	5	,,
8 Cinque Ports	16	,,
12 Welsh Boroughs	12	,,

Included in this enumeration of the cities and boroughs in England and Wales, there were nineteen constituencies which were counties in themselves. Ten were cities and nine were boroughs. These were communities which, like the county boroughs of the present day created by the Local Government Act of 1888, were for local government purposes cut out of the counties in which they were situated. They had sheriffs of their own; law-courts of their own; they raised their own quota of militia; and in other particulars they enjoyed special privileges in their municipal government. To these cities and boroughs the Lord Chancellor's writs for a Parliament went direct. They were not received, as were the precepts for all other boroughs, except for those of the County Palatine of Lancaster, for the Cinque Ports and for Berwick-on-Tweed, from the sheriffs of the counties in which the boroughs were situated. *Cities and Boroughs of Counties.*

These cities of counties and boroughs of counties, with the exception of London, which owed its place in the list to prescription, all had their origin in charters dating subsequent to 1373, when Bristol received its charter from Edward III. The object of the creation of the other seventeen cities or boroughs of counties was much the same as led to the Bristol charter. This *Charters.*

---

[1] Each returning two members, with the exception of London, which returned four.

[2] Abingdon, Banbury, Bewdley, Higham Ferrers, and Monmouth.

was to make them as self-contained as possible for local government. The Bristol charter was granted to save burgesses, concerned with public business, from the necessity of travelling to
Gloucester or Ilchester, then the county seats of Gloucestershire, and
"distant thirty miles of road, deep (in mud) especially in winter
time, and dangerous to passengers[1]." The last of these charters
was granted to Worcester in the reign of James I.

Freeholders
in Cities and
Boroughs of
Counties.
Many of these cities and boroughs of counties had interesting
electoral histories, due to the peculiar and unconstitutional position
of the freeholders, who in most of them could neither vote at the
borough elections, nor for the knights of the shire for the counties
from which these cities of counties and boroughs of counties had been
severed. As a result, in the last two centuries of the unreformed
House of Commons, from the time in fact when votes became of
value and added to a man's local consequence, there were movements in most of them, successful in a few, but unsuccessful to
the last in others, on the part of the freeholders to join with the
townsmen exercising the franchise, as established by municipal
usage and determined by election committee decisions, in electing
members to the House of Commons. In six of these cities of
counties or boroughs of counties the freeholders had grafted themselves on the local electorates, and were enjoying the right of voting
when the reform of 1832 was accomplished. These were Bristol,
Haverfordwest, Lichfield, Norwich, Nottingham and Carmarthen[2].
In Canterbury, Poole and Southampton[3] the freeholders were in
possession of the right to vote at elections for knights of the shire
for the parent counties. In the City of York part of the freeholders exercised a similar right; while in nine of these constituencies, Chester, Coventry, Exeter, Gloucester, Kingston-upon-Hull,
Lincoln, London, Newcastle-on-Tyne and Worcester, the freeholders, as such, could not vote either at the borough or the county
elections. These freeholders were paying land tax and bearing
all county and municipal charges[4]; and for ninety years prior
to 1832, election laws[5] applicable to forty-shilling freeholders
in counties had been made to apply to county boroughs; yet

[1] Seyer, *Charters of Bristol*, 40.

[2] Corbett, *County Boroughs*, 20–28; Hansard, xv. 634.

[3] Corbett, *County Boroughs*, 20.

[4] Cf. Mackenzie, *Hist. of Newcastle*, i. 659–661; Oldfield, *Representative
Hist.*, v. 277.

[5] 13 Geo. II, c. 20; 19 Geo. II, c. 28.

freeholders in at least half of these places were, as long as the old system survived, completely cut off from the exercise of the Parliamentary franchise. In county boroughs where they were thus excluded, the freeholders were in a worse constitutional position than the freeholders in the most exclusive corporation or freeman boroughs; because in these boroughs, while they might not be able to vote at the borough election, they could vote at the county election. They were worse off too than the freeholders in such unenfranchised towns as Manchester or Leeds; because the freeholders of Manchester voted at the election for the County of Lancaster, while those of Leeds, Bradford and Sheffield had necessarily in the closing decades of the old representative system, when commerce and industry were extending, a large influence in the election of knights for Yorkshire. Especially was this so during the last ten or eleven years of the unreformed Parliament, when the County of York had profited by the disfranchisement of Grampound.

CHAPTER II.

THE COUNTY FRANCHISE.

Contrast with Borough Franchise.

THE county franchise of the unreformed Parliament had a less eventful history than the borough franchises. It underwent much less change. Election committees of the House of Commons were not able to leave their trail on the franchise in the counties, because the statutory enactments governing the county franchise from the fifteenth century made impossible manipulations like those which mark the history of the borough franchises.

Early County Franchise.

The landmark in the history of the county electorate between the thirteenth century and the Reform Act of 1832, is the Forty-Shilling Freeholder Act of 1430[1]. Prior to the reign of Henry VI, made memorable in electoral history by this Act of 1430, there is abundant evidence to warrant the statement that every free inhabitant householder, freeholder and non-freeholder, could vote at election of knights of the shire[2]. Freemen, who were not freeholders, were up to 1430 assessed for the payment of wages of knights of the shire[3]. As long as sheriffs were elected, freemen voted at these elections[4]. Local offices were held by non-freeholders[5]; and in the first century of the House of Commons, service

---

[1] 8 Henry VI, c. 7.

[2] Cf. Longman, *Edward III*, I. 351; Merewether and Stevens, *Hist. of Boroughs*, Introd. vi, xxxiii; Selden, *Table Talk*, 141; Merewether, "An Address to the King, Lords and Commons on the Representative Constitution of England," 45.

[3] Cf. Prynne, *Parl. Writs*, IV. 381.

[4] 28 Edward I, c. 13.

[5] Cf. Toulmin Smith, *English Guilds*, 135, 136.

there, either as the representative of a county or of a borough, was
not held in higher esteem than any local office. In subsequent
centuries the meaning of the term 'freehold' as used in the Act
of 1430 was greatly extended; and it was on the later seventeenth and eighteenth century uses of the word that election
committees, dealing with controverted cases from the counties,
had chiefly to pass judgment, and on which their determinations
were of lasting significance.

Early in the fifteenth century seats in the House of Commons Limiting the
for counties were in demand. Men were willing, as they were at Freedom of
the same period in the boroughs, to serve the counties as knights Election.
of the shire without pay; and were by this time scheming and
working to secure election. By the time the fifteenth century was
half-way through, it was a grievance with the followers of Jack
Cade, the earliest popular advocate of Parliamentary or electoral
reform of whom there are authentic records, that " the freedom of
election for knights of the shire hath been taken from the people
by the great men who send letters to their tenants to choose
such men as they approve not[1]." Pressure by landlords on tenants
had begun thus early. The practice was well established before
the end of the sixteenth century[2], and it was continued after the
Reform Act of 1832. It survived, in fact, until in most counties
the forty-shilling freeholders and the voters on the fifty-pound
occupation qualification, one of the creations of the Act of 1832,
were swamped by the extension of the county franchise to the
labouring population by the Act of 1884, and the county electorate
so largely increased that pressure on tenants from landlords was no
longer of much avail.

By 1441 candidates at county elections were scheming to get The Struggle
the writs into their possession[3] to enable them to forestall rival for County
candidates; and by this time, alike in counties and boroughs, Seats.
there had begun the irregularities in the issue and conveyance of writs which were not corrected until 1813[4], when an Act
was passed under the provisions of which all Parliamentary writs
were conveyed and delivered by the post office. This irregularity
in the delivery of writs, which can be dated from the middle years

---

[1] Parry, 186.
[2] Cf. *Hist. MSS. Comm. 10th Rep.*, pts. ii. and iii. 72.
[3] Cf. *Paston Letters*, No. 408, ii. 36.
[4] 53 Geo. III, c. 89.

of the fifteenth century, is not only proof that seats in the House
of Commons were thus early in demand; it is significant for
another reason. It was this eagerness to obtain early possession
of writs that, by usage, first fastened upon Parliamentary candidates fees in connection with elections. The early possession of a
writ frequently went to the candidate who would bid most for
its possession. For a long time previous to the reform of 1813,
the messenger of the Great Seal collected a fee of five guineas for
a writ for a borough, and ten guineas for a writ for a city or
county[1]; and when the Act of 1813 turned the delivery of writs
over to the general post office, the messenger of the Great Seal was
liberally compensated for the loss of these fees.

The Struggle for the Franchise.

As early as 1467 candidates at county elections were enter-
taining the freeholders[2]; so that long before the end of the fifteenth
century, pressure on tenants, bribery, and intriguing for early
possession of writs had all begun. By about 1450 non-residents
were seeking to vote at county elections[3]. But in this century
and also in the sixteenth century, although seats in the House
of Commons were becoming more and more in demand, and county
elections were being contested with increasing spirit by territorial
families, I have not been able to discover any evidence of enlargement of the electorate by the subdivision of freeholds, solely
to qualify voters. The faggot voter, so far as I can trace him,
dates only from the early years of Charles I. There are un-
mistakeable indications that the faggot voter had come into
existence by 1628[4]; and from that time the multiplication of
forty-shilling freeholds and the wider interpretations of the meaning of a freehold added largely to the number of votes based on
the Act of 1430.

The Multi-plication of Freeholds.

Before the Revolution men were voting in counties in respect
of annuities and rent-charges; as trustees and mortgagees; as leaseholders for life; and in respect of the dowers of their wives. Later
on such properties as pews in churches carried with them the right
to vote at county elections. When, soon after the Restoration,
the electoral rights of clergymen of the Church of England had
received statutory recognition, preferment and offices in the Church,

---

[1] Hansard, *Debates* (1807) ix. 976, 977.
[2] Cf. Eden, *Hist. of the Poor*, App., xxxix.
[3] Cf. Prynne, *Brevia Parliamentaria*, 159.
[4] Cf. *Cal. State Papers*, 1628–1629, p. 6.

as well as offices connected with the judiciary system of which the tenure was for life, were held to confer the county franchise; and as the eighteenth century advanced, and as knowledge of the fact that these offices conferred votes became more general, the number of these voters steadily increased. Incumbents voted on such qualifications; so did the holders of lectureships; so did school-masters; and so did clerks of the peace.

As soon after the discovery of this new avenue to the franchise as 1693, a chorister of Ely Cathedral voted at an election for the County of Cambridge in respect of his office[1]; and in 1803 the brewer and butler of Westminster Abbey, the bell-ringer, the gardener, the cook and the organ-blower all voted in respect of their offices[2]. In this case these votes were disallowed by a Grenville committee. But the fact that these servants of the Abbey were permitted to poll at the election for the County of Middlesex is an indication of the wide interpretation which, in the last century of the unreformed Parliament, was popularly put upon the meaning of the forty-shilling freeholder Act of 1430. In the closing decades of the unreformed electoral system votes were claimed in respect of purchases of the land-tax; and in 1811, doubts having previously arisen as to the right of these claimants to vote, an Act[3] was passed, confirming the right, and making it unnecessary for voters in respect of land-tax purchases to register any memorial of contract, or certificate of purchase with the clerk of the peace, as voters in respect of annuities, fee farm rents, or rent charges had long been required to do.

For four centuries the county franchise remained on the statutory basis on which it was placed by the Act of Henry VI. But after the electoral system had been reformed in 1832, when the forty-shilling franchise was continued in its old form, with the addition of only one new county qualification, a fifty-pound occupation franchise, and right of voting in the boroughs had at last been made uniform, there were no fewer than eighty-five avenues[4] through which the Parliamentary franchise could be reached. Some of these many avenues were in the boroughs in which the franchises, existing prior to 1832, were continued for the lifetime of the then holders of them. But most of them led only to the county

Electoral Qualifications in 1832.

---

[1] *H. of C. Journals,* xi. 93.

[2] Peckwell, *County Election Law,* ii. 102.

[3] 51 Geo. III, c. 99.

[4] Cf. Hansard, Series iii. Vol. xcix. 893.

franchise, and were the avenues which had been opened up by the wider interpretations of the Act of 1430.

Residential Qualification.

Between the date of the forty-shilling freeholder Act of 1430 and that of the Reform of 1832, the county franchise had undergone three important changes. One was due to usage, the others to Parliamentary enactment. Before the Act of 8 Henry VI, the law directed that "choosers of knights of the shire be resident within the same shire, the day of the date of the writ of summons of Parliament[1]"; and by the law which established the forty-shilling freehold qualification, it was directed that the knights should be "chosen by people dwelling and resident in the same counties." Exactly when this residential qualification of county voters became of non-effect it is impossible to determine. It gradually fell into desuetude; and the probability is that it was no longer in operation when, in 1620, the residential qualification for members of the House had admittedly become a condition of the past. By 1679 there is adequate proof that it was no longer necessary to regard the law, for in that year more than four hundred non-resident voters, many of them students from Cambridge, polled at an election for the County of Norfolk[2]; and two or three years later, when Dalton wrote his handbook for the use of sheriffs, for the men with whom rested in the first instance the determination of who should and should not vote at county elections, his dictum was in favour of non-residents. "If," Dalton wrote, "a man have two dwelling-houses in several shires, and a family or servant at each home; or if a man keep his family in one county, city, or borough, and abideth in service in another county, in both cases he may be a chooser of knights of the shire, or of the citizens or burgesses of the city or borough where he keepeth his family[3]." It may thus be concluded that the residential qualification had gone before the faggot voter arrived, and before those wider interpretations were given to the Act of 1430 which by 1832 had opened so many new gateways to the county franchise.

Tax-paying and Time Qualifications.

At the time the forty-shilling freehold franchise was established, its exercise was contingent on the payment of neither national nor local charges. Residence in the constituency and the possession of

[1] 1 Henry V, c. 1.
[2] Works of Sir Thos. Browne, i. 240, 241, Ed. 1846.
[3] Dalton, *Office of Sheriff*, 332, Ed. 1682.

a freehold were by the Act of 1430 the only conditions necessary to a county vote. From the time the residential qualification fell into desuetude until 1712, possession of a freehold of the requisite value was the only condition necessary to a vote. In 1712 the exercise of the county franchise was made contingent upon the assessment of the lands or tenements in respect of which the vote was enjoyed to the " public taxes, church rates, and parish duties." With this new condition, which in this respect assimilated the county franchise to the franchises in the scot and lot boroughs, where the vote was dependent on the payment of poor rate or church rate, there was also established an additional condition in the nature of a time qualification. Both these new conditions were created by the same Act of Parliament[1]. As to the time quali-fication, the Act of Queen Anne provided that no person should vote in respect of lands or tenements for which he should not have received the rents or profits for one year before the election. An exception was made in the case of lands or tenements coming to a person " within the time aforesaid by descent, marriage, marriage settlement, devise or presentation to some benefice in the church, or by promotion to some office unto which such freehold is affixed." These conditions as to national and local burdens attaching to the county franchise were continued until 1781. Then the right to vote was made dependent on a charge or assessment made within six months before the election " towards some aid granted or to be granted to His Majesty by a land-tax, on an assessment in the name of the person claiming to vote[2]." These enactments of the reign of Anne and George III, by which certificates of payment of land-tax became the title of an elector to vote, made the only statutory changes in the conditions attending the forty-shilling freeholder franchise during the four hundred years in which none but freeholders, using the term in its wider eighteenth century acceptance, were of the county electorate.

Although these are the only noteworthy enactments which per-manently affected the county electoral system between the reign of Queen Anne and the Reform Act of 1832, the conditions under which the county franchise was exercised were frequently before Parliament during the last twenty years of the eighteenth century, and in particular much attention was given to the question of the registration of county voters. The system under which the county

Registration of County Voters.

---

[1] 10 Anne, c. 31. [2] 20 Geo. III, c. 17.

elector carried his receipt for the payment of land-tax to the polls never worked satisfactorily. It involved much delay at elections. Furthermore the owners of many estates did not directly pay the land-tax. Small freehold properties carved out of larger estates were often sold free of land-tax. In these cases agreements were made under which the owner of the principal estate paid the tax for the whole after its dismemberment, and was assessed for it. The result of transfers of land so made was that, as time went on, it often became difficult for the owners of the smaller properties to furnish documentary proof that their lands had been assessed. The system also afforded opportunities for sharp practices at elections; opportunities for taking advantage of legal technicalities, which, it is on record, were not overlooked by men who controlled political influence in the counties. Of such men in the last half of the eighteenth century, Sir James Lowther, afterwards Earl of Lonsdale, may be taken as a typical representative; and of Lowther it is recorded that, at the Cumberland election in 1768, he "nobbled the sheriff, who rejected a large number of votes on the ground that the land-tax lists, which were the registers of voters, were in many cases signed by only two commissioners and not by three," as the law required[1].

Publication of Voters' Lists. There was an amendment to the land-tax system of registration in 1781[2], under which assessors of the tax in the parishes were required to publish preliminary lists of their assessments before sending them to the land-tax commissioners for the counties. These lists were to be placed on the door of the church or chapel of the parish for which the assessment was made, a mode of publication continued by the registration system established by the first Reform Act; and it was then open to any freeholder who was not on these parochial lists, to appeal to the commissioners of the land-tax of the county, and, if necessary, from the commissioners to the magistrates in quarter sessions.

An Abortive Registration Act. In order to simplify polling in counties, Parliament in 1788 passed an Act[3] to establish an elaborate system of registration. Under this Act of 1788 the lists of freeholders were to be printed by the King's Printer in London, and the collectors of the land-tax were to be the custodians of the electoral lists in each parish. The preamble of the Act set forth that "it would

---

[1] Ferguson, *Hist. of Cumberland*, 168.
[2] 20 Geo. III, c. 17.
[3] 28 Geo. III, c. 36.

be much for the ease and convenience of the generality of freeholders, if they were enabled to cause their names to be enrolled"
on the register of freeholders, " without being obliged to travel a
great distance from their respective habitations for the purpose";
and the machinery which has here been briefly described, and much
other machinery, was created to bring about a uniform system of
registration, and to make the lists of electors open and available
for all public purposes. The first step under the Act was to be
taken by the clerks of the peace, who on or before the 5th of
April, 1789, were to deliver to the register keepers notices which
were to be delivered to freeholders and otherwise published, an-
nouncing that the register keepers would be ready on the first
Monday in May to begin the enrolment of freeholders in pursuance
of the Act. Between the passing of the Act of 1788 and the
distribution of these notices in April, 1789, it had been realized
that the expense of carrying the Act into effect,—which promised
to be considerable, for the printer's bill alone was estimated at
£55,000[1], and there were to be local charges in addition,—was to
be defrayed out of the county rates. When Parliament assembled
in 1789 petitions were presented for the repeal of the Act. Some
of them were from the magistrates in quarter sessions. Others
were from the " gentlemen, clergy and freeholders" of the counties.
One, from the County of Warwick, was from the unenfranchised
copyholders, who complained that they would have to bear their
share of the increased county rate, but would obtain no advantage
from registration[2]. In most of the petitions, stress was laid on the
cost attending the working of the Act. But it was further objected
that many freeholders would be deprived of rights and immunities
by being deterred from registering " merely from the apprehension
of subjecting themselves to the inconvenience and expense of suits
in a court of justice, as it is oftentimes difficult to determine the
validity of votes of a doubtful nature[2]."

Between February 16th and March 12th, 1789, nearly twenty *Repeal of*
of these petitions were presented. On the 12th of March the *the Act.*
House of Commons went into committee on them, with the
result that a bill was reported on the 8th of May for the
repeal of the Act. The preamble of this bill declared that
the operation of the Act of 1788 " would be attended with a

[1] Cf. *H. of C. Journals*, XLIV. 128.
[2] *H. of C. Journals*, XLIV. 280.

great and continual expense, and be productive of many hardships and inconveniences to freeholders and others"; and furthermore that the "said Act would be inadequate to answer the purposes thereof[1]." This was one of three noteworthy occasions in the eighteenth century on which Parliament, in response to public agitation, repealed in one session an Act which it had passed in a preceding session. In consequence of the protests from quarter sessions and from other meetings of freeholders, Parliament in 1789 turned to the right-about as quickly on the registration Act of 1788 as it had done on the excise Act in 1733, and on the Act for the naturalisation of Jews in 1754.

The Old System Resumed.

With this abandonment of a uniform system of registration, a system which had not even been tried, there was a reversion to the land-tax commissioners' lists, and this unsatisfactory system, with its delays, confusion and contentions at elections, with the expense which it entailed on Parliamentary candidates for counties in barristers' fees, and with the responsibility it threw on sheriffs in respect to doubtful votes, was continued until after the Reform Act of 1832. Then a system of registration, in its main features similar to that created by the abortive Act of 1788, was established, and with but little alteration has since been continued for both counties and boroughs.

[1] 29 Geo. III, c. 13.

CHAPTER III.

THE BOROUGH FRANCHISES.

In this chapter, which aims to give a sketch of the electoral Classi- system as it had been developed between the thirteenth century fication of Boroughs. and the first thirty years of the nineteenth century, I have classed all the constituencies in England, other than the counties and the universities, as boroughs. In this category therefore must be understood to be included (1) cities and boroughs which were counties of themselves; (2) cities; (3) boroughs; (4) the cinque ports and their three dependent ports; and (5) the four delinquent boroughs which subsequent to 1770 were thrown into the hundreds. Of the 489 representatives of England in the last unreformed Parliament, 86 were returned by the 40 counties and the universities of Oxford and Cambridge. The other 403 were from constituencies which are here classed as boroughs.

Of these English borough constituencies the number was 203. Four Groups. Excepting the City of London, which had four members, and Abingdon, Banbury, Bewdley, Higham Ferrers, and Monmouth, which were single-member boroughs, all these constituencies returned two members each to the House of Commons. This was the only point on which there was then any uniformity in borough representation. In the franchises of the boroughs there was no uniformity; and while it is possible to group the boroughs in four distinct classes, there was in the boroughs within these several classes, except as regards the period of residence in the scot and lot boroughs, no uniformity as to the conditions on which the exercise of the franchise was dependent. Taking the four groups of boroughs in the order in which they stood as regards nearness to the franchise on which the House of Commons was elected in the thirteenth and fourteenth centuries, before it was to the interest of municipal oligarchies or of the landed aristocracy to narrow the borough franchises, they were (1) scot and lot boroughs, including the inhabitant householder boroughs in which the ancient scot and lot qualification had disappeared; (2) burgage boroughs; (3) corporation boroughs; and (4) freeman boroughs.

Order of Groups.

The scot and lot boroughs were nearest to the thirteenth and fourteenth century franchise, because the vote in them to the last depended on residence and contribution to the charges of municipal government. The burgage boroughs come next in this grouping; because the franchise in them, while narrowed by usage and tradition, still retained some of the characteristics of borough representation in its early days. The corporation boroughs and the freeman boroughs, especially those boroughs in both groups in which non-residents were of the corporation, or in possession of the freedom, were the farthest removed from the early borough franchise; and their constitutions showed most obviously the changes which had been wrought from the period when seats in the House of Commons first became in demand, and when the landed aristocracy began to possess themselves of the control of borough representation.

Numbers in each Group.

In the scot and lot group there were fifty-nine boroughs; in the burgage group thirty-nine; in the corporation group forty-three; and in the freeman group sixty-two. Within these groups, except in the scot and lot boroughs, where there was a six months residential qualification, there was no uniformity in the conditions governing the exercise of the franchise. Much depended on local usages and customs which, in more than half the boroughs by the end of the eighteenth century, had been sanctioned and stereotyped by last determinations of election committees, and fastened on the boroughs by the Act of 1729.

(1)   *Scot and Lot and Potwalloper Boroughs.*

Scot and Lot Boroughs.

The scot and lot boroughs ranged in population from Gatton, where there were on the eve of the Reform Act only 135 inhabitants in the borough and parish[1], while in the borough, according

---

[1] Lewis, *Topographical Dictionary of England*, II. 217.

to another authority writing in 1816, there were only six houses[1];
to such populous places as Westminster and Southwark, and to
such large industrial towns as Northampton and Preston. In
these scot and lot boroughs, the only uniformity was as to length
of residence necessary to qualify for a vote, a uniformity which
had been lacking until, after an unsuccessful attempt of the
House of Commons to establish a qualification in 1739[2], a six
months qualification was imposed by Act of Parliament in 1786[3].

In some of these boroughs the vote depended on the payment
of poor rate or church rate, the equivalents of scot and lot.
In others the only condition other than residence was that the
voter was self-sustaining, that he had not been a charge on the
poor rate. The potwalloper boroughs formed this subdivision
among the boroughs in which the franchise was in the possession
of the inhabitants generally as distinct from burgage holders,
corporations or freemen; for the potwalloper's vote depended on
proof that he provided his own sustenance, that he was master
of a fireplace at which he could cook it[4], and that he was in
control of a doorway leading to his dwelling. An eighteenth
century Parliamentary definition of a potwalloper was "every
inhabitant in the borough who had a family and boiled a pot
there," and in the case of Honiton, the borough in respect of which
this definition was made, it was held that the inhabitants who
came within this definition had a "right to vote equal with the
rest of the inhabitants whether they paid or did not pay scot
and lot[5]." *Potwalloper Boroughs.*

The potwalloper was the quaintest of the old borough
franchises, and in its seventeenth and eighteenth century modes of
claim and proof was the most picturesque and the most reminiscent of medieval borough life. It went back to the days of
serfdom, when serfs and freemen mingled in the urban communities, and when freemen occasionally took their meals in public,
in some places in the kitchens which before the Reformation
were attached to the churches, to prove to their neighbours
that they were free and self-sustaining and ate as dependents at
no lord's table. In the seventeenth and eighteenth centuries, *The Pot-walloper.*

---

[1] Oldfield, *Representative Hist.*, ii. 606.
[2] *H. of C. Journals*, xxiii. 505.
[3] 26 Geo. III, c. 100.
[4] *H. of C. Journals*, xi. 492.
[5] *H. of C. Journals*, xx. 366.

when votes had become of value, in some boroughs the claimants
to the potwalloper franchise set out tables in the street in front of
their houses to prove that they were self-sustaining and entitled
to the franchise [1].

Restriction
of Borough
Areas.

    In one other important respect there was a lack of uniformity
in the boroughs in which the franchise remained to the end where
it was when the representative system came into being. In many
of the boroughs, where the inhabitant householders voted, the
Parliamentary borough was not co-extensive with the town. It
had not been permitted to extend with the growth of the town.
The Parliamentary borough was restricted in area; and this
restriction, there is good ground for believing, dated back to
the early years of the seventeenth century, by which time seats
in the House of Commons were much in demand, and Parliamentary candidates were ready to bestow advantages, entertainments, or bribes in kind or in money, on electors who would
vote in their interest. These restrictions could hardly have
existed in the days when members of the House collected their
wages and their travelling charges from their constituents; for
these charges had usually to be met by a special levy, and
it was to everybody's interest that the largest number of townspeople should come within the reach of the collector of the
assessments. At Taunton, when the electoral system was reformed
in 1832, the Parliamentary borough had long been smaller than
the town [2]. It was the same at Bridgwater, where the inhabitants
of the eastern and western divisions were excluded from the
franchise [3]; and to name only two more instances, similar conditions existed at Southwark [4] and at Guildford [5].

Control
of these
Boroughs.

    The restriction of the Parliamentary area of boroughs had
far-reaching effects on their electoral history. It helps to explain
why boroughs, where the vote was in the hands of the inhabitant
householders, fell under the control of the landed aristocracy almost
as quickly and as completely as the burgage or the corporation
boroughs. The existence of these boroughs of restricted area

[1] Cf. Defoe, *A Tour through the Whole Island of Great Britain*, II. 19,
Ed. 1738; Fraser, *Election Committee Reports*, II. 269, Ed. 1793; Russell,
England Displayed, I. 44; Farrer, *Hist. of Ripon*, 46, 47.

[2] Lewis, IV. 271.

[3] Oldfield, *Representative Hist.*, IV. 445.

[4] Oldfield, IV. 587.

[5] Lewis, II. 281.

shows moreover conclusively that the same forces and influences were at work in them as were responsible for the narrowing of franchises in boroughs of the burgage, the corporation, or the freeman group. In the corporation and freeman boroughs, it was usually a handful of electors who arrogated to themselves the exclusive right to elect members of Parliament. In the inhabitant householder boroughs neither corporations nor freemen completely usurped the franchise; but those who possessed the franchise were on their guard against its extension to new-comers; and as the records of controverted elections in the Journals of the House of Commons make clear, those who exercised the franchise as inhabitant householders, were not unwilling to act with a municipal corporation or a local landed proprietor to whose advantage it was that a larger electorate should not come into existence with the extension of the town.

These boroughs of restricted area were easier of control and manipulation by borough owners than either corporation boroughs or freeman boroughs. Next to the burgage boroughs, they were the easiest of control. In the inhabitant householder boroughs of restricted area the borough owner was seldom called upon to intrude himself into municipal politics, or subject himself to the whims and caprices of either aldermen or freemen. If he had once possessed himself of the larger part of the property within a restricted Parliamentary area, as was done, to quote two instances, at the Yorkshire borough of Aldborough, and at Steyning[1], all that was necessary was to fill the houses with tenants, who would obey his instructions as the recurring Parliamentary elections came round.

Ease of Control.

(2) *Burgage Boroughs.*

In boroughs in the burgage group there was the same lack of uniformity in the conditions governing the exercise of the Parliamentary franchise as in the inhabitant householder boroughs. In nearly all these boroughs the electorates were small. Burgages had gradually been appreciating in value from the second half of the sixteenth century. Consequently when, in the seventeenth and eighteenth centuries, burgages began to be acquired in groups by the landed aristocracy or by other controllers of burgage

Small Electorates.

[1] Cf. Oldfield, v. 329 and 45.

borough interests, the holders, whether of single burgages or of groups of burgages, found it to their advantage to restrict the number of properties to which the right to vote at a Parliamentary election was attached.

Value
attached to
Burgages.

Burgages were not peculiar to the Parliamentary boroughs. They existed in towns which never sent members to the House of Commons, and also in boroughs which were represented, but in which the Parliamentary franchise was not based on the ownership or occupation of burgages. It was only in those Parliamentary boroughs where the right to elect was attached exclusively to burgages, that from the Stuart period to the electoral reform of 1832, burgages were of great value and could command a ready market. In other cities and boroughs where burgages existed or had existed, as in the City of London, in Liverpool, Carlisle and Cambridge, in all of which the right to elect was in the freemen, these properties had only an antiquarian interest.

Residential
Quali-
fication.

In the boroughs where the franchise was in the burgage holders, the conditions, other than possession or occupation, varied according to local usage, which in most boroughs had the seal of a last determination; for from the time the House of Commons possessed itself of the right of determining controverted elections until the end of the old electoral system, elections in burgage boroughs contributed more than those in boroughs in any of the other three groups to the work thrown on committees of privileges and elections and, later, on committees chosen under the Grenville Acts. Residence was necessary to the exercise of the franchise in some of the burgage boroughs. This was the rule at Cricklade, where a residence of forty days prior to an election was part of the qualification of a voter[1]. Residence was also necessary at Haslemere, a Surrey borough which in the reign of George III was in the possession of the Earl of Lonsdale who, first as Sir James Lowther and later as the Earl of Lonsdale, was the most powerful and notorious unofficial election undertaker of the period. The Earl settled at Haslemere a colony of Cumberland miners, whose only business was to occupy the burgage houses, and obey Lonsdale's behests at the elections[2].

---

[1] *H. of C. Journals,* xxxviii. 869.
[2] Cf. Allen, *Hist. of Surrey and Sussex,* ii. 70 ; Oldfield, iv. 599, 600.

In other of the burgage boroughs there was no fixed period of residence. At Bedwin it was the custom to let the burgage houses four or five days before an election [1]; at Weobly, if the owners of the "vote houses," to quote the contemporary description of burgages from the Journals of the House of Commons, were resident overnight, they could vote at an election next day [2]. Until 1832 it must have been possible for an observant traveller to ascertain from the outside seat of a stage coach in which burgage boroughs there was some vestige of a residential qualification, and in which any such qualification had completely fallen into desuetude. In the occupation boroughs, when controverted election cases came before the Parliamentary committees, much stress was usually laid on the existence of chimneys. The chimney had an important part in the constitutional history of these boroughs; for wherever there was retained a vestige of an occupation qualification, it was necessary for the owner of a vote house, no matter how wretched a hovel it might be, to prove that it could be occupied; and one of the conclusive proofs of this, and one frequently submitted to election committees, was the existence of a chimney. Where occupation was necessary, the chimneys of the burgage hovels were usually carefully preserved. They constituted part of the title to a vote.

In many of the burgage boroughs residence was not necessary to the exercise of the Parliamentary franchise. Under the peculiar conditions which existed in some of them it would have been impossible. The possession of title-deeds to particular parcels of land—"snatch papers," as they were commonly called in the burgage borough phraseology of the eighteenth century from the celerity with which they were transferred and re-transferred at elections [3]—or registration in the records of a manor was all that was essential. At Old Sarum, which James I in 1624 had pointed to as a borough which must soon be deprived of its members, ploughed fields gave the vote. There were seven votes in all at Old Sarum [4]. As long before the Reform Act of 1832 as 1776, the borough or rather the area which in far-off ages had been the site of the old city of Salisbury was described

[1] *H. of C. Journals*, xxi. 294.

[2] *H. of C. Journals*, xxii. 796.

[3] Lambert, "Parl. Franchises Past and Present," *Nineteenth Century*, Dec. 1899, p. 942.

[4] Oldfield, v. 217.

by Samuel Curwen, an American who was in England from 1775 to 1783, as without a house. "This spot," he wrote, "which in former days was the site of Old Sarum, containing about sixty acres, unless I am misinformed, without one house on it, is now entitled to send two members to Parliament. On the lower plain, and bordering on the slope, stands one house, where dwells a family supplying the curious who visit there with punch, wine and tea[1]." Curwen's description is borne out by the fact that as long as Old Sarum returned its two members to the House of Commons, it was necessary to erect a tent within the area of the old borough to shelter the returning officer and others who took part in the formality of electing these representatives.

Droitwich.   At Droitwich, which I have included in the burgage group, it was "a necessary qualification that each elector should be seised in fee of a small quantity of salt water arising out of a pit[2]." In the early days of the borough, which was re-enfranchised in 1554 after having permitted its right to lapse, what was known as the old pit was open. It was the only salt pit in the borough at this time, and was "under the care of persons appointed to deliver the brine to each manufacturer according to his property in the pit[3]." The Parliamentary franchise had from 1690 been exclusively in the possession of the owners of this salt pit, these "burgesses of the corporation of the salt springs," as they were described in the Journals of the House; although it was testified before a committee of privileges in 1747 that the springs had been dried up for forty years prior to that time; that since then there had been no visible enjoyment of the property; and that it could not then be known "who has or has not property in them, otherwise than by title-deeds[4]." These title-deeds were always forthcoming at an election, and by votes founded on them Droitwich returned two members until 1832.

Downton.   At Downton, another burgage borough, an occupation qualification in respect to some of the burgages would have been as impossible as it was at Droitwich. When the Reform Bill was before the House of Lords, Lord Radnor, who was supporting the bill and whose borough members, by his instructions, had

---

[1] Samuel Curwen, *Letters and Journals*, 67.

[2] *H. of C. Journals*, xxxix. 361.

[3] *H. of C. Journals*, xxxix. 361.

[4] *H. of C. Journals*, xxv. 471.

supported it in the House of Commons, stated that he was the proprietor of ninety-nine out of the one hundred burgage tenures in this Wiltshire borough, one of the earliest boroughs which the House of Commons had proposed to throw into the hundred to eradicate its eighteenth century corruption, and that "one of the properties that gave a vote was in the middle of a water-course [1]."

All through the eighteenth century the boroughs in the burgage group had many alert friends in Parliament. Whenever any attempt was made to establish fixed and uniform residential qualifications in the inhabitant householder boroughs, or to make any slight reform in the borough electoral system, the burgage boroughs were most jealously guarded. In an abortive bill which was before the House of Commons in 1739, a bill which had for its object the establishment of a six months residential qualification in the inhabitant householder boroughs, an exception was specifically made in favour of the burgage boroughs and their snatch-paper voters [2]. Again in 1746, when an Act was passed making forty-shilling freeholders, who in cities of counties or boroughs of counties had grafted themselves on the local franchises, subject to the same conditions as to payment of land-tax as had long existed in connection with the county franchise, there was added after third reading, a clause excepting "where the right of voting is for or in respect of burgage tenure [3]." In 1786, when it had been proved to Parliament that the residential qualification at Preston, widened beyond all precedent as the result of a contest between the corporation and the inhabitants in 1661 [4], had long been so loosely interpreted that there was nothing to hinder a regiment of soldiers from marching into the town one night, and voting at an election the next morning, the Act [5] was passed which created a six months qualification in all the inhabitant householder boroughs. In this Act there was embodied, as it was proposed there should be in the bill of 1739, an exemption of the burgage boroughs. And so it came about that until the Reform of 1832 finally cut the burgage boroughs out of the

[margin: Burgage Interests in Parliament.]

---

[1] Hansard, 3rd Series, vii. 1394.
[2] Cf. *H. of C. Journals*, xxv. 505.
[3] *H. of C. Journals*, xxv. 151, 161.
[4] *H. of C. Journals*, viii. 36.
[5] 26 Geo. III, c. 100.

electoral system, burgages under water-courses ; ploughed fields like those at Old Sarum ; deeds which could not convey any property which could be seized either for taxes or for debts, like those at Droitwich ; coal-houses, pigeon-lofts and pig-styes, on which burgage franchises were based at Richmond[1]; and plots of land at Ludgershall so small that they might be covered with a hearth-stone[2], continued to confer the right to vote for members of the House of Commons.

Persistence of the Burgage Borough.

To the last, in days when England had a well-established daily newspaper press, and the railway era had begun, as from the early days of the Stuart period, House of Commons election committees were burdened and vexed with the miserable local squabbles of the burgage boroughs, and the desperately-waged contests of rival claimants to borough influence in these long notorious rotten branches of the borough electoral system. To the last, in days when the back row in the gallery in the ancient chapel of St Stephen's was occupied by shorthand reporters, turning out verbatim reports of the proceedings on the floor below, which from quick printing presses were scattered broadcast over the land, and when select committees were busy in adjacent committee rooms listening to the evidence of Stephenson and Brunel, Grenville committees were spending arduous days in rooms thronged by barristers expert in burgage borough election law and burgage borough lore and tradition, by borough attorneys equally well equipped, and by oldest inhabitants, men and women, brought to London as witnesses from burgage boroughs in distant counties, solely to determine just such questions as had presented themselves to election committees in the seventeenth century.

Disputes concerning Burgage Rights.

From the time when the House of Commons took into its own hands the determination of controverted elections, the cases from the burgage boroughs had called for determination on such questions as whether the Widows' Row at Petersfield really stood upon the old foundation of six houses, which in the reign of William III conferred the Parliamentary franchise[3]; or whether new houses built on old foundations at Great Bedwin and Steyning gave votes[4]. Landed proprietors who were borough

---

[1] Clarkson, *Hist. of Richmond*, App., liii.

[2] Oldfield, v. 215.

[3] *H. of C. Journals*, xx. 860.

[4] *H. of C. Journals*, xxi. 294 ; Fraser, *Election Reports*, ii. 339.

owners, mortgaged their lands to carry these and similar questions to London for determination by the House of Commons and its committees. They were carrying these cases to London before the Commonwealth. They were still taking them there when the stage coach had disappeared, and the oldest inhabitants, who from the seventeenth century invariably had had their place in these contests and whose evidence, as spread out in the Journals of the House of Commons, throws such peculiarly interesting light on municipal and local political life in the pre-reform period, could be carried to the metropolis in railway trains, of which Parliament had determined the speed and the fares for passengers. Slavery in the United States could not have long survived the era of the railway, the telegraph, and the Hoe printing press. Similarly, these English burgage boroughs, entrenched as they were in the electoral system, and supported in Parliament by powerful interests, like those which so effectually guarded them in 1739, 1746 and 1786, could not have survived the era of cheaper and more general travel, which came in with the railways, coupled as this great change was with the influence of a newspaper press freed from governmental control.

While in many of the boroughs in the burgage group the Vestiges of changes which had occurred in the two-and-a-half centuries in the early which all Parliamentary franchises had been appreciating in value Franchise. and seats in the House of Commons had become increasingly prized, had carried the conditions governing the exercise of a vote far from where they stood when the Parliamentary vote was no more valued than the vote for tithing man, and when manucaptors were still appointed at elections; in at least some of the burgage boroughs, other vestiges of the early conditions, besides easy and ill-defined residential qualifications, survived until the last. These survivals existed where the residential qualification was in force in what may be described as the chimney burgage boroughs. In some of them, as at Whitchurch[1], a burgage holder must have paid scot and lot or its equivalent before he could vote; and in others, receipt of poor law relief was a disqualification.

In the boroughs in the burgage group the electoral privileges Women in of women were more direct and more valuable than in those in the Borough Elections. freeman group, the only other group in which women had any electoral privileges assured to them. It does not seem possible to

---

[1] Cf. *H. of C. Journals*, xv. 548.

trace that women ever voted at Parliamentary elections in boroughs. They undoubtedly had their part in electioneering, a part which is easily traceable in reports of election committees in the Journals of the House, in the municipal records, and in the letters and memoirs of the seventeenth and eighteenth centuries. Oftentimes it must be conceded it was a discreditable and sordid part; for women were frequently the channels between the bribers and the bribed. Especially was this so in the inhabitant householder boroughs, and in the corporation boroughs, in which the wives of voters and of members of municipal corporations controlling elections often figured in these sordid electioneering bargains. In these two groups of boroughs, inhabitant householder and corporation, whatever part women had in politics or in electioneering was extra-constitutional. Only in the burgage and freeman boroughs had women places recognized by custom and by the determination of election committees.

Women's Burgage Rights.

In the burgage boroughs, women who were burgage holders, were permitted to transfer their right to vote to their husbands, their sons, their sons-in-law or their nephews. In fact, a woman burgage holder could transfer the right she enjoyed to any man possessed of the qualifications made necessary by usage in the particular borough in which the transfer was made. Men were voting in respect of burgages owned by their mothers or their wives at Pontefract and Corfe Castle as early as 1699[1], and at Westbury and Whitchurch in 1702[2]. By 1729 widows at Great Bedwin were transferring their right to their neighbours[3]. The practice was for the non-burgage owning neighbour to exchange houses with a widow owning a burgage from a date three weeks before an election until a fortnight afterwards. A similar practice had been established at Steyning by 1734[4]. At Westbury, where on the eve of the Reform Act there were only sixty-one burgage voters[5], a transfer of this kind in 1747 was worth one hundred pounds to a widow[6], an incident which, as told in detail in the Journals of the House, coupled with such later incidents as the migration of the Earl of Lonsdale's colliers from Cumberland to Surrey, helps to

[1] Cf. *H. of C. Journals,* xiii. 127, 128 and 249.
[2] Cf. *H. of C. Journals,* xiv. 25, 62.
[3] Cf. *H. of C. Journals,* xxi. 295.
[4] Cf. Fraser, *Reports,* ii. 295.
[5] Cf. Lewis, iv. 428.
[6] *H. of C. Journals,* xxv. 577.

explain why all through the eighteenth century electoral influence
in the larger burgage boroughs, in which there were still any
vestiges of a residential qualification, was the most expensive
which a borough patron could set out to acquire and maintain.
Not only were the individual burgages held for high prices; but
the borough patron had to stand ready to carry any dispute to the
House of Commons; for although a last determination might, and
in most cases did, reserve the right to the burgage owners, there
were continual contentions as to which properties were burgages
and which were not. It was in these boroughs, so far as their
electoral history can be traced in the Journals of the House and in
the later unofficial reports of proceedings before the Grenville
committees, that women, who were burgage holders, as distinct
from women of the territorial families who at times controlled
some of the burgage boroughs outright, had from the Revolution
to 1832, their most frequent, most conspicuous, and most direct
part in the old representative system.

(3) *Corporation Boroughs.*

Corporations, or before the era of corporation charters select *Election by* bodies, were electing members to the House of Commons before *Corporations.* burgages became of value by reason of their place in the electoral system, before votes in inhabitant householder boroughs were prized, and before seats in the House of Commons were generally in demand. Prynne, with good reason, dates Parliamentary elections by municipal corporations to the period when the final stages of borough elections took place not within the boroughs themselves, but at the shire towns where the county court was held at which knights of the shire were chosen[1]. It was because Parliamentary elections in those days occurred with such frequency, because votes were not yet of value, because no one was yet canvassing for them, and no one was yet willing to bestow advantages on voters who would exercise the franchise in their favour, that the municipal corporations fell into the habit of electing the members to the House of Commons with little or no consideration for the townspeople to whom they were responsible for the administration of municipal government.

At this period the inhabitants of many boroughs either waived *Borough* their right of election, or implicitly delegated it to the select *Elections after 1444.*

---

[1] Prynne, *Brevia Parliamentaria*, 256.

bodies[1]. The final stages of borough elections took place in the
county courts from 1374 to 1444, when by Act of Parliament[2] it
was directed that the sheriff should send his precepts to the
boroughs; that all the stages of an election should take place
within the borough itself; that the boroughs should cease to have
any part in the county court; and that their elections should be
made complete by the return of the precept to the sheriff.

Early
Elections
by Select
Bodies.

There are proofs that before 1444 select bodies in the municipalities were electing the members to the House of Commons.
Members were so elected at Northampton in 1381; and moreover
at a congregation held in the church on Tuesday of Easter week of
that year, the mayor had been so chosen as one of the members to
Parliament, which was to meet on the 7th of May, 1381; and it
had been ordained " that every one last holding the office of mayor
of Northampton should be hereafter elected burgess of Parliament,
if he shall not have discharged the office of burgess before, the
office of mayoralty aforesaid being no hindrance[3]." At Lynn, in
1432, the election was by a very limited number not exceeding
twelve, to the exclusion of the mass of the people[4]. Elections by
select bodies during this period were, however, not general; for in
some places, notably at Shrewsbury, instead of the election of
members of the House of Commons being made by the corporation,
there were municipal ordinances which directed that "the commons
assembled together on the ringing of the common bell shall choose
the members to Parliament[5]."

Seats in the
House of
Commons in
Demand.

Before borough elections were entirely dissevered from any connection with the county court by the Act of 1444, membership of
the House was appreciating in value. The Act itself is proof of
this, for it was intended to check irregularities on the part of
sheriffs, who in the past had returned men " which were never duly
chosen, and other citizens and burgesses than those which, by the
mayor and bailiffs, were to the said sheriffs returned[6]."

The Right
to Elect
considered
of Value.

As seats in the House of Commons appreciated in value, it
began to be to the advantage of the select bodies, or corporations, to restrict the right of election to themselves. At the time

---

[1] Merewether and Stephens, *Hist. of Boroughs,* II. 1331.

[2] 23 Henry VI, c. 14.

[3] *Northampton Borough Records,* I. 248, 249.

[4] *Archæologia,* XXXIV. 317.

[5] Merewether and Stephens, *Hist. of Boroughs,* III. 2099.

[6] Cf. *Official List,* pt. I. 225.

that all the procedure of borough elections was transferred to within the boroughs by the Act of 1444, it was declared that the elections were to be by the citizens and burgesses. But who were such was still left to usage, as it had been since the boroughs were first represented in Parliament; and the borough records and State Papers between 1444 and the end of the Tudor period put it beyond doubt that in scores of boroughs the elections continued to be made by the corporations, and that corporations now so valued the power they had acquired, that they were intent on having the right to elect members to the House of Commons secured to them by charter.

How numerous were the elections thus made in Queen Eliza- beth's reign, and how well-established was the idea that to the corporations belonged the right of election, may be gathered from Hooker's statement of English Parliamentary procedure, submitted to the Irish House of Commons in 1569. Hooker was of the Irish Parliament. He had been of the Parliament at Westminster. He was a lawyer; he had been chamberlain of Exeter; and was well known as an antiquary. When he was of the Irish House of Commons, as member for the borough of Athenry, he sought to assimilate the procedure of the Parliament in Dublin to the procedure of the English House of Commons. In a paper which gives one of the fullest contemporary descriptions of procedure at Westminster in Queen Elizabeth's reign, Hooker explained the procedure at borough elections in England, evidently with the intention that a similar procedure should become the usage at borough elections for the Irish Parliament. "The sheriff of every county," he wrote, "having received his writs, ought forthwith to send his precepts and summonses to the mayors, bailiffs, and head officers of every city, town, corporate borough, and such places as have been accustomed to send burgesses within his county, that they do choose and elect among themselves two citizens for every city, and two burgesses for every borough, according to their ancient custom and usage"; and "the head officers," continued Hooker in a part of his paper which is of value as showing how so high an authority regarded elections by corporations, "ought then to assemble themselves and the aldermen and common council of every city and town, and to make choice among themselves of two able and sufficient of every city or town to serve for and in the said Parliament[1]."

Evidence of Right of Corporations to Elect.

[1] Hooker, *Statement of English Procedure*; Lord Montmorres, *Ancient Irish Parliaments*, I. 93.

That the feeling, thus expressed by Hooker, that the corporations had the right to elect, survived his time and at a later period was held by men familiar with election procedure, and with the House of Commons, is shown by a letter from General Sir Edward Cecil to Lord Zouch, Warden of the Cinque Ports, written in 1624. Cecil was writing to Zouch concerning two members of the House of Commons who at the instance of the Lord Warden had been chosen for Dover. Their election had been declared void, and they had been "put out of the House of Commons as not being elected according to ancient law by the commons" of Dover. "If this law were generally followed," wrote Cecil, who was one of the unseated members, "few would be left to sit in Parliament[1]."

The Awakening of Popular Interest.

However complacently the free inhabitants of the period between 1374 and 1444 may have regarded the elections by select bodies, however indifferent they may, in those days, have been as to who represented their boroughs in the House of Commons, and as to how and by whom these representatives were chosen, the indifference was coming to an end by the time Hooker submitted his suggestions as to the reform of procedure in the Irish Parliament. Even nearly a century earlier than the date of Hooker's paper, there can be traced an awakening of popular interest. As early as 1474, only thirty years after all the procedure and formalities at borough elections had been transferred from the county court, over which the sheriff presided, to the guildhalls, to the market crosses, and to the churches within the boroughs, there was a measure of electoral reform at Ipswich. It came from inside the borough. Parliament had no part in it. It was brought about by a municipal ordinance, which declared "that all burgesses resident, and no others, shall have their free votes in the election of bailiffs and other officers of the town, according to the ancient custom, upon the day of the Nativity of the Virgin; and their free election of burgesses of the Parliament, whensoever the same shall be[2]."

Excuses for Corporation Monopoly.

Similar movements were going on in the boroughs in the closing years of the Tudor dynasty, not always with the same success as at Ipswich; for as late as 1621 select bodies were still appropriating the right to elect members to the House of Commons.

---

[1] *Cal. State Papers,* 1625, p. 200.

[2] *Annalls of Ipswiche,* by Nathaniel Bacon, serving as Recorder and Town Clerk, A.D. 1654, p. 135.

But in the Stuart period it was not the indifference of the inhabitants to Parliamentary elections which permitted these exclusions of the townspeople from the electoral franchise. The plea which the select bodies put forward to justify these exclusions proves that there was no longer any popular indifference, and shows that the inhabitants were now no longer willing that the municipal corporations exclusively should have the right, and exercise it at their sole discretion. The plea on which these exclusions were now urged or defended was " the avoidance of popular tumults common at elections." This was the ground on which the mayor, jurats and council at Sandwich in 1621 assumed the right to elect; and the inhabitants so keenly resented the exclusion, that Lord Zouch, the Warden of the Cinque Ports, through whom the writs went to these constituencies, was informed that it was "the intention of the commons of Sandwich to present a bill to Parliament for the restoration of their former privileges of having a voice at elections, and for disannulling the late choice of burgesses[1]," the choice which had been made by the mayor, jurats and council. In 1628, when Huntingdon obtained a new charter, a charter under which " it sank rapidly into the spiritless condition of a rotten borough, in which it continued until the passing of the Reform Act," the reason set out in the new instrument for effacing the democracy in municipal government, and in the election of members of the House of Commons, was that it was necessary to prevent " popular tumult, and to render the elections and other things and the public business of the said borough into certainty and constant order[2]."

There were men of the corporations to whom it was personally advantageous that the corporations should have these exclusive rights; and outside these municipal oligarchies, there were men of the local territorial families who also had a direct and an appreciating interest in helping to place and keep electoral rights in the hands of as few borough inhabitants as possible. These outsiders were the forerunners of the borough patrons, although the phrase borough patron was not in vogue in the sixteenth and seventeenth centuries. As yet, the landed aristocracy who had their hands on the boroughs had not fully arrived at the position of

The Coming of the Borough Patron.

---

[1] *Cal. State Papers*, 1616–1623, p. 219.

[2] John Bruce, " An Unnoticed Incident in the Early Life of Cromwell," *Athenæum*, October 13th, 1855.

patrons. As yet they could not dictate to the townspeople in the inhabitant householder and the corporation boroughs. Their letters were still those of suppliants for favours. They were not couched in the commanding tones which characterised the correspondence between borough owners and subservient borough corporations in the eighteenth and nineteenth centuries; and it was not until the eighteenth century that the term patron, as applied to a man who controlled borough influence and borough elections, generally found its way into literature, into memoirs and letters, into county histories, and into gazetteers. Even in *England Displayed*, an ambitious and useful work in folio published as late as 1759, and one of the best precursors of Lewis's *Topographical Dictionary of England*, the fullest and most complete gazetteer published prior to the Reform Act of 1832, it is not possible to find any references to patrons of Parliamentary boroughs. In Lewis the patrons of boroughs are named, as to-day the Clergy List publishes the names of the patrons of church livings.

Develope-ment of the Patron.
During the Tudor and early Stuart periods, the patron was still only in developement. But even then, and more so than in the eighteenth century when his hold on the boroughs had become secure, he was always ready at Court or in Parliament to serve a borough on which he was fastening himself; and whenever there was a new charter by which the right of election was transferred to a corporation, like that at Huntingdon in 1628, it is safe to assume that in that borough the predecessor of the eighteenth and nineteenth century patron was already on the scene[1].

Corporations securely in Possession.
In a borough whose charter dated earlier than the Restoration, a corporation in possession of the exclusive right of electing members was entrenched in an almost impregnable fort. It was advantageously placed for discouraging, if not for preventing, a movement within the borough for a wider franchise. If such a movement were begun and persisted in, and carried to the House of Commons, a corporation with a charter had not much to fear from a contest at Westminster, even in the early days of Charles I, when as General Sir Edward Cecil, from whose letter of 1624 quotation has already been made, affirmed that the House of Commons "is violent for free elections[2]"; when Eliot, who was "always ready to oppose all unfair tampering with the rights of

---

[1] Cf. Bruce, *Cal. State Papers*, 1829–31, Introduction, viii.
[2] *Cal. State Papers*, 1623, 1625, p. 192.

electors," and Hampden, who helped in and sympathized with Eliot's work as an electoral reformer[1], were of the committee of privileges. But the committee of the Parliament of 1628, of which Eliot and Hampden were members, while declaring in one of its resolutions that " the election of burgesses in all boroughs did of common right belong to the commoners, and that nothing could take it away from them," made an exception which afforded a cover for boroughs with charters, and in some instances for boroughs which had none, by adding " but a prescription and a constant usage beyond all memory to the contrary[2]." Some of the boroughs had both usage and charter to uphold the exercise of the exclusive right of election by the corporation ; for the men within and without the corporations, interested in the continuance of this right, had protected their interests by obtaining charters.

The contests between the advocates of popular franchises and the corporations in exclusive possession in non-charter boroughs, which went on from Queen Elizabeth's reign until shortly before the Revolution, especially from the beginning of the reign of Charles I to 1640, were, however, not in vain. While Eliot and Hampden were of the committee of privileges, and when, in all controverted election cases, Eliot " took earnest share and never but in behalf of a more extended franchise[3]," " the common sort of burgesses," those who in the earliest days of English municipal life did watch and ward, paid scot and lot, and within whose right it was to vote for members of the House of Commons, as it was their burden to pay their members' wages so long as the payment of wages lasted, had their electoral rights restored at Warwick, Colchester, Boston, Bridport and Lewes[4]. In these boroughs, municipal oligarchies in the form of the mayor and common council at Warwick ; bailiffs, aldermen and common council at Colchester ; two bailiffs and thirteen capital burgesses at Bridport ; and at Lewes a small number of constables, were all denied the exclusive right of electing members for these several boroughs.

The committee of privileges of this Parliament of 1628,

Some Restoration of Popular Rights.

---

[1] Cf. Forster, *Life of Eliot*, i. 557 and ii. 271.

[2] *H. of C. Journals*, xvii. 143 ; Waylen, *Hist. of Devizes*, 347.

[3] Forster, *Life of Eliot*, ii. 273, 274.

[4] Colchester, March 28th ; Lewes, March 29th ; Bridport, April 12th ; Boston, May 7th ; Warwick, May 31st, 1628 ; *H. of C. Journals*, 1628.

a Parliament nearly as memorable as the one that succeeded it, left
its impress on the representative history of England.   By its work
in the interest of electoral reform it gave an impetus to popular
movements within the boroughs for a restoration of wider Parliamentary franchises, an impetus which made itself felt at the
Restoration, and again at the calling of the Convention Parliament
of 1688.   It had not spent itself when it was checked and almost
lost for two generations by the Last Determinations Act of 1729.
In boroughs whose franchises had been passed upon by election
committees, no matter how remote the determinations, this Act
ended all these local popular agitations, these contests with corporations, corporations now grown more daring, more arrogant,
and now frequently dominated by outsiders with no direct *bona fide*
interest in the boroughs, who had become of the municipal
corporations solely to advance and conserve the Parliamentary
interests of the territorial families under whose patronage the
boroughs had passed.

At the Restoration, when the general electoral reform which
had been made by Cromwell was reversed, and the House of
Commons was to be elected again on the old representative system,
there were many contests in the boroughs between the exclusive
groups which before the Commonwealth had claimed the right of
election, and the inhabitants who saw in the calling of a Parliament
on the old model an opportunity for possessing themselves of the
franchise.   There were so many of these local contentions, so many
of these popular assaults on the corporations, that the corporation
of Northampton, fearing the ill success of an isolated defence,
passed an ordinance declaring the intention of Northampton to
" unite with any other corporation of the neighbourhood for the
maintenance and continuance of their constancy in the choice of
burgesses to serve in Parliament by the mayor, bailiffs and burgesses[1]."

Nearly forty election contests were carried to the House of
Commons in the Parliament of 1660 ; and, as the Journals show,
most of these disputes were due to local agitation for a wider
franchise.   Seventeen of these cases were determined before the
first Parliament of Charles II was dissolved on the 29th of
December, 1660.   Some of the determinations were in favour of
the wider franchise ; as in several of the boroughs, notably at

[1] *Northampton Borough Records,* II. 498.

Plymouth[1], at Northampton[2], and at St Ives[3], corporations or select municipal groups failed to maintain their hold on the right of election. On the other hand, corporations succeeded in doing this at Truro[4]; at Buckingham[5]; and at St Michaels[6]; so that by the determinations of the first Parliament of Charles II, there was but slight change in the number of the corporations which were exercising the right of election. The agitations for wider franchises were renewed at the elections for the Parliament of 1661; but in the determinations which were made in contested elections by the House of Commons in 1661 and 1662, there were only two instances in which municipal corporations lost the right they had hitherto enjoyed. These were at Preston and Ludlow[7].

The outcome of the determination in respect to Preston was remarkable; for under this determination of 1661 there was established one of the most extraordinary franchises on which members of the House of Commons were ever elected, a franchise which was directly responsible, one hundred and twenty-five years later, for the first Act of Parliament establishing a residential qualification in the popular boroughs,—in all the boroughs in which members were chosen otherwise than by burgage holders, freemen, or corporations. Until the Restoration the right of electing at Preston had been exercised by the corporation. The determination of 1661 was, to quote the Journals, "in favour of all the inhabitants"; and the determination was so loosely rendered, and afterwards so widely interpreted, that until 1786, neither residence in the ordinary acceptance of the term, nor any payment to local taxation was necessary to the exercise of the Parliamentary franchise. Any man who had been overnight in Preston could vote at a Parliamentary election there, until the six months residential qualification for all inhabitant householder boroughs was established by the Act of 1786. The franchise at Preston from 1661 to 1786, so favourable to fugacious electors, was thus wider than in the popular boroughs in which no

Wide Franchise at Preston.

[1] Cf. *H. of C. Journals*, VIII. 59.
[2] Cf. *H. of C. Journals*, VIII. 70.
[3] Cf. *H. of C. Journals*, VIII. 90.
[4] Cf. *H. of C. Journals*, VIII. 69.
[5] Cf. *H. of C. Journals*, VIII. 87.
[6] Cf. *H. of C. Journals*, VIII. 92.
[7] Cf. *H. of C. Journals*, VIII. 336, 373.

contribution to local taxation was necessary to a vote; for in these boroughs some period of residence was required, and the term residence had not in them the elastic meaning which it had at Preston. Moreover in these popular boroughs, even if a voter did not pay poor rate or church rate, he was usually disqualified if he had received help from the poor rate. Many curious anomalies resulted from the determinations of election committees; but none more curious or more at variance with constitutional usages than resulted from the determination under which Preston was freed from its municipal oligarchy, and the right of election thrown into the possession of "all the inhabitants."

Charles II and Corporation Boroughs. At the Restoration the Crown was no more favourably disposed towards open boroughs than it was in the years that intervened between the Restoration and the Reform Act of 1832; for in 1661, when local reformers were still busy with the contests for wider franchises which marked the calling of the first Parliament of Charles II, and election committees were making occasional determinations in favour of the inhabitants and against the local bodies which had been in control, instructions in a contrary direction were being issued from Whitehall in respect to new municipal charters. These were that when new charters were granted for boroughs, there should be "express reservation to the Crown of the first nomination of aldermen, recorders and town clerks"; and also that "there be a provision for elections to Parliament to be made by the common council only [1]," instructions which foreshadowed the coming struggle between the last of the Stuarts and Parliament.

Corporations assailed in 1688. At the Revolution, which the manipulation of the boroughs by Charles II and James II had done so much to bring about, local reformers in the Parliamentary boroughs entertained the same expectation of success and of the widening of franchises that they had held when the Parliament of 1660 was called. In spite of the fact that the letters issued for the Convention Parliament contained a clause directing that the elections should be by "such persons only as according to the ancient laws and customs of right ought to choose members for Parliament [2]," the unenfranchised inhabitants of the boroughs, where select groups had hitherto been in control, again pressed their claims

---

[1] *Cal. State Papers*, 1660–61, p. 582.
[2] Stephens, *Intro. to De Lolme*, I. 479.

to vote, as they had done at the Restoration; and again many of these contests were carried for final settlement to Westminster. Portsmouth then obtained a wider franchise[1]; but the success of these local agitations at the Revolution was even less than at the Restoration; and between the Revolution and the Last Determinations Act, few changes were made in the position of the boroughs in which the corporations were in control.

The demand for seats in the House of Commons was greater during the lifetime of the Parliament which was elected in 1661 and continued until 1678, than in any preceding Parliament. This demand is evident from the number of candidates who presented themselves at by-elections[2], and from the more general use of bribes which marked the elections to the second Parliament of Charles II[3]. It is clear also from the intimidations which some members of the Pensioner Parliament used towards their constituents, when at last this long-drawn out Parliament was coming to a close. One member of this Parliament, Andrew Marvell, is authoritatively known to have received wages from his constituents at Kingston-upon-Hull. But while there had been isolated instances of local payment of wages during the Commonwealth, as for instance at Newcastle-on-Tyne in 1654[4], such payment had long ago generally disappeared, and it may be concluded that Marvell was the last member of the House to receive wages, regularly and freely paid by his constituents. Claims for wages were threatened by many members of the Pensioner Parliament, but the fact that these threatened claims were made with a view to their use as levers to secure easy re-election[5], led to the introduction of a bill to put a formal and statutory end to wages[6]. The bill did not become law; nor has any such measure ever been passed. But that there were threats of a revival of the old law, and that these threats were, according to Marvell's understanding of them, solely to give opportunities for bargains for re-election, is another proof of the extent to

Demand for seats in Parliament of 1661-78.

---

[1] *H. of C. Journals,* xi. 411.

[2] There were six at Aldborough in 1673. Cf. Reresby, *Memoirs,* 177.

[3] Cf. Saville, *Correspondence,* 113.

[4] Cf. Mackenzie, *Hist. of Newcastle,* ii. 650.

[5] Cf. Marvell, *Works,* ii. 518.

[6] Cf. Somers, *Tracts,* viii. 396, 397.

which seats were in request between the Restoration and the Revolution.

Enhanced Value of Votes.

The increased demand for seats and the larger bribes which from the Restoration began to be distributed among constituents, enhanced the value of exclusive rights of election, whether exercised by municipal corporations, by burgage holders, by the modern freemen to the exclusion of the inhabitants who were not freemen, or by the voters in scot and lot constituencies, where the Parliamentary borough was not co-extensive with the municipality. At the Revolution, in the boroughs and also among the territorial families which controlled or were seeking to control borough elections, there had already been long at work those interests which either schemed for the Last Determinations Act of 1729, or heartily welcomed that measure when it was placed on the statute book.

Unrecorded Contests.

When it is remembered how general was Parliamentary election by municipal oligarchies up to the end of the Tudor period ; when statements like those of Hooker and Sir Edward Cecil indicating the extent of this usage in the reigns of Elizabeth and James I are recalled, it becomes obvious that after seats became in demand, and the Parliamentary franchise began to be prized, there must have been many local contests between municipal oligarchies and larger bodies of inhabitants for the possession of the right to elect members to Parliament, which went against the oligarchies, but which are not recorded in the Journals of the House. Some of these contests, like that at Ipswich in 1474, where the inhabitants reasserted themselves, were doubtless settled in favour of a wider franchise, and settled as the Ipswich contest was, without any interference from the outside ; for when the end came in 1832, there were only forty-three boroughs, as far as I can trace them, out of a total of 203 in England and Wales, in which the corporations had by usage or by charter the exclusive right to elect.

Indirect Corporation Control.

Forty-three does not represent the total number of boroughs in which the control of Parliamentary elections was in the hands of corporations. Corporations were in control in many boroughs in which they had not the exclusive right of election. They were in control in some of the freeman boroughs, and in some of the scot and lot boroughs. In the freeman boroughs the corporations possessed control chiefly by the exercise of the right to make freemen, either resident or non-resident, as the

usage of the borough allowed, and by their use of the corporation property and revenues[1]. In the scot and lot boroughs
they exercised control through their local political power, helped
in some places by the manipulation of the poor law in their
interest by the overseers of the poor, and often, as was the
vogue in freeman boroughs, by the use of local charities for
electioneering purposes[2]. But in boroughs controlled by corporations in this way, in these freeman and scot and lot
boroughs, the inhabitants, or some portion of them, were in
possession of the franchise, and the corporations obtained and
held control of Parliamentary elections, and often acted as sub-
agents of borough patrons, by alliance with the electors.

In the boroughs I have included in the category of corporation boroughs, this was not the case. In these boroughs the
corporations were exclusively in possession of the right to elect,
and needed no outside help or alliances. The right had been
acquired and maintained through many generations, and in these
boroughs the elections were made solely by the corporations ;
and the inhabitants, well-to-do and poor alike, were as completely
ignored in the choice of members to Parliament as though they
had been dwelling on another continent. Neither borough patrons
nor members of the House of Commons in these constituencies
had any political relations with the inhabitants who were not of
the corporations ; and from within a few years after the Revolution, it was usual, as is evident from the letters and memoirs
and the Parliamentary reports of the eighteenth century, for a
member who represented a corporation borough to speak, not
as nowadays " of my constituents," but of " my corporation[3]."
It was in these boroughs that it was often in the power of the
mayor to tell Parliamentary candidates or local electoral reformers,
and to tell them with truth, as the bailiff of Haslemere did
in 1661, that "it lay in his little pate to return whom he
pleased[4]."

Complete Corporation Control.

In these borough corporations there was as little uniformity
as to residential qualification for members of the corporation, as

Non-resident Mayors.

---

[1] Cf. *H. of C. Journals*, xii. 527.

[2] Cf. *H. of C. Journals*, xvi. 477; *Mirror of Parliament*, 1835, ii. 1505;
Municipal Corporations Comm. 1st Rep., pt. iv. p. 2496.

[3] Cf. *Hist. MSS. Comm. 15th Rep.*, App., pt. iv. 94; Sir John Bland
to Robert Harley, June 20th, 1704.

[4] Oldfield, iv. 595.

there was in regard to residential qualification for voting in the burgage boroughs. In many of them the members of the corporations were non-resident. These corporations were supposed to exist for municipal government; but few of them were responsible to the community. Most of them were self-elected; and they were kept together, not primarily with a view to the well-being and good administration of the boroughs, but as organisations for returning members to the House of Commons, and for defending and maintaining the exclusive right to make these elections. Usually this was the sole object of the non-residents who were of the corporation. Non-residents were frequently chosen as mayors, or to the offices which corresponded to that of mayor. They had no interest in the municipal government of the borough. Oftentimes these mayors were not in the boroughs, at the head of whose municipal governments they had been placed, from one year's end to another[1]. They took the office because in nearly all the boroughs the mayors were the returning officers. They, or their deputies, conducted the formalities connected with the Parliamentary elections; and when a borough was in the control of a patron, it was necessary that the patron should have as mayor a man on whom he could absolutely rely, to act steadfastly in his interest at the Parliamentary elections.

Patrons of Corporation Boroughs. From the time when seats in the House of Commons became generally in demand, the landed families who were fastening themselves on the boroughs, and who in later years were to become their patrons, thrust themselves into municipal politics and subsequently into the municipal corporations. Their concern in municipal politics was always their Parliamentary interest. The intrusion of outsiders into the municipal corporations was solely to this end. They were there only as the guardians of the electoral influence of the borough patrons[2].

Pernicious Effects on Municipal Life. Throughout the eighteenth century men of the landed classes were thus active in municipal politics, and they pushed themselves not only into the corporations in boroughs in which the corporations were in exclusive possession of the right to elect members to Parliament; but also into the corporations in those scot and lot and freeman boroughs in which the corporations had control

---

[1] Cf. *Municipal Corp. Comm. 1st Rep.*, p. 37.
[2] Cf. *Mirror of Parliament*, 1835, ii. 1249.

by their alliance with the inhabitants in whom the Parliamentary franchise was vested. The whole character and purpose of municipal corporations was altered, and altered for the worse, in nearly every borough in which the corporations possessed the right of election, or exercised it through influence over the local electorate. It is of the corporations in the period between the Revolution and the Reform Act, in the period of their most rampant rule, when they were permitted to make what by-laws they liked, and spend the borough revenues as they chose, that Professor Maitland writes, " There was a vicious circle. The corporation was untrusted because untrustworthy, untrustworthy because untrusted." "For what end then," Professor Maitland asks, after showing that the corporations were fulfilling none of the new duties that were to answer new urban needs, "did its property exist?" "For," he answers, "the election of the patron's nominee, and then for the common good of the corporators, and that may mean dinners or a division of the income or even of the lands among themselves [1]."

The boroughs in which the corporations had exclusive right of election have another claim on the student of the history of the English representative system. Dissenters from the Church of England were never incapacitated from being of the House of Commons, or from being freemen. The Test and Corporation Acts did not apply to members of Parliament; but they did apply to municipal corporations, and from nearly all of them dissenters were rigorously excluded. *Dissenters in Corporation Boroughs.*

Three years after the Parliamentary electoral system was reformed in 1832, these old borough corporations were also reformed. Their reform came quickly after the Act of 1832. It was largely due to the democratic movement which was developed by the Reform Act. But even had the reforming spirit not so soon reached the corporations which had for more than a century made a travesty of municipal government and so long affronted the people whom they were supposed to serve, the old municipal corporations could not have survived the downfall of the old representative system. They were bound up with this system. They were part of it. The two systems, the Parliamentary electoral system and the system of corporation misrule, were so interwoven, so interdependent, that after the *The End of the Corporations.*

---

[1] Maitland, *Township and Borough*, 95. Cf. *Municipal Corp. Comm. 1st Rep.*, p. 49.

electoral system had been remodelled, the old corporations, if left untouched by Parliament, must soon have toppled over of their own weight. Patrons no longer had any need of them. They no longer paid salaries to those resident members of the corporation who had hitherto locally safeguarded their Parliamentary interests. Outsiders were no longer desirous of being of the corporations. The mission of these outsiders, who for the most part had not the remotest interest in the real municipal life of the boroughs with which they had been officially and closely connected, was at an end as soon as these corporations could no longer of their own exclusive right, or through their influence with scot and lot voters, or with freemen, elect members to the House of Commons.

No more Advantages for Members.

Landed proprietors who were borough patrons, or borough patrons who were of the commercial classes, ceased to trouble themselves with offices within the municipal corporations after 1832. Bribes to members of the small corporations, which in amount sometimes reached a thousand guineas[1]; government patronage which from soon after the Revolution had gone increasingly to members of municipal corporations and to their sons and sons-in-law ; crown livings, clerkships in the State Departments in London, cadetships in the Navy and in the India service, and appointments under the Post Office and the Customs and Inland Revenue Boards,—this stream of good things, which patrons and members of the House of Commons who were supporters of the Government had directed to their corporations, was abruptly stopped. "The tumultuous and merry election ball," to quote Croker's description of the dance he had to attend after his election at Lord Dunstanville's nomination borough of Bodmin in 1820[2], was now a thing of the past. These balls were no doubt " at once tiresome and foolish," as Croker, who had a close connection with two other corporations in another part of the country[3], described the Bodmin ball. To Parliamentary candidates they must have been tedious and fatiguing ; but they added to the social distinction of the wives and daughters of members of the corporations, and attendance at them was part of the price that men in high official position, like Croker, had to pay for a seat in the unreformed House of Commons.

[1] At Malmesbury in 1722 ; *H. of C. Journals*, xx. 78.
[2] Croker, *Papers*, i. 152, 153.
[3] *Mirror of Parliament*, 1835, ii. 1249.

Bribery did not disappear with the old electoral system. It was as rampant at Stafford at the first election after the Reform Act, as it had been in any of the four boroughs which for their deep-seated corruption were thrown into the hundreds between 1770 and 1832. At the Stafford election, out of 1049 voters, 852 were bribed[1], and the electoral condition was so bad that the early eighteenth century remedy of withholding writs was applied to the borough; and in the session of 1835 a bill was introduced for its disfranchisement[2]. But while bribery continued under the new electoral system, and the evil was not completely eradicated until after the passing of the Corrupt Practices Act of 1883, there were no longer, after 1832, the heavy bribes, douceurs which went into hundreds of pounds, to the members of municipal corporations. Every advantage, except that of dividing among themselves the municipal revenues and the municipal lands, disappeared after the corporations were deprived of their exclusive right to elect members to the House of Commons, or of their great influence in bringing about these elections; and if Parliament in 1835 had passed an Act merely depriving the corporations of the right to do what they liked with what they regarded as their own, instead of sweeping two hundred corporations out of existence, the end would not have been long in coming. Divorced from their old place in the Parliamentary electoral system, the cohesion of the municipal oligarchies was gone. The corporations had taken on all the exclusiveness, all the utter disregard of the real purpose for which they existed—they had taken on all the worst features which marked the last century and a half of their history, from their close and interested connection with the election of members of the House of Commons. They were held together chiefly by the gain of this connection; and the reform of the House of Commons, which abruptly cut them out of the electoral system, left them lower than ever in local esteem, stranded or derelict, and totally unable to withstand even a much less violent storm than that which overtook them and to which they gracelessly succumbed in 1835.

[1] *Mirror of Parliament,* 1835, ii. 1932.
[2] *Mirror of Parliament,* 1835, i. 937.

(4)   *Freeman   Boroughs.*

Warping of
the Freeman
Franchise.

The freeman boroughs have been placed last in the grouping of the old English boroughs which has been here adopted, because in so many of them the Parliamentary franchise on the eve of the Reform Act was more remote than in any of the other three groups of boroughs from the franchise which existed when the House of Commons of the thirteenth and fourteenth centuries was elected—a franchise which could be exercised by any freeman who was a householder, who obeyed the curfew bell, did watch and ward, and bore the other burdens of municipal life.   Burgages had a close connection with this early Parliamentary franchise, for each burgage may be taken to have represented a home, an occupied house within a borough[1]. It is not difficult to trace how corporations drew to themselves the exclusive right of electing members to the House of Commons, when the franchise was still unprized and few men were desirous of being of the Parliament.   But only the exigencies of the control and management of Parliamentary elections, such as confronted borough managers from the closing years of the Tudor regime, could account for the extraordinary and utterly unconstitutional position in which the electoral franchise stood in the freeman boroughs, when Parliament at last seriously turned its attention to the reform of the representative system in 1832.

Extensions
and Re-
strictions of
the Fran-
chise.

In thirty-eight boroughs in which hosts of honorary and non-resident freemen were permitted to vote at Parliamentary elections, this wide difference between the early borough franchise and the franchises in the freeman boroughs in 1832 was especially marked.   Even in some of the freeman boroughs in which the residential qualification survived to the last, or in which electors had to pay scot and lot, or poor or church rates, there had been departures from the early borough franchise.   These were due to local usages which, with the appreciation of the Parliamentary vote, had gradually come into existence, and which restricted the number of freemen, thus withholding the franchise from all the inhabitant householders who could not comply with them.   A restriction of this kind, which was typical of those in other freeman boroughs, existed at Carlisle.   It excluded to the

[1] Cf. Merewether and Stephens, *Hist. of Boroughs*, II. 830; Bacon, *Annalls of Ipswiche*, 146.

last inhabitants who were not of the trade guilds[1]. In the
eighteenth century, and as long as the old electoral system
continued, clergymen, lawyers, doctors and bankers were excluded
from the franchise, because they were not of the guilds; and
none of these inhabitants could vote at the elections at Carlisle,
unless they managed to ally themselves with the oligarchy in
control, and were made honorary members of the trade guilds,
and through this avenue obtained the right to the franchise.
In London, and in many other freeman boroughs, the usage was
the same. Only through the trade guilds, or by their special
favour, could men obtain the Parliamentary franchise in the
cities and boroughs in which the right of election was in the
freemen, and in which the corporations did not possess entire
power over the creation of freemen.

These usages,—which dissevered a man unless he were a Freemen.
freeman from any recognized share in the municipal life of
the town in which he lived, and which denied him trading,
educational, and other local privileges of more immediate value
than a participation in local politics,—became general in the
boroughs after the word ' freeman ' had ceased to be used to mark
the difference in social status of bond and free, between villeins
and those who had lived free a year and a day in a borough,
and thereafter owned no man as their lord. The term freeman
as it was used in the last two centuries of the unreformed
representative system, as distinguished from its medieval signification, dates from long after serfdom had entirely disappeared
from English social life; for until the early years of the seventeenth century so far from there being any restrictions to limit
the number of freemen, men were compelled by municipal ordinances to assume the freedom and the municipal obligations
which went with it[2]. But by this time the appellation of freeman
was becoming more connected with trade, more special to the
men who were of the trade guilds, as distinct from men who
owned no lord, and the general term ' inhabitants,' which entirely
overlooked the distinction of bond and free, was coming into
use[3]. These were the freemen whose claims to the exclusive
possession of the electoral franchise, or sometimes to a share

[1] Cf. Lonsdale, *Life of John Heysham, M.D.*, 26; *H. of C. Journals*, xvii.
107.

[2] Cf. Ipswich, *Ordinance of* 1608; Bacon, *Annalls of Ipswiche*, 433.

[3] Cf. Merewether and Stephens, *Hist. of Boroughs*, iii. 1554.

with a corporation in the right of electing members to Parliament, now began to occupy the attention of committees of privilege or of the House itself. These were the freemen, the men of the trade guilds, who in so many boroughs from the later days of the Tudor sovereigns were in attendance at guildhall to elect the mayor and aldermen, as well as the representatives of the borough to the House of Commons; and it was these men who in some of the boroughs wrested the right of election of members of Parliament from the municipal corporations.

Honorary Freemen.

In the first two or three decades of the seventeenth century the freeman voters may be taken to have adequately represented the constituencies in which they exercised the Parliamentary franchise; to have been nearly as representative of the inhabitants of the freeman boroughs, as the scot and lot voters or the potwalloper voters were of the boroughs in which the Parliamentary franchise was based on these popular qualifications. It was only when seats in the House of Commons became generally in demand that there would be any political reasons for restricting the number of freemen entitled to vote at Parliamentary elections. As soon, however, as that demand became general, as soon as Parliamentary candidates were willing to bribe freemen to vote, two changes took place in the freeman boroughs. In some of the boroughs the corporations began to manœuvre to keep down the number of freemen; and in other boroughs there was begun the practice of making honorary freemen, a practice which, before the eighteenth century was far advanced, had been extended to many of the boroughs in which members of the House of Commons were chosen wholly or partly by freeman electors.

Members made Freemen.

The earliest of the non-resident freemen were outsiders who represented the freeman boroughs in Parliament. These men were made freemen either to comply with the old law which directed that members should be of the constituencies they represented, or to comply with local ordinances and usages[1], established after seats were in demand, which decreed that only freemen should represent the borough in Parliament. This custom of making non-residents freemen had certainly begun as early as the reign of James I; for at Rye in 1624, Sir Edward Conway and John Angell were chosen to represent the port, and with the intimation to them of their choice there went a request " to

[1] Cf. Norwich, 1640, *H. of C. Journals*, xv. 55, 56; Barnstaple, 1685, *Pinecoffin MSS., Hist. MSS. Comm. 5th Rep.*, App., 371.

come down to be sworn in as freemen and to receive requisite information" on what was to be done in Parliament for the benefit of the constituency[1].

In 1640 there was an instance of this kind, a case in which an outsider was made a freeman in order that he might represent a borough in Parliament, which in its results had a memorable effect on the course of English history in the seventeenth century. Early in 1640 Cromwell was again contemplating entering the House of Commons; this time as one of the members for the borough of Cambridge. He had already been of the House as member for the borough of Huntingdon; and at the time it was suggested to him that he should become a candidate for Cambridge, he was living at Ely. There was a difficulty in the way of his standing for Cambridge in that he was not a freeman of that borough. This objection was surmounted by the mayor bestowing on him the freedom. Cromwell was made a freeman " gratis, on the payment of one penny for the poor "; and on the 25th of March he was elected to the first Parliament of 1640[2]. Cromwell made a Freeman of Cambridge.

After an end had been temporarily made to the House of Lords in 1649, the Earl of Salisbury was similarly made a freeman at King's Lynn[3]. He was elected to the Parliament of the Commonwealth, and served as member for King's Lynn until 1654, when he became member for the County of Hertford[4]. Salisbury was the first non-resident to represent King's Lynn in the House of Commons, and one of the earliest unpaid members for that borough[5]. Another Instance.

From the Restoration such bestowals of the freedom as that on Cromwell at Cambridge, and on the Earl of Salisbury at King's Lynn, became frequent; and with the increasing pressure from candidates on borough constituencies, corporations in freeman boroughs began more generally to pass ordinances decreeing that none but freemen should represent them in the House of Commons. With pressure from candidates, these bestowals of the freedom ceased to be made in good faith. They ceased to be made with a view to securing eligible candidates, and were often made solely for the purpose of extorting tribute; for it was the rule in most boroughs Payments for the Freedom.

---

[1] *Cal. State Papers*, 1623–25, p. 152.

[2] Cf. Sandford, *Studies and Illustrations of the Great Rebellion*, 267.

[3] Doyle, *Official Baronage*, III. 250.

[4] Doyle, *Official Baronage*, III. 250.

[5] *Archaeologia*, XXIV. 327.

that until this tribute had been paid, a candidate was not to be permitted even to try his fortunes at the polls.

Aristocratic Freemen.

At the time boroughs were thus making freemen of outsiders who desired to represent them in the House of Commons, they were also making two other innovations in connection with the freedom. They were using their power to confer the freedom on men who desired to become patrons of the boroughs in order to nominate their Parliamentary representatives ; and also on men who desired to be freemen to help patrons to secure control, and whose only interest in the boroughs centred in the Parliamentary elections. The first of these two classes of outsiders, who were now being made honorary freemen, were men of territorial families. In boroughs in which the corporations exercised the exclusive right of election, as distinct from the boroughs in which the corporations exercised control through their influence with the freemen, these men became of the municipal oligarchies, and held the office of mayor or recorder, in order to guard their Parliamentary interests. In the reign of Charles I men of the landed classes, men who in many cases were already of the peerage, were being made honorary freemen in order that they might have a part in municipal politics, so far as such politics had any direct connection with the representative system, and thereby be enabled from inside the corporations, to advance and safeguard the claims they were now making, claims which in this reign were being generally conceded, to nominate members of the House of Commons.

Freemen at Worcester.

In 1639 Lord Windsor, whose family had long been established at Hewell Grange, near Worcester, was made an honorary freeman of this city, under circumstances which suggest that his interest in the city was Parliamentary, as distinct from municipal. Lord Windsor was evidently desirous of becoming a freeman, for " he promised upon his honour not to claim exemption of toll, and to pay like a foreigner "; and from the time he was admitted on these terms, honorary freemen continued to be admitted and to vote at Parliamentary elections at Worcester for more than a century. In 1746, with a view to an election which took place in 1747, one hundred freemen were made at Worcester. This election was controverted, and the House of Commons, acting in a different spirit from the House which in 1701 upheld the right of honorary freemen at Hertford[1], set

[1] *H. of C. Journals,* XIII. 709.

aside the right of the honorary freemen at Worcester[1]. But until the end of the old representative system, outvoters resident in London, Birmingham, Kidderminster and other places, freemen who had left Worcester, were carried there at the expense of Parliamentary candidates to vote at elections.

These non-resident freemen were a distinct class from honorary freemen. They were men who had complied with the conditions necessary to the freedom of Worcester, who had obtained the freedom by birth, by servitude, or by redemption ; men who had once had a local connection with the city, but who had moved away after admission to the freedom. By their removal they did not lose their right to the franchise, as Worcester was one of the boroughs in which the only qualification for voting was the negative one that the freeman had not been in receipt of alms. The determination of the House of Commons of 1748 was special to Worcester. In other freeman boroughs honorary freemen continued to exercise the Parliamentary franchise until 1832 ; and in most of the freeman boroughs in which there was not a residential or a scot and lot paying qualification, there were to the end of the old freeman franchises two classes of non-resident voters. These were the honorary freemen, who need never have had, as was the case with most of them, any connection with the boroughs, other than that of voting at Parliamentary elections, and non-resident freemen who had had a local connection, but who, for trade or other reasons, had left the city, and had ceased to have any connection with it except at election times. Then they were sought out in London, in Birmingham, or elsewhere, and carried to their old home to exercise the Parliamentary franchise. So many freemen had drifted to London, that in the closing years of the old electoral system a Parliamentary candidate would call a meeting there of the freemen of the constituency he was about to contest, to canvass for their votes, and arrange for their conveyance to the constituency[2]. Rival candidates occasionally came to an agreement to refrain from bringing in at their expense the non-resident freemen[3].

After the Restoration the making of honorary freemen was the most general method by which corporations, usually working in the

[margin note: Non-resident Freemen.]

[margin note: At Dunwich.]

[1] Cf. Charles Gray, *Parliamentary Notebook, Hist. MSS. Comm. 14th Rep.,* App., pt. IX. 311, 312.

[2] Cf. *Dict. Nat. Bio.,* LXI. 208; Colchester, *Diary,* I. 62.

[3] Cf. Cromwell, *Hist. of Colchester,* 292.

interests of patrons, secured the control of Parliamentary elections.
In 1670 five hundred non-resident freemen were made at Dunwich[1],
a Suffolk borough which had almost as remarkable a place in the
old representative system as the more notorious boroughs of Gatton
and Old Sarum.   Like Old Sarum, Dunwich had once been the
seat of a Bishop's see.   In the reign of Henry II it was described
by William of Newburgh as a wealthy and famous seaport[2].   But
in 1670, when five hundred honorary freemen were made there,
there were only forty resident in Dunwich[3], as for centuries past
the German Ocean had been encroaching on this part of the
Suffolk coast.   In the eighteenth and nineteenth centuries the
encroachments of the ocean were still going on; and in 1816
Oldfield described Dunwich as consisting of only forty-two houses
and half a church; and suggested that the encroachment would
probably in a few years oblige the constituent body to betake itself
to a boat whenever the King's writ summoned it to the exercise of
the electoral franchise[4].

Other
Instances.
    At Grantham, in 1685, there is good reason for believing
that freemen were being made in the interest of the Earl of
Rutland's control of the borough[5].   On the eve of the election
of the first Parliament of James II, the mayor and aldermen
of Hertford " did arbitrarily make great numbers of persons
who were neither inhabitants of the said borough or parishes "
freemen or free burgesses, who polled at that election and again
for the first Parliament of William and Mary[6].   Before the
Revolution honorary freemen were voting at East Grinstead[7].   At
Colchester, in 1706, two days before an election, the mayor
" without the consent of the common council made one hundred
foreigners free, and swore them in the night time in alehouses and
taverns without the town clerk, who ought to swear them publicly
in the town hall[8]."   At Carlisle the practice of making freemen to
carry elections, which was continued in that city until the end of
the old electoral system, had begun as early as 1711[9].   In 1727
outsiders were pressing in at King's Lynn[10].   In 1773 three

[1] Stephens, *Intro. to De Lolme*, I. 481.   [2] Lewis, II. 87.
[3] Stephens, *Intro. to De Lolme*, I. 481.   [4] Oldfield, IV. 561, 562.
[5] Cf. *Hist. MSS. Comm. 12th Rep.*, App., pt. v. 87.
[6] *H. of C. Journals*, XIII. 655.
[7] *H. of C. Journals*, XIII. 493.
[8] *H. of C. Journals*, XVI. 470.
[9] Merewether and Stephens, *Hist. of Boroughs*, III. 2132.
[10] Phillips, *Election Cases*, 351.

hundred and ninety-six freemen were made on the eve of an
election at Northampton, " the great majority of whom were utter
strangers to either the town or shire of Northampton[1]"; and in
1734 five hundred freemen were made at Liverpool in order to
constitute it a court borough[2].

These practices so begun, except for isolated checks like that at A Check to the making of Freemen.
Worcester in 1748, went on without any interference from Parlia-
ment until 1763; and until that time in many boroughs, scores,
sometimes hundreds, of honorary freemen were often made on the
eve of an election; some of them after the writs for a new Parliament or for a by-election were out.   At an election for the City of
Durham in 1762 two hundred and fifteen freemen, most of them
non-residents, were so made, all after the date of the teste of the
writ[3].   The election was disputed, and the resident freemen petitioned against this wholesale invasion of their rights.   The House
of Commons was in a virtuous mood, like that of 1748, when it
denied the right of the honorary freemen to vote at Worcester;
and the exposure of the practice of making non-resident freemen
at Durham led to the unseating of the member in whose interests
the freemen had been made; and between the 25th of February
and the 21st of March, 1763[4], a bill intended to check this abuse
passed all its stages in the House of Commons.   It was passed by
the House of Lords, and became a law which is as memorable in
the history of the old representative system as the Act of 1786,
which was the outcome of the loose interpretation of the determination of 1661, under which every tramp who was in town could,
until 1786, vote at an election in Preston.

By the Durham Act[5] the right to vote was withheld from The Durham Act.
honorary freemen who had been admitted within twelve months of
the first day of an election.   The right of the ordinary freemen,
those who were admitted by the custom of the borough, was not
interfered with; and to the last these freemen could be admitted at
any time previous to an election, and could take up their freedom
while an election at which they were to vote was proceeding.   As
admission to the freedom was, in the eighteenth and nineteenth
centuries, chiefly with a view to what the commissioners, who in

[1] Northampton, *Borough Records*, ii. 501.
[2] *Hist. MSS. Comm. 15th Rep.*, App., pt. vii. 122.
[3] *H. of C. Journals*, xxix. 332.
[4] *H. of C. Journals*, xxix. 500, 599.
[5] 3 Geo. III, c. 15.

1834–35 inquired into the conditions of the municipal corporations, described as "the lucrative exercise of the franchise," the admissions were abnormally swelled whenever a Parliamentary election was about to take place. At Bristol, in 1812, seventeen hundred and twenty freemen were admitted with a view to an election in the autumn of that year. At Malden, in 1826, one thousand freemen were admitted during an election; and that admission at election times or when elections were pending was general in all the freeman boroughs is conclusively shown by the statistics of freeman admissions, which were collected and compiled for presentation to Parliament while the Reform Bill of 1832 was pending[1]. The Act of 1763, which first went into effect at Bewdley in 1769[2], was one of the many half-measures which Parliament from this time began to pass for dealing with electoral irregularities and anomalies, and for punishing incorrigibly corrupt boroughs. The Act left undisturbed the right which many corporations had usurped, of making honorary freemen, and it left untouched the right of non-resident freemen to return after years of absence to vote at Parliamentary elections, a practice which was as much without any constitutional warrant, as was that of making honorary freemen by the corporation.

Honorary Freemen still made. After the Durham Act honorary freemen continued to be made in as large numbers as heretofore, but usually they were so made as to comply with the conditions now imposed. At Bedford, in 1769, where at this time there were only five hundred and forty householders, five hundred freemen were made, "most of them strangers and foreigners," who "never served any corporate office, nor exercised any trade, nor contributed to any rate"; but were made for the sole purpose of voting at elections for members of Parliament[3]. At Gloucester in 1779, five hundred and thirteen freemen were made in one day; a gross abuse of the power of the corporation which led to a petition from the citizens and burgesses of Gloucester, and to the introduction of a bill to check the abuse. The citizens of Gloucester in their petition asked for the exclusion of "all honorary freemen and others than such as are free by birth and servitude[4]." At Derby, a borough long controlled by the Cavendish family, largely by the aid of honorary freemen[5], in 1779,

---

[1] *Mirror of Parliament*, 1835, ii. 1474.
[2] *H. of C. Journals*, xxxii. 135.
[3] *H. of C. Journals*, xxxv. 315.
[4] *H. of C. Journals*, xxxvii. 391.
[5] *Mirror of Parliament*, 1835, ii. 1253.

four hundred and twenty-six freemen were similarly made for election purposes; and a complaint like that from Gloucester was lodged with the House of Commons[1].

But the corporations which exercised the right of making honorary freemen had nearly as many friends in Parliament as burgage boroughs, and boroughs in which the corporations were exclusively possessed of the right to elect members. In 1773 there was an abortive attempt to set up a residential qualification in all freeman boroughs[2]. In 1779, the year of the Gloucester petition, and growing out of it, a bill was introduced in the House of Commons to stop the making of honorary freemen. It was read a second time[3], but did not make any further progress. In 1780 there was a proposal that a stamp duty should be imposed when honorary freemen were made. This proposal was embodied in a bill which also went no further than second reading stage[4]. In 1787 there was a bill to prevent occasional freemen from voting at elections. This bill was, however, withdrawn[5]; and the Durham Act was the only one between 1763 and 1832, passed with the object of correcting the abuses which had become rooted in the freeman boroughs since the reign of Charles I; and to the last the outsitters, as the honorary and non-resident freemen were called, swamped the resident electors in many of the boroughs in which the freemen were in possession of the franchise.

Unsuccessful Attempts at Reform.

Until 1832 Parliamentary elections at Cambridge, one of the last boroughs to be invaded by outsitters, were controlled by the honorary freemen, who had first made their appearance in large numbers only in 1783[6]. At the general election which preceded the reform of 1832, two hundred and thirty-five out of the four hundred and twenty-six freemen who voted at Coventry were non-resident[7]. Out of five hundred freemen who polled at the same general election at Barnstaple, only two hundred and seventy-eight lived at Barnstaple, or within twenty miles of the borough[8]; while

Persistence of the Abuse.

---

[1] *H. of C. Journals*, xxxvii. 399, 407.

[2] *H. of C. Journals*, xxxiv. 202.

[3] *H. of C. Journals*, xxxvii. 407.

[4] *H. of C. Journals*, xxxvii. 624, 920.

[5] *H. of C. Journals*, xlii. 703.

[6] *H. of C. Journals*, xxxix. 176 ; Pryme, *Autobiographic Recollections*, 138, 139.

[7] Hansard, 3rd Series, i. 128.

[8] Gribble, *Hist. of Barnstaple*, 254.

at Colchester, where honorary freemen in large numbers were made as early as 1706[1], at the same general election in 1831 there were nine hundred of these outsitters[2].

Local Safe-guards to the Freeman Franchise.

Not all the freeman boroughs were swamped at Parliamentary elections by honorary or non-resident freemen. In twenty-four out of the sixty-two boroughs in which freemen exercised the Parliamentary franchise, there were either residential or rate-paying qualifications which usually excluded the honorary and non-resident freemen. In these boroughs the qualifications were due to usages which were in keeping with the conditions under which the franchise was exercised in the days before seats in the House of Commons were in demand; and in keeping also with the medieval usage by which, if a freeman were absent from his borough for a year and a day, he forfeited the privileges that went with the freedom. In some boroughs these qualifications had only usage to uphold them. In others the usages had come to have all the force of enactments, because they had been confirmed by determinations of the House of Commons in controverted election cases. In some of the boroughs the usages as to freemen had been embodied in local Acts of Parliament.

The Franchise at Lichfield.

Lichfield was a good example of a borough where outsitters were excluded by a last determination. In 1718 non-resident freemen voted there. The election, however, was disputed, and the member who had been returned sought to justify the votes of the non-resident freemen which had been polled in his favour. It was the usage at Lichfield at this time that freemen who voted at Parliamentary elections must have paid scot and lot. The outside freemen had not paid scot and lot; but to make good their votes, the plea was advanced that they had paid scot and lot in the places in which they were living. The House of Commons refused to accept this plea. The committee which heard the case came to the determination that the right was in the bailiffs, the magistrates, the forty-shilling freeholders, in all that held by burgage tenure, and "in such freemen only of the said city as are enrolled, paying scot and lot there[3]." After this determination the sitting member waived his election; and although from 1718 to 1832 Lichfield had the most composite electorate of any borough returning

[1] *H. of C. Journals*, xvi. 470.
[2] Hansard, 3rd Series, iv. 962.
[3] *H. of C. Journals*, xix. 35.

members to the House of Commons, it was not sufficiently comprehensive to admit of the exercise of the franchise by freemen who
had ceased their connection with the city.

The City of London was a good example of a freeman constituency in which some of the old democratic conditions of the
early franchise were preserved intact by an Act of Parliament. By
an Act of 1724[1], an Act which, unfortunately for the reputation
and the more wholesome social life of the freeman boroughs, was
special to the City of London, no freeman could vote who had
received alms; nor could he vote, unless he swore before he polled
that he had been a freeman for twelve calendar months. The
freeman usages at Coventry were confirmed by a last determination
of the House of Commons in 1722[2], and by an Act of Parliament
in 1781. Under these measures, both of equal importance as
regards their statutory value, the franchise was in such freemen as
had served seven years' apprenticeship to one and the same trade,
and did not receive alms or weekly charity. The Coventry Act of
1781 further strengthened the determination of 1722 by the
declaration that none were to be admitted freemen without pro-
ducing their deeds of apprenticeship[3]. The Coventry usages and
the subsequent enactments protected the borough from the inroads
of honorary freemen; but did not, as has been shown by the
election figures for 1831, protect the constituency against the
practice of freemen, who had left the borough, swamping the
resident freemen at elections.

One of the most remarkable usages connected with freeman
boroughs, perpetuated by an Act of Parliament, was at Norwich,
where from 1730[4] it was legal for the representatives of the
returning officer to go into the city jail to take the votes of
freeman prisoners. It did not need the authority of an Act of
Parliament to secure to freemen, who happened to be in jail
at the time of an election, opportunities to vote. If the freemen, thus unable to be at large, could be counted upon by the
corporation and the magistrates who were associated with the
corporation in the Parliamentary control of the borough, they were
parolled to vote. As late as 1816 two of the magistrates of
Carlisle, one a doctor of divinity and the other of medicine, both
active partisans in the Lowther interest, "permitted a felon to

(marginal notes) London and Coventry.

Freemen voting from Jail.

---

[1] 11 Geo. I, c. 18.
[2] *H. of C. Journals*, xx. 60.
[3] 21 Geo. III, c. 54.
[4] 3 Geo. II, c. 8.

come out of Carlisle jail, to give his vote in favour of a Lowther candidate against the renowned Whig, John Christian Curwen[1]." Similar usages must have existed in other freeman boroughs; for when the Municipal Reform Act of 1835 was before the House of Commons, and the Tory Opposition was seeking to secure to the freemen their old right to the municipal franchise, Sir John Campbell, Attorney-General of the Melbourne Administration, objected. He urged that " in various places the majority of the freemen pay no rates, have no property, do not pay scot or bear lot." " Some instances there are," Campbell added, " of freemen having no home except the common jail, in which they pass the greater part of the year, and from which they are withdrawn on the approach of a contested election, municipal or Parliamentary, for the purposes of giving their votes for a bribe[2]."

Corporations and the Freeman Franchise.
The freeman boroughs which were controlled by corporations can be divided into two groups. In the first were the boroughs in which corporations made freemen wholesale. In the second were the boroughs in which corporations restricted the number of freemen, and had been so restricting the number from the time members of the municipal bodies found it to their advantage to turn over a borough to a patron, or to market its Parliamentary representation without the intervention of a patron.

Oxford and Cambridge.
Professor Maitland, in summing up his story of the decline and fall of the old municipal corporations, a story which he characterises as " curious, if not disgraceful," describes the condition of the boroughs of Oxford and Cambridge in the decades which preceded the Municipal Reform Act of 1835. " The constitutions of Oxford and Cambridge," he writes, " were closely similar on paper. They went to the bad in different ways. The freemen of Oxford were numerous; the freemen of Cambridge few. Too many of the Oxford corporators lived in the workhouse; too many of the Cambridge corporators lived near Cheveley. It is of beer and mob rule that we read in the one town; in the other of oligarchy and wine—' excellent wine,' said an unregenerate alderman, ' and plenty of it[3].' "

Cambridge Freemen.
Cambridge was one of the freeman boroughs in which the outsitter had a dominating influence; but the outsitter came in only during the last half-century of the unreformed House of

---

[1] Lonsdale, *Life of John Heysham, M.D.*, 99.
[2] *Mirror of Parliament*, 1835, II. 1502.
[3] Maitland, *Township and Borough*, 95.

Commons. An outsider had been brought in as early as Cromwell's time[1], and honorary freemen were made there in the reigns of Charles II and James II[2]. These, however, seem to have been exceptional instances; and at Cambridge, outsitters never swarmed in as they did for more than a century at Colchester, or at Carlisle. There was none of the squalid electioneering at Cambridge which marked electioneering at Norwich or Liverpool. During the greater part of the time when outsitters were dominating Parliamentary elections at Cambridge, the borough was managed by a local banker named Mortlake, first in the interest of the Duke of Portland; later in that of the Duke of Rutland. This Cambridge borough manager had no sympathy with the kind of electioneering which necessitated the making of freemen in alehouses and from among alehouse frequenters. Fox, who was a freeman of Cambridge, was one of his creations[3]; and Mortlake kept his honorary freemen down to such a manageable number, seldom more than eighty, and these mostly chosen from the tenants and friends of the Duke of Rutland[4], that he was not driven to the necessity of conferring the freedom on men who were so needy that they had to be carried to the elections at the expense of the candidates, and paid in one form or another, but always paid, for the trouble they took in going to vote. Cambridge was not of the freeman boroughs in which men were taken out of jail to vote, and in which the alehouses at election times were thronged with outsitters.

Oxford and Cambridge, as characterised by Professor Maitland, Withholding may be taken as typical of the freeman boroughs in which the Freedoms. corporations had control through the outsitters, and of the boroughs in which the corporations controlled the representation by reducing the electorate. On the eve of the Reform Act the electors in the freeman boroughs varied in number from six at Rye and fourteen at Dunwich—where the seventeenth century method of swamping the constituency by large creations of outside freemen had long been abandoned in favour of quieter and more certain methods of control—to six thousand at Bristol and twelve thousand in the City of London. When the freemen were few the corporations retained control by keeping the electorate stationary in numbers or by reducing it; and the most common method of keeping it stationary

[1] Sandford, *Great Rebellion*, 267.
[2] *H. of C. Journals*, xvi. 300, 301.
[3] Oldfield, iii. 126.
[4] Pryme, *Recollections*, 139.

was by throwing obstacles in the way of men who, by birth or servitude, were entitled by the custom of the borough to their freedom. This method of securing control seems to have been adopted later than the plan of making honorary freemen, which was in frequent use soon after the Restoration. It does not seem possible to find traces of the restrictive method of freeman borough control earlier than the close of the seventeenth century. It was in use in 1698 at Ludlow[1], and at East Retford in 1701[2].

Instances.

At Ludlow the right of election in 1698 was in the municipal body, and in the resident common burgesses; in other words in the freemen; and the sons of burgesses and men who married the daughters of burgesses had a right to the freedom. In accordance with a by-law made in 1663 the burgess-right was conferred on demand by petition, a petition which the claimant had to lodge with the head bailiff, who submitted it to the corporation, in which body a majority of nineteen was necessary on the motion to confer the burgess-ship. Until the time of James II these petitions were seldom refused; but in 1698, as a witness informed an election committee, " there was about three-score pocketed, and not presented by the head bailiff[3]." Petitions for the freedom were being similarly treated by the bailiffs at East Retford in 1701[4]. At Plympton, where there were only about forty freemen in the last twenty years of the borough[5], the magistrates began as early as 1702 to refuse the freedom to freemen's sons, because they would not vote as desired[6]; and at Launceston, about the same time, the members of the corporation took upon themselves to refuse " all but their own party, and to swear those they admitted never to be against the mayor and corporation[7]." At Hastings, in 1708, there is on record an agreement between the mayor and jurats and the justices of the peace that " only two freemen be made in each year, the one nominated by the mayor, and the other by the majority of the bench[8]."

The Legal
Remedy.

Men from whom the freedom was withheld in this way might have appealed to the courts. They might have obtained a mandamus

[1] *H. of C. Journals*, xii. 537.
[2] *H. of C. Journals*, xiii. 494.
[3] *H. of C. Journals*, xii. 537.
[4] *H. of C. Journals*, xiii. 494.
[5] Oldfield, iii. 324.
[6] *H. of C. Journals*, xiv. 149.
[7] Merewether and Stephens, *Hist. of Boroughs*, iii. 2007.
[8] *Hist. MSS. Comm. 13th Rep.*, App., pt. iv. 363.

compelling compliance with the custom and usage of the borough[1]. But this remedy was hopelessly out of reach of the men who were denied their freedom; and although much the same procedure as that at Ludlow, East Retford, Plympton, Launceston, and Hastings was adopted in other freeman boroughs as the eighteenth century went on, there are few recorded cases in which the law courts were appealed to for intervention.

Where the number of freemen was small, much pressure could be put by corporations on men whom it was not possible to manœuvre out of the franchise. Corporations could threaten men, who were indisposed to vote in their interest, with impressment for the naval or the military forces. Threats of a similar kind, threats to press the servants and carts of voters acting contrary to the wishes of the bailiff of East Grinstead, were used as early as 1640[2]. East Grinstead was a burgage borough. But what was possible on the part of a municipal oligarchy in a burgage borough, was just as possible in a freeman borough; and at Okehampton, which was a freeman borough, a case occurred in which, in 1705, a man was forced into the army, and offered his discharge if he would vote for Sir Simon Leach, who subsequently represented the borough in the House of Commons[3]. At this time, and throughout the eighteenth century, a man who was a voter, a freeholder in a county, a freeman, or a voter on any other franchise in a borough, had statutory protection against impressment for the army[4]. But this protection was not invariably a safeguard against threats, for corporations which were sufficiently daring to keep men out of municipal privileges to which they were entitled by birth or servitude, would not hesitate to take the small and uncertain risk of treating a voter as the freeman of Okehampton was treated in 1705 to secure his vote for Sir Simon Leach.

Pressure on Freemen Voters.

In the smaller as well as in the larger freeman boroughs, and in fact in most of the boroughs in which corporations were seeking or maintaining control of Parliamentary elections, the corporations usually had it in their power to use the local charities to buttress their electoral influence. Charities were so used at Shrewsbury as early as 1707[5]. At Guildford, in 1710, money,

Charities and Electioneering.

---

[1] In 1772, by 12 Geo. III, c. 21, the common law was reinforced by a statute making procedure easier and giving costs to a successful plaintiff.

[2] *H. of C. Journals,* II. 10.   [3] *H. of C. Journals,* XV. 73.

[4] 2 and 3 Anne, c. 13; 18 Geo. III, c. 53.

[5] *H. of C. Journals,* XVI. 248.

which was intended for charitable purposes, was being diverted to electioneering[1]; and the practice, which can be traced back to these years, and which probably existed at an earlier period, did not come to an end even after the Reform Act of 1832.

The Use of Patronage.

Another source of influence, long used by corporations in the larger and smaller freeman boroughs, was municipal and government patronage. At Carlisle, in 1786, the corporation officials, from the recorder and town clerk down to the sword-bearers, bellmen and scavengers, were all voters[2]. It was much the same in the smaller freeman boroughs; and in these boroughs, especially in those on the coast, the customs house officers, and the men engaged in the preventive service and in the collection of excise, owed their appointments to local borough managers, who had the disposal of this patronage placed in their hands, either by borough patrons or by borough members who had influence with the Government.

Disfranchisement of Officeholders.

As early as 1694 there was a statute making liable to a penalty of one hundred pounds any collector of excise who should by "word, message, or writing, or in any manner whatsoever, endeavour to persuade any elector to give, or to dissuade any elector from giving, his vote for choice of any person" to be of the House of Commons[3]. In 1710 there was a similar enactment[4] with respect to postmasters; but neither of these statutes disfranchised any officials in the excise or post office departments. Dowdeswell sought to pass an Act disfranchising them in 1770[5]; but men continued to be appointed to places in the excise, the customs, and the post office, as rewards for services at elections, and office-holders continued to vote at elections, until the Act of 1782[6]—passed by the Rockingham Administration at the instance of Crewe, who had taken up Dowdeswell's mission of reform—disqualified voters who held offices in the customs, the excise, and the post office. How generally these offices were then held by voters is shown by Lord Rockingham's statement that seventy elections depended chiefly on such votes, and that eleven thousand five hundred officers of customs and excise were electors[7].

---

[1] *H. of C. Journals*, xvi. 477.

[2] Ferguson, *Cumberland and Westmorland Members of Parliament*, 202.

[3] 5 and 6 W. and Mary, c. 20.

[4] 9 Anne, c. 5.

[5] *Parl. Hist.*, xvi. 834.

[6] 22 Geo. III, c. 41.

[7] *Parl. Hist.*, xxii. 95.

In one Cornish borough, the mean fishing village of Bossiney, the list of voters was reduced by the Crewe Act to a single elector[1].

It was in boroughs of the Bossiney type that the elections to which Lord Rockingham referred were in the hands of customs and excise officers; for it was in these small boroughs, with no commerce and no industries, that so much of the patronage of the customs and excise boards passed through the hands of borough managers and was bestowed by them with a view to elections. Patronage continued to pass through these hands after the Act of 1782. Borough patrons and borough members still continued to dance attendance on the commissioners in London, who in the first instance had the bestowal of these offices, and they continued their attendance on these commissioners and on the patronage secretary of the Treasury as long as such constituencies as Bossiney and Queenborough were of the electorate. Queenborough was a Kentish borough, whose voters, prior to the Crewe Act, had enjoyed as large a part of the patronage of the Ordnance Department and the Admiralty, as those of Bossiney had enjoyed of the Customs Department. After the Act of 1782 much of the government patronage was put in trust for the freemen and the other voters in these Bossineys and Queenboroughs. Instead of offices being bestowed on freemen, or on members of the corporation who were electors, they were given to the sons and the sons-in-law of these voters; or freemen, to save their right to vote, which was sometimes as valuable to them as the pay attaching to a customs, an excise, or an admiralty appointment, would transfer their government offices to non-voters, who entered into agreements to pay them annuities[2]. Such practices for circumventing the Act of 1782 can be traced as late as 1803[3]; and there is reason for assuming that they survived as long as these freeman and corporation boroughs had a place in the representative system.

Much more tangible and permanent rewards fell to voters in small freeman boroughs than the bribes of a few guineas each and the alehouse treats which were the lot of the freemen in boroughs like Norwich and Carlisle. The possession of a vote in one of the small freeman boroughs, like membership of a municipal corporation in a town where the right of election

Indirect Use of Patronage.

Rewards to the Voters.

---

[1] Cf. Courtney, *Parliamentary Representation of Cornwall to 1832*, Preface, xix.

[2] Oldfield, v. 379.

[3] Peckwell, *Controverted Election Cases*, I. 397.

was exclusively in the corporation, was almost sufficient to put a man beyond the need of any other business than politics. Moreover the possession of a vote in these places carried with it provision for the sons and sons-in-law of the voters, in the shape of government offices, commissions in the navy, and not infrequently benefices in the Church[1]. In these boroughs the relations between the electors and the patrons or members, principally between electors and patrons, were much more close and individual than in the boroughs in which freemen were numbered by the thousand, and were brought to the polls from all parts of the kingdom. They were as close as the relations were between the patrons and voters in the corporation boroughs, and to these freeman boroughs Professor Maitland's description is as applicable as it was to Cambridge. "It is of beer and mob rule," to apply Professor Maitland's characterisation of Oxford to other freeman boroughs, "that we read" concerning the constituencies such as Norwich, Colchester, Liverpool and Carlisle; while it is "of oligarchy and wine, and plenty of it," that we read in boroughs such as Winchelsea, Rye and Dunwich, where the electors, for many years before the end came in 1832, were so few that they could have been gathered round a dining table when they met the patrons or the members for their boroughs.

Cost of Borough Control.

It was in these boroughs, where members and constituents could thus meet in the parlour of an inn, that elections were quietly and cheaply managed. All through the eighteenth century, any man who assumed the patronage of a borough had to be much on the alert, to submit to many personal inconveniences and annoyances, and to spend freely to maintain his influence. But in these smaller boroughs much could be done with the aid of government offices; and a thousand or two thousand pounds accomplished much in boroughs in which there were fewer than twenty freemen. It was in the freeman boroughs at the other end of the scale, those famed like Oxford for beer and mob rule, that eighteenth and early nineteenth century electioneering was so inordinately expensive. In 1790 Lord Penrhyn spent nearly thirty thousand pounds in unsuccessfully contesting Liverpool, at an election when nineteen hundred and sixty-seven freemen voted[2]; and at an election there forty years

---

[1] Cf. *Mirror of Parliament*, 1835, ii. 1249.

[2] Picton, *Memorials of Liverpool*, i. 231.

later, when the freemen had become much more numerous, eighty thousand pounds were expended, and two thousand and sixty freemen were bribed[1]. At Carlisle in 1820, Mr James, also an unsuccessful candidate, spent thirteen thousand pounds[2].

Next to a county in which territorial families, politically opposed, were fighting for supremacy and control, there were no election contests which involved more wear and tear on Parliamentary candidates and larger drafts on bank accounts than those in freeman boroughs in which electors were counted by the thousand. This was especially so when half of the freemen had to be carried from remote parts of the country to exercise a franchise for which there was no constitutional warrant, a franchise which would never have been theirs, after they had once removed from the town of which they enjoyed the freedom, had it not been for the exigencies which confronted borough patrons and men anxious to be of the House of Commons in the last forty years of the seventeenth century. *In Large Freeman Boroughs.*

Much of the warping of the representative system from the lines on which it was first drawn, much of the wide and deep-seated corruption of the borough constituencies has been erroneously dated from the unprecedented demand for seats in the House of Commons in the first two Parliaments of Charles II. But the warping of the representative system and electoral corruption were of a much earlier date than the Restoration. These evils only became deeper and more widespread after the Restoration, and as a result of the much enhanced value of a seat in the House of Commons; and the only new departures of significance in borough electioneering which marked the reigns of the last two Stuart sovereigns, were the wide extension of the practice of making honorary freemen, and the practice of permitting freemen who had long been absentees to return to vote at Parliamentary elections. The outsitter, whether an honorary or a non-resident freeman, was a memorial of the warping of municipal usages for the sake of the Parliamentary franchise, begun on a large scale after the Restoration; and the Parliamentary candidates, who in the closing decades of the old House of Commons had to spend thirteen thousand pounds at Carlisle and thirty thousand at Liverpool, could, had they only known it, have fixed the original responsibility for such large *Corruption at the Restoration.*

[1] *Mirror of Parliament*, 1835, ii. 1847.
[2] Bean, *Parl. Hist. Northern Counties*, 40.

outlays on electioneering on the borough managers and borough patrons of the time of Charles II and James II.

Women and the Freedom.   The position of women in the freeman boroughs has been touched upon in treating of the place of women in the burgage boroughs. Their connection with the Parliamentary franchise was more general, but less direct, in the freeman than in the burgage boroughs, in which the usage was to permit women to transfer, as often as they pleased and under the easiest conditions, the right, inherent in their burgages, to vote at Parliamentary elections. In the freeman boroughs marriage with a freeman's daughter, and in many of them marriage with the widow of a freeman, carried with it the right to the freedom, with which usually went the right to vote at Parliamentary elections. With respect to these rights which daughters and widows of freemen transmitted to their husbands, there was no usage which held good in all the boroughs. Local usage, oftentimes given the force of law by a last determination, governed each borough. At Dover the husband of a freeman's daughter was of the freedom by virtue of his marriage only while his wife was alive[1]; and at Hertford marriage with a freeman's eldest daughter transmitted the freedom to the husband only when the father-in-law had no son[2]. The usage was least restricted at Bristol[3], and at Grimsby[4], where marriage with a daughter of a freeman transmitted the right to the franchise.

Value of the Right to the Freedom.   These usages added to the social status and local consideration of the families of freemen. In many boroughs the right to transmit the freedom was practically a dower to a freeman's daughter, and conveyed to the new family the social status, local consideration, and in many boroughs the pecuniary gains from elections enjoyed by the family from which the bride was taken. " I have heard," wrote the town clerk of Bristol in 1889, "that in former days, when the advantages of a Parliamentary vote were tangible, the prospect of an election would bring hesitating or lagging swains to a sense of the desirability of prompt action[5]"; and there can be no doubt, in view of the money value attaching

---

[1] *H. of C. Journals*, xxxii. 780.   [2] Lewis, ii. 366.

[3] Lambert, "Parliamentary Franchises Past and Present," *Nineteenth Century*, Dec. 1889, 947.

[4] Lewis, ii. 264.

[5] Lambert, " Parliamentary Franchises Past and Present," *Nineteenth Century*, Dec. 1889, 948. Cf. *Municipal Corporations Comm. 1st Rep.*, pt. iv. 2440–2442.

to a freeman vote during the last one hundred years of the old representative system, that the traditions of Bristol recalled in 1889 by the town clerk, are well-founded. In boroughs where the freemen were counted only by the hundreds, the bribes to freemen were often sufficiently large to pay for the furnishing of a house.

From the early years of the eighteenth century, by which time freemen were obtaining large bribes for their votes, bribes which depended in amount on the number of freemen and the exigencies of each particular election, it became customary for Parliamentary candidates to give smaller douceurs to the wives and daughters of freemen. Early instances of this consideration on the part of Parliamentary candidates for women in freeman boroughs occurred at Malden in 1690[1], and at Winchelsea in 1711 ; in the latter borough at this time thirty pounds were paid for freemen's votes[2]. *[margin: Bribes to Freemen's Wives and Daughters.]*

Long before the reform of 1832 freemen's wives, widows and daughters had come to appreciate their right almost as highly as though it had been the right to vote ; and when the second reform bill was before Parliament, the House of Lords, which was then defending the assailed freemen, was petitioned by the wives and daughters of the freemen of Great Grimsby, that their rights and those of their children and their future husbands, might be preserved to them[3]. Again in 1835, when the municipal corporations were being reformed by Parliament, and the Opposition in the House of Commons, led by Sir Robert Peel and Sir William Follett, was making its last stand for the freemen, there was an effort also to save the rights of the daughters of freemen[4]. These rights had not been interfered with by the Act of 1832. Then the House of Lords was sufficiently powerful to safeguard at least the resident freemen from the disfranchisement at first proposed by the Grey Administration ; and with the rights of the resident freemen there were preserved the rights of the widows and daughters of freemen. But in 1835, when municipal corporations lost the power of making freemen, a power which was not restored to them until 1885, and then only under conditions which protected both the *[margin: Efforts to preserve the Rights of Women.]*

---

[1] *H. of C. Journals*, xi. 63.
[2] Oldfield, v. 413.
[3] *Mirror of Parliament*, 1831, iii. 197.
[4] *Mirror of Parliament*, 1835, ii. 1547.

municipal and Parliamentary franchises[1], the political privileges in connection with both the Parliamentary and the municipal franchise, which women had so long enjoyed in most of the freeman boroughs, disappeared altogether[2].

Electioneering and Municipal Life.

In the boroughs in which the exclusive right of election was in the corporations, municipal business for generations before 1832 had been subordinated to the management and control of Parliamentary elections. It was the desire to take part in these elections and to share in the gains directly and indirectly accruing from them, that impelled local men to become of the corporations. When outsiders became of these oligarchies, they went in avowedly with a view to political control, and without the least regard for the municipal welfare of the borough. In the freeman boroughs, from the time when these boroughs began to play an important part in the electoral system, the time when the outsitters were dominating the elections, municipal business also became subordinate to Parliamentary electioneering[3]. This was particularly the case in those boroughs in which the corporations made honorary freemen; for, with the majority of the corporation ready to support the making of freemen, the elections to the House of Commons were in the hands of the corporations almost as completely as they were in the boroughs in which the electoral right was vested in the corporations. In such constituencies the borough patrons were usually active in municipal politics; as their hold on the boroughs lay in their ability to keep a majority in the municipal councils when honorary freemen were to be made. In the freeman boroughs, whether of the Winchelsea and Oxford type, or of the Norwich and Carlisle type, it was essential to the borough patron that the mayor should be on his side; for the mayor, or the head bailiff where there was no mayor, was the returning officer. He received and returned the writs or the precepts, and he was in a position of exceptional power at election times.

The Aristocracy in Municipal Politics.

From the Restoration to 1832 members of the landed aristocracy, barons, viscounts, marquises, earls and dukes, were more actively concerned in English municipal politics than at any period before or since. Their activity was not disinterested. It

---

[1] 48 and 49 Vict., c. 29.

[2] 5 and 6 W. IV, c. 76.

[3] Cf. *Municipal Corporations Comm. 1st Rep.*, 34.

had no altruistic motive; for in most instances in which a peer or a commoner of landed family was of a municipal corporation, his association with it grew chiefly out of his Parliamentary interest in the borough[1].

In the early years of the period which intervened between the Restoration and the Reform Act of 1832, and in some places even earlier than the Restoration, members of landed families went into municipal government in order to insinuate themselves into the Parliamentary control of the boroughs. In the second half of this period, they were of the municipal corporations to safeguard what they had come to regard as their own. They were there to protect their power of nominating the members for the boroughs of which they were patrons, a power frequently transmitted to them by their predecessors in the peerage; and by 1832 they had enjoyed this power so long, and had been so indisputably in possession of it, that when the representative system was remodelled there was a feeling on the part of William IV[2], that the least the Government could do was to follow the Irish precedent and make liberal compensation to patrons whose hold on the boroughs was now to be loosened, if not entirely shaken off. This feeling was shared by many of the borough patrons, and by their partisans in Parliament and in the press[3]; and that borough owners should be ·compensated was an opinion held by Lord North as far back in the history of the movement for Parliamentary reform as 1776, when Wilkes urged the enfranchisement of Manchester, Leeds, Sheffield and Birmingham.

The Right of Borough Patrons.

In freeman boroughs with large electorates the corporations drew on the municipal treasuries[4], mortgaged borough property[5], and used their other varied powers to secure the control of Parliamentary elections. Although these elections ordinarily came only once in five or six years, the Parliamentary contests were usually uppermost in the municipal elections.

Parliamentary Interests in Municipal Elections.

Two contemporary pictures of the spirit and actuating motives in municipal elections will serve to show how these contests

At Norwich.

---

[1] Cf. Picton, *Memorials of Liverpool*, I. 129; Grenville, *Papers*, IV. 451; Hervey, *Letter Books*, II. 379; *Letters of Humphrey Prideaux*, 105.

[2] Parker, *Sir Robert Peel*, II. 179.

[3] Oliphant, *Wm. Blackwood and His Sons*, I. 247.

[4] Hansard, XIX. 1297, 1646, 1647.

[5] *Municipal Corporations Comm. 1st Rep.*, 43.

were interwoven with those for the election of members of the House of Commons. They are both from Norwich; and are pictures of municipal elections in the closing half-century of the old representative system, when there were at Norwich some three thousand Parliamentary electors. "These elections," writes one of the historians of Norwich, in describing the Parliamentary contests, "and even those for the nominees of the wards, are carried on with a spirit which is surpassed in no other place. The ward elections are considered as trials of strength between the different parties; and if they chance to occur at a period when a general election may be supposed not far distant, the money expended on the occasion seems to a stranger quite incredible. It has been asserted, and from very good authority, that no less a sum than sixteen thousand pounds was dissipated in the contest for a single ward in the year 1818[1]."

Municipal Demoralisation.

The second picture is from the report of the Municipal Corporations Commission of 1833–34, and is part of the evidence tendered to the Commissioners, when they visited Norwich, by the editor of a Norwich newspaper. "The prosperity of the city and private intercourse of society," said this witness in reviewing his fifty years' experience of Norwich politics, "are poisoned by party spirit, engendered at the municipal elections. I attribute these consequences to their frequency and the nature of the constituency. We have three elections every year, and there is no cooling time. During the cleansing week, the period of the ward elections, the city is in a state of intoxication. I cannot express strongly enough my sense of the ill effects on the morals, trade and society[2]."

A Municipal Election at Oxford in 1695.

Municipal elections contested in order to gain Parliamentary control of the borough had begun at Oxford as early as 1695, three or four years earlier than the date when the freemen succeeded by a determination of the House of Commons in wresting the right to elect members of the House of Commons from the corporation[3]. These turbulent municipal contests dated from the time when Thomas Wharton, member for the County of Buckingham, and afterwards Marquis of Wharton and Malmesbury[4], was busy, as Le Fleming writes in a letter to his brother, in

[1] Stacy, *Hist. of Norwich*, 36.
[2] *Municipal Corporations Comm. 1st Rep.*, App., pt. IV. 2498.
[3] *H. of C. Journals*, XIII. 191, 1699.
[4] Doyle, III. 661, 662.

"the greatest canvassing for the new mayor that has been perhaps in the memory of man." Wharton was at this time borough-manager-at-large for the Whigs, and took a pride in making freemen drunk on the best ale[1]. In this municipal canvass, Le Fleming avers[2], the purses of candidates were "bleeding as freely" as the purses of Parliamentary candidates had to bleed at Clitheroe, a borough with which both Le Fleming and his brother, as members of the Westmorland family of Le Fleming, had a political connection.

"Beer and mob rule" were peculiar neither to Oxford nor Norwich. Municipal elections elsewhere were similarly charac-terised in the days when municipal politics were so closely inter-woven in the Parliamentary system. Had the historian of Norwich looked further afield, he would have discovered other large freeman boroughs, and several large scot and lot boroughs, which, although not surpassing Norwich in the spirit which characterised their municipal elections, at least equalled it. He would also have discovered that in these other boroughs, control of the Parliamentary elections was the underlying source of the spirit which was infused into the municipal contests. After the outsitters, honorary and non-resident, were disfranchised by the Act of 1832, and the resident freemen to whom the right to the Parliamentary franchise was reserved had to a large extent been merged into the ten-pound householder electorate, there was in most boroughs an end to such municipal contests as that at Norwich in 1818. These municipal contests came to an end because, with the swamping of the freeman vote, and the diminu-tion, if not the actual disappearance, of corporation control in Parliamentary elections, it was no longer to the interest of borough patrons or borough members actively to concern themselves with municipal politics, and to furnish the money which infused zest and temper into the municipal elections. *(margin note: Demoralising Influences of Elections.)*

After this change, and the reform of the municipal corpora-tions in 1835, the close and active interest of the aristocracy in municipal corporations came to an end. There was no revival of it until sixty years later, when, in nine or ten municipalities, councils, acting under the clause in the Act of 1835 which gives them the power to choose the mayor from within or without *(margin note: The End of the System.)*

---

[1] *Dict. Nat. Bio.* LX. 422.

[2] Le Fleming, *Hist. MSS. Comm. 13th Rep.*, App., pt. VI. 338.

the council, went outside their body and elected as mayors the
heads of landed families long established in their neighbourhood.
The peers so chosen lacked knowledge of local detail, and also the
training in municipal work essential to the discharge of the duties
of the mayor.

Modern
Aristocratic
Mayors.

No really useful purpose was served by these elections; but
the choosing of peers as mayors, fortunately for the well-being
of English municipal life, was only a passing fad; and the peers
who in 1896 and 1897 served as mayors, unquestionably were
not actuated by any motives of self-interest. Unlike the peers
who were actively interested in the old municipal corporations
from the days of the Stuarts to the reform of the House of
Commons in 1832, who were of the municipal corporations when
these institutions were at their worst, the later nineteenth century
mayors who were of the peerage had no designs on Parliamentary
influence within the boroughs. They could do these boroughs
small practical service, but in rendering the little that lay within
their power, they gratuitously took upon themselves some new
duties and incurred some inconveniences; while there was nothing
which was reminiscent of the bygone connection of the peerage
with municipal life in the passing and almost wholly ornamental
aristocratic mayoralties which faintly marked the municipal life of
Liverpool, Sheffield and half a dozen other towns in the last decade
of the nineteenth century. The later connection had advantages
neither for the peerage nor for the municipalities. Political
conditions, municipal and national, had so altered in the sixty
years following the Reform Act of 1832, that there could be
no advantages like those which marked the earlier connection,
advantages then mostly on the side of the aristocracy, and when
on the side of the municipality, personal to the members of the
corporation, rather than belonging to the municipality as a whole.

CHAPTER IV.

THE ELECTORAL MAP IN 1832.

UNDER the old representative system the geographical distri- Unequal Distribution of Electoral Power. bution of the two hundred and three boroughs among the forty counties of England, was as remarkable and as anomalous as the variety of franchises on which the four hundred and three members for these Parliamentary constituencies were returned. Many of the anomalies in the borough franchises were due to the positive action of Parliament. They were due to the determinations of committees of the House of Commons, and to the Act of 1729, which gave so many of these determinations the force and effect of law. The unequal distribution of electoral power, manifest even as early as the Commonwealth, and increasingly manifest throughout the eighteenth and the first thirty years of the nineteenth century, was due to the lack of any action on the part of Parliament. Yet remarkable as was this distribution, unrelated as it was to the distribution of population in England from the reign of Charles II to the reign of William IV, and glaringly obvious as were its inequalities, it is comparatively easy to understand how it arose, and why it had been perpetuated.

The distribution of electoral power prior to 1832 presents no No Law Governing Distribution in England. mystery when the social and industrial conditions of England up to the reign of Elizabeth are borne in mind; and when also it is remembered that, during the entire existence of the unreformed House of Commons, from the memorable time when Edward I, "consciously or unconsciously—by genius or good luck," became

"famous for all time as the propounder of the great idea," that
"that which touches all shall be discussed by all[1]," until 1832,
Parliament had not passed a single reform Act, general in its scope.
Nor had it in these five-and-a-half centuries enacted a single
general measure for the redistribution of electoral power.

Acts for
Wales, Scot-
land and
Ireland.

During the Protectorate there was a redistribution of electoral
power which corrected many of the inequalities; but Cromwell's
redistribution did not outlast the Commonwealth. When Wales
was brought within the representative system, in the reign of
Henry VIII, the counties and the boroughs which were to return
members to the House of Commons were named in the Act[2].
When Scotland came in, in 1707, one of the measures for the
Union named the constituencies in Scotland which were to be
represented in the Parliament at Westminster. Again, at the
Union of Ireland with Great Britain, the constituencies to be
represented in the United Parliament were named in the Act of
Union of 1800. For Wales, Scotland and Ireland, Parliament had
thus passed Acts, under which electoral power in those countries
was specifically distributed; while for England there had never
been an Act which specifically named all the constituencies which
were to elect members to the House of Commons.

First Redis-
tribution
Act.

Just prior to the Act of 1832, in the years which preceded the
great reform, the fringe of the question of the distribution of
electoral power in England had been touched by Parliament.
When Grampound was disfranchised in 1821, and its right to elect
two members to the House of Commons was transferred to the
County of York, there was passed the first Act in which any
recognition was given to the demand of the populous parts of
the country, that they should be more directly and adequately
represented in the House of Commons. "It does little, but it
promises much," was the entry which Heron, a member of the
House who had long advocated Parliamentary reform, made in his
diary after Lord Castlereagh, on February 18th, 1820, intimated
for the Government that he was willing to accept Lord John
Russell's proposal to disfranchise Grampound, and to transfer to
Leeds Grampound's long abused right to elect representatives[3].
"We all expected," continues Heron in his note on Lord John
Russell's proposal, "to be treated with derision. Sir Henry Ward

[1] Jenks, *Law and Politics in the Middle Ages*, 44.
[2] 34 and 35 Henry VIII, c. 26.
[3] Heron, *Notes of Public Life*, 110. Cf. Hansard, XLI. 1616.

was supposed to be ready, and Canning evidently so. Suddenly Lord Castlereagh yields this question, as far as it goes, of radical reform."

After much delay Grampound was disfranchised. Its franchise went, not to Leeds directly, but to Yorkshire, and so indirectly to Leeds, whose numerous forty-shilling freeholders were of the newly-created Parliamentary division. Over the question as to whether Grampound should be totally disfranchised, or be thrown into the hundreds after the eighteenth century precedent of Shoreham, Cricklade, and Aylesbury, Lord John Russell and the advocates of reform gained their first signal Parliamentary success. "At this time," wrote Lord John Russell, in alluding to an earlier day than that which witnessed the scene in the House of Commons described by Heron, "Lord Castlereagh, who had always been personally very kind to me, invited me to speak to him on one of the benches behind the Treasury Bench. He told me that the Government would cordially support me, if I would content myself with extending the right of voting for Grampound to the neighbouring hundred. I answered him that I could not agree to that proposal, and that I must persist in proposing that the franchise of Grampound should be transferred to the town of Leeds. After a long conversation, Lord Castlereagh persisted in his view and I in mine. This was in fact the whole principle at issue between the Government and the reformers. The hundreds of Cornwall represented the stationary policy of the ministry, Leeds the new population which I sought to admit, and with them the principle of reform[1]."

At this time Lord John Russell could not be classed as a Parliamentary reformer in the general and early nineteenth century sense of the term. He did not at this time go even so far as some of his Whig colleagues; for while the question of Grampound was pending in 1819, he told the House of Commons, in the debate on Burdett's motion for a committee of inquiry into the franchise, that "he could not pledge himself to support a measure that went the length of proposing an inquiry into the general state of the representation, because such an inquiry was calculated to throw a slur upon the representation of the country, and fill the minds of the people with vague and infinite alarms[2]." To the surprise of the Parliamentary reformers, Castlereagh gave way, when Lord John Russell's bill to disfranchise

Marginal notes: Grampound and Reform.   Transfer of a Franchise a new Departure.

[1] Earl Russell, *Recollections and Suggestions,* 1813, 1873, p. 32.
[2] Hansard, XL. 1496.

Grampound came up for second reading in the House of Commons, on the 18th of February, 1820. There was then a departure by the Government from the eighteenth century precedent of penalising boroughs, which were irremediably corrupt, by throwing them into the hundred.

Importance of the New Departure.

In the end the franchise of Grampound did not go to Leeds. It was diverted by the House of Lords to Yorkshire[1]. But the difference between Leeds and Yorkshire mattered little. The need of a redistribution of electoral power had at last been admitted. The case of the Parliamentary reformers had been practically conceded. It was now no longer possible for the law officers of the Crown in the House of Commons to quote Vatel, to answer Parliamentary reformers that "all legitimate authors who have written on the constitution of government invariably hold that when a government is settled and established—the great desideratum in a state—and it fulfils the ends and purposes of its institution, nothing can justify an alteration in the slightest part of its constitution[2]." It was no longer possible to dwell on the danger and mischief of unsettling the public mind, and of removing ancient landmarks. Mill and the philosophical Radicals might treat the disfranchisement of Grampound "as a display of virtue on the part of the Government and the Tories costing nothing[3]." But men like Spring Rice, who were of the House of Commons, who knew its inner life and the forces which inside and outside by 1820 were at work, were more far-seeing than Mill and the men of his school. "Reform is now carried" was the feeling of the men in political life among whom Rice moved[4]; and Grampound was in fact the beginning of the end of the old representative system.

Suggestions for further Redistribution.

In 1829, when East Retford was marked out for treatment like that meted out to Shoreham, Aylesbury, Cricklade and Grampound, even Tories like Croker admitted, in their intimate correspondence, that the wise plan was not the old one of throwing the borough into the hundred, as was ultimately done in that year in the case of East Retford. They urged that the best way of averting a worse and wider reform would be to transfer the franchises to Birmingham, Manchester and Leeds, as cases of flagrant corruption might

[1] 1 and 2 Geo. IV, c. 47.
[2] Cf. Castlereagh, *Correspondence*, iv. 413.
[3] Bain, *Life of J. S. Mill*, 320.
[4] Pryme, *Autobiographic Recollections*, 179.

arise in the small boroughs[1].   From the time when the franchise of
Grampound was transferred to Yorkshire, only the Tories who relied
on such arguments as that furnished by the Irish Attorney General
about this time to Lord Castlereagh, to combat Catholic Emancipation—the argument from Vatel already quoted—now opposed
all reform.   Only such as these would have endorsed the Duke of
Wellington's declaration in the House of Lords that he had
"never heard or read of any measure up to the present moment,
which could in any degree satisfy him that the state of the representation could be improved or rendered more satisfactory to the
country at large than at the present moment[2]."

Important as the Grampound Act is as a landmark in the long The Only
movement for Parliamentary reform, standing out as it does as the Change in
only approximation to a redistribution Act passed for England the Map.
prior to 1832, and singularly interesting as are the circumstances of
its enactment to the student of British constitutional history, the
Grampound Act, after all, effected only a microscopic change.   It
wrought only one alteration in the map of the Parliamentary constituencies of England between the enfranchisement of Newark in
the reign of Charles II, and the memorable Act which in 1832 was
piloted through the House of Commons by Lord John Russell,
who, on the eve of his Grampound success, had hesitated to
propose an inquiry into the general state of the representation,
because such an inquiry was calculated "to throw a slur upon the
representation of the country, and to fill the minds of the people
with vague and infinite alarms."

When once the first alteration in the map of the constituencies Effect of the
had been made, the movement for reform travelled at a rapid pace. Change on
In 1832 sixty boroughs disappeared entirely from the map, and ment for
twenty-one hitherto unrepresented towns were placed upon it.   In Reform.
1867 four of the old boroughs which had unworthily survived the
Act of 1832 disappeared, and thirteen hitherto unrepresented
towns henceforward had places on the map.   In 1885 there were
other and more extensive changes, again affecting old boroughs
which had survived the Reform Acts of 1832 and 1867, but
chiefly affecting the counties.   The counties were now generally
divided into electoral divisions, a change made necessary by the
greatly enlarged county electorates due to the Reform Act of 1884.
The result of all these changes from 1832 to 1885—the disfranchise-

---

[1] Cf. Croker, *Papers*, I. 124.   [2] Hansard, 3rd Series, I. 52.

ment of sixty-four boroughs, and the creation of thirty-four new borough constituencies, and the throwing of other small boroughs into county divisions by the Act of 1885—was that the electoral map of England, when the twentieth century began, was as unlike the electoral map when the nineteenth century opened, as was the social and industrial condition of England in the closing years of the reign of Queen Victoria to the England of the days of Queen Elizabeth.

The Grouping of the Parliamentary Boroughs.

The striking feature of the electoral map of England as it stood on the eve of the First Reform Act, was the number of Parliamentary boroughs in the maritime counties extending along the coastline southward from the Wash to Dungeness, thence westward to Land's End; and from Land's End north-eastwards to the estuary of the Severn. The counties of Norfolk, Suffolk, Essex, Kent, Sussex, Hants, Dorset, Devon, Cornwall, Somerset and Gloucester, are all on the coastline from the Wash to the Severn; and although Wiltshire has no coastline, it is near enough to both the English Channel and the Bristol Channel to have been affected in its early economic conditions by its contiguity to the sea-board. In these twelve counties, which had a population in 1821 of 3,666,683, out of a total population for England and Wales of 12,000,326[1], there were, excluding Grampound but including the Cinque Ports and their dependent ports, one hundred and fifteen out of the total of two hundred and three Parliamentary boroughs distributed over the forty counties of England.

Boroughs on the Sea-board.

Nearly half of these hundred and fifteen boroughs, or fifty-six, to be exact, were on tide-water; and most of these fifty-six boroughs had at some period of their history been places of importance in maritime trade. During the period when boroughs which had allowed the right to choose members to lapse were coming back into the representative system, and towns which had never sent members to Parliament were seeking to come in, the influence exercised with the Crown by territorial families, and the Parliamentary exigencies of the Crown, had much to do with the choice of the boroughs readmitted or newly enfranchised. But the grouping of Parliamentary boroughs in the eastern, southern, and south-western counties was only partly due to these causes. These counties owed their pre-eminent place in the representative system, as it stood until 1832, to the fact that in the formative period of

---

[1] Census of 1821, on which the Reform Act was based.

the system, population and trade were mostly to be found on the sea-board. When England was still sparsely populated, it was in keeping with social and economic development that population should be densest and towns most numerous along the south-eastern and southern sea-board, and on the navigable rivers which gave access to the sea. The same characteristic in the distribution of population marked the American colonies until the Revolution of 1776, and even after the Revolution the predominance of the representatives of the sea-board counties was noticeable in the various State Legislatures.

Cornwall had the tin-mining industry long before the birth of the representative system; and of its twenty-one boroughs, most are named in Domesday Book[1]. Wiltshire and Somerset were seats of the woollen trade as early as the reigns of Richard II and Henry IV[2]. Long before Defoe made his tour, the woollen industry in these western counties had reached the factory stage; and Defoe wrote of the counties in which the woollen trade was established, as " full of rivers and towns, and infinitely populous, in so much so that some of the market towns are equal to cities in bigness, and superior to many of them in numbers of people[3]." The harbours and quays which survived in what were even the most miserable of the Cornish boroughs in the eighteenth century, were proofs that these places had once been of trading importance. Another proof that population was densest in the maritime counties from the Wash to the Severn, and that this population was stirring and fairly well-to-do, is found in the large number of emigrants from these counties, particularly from those in the west, who settled in New England in the seventeenth century, and whose descendants now trace their genealogies back to the maritime counties of many Parliamentary boroughs.

Economic Influences on Population.

For a century and a half before 1832 Cornwall was proverbial for its many rotten boroughs. Some of these boroughs, as also some in other parts of England, were already rotten when they were enfranchised. The names of some have gone into the English language as synonyms for electoral rottenness; synonyms which are used to-day by members of American Legislatures who have never been in England. These Cornish boroughs were

The Decay of Boroughs.

[1] Merewether and Stephens, *Hist. of Boroughs*, I. 172.
[2] Bischof, *Hist. of Woollen and Worsted Manufactures*, II. 424.
[3] Defoe, *Tour*, 11, 35, Ed. 1753.

perpetuated for centuries, partly from the interested motives of men who were turning them to profit, and partly from the lack of the touch of supreme authority of Parliament, so long required to set the electoral system in order, a touch which was withheld owing to the influence which men, interested in the continuance of the old order, exercised in and over Parliament. But Cornish boroughs, when they first sent members to Parliament, were as populous and important as the towns in other parts of England which were represented there; and the responsibility for Cornwall's eighteenth century notoriety rests not with the county, but with Parliament, which never, prior to 1832, made a single general determination as to the franchise on which members from boroughs were to be returned, nor a revision of the English boroughs electing members to the House of Commons.

Clusters and Pairs of Boroughs.

Turning from the general characteristics of the electoral map to some of its minor incongruities, one of the most noticeable of these was the clustering of boroughs in Cornwall, which necessarily grew out of their large number, and the juxtaposition of boroughs in pairs in the counties of Devon, Dorset, Sussex and York.

The Cornish Boroughs.

Within the area in Cornwall of which Liskeard is the centre, and which extends twenty-eight miles from east to west, and twelve miles from north to south, an area which since 1885 has formed but one Parliamentary division, and is represented by only one member, there were until 1832 nine Parliamentary boroughs returning eighteen members. In this area, on the eve of the Reform Act, there was a population of only 14,224, "of whom," writes a historian of Liskeard, "probably not more than one-fortieth were electors[1]." Two boroughs of this Liskeard group, West and East Looe, one with a population in 1821 of 593, and the other with a population of 865, were divided by the river Fowey, which was spanned by a bridge of fifteen arches. Fowey, which had a population of 1,767 in 1821, was only five miles distant from Lostwithiel, which had a population of 1,074; while outside the area of which Liskeard was the centre, in the more western parts of Cornwall, Tregony was only three miles from the disfranchised borough of Grampound. Newport was the same distance from Launceston. Camelford was but two miles from Helston; and there was only a mile between Falmouth and St Mawes.

---

[1] Allen, *Hist. of Liskeard*, 316, 317.

How, in the middle years of the eighteenth century, this Moral Evils. county of many Parliamentary boroughs was socially affected by so much electioneering of the character for which all Cornish boroughs were notorious, has been recorded by Dr Borlase, one of the historians of the county, who was for over half a century rector of Ludgvan, a small village, with the Parliamentary borough of St Ives a few miles distant to the northward, and with St Michaels less than three miles to the southward. Writing in 1758 of the "low luxury and drunkenness" which characterised social life in the tin-mining country, Dr Borlase expresses his regret that these evils were not confined to the mining centres of Cornwall. They prevailed in the towns and villages, where their existence in his opinion was surely attributable "to the present too general, but it is to be hoped short-lived, corruption of our boroughs at the electing members of Parliament." "This fatal, infamous traffic," he continues, "begins with intemperance and riot; these dissipate every generous sentiment of freedom, love of our country, and inclination to industry. Venality naturally succeeds; and is followed by extravagance and idleness. These by poverty and poverty (such is the round!) by abandoning themselves to intemperance again on the first opportunity, and repeating the basest prostitution of the highest privilege. A corruption this, both of principle and practice; of patriotism and morality; infesting more counties than one, but so much the more to be lamented in Cornwall, as this county has so much a greater number of boroughs than any other in Great Britain and sends as many almost as the kingdom of Scotland itself. However the whole disgrace of this iniquity cannot rest upon my countrymen. It is the much to be lamented vice of the nation, and not of the vulgar. The part of the corrupted is indeed most shameful, for so the world will have it; but that of the corrupter is at least equally guilty, and ought to share our detestation[1]."

The juxtaposition of boroughs was not peculiar to the county A Pair of most notorious for its over-representation in the House of Commons Boroughs. and for the squalid political life which Dr Borlase describes. Weymouth and Melcombe-Regis in the County of Dorset, geographically divided by the harbour on the Wey, were administered municipally as one borough from the reign of Elizabeth, when the Lords of Council, "wearied by the continual disputes of the twin

[1] Borlase, *Hist. of Cornwall*, 308, 309.

towns, by the advice of Cecil, Lord Treasurer, united them into one borough[1]." Although Weymouth and Melcombe were united for local government, the electors continued to vote for four members of the House of Commons, who were returned in two different indentures as burgesses for Weymouth and burgesses for Melcombe-Regis[2]. This Parliamentary borough, so constituted and doubly represented in the House of Commons, a double representation sanctioned by the House in 1597[3], and affording one of many proofs that seats were in demand at the time these towns were united, subsequently earned notoriety in the old representative system.

Electioneering at Weymouth.

Notoriety accrued to Weymouth for a variety of reasons. It was one of the boroughs of counties in which the forty-shilling freeholders early superimposed themselves on the franchise, and shared the right of election with "the mayor, aldermen and capital burgesses inhabiting the borough[4]." Were it conceivable that news of the way in which the freehold franchise at Weymouth was manipulated could have reached other boroughs of counties or cities of counties, where the freeholders were denied the privilege of the franchise, it might have accounted for the opposition of the freemen in these cities, continued to the last, to the admission of forty-shilling freeholders. Electioneering at Weymouth and Melcombe, in Queen Anne's reign, was known as the "Game of All Fours[5]"; and as early as this time, Weymouth had become more notorious than any other borough of county, or city of county, for the splitting of freeholds, and fraudulent conveyances to make votes, and for the incursions of hosts of outsiders who, to quote the words of the Journals of the House of Commons, went to poll there "with conveyances just wrote—no consideration money having been paid, nor any possession had under them[6]."

A Notorious Borough Manager.

Further notoriety accrued to Weymouth and Melcombe in the middle years of the eighteenth century, from the association of Bubb Dodington with them. They were long under the electoral control and close personal management of Dodington, who at the same time was similarly, but less successfully, associated with the borough of Bridgwater. Dodington was a political adventurer of about as bad a type as the politics of the first half-century of

[1] Lewis, iv. 442.   [2] *England Displayed*, 67.
[3] Oldfield, iii. 377.   [4] Lewis, iii. 383.
[5] *H. of C. Journals*, xvi. 558.   [6] *H. of C. Journals*, xvii. 645.

the Hanoverian dynasty produced. But students of the history of the English representative system will readily forgive this most sordid and self-seeking of borough hucksters, who died as Lord Melcombe, for the sake of the remarkable diary he left behind him. Dodington's story of how he managed Weymouth and Melcombe, and of his endeavours to establish himself as the patron of Bridgwater, is told with much openness and much bluntness of language. With equal frankness he tells how at Whitehall he disposed of his "marketable wares," as he describes his borough interests; what he demanded for them; and what he got for them[1]. Dodington's experiences were confined to three or four boroughs; yet his diary throws more direct light on borough management, and on government methods of House of Commons control in the eighteenth century, than any other printed volume in the vast library of the literature of the representative system, except the letters of George III to North, and Torrens' much more recent *History of Cabinets.*

Sussex and Yorkshire had examples of hyphened boroughs Steyning and nearly similar to those of Dorset. Steyning and Bramber in Bramber. Sussex were in even closer proximity than Weymouth and Melcombe; and for generations before these Sussex boroughs were disfranchised in 1832, both had been mean and inconsiderable places only noted for moated ruins of a castle and of a bridge, suggesting former importance, and for the peculiar place they had in the representative system. The constitutional history of these Sussex boroughs was different from that of Weymouth and Melcombe. The Dorset towns had been united for municipal government, and, when united, had managed to keep a double representation in the House of Commons. Bramber and Steyning do not seem ever to have been municipally united; but from 1279 to 1472 they had been joined in one Parliamentary writ, and had sent only two members to the House of Commons[2]. From 1472, although one part of Bramber was in the centre of Steyning[3], each borough sent two members to the House of Commons; and in the closing years of the old representative system, the members were elected on a different franchise in each town. When the end came in 1832, the members for Steyning were being elected on a scot and lot franchise, exercised by about eighty of the inhabitants[4];

[1] Dodington, *Diary,* 308.
[2] *England Displayed,* 120.
[3] Lewis, IV. 173.
[4] Oldfield, IV. 41.

while the members for Bramber were being chosen by burgage holders, of whom in 1831 there were about twenty[1].

The Franchise at Steyning.

From 1715 to 1791 Steyning, like Bramber, was a burgage borough. It was, however, one of the few boroughs which gained an advantage from the Act passed in 1788, which gave persons claiming to be electors a right to petition against determinations of Grenville committees. The franchise at Steyning had long been the subject of much contest; and when in 1792 there was a petition against a determination of 1791, the petitioners made good their case, and it was decided that the determination of the preceding session in favour of the burgage holders, who had been in possession since 1715, was "not the right of election for the said borough, but that the right of election was in the constable and householders, inhabitants within the said borough paying scot and lot, and not receiving alms[2]," a determination which gives Steyning still another claim on students of the old Parliamentary system.

Aldborough and Boroughbridge.

The Yorkshire boroughs which, on account of their proximity and different franchises, presented much the same features of interest as the Sussex boroughs of Bramber and Steyning, were Aldborough and Boroughbridge. They were in the same parish, and only half a mile apart. At Boroughbridge on the eve of the Reform Act there were eighty-six inhabitants. The right to elect was in the burgage holders, and the Parliamentary electorate numbered sixty-five[3]. On the other side of the river Ure, in Aldborough, there were in 1831 four hundred and eighty-four inhabitants within the borough. The right of election was in the inhabitants paying scot and lot, who numbered about fifty[4]. Boroughbridge and Aldborough had both been electing members to the House of Commons since the reign of Mary; and in the case of these two boroughs, as in the case of Weymouth and Melcombe, and of Bramber and Steyning, the fact that these small and contiguous places were enfranchised and each permitted to send two members, affords proof of the early period at which seats in the House of Commons were in demand.

Landmarks on the Map.

While the electoral maps of Cornwall, Dorset, Sussex and York were marked by these small hyphened boroughs, these boroughs whose inhabitants worshipped in the same parish church, or had a common use of the same harbour, or were connected by a bridge

[1] Lewis, i. 211.
[2] Oldfield, v. 43, 44.
[3] Lewis, i. 188.
[4] Lewis, i. 16.

or by half a mile of country road, the electoral maps of other
English counties had also ancient landmarks, which the opponents
of Parliamentary reform, from the American Revolution to 1832,
so dreaded to remove. Wiltshire had its Old Sarum, a borough
within whose limits there was not a permanent house in which
to shelter the returning officer at elections. It also had its Downton,
where some of the burgages were under water. Essex had its
Dunwich, which was gradually being swept away by the encroachments of the German Ocean. Shropshire had its Droitwich brine
pit, which had yielded no salt for two centuries before the disfranchisement of the parchment voters who derived their right to vote
from their interest in the pit.

Lancashire had its Newton, a borough of one street, and a Newton.
borough with several claims to distinction. It is historically famous
from the fact that in connection with it there is recorded one of
the earliest instances of the right to elect members to Parliament
being sold with a manor. This borough, which, from the time
it was enfranchised in 1558 to 1832, was in possession of only
three families, the Langtons, the Fleetwoods—who purchased the
right to "the nominacion, elecion, and appointment" of two
burgesses to Parliament with the manor in 1594[1]—and the
Leghs, was also remarkable from the fact that it was the only
borough in England in which the forty-shilling freehold franchise
was the sole and uniform qualification for a vote. Newton was
remarkable also from the fact that there was no determination
of its franchise until within twenty-five years of the complete
disfranchisement of the borough in 1832.

Surrey had its Gatton, memorable in the history of the repre- Gatton.
sentative system alike from the fewness of its electors, who for
centuries never numbered more than half a dozen, and from the
fact that in connection with it there is recorded one of the earliest
instances of a woman becoming possessed of the right to elect
members to the House of Commons as part of her jointure. She
exercised this power as early as 1558[2], as absolutely of her own will
as ever a Newcastle or a Lowther of the eighteenth century returned
members to the House of Commons when borough patrons and
would-be borough patrons were nearly as numerous as Parliamentary boroughs.

[1] **Deed of Sale, Earwaker,** *Local Gleanings Relating to Lancashire and
Cheshire,* II. 184.

[2] *Loosely MSS.,* 242.

Somerset had the potwalloper boroughs of Taunton and Ilchester. Oxfordshire, in Banbury; Northamptonshire, in Higham Ferrers; and Berkshire, in Abingdon, had each an example of the single-member Parliamentary boroughs first created in the reign of Mary. Sussex, Buckingham, Wilts and Nottingham had each their hundred, into which a delinquent borough had been thrown, with the composite franchises and plural voters which resulted from these ineffectual efforts at electoral reform, made by Parliament during the last sixty years of the unreformed House of Commons. In the counties of Chester, Derby and Durham, the map showed but one city or borough, electing members; while the counties of Oxford and Cambridge were distinguished by university seats, each returning two members. And so through the list of English counties; for in nearly all of them there existed in one form or another those ancient landmarks for which the eighteenth and nineteenth century opponents of electoral reform had so much tenderness and veneration.

CHAPTER V.

UNIVERSITY REPRESENTATION.

Two other constituencies still remain to be noticed in this Petitions for Enfranchisement. survey of the Parliamentary system in England, as it existed on the eve of the Reform Act. These are the universities of Oxford and Cambridge. Both were enfranchised by James I in 1603; and each from that time was represented by two members. The universities had long and persistently sought direct representation in the House of Commons. Between 1570 and the end of the reign of Elizabeth there were six petitions for enfranchisement from one or other or from both of them[1]. In one of these petitions, addressed in 1572 to Lord Burleigh, the University of Cambridge urged " that the universities have two burgesses in Parliament, which Mr Speaker and others think requisite; as they will not always have such as your Lordship to assist them, not having any burgesses in the House who can so aptly answer objections against the universities as they that remain in them and best know their present state[2]."

Representation was not granted until the first year of James I, Reasons for Representation. when both Oxford and Cambridge again petitioned. The reasons for granting the privilege were set forth in the charters of enfranchisement. " As in the colleges of our university," reads the Cambridge charter, " there are many local statutes, constitutions, etc., and as in past times, and especially of late, many statutes and acts of Parliament have been made concerning them, it therefore appears to us worth while and necessary that the said university should

---

[1] Cooper, *Annals of Cambridge*, ii. 269, 401, 435, 460, 585; *Cal. State Papers*, 1569–79, 440.

[2] *Cal. State Papers*, 1569–79, 440.

have burgesses of its own in Parliament, who from time to time
may make known to the supreme court of Parliament the true
state of that university; so that no statute or act may offer any
prejudice or injury to them, or any of them severally, without just
and due notice and information being had in that respect [1]."

Advice concerning the First Election.

Lord Cecil, who at this time was Chancellor of the University
of Cambridge, and Sir Edward Coke were chiefly instrumental in
procuring this privilege for the universities.   On Sir Edward Coke,
in his capacity of Attorney-General, devolved the duty of communicating to them that their plea for representation had been
granted.   Coke, in his letter to the Vice-Chancellor of Cambridge,
went over the arguments which had been put before the King on
behalf of university representation.   Chief among these was Coke's
own experience, when Speaker of the House of Commons of 1593, of
the necessity for the universities to have burgesses in Parliament.
Coke then offered some advice to the university in making its first
election.   He counselled that choice should be made " of some that
are not of the Convocation House," because of the likelihood that
objection would be taken in the House of Commons to members of
Convocation ; and that professors of civil law should be chosen as
the first members for the university [2].

The First University Members.

Coke's advice was heeded, and the two first members for Cambridge were Henry Mowtlow, LL.D., of King's, Public Orator of
1589, and Nicholas Steward or Styward, LL.D., of Trinity [3].
Similar advice would seem to have been given to Oxford; for
that university in the Parliament of 1603–4 was represented by two
doctors of civil law [4].

Wages for University Members.

In the charters it was provided that the burgesses were to be
" two of the more discreet and sufficient men of the university for
the time being "; and that the burgesses were to be " at the charge
and costs of the chancellor, masters and scholars."   Both these
provisions were complied with by Cambridge at the election to the
Parliament of 1603–4 ; for Mowtlow and Steward were allowed
five shillings a day for their expenses [5].   Parliamentary wages were
at this time ceasing to be paid by most of the boroughs.   It is
doubtful whether the practice begun at Cambridge in 1603 survived

---

[1] Huber, *English Universities*, III. 421.   Cf. Cooper, *Annals of Cambridge*,
III. 3, 4.

[2] Mullinger, *University of Cambridge*, 459, 460.   [3] Mullinger, 461.

[4] *Official List*, pt. I. 445.

[5] Mullinger, 461.

the reign of James I; for by 1624 the university was easily under the control of the court[1] and with court or any other outside control, Parliamentary wages invariably disappeared. In 1617 Sir Robert Nauton became principal secretary of state to James I; and in 1624 Nauton wrote to the Duke of Buckingham that "the King having expressed a wish to use his (Nauton's) services in Parliament, the University of Cambridge, at the Lord Keeper's request, has chosen him their member[2]."

The court influence exercised in the reign of James I was continued in the early years of the reign of Charles I. When the Parliament of 1628 was being chosen, Robert Mason, a fellow of St John's, a proctor of the university, who was long secretary to the Duke of Buckingham[3], wrote asking what choice the Duke "directs the University at this election." This letter was dated March 3rd, 1628. Four days later the university was still waiting the directions of Buckingham, who was then its Chancellor[4]. The correspondence between Mason and Buckingham suggests that Cambridge University may be grouped with the constituencies which, according to the Lord Keeper Williams's hint to Charles I when the King was about to meet his first Parliament in 1625, it had been customary in the preceding reign to allow the King's trusted friends "to deal with where they were known to procure or promise for their elections[5]." Mason, from the nature of his correspondence with Buckingham at the election of the Parliament of 1628, was clearly one of the King's trusted friends in the University of Cambridge. *Influence of the Crown.*

As regards Parliamentary representation the English universities have a much less eventful history than most of the English borough constituencies. Political life in them ran even more smoothly than in the University of Dublin, which from the reign of James I until the Union elected two members to the Irish House of Commons. Oxford City and the borough of Cambridge, which James I refused to raise to the dignity of a city, with the freeman mob at Oxford and the honorary freemen at Cambridge, are infinitely more interesting to students of the developement and working of the representative system than either the University of *An Uneventful History.*

[1] *Cal. State Papers,* 1623–25, 143.
[2] *Cal. State Papers,* 1623–25, 148.
[3] *Dict. Nat. Biog.,* xxxvi. 436.
[4] *Cal. State Papers,* 1628–29, 5, 9.
[5] D'Israeli, *Commentaries on the Life of Charles I,* i. 246.

Cambridge or that of Oxford.   Cambridge in the last half century of the unreformed House of Commons was represented by Pitt. Oxford during the same period was represented by Abbot and Peel. Abbot was Speaker from 1802 to 1817, and his name stands out in the history of Parliamentary reform by reason of the sincere and spirited part which he took in 1809 in support of Curwen's bill for preventing the sale of seats in the House of Commons[1].   But except for the distinction arising from the choice of members whose names are prominent in Parliamentary annals, and apart from the traditional Toryism of Oxford, there is little in the representative history. of the universities to command attention.

**Few Contro-
verted
Elections.**   From the nature of the franchise there were necessarily few controverted elections.   There could be few such cases from constituencies in which there were no openings for disputes as to who were entitled to the franchise, and in which the name of every elector was enrolled for other purposes than as a voter at Parliamentary elections.   From the time the universities were enfranchised, their elections added nothing to the work of the committees of privilege.   Controverted elections were so exceedingly rare that the Journals of the House of Commons may be searched in vain for information as to election usages in the university constituencies.

**Mode of
Election.**   The Vice-Chancellors acted as the returning officers.   The franchise in each university was based on membership of the Senate, not on the ownership or the occupation of property ; and this academic qualification differentiated the electors of the universities from the forty-shilling freeholders in the counties and from the variously qualified electors in the boroughs.   Nowadays electors for the universities can send their votes by post.   Attendance at the poll was necessary under the old system.   Each elector carried to the Vice-Chancellor the names of the candidates for whom he voted, written on a slip of paper.   This mode of election was nearest to the present-day method of voting by ballot ; and it is remarkable that in the early days of the movement for Parliamentary reform it was a grievance with reformers at Cambridge that, while in all other constituencies electors were called upon publicly to say for whom they polled, at university elections voting was secret[2].

---

[1] Cf. Hansard, xiv. 837, 851 ; Colchester, *Diary*, ii. 193; 49 Geo. III, c. 118.

[2] *The Poll for the Election of Two Representatives in Parliament for the University of Cambridge*, 1780, iv.

Bishops, peers and minors who were of the Senate were disqualified from voting[1].

As far as can be ascertained from the records of elections at Cambridge it was not until after the Revolution that the right to vote at university elections was much valued. In the eighteenth century there was more interest in the elections, as is shown by the increase in the number of voters. In 1727 at Cambridge only 377 electors polled[2]. In 1784, when Pitt was one of the candidates, 588 out of 735 electors went to the poll[3]. From this time interest in the elections became more manifest. Electors now came from remote parts of the country, and pressure was apparently exercised by the heads of territorial families who had church patronage in their gift to induce their parsons to go to Oxford or Cambridge to exercise their right to vote at the Parliamentary elections[4]. At the general election in 1826 there were 1293 voters at Cambridge, and four days were occupied with the polling[5].

Increase of Interest in Elections.

At Oxford it was a rule that candidates were not to canvass. They were even forbidden to come within ten miles of the jurisdiction of the university when an election was pending[6]. There was also a usage that the representatives should be put to no expense in connection with their elections[7].

An Oxford Usage.

The representatives of the universities from the time property qualifications were imposed on members in 1710, until all property qualifications were abolished in 1858, were specially favoured. They were not required to possess landed or personal property as a qualification for a seat in Parliament. From the first the universities by the terms of their charters were obliged to return members of their own bodies. In this one respect the conditions of university representation were similar to those of county and borough representation in the early days of the House of Commons, and when the great reform was made in 1832 the universities were the only English constituencies for which it was not possible for outsiders to be elected.

Special Qualifications.

---

[1] *The Poll for the Election of Two Representatives in Parliament for the University of Cambridge,* 1780, iv.

[2] Cooper, *Annals of Cambridge,* iv. 194.

[3] Cooper, iv. 412.

[4] Cf. *Hist. MSS. Comm. 13th Rep.,* App., pt. vii. 135, 219.

[5] Cooper, iv. 552.

[6] Oldfield, iv. 362.

[7] *Oxford during the Last Century,* 1859, 18.

CHAPTER VI.

THE REPRESENTATION OF WALES.

County and
Borough
Represen-
tation.

THE representative system as it existed in Wales until the Reform Act of 1832 differed in two essentials from the system in England. In England the counties, with the exception of York-shire, where there had been a recent innovation due to the disfranchisement of Grampound in 1821, returned two knights of the shire. The counties of Wales, if Monmouth is excluded, returned only one member each. Borough representation in the Principality also differed from borough representation in England in that several boroughs were associated in a group for the purpose of returning one member; while all the English boroughs were as self-contained for Parliamentary purposes as they were for municipal administration, and with five exceptions returned two members each. This grouping of Welsh boroughs, in some of its aspects not unlike the grouping of boroughs in Scotland for the election of members to the House of Commons, dated from the reign of Henry VIII, when Wales was first included in the repre-sentative system. It survived the Reform Act of 1832, also that of 1867; and did not entirely disappear even after the counties were divided into electoral divisions by the Redistribution Act of 1885.

Wales
brought
into the
Electoral
System.

Two Acts of Parliament, passed with an interval of only a few years, were necessary to the establishment of the repre-sentative system in Wales on the basis on which it stood in 1832. The first, passed in 1535–36[1], enacted that one knight should be returned for every county, and one burgess for each county town

[1] 27 Henry VIII, c. 26.

except Merioneth. All that is stated in this Act as to the electoral franchise is contained in a clause which reads " and the election to be in like manner, form and order, as knights and burgesses of the Parliament be elected and chosen in other shires of this realm." With this extension to Wales of the form and order of Parliamentary elections in England, an extension which *inter alia*, established the English forty-shilling franchise in the counties of Wales, there was a provision that Welsh members should be paid, as members in England were paid. The Act directed that the knights' fees should be " levied and gathered of the commons of the shire that they be elected in," and that the fees of burgesses " be levied and gathered as well of the boroughs and shire towns, as they be burgesses of, as of all other boroughs " within the shire. In the English constituencies in 1535 wages for members of the House of Commons had long ceased to be generally paid. Their payment at this time was the exception.

In 1543–44 there came the second Act dealing with the Parliamentary representation of Wales[1]. It was practically an Act for the extension of the borough franchise in Wales, or for making assured the more extensive franchise which had been only inferentially established by the clause in the Act of 1535–36 making towns, other than the shire towns, liable to contribute to the wages of the representatives of the shire towns. This second Act for Wales is noteworthy in two respects. It was passed evidently in response to a popular demand for a definite extension to the contributory towns of the right to elect, given by the Act of 1535–36 specifically only to the shire towns. It is also remarkable in the history of the representative system as being the last Act confirming or continuing earlier enactments providing for the payment by constituencies of wages to their representatives in the House of Commons. Durham was the only county which came into the representative system later than the enfranchisement of Wales. But while the preamble of the Durham Act of 1672[2] is as democratic in spirit as the memorable statute of Edward I[3], which, if authentic, must be taken as the basis of the whole representative system, the Durham Act makes no mention of the payment of wages. Nor was there, subsequent to 1672, any Act of Parliament in the least degree suggestive of the fact that constituents were ever liable for the

The Borough Franchise.

[1] 34 and 35 Henry VIII, c. 26. [2] 25 C. II, c. 9.
[3] 34 Ed. I, c. 1.

wages of their representatives at Westminster. There were abortive bills for putting an end to wages, but no enactments later than the Welsh statutes confirming the right of members of the House of Commons to payment for their services.

The Franchise and the Payment of Wages.
For the boroughs tributary to the shire towns in Wales the wages clauses of the Act of 1535–36 and, more especially, the later Act of 1543–44, were of much significance; for it was on the statutory liability of these towns for Parliamentary wages that their right to a part in the borough elections of the shire towns depended. I have not been able to trace that wages were ever generally paid to the representatives of the Welsh boroughs. The probability is that they were never so paid, and that there were no general or persistent efforts on the part of Welsh borough members to obtain the necessary certificates from the clerk of the House, and to put the wages enactments of 1535–36 and 1543–44 into effect. These enactments as to wages were none the less the charters of enfranchisement for the towns not named as shire towns in the first Act of Henry VIII.

The Contributory Towns.
The Act of 1543–44 was particularly valuable to these towns. " As the inhabitants of all the cities and boroughs in every the said twelve shires within Wales...not sending burgesses for the Parliament themselves must," the Act declares, " bear and pay the burgess wages within the shire towns of and in every the said twelve shires...the burgesses of all and every the said cities, boroughs and towns which be, and shall be contributory to the payment of the burgess wages of the said shire towns shall be lawfully admonished by proclamation or otherwise by the mayors, bailiffs or other head officers of the said town, or by one of them, to come and to give their elections for the electing of the said burgess at such time and place, lawful and reasonable, as shall be assigned for the same intent by the said mayors, bailiffs and other head officers of the said shire town, or by one of them, in which elections the burgesses shall have like voice and authority to elect and choose the burgess of every said shire town, like and in such manner as the burgesses of the said shire towns have or use."

The County Franchise.
It was easy to adopt the form and order of English county elections in the Welsh counties, because the forty-shilling free-holder franchise was the uniform one on which knights of the shire in England were elected. When Wales came into the representative system the forty-shilling freeholder Act of 1430 had not begun to be interpreted with the elasticity and comprehensiveness which

gave such variety to the forty-shilling freehold qualification from the Restoration to the Reform Act of 1832. Pressure on tenants, treating, and the exertion of other influences to affect the votes of forty-shilling freeholders, antedate the inclusion of Wales. But as far as my research goes, it would seem that not until eighty or ninety years later than the enfranchisement of the counties and boroughs of the Principality did the practice of splitting freeholds to create county votes begin. In the reign of Henry VIII the Act of 1430 had not begun to open pitfalls for sheriffs, or to call for the attendance of gentlemen of the long robe to aid the sheriff in determining what did or did not constitute a forty-shilling freehold, and entitle the possessor to vote for knights of the shire. It would be a comparatively simple matter, therefore, when Wales began to elect members to the House of Commons, to choose the knight for each shire in consonance with the forty-shilling freeholder Act of 1430.

In the boroughs the mandate of the Act of 1535–36 that the elections should be " in like manner, form and order " as the elections in England, would be more difficult to fulfil; because even at this time the distinctive groups into which English boroughs can be divided from the early years of the reign of Charles I were already in formation. In many of the boroughs in the reign of Henry VIII the right to elect was exclusively in the hands of the corporations. As yet there had been no determinations of the House of Commons in favour of the exclusive right of burgage holders. There could have been none; for in the reign of Henry VIII the judges of assize were still hearing disputed election cases. But already many municipal privileges were in the hands of burgage holders, and burgages were gradually nearing their future importance in the representative system, even if definite proof is lacking as yet that burgage holders were electing members to the House of Commons. The probability is that they already had this right in the reign of Henry VIII ; while in other boroughs the Parliamentary franchise was undoubtedly being exercised by the inhabitant householders. There was consequently in England in 1535–36 no uniform borough franchise which could be easily and uniformly adopted in Wales, as the forty-shilling freeholder franchise was adopted in the Welsh counties. Neither of the enfranchisement Acts for Wales declared who should vote at borough elections. But the Act of 1543 distinctly states that " the inhabitants of all the cities and boroughs must bear and pay the wages " of the

[margin note: An Inhabitant Householder Borough Franchise.]

borough representatives; and the outcome of this declaration of the liability of all for the wages of the members of the House of Commons was the establishment in the early years of the representative system in Wales of an inhabitant householder franchise in the boroughs.

Changes in the Borough Franchise.
Nearly three centuries intervened between the enfranchisement of Wales and the Reform Act of 1832. In these three centuries, as was only to be expected in view of what was taking place in the English boroughs, there were some changes in the borough franchise in Wales, similar in character to those which marked so many of the English boroughs in the same period. The corporation borough, with the corporation in exclusive possession of the right to elect the burgesses to Parliament, came into existence in at least one instance. The honorary burgess, with merely a recurring interest in the Welsh towns like that of the honorary freeman in the English freeman boroughs, came on the scene, and troubled the resident electors as he did in England. There was also successfully adopted in two shire towns the device of contracting the area of the constituency, and excluding what was constitutionally a part of it from the exercise of the Parliamentary franchise. The burgage borough, in its seventeenth, eighteenth and early nineteenth century acceptance of the term, the burgage boroughs that were fought over before committees of privilege and Grenville committees, never had any place in the representative system of Wales. Nor were there freeman boroughs of the exact type that existed in England. The nearest approximations to them in Wales were the boroughs in which non-residents, honorary burgesses they were called, exercised the Parliamentary franchise.

Controverted Elections.
As in England, the county franchise in Wales gave committees of privilege and Grenville committees little work ; and, while most of the controverted elections were from the boroughs, the determinations of election committees established an important change in respect to only one group of boroughs. There were numerous controverted elections from the boroughs ; but the questions raised concerned not the actual franchise so much as election irregularities, and the right of the contributory boroughs to the place in the representative system assigned them by the Act of 1543–44.

Shire Towns versus the Contributory Towns.
There were many contests between the shire towns and their contributory towns. On the part of the shire towns, the object of these contests was to cut themselves loose from the contributory towns, so that the shire towns should have the exclusive right of

electing the burgess. There was a typical, and for the shire town, a successful contest of this nature in 1728, when Montgomery freed itself, for Parliamentary election purposes, from its contributory towns of Llanidloes, Welshpoole, and Llanvylling. The case of Montgomery against its contributory towns was that they had forfeited their rights under the Act of 1543–44 by their failure to contribute to the wages of the burgess. But Montgomery could not prove that it had ever paid wages to its representatives in the House of Commons. To support its case it carried to London an old man who "had heard old men say" that none but burgesses of Montgomery voted, and that money for the wages of the burgess was collected at Montgomery in the reign of Charles II[1]. Further, to support its claim to be free from the contributory towns, Montgomery also carried to London Charles Mason, who represented it in the Parliament of 1705[2]. Mason had excused the burgesses of Montgomery because "they were his friends"; but he had demanded wages from the bailiff of Welshpoole who had refused to pay. Mason, when cross-examined, had to admit that he had no certificate from the clerk of the House, as required by the early enactments covering the payment of wages; and this omission, and his excusing the burgesses of Montgomery, because they were his friends, strengthens the probability that wages were never generally claimed by the members for either the counties or the boroughs of Wales.

Poor as the evidence was in the Montgomery case, it served to free the shire town from its contributory towns, all subsequently much more populous and more important than itself; for the determination of the committee was "that the right of election is in the burgesses of the said shire town only," and the candidate who had been returned by the votes of Montgomery triumphed over the candidate who had been returned by the votes of the contributory boroughs[3]. The Montgomery case is typical of many of the contests from the Welsh boroughs after the Restoration; but it stands out in the history of the representative system in Wales as the only instance in which a shire town was able, through a controverted election determination, to free itself from its contributory boroughs, and so greatly narrow the area of the

Victory for a Shire Town.

---

[1] *H. of C. Journals*, xxi. 137.

[2] *Official List*, pt. ii. 8.

[3] *H. of C. Journals*, xxi. 138.

constituency as established by the Acts of Parliament of the reign of Henry VIII.

In these contentions between the shire towns and the contributory towns the shire towns were not invariably the aggressors. Denbigh, as a shire town, had associated with it the boroughs of Ruthen and Holt, a group which remained intact after 1832 and was known in modern Parliaments as the Denbigh boroughs. As early as 1691 Denbigh, the shire town, and Ruthen, one of the contributory towns, had a complaint against Holt, the statement of which, as laid before the House of Commons, together with other evidence to be found in the Reports of the Historical Manuscripts Commission, shows that at least as early as the reign of William and Mary, the counterparts of the honorary freemen of the English boroughs, and the Parliamentary candidates and election managers who could utilize them, had established themselves in the economy of at least two of the boroughs in Wales. These were Holt and Radnor[1].

The petition of the aggrieved Parliamentary voters of Denbigh and Ruthen in 1691 recited that the vill of Holt had only in conjunction with them the right of voting for burgess; "yet," proceeds the petition, "the said vill hath assumed the power of making a great number of inhabitants of other counties burgesses of the said vill, contriving merely to outvote the legal electors of the aforesaid borough in prejudice to their rights and freedoms[2]." No redress was forthcoming from the House of Commons for the electors of Denbigh and Ruthen. They were again swamped by the outvoters in 1698, when "above four hundred foreigners and strangers, brought hither by the interest of Sir Robert Cotton of Cheshire, were made burgesses of Holt[3]."

Even earlier than the petition of the burgesses of Denbigh and Ruthen in 1691, the honorary burgess had established himself at Radnor; for in 1688–89 Robert Harley wrote to Sir Edward Harley, who had been connected with the borough since 1678, " I intend to go to Radnor on Monday, to be sworn common burgess in your right[4]"; and the making of honorary burgesses, evidently a matter of ordinary occurrence at Radnor in the closing

---

[1] *H. of C. Journals*, x. 554; *Hist. MSS. Comm. 14th Rep.*, pt. ii. 425, 426.

[2] *H. of C. Journals*, x. 554.

[3] Oldfield, vi. 62.

[4] *Hist. MSS. Comm. 14th Rep.*, pt. ii. 425, 426.

years of the seventeenth century, was still the custom in 1779[1], when the inhabitants complained of it to the House of Commons. This complaint was addressed to the House about the time that Derby and Gloucester complained that they were swamped by honorary freemen; complaints which led to the introduction of a bill to prevent the making of these outvoters. The bill failed; and subsequent to the appeal to the House from Radnor by petition, the right of non-residents of Radnor to exercise the franchise there was contested before a Grenville committee. The determination was in favour of the non-residents[2]; and as in the other Welsh boroughs in which honorary burgesses had established themselves, these outvoters, resident in neither the shire towns nor the contributory towns, continued to exercise the franchise until they were disestablished by the residential qualification for freeman voters set up by the first Reform Act.

Beaumaris was the only borough in Wales in which a corporation secured to itself and long exercised the exclusive right of electing a member to the House of Commons[3]. Newborough was the only contributory borough of Beaumaris, the shire town of Anglesea. Early in the reign of Edward VI, when the holding of the assize was transferred from Newborough to Beaumaris by Act of Parliament, Newborough was discharged by the court of grand sessions from contributing to the payment of wages of the burgess of Beaumaris. With its freedom from this liability there lapsed the right of the inhabitants of Newborough, so specifically secured to all the contributory towns by the Act of 1543–44, to " be lawfully admonished by proclamation or otherwise" by the mayor of the shire town, "to come and give their elections for the electing of a burgess" for Beaumaris. Freed from any electoral connection with Newborough, Beaumaris became thus a self-contained borough for Parliamentary purposes. It was the first Welsh borough to secure this afterwards much desired self-containedness; and Beaumaris and Montgomery, which was made similarly self-contained by the determination of the House of Commons in the controverted election case of 1728, were the only Welsh boroughs which managed to sever themselves from their contributory towns between the reign of Henry VIII and the end of the old representative system.

The Two Self-contained Boroughs.

---

[1] *H. of C. Journals,* xxxvii. 399. [2] Oldfield, vi. 118.

[3] Oldfield, vi. 15.

Newborough
loses the
Right to
Elect.

It is not possible to determine whether Beaumaris was desirous that Newborough should be excluded from its statutory part in the franchise. The probability is that Newborough broke the connection in a fit of ill-humour, due to the transfer of the assizes to Beaumaris ; or that it was freed from its statutory liability to contribute to wages, as a solatium for the loss of the assizes ; for the question as to which should be the shire town had already in the reign of Edward VI for fifty years been a subject of fierce contention between the two boroughs. But as time went on, as seats in the House of Commons became in demand, and votes appreciated in value, the electors of Beaumaris, if subject to the same influences which were at work in the English boroughs, must have been hostile to any attempt of Newborough to come again into the Parliamentary constituency.

The
Beaumaris
Charter of
1562.

Only from the Act of 2 and 3 Edward VI, when Newborough lost the assizes, to 1562, could Newborough have had a fair field for agitations for the recovery of its Parliamentary franchise. After 1562 attempts on the part of Newborough to re-assert its electoral rights, and to resume its statutory place in the Beaumaris constituency, were almost necessarily in vain ; for in that year, Beaumaris received from Queen Elizabeth a new charter[1], by which the right of election was vested in the municipal corporation.

Newborough
seeks to
regain the
Franchise.

At the Restoration, and again on several occasions prior to the Last Determinations Act of 1729, Newborough sought to regain its former place as a contributory borough. The burgesses of Newborough sought to exercise the franchise at the election in 1708. Their claims were ignored by the returning officer at Beaumaris. Petitions to the House of Commons followed the election ; and old residents were carried to Westminster as witnesses in support of the claim of Newborough. One witness, named Rowland, who had known the contributory borough for fifty years, told the committee that its inhabitants had claimed to vote for member of Parliament for Beaumaris for forty-eight years[2], testimony which proves that the popular local agitations for wider franchises, which marked the Restoration in England, extended to Wales. The evidence of this witness from Newborough is but briefly recorded in the Journals ; but besides establishing

[1] Cf. *Municipal Corporations Comm. 1st Rep.*, App., pt. iv. 2586.
[2] *H. of C. Journals*, xvi. 323.

the fact that the local agitations at the Restoration extended to the one Welsh borough in which the corporation was exclusively in possession of the right to elect, it shows that the corporation of Beaumaris was as alert and as resourceful as any English corporation of that and later times, in suppressing a threatening agitation likely to disturb its electoral privileges.

In 1698 Newborough had already made a determined effort to regain its rights under the Acts of 1535–36 and 1543–44, the second effort of which there is a record between the Restoration and the appeal of the inhabitants of Newborough after the election of 1708. Owen Hughes, who was then the mayor of Newborough, led the movement of 1698. He was the Parliamentary candidate of the popular party there, and to support him he summoned the would-be electors of Newborough to attend him at the poll at Beaumaris. "About thirty of them," to quote the evidence of Rowland, the old resident who was at Westminster in 1709 to support Newborough's claim, "went thither accordingly; but when they came, Mr Hughes thanked them, and desired them to go home, for that the election was agreed." Owen Hughes might not have been the candidate whom the twenty-four members of the corporation of Beaumaris would have preferred to honour with their choice, but he was elected member for the borough[1]. A threatening agitation was at an end so far as the election of 1698 was concerned, and the right of the Beaumaris corporation remained intact.

Bargains like that at Beaumaris were common in English borough elections. They were made by borough patrons, as well as by municipal corporations, when it was deemed more expedient to concede one election than to risk a contest, either locally or at Westminster, which might endanger their future hold on the borough. The contest at Westminster in 1709 between the inhabitants of Newborough and the corporation of Beaumaris, which produced this singularly interesting first-hand evidence—a contest in which the burden of defending the exclusive right of the corporation fell on Henry Bertie, who had been chosen by the corporation[2]—brought no gain to Newborough. It was only necessary for counsel for Bertie to submit to the committee the charter of Elizabeth to ensure the determination "that the right of election of a burgess to serve for this borough is in the

[margin note: Beaumaris buys off its Assailant.]

[margin note: The Outcome of the Contest in 1709.]

---

[1] *Official List*, pt. i. 585. [2] *Official List*, pt. i. 8.

mayor, bailiffs and capital burgesses of Beaumaris only," with the resultant determination "that Henry Bertie is duly elected for said borough," and to these determinations the House agreed[1].   As yet the Last Determinations Act of 1729 was not on the statute book, so that the determination of 1709 did not finally settle the long drawn out contest between the disfranchised inhabitants of Newborough and the corporation of Beaumaris—a corporation already apparently under the influence of the Bulkley family, which remained in control for more than a century afterwards[2].

Further Attacks by Newborough.   In 1722 there was begun another contest at Westminster, in which the question at issue was again the rights of the inhabitants of Newborough.   There was no determination on this occasion, or rather there is no report of a determination, a circumstance which suggests that the inhabitants of Newborough for the time wearied of the contest and abandoned the petition.   But in 1728–29 there was a third contest, when the determination was, as in 1709, that the right was "in the mayor, bailiffs, and capital burgesses of Beaumaris only."   By this time the Last Determinations Act was on the statute book, and it made an end to the assaults on the position of the Beaumaris corporation, either from the inhabitants of Beaumaris or from those of Newborough.   The inhabitants of Newborough were now in the position of the agitators for wider franchises in scores of the English boroughs. They were helpless in face of the Act of 1729; and although the Act of 1788, making it lawful to petition the House of Commons against the finality of determinations as to franchises by Grenville committees, gave Newborough an opening—only a narrow one, in view of the Beaumaris charter—Beaumaris continued a corporation borough until, in 1832, all borough corporations in England and Wales were dispossessed of the right to elect members to the House of Commons.

Beaumaris sustained by its Patrons.   Like most of the corporation boroughs in England, Beaumaris was long under the control of a patron.   Without a patron prepared to spend freely to uphold the corporation, unless its representative were equally prepared to spend to maintain his connection with the borough, it is not easy to conceive how the corporation of Beaumaris—notwithstanding the custom of corporations of doing what they liked with what they regarded as their own—could have withstood the successive contests with Newborough, which were waged locally and at Westminster between the Restoration and that welcome measure of relief for assailed corporations, borough patrons and the upholders of narrow franchises generally, the Last Determinations Act of 1729.

In two of the Welsh boroughs, in the period between 1535–36 and 1832, there had thus been obvious departures from the borough franchise, which was originally based on the liability of all the inhabitants to contribute to the wages of their representatives in the House of Commons. Beaumaris had not only freed itself from its contributory borough, but the electoral franchise in the original Beaumaris group of boroughs had been greatly restricted by vesting it exclusively in the corporation of Beaumaris. By means of a determination of the House of Commons, Montgomery had severed itself from its contributory towns, and had thereby become as self-contained a Parliamentary borough as Beaumaris had been from the reign of Edward VI. Beaumaris owed its first period of electoral independence to the Act of the reign of Edward VI; but its great defence in the period when votes were appreciating in value, and when consequently the inhabitants of Newborough were anxious to renew the early partnership, was the charter of Queen Elizabeth's reign. Montgomery owed its exclusive possession of the right of election and its severance from towns which, in the eighteenth century, were larger and more important than itself, to one of the many determinations of election committees, applicable to individual boroughs, which distorted borough franchises in both England and Wales, and to the personal and interested motives of men either possessed of or seeking borough interest and borough control.

Another departure from the franchise based on liability to contribution towards members' wages, was the creation of honorary burgesses in such boroughs as Radnor and Holt. In Flint there had come into existence between the enfranchisement of Wales and 1728 a scot and lot qualification[1]. Flint was the only Welsh borough in which such a qualification was established; but this qualification involved no departure from the usages in English boroughs in which the franchises had survived in their early democratic form.

An examination of the lists of men who represented the Welsh boroughs in the House of Commons, and of their biographies as

Modifications of the Borough Franchise.

A Scot and Lot Qualification.

Welsh Patrons.

---

[1] Oldfield, VI. 71.

given in Williams' *Parliamentary History of Wales*, warrants the
inference that from the earliest years of their enfranchisement,
these boroughs elected many outsiders, courtiers and lawyers, and
generally men of the same classes as those who, during the Tudor
regime, were securing election in the boroughs in England. Oldfield,
who as a borough attorney—one of the busiest and most notorious
borough attorneys concerned in the sale of seats in Parliament in
the last thirty or forty years of the unreformed House of Commons[1]
—knew the condition of the English and Welsh boroughs better
perhaps than any man outside the Treasury, states in his history of
the Welsh counties and boroughs that Beaumaris and Montgomery
were the only boroughs which, when he wrote in 1816, could be
said to be under absolute control. " The influence which prevailed
in the other towns," he adds, " is not the produce of corruption ;
but arises from the popularity and hospitality of men of considerable property, whose residences are contiguous to them, and
who are ready to serve them with that assistance and advice which
the exigencies of their situation may require[2]."

Control by
Patrons at
Flint.

Whatever may have been the actual control exercised by
neighbouring landowners over the Welsh boroughs, and whether
this control was acquired by bribery or in the way described
by Oldfield, there is proof that territorial control was exercised
over some of the boroughs at a comparatively early period in the
representative history of Wales. As early as 1620 the Earl of
Bridgwater was arranging to obtain a blank indenture from Flint.
He was anxious that his cousin, William Ravenscroft, should be
of the House of Commons; but as there was a probability that
Ravenscroft might be chosen for some other borough, he desired
Thomas Ravenscroft, George Hope, and Robert Davies, all concerned in the election at Flint, to send him an indenture with
a blank, so that if he provided for William Ravenscroft in the
meantime, " the town may be furnished with another of his nomination." Should the burgesses of Flint hesitate to trust him
with a blank indenture, Bridgwater's instructions to his correspondents in Flint were " to put in William Ravenscroft[3]," who
was subsequently returned for the borough[4]. At this period in the
reign of James I—with the exception of a few boroughs, such as

[1] Cf. Hansard, 2nd Series, xvii. 693, 1210.
[2] Oldfield, i. 1.
[3] *Hist. MSS. Comm. 3rd Rep.*, 258.
[4] *Official List*, pt. i. 455.

Gatton and Newton, which were owned absolutely by the territorial families controlling them, and had been so owned since the reign of Elizabeth, and which had already been bequeathed by will or transferred by purchase—there were no boroughs in England more completely under the dictation of a patron than Flint must have been when the Earl of Bridgwater was instructing his election agents there.

On the eve of the Revolution other Welsh boroughs were under similar control; for in September, 1688, when Sunderland, just before his downfall and flight, was writing from Windsor, recommending candidates by the hundred for the Parliament which James II had declared his intention to convene on the 27th of September[1], Brecon and Cardiff, as well as the county of Flint, were of the constituencies which, from Sunderland's letters, were apparently at this time under territorial rule[2]. *Control in other Boroughs.*

In some noteworthy particulars the Welsh boroughs were unlike many of the English boroughs. I have met with no instances in which the right to elect members of the House of Commons was so absolutely treated as property to be bought or sold, to be bequeathed or given as part of a marriage portion, or to be quarrelled over by families, as was the case in respect to the right to elect in so many of the smaller English boroughs. During the three centuries of the continuance of the representative system of Wales on the basis on which it was established by the enactments of the reign of Henry VIII, there were developed narrowed borough constituencies such as Beaumaris and Montgomery, and there were such warpings of the franchise as brought into existence the honorary burgesses at Radnor, where in 1776 the right to make burgesses was sold at auction in connection with the lordship of Kevenllesce[3]. But the Welsh representative system produced neither a Shoreham nor an Aylesbury; neither a Grampound nor an East Retford. The electoral map of Wales was not marked by a hundred into which a borough had been thrown to punish and perhaps eradicate the deep-seated and long-standing corruption of the borough electorate. Nor was it ever marked by a Droitwich, with the electoral franchise based on nothing but parchment qualifications; or a Downton, with burgages which, although under water, continued for generations to serve as qualifications for a *A Creditable Electoral History.*

---

[1] Parry, 600. [2] *Brit. Mus. Add. MSS. 34516,* Folio 50.
[3] *H. of C. Journals,* xxxvii. 399.

Parliamentary vote.　Wales had no Old Sarum.　It had no double representation boroughs like Weymouth.　It had no boroughs dovetailed one into the other as were Bramber and Steyning, each miserable little borough returning two members.　It had no freeman boroughs, long notorious for squalid and tumultuous municipal and Parliamentary electioneering like Liverpool or Norwich.　Nor has Wales a county historian who has had to make admissions like those of Borlase, the historian of Cornwall, concerning the social demoralisation due to the political conditions of that county of many boroughs.

Welsh Municipal Life.　　In Wales, Parliamentary representation was much less interwoven with the municipal system than in England ; and municipal and social life did not suffer as they did in England from the connection of the municipalities with Parliamentary electioneering. The Welsh boroughs necessarily presented fewer opportunities for borough patrons than the English boroughs from the Restoration to 1832.　The Welsh single-member constituencies were not such valuable possessions as the doubly-represented boroughs in England ; and moreover the electorates in the Welsh boroughs, except at Montgomery and at Beaumaris, were comparatively large. The franchise was on a popular basis.　Owing to the grouping of the boroughs the electors were scattered ; and in such constituencies, as in populous constituencies in England, a borough patron would be less secure of his hold, and would be concerned in a more hazardous speculation than when he essayed control of a corporation or of a burgage borough, or even a freeman borough in which he could keep the corporation on his side.

PART II

RELATIONS BETWEEN MEMBERS AND
CONSTITUENTS.

CHAPTER VII.

RESTRICTIONS ON THE CHOICE OF CONSTITUENCIES.

AT no time in the history of the unreformed Parliament, Restrictions of Different Periods. certainly at no time subsequent to 1372, had constituencies an unrestricted choice in electing representatives to the House of Commons. There was never a period between the reigns of Edward III and William IV, in which there were not on the statute books laws imposing restrictions on the choice of electors. First came the law of 1372, which excluded sheriffs of counties, " who are common officers for the people, and ought to be abiding in their office for doing right to everyone[1]." Then came the laws which restricted the choice of constituencies to men dwelling in their midst; next a series of enactments imposing religious tests; and concurrently with these there were laws imposing oaths for the protection of the Crown, and subsequently of its settlement as determined at the Revolution. Later still there was gradually enacted a code which made many office-holders ineligible; and about this time came the enactments which imposed property qualifications and were intended to restrict the choice of electors to men of means or of assured position. Some of these laws survived the Reform Act. Those excluding office-holders under the Crown still survive, as also the laws, of which that of 1372 was the forerunner, making sheriffs and mayors ineligible for the representation of their own counties and boroughs. But to-day these are the only survivals of the code which is almost as old as the House of Commons; and since 1858, when it became possible for Jews to vote as well as sit in the House, and all property qualifications for membership were abolished, the electors have had, so

---

[1] 46 Ed. III.

far as the statute law is concerned, a much freer choice than at any time in the history of the representative system.

The Residential Quali- fication. The earliest general restrictions grew out of the laws which enacted that "knights of the shire and citizens and burgesses should be dwelling and resident" within the constituencies they represented[1]. How and why these laws were evaded, and how, long before the end of the sixteenth century, they had fallen into desuetude, has been told in the preceding chapters in tracing the evolution of the franchise in the boroughs. In treating of these laws here in these chapters on the relations of electors and elected, it is only necessary to repeat that by 1620 the residential qualification had obviously been so long in desuetude that a committee of the House of Commons proposed that the laws of 1413, 1429, 1432, and 1444–45 should be repealed. The repeal did not come in 1620; and it was not until 1774 that Parliament declared that the provisions as to residence of these Acts "have been found by long usage to be unnecessary and have become obsolete"; and that, in order to "obviate all doubt that may arise upon the same," the statute book was cleared of all the enactments relating "to the residence of persons to be elected to serve in Parliament, or of the persons by whom they are to be chosen[2]."

Social Status of Members. In the period when these early Acts were observed, eldest sons of peers were excluded from the House. By one of the Acts[3] also no man could be a knight of the shire unless he were of the "notable esquires and gentlemen"; but the social qualification set up by the Act of the reign of Henry VI was not long, if ever, generally demanded of men elected to represent the counties. The enactment was for a temporary purpose, "to prevent the growth of a levelling party, then tumultuously opposing the nobility, knights and gentry in most counties[4]"; and as far as can be traced there was no attempt to disqualify a representative of a county for lack of the qualification set up by 23 Henry VI after 1450, when the law was invoked against Henry Gymber. Gymber had been elected for Huntingdonshire[5]; but his election was declared void, because his coat of arms could not be discovered at the Heralds' Office, and the Garter King would not certify that he was of gentle birth.

[1] 1 Henry V, c. 1; 8 Henry VI, c. 7; 10 Henry VI, c. 2; 23 Henry VI, c. 14.
[2] 14 Geo. III, c. 58.   [3] 23 Henry VI, c. 14.
[4] Prynne, *Brevia Parliamentaria*, 161.
[5] Prynne, *Brevia Parliamentaria*, 161; *Official List*, pt. i. 344.

The usage, or law of Parliament, excluding eldest sons of peers Exclusion of Eldest Sons of Peers. broke down in 1549, when Sir Francis Russell, then member for Tavistock, became heir apparent to the Earl of Bedford, and by vote of the House was permitted to continue as a member[1]. The same question came up again in 1575, when it was ordered " that Lord John Russell, son and heir apparent to the Earl of Bedford, being a burgess for the borough of Bridport, in the County of Dorset, shall continue a member for this borough according to the like former precedent in the like case, had heretofore of the said now Earl of Bedford[2]."

With these votes of 1549 and 1575 the custom of Parliament The House admits and honours Peers' Sons. excluding the eldest sons of peers came to an end ; and within the next half century the House went to the other extreme in its treatment of them. It accorded them the privilege of seats on the benches to the right of the Speaker's chair, where sat the privy councillors. Denzil Hollis was seated on the privy councillors' bench on the 2nd of March, 1629, the day on which he and Valentine pushed Finch, the Speaker, back into the Chair whilst Eliot read his memorable resolutions, and in explaining his part on that epoch-making day in the House, Hollis said " the place he had so taken," on the seat to the right of the Chair, " he had before frequently occupied, being entitled to it as an Earl's son[3]."

About the time the Acts imposing residential qualifications Exclusion of Sheriffs and Mayors. were falling into desuetude, there was a re-enactment of the law of 1372[4] excluding sheriffs. It was passed in the twenty-third of Henry VIII ; and in the thirty-eighth of Henry VIII it was made to apply to mayors of boroughs[5]. But as late as 1604 there were doubts as to how far the law really applied to mayors; and a member then " moved to know the opinion of the House, whether the mayor of a town might be lawfully returned and admitted to serve as a member here." At this time summaries of debates were embodied in the Journals of the House, and the discussion on the eligibility of mayors is recorded in some detail. " By some," reads the report, " the great inconvenience was urged that mayors to whom the writs were directed should be admitted burgess, seeing for the most part their power was such that they might procure

---

[1] *H. of C. Journals*, Jan. 21st, 1549.

[2] Ferral, *Law of Parliament*, 207; *Order and Proceedings of the House of Parliament*, 1641, Harleian MSS., iv. 559.

[3] Forster, *Life of Eliot*, 447, 448.   [4] 46 Ed. III.

[5] *H. of C. Journals*, i. 246.

themselves to be chosen." " By others," continues the summary in
the Journals, " a difference was taken. If the mayor-elect procure
himself to be chosen, then with good reason doth he stand incapable;
but if he be freely and indifferently chosen, or elected burgess of
another borough, whereof he is not mayor, that then he might
lawfully be returned and fitly admitted to serve as a member of
this House." In the end it was resolved, and the clerk of the
House was commanded to enter it accordingly, " that from and
after the end of this Parliament, no mayor of any city, borough, or
town corporate, should be elected, returned or allowed to serve as
a member of this House, and if it did appear that any mayor were
returned a burgess, that presently a new writ should be awarded
for the choice of another in the room and place of the said mayor;
and this to continue as an act and order of this House for ever."
It was resolved also at this time that if a mayor of a town were
chosen for a county, then he might serve[1]; and in general it may
be said that this order of 1604 has continued ever since; for to-day,
as in the unreformed Parliament, sheriffs cannot be chosen for their
own counties, nor mayors for their own boroughs.

A Period of less Restricted Choice. The period in the unreformed Parliament in which constituencies
had the greatest range of choice was between the breakdown of the
laws imposing residential qualifications and 1563. Then the oath
of supremacy was imposed on members of the House, and there
was begun the system of exclusion based on religious tests which
in a greater or less degree survived until 1888, when the late
Mr Bradlaugh was instrumental in carrying through Parliament
the Act which directs that " a solemn affirmation may be made in
lieu of an oath by every person who states as a ground of such
objection either that he has no religious belief, or that the taking
of an oath is contrary to his religious belief[2]." The disregard of
the laws imposing residential qualifications was at first gradual.
It was most general in the boroughs; and between the breakdown
of these laws, and the beginning of the era of exclusion due to
religious tests, constituencies had in practice, though not in law,
an even more unrestricted choice than that enjoyed by electors
under the reformed representative system at the close of the
nineteenth century.

Restrictions before 1563. To take the case of a borough as an example. In this period
previous to 1563, when its electors were agreed that they need pay

---

[1] *H. of C. Journals*, i. 246.   [2] *House of Commons Rules*, 1891, p. 9.

no heed to the enactments imposing a residential qualification, the classes of men they had to rule out in making their election were extremely few.   After 1547 they could not elect their mayor. Infants, men of unsound mind, aliens, peers and clergymen were also ineligible.   Apart from these exceptions the choice of the electors was unrestricted.   They were in practice no longer compelled to choose one of themselves; and when an outsider offered, it was not necessary to inquire of him to what church he belonged, or what oaths he could or could not take, for until 1563 there were no tests standing as barriers between a man who had been elected and his seat in the House of Commons.   It was not necessary to inquire whether he held an office under the Crown or whether he had an assured income.   Never in the history of the unreformed representative system was it more open to electors to go out into the highways and by-ways to seek men to represent them at Westminster than in the century which preceded the era of religious tests.

In this period of so much freedom of choice, clergymen were on the excluded list, at least from 1553, and they have been ineligible ever since.   They were not eligible at this time, for the same reason that until after the Restoration they were not recognized as of the electorate.   They were not electors, and they could not be chosen; because as clergymen they were represented in Convocation and taxed by Convocation.   Prior to the reign of Henry IV clergymen were occasionally of the House[1].   A select committee, reporting in 1801, stated that later than the eighth of Henry IV they could not find that clergymen were ever admitted; while in the period from the reign of Mary until the Restoration, there are three recorded cases in which clergymen who had been elected were not permitted to take their seats.   The first of these was the case of Dr Alexander Nowell, Prebendary of Westminster, who was elected burgess to the first Parliament of the reign of Mary from West Looe in Cornwall.   To consider his eligibility a committee of six was appointed on the 12th of October, 1553.   It reported on the 13th, that " A. Nowell, being a prebendary in Westminster, and thereby having a vote in the Convocation House, cannot be a member of the House."   The House of Commons concurred in this report, and a new writ was ordered for a burgess in Dr Nowell's

Clergymen Excluded.

---

[1] *Rep. from Select Comm. respecting the Eligibility of persons in Holy Orders to sit in the House,* April 2nd, 1801.

place[1]. John Robson, elected for Morpeth, was excluded in 1621, "he being a clergyman[2]"; and on the 9th of January, 1661-62, on the eve of the admission of clergymen to the electorate, Sir James Cradock, who had been chosen for Richmond in Yorkshire, was denied a seat because he was in holy orders. In this case—the last on record in which a clergyman was declared ineligible by a vote of the House—the objection to his election was made by a defeated candidate, John Wandesford, who on Dr Cradock's exclusion succeeded to the seat without another election[3].

The Exclusion of Clergy by Statute.

The statutory exclusion of clergymen, which dates from 1801[4], owes its origin to the election of Horne Tooke for the borough of Old Sarum, on the 14th of February, 1801. At the time of his election Tooke had long held no benefice in the Church; but in law he was still in holy orders. For twenty years he had been associated with the movement for Parliamentary reform, and other movements for constitutional change, and had rendered valuable literary services to these constitutional agitations. He was objectionable to George III and the Government for this reason; and as the right of a clergyman to a seat in Parliament was held to be in doubt, and as the question had been raised anew as recently as 1784, when Edward Rushworth, who was in deacon's orders, had been allowed to take his seat for Newport[5], the Government, as soon as Tooke was elected, moved for a committee to inquire into the precedents. These were held not to warrant the exclusion of Tooke. None of the exclusions of men in holy orders was subsequent to the law of the Restoration Parliament by which the clergy became liable to taxation with the laity, instead, as in the past, of being taxed separately by Convocation; and following the report of the committee, a bill was carried through Parliament in which it was enacted that no person who had been ordained "to the office of priest or deacon, or being a minister of the Church of Scotland, is or shall be capable of being elected to serve in Parliament as a member of the House of Commons[6]."

The Plea for the Horne Tooke Act.

The old constitutional ground for the exclusion of clergymen of the Church of England, that they were taxed by Convocation and

---

[1] *H. of C. Journals*, I. 27.

[2] Whitworth, *Succession of Parliaments*, 194; *Cal. State Papers*, 1623, 21.

[3] *H. of C. Journals*, VIII. 341, 346; Clarkson, *Hist. of Richmond*, App. 1.

[4] 41 Geo. III, c. 62.

[5] Anson, *Law and Custom of the Constitution*, pt. I. 73.

[6] 41 Geo. III, c. 63.

represented in Convocation—the ground on which Prebendary Nowell was excluded in 1553—was not tenable in 1801, when it was deemed expedient to keep Horne Tooke out of the House. The new ground of exclusion, on which the Act of 1801 was justified by the Addington Administration, was that as the benefices of a great number of the clergy were in the direct gift of the Crown, or of the nobility, the admission of clergymen would diminish the purity and impair the independence of the House of Commons[1]. The Act was not retroactive, and for the short remainder of the Parliament of 1796–1801, Tooke was able to harrass and perplex the ministry by his ingenuity and dexterity in debate[2].

The celebration of divine service according to the rites of the Church of England or the Church of Scotland, in any church or chapel consecrated or set apart for public worship, was "to be deemed and taken to be *primâ facie* evidence of the fact of such person having been ordained to the office of a priest or deacon, or of his being a minister of the Church of Scotland within the intent and meaning of this Act." The Act of 1801 put clergymen of the Established Church in England, Ireland and Scotland on the excluded list; and in 1829, when, after an exclusion which in the case of England dates back to the reign of Elizabeth, Roman Catholics again became eligible as members of the House of Commons, a clause was inserted in the Relief Act[3] adding priests of the Church of Rome to the list of persons incapable of election to the House of Commons. At the time that Horne Tooke's election determined the Addington Administration to settle by enactment the constitutional status of clergymen of the Church of England, a man who had been ordained could not renounce holy orders. Long after the representative system was reformed, the laws as to ordination were amended, and it is now possible for a clergyman formally to renounce his orders. Thereafter he is no longer disqualified by the Act of 1801, which, by reason of its special purpose, has long been known in the literature of statute law as the Horne Tooke Act.

For nearly three centuries after the representative system came into existence, constituents had no concern with the religious beliefs of candidates for their suffrages; for until the Act of Supremacy was passed[4] no restrictions were by law imposed on

(margin notes: Roman Catholic Clergy Excluded. The Oath of Supremacy.)

---

[1] *Parl. Hist.*, xxxv. 1331.   [2] Cf. Gunning, *Reminiscences*, 245.

[3] 10 Geo. IV, c. 7.   [4] 5 Eliz., c. i.

their choice other than those which have been described earlier in this chapter. The Act was passed in the first year of the Parliament of 1563–67[1]. Prynne is the authority for the statement that the oath was not administered until 1566[2]. Its imposition was deemed necessary by "reason of the manifold plots and treasons of the Pope and the Papists, against the Queen's person, crown and realm[3]." Its purpose was "to abolish the Pope's usurped supremacy and prevent his and his instruments' traitorous attempts against the Queen's person, crown, and kingdom ; discover persons popishly affected ; and seclude them from sitting or voting in the Commons House[4]."

Provisions of the Act.   The Act directed that every person "who shall be hereafter elected or appointed a knight, citizen or burgess, before he shall enter into the Parliament House, or have any voice there, shall openly receive and pronounce the said oath before the Lord Steward, his deputy or deputies." Before a member could take his seat, he had by this oath to declare that in his conscience the reigning sovereign was the only supreme governor of the realm, "as well in all spiritual or ecclesiastical things or causes as temporal; and that no foreign prince, person, prelate, state or potentate hath, or ought to have, any jurisdiction, power, superiority, pre-eminence or authority, ecclesiastical or spiritual within this realm." A person elected who did not take the oath was to be to all intents, constructions and purposes, as if he had never been returned or elected, and liable to "suffer such pains and penalties as if he had presumed to sit in the House without election, return, or authority."

Opposition to the Act.   This harsh statute, especially harsh when it is remembered what control the Crown could exercise over the electorate and the House of Commons in the sixteenth century,—a statute which was the forerunner of a series of enactments by the Parliaments of England, Scotland and Ireland by which Catholics were rendered ineligible for seats in the popularly elected chambers until the eve of the Reform Act of 1832,—was not passed without opposition in both Houses of Parliament. "Two speeches against it," writes Hallam, "have been preserved, one by Lord Montagu in the House of Lords, the other by Mr Atkinson in the Commons, breathing such generous abhorrence of persecution as some erroneously imagine to have been unknown to that age, because we rarely meet with it in

[1] Parry, 215.   [2] Prynne, *Survey of Parl. Writs*, 407.
[3] Prynne, *Survey of Parl. Writs*, 406.
[4] Prynne, *Survey of Parl. Writs*, 408.

theological writings[1]." " This law," said Lord Montagu, " is not necessary; forasmuch as the Catholics of this realm disturb not, nor hinder the public affairs of the realm, neither spiritual nor temporal. They dispute not; they preach not; they disobéy not the Queen; they cause no trouble nor tumults among the people; so that no man can say that thereby the realm doth receive any hurt nor damage by them. They have brought into the realm no novelties in doctrine and religion. This being true and evident, as it is indeed, there is no necessity why any new law should be made against them. And where there is no sore nor grief, medicines are superfluous and also hurtful and dangerous." This speech by Montagu is indeed generous in spirit, in view of the fact that the oath of supremacy was not to be taken by the members of the House of Lords[2]. Several peers of great weight and dignity were still Catholics. But the Queen, in the Act of 1563, declared her full confidence in the House of Lords; and for one hundred and fifteen years to come, there was no Act establishing oaths which had the effect of excluding Catholics alike from the Representative Chamber and from the Upper House.

From the Parliament which established the oath of supremacy there can be traced the beginning of the practice at the opening of a new Parliament, of the House of Commons attending to hear a sermon at Westminster Abbey; and there was also begun in this Parliament the use of prayers at the opening of each day's sitting of the House. In the Journals of the Parliament of 1563–67 there is no record of daily prayers; but immediately after the Speaker of the Parliament of 1571 had been chosen, the House passed a resolution directing that " the litany shall be read every day as in the last Parliament, and also a prayer said by Mr Speaker as he shall think fittest for this time, to be begun every day at half-past eight a.m., and that each then making default shall forfeit for every time fourpence to the poor man's box[3]." *Prayers in the House of Commons.*

The usage of attending the Abbey at the opening of a new Parliament was continued into the seventeenth century. In this period it was the rule for the members, after attending service there, to return to " the great room called the Court of Whitehall, or the Court of Request," where the Lord Steward of the King's Household, or his deputies, were in waiting to administer the oath *Commons attend Service.*

[1] Hallam, *Constitutional Hist. of England*, i. 124, 125, Ed. 1862.
[2] Prynne, *Parl. Writs*, 407.   [3] Parry, 217.

of supremacy to members before they betook themselves to their own Chamber for the election of the Speaker[1].

The Oath of Allegiance and Abjuration. For almost half a century, from 1566 to 1610, the oath of supremacy was the only oath demanded of members of the House of Commons. Following the popular alarm arising out of the popish conspiracy in 1605 to blow up the Houses of Parliament, there was passed in 1606[2] an Act empowering a justice of the peace or a judge of assize, to tender a new oath aimed against popish recusants to any person above the age of eighteen; also empowering the Lords of the Privy Council to put the same oath to any nobleman or noblewoman suspected of being a papist. In 1610 the Act of 1606 was so extended as to compel men elected to the House of Commons to take this new oath[3], since known in history as the Oath of Allegiance and Abjuration. This early seventeenth century oath, like the oath of supremacy, had to be taken before members went into the House, and taken before the Lord Steward, which was considered as taken before the sovereign himself, represented by his officer[4]; and from 1563 until after 1829 a man elected to the House of Commons had in law no right within the Chamber, no status as a member of the House, until he had taken oath in one of the outer halls.

Members ordered to take the Sacrament. A second religious test was imposed on members by an order of the House of 1614. The order was adopted on the opening day of the Parliament, and directed "that every member of the Commons shall take the sacrament at St Margaret's Church," "which," continues the record, "not one refuses[5]." This order of 1614 must have been embodied in the standing orders of the House of the Parliament of 1621; for the usage of 1614 was continued, and on the 6th of February the Speaker acquainted the House that the Dean and Chapter of Westminster refused to receive them there, "because they were not first asked, and because the preacher was not one of themselves; but that if they would appoint a canon preacher they might receive the communion with the ordinary bread." The House resented this dictation from the Dean and Chapter, and chose the Temple Church as that at which members should receive the communion[6].

House insists on the Order. The taking of the communion imposed only by order of the House differed from the taking of the oath of supremacy imposed

---

[1] Cf. *H. of C. Journals*, i. 140.　　[2] 3 and 4 James I, c. 4.

[3] 7 James I, c. 6.　　[4] Hansard, 3rd Series, v. 92.

[5] Parry, 262.　　[6] *Cal. State Papers*, 1619–23, 221.

by statute, in that a member could be of the House, and could vote for the Speaker, or for or against the order before he was called upon to take the communion. But in the reigns of James I and Charles I the House was insistent on members taking the communion. If a member failed to take it on the appointed Sunday he was permitted to remain in the House only on promising to take the communion on the following Sunday. A typical entry in the Journals covering cases of this kind is that of August 9th, 1625. " Mr Fynes enforced the last Sabbath to go out of town," it reads, " is licensed to come into the House, till he can conveniently receive the communion[1]."

In the first Parliament of 1640 the House was especially insistent on members receiving the communion, and took more precautions than at any time since 1614 to secure a general compliance with the order. By an order passed on the 23rd of April, 1640, it was directed that all members "shall receive the communion at St Margaret's Church in Westminster upon Sunday next come sevennight in the forenoon; and whoever shall not then and there receive the communion, shall not after that day come into the House until he shall have received the communion in the presence of some or one of the persons hereafter appointed to that purpose, and the same be certified and the certificate thereof be allowed by this House[2]." For the better discovering on Sunday, April 26th, "who shall then receive the communion and who not," it was further ordered that Sir Arthur Ingram, Sir Walter Erle, Sir William Masham, Sir Jo. Ray, Mr Rowse, Mr Cage, Mr Godfrey, and the two burgesses for Westminster, shall take special notice of all such as shall then and there receive the communion; and "that every member of this House shall then bring with him a note in writing containing his name and the shire whereof he is knight, or the borough whereof he is burgess, which note he shall in the same church, and when the same shall be demanded of him, deliver unto the said parties before particularly mentioned, some or one of them, and the persons so appointed are likewise to take particular notice of every member of this House at such time as he receiveth the communion[3]."

The new stringency as to the communion was intended "for the discovery of Papists among us." Some who took the oath of

Further insistence in 1640.

Efforts to discover Papists.

[1] *H. of C. Journals,* I. 812.
[2] *H. of C. Journals,* II. 12.
[3] *H. of C. Journals,* II. 12.

supremacy were at this time suspected, because their wives were Papists[1]. Judging from the Journals, few men who were of the Church of Rome sought election to the House subsequent to the enactment of the oath of supremacy, or at any rate few were successful at the elections. In 1620 Sir Joseph Leedes, who was chosen for Hindon in Wiltshire, did not take the oath and a new writ was issued[2]. Sir Thomas Gerrard, who belonged to a South-west Lancashire Catholic family of long standing, then as now well known for its adhesion to the old faith, was elected for Liverpool to the Parliament which met in 1624. As he could not take the oaths, he desired that a new writ should issue. But the House was not disposed to let Gerrard off thus easily. It was objected that he was a recusant, and an order was made that he appear next day to take the oaths of supremacy and allegiance, and that thereafter he receive the communion[3]. Next day, the sergeant-at-arms reported " that Sir Thomas Gerrard hath changed his lodgings, where he lay, and they either will not or cannot tell where he lieth." On this report, the House made a second order "that the sergeant-at-arms search for him, attach him, and bring him hither to-morrow morning[4]."

Covenant as a Test.

In the Long Parliament, when in 1645 writs were to be issued for new elections at Southwark, Bury St Edmunds, and Hythe, the order of the House to the Speaker to issue his warrants directed that "none to be chosen and sit unless they took the Covenant[5]."

Taking the Communion after the Restoration.

After the Restoration, when the House of Commons was again chosen on the representative system in existence up to the time of the Commonwealth Parliaments, all the old usages of the House were restored. The Lord Steward on June 4th, 1660, was reinstated in the lobby to administer the oaths of supremacy and allegiance[6]; and the taking of the sacrament by orders of the House was for some years continued[7]. In 1661 there was an objection to it, and Sir Ralph Ashton sought to raise a debate on the order so that he might explain why he could not with a good conscience receive the sacrament. But the House would not debate the question[8]; and Sir Ralph Ashton, who had been elected for the Lancashire borough of Clitheroe, was soon afterwards unseated on a petition. In the session of 1661 the House was insistent on members taking

---

[1] *H. of C. Journals,* ii. 34.
[2] *H. of C. Journals,* i. 516.
[3] *H. of C. Journals,* i. 679.
[4] *H. of C. Journals,* i. 680.
[5] Whitelock, *Memorials,* i. 498.
[6] *H. of C. Journals,* viii. 53.
[7] *H. of C. Journals,* viii. 247.
[8] *H. of C. Journals,* viii. 258.

the communion; and, following the precedent of 1640, appointed commissioners to see that the order as to communion was obeyed. In July, 1661, it was reported that there were about thirty members who had not communicated; and following this report there was a resolution that Mr Love " be suspended from sitting in this House until he shall communicate and bring certificate thereof from the said commissioners according to the former order[1]." Love, like Ashton, apparently had a conscientious objection to taking the communion; for in the next session he was again reported as a defaulter, and was given a month in which to comply with the order of the House[2]. As late as 1666 members were still called upon by order of the House to take the communion at the beginning of the session[3]; and in 1666 there was again a motion like that offered by Sir Ralph Ashton in 1661. This time leave was asked " for speaking against the orders made to receive the sacrament." It was refused by ninety-eight votes to fifty-four[4]. By 1672 orders as to the sacrament cease to appear in the Journals; and in this and in succeeding years the House was occupied with bills to exclude Dissenters[5]; with hunting out members like Mr Pepys, who were reported to have altars with crucifixes in their homes[6]; and with bills to prevent Papists from sitting in Parliament[7].

The spirit of exclusion on account of religious or theological beliefs was rampant between 1672 and 1678. The barrier excluding Roman Catholics was made stronger, and there were also ineffectual endeavours to establish a test which should exclude Protestant Dissenters from the House.

Further Religious Tests.

On March 17th, 1672, " a bill was tendered and delivered in by Sir Thomas Meeres, in pursuance of the order of the House, for making dissenters in matters of religion from the Church of England incapable of being elected to serve in Parliament[8]." This bill failed; and in 1673 there was another endeavour to impose tests on members[9]. It also failed. These proposed enactments would have been tantamount to the orders of 1614, 1640, 1661 and subsequent years, compelling members to receive the communion, for by the Test Act of 1673, receiving the communion was made

Proposed Laws to exclude Dissenters.

---

[1] *H. of C. Journals,* VIII. 289.
[3] *H. of C. Journals,* VIII. 643.
[5] *H. of C. Journals,* IX. 270, 314.
[7] *H. of C. Journals,* IX. 337, 341.
[9] *H. of C. Journals,* IX. 314.

[2] *H. of C. Journals,* VIII. 444.
[4] *H. of C. Journals,* VIII. 659.
[6] *H. of C. Journals,* IX. 306.
[8] *H. of C. Journals,* IX. 270.

the test of adherence to the Established Church. A test imposed on members by statute would have become operative at an earlier stage after an election than the tests imposed only by orders of the House. These could not become operative until after the Speaker had been chosen and the House had reaffirmed an order made in a preceding Parliament, or had adopted a new one. The Test Act, which was aimed at Nonconformists, excluded them from municipal corporations until 1828, except in a few instances in which Dissenters availed themselves of the Indemnity Acts, which in the eighteenth century were annually passed by Parliament. Where Nonconformists did not avail themselves of these annual Acts, the Test Act of the reign of Charles II excluded them from any part in electing members to the House of Commons in the numerous municipalities in which the right was by usage or by charter in the corporations.

Test Act of 1673 not applicable to Members. The test imposed by the Act, which required the reception of the communion according to the rites of the Anglican Church, was however neither in the Parliament of 1661–78, nor in any subsequent Parliament, made applicable to members of the House of Commons; and the only Protestant Dissenters at this time excluded from the House were Quakers and Moravians. Their refusal to take any oaths rendered them ineligible and also excluded them from the electoral franchises, except in instances such as that at the election of a knight of the shire for Brecon in 1693, when there were agreements between the candidates that Quakers "that could make out their estates should vote[1]."

A Quaker elected in 1699. After the amendment of the law in 1796, which made it possible for Quakers to exercise the franchise without being called upon to take an oath, one Quaker, John Archdale, was elected to the House of Commons. He was chosen to the Parliament of 1698–99 by the Buckinghamshire borough of Chipping Wycombe. On the 3rd of January, 1698–99, there was a call of the House. The oaths administered by the Lord Steward kept Archdale without the Chamber; and he responded to the call by addressing a letter to the Speaker. He reminded the Speaker that upon a call it would appear that he was duly chosen and returned for Chipping Wycombe, "therefore," continued Archdale's letter, "I request of thee to acquaint the Honorable House of Commons, the reason I have not yet appeared, which is—That the burgesses being voluntarily inclined to elect me, I did not oppose their inclinations, believing

---

[1] *H. of C. Journals,* xi. 463.

that my declaration of fidelity might in this case, as in others where the law requires an oath, be accepted. I am therefore ready to execute my trust if the House thinks fit to admit me thereupon, which I do humbly submit to their wisdom and justice, and shall acquiesce with what they will be pleased to determine therein. This is all at present.—I remain, Thy real and obliged friend, John Archdale[1]." " Ordered to attend next Friday morning" is the only entry in the Journals of January 3rd concerning Archdale's petition. On the 6th of January Archdale was at the bar. By direction of the House the Speaker asked him whether he had taken the oaths, the three now prescribed by 30 Charles II, 1 William and Mary, and 7 and 8 William and Mary, or would take them. " To which he answered That in regard to a principle of his religion, he had not taken the oaths, nor could take them." Archdale then withdrew, and the House ordered a new writ for Chipping Wycombe[2].

Quakers in the closing years of the seventeenth century, as in later days, were usually prosperous and well-to-do people. The frequency with which questions as to Quaker votes occurred in county election petitions, between the Restoration and the end of the seventeenth century, is testimony to the fact that many Quakers were freeholders[3]. The staid brethren in drab understood also how to agitate so as to secure their constitutional rights without sacrificing their religious scruples; so much so that the statute books from the Revolution to the reign of Queen Victoria are replete with clauses inserted in an almost endless variety of enactments each protecting the right of Quakers to affirm instead of taking oath, and each a testimony to the pertinacity and alertness of that body in securing their rights as citizens, and at the same time preserving to the full the principles of their religion. *Quakers and the Franchise.*

The attitude of Quakers towards the oaths, which, at the time Archdale wrote his dignified letter to the Speaker, excluded them from the House of Commons, is set out in a contemporary petition or manifesto. " We are not," it reads, " such as do wilfully and obstinately disobey any law of men, but for conscience sake, and that we may not sin against God nor offend his witness in us. Therefore we cannot obey laws contrary to our consciences, *Quakers and the Oaths.*

---

[1] *H. of C. Journals*, xii. 386.

[2] *H. of C. Journals*, xii. 388.

[3] *H. of C. Journals*, x. 76; xi. 83, 463; xiii. 78; Bramston, *Autobiography*, 392.

whatsoever we suffer, which we resist not nor rebel against, so that
our principles and practices are to obey every law and government,
either by doing or suffering. And though we disobey such laws as
are not according to the law of God, and rather do choose to
suffer, yet herein we are justified by the law of God and the Holy
Scriptures[1]."

Antagonism
of the
House to
Quakers.

Seven years earlier than the issue of the new writ for Chipping
Wycombe, due to Archdale's refusal to take the oaths, the Quakers
had petitioned the House of Commons for relief. They asked for
a bill providing " that their solemn answer may be accepted instead
of an oath," because " by reason of their tender consciences," they
could not take an oath in any case[2]. Their petition went to a
committee, which reported in favour of a bill, and asked leave to
introduce one, a request which was denied by the House[3]. This
was in 1692. In 1694 the feeling of the House was still so much
against the Quakers that a bill was introduced which would have
disabled all persons from voting at Parliamentary elections who
should refuse to take the oaths[4]. Had this measure passed it would
have put an end to agreements between candidates to permit
Quakers to poll without taking the oaths, and would have made it
no longer possible for returning officers good-naturedly to ignore
the prerequisite oaths, as the sheriff of Essex was disposed to do in
1695, when Sir Francis Masham, who was then a candidate, desired
to poll the Quakers, " who were come in great numbers[5]."

Quakers
relieved of
Disabilities.

In 1695 there was another petition from the Quakers on the
lines of that of 1692. Again there was a motion for leave for
a bill. This time leave was given, by 189 votes to 143[6]. The
bill was read a first time on the 19th of February, and encountered
so little opposition that by March 10th it was reported from
committee[7]. There were divisions on the remaining stages, but all
in favour of the bill. In the Lords the measure was amended in
some particulars[8]. The Commons accepted these amendments[9].
The bill received the royal assent, and thereafter it was possible
for Quakers to affirm in cases where people of other religious faiths
were required to take oaths[10]. Thus by Parliamentary agitation
extending over less than ten years, the Quakers freed themselves

[1] Sewell, *Hist. of the Quakers*, I. 557.
[2] *H. of C. Journals*, x. 714.
[3] *H. of C. Journals*, x. 734.
[4] *H. of C. Journals*, xi. 264, 303.
[5] Bramston, *Autobiography*, 392.
[6] *H. of C. Journals*, xi. 434.
[7] *H. of C. Journals*, xi. 502.
[8] *H. of C. Journals*, xi. 558.
[9] *H. of C. Journals*, xi. 560.
[10] 7 and 8 W. III, c. 24.

from the oaths which had disfranchised them in the constituencies.
The Act of 1696 was renewed from time to time; in 1722, not
without opposition from the bishops in the House of Lords[1].
In the reign of George II it was made permanent, and the privilege
enjoyed by Quakers since 1696 was then extended to Moravians[2].
Not until 1833, however, did the House of Commons so interpret
the Acts permitting Quakers to affirm instead of taking oaths as to
admit a Quaker into Parliament[3]. Until 1829, therefore, exclusion
from the House and the consequent restrictions on the choice of
constituencies based on religious beliefs, affected Roman Catholics,
Quakers and Jews.

Between the reign of Elizabeth and the Restoration Catholics, Barriers
as has been shown, were excluded from the House of Commons by against Roman
reason of their inability to take the oaths of supremacy and Catholics.
allegiance. During this period no man could take his seat until,
before the Lord Steward, he had taken (1) the oath of supremacy,
and (2) the oath of allegiance, which denied the authority of the
Pope to depose the sovereign; and (3) declared that he did from
his heart " abhor, detest and abjure, as impious and heretical, the
damnable doctrine and position that princes which be excommunicated or deprived by the Pope, may be deposed or murdered
by their subjects, or any other whatsoever[4]." The oath of
supremacy, with its denial that the Pope had " any jurisdiction,
power, superiority, pre-eminence or authority, ecclesiastical or
spiritual, in this realm " was in general sufficient to exclude Roman
Catholics from the House. But from 1678 a more direct test, one
raising an almost insuperable barrier against Roman Catholics, was
imposed to disable " Papists from sitting in either House of
Parliament." It was a test which no good Catholic could stand;
and was established by Act of Parliament[5], not by order of the
House, like the communion test of the Parliaments between 1614
and 1672.

The new test was a declaration against transubstantiation, Declaration
which every person elected to the House had to make, after taking against Transub-
the oaths of allegiance and supremacy, and until it had been made stantiation.
no person so elected was to vote in the House, or sit there during
any debate after the Speaker was chosen. Each member had " to

---

[1] *Parl. Hist.*, vii. 938, 946.   [2] 22 Geo. II, c. 30.
[3] May, *Constitutional Hist.*, iii. 177.   [4] *H. of C. Journals*, viii. 55.
[5] 30 C. II, *St.* 2.

make, subscribe, and audibly repeat" this declaration :—" I, A. B.,
do solemnly and sincerely in the presence of God, profess, testify
and declare that I do believe that in the sacrament of the Lord's
Supper there is not any transubstantiation of the elements of bread
and wine into the body and blood of Christ at or after the
consecration thereof by any person whatsoever; and that the in-
vocation or adoration of the Virgin Mary or any other saint, and
the sacrifice of the mass, as they are now used in the Church of
Rome, are superstitious and idolatrous." This Act, over which
there had been much controversy between the two Houses, and
much unusual pressure exerted by the House of Commons on the
House of Lords to hasten its several stages in the Lords[1], received
the royal assent on the 30th of November, 1678; and on the same
day members of the House of Commons began making the new
declaration, and were so occupied on three successive days[2].

The Oaths after the Revolution.   By the Act of Settlement at the Revolution the oaths of
supremacy and allegiance, in the form in which they had respectively
stood since the reigns of Elizabeth and James I, were abrogated.
The new oath of allegiance was a simple declaration that the person
taking it would be faithful and bear true allegiance to the King
and Queen.   The oath of abjuration, and the declaration that " no
foreign prince, person, prelate, state or potentate, hath, or ought
to have, any jurisdiction, power, superiority, pre-eminence or
authority, ecclesiastical or spiritual within this realm" were continued.   So was the declaration of the Act of 1678 against
transubstantiation; and in 1689 Sir Henry Mounson and Lord
Fanshawe were excluded from the House of Commons because they
would not take these oaths and make the declaration[3].

Roman Catholics excluded until 1829.   In the eighteenth century, there was a new oath in support of
the Revolution settlement of the Crown, and there were several
changes in the older oaths; but the oaths and declarations of 1678,
which excluded Roman Catholics, survived until the Relief Act of
1829, and from the reign of Elizabeth to that of George IV
conscientious Catholics had to stand aside when constituencies were
electing men to represent them in the House of Commons.   They
were prevented from coming forward first by the oath of supremacy
of 1563, and for the last century and a half of the unreformed

[1] Cf. *H. of C. Journals,* ix. 538, 541.
[2] *H. of C. Journals,* ix. 551.
[3] Cf. *H. of C. Journals,* x. 131.

Parliament by the declaration against transubstantiation. Denials of the "damnable doctrine and position that princes excommunicated might be deposed or murdered," and the declarations against the jurisdiction of the Pope "ecclesiastical or spiritual within this realm" might not have been an obstacle to all conscientious Roman Catholics. But it was impossible for any Roman Catholic, true to his faith, to make the declaration against transubstantiation; and this was the great barrier against Roman Catholics in the period between the abrogation of the old oaths of supremacy and allegiance in 1689, and the Relief Act of 1829.

The Earl of Surrey, whose father, the Duke of Norfolk, was the first Catholic nobleman since 1678 to sit in the House of Lords[1], was the first Roman Catholic to enter the House of Commons after the passing of the Act of 1829. The Norfolk family, which was possessed of extensive property in Sussex, had long controlled several boroughs in that county. Although the Dukes of Norfolk, between 1678 and 1829, could not sit in the House of Lords, the political influence indirectly exercised by the Howards had long been considerable. The Duke of Newcastle, when he was managing the general election of 1734, appealed to the Duke of Norfolk of that day for his support[2]; while a later Duke of Norfolk kept such a strict control over the members whom he returned for his boroughs, that it was customary with him to send the agent of his estates to the House of Commons with orders to his members as to how they were to vote[3].

The first Roman Catholic in the House in 1829.

As soon as the Relief Act of 1829 received the royal assent on the 13th of April, one of the Duke of Norfolk's members applied for the Chiltern Hundreds; and on May 4th, 1829, the Earl of Surrey, heir apparent to the Duke, was returned for Horsham, where the vacancy so created had occurred. The new member took his seat on the 6th of May. "This being the first admission of a Roman Catholic to the House since the passing of the Relief Act," reads a contemporary report of the Earl of Surrey's reception by the House, "the circumstance occasioned some sensation, and the noble lord was warmly greeted by many of his friends[4]."

The Earl of Surrey's Election.

[1] May, ii. 173.
[2] Basil Williams, "The Duke of Newcastle and the Election of 1734," *Eng. Hist. Review*, xii. 460.
[3] Cf. Hansard, 3rd Series, v. 373.
[4] Hansard, xxi. 1105.

O'Connell
and the
Relief Act.

O'Connell, the first Catholic to represent an Irish constituency in the House of Commons of the Imperial Parliament, had been elected in 1828. His election for County Clare had resulted in the Relief Act of 1829. O'Connell did not claim to sit until the Relief Act was passed. The Earl of Surrey had taken his seat for Horsham before O'Connell claimed his on the 15th of May. As O'Connell had been elected prior to the Relief Act, the question was raised as to whether he was entitled to take the new oath. After two nights' debate, and a division in which, with a spirit little less than vindictive, the Government threw the weight of its influence in the scale against O'Connell[1], the House decided that O'Connell was not entitled to his seat unless he took the old oaths. As O'Connell refused to do so, his seat was declared vacant[2]. At this juncture a borough patron offered O'Connell a seat free of expense[3]. O'Connell declined the offer, and again contested County Clare. He was again returned; but he did not take his seat in the House until the session of 1830.

Disabilities
of Scotch
Roman
Catholics.

In Scotland, by an enactment of the Scotch Parliament, an enactment continued at the union in 1707, the disqualification of Roman Catholics as Parliamentary candidates was positive and direct. There a Roman Catholic was specifically disqualified because he was a Catholic, and not as in England in consequence of his inability to take the oaths or make the declaration[4]. The disability of Roman Catholics in Scotland was removed in 1829. But as late as 1891 not a single Roman Catholic had ever been returned by a Scotch constituency[5].

The Con-
stitutional
Position of
Jews.

Until a quarter of a century after the Reform Act of 1832 it was not possible for Jews to sit and vote in the House of Commons. But it is not likely that Jews were candidates for Parliament earlier than the Revolution. In the first two and a half centuries of the representative system, Jews were to be found only in a few of the larger trading centres. There they were a class apart, treated as aliens. From the reign of Elizabeth to the Protectorate they were banished from England[6]. On their return during the

---

[1] Cf. Fitzpatrick, *Correspondence*, Daniel O'Connell, ii. 188.

[2] Cf. Fitzpatrick, *Correspondence*, Daniel O'Connell, ii. 184, 185.

[3] Cf. Fitzpatrick, *Correspondence*, Daniel O'Connell, ii. 189.

[4] Cf. Peel, *Memoirs*, i. 300, 301.

[5] Cf. May, iii. 176.

[6] Heywood, *County Election Law*, 217, 218; Goldsmid, *Remarks on the Civil Disabilities of the British Jews*, 9.

Protectorate, there was still on the statute book the Act of the reign of James I, which denied naturalisation to any alien who did not receive the sacrament of the Lord's Supper, before his application for naturalisation[1]. With this enactment still in force a Jew could have no place under the Constitution. He could neither vote at a Parliamentary election, nor be a candidate for the House; and between the return of the Jews in Cromwell's time, and the closing years of the reign of George II, popular feeling continued so hostile to them as to compel Parliament to recall a measure of relief,—to repeal in one session an Act which had been passed in the previous session.

In 1753 the orderly and loyal demeanour of the Jews, both in England and in the British colonies in America, induced the Government to propose to Parliament an Act repealing that part of the statute of James I which compelled Jews to receive the sacrament before petitioning Parliament for naturalisation. It was introduced in the Lords. It encountered no opposition there, not even from the bishops, who were usually jealous of the slightest inroad on the code under which religious tests were then imposed. In the House of Commons, however, an alarm was spread that the measure was covertly intended against the Established Church. The bill was strongly opposed by the Tories; and in and out of the House religious feeling was invoked against what was stigmatised as the bartering of a Christian people's birthright for some clandestine gain which the Government dared not own. But in spite of the clamour, the opposition in the House of Commons could muster only fifty-five votes against the measure, which received the royal assent[2]. Unfortunately for the Jews, the clamour outside Parliament did not cease with the end of the session. It was kept up during the recess; and in 1754 the Act was repealed, " because it had given occasions to discontents," and had disquieted " the minds of many of His Majesty's subjects[3]." *The Jewish Relief Act of 1753.*

Such being the position of Jews in England in the middle years of the eighteenth century, and such the popular feeling towards them, it is reasonable to assume that up to this time Jews were well outside the range of choice of constituencies seeking Parliamentary candidates. Until as late as the reign of George II, a Jew must have been as much outside the limits of choice as a *Jews outside of Political Life.*

[1] 7 James I, c. 2.
[2] Torrens, *Hist. of Cabinets*, II. 165, 167 ; 26 Geo. II, c. 26.
[3] 27 Geo. II, c. 1.

negro is to-day in a Congressional district in a Northern or Western State in America, or in a Congressional district of a State of the Black Belt, where the white electors are politically dominant. Had there been no racial feeling at this time, the conditions of naturalisation, imposed by the Act of James I, would have disqualified Jews both as electors and as Parliamentary candidates.

An Awakening of Jewish Ambition. I have not been able to discover that Jews manifested any ambition for Parliamentary life much earlier than 1741. It is recorded of William Mellish, who was elected in that year for the borough of Retford, that in early life he was betrothed to a Jewess of considerable wealth; but that "by a curious clause in the will of her father, her husband could not inherit, until he was chosen member of Parliament." "Accordingly," to give this story in the language of the local historian whose book has perpetuated it, "he offered himself for Retford, and his wife was so overjoyed on his election, that she fell into hysterics and died from the effects[1]." William Mellish was returned in 1741 for Retford[2]; and this is the only evidence I have been able to find in any way corroborating the Retford story. But if the story be true, it proves only that the House of Commons in the reign of George II was coming to have attractions for Jews, and that they recognized that there were bars to their admission. Thomas Thompson, "natural son of Levi, a Jew well known in the city and upon 'change, was elected for Evesham" in 1790[3]. But Thompson's mother could not have been of the Jewish religion. At any rate Thompson must not have regarded himself as a Jew; for he took the oaths, was admitted to the House, and sat in two Parliaments[4]. Had he been an orthodox Jew, he would have discovered that his entry to the House was barred, if by nothing else, by the oath of abjuration[5], and in particular by the words in that oath "on the true faith of a Christian." No orthodox Jew could take this oath.

Exclusion of Jews from House of Commons. In the early years of the nineteenth century, and especially after the Acts of 1828 and 1829 abolishing tests, it was maintained by the advocates of Jewish relief measures that the exclusion of Jews was accidental, and that Parliament in the seventeenth and eighteenth centuries had not legislated directly for the exclusion of Jews from the House of Commons. It was argued that

[1] Piercy, *Hist. of Retford*, 74.
[2] *Official List*, pt. ii. 90.
[3] May, *Hist. of Evesham*, 292.
[4] *Official List*, pt. ii. 196, 209.
[5] 6 Anne, c. 23.

the Acts of Elizabeth and James I, which required oaths to be taken on the Evangelists, a form of oath which it was impossible for Jews to take, could not have been inserted to exclude Jews, since in the days of Elizabeth and James I no Jews resided in England[1]. "Nothing," wrote Goldsmid, one of the foremost advocates of relief measures for Jews, "can exceed the simplicity of the instruments by which so much hardship is produced. The first and principal of these consists of the words 'upon the true faith of a Christian,' which occur in the abjuration oath, and which also form part of the declaration prescribed by the law of 1828[2]. It appears neither from the words of the statutes establishing the abjuration oath and the declaration, nor, as far as I am aware, from the debates which occurred on the latter of them, that the phrase 'upon the true faith of a Christian' was originally designed by those who introduced it to affect the condition of the Jews[3]."

The probability is that when the abjuration oath was first *Attitude of* enacted in 1610, and re-enacted in the reign of Queen Anne, *Parliament towards* Parliament had not Jews in mind. But there can be no doubt *Jews.* about the attitude of Parliament towards Jews, as Parliamentary candidates, in the middle years of the eighteenth century. Its intention then was unmistakeably against their eligibility for·seats in the House of Commons; for in the Act of 1753, by which Jews were enabled to naturalise, there was a clause which provided "that no person shall hereafter be naturalised, unless in the bill exhibited for that purpose, there be a clause or particular words inserted to declare that such person shall not thereby be enabled to be of the Privy Council or a member of either House of Parliament[4]."

A few men of the Jewish race were of the House of Commons *Converted* between 1753 and 1832. Two of them, Sir Gideon Sampson and *Jews in the House.* Sir Manasseh Lopes, were long of the House, and both obtained notoriety as borough-mongers. But these men, and the others of the Jewish race who were elected to the unreformed Parliament, were not of the Jewish religion; and no orthodox Jew was ever of the unreformed House of Commons.

[1] Goldsmid, *Civil Disabilities of British Jews,* 9.
[2] The declaration which was embodied in the Act of 1828, for the relief of Dissenters.
[3] Goldsmid, *Civil Disabilities of British Jews,* 9.
[4] 26 Geo. II, c. 26.

Jews admitted by Sessional Order in 1858.

To the end of the old electoral system Jews were outside the range of electoral choice, and the agitation for their admission to the House, begun in 1830, was attended with no success until 1858. From 1858 to 1866 the House of Commons was open to Jews in consequence of a change in the form of the oath, made by sessional order. This new order was made possible by an Act which was the outcome of a compromise with the House of Lords, a compromise under which it was put in the power of the House to admit a Jewish member, while it remained possible for the Lords to exclude a Jewish peer[1].

The End of the Struggle.

Between 1830 and 1858 the attitude of the House of Lords towards Jews was much the attitude of the Parliament of 1753 which passed the Act under which the naturalisation certificate of every Jew was to have written across its face the statement that the holder was ineligible as a member of Parliament. The compromise of 1858, brought about by the election of Baron Lionel Nathan de Rothschild for the City of London in 1847[2], was unsatisfactory, in that a sessional order carried with it no guarantee of permanence. The House in one session could admit Jews; in the next it could refuse them. Constituencies had thus no abiding guarantee that a candidate whom they had elected would be seated. In 1860, however, the sessional order was made a standing order, and thus given a more permanent character. This standing order of 1860 served until 1866. Then a new oath was established[3]. From the new oath the words " on the true faith of a Christian " were at last omitted. Thus, as the result of an agitation extending from 1830 to 1866, the constitutional barrier against the Jews finally disappeared; and from 1858 to 1888 men of no religious faith, who could not conscientiously take any oaths, were the only persons excluded from the House of Commons by religious tests.

[1] 21 and 22 Vict., c. 48.   [2] *Official List*, pt. ii. 402.
[3] 29 and 30 Vict., c. 19.

CHAPTER VIII.

RESTRICTIONS ON CHOICE FOR THE PROTECTION OF THE CROWN.

FROM the reign of Elizabeth the choice of constituencies was restricted by oaths imposed on members as a protection to the Crown. All the oaths taken within the walls of Westminster Palace, but not inside the Chamber, come within this category. The power to administer these oaths was given to the Lord Steward in 1563, for the satisfaction of the Crown, which at that time, and as long as these oaths taken before the Lord Steward survived, was or was held to be not sufficiently safeguarded by the oaths taken at the table of the House of Commons[1]. Oaths administered by the Lord Steward.

All the oaths so administered from the reign of Elizabeth to that of William III had one object. They were intended as a protection to the Crown against the claims and aggression of the Papacy. After the death of the deposed King, James II, there were established additional oaths for the safeguarding of the Parliamentary settlement of the Crown made at the Revolution; so that from the reign of William III to that of Victoria, oaths were required from members as safeguards to the settlements of both the Reformation and the Revolution. Safeguarding the Crown.

The first of these two sets of oaths, the oaths of supremacy and allegiance, dating respectively from 1563 and 1610, have been dealt with in the preceding chapter. They have their place there because, during the greater part of the long period in which they were demanded from members, the oath of supremacy, at The Oath of Allegiance.

---

[1] Cf. Peel's Speech on the case of Mr O'Connell, *Mirror of Parliament*, 1829, III. 1685.

least, was in practice a religious test, rather than an oath which afforded any needed protection to the Crown. The oath of allegiance could be taken by Roman Catholics. In the seventeenth century it was taken by Roman Catholics in Ireland; and by the British North America Act of 1774[1] this oath was all that was demanded of the French Roman Catholic population of Canada. But in England and Ireland the oath of supremacy served as a constitutional dividing line between Protestants and Roman Catholics. For that reason I have included it among the religious tests which, from 1563 to 1888, had the effect of restricting the choice of constituencies in electing members to the House of Commons. From 1689 to 1696 the shortened and simplified oath of allegiance[2] was all that was required from members of the House of Commons, as a safeguard to the settlement of the Revolution. In this oath there was no mention of the Revolutionary settlement of the Crown. All that was required from a candidate elected to Parliament between the Revolution and 1696 was an oath that he would be faithful and bear true allegiance to their Majesties, William and Mary.

The Oaths after the Revolution. In these years the oaths safeguarding the Crown were fewer, shorter and simpler, than at any time since 1563, or in the subsequent history of the House of Commons prior to 1868. In this period, from 1689 to 1696, there were taken before the Lord Steward or his deputies, (1) the simple and shortened oath of allegiance; and (2) the remodelled oath of 1689, declaring abhorrence of the "damnable doctrine and position" that excommunicated princes might be deposed or murdered by their subjects, and also declaring that "no foreign prince, person, prelate, state or potentate, hath or ought to have any jurisdiction, power, superiority, or pre-eminence or authority, ecclesiastical or spiritual, in these realms." During these seven years the oaths taken outside the Chamber were so tersely expressed that they could have been printed on a post-card. Inside the Chamber a member had to repeat these oaths, and had also to make the declaration against transubstantiation established by the Act of 1678.

Association Pledge. In 1696 there was an addition to these oaths, and a new political test was established. By an Act passed in this year, members of the House of Commons were required to subscribe to the association pledge, to declare that King William was the

---

[1] 14 Geo. III, c. 3.   [2] 1 W. and M., c. 2.

rightful and lawful sovereign; to engage to stand by each other in support and defence of " His Majesty's most sacred person and government, against the late King James, and all his adherents "; and, in case His Majesty came to a violent or untimely death, to oblige themselves " to unite, associate, and stand by each other, in revenging the same upon his enemies and their adherents," and in supporting and defending the succession of the Crown according to the Act made in the first year of King William and Queen Mary[1]. From 1696 to the death of the King in 1702, all members of the House were thus compelled to proclaim their adherence to William III, and pledge themselves to the defence of his person and government.

The first oath—other than the association of 1696—imposed as a protection to the Crown against any other special danger than that of Rome, was established in 1701. In September of that year James II died at St Germains. On the day of his death Louis XIV proclaimed James's son, James Frederick Edward, James III of England. Immediately all England burst into a storm of indignation against the French King for having thus dared to acknowledge as King of England a boy whose title had been rejected by the English Parliament and nation. William III dissolved Parliament. A new House of Commons was elected. The army was raised to forty thousand men. A large grant was made for the navy, and further to meet the exigencies due to the action of the King of France and to safeguard the Revolution settlement there was passed the Act[2] by which the new oath of 1701 was established. *The Pretender and the Oath of 1701.*

By this oath of the last year of William III every person elected to the House of Commons had to "acknowledge, profess, testify and declare" in his conscience before God and the world, that King William was lawful and rightful king, and to declare his belief that "the person who pretended to be the Prince of Wales during the life of the late King James, and, since his decease, pretending to be and taking on himself the style and title of King of England by the name of James III, hath no right or title whatsoever to the crown of this realm or any other the dominion thereto belonging." The person sworn had also to renounce, refuse, and abjure any allegiance or obedience to the Pretender, and to swear to maintain and defend "the limitation *The Terms of the Oath.*

---

[1] 7 and 8 W. and M., c. 27. [2] 13 and 14 W. III, c. 6.

and succession of the crown against him, the said James, and all other persons whatsoever, as the same is and stands limited" by the Act "declaring the rights and liberties of the subject and settling the succession of the crown." It was directed by the Act establishing this new oath that the oath should be taken " between the hours of nine in the morning and four in the afternoon," at the table in the middle of the House, "whilst a full House of Commons is there duly sitting with their Speaker in the chair"; and that until he had taken the oath no member was to sit in the House " during debate after the Speaker is chosen."

Changes in the Oath.   This oath—in which, as in the oath of allegiance of 1610, there were embodied the words "upon the true faith of a Christian," which in the nineteenth century long served as a barrier to keep Jews out of Parliament—underwent several alterations in the eighteenth century. These were consequent upon the deaths of the Chevalier de St George in 1765; and of Charles Edward, the last of the Stuart Pretenders, in 1788. On the death of the Chevalier de St George the abjuration was directed against "the person who pretended to be the Prince of Wales[1]"; and after the death of Charles Edward in 1788 it was directed against "any of the descendants of the person who pretended to be the Prince of Wales."

The Oaths of 1866 and 1868.   The oath so originating in 1701, and so amended in 1766, survived the unreformed Parliament, and was taken by members of the House of Commons until 1866. Then the oath of supremacy, traceable to 1563; the oath of allegiance, dating back in one form or another to 1610; and the oath of abjuration, dating from 1701, were all remodelled, or rather there was substituted for them a single oath, by which a member of the House of Commons swore that he would be faithful and bear true allegiance to Her Majesty Queen Victoria, and undertook to "maintain and support the succession to the Crown, as the same stands limited and settled by virtue of the Act passed in the reign of William III, entitled ' an Act for the further limitation of the Crown, and better securing the rights and liberties of the subject[2].'" The oath of 1866, the shortest and simplest oath since that of the period between 1689 and 1696, and the first oath since 1563 which embodied no allusion to the Papacy and its claims, was short-lived. It was abandoned in 1868 for the present oath, by which the person taking it swears

---

[1] 6 Geo. III, c. 53.   [2] 29 and 30 Vict., c. 19.

simply that he will be faithful and bear true allegiance to His Majesty King Edward VII, his heirs and successors according to law[1]. But these nineteenth century changes were made subsequent to the reform of the representative system in 1832; and from 1696, electors, in making their choice of representatives to the House of Commons, had to put aside men who were unable to pledge themselves by oath to the two Parliamentary settlements affecting the Crown, the one growing out of the Reformation and the other out of the Revolution.

Scotland had a peculiar place in respect to these various laws establishing restrictions of choice on the Parliamentary constituencies. As has been shown in the chapter dealing with restrictions on choice due to religious tests, Roman Catholics were on the excluded list in Scotland by specific mention as such in the enactments, and not, as were Roman Catholics in England, because of their inability to take oaths or make the declaration against transubstantiation. Scotland, in the same way, had a peculiar place in the eighteenth century legislation intended to keep out of the House of Commons men who might be disloyal to the Revolution settlement. After the Revolution the Scotch Episcopal Church, which owed its establishment to Charles II, became a stronghold of the champions of the deposed Stuarts, and men who were of this church and avowed themselves as nonjurors were long in close correspondence with the adherents of the exiled family. In the reigns of George I and George II there were laws passed to check this power for mischief of the Episcopal Church. Among these was an enactment passed in 1746[2], which directly touched the representative system, and affected both electors and Parliamentary candidates. It declared that no person should be capable of being elected or voting at a Parliamentary election in Scotland, who should be present twice in the same year at divine service in any episcopal church " whereof the pastor or minister thereof shall not pray in express words for His Majesty by name, and for His Majesty's heirs or successors, and for all the royal family." Under this enactment it was competent for a candidate at a Scotch election, or for any person who could vote at an election, to object against a candidate or voter that he had attended services at which the King was not prayed for, and to prove the charge by witnesses

The Scotch Protection of the Revolutionary Settlement.

---

[1] 31 and 32 Vict., c. 72.　　　[2] 19 Geo. II, c. 38.

on oath; or to put the candidate or voter against whom the objection was made on oath. In 1792 there was a measure for the relief of the Scotch Episcopal Church from the severe legislation affecting it which had been passed in the first half of the eighteenth century. But in the new Act there was continued the clause incapacitating as members of Parliament men who had attended services at which the King and the royal family went unmentioned in the prayers, and the clause was still on the statute books when, in 1832, the Scotch representative system was reformed.

CHAPTER IX.

MEN WITHOUT MEANS EXCLUDED FROM THE HOUSE OF COMMONS.

FROM 1710 until 1858 men who could not furnish proof that they were possessed of assured incomes were by statute excluded from the House of Commons. But the exclusion, established by law in 1710 and maintained for nearly a century and a half, was not a new discrimination against men without means, although it was then first brought about by statute. For at least a century earlier than the Act of Queen Anne's reign which disqualified men who had not settled incomes derived from landed property, men who were not possessed of means, men who were unable to serve without pay, and, later on in the seventeenth century, to expend money freely to secure election, had been very generally compelled to stand aside when constituencies were choosing representatives to Parliament. Usage, as distinct from statute, brought about this earlier discrimination. In this respect, however, usage gradually became buttressed by law ; and the laws which grew out of the usage in accordance with which candidates paid election charges, have survived the greater part of the exclusion code of the pre-reform period ; and in the opening years of the twentieth century these laws, throwing the official costs of elections on candidates, coupled with the fact that members of the House of Commons serve without pay and have to meet many financial calls from the constituencies, constitute one of the great barriers between England and democracy.

The most obvious barrier is the House of Lords. The three great Reform Acts of the nineteenth century have left the House of Lords untouched. Excepting the exclusion of bishops of the

Laws and Usages excluding Men without Means.

The Barriers between England and Democracy.

Church of England in Ireland, brought about by the Irish Church Disestablishment Act of 1868[1], and the inclusion of life peers subsequent to 1856[2], the constitution and powers of the House of Lords are to-day what they were before the House of Commons underwent the great reform of 1832. The manner of creating peers has not been changed; while, by successive reforms in the system of Parliamentary representation, a share in the electing of the Commons has been made possible to every man not of the peerage, who for twelve months has had a settled abode and has made no call on the poor law funds. Except for the possibility of plural voting, so far as the franchise is concerned, England is to-day a democracy. But England is not a democracy in the same sense as the United States, or even Canada; for apart from the House of Lords, which forms a second line of defence, there is the other great barrier against democracy—the barrier built up by usage from the sixteenth century to the eighteenth, and in the eighteenth and nineteenth centuries legalised and strengthened by Parliamentary enactment.

The Building Up of the Barrier.
The erection of this barrier, which has had the effect of putting men who are not possessed of means on the list of those from whom the constituencies cannot choose representatives, was brought about by slow stages. Its foundations were laid as soon as men were willing to accept election to the House of Commons without pay from their constituents. The barrier was raised a tier higher when men became so eager to be of the House that they would bribe electors individually and in the aggregate to choose them, and when they became willing also to defray all charges, official but as yet not statutory, at Parliamentary elections. The barrier had reached this height without any aid from Parliament before the seventeenth century came to an end.

Election Expenses thrown on Candidates.
Early in the eighteenth century Parliament began to concern itself with raising the barrier. The first addition was the Act of 1710, disqualifying men who had not incomes derived from land. From the following year it began to pass enactments throwing official expenses on Parliamentary candidates. In the early years of the eighteenth century the charges thus thrown by law on candidates were small. There were wide intervals between the first of these eighteenth century laws, and the later ones of the same century; and there was no law prior to the reform of 1832 which

---

[1] 32 and 33 Vict., c. 42.   [2] May, i. 295.

threw all official charges on candidates. Candidates paid all the expenses of the pre-reform period; but they paid most of them because it was customary to do so, not because there were laws which directed that all the returning officers' charges should be paid by candidates[1]. But in the middle years of the eighteenth century enactments were passed which established the principle that expenses at elections were chargeable on candidates; and after the House of Commons had been reformed in 1832, it was made possible for returning officers to collect at law many charges upon candidates which in the earlier history of the representative system had had nothing but usage to support them.

Wages hardly survived the sixteenth century. Devizes paid as late as 1641[2]; King's Lynn as late as 1643[3]; and Andrew Marvell, to cite a much quoted instance, received wages from Hull until his death in 1678[4]. But while it is possible to cite these and a few earlier seventeenth century instances of payments to members, it would be equally easy to cite ten times as many instances, prior to the last payment to Marvell, in which at the time of election constituencies exacted written pledges from members that they would not charge the statutory wages and expenses. "Provided always," reads an agreement of this kind made between the borough of Northampton and Henry Hickman and Francis Tate, who represented the borough in the Parliament of 1601, "that both of them bear and defray their own charges in all things, without any allowances or recompense from this town or inhabitants thereof, or any of them in this behalf[5]." Such agreements had been frequent in the sixteenth century. They became increasingly common in the seventeenth century. Hundreds of them are to be found among the records of old Parliamentary boroughs. As regards most borough constituencies, it may therefore be inferred that from the reign of James I the man who could not afford to pay his own expenses to and from London and bear all his own charges there was on the exclusion list, and, whether a resident or a non-resident of a borough, had little prospect of becoming of the House of Commons.

The position of men who were not wealthy became more

The last Payments of Wages.

[1] Cf. *Rep. Select Committee on Election Expenses*, 1834, xix, xxii.
[2] Waylen, *Hist. of Devizes*, 153.
[3] *Hist. MSS. Comm. 11th Rep.*, App., pt. iii. 181.
[4] Marvell, *Works*, ii. xxxv, xxxvi.
[5] *Northampton Borough Records*, ii. 493.

Expenses
become
heavier.

disadvantageous as the seventeenth century progressed. In the boroughs money bribes were now becoming general[1]. Returning officers were charging fees and out-of-pocket expenses to candidates[2]. The Clerk of the Crown was collecting fees on the return of writs[3]; and with the numerous oaths which electors might be compelled to take subsequent to the Restoration, new charges were thrown on candidates, and it became necessary for them to hire agents, lawyers and others, to watch their interests at the polls.

Bribing Con-
stituencies.

Treating and bribing of individual electors in the boroughs in the seventeenth century made it next to impossible for a candidate to go into an election, unless he were possessed of a long purse, and prepared to spend freely. But in no way is the growing expense attendant on the representation of a borough in the seventeenth and eighteenth centuries better illustrated than by the practice which came into existence in the seventeenth century of bribing constituencies in the aggregate. Even more than the nefarious practice of individual bribery, it shows the attitude of constituencies towards Parliamentary candidates. It accentuates the difference in popular sentiment between the fourteenth and fifteenth centuries, when constituencies paid the wages and travelling expenses of their representatives, and the seventeenth and eighteenth centuries, when the popular idea was that a man who desired to represent a constituency must be prepared to pay well for the honour or advantage he sought.

Payments
for the
Freedom.

The beginning of the practice of positive bribery for constituencies in the aggregate can be traced back to as early a period as the reign of Charles I. It doubtless had its beginning in the practice by which candidates in the sixteenth century were made free of boroughs in order technically to comply with the old law that a member must be of the constituency he represented in Parliament. At first such freedoms were granted without charge[4]; but between the Restoration and the Reform Act, in many boroughs heavy fees were demanded for admission to the freedom[5], and by-laws were made to prevent a candidate going to poll unless he had been admitted.

---

[1] Cf. Marvell, *Works,* III. 538.

[2] Cf. Ballard, *Chronicles of Woodstock,* 318; Burton, *Chronology of Stamford,* 26.   [3] *H. of C. Journals,* XII. 484.

[4] Cf. Bacon, *Annalls of Ipswiche,* 340; Whitelocke, *Notes on the King's Writ,* I. 502; Izacks, *Antiquities of Exeter,* 127.

[5] Cf. *Municipal Corporations Comm. 1st Rep.,* App., pt. IV. 2927.

The earliest instances of bribing constituencies in the aggregate Bargains for Reduced Wages. were those in which representatives accepted service for less than the statutory rate of wages, fixed in 1323[1], at four shillings a day for every knight of the shire, and two shillings for every citizen or burgess; or those in which, with a view to lessening the drafts on the municipal treasuries, members stole away from Parliament before the session had come to an end. As an instance of the first kind may be cited the case of Rochester, which in the reign of Henry IV, made an agreement with a newcomer, "a foreigner" in the phraseology of the period, that if he would serve in Parliament free of all expense, he should be made free of the borough[2]. Special agreements were sometimes made for less than the statutory money payment, and sometimes for payment in kind. In 1463 the bailiffs of Weymouth agreed with John Sackvylle that he should serve the borough in Parliament for a cade of five hundred mackerel[3]; and in 1465 there was an agreement between the bailiffs of Dunwich and John Strange by which Strange pledged himself to give service in the Parliament of 1465 "for a cade of full herring," whether the Parliament "holds long time or short[4]." In 1472 there was an agreement with the town of Ipswich by which William Worsop covenanted to serve for five shillings a week, and John Walworth for three-and-fourpence a week[5].

In the fourteenth century, while boroughs still regarded repre- Curtailing Attendance on Parliament. sentation in the House of Commons as a burden to be evaded or shirked whenever possible, and when cities of the trading and commercial importance of Bristol had clauses inserted in their charters providing that they should "not in any wise be burdened to send more than two men only to the Parliament[6]," the members who stayed the shortest time in attendance on the House of Commons "afforded the greatest amount of satisfaction to themselves and their fellow townsmen[7]." As late as 1532, long after seats in the House were becoming objects of ambition, Canterbury gave John Bridges, one of its representatives, a sum of money, "towards a bonet for saving the wage that he should have had of

---

[1] 16 Ed. II.

[2] Palgrave, *Dormant Parl. Boroughs*, 14, 15.

[3] Ellis, *Hist. of Weymouth*, 163.

[4] *Archæologia*, I. 225.

[5] Bacon, *Annalls of Ipswiche*, 133.

[6] Corbett, *Election Franchise for Corporate Counties*, 30, 31.

[7] Roberts, *Social Hist. of the Southern Counties*, 469.

the city, by reason of his being at home from the Parliament after Easter term[1]." Canterbury's representative may have stayed away from London on account of the plague, which made a break in the session of the Parliament of 1532–33[2]. But evidently such desertions of Parliamentary service, which can be traced back as early as 1323, when a burgess from Lyme Regis came home after four days[3], were quite common; for in 1514–15 there was an Act of Parliament to put an end to them[4].

An Act to stop the Practice.

The preamble of this Act of 1514–15 describes the practice which the Act was aimed to prevent. "Forsomuch as commonly in the end of every Parliament," reads the preamble, "divers and many great and weighty matters, as well touching the pleasure, will and surety of Our Sovereign Lord the King, as the common weal of this his realm and subjects, are to be treated, communed of, and by authority of Parliament to be concluded, so yet is that divers knights of shires, citizens for cities, burgesses for boroughs, and barons of the Cinque Ports, long time before the end of the said Parliament of their own authority depart and goeth home to their counties, whereby the said great and weighty matters are many times greatly delayed." It was accordingly enacted that from henceforth "none of the said knights, citizens, burgesses and barons, nor any of them that hereafter shall be elected to come or be in any Parliament, do depart from the same Parliament, nor absent himself from the same, till the same Parliament be fully finished, ended or prorogued, except he or they so departing have license of the Speaker and Commons in the same Parliament assembled, and the same license be entered of record in the book of the Clerk of the Parliament * * * upon pain to every of them so departing or absenting themselves to lose all those sums of money which he or they should or ought to have had for his or their wages, and that all the counties, cities and boroughs, whereof any such persons shall be so elected, and the inhabitants of the same, shall be clearly discharged of all the said wages against the said person and persons, and their executors for evermore."

Reducing Travelling Allowances.

Members, while not foregoing wages or attempting to cut down the number of days of attendance in Parliament. seem sometimes to have agreed to accept less than the statutory mileage allowances.

---

[1] *Hist. MSS. Comm. 9th Rep.*, App., 152; *Official List*, pt. i. 60.
[2] Parry, 202.
[3] Roberts, *Southern Counties*, 469.
[4] 6 Henry VIII, c. 16.

Twenty miles a day in winter, and thirty in summer, were in the sixteenth century reckoned in official accounts a day's journey. Members of Parliament were paid on this basis[1]. But in 1462 York compounded with its Parliamentary representatives; and since the distance between Westminster and York was a hundred and ninety miles, the citizens stipulated that their members should be content with twelve days' travelling expenses, instead of requiring payment for twenty days, the full legal period for which the journey money could be demanded[2].

Following bribes of this negative kind to constituencies came other bribes still of a negative character, which took the form of foregoing wages and travelling expenses altogether. Agreements for part wages and reduced travelling expenses were made almost invariably by resident members. Non-resident members went a step further and entered into agreements to serve altogether without pay[3]. Such undertakings on the part of candidates were really bribes to constituencies as a whole, as were agreements for part wages; for if wages and expenses were reduced or not paid at all, local taxation to cover these statutory charges was less, or had not to be levied. *Serving without Pay.*

The first instance I have traced of positive bribery of a constituency as a whole, an instance in which the candidate offered to do more than free the town of all expense attendant on its representation at Westminster, occurred at Hastings in 1640. Thomas Rede, when seeking election there, undertook "that if the mayor, jurats and freemen would be pleased to make choice of him for one of the burgesses, he would do them the best service he could, and moreover would give to the poor of Hastings twenty pounds down, and ten pounds a year during life, besides two barrels of gunpowder yearly for exercising the youths[4]." Rede had gone to Hastings "with letters of recommendation from certain noblemen." His proposal evidently found favour with the mayor and jurats, for he represented the port in two Parliaments[5]. *An Early Instance of Positive Bribery.*

Although this is the first case that I have been able to trace in which a member thus bought his seat of the electors, *"Something for the Corporation."*

[1] Mountmorres, *Ancient Parliaments of Ireland,* i. 87.

[2] Davies, *York Records,* 15; cf. pp. 45, 67.

[3] Cf. *Hist. MSS. Comm. 14th Rep.,* App., pt. viii. 254, 256; *11th Rep.,* App., pt. iii. 151, 166; *10th Rep.,* App., pt. iv. 403; Howard, *Hist. Anecdotes of the Howard Family,* 90.

[4] *Cal. State Papers,* 1639–40, p. 565.   [5] *Official List,* pt. i. 362, 391.

there is good ground for believing that boroughs, as early as James I, were demanding "something for the corporation" as a return for electing members to the House of Commons. In 1609, when Sir Robert Cecil was seeking to get control of the nomination at Hedon, it was given him together "with a plain intimation that previous members had not only served without expense, but had done something for the corporation[1]." In 1646 Colonel Edward Rosseter was made a free burgess of Grimsby previous to his being chosen to represent the borough, "and he gave ten pounds to the town chamber, also a bond indemnifying the town against any expense in the matter[2]." In this case the payment to the town chamber was clearly for Rosseter's admission to the freedom.

Bribing Constituencies becomes more general.   After the Restoration, when men were more eager to be of the House of Commons than at any time in its previous history, this practice of bribing borough constituencies as a whole became much more general. In 1671 William Leman, "being chosen a burgess to serve in Parliament for the borough of Hertford, did give one hundred pounds to pay the town tolls." In 1672 Sir Thomas Pye, the other burgess, gave the borough fifty pounds towards the discharge of the town debts[3]. In 1675 Pye, while still member for Hertford, writing from Lincoln's Inn, remitted money to the mayor "for disposal after an election[4]." Sir Joseph Williamson, who sat for Thetford from 1669 to 1687, in 1669 gave twenty-six pounds towards the expense of obtaining an Act of Parliament to make the river navigable from Brandon to Thetford. In 1678 Williamson bore the expense of an addition to the guildhall. He also gave a sword and mace to the corporation, which in the nineteenth century were insured for a thousand pounds, and were regarded as the most valuable part of the corporation insignia. Williamson is also credited with having restored a bridge at Thetford at his own expense[5].

Various Instances.   These gifts were all after Williamson's first election. Oftener the bribes to constituencies were made at an earlier stage; as at Dover in 1673, when Admiral Sir Edward Sprague offered three hundred pounds to the town provided he was elected[6]. In 1688,

---

[1] Cartwright, *Old Yorkshire*, 277.

[2] *Hist. MSS. Comm. 14th Rep.*, pt. VIII. 283.

[3] Turnor, *Hist. of Hertford*, 134.

[4] *Hist. MSS. Comm. 14th Rep.*, App., pt. VIII. 162.

[5] Millington, *Life of Sir Joseph Williamson*, 16.

[6] Papillon, *Memoirs of Thomas Papillon*, 127.

when Sir Nathaniel Napper was anxious to be elected for Poole, he undertook to settle fifteen pounds a year on the town, and was at the charge of obtaining a new charter[1]. In 1693 a candidate seeking election at Wigan offered to build "a conduit in the market place and bring water to it to supply it, at his own charge[2]." New Lymington in 1694 obtained from one of its members fifty pounds towards repairing the quay[3]. In 1695 it was stated before an election committee determining a case from Sandwich, that the member petitioned against had intimated that if he were elected to the House and were appointed to office, he would give half of his official salary to the corporation[4]. More definite offers from the same candidate were promises of twenty pounds a year for the poor of Sandwich, and a treat to the corporation on the anniversary of his election.

In the eighteenth century largess to constituencies became still more general and was bestowed in an increasing variety of ways. In many instances boroughs did not wait until candidates appeared with their offers, but sought out men willing to pay well for the privilege of seats in the House of Commons. In 1701 it was ascertained by an election committee that Andover had endeavoured "corruptly to set to sale the election of a burgess"; and a resolution was passed by the House declaring "that the lending of money upon any security to a corporation, and remitting the interest with intent to influence the election of members to Parliament, is an unlawful and dangerous practice[5]." In the same year it was also testified before an election committee that one of the candidates at Lichfield had promised that, if the city would choose him, he would make the markets free from tolls[6]; and about the same time it was elicited in the hearing of a petition case from Winchester, that a candidate there had pledged himself "to set up a fund out of which money was to be lent to poor tradesmen without interest[7]." At the same general election a candidate contributed fifty pounds towards the purchase of allotments for the poor at Higham Ferrers[8]. At Sudbury, a candidate offered

Consti-tuencies become demanding.

---

[1] Merewether and Stephens, *Hist. of Boroughs*, III. 1848.
[2] *Hist. MSS. Comm. 13th Rep.*, App., pt. IV. 278.
[3] Barbe, *Lymington Records*, 44.   [4] *H. of C. Journals*, XI. 421.
[5] Beatson, *Chronological Register*, I. 385—86.
[6] *H. of C. Journals*, XIII. 528.
[7] *H. of C. Journals*, XIII. 581.
[8] *H. of C. Journals*, XIV. 147.

two hundred pounds towards making the river Stour navigable, and two hundred pounds more for a workhouse[1]. At Rye a promise was made that if the electors chose Edward Southwell, the court candidate, they should have a good harbour and have convoys and protection for shipping[2]. In 1719 Boston raised the fee for the admission of Parliamentary candidates to the freedom to fifty pounds. In 1790 it was again raised to one hundred pounds, and again in 1800 to one hundred and thirty-five pounds. Before the Revolution, the fee had been only five pounds, from which it was raised to twenty pounds in 1700[3].

Patronising Local Industries. Douceurs to constituencies occasionally took the form of orders for local industries. This form of bribe can be traced from the closing years of the seventeenth century. At Newport, Isle of Wight, in 1698, after Lord Cutts and Sir Robert Cotton were elected, it was complained by petition in 1699, that their election was due to the fact that through the interest of the clerk of the rope yard at Portsmouth, thirty-five tons of junk had been sent to Newport to be made into oakum. The municipality received three-and-fourpence per hundredweight for converting junk. They paid the people who picked the oakum, three-and-twopence a hundredweight; and it was insisted that this work, sent from the Royal Dockyard at Portsmouth, "was an ease to the electors in point of the poor's rate, for that a great many must have been relieved by the town, if not for the benefit they had by picking oakum, and that some were taken off the rates on that account[4]."

Orders for Shoes. In a petition case from Ilchester, in 1709, it was stated that the sitting members ordered two thousand pairs of shoes, and that all the shoemakers in the town were employed on the order[5]. In a similar case from Carlisle in 1711, it was testified that Colonel Gledhill, "who wanted to get into Parliament, and get a regiment," told the shoemakers' guild after he had been made a brother, and had asked his newly-made brethren for their Parliamentary votes, that "he should, after a while, have occasion for seven hundred pairs of shoes for his regiment, which the shoemakers in the town should make[6]."

Buildings and Gifts. Two of the candidates at Weymouth in 1713 built a bridge there. Work was given out in such a way as to influence votes. One elector told an election committee that he voted for the

---

[1] *H. of C. Journals*, xiv. 120.　　[2] *H. of C. Journals*, xiv. 89.
[3] Thompson, *Hist. of Boston*, 307, 451.　　[4] *H. of C. Journals*, xiii. 112.
[5] *H. of C. Journals*, xiv. 47.　　[6] *H. of C. Journals*, xvii. 108.

donors "because they built him a good bridge to walk over[1]."
Sir James Thornhill, Sergeant Painter to George I, who was of the
House of Commons of 1722-27 for Weymouth's twin borough,
Melcombe Regis, built almshouses there, and contributed an altar-
piece to the church. But in this case the gifts may have been due
to personal as well as political reasons, for Thornhill was a native
of Melcombe Regis[2].

The attitude of corporations towards candidates for Parliament
during the reigns from George I to George III is well illustrated
by episodes in the representative history of Banbury, Tewkesbury
and Oxford. In 1722, when the mayor and aldermen of Banbury
were asked for their suffrages, they answered "that most other
corporations made a considerable advantage of their elections, and
they knew no reason why they should not do it as well as their
neighbours; that they wanted to have their streets paved; an
augmentation to their vicarage, and a school built; and that the
person who should be chosen should be at that expense, which in
all might amount to five or six hundred pounds[3]."

Expectations of Constituencies.

At Tewkesbury in 1754 Lord Gage and his son General Gage
were defeated at a Parliamentary election. After they had left the
town Lord Gage addressed a letter "to the gentlemen, clergy, and
voters, remonstrating on an illegal association of the electors to
sell their votes to mend their roads[4]." This letter, with other
evidence, warrants the inference that the successful candidates
must have concurred in a scheme for bribing the constituency as
a whole. A petition followed the defeat of the Gages, and it was
stated in support of the petitioners' case that "some persons of
property in and about the town of Tewkesbury and leading men
of the said borough" made it known that "no persons could be
elected unless they would advance fifteen hundred pounds each for
the repair of the roads." "After the projectors had thus settled
and prepared matters," continued the petition, "the sitting members
made their public entry into the town with pickaxes and shovels
carried before them, and flags with inscriptions thereon of 'Calvert
and Martin' on one side, and 'Good Roads' on the other, in order
to give the town and voters notice that they were the persons who
were to agree to give the three thousand pounds for the repair of
the roads." The electors, however, were warned that they were

Good Roads for Tewkesbury.

---

[1] *H. of C. Journals*, XVII. 648.   [2] Ellis, *Hist. of Weymouth*, 178.
[3] *Parl. Hist.*, VII. 964.   [4] Bennett, *Hist. of Tewkesbury*, 258.

not individually to expect anything from the candidates; that the constituency was being bought as a whole, and that there was to be no buying in detail[1].

A Rebuke for Oxford.

As late as 1766 Oxford was following the example of Andover of 1701, in seeking to utilise its privilege of returning two members as a means for raising a municipal loan without interest[2]. Oxford had then a debt of £5,670, and it offered to elect any two persons who would advance four thousand pounds. These overtures were reported to the House, which this time adopted more drastic measures than it had done in the case of Andover. Then the House contented itself with a condemnatory resolution. In the Oxford case the mayor and other corporation officers were summoned to the bar, and reprimanded from the chair. " A more enormous crime," said the Speaker, who must have well known that on each side of him sat scores of members who had purchased their seats, " you could not well commit, since a deeper wound could not be given to the constitution itself than by the open and dangerous attempt which you have made to subvert the freedom and independence of this House[3]."

Bribery in the Aggregate *versus* Bribery in Detail.

After this reprimand from the chair in 1766, corporations may have been more cautious and circumspect in their overtures to Parliamentary candidates. But there were still candidates to make overtures to corporations. At the general election in 1768 a candidate at Poole, who was subsequently elected, called on the mayor with an offer of a present of one thousand pounds to be applied to local public uses[4]. Political morality in Andover, Banbury, Tewkesbury and Oxford was no worse than in other boroughs in the eighteenth century. At the time these cases came before the House, it was apparently higher than in those boroughs which sold their representation to a patron, or dealt at first hand with candidates, and in which the proceeds of the sale went only to the advantage of the individual members of the corporation or to little groups of freemen. At Andover, Banbury, Tewkesbury and Oxford, there was some municipal spirit; at least when the boroughs had a valuable asset to sell, the money accruing went to the municipality as a whole. At a time when the representation of most boroughs was sold, and payment made either in bribes to individual electors, or to electors in the aggregate,

---

[1] *H. of C. Journals*, xxii. 27.   [2] Cf. *supra*, 159.
[3] *Parl. Hist.*, xvi. 400.   [4] *H. of C. Journals*, xxxii. 197.

Tewkesbury stands on a high plane of political morality; for in 1754, when it bartered its representation for good roads, it was with the distinct understanding that this payment was all that was to be expected from the candidates, and that there were to be no bribes to individuals.

As long as the old representative system lasted, largess from borough representatives to constituencies as a whole survived. The histories of the old Parliamentary boroughs show that many of them in the eighteenth century and in the early years of the nineteenth were indebted to their representatives in the House of Commons for their public buildings and public improvements. In 1771 Woodstock received one hundred pounds from one of its members towards the cost of a workhouse[1]. Tewkesbury, which put its representation to auction in 1754 in order to raise money to repair its roads, in 1790 received eight hundred pounds from its members for a similar purpose[2]. It also owed a new town-hall to Sir William Codrington, who represented the borough from 1771 to 1792[3]. Sir Benjamin Hammet, who represented Taunton in four Parliaments subsequent to 1782, according to a local historian greatly benefited the town. "He opened up the beautiful tower of St Mary Magdalen, by the erection of the street that now bears his name, and he also greatly assisted in the restoration of Taunton Castle[4]."

At Helston, in 1796, there was manifested on the part of the electors something of the spirit displayed at Tewkesbury in 1754. "We had been previously desired," writes Lord Colchester, who in 1796, as Charles Abbot, was chosen one of the burgesses for Helston at an election attended by sixteen voters, "not to give any election entertainments; but to commute that expense for a subscription of one hundred guineas each, to remove the Cornage Hall, and rebuild it in a more convenient part of the town[5]." About 1805 the representatives of the borough of East Looe rebuilt and decorated the chapel-of-ease there[6]; while as near to the Reform Act as 1825, the members for Devizes paid the expenses of procuring an improvement Act, and contributed three thousand

Later Eighteenth Century Instances.

Municipal Patriotism at the Expense of Candidates.

---

[1] Marshall, *Hist. of Woodstock Manor*, 274.
[2] Bennett, *Hist. of Tewkesbury*, 179.
[3] Dyde, *Hist. of Tewkesbury*, 14.
[4] Jeboult, *Hist. of Taunton*, 45.
[5] Colchester, *Diary*, I. 59.
[6] Bond, *Sketches of East and West Looe*, 15.

pounds towards the municipal undertakings so authorised by Parliament[1].

Survivals of the Practice of Bribing Constituencies.

In this way, and as early as the reign of Charles I, there was begun the usage under which constituencies, in addition to demanding services in Parliament without pay, began to expect, often to demand, that the men who sought their suffrages should bear some of the charges for municipal undertakings which ought to have been charges on the community as a whole. In another form the usage so originating has survived all the reforms and all the bribery legislation of the nineteenth century. Enlarged electorates—due principally to the Reform Acts of 1867 and 1884— the Ballot Act of 1872, and the Corrupt Practices Act of 1883, coupled with an enlightened and more wholesome public opinion, have all worked to the suppression of individual bribery at Parliamentary elections, an evil with which Parliament grappled from the reign of William III[2] to that of Victoria, and which is now at an end.

Changes in the Form.

Municipalities nowadays do not expect their representatives in the House of Commons to advance loans without interest; to pay the costs of carrying local improvement Acts through Parliament; or to contribute to the building of bridges, the deepening of rivers, the widening of narrow streets, the paving of streets, or the building of market-houses, town-halls, and workhouses. All these municipal undertakings have long been accepted as charges on municipalities. But while legislation and public opinion have completely suppressed individual bribery, and while the developement of the municipal spirit has made communities independent of individual contributions to municipal enterprises, other financial claims are still pressed on members of the House of Commons, now however in behalf of groups of constituents, rather than of constituencies as a whole. To-day it is nearly as essential as it was in the seventeenth and eighteenth centuries, that a man who seeks election to the House of Commons should be possessed of a long purse, because, although he is not expected to build town-halls or bridges, he is still expected to meet many claims from churches and philanthropic and social organisations within his constituency.

Modern Demands on Members.

As late as 1898 it was estimated by an ex-member of the House of Commons, who had sat in two Parliaments subsequent

---

[1] Waylen, *Chronicles of Devizes*, 168.
[2] First Bribery Act, 7 W. III, c. 4.

to 1884, that these claims on members by constituents—not as individuals or en masse, like the claims on the eighteenth century representatives of Banbury and Tewkesbury, but as associated groups—could not be met for less than five hundred pounds a year[1]. In the issue of the newspaper in which this estimate of the pecuniary calls on members was published, there was also a report of a political meeting at Oldham at which one of the members for the borough produced a roll over twenty feet long, containing requests for subscriptions to religious, philanthropic and social organisations; and it was stated by the member, who had thus tabulated the calls upon him, that one of his fellow-members in the Parliament of 1895–1900, who sat for a Lancashire county division, had in one year been asked for subscriptions to the amount of twenty-seven thousand pounds[2].

These calls on members, in the form in which they are still being made in the opening years of the twentieth century, are a survival of the practice which I have traced back to 1640; to the day when Robert Rede, bent on being chosen for Hastings, pledged himself that he would give to the poor twenty pounds down, and ten pounds a year during life, besides two barrels of gunpowder yearly " for exercising the youths." Rede's contributions to the poor of Hastings have their modern equivalents in the calls on members for contributions to churches and philanthropic organisations; while as equivalents for Rede's barrels of gunpowder, there are the calls for cricket, football and bowling clubs. In the last Parliament of the nineteenth century there were a few members of the House of Commons who consistently refused to meet these calls. They interpreted the Corrupt Practices Act of 1883 as freeing them from all such obligations. But the majority of members were still responding to these calls when the nineteenth century closed: and by so doing were helping to perpetuate that barrier against democracy which was first erected in the sixteenth century, and which from that time has been maintained solely by usage—a usage due to the ambition of men to be of the House of Commons, and to a feeling on the part of electors that in choosing a man to represent them in Parliament, they were doing him a service for which he could not make full and adequate return simply by the fulfilment of his Parliamentary duties.

The Practice due to the Desire for Seats.

[1] Letter from Mr W. S. Caine, *Manchester City News*, Jan. 15th, 1898.
[2] *Manchester City News*, Jan. 15th, 1898.

PROPERTY QUALIFICATIONS FOR MEMBERS.

Statutory
Exclusion
of Men
without
Means.

With the payment of wages in desuetude for a century or more, with the practice well established of bribing electors as individuals and in the aggregate, and with the payment of election expenses thrown by custom on candidates, it cannot be affirmed that the legislation of Queen Anne's reign, imposing property qualifications on members, and making candidates liable for certain charges at elections, began the erection of the barrier between poor men and the House of Commons. This legislation, and in particular the Act of 1710 making it a prerequisite to service in the House that a knight of the shire should possess an income of six hundred pounds a year derived from land, and a burgess an income of three hundred, was in antagonism to the early principles of the representative system. It was as much in antagonism to these principles as were the determinations in controverted election cases which legalised the votes of non-resident freemen in boroughs. But while this is so, legislation was never wholly responsible for the fact that men without fairly ample means were excluded, and stood with aliens, with men who could not take the oaths, with clergymen and office holders, in the list of men who could not be of the House of Commons.

Arguments
for such
Exclusion.

An agitation which began in 1695 or 1696 preceded the enactment of the statute of 1710, excluding men without property qualifications from the House of Commons. Although the agitation for a bill on these lines did not begin until that time, the subject had been engaging attention before the Revolution. In Shaftesbury's treatise on the regulations for elections, published about 1688, there is an argument in favour of restricting membership of the House to men of assured wealth. " As the persons electing ought to be men of substance," wrote Shaftesbury, " so in a proportioned degree ought also the members elected. It is not safe to make over the estates of the people in trust to men who have none of their own, lest their domestic indigencies in conjunction with a foreign temptation should warp them to a contrary interest, which in former Parliaments we have sometimes felt to our sorrow. Wealth and substance will also give a lustre and reputation to our great council, and a security to the people ; for their estates

are then pawned and so many pledges for their good behaviour, becoming thereby equal sharers themselves in the benefit
or disadvantage which shall result from their own acts and
councils[1]."

The Convention Parliament showed no inclination to adopt
any of the reforms recommended in the treatise, and it was not
until 1696 that the Tories in the House of Commons began to
make headway with the ultimately successful movement to restrict
membership of the House to men of the landed classes. The
Tories were then working to make sure of the next Parliament,
and with this aim in view they sought to drive their bill furiously
through the House of Commons[2]. The bill was read a first time
on the 12th of November. Within two weeks petitions against it
were received from Oxford, Taunton, Bridgwater and Plymouth.
The aldermen, common council, freemen and freeholders of Oxford
objected against the bill that it would exclude " many persons
who had not estates in land, though great personal estates,"
and that it would render " prudent citizens" incapable of serving
in Parliament. The petitioners also complained of the bill as
an inroad on the ancient rights and privileges of Oxford, and
prayed that these might be preserved[3]. After second reading by
fifty votes to forty-two, there came the petitions from Taunton,
Bridgwater and Plymouth. Those from Taunton and Bridgwater were to the same effect as that from Oxford[4]. The
petition from Plymouth set forth that that borough chiefly
subsisted by trade, and that if the bill became law the people
of Plymouth might never " send one of their own inhabitants
who knows their circumstances, though wise and greatly rich
in personal estate," and " must choose a stranger to represent
them, who knows not their occasions, which is to restrain the
liberty of the subject[5]."

After the bill had been sent to committee and its provisions
became more generally known, the City of London, Southwark,
Shafton, Poole, Ashburton, Weymouth and Melcombe Regis,
Nottingham, Rye and Honiton all petitioned against it[6]. The
grievance of the City of London was that the bill would much

Opposition to the Movement in 1696.

Petitions against the Bill.

---

[1] Somers, *Tracts*, viii. 369.
[2] Cf. *Vernon Correspondence*, i. 86.
[3] *H. of C. Journals*, xi. 590.
[4] *H. of C. Journals*, xi. 597.
[5] *H. of C. Journals*, xi. 598.
[6] *H. of C. Journals*, xi. 599–631.

restrain the ancient privileges of its citizens, " by rendering many
eminent and fit merchants and traders of great personal estate
incapable to serve in Parliament." The London petitioners also
asked that they might be heard at the bar of the House of
Commons against the bill[1]. This request and similar ones from
Shafton and Lyme Regis were refused[2]. Poole complained that if
the bill became law it would be compelled " to choose such men
as are strangers to the constitution of their corporation, and
unskilful in the mysteries of trade," and that it " would hinder
those among them of sound understanding and having great
personal estate, of their birthright to be elected[3]."

The Bill passes the Commons. There was much obstruction from the opponents of the bill at
committee stage[4]; when it was proposed that a man should be
eligible, who had a " clear personal estate of five thousand
pounds," and made oath to that effect before a magistrate or
before the returning officer. But the landed interest would accept
no amendment of this character at this stage, and the motion
for the engrossment of the bill was carried on the 3rd of December,
1696, by 183 to 167[5]. At third reading an amendment was
accepted making eligible a merchant with three thousand pounds
in real and personal estate. But such an exception was to apply
only in boroughs where the merchant had a right of election;
and it was expressly provided that no person was to be " esteemed
as a merchant for having any money in the bank, or any other
company, only by reason of such adventure[6]." Third reading was
carried by two hundred to one hundred and sixty[7], and the bill
was sent to the Lords.

It is rejected by the Lords. William III was known to be unfavourable to the bill[8]. Its
fate in the Lords has been narrated by Burnet. " The Lords,"
he writes, " rejected it. They thought it reasonable to leave the
nation their freedom in choosing their representatives in Parliament. It seemed both unjust and cruel that if a poor man had
so fair a reputation as to be chosen, notwithstanding his poverty,
by those who were willing to pay him wages, that he should be

[1] *H. of C. Journals*, xi. 599.   [2] *H. of C. Journals*, xi. 601.
[3] *H. of C. Journals*, xi. 607.   [4] *H. of C. Journals*, xi. 601.
[5] *H. of C. Journals*, xi. 612.   [6] *H. of C. Journals*, xi. 632, 633.
[7] *H. of C. Journals*, xi. 632.
[8] *Hist. MSS. Comm. 12th Rep.*, App., pt. vii. 345.

branded with an incapacity, because of his small estate. Corruption in elections was to be apprehended from the rich rather than from the poor[1]." The debate in the Lords occupied some hours on the 23rd of January, 1696, and ended with the division rejecting the bill by sixty-two against thirty-seven[2].

In 1702–3 the bill was again introduced in the House of Commons, and on the 8th of February, 1702–3, was again sent to the House of Lords[3]. The members of the Commons then most intent on insisting that the " choice shall lie in a very narrow compass," and on creating what Vernon describes as " a senate of patricians[4]," were Mr Howe, Sir John Leveson Gower, Sir Roger Mostyn, Sir Richard Onslow, Sir George Warburton, the Marquis of Hartington, and Sir Thomas Powis[5]. The Lords once more rejected the bill[6]. After the Tories came into power in 1710 the movement of 1696 and 1702–3 was again renewed in the House of Commons. With the Ministry in its favour, success soon attended it, and in February, 1710–11, the bill became law[7]. *Finally becomes Law in 1710.*

In the measure which was thus enacted there were no exceptions in favour of merchants. Scotland was not included within its provisions. Ostensibly Scotland was exempted on the ground that estates were much smaller there than in England; but more probably on account of an apprehension that the Scotch peers and the Scotch members would resent an interference with the settlement of the representative system made by the Scotch Parliament on the eve of the Union. Members from Scotland were most tenacious of any advantages secured to them at the Union; and about this time Scotch votes were needed both in the House of Commons and in the House of Lords. The universities were excepted. Exceptions were also made in favour of heirs of men qualified to be knights of the shire, and of heirs of peers. For the rest, every member of the House of Commons between 1710 and 1838, when the law of Queen Anne's reign was amended in the interest of men deriving incomes from personal property[8], was compelled to furnish proof if required to the returning-officer at his election[9] *Exceptions in Favour of Scotland, of the Universities, and of Heirs of Men of Landed Estates.*

---

[1] Burnet, *Hist. of His Own Times,* iii. 231.
[2] *Vernon Correspondence,* i. 182, 183.
[3] *H. of C. Journals,* xiv. 184.   [4] *Vernon Correspondence,* i. 87.
[5] *H. of C. Journals,* xiv. 95.
[6] Luttrell, *Brief Relation of State Affairs,* v. 270.
[7] 9 Anne, c. 5.   [8] 1 and 2 Vict., c. 48.
[9] Simeon, *Election Law,* 51.

and after 1760 also to the clerk at the table on his taking his seat, that he had an income from landed property.

Swift's Argument for the Act.

The petitions from the cities and boroughs express the popular opposition to the Qualification Act. The Tory view of it and the Tory reasons for pushing it through Parliament were put on record by Swift. " At present," he wrote in March, 1711, after the bill had become law, " the House of Commons is the best representative of the nation that has ever been summoned in our memories; so they have taken care in their first session, by that noble bill of qualification, that future Parliaments should be composed of landed men, and our properties be no more at the mercy of those who have none themselves, or at least what is only transient or imaginary. If there be any gratitude in posterity the memory of this assembly will be always celebrated[1]." In a later number of the *Examiner*[2], Swift described the Act " as the greatest security that was ever contrived for preserving the constitution, which otherwise might in a little time be wholly at the mercy of the moneyed interest." These sentiments, expressed in the *Examiner*, were in keeping with Swift's opinion uttered ten years after the Act of 1710, that " there could not be a truer maxim in our government than this, that the possessors of the soil are the best judges of what is for the advantage of the kingdom[3]."

The Act in Operation.

While technically the law was stringently enforced, it never restricted membership to the possessors of the soil. Between 1711 and 1760, when it was amended so as to compel all members to take oath in the House as to their qualifications, and to lodge with the clerk at the table a statement of their qualifying property, it was technically enforced chiefly because its provisions gave unsuccessful candidates opportunities of harassing men by whom they had been defeated. It was put to this use in a number of cases after the general election of 1713. But the petitions based on allegations that the members returned were not qualified mostly failed; because the onus of proof as to lack of qualification fell on the petitioners[4]. In 1717 a standing order was made which required petitioners to lodge with the clerk a statement of their own qualifications[5]. This order gave a new protection to members who were

---

[1] *Examiner*, xxxi.   [2] *Examiner*, xlv.
[3] Swift, *Letter to Pope*, Jan. 10th, 1721.
[4] Hansard, 3rd Series, xxxvi. 525.
[5] *H. of C. Journals*, xviii. 629

petitioned against on the ground that they were not qualified; because if a petitioner failed to make out his own qualification the election committee would proceed no further with a petition based only on this objection. A petition case from Shaftesbury collapsed on this account in 1722[1].

By 1722 the practice of creating fictitious qualifications was well established. Archibald Hutchinson, member for Hastings, who introduced a bill for amending the law, one of many that were rejected between 1711 and 1760, declared in 1722 that there was much fraud under the Act, and that men who possessed themselves of qualifications on the eve of an election, parted with them as soon as they had taken their seats[2]. That the practice exposed by Hutchinson in 1722 was prevalent is suggested by the fate of the bills for making the Act more workable and more stringent, and also by the fate of a motion made in 1731 after one of these bills had been rejected, directing that a committee should be appointed to inquire whether any members of the House sat there contrary to law. Such an inquiry, midway in a Parliament, would have been embarrassing to men who had held qualifying properties only long enough to enable them to take their seats; and it was rejected by eighty-three votes to thirty-seven[3].

Fictitious Qualifications.

There were many cases during the first twenty-five years of the Act in which it was objected on petition that members returned did not possess landed qualifications. Under the Act, as it stood until 1760, the test came at this stage. But I have discovered no instance earlier than 1735 in which a member was unseated because he was not qualified. At the general election in 1734 John Boteler was returned for Wendover. Lord Limerick, on petition, objected that Boteler was not qualified, and on that ground the election was declared void. A new writ was issued, when Lord Limerick, the successful petitioner, was returned[4]. The fact that in this period, that is, prior to 1760, a candidate could be required to take oath as to his qualifications at the election, and might also need documentary evidence of them in the event of a petition, made it essential that candidates should possess themselves of qualifications which would serve them until they were safely in their seats. If a candidate failed to take the oath

The Working of the Act before 1760.

[1] *H. of C. Journals,* xx. 130.
[2] *Parl. Hist.,* vii. 951.
[3] *H. of C. Journals,* xxi. 359.
[4] *H. of C. Journals,* xxii. 335, 468; Beatson, *Register,* i. 13.

as to his landed qualifications at the election, it was usual for the agents of the opposing candidates to tell each voter as he came to poll that the candidate who had so failed was disqualified, and that votes given for him would be lost[1].

The Amendment of 1760.

Until the law was amended in 1760[2], it was evaded chiefly by a candidate possessing himself of a title to the required landed property before an election and retransferring it as soon as he was safely of the House. After the amendment of the Act in 1760, these temporary transfers to create qualifications were no longer possible. Members had now to swear to their qualifications at the table; and moreover they had to file with the clerk a signed schedule describing the qualifying property, with almost sufficient detail to serve as a memorandum for an auctioneer's advertisement. Under this arrangement impecunious members must often have been in the position of Anthony Storer, who, in 1781, was chosen by the Earl of Carlisle for Morpeth, one of his lordship's boroughs. A member chosen by a patron who was in easy control of a borough, had of course no difficulty with the qualification oath at the election; for often members so chosen were not in the boroughs for the election. Still, even a member with a powerful patron behind him and in no dread of a petition, had to undergo the ordeal at the table, and to the impecunious member the oath and the schedule undoubtedly had their terrors. " I arrived in town this morning," wrote Storer to Carlisle, on the 26th of November, 1781, " time enough to do all in my power to send to Gregg to try if I can get a qualification to take my seat to-morrow. My qualifications have been always embarrassing to me[3]." But to a member who could command a little ready money, and take the oath at the table with no qualms of conscience, the lack of landed property caused little of the embarrassment which was so disturbing to the Earl of Carlisle's nominee for Morpeth.

Instances of Exclusions.

Subsequent to 1760, exclusions due to non-possession of property qualifications were hardly more frequent than from 1711 to 1760. In 1781 an election at Honiton was voided on that account[4]; and in 1784 Christopher Potter was unseated for Colchester because he had no qualification[5]. But Potter had been declared a

[1] Simeon, *Election Laws*, 4.

[2] 33 Geo. II, c. 20.

[3] *Hist. MSS. Comm. 15th Rep.*, App., pt. vi. 535.

[4] Oldfield, iii. 454; *Official List*, pt. ii. 164.

[5] Oldfield, iii. 447; *Official List*, pt. ii. 178.

bankrupt in April, 1783[1], only a year before the election; and as a bankrupt he could not have obtained the qualification either from friends, or from the bankers and attorneys, who in the last three-quarters of a century of the old representative system made a business of furnishing landed qualifications for members of the House of Commons.

From 1760 to 1838, men who qualified under the Act of Queen Anne may be divided into three groups. In the first were those who bonâ fide were the owners of the landed estate of which they swore themselves possessed at the table before taking their seats. In the second group were the men who had had transferred to them by relatives or friends sufficient landed property to qualify them; while in the third group were men who had obtained their qualifications for a consideration from bankers and attorneys. Knights of the shire were usually of the first group; so generally were the younger sons of peers, as, subsequent to the Act of 1710, peers with younger sons were usually careful, in the settlements of their families, to provide these sons with a sufficient income derived from land to furnish the requisite passport into the House of Commons[2]. *Methods of Qualifying.*

Many of the men whose names stand out in the Parliamentary history of the eighteenth century were of the second group, and owed their qualifications to the kindness of friends. Philip Yorke, afterwards Earl of Hardwicke, and Lord Chancellor from 1737 to 1756, had no landed qualification of his own when he was elected for the borough of Lewes in 1719; but "a wealthy relative enabled him to overcome this difficulty by granting him a rent-charge out of his estate, of the amount requisite for this purpose[3]." In later times Burke, Pitt, Fox and Sheridan were similarly qualified[4]. Wilkes owed his qualification to Earl Temple, who granted him a freehold estate of six hundred pounds a year for life[5]. Roebuck was not of the unreformed Parliament; but he represented Bath in the first reformed House of Commons, while the Act of Queen Anne's reign was still in force; and the history of his landed qualification illustrates the working of the law in the unreformed Parliament. Roebuck was indebted to Joseph Hume for his qualification. Roebuck's father-in-law nominally *Qualifications provided by Friends.*

[1] Oldfield, III. 453.
[2] Cf. *Harcourt Papers*, VI. 53.
[3] Harris, *Life of the Earl of Hardwicke*, I. 91, 92; Doyle, II. 122.
[4] Hansard, 3rd Series, XXXVI. 526.
[5] Nicholls, *Recollections*, I. 30.

gave him a fine painting of a race-horse by Sir Joshua Reynolds. For this picture Hume made over to Roebuck, also nominally, the title to some of his landed property in Ireland, and on a qualification so obtained Roebuck first found his way into the House of Commons[1].

Business of making Qualifications.
The methods by which landed qualifications were obtained after the amendment to the Act of 1710 in 1760, were explained in the House of Commons in the debates on the Act of 1838, by which the Acts of 1710 and 1760 were repealed, and personal as well as landed property was made to serve as Parliamentary qualification. " Nothing can be easier," said Sir William Molesworth, " than to obtain a fictitious qualification. Any gentleman who has a sufficient sum at his bankers can obtain from his banker a rent-charge as a mere matter of business; for most of the largest London bankers possess landed property. If the gentleman who desires to be qualified does not possess a sufficient sum at his immediate disposal, he then applies to a friend or to an attorney, who generally can find among his clients some person of landed property willing to grant a fictitious qualification. A deed is drawn up conveying the rent-charge required, which deed never goes out of the possession of the attorney. In the presence of two witnesses, unacquainted with the nature of the transaction, a seeming payment is made of the sum of money which would be required to make the transaction a real one. If there should be a petition, then the nature of the deed and the consideration are stated to the committee, and the witnesses prove the transaction to be a bonâ fide one[2]."

A Retrospect of the Working of the Act.
Sir William Molesworth declared, and no one in the House of Commons controverted his statement, that it was well known " that one-half the members, if not more, do not in reality possess the amount of landed property required; but sit here in virtue of fictitious qualifications[3]." In support of this statement Molesworth read a letter from a London lawyer whom he described as " an eminent attorney well acquainted with his subject," in which the working of the laws of 1710 and 1760 was reviewed. " If the law were effective," wrote Molesworth's correspondent, " it would unquestionably have deprived the community of the services

---

1 Interview with Samuel Bartlet, Roebuck's first election agent, *Manchester City News*, April 30th, 1895.

2 Hansard, 3rd Series, xxxvi. 526.

3 Hansard, 3rd Series, xxxvi. 526.

of many of our past and present public men. Certainly many of
the old luminaries would never have shone in the British Legislature. Burke, Pitt, Fox and Sheridan in my early days were
always notoriously fictitiously qualified. The law has been nearly
inoperative as an exclusion. Some few conscientious men have
refused to enter the House of Commons on a fraudulent qualification. Perhaps a few men of considerable talent have been unable
to obtain a fictitious qualification. Of the latter, there is known
only one instance, but he would, if qualified, have represented
the largest town in England. Of the number of the House of
Commons not legally qualified * * * it is generally believed that
one-third at least have no bonâ fide qualification. On the eve
of a dissolution of Parliament, dozens of sham qualifications are
made by solicitors, often drawn and settled by counsel. One
solicitor in London is known in fashionable circles as a gentleman
who will 'qualify' any candidate respectably introduced for one
.hundred pounds, including the stamps. But solicitors of the
highest station and unquestionable integrity do not scruple to
manufacture qualifications. * * * Candidates on the hustings notoriously swear to and state ambiguously-described qualifications,
and have shifted them when lodged in the House. Many .sham
qualifications are made after the returns and before members take
their seats, their consciences being tender as to declaring themselves
qualified on the latter occasion[1]."

I have not succeeded in obtaining any clue to the man of
considerable talent referred to by Molesworth's correspondent who
might, had he possessed a borough qualification, have represented
the largest town in England; and the only instance I have traced
in which a man, who had been elected to Parliament, voluntarily
declined his seat on the ground that he had not the requisite
property qualification, is the historic case of Southey. He was
returned for Downton in Wiltshire, on the 11th of June, 1826.
The new Parliament met on the 25th of July; and from Keswick
on the 15th of November, Southey communicated to the Speaker
his reason for not having taken his seat. "Having while I was
on the continent," he wrote, "been, without my knowledge, elected
a burgess to serve in the present Parliament for the borough of
Downton, it has become my duty to take the earliest opportunity
of requesting you to inform the honourable House that I am not

Southey's Lack of a Quali- fication.

---

[1] Hansard, 3rd Series, xxxvi. 526, 528.

qualified to take a seat therein, inasmuch as I am not possessed
of such an estate as is required by the Act passed in the ninth
year of Queen Anne[1]."

The Amendment of 1838.

Molesworth's speech, which has been quoted, was made in
1837 in support of an amendment to Warburton's bill, the bill
which subsequently became law, making personal as well as real
property a qualification for a seat. The purpose of the amendment
was to abolish all property qualifications. It was defeated by
133 votes to 104[2]. At this time a proposal was made that professional incomes should also serve to qualify. Peel, who was then
prime minister, was favourable to some amendment of the law of
Queen Anne, but he would not accept this suggestion[3]; and the
only change in the eighteenth century enactments brought about
by Warburton's Act was that personal estate was made to rank
with landed property as a qualification. For the rest the old
law was continued. Knights of the shire, as from 1710 to 1838,
were required to possess incomes of six hundred pounds; and
burgesses three hundred pounds a year. The universities were again
exempted; so were the eldest sons of peers, and of men qualified
to act as knights of the shire. Candidates still remained liable
at elections to the oaths as to qualifications, and, as from 1760,
members were required to take oath as to their qualifications at
the table of the House, and to file particulars with the clerk.

Fictitious Qualifications still made.

With personal property now serving as a qualification, there
was obviously less need for resort to the methods in vogue between
1710 and 1838 for obtaining fictitious qualifications. But the
clients of the qualifying attorneys did not disappear with the
Act of 1838; although their fees for procuring qualifications fell
from one hundred pounds to eighty pounds[4]. There also came
into vogue a usage under which the titles constituting these
fictitious qualifications were deposited with the librarian of the
House of Commons, and at the end of the Parliament were returned to the members in whose interest they had been drawn,
so that the property covered by them might be reconveyed to
its real owners. " It was so broad a farce," said Mr M. T. Baines,
member for Leeds, in describing in the House of Commons in
1865, the working of the Qualification Act of 1838, " so ridiculous

[1] Hansard, 2nd Series, xvi. 111.
[2] Hansard, 3rd Series, xxxvi. 552.
[3] Hansard, 3rd Series, xl. 929.
[4] Hansard, clxxviii. 1385.

and contemptible, that the House entirely repealed the property qualification[1]."

The repeal came in 1858. It was precipitated by the case of Edward Auchmuty Glover, who at the general election in 1857 was returned for Beverley. There was a petition against Glover; and on the 11th of August, 1857, his election was declared void, because he had not the necessary property qualification. He had, however, made a declaration at the table that he was qualified, and after he had been ousted, criminal proceedings were instituted against him by order of the House for making a false declaration[2]. He was tried at the Old Bailey, found guilty, and sentenced to three months' imprisonment as a first class misdemeanant: although he had been recommended to mercy by the jury, on the ground that his prosecution was the first for this offence, and because of the notoriously loose way in which declarations as to the possession of qualifying property were made[3].

The Case of Mr Glover.

The Act of Queen Anne had been in force nearly a hundred and fifty years. There is abundant testimony that during this long period it was notoriously evaded, and that hundreds of members swore to the ownership of property which they had never possessed. Instances of exclusion by reason of the non-possession of qualifying property in the days of the unreformed Parliament have been cited. After the Reform Act, in 1837, two members from Ireland were similarly excluded[4]. In 1848 an election at Harwich was declared void on this account[5]; and in 1853 a candidate returned for Tavistock was unseated, because he had not the necessary property qualification[6]. Including the six exclusions subsequent to 1832, I have not been able to trace more than ten instances between 1710 and 1858, in which candidates who had been returned were excluded under the property qualification Acts. While it was notorious, from as early as 1722, that members swore to the possession of qualifications which they had not, the case of Glover was the only prosecution for making false declarations during the century and a half in which the

The Uselessness of the Qualification Acts.

---

[1] Hansard, CLXXVIII. 1385.

[2] Hansard, CXLVIII. 385.

[3] *Annual Register,* 1858, c. 69; White, *Inner Life of the House of Commons,* I. 54, 56.

[4] Hansard, 3rd Series, XXXVI. 538.

[5] *Official List,* pt. II. 400; Hansard, CL. 1426.

[6] *Official List,* pt. II. 415; Hansard, CL. 1837.

qualifications Acts were on the statute books[1]; and Southey's letter is the only communication I can discover in the Journals expressing inability to serve in the House by reason of the non-possession of the statutory qualification.

The Abolition of Property Qualifications.

The abolition of the property qualification in 1858 was brought about by a private member's bill introduced by Locke King, who, during his service in the House, secured the repeal of one hundred and twenty dormant statutes[2]. The notoriety of the evasion of the law helped the agitation for its repeal, as did the experiences of members who had served on election committees, in cases in which objection was made that a candidate returned had not the necessary qualification. Such cases involved protracted and wearisome inquiries as to the validity or invalidity of deeds, and the determination of the nicest questions in equity[3].

Opposition to the Abolition.

There was some opposition in the House of Commons from old-school Tories such as G. W. P. Bentinck, then knight of the shire for Norfolk; and as was inevitable, in view of the changed political character of the House of Lords between the reign of William III, when it opposed qualification bills, and the reign of Queen Victoria, Locke King's bill encountered much opposition there. The Earl of Clancarty opposed it from an apprehension that the Chartists, who at this time were still engaged in their agitation, would regard it as of "marked significance and a concession of one of the points of the Charter[4]." Earl Grey, son of the Earl Grey who had been the foremost member of the House of Commons identified with the movement of the Friends of the People of 1792, and afterwards prime minister of the Whig Administration which carried the Reform Act in 1832, defended the principle of the Act of 1710, and repudiated the idea that by the law of Queen Anne's reign there was any invasion of the natural rights of electors[5]. Lord Denman moved a resolution, which was tantamount to the rejection of the bill[6]. But the opposition in the House of Lords did little more than delay by a few days the passage of the bill; and from the end of June, 1858, electors ceased to have any concern as to whether a man who sought their suffrages was possessed of an assured income of an

[1] Hansard, cl. 1831; *Annual Register*, 1858, c. 69.
[2] *Dict. Nat. Bio.*, xxxi. 148.
[3] Cf. Hansard, 3rd Series, xxxvi. 525.
[4] Hansard, cl. 2092.   [5] Hansard, cl. 1848.
[6] Hansard, cl. 2096.

amount required by law to make him capable of serving as their representative in the House of Commons.

During the hundred and fifty years in which the Act of Queen Anne's reign was in force, the question whether a candidate was qualified had particularly affected the electors in boroughs. Occasionally, as in the case of Wilkes, when he was a candidate for Middlesex, there may have been candidates for counties not possessed of the necessary six hundred pounds income qualification. But territorial and social conditions in the counties were always overwhelmingly against the candidature of a man who was not possessed of landed property; and a man who had no territorial connection with a county, no matter what his fame, was looked upon as Brougham was in 1830, when he contested Yorkshire. Then even Brougham's political friends, Earl Fitzwilliam and Lord Milton, expressed their repugnance to an outside candidate by calling him a "foreigner[1]." The dislike of outsiders continued until counties were divided into Parliamentary divisions by the Redistribution Act of 1885. In the industrial and thickly populated counties this Act, which put an end to the old social distinctions in favour of knights of the shire, and to the medieval ceremony of girding the knights with swords, made a much greater inroad into the customs and usages of county electioneering than the Reform Act of 1832. So long as the old conditions survived, a man of no landed property had only the remotest chance of becoming a knight of the shire, and his chance would seldom have been any better had there been no Qualification Act from 1710 to 1858.

The Act of 1710 was aimed by the Tories against members from the boroughs, from which moneyed men found their way into Parliament. It gave a legal sanction to the exclusion of men without means which, by usage and custom, was increasingly practised by constituencies from the reign of Queen Elizabeth to that of Queen Anne. But for the man who from lack of means was already on the exclusion list, the Act of 1710 created no new barrier to the House; at most it only strengthened an existing barrier. Borough constituencies were more rapacious in their demands on Parliamentary candidates between 1710 and 1832 than they had been in the seventeenth century; so that, apart from the Qualification Act, a man not possessed of means, but desirous of being of the House of Commons, must have found

The Qualification Acts superfluous in Counties.

No new Barrier in the Boroughs.

---

[1] Roebuck, *Hist. of the Whig Administration*, i. 350.

himself in an increasingly disadvantageous position as the eighteenth century advanced, as Indian nabobs came into the political arena, and as, with the increase of wealth due to the developement of commerce and industry, seats in the House became more and more in demand.

Nor did the Act serve to keep out of the House of Commons political adventurers on the hunt for spoils, such as offices or military commands, who had sufficient money to meet the rapacity of borough constituencies or to pay the price demanded by borough patrons for nominations which were equivalent to election, but who were not possessed of assured incomes from land. Temporary transfers of landed property served the purpose of these men during the half century when it was necessary to hold a qualification only long enough to take oath before the returning officer, or fight off an election petition. After the oath at the table was instituted by the Act of 1760, transfers of landed property which would stand a little more scrutiny and serve for the lifetime of a Parliament were substituted for the briefly held qualification in use before that year. But in this later period, he must have been a poorly equipped political adventurer, an adventurer likely soon to come to grief with greedy borough electors, who could not find the fee for the services of an attorney, which were necessary to safeguard his progress from the hustings to his seat in the House of Commons, by way of the table at which the qualification oath had to be taken. With men without means already thrust aside, and with devices for circumventing the Act of 1710 soon to hand, it may be concluded that the qualification laws had really little effect in limiting the choice of constituencies; and that between 1710 and 1832 it was only here and there that a man, not already excluded by the rapacity of electors, was compelled by the law to stand aside and abandon all hope of a seat in the House of Commons.

No matter how needy a man might be, if he had a powerful borough patron behind him the barrier against men without means was inoperative. A member returned by a patron who was in absolute control of a borough, a member who went into the House subject to the expressed or implied condition that he was to obey his patron's instructions, usually had no financial dealings with the electors who chose him. His patron satisfied their claims; and if the patron had the borough in easy possession, there was little likelihood of an election petition with its attendant risks for the member who was not properly qualified. The barrier built up by long usage and strengthened by law operated not against the nominee of the borough patron, but against the independent man of small means, who could not satisfy the greed of electors and who was not willing to perjure himself.

ELECTION EXPENSES THROWN ON CANDIDATES.

The code saddling official costs at Parliamentary elections on candidates, the foundations of which were slowly laid between 1712 and 1832, has a much less interesting history than the Qualification Acts. But this code, from a constitutional point of view, is of great significance. It was developed from the eagerness of men to be of the House of Commons; from the willingness to gratify all who could in any way help them to reach that goal. Along with the custom, now of three centuries standing, that members of the House shall not be paid—a custom still unsupported by a single enactment, and equally due to the eagerness of men to be returned to the House of Commons—this code has survived all the constitutional changes of the nineteenth century. Origin of the Code.

Subsequent to the important changes brought about by the Act of 1832 the code was considerably strengthened, and along with the custom which decrees that there shall be no pay for Parliamentary representatives out of public funds, it has preserved to the House of Commons one of the most remarkable of its seventeenth and eighteenth century characteristics. In those centuries none but men of means could be of the House; and to-day, although the twentieth century franchise has—except in a few inhabitant householder constituencies, such as Westminster, Southwark, and Taunton—no resemblance to the borough franchises of the seventeenth and eighteenth centuries, the modern franchise with its uniformity and its democratic features has brought no change in this characteristic of the personnel of the House. Trade and commerce and the learned professions are much more numerously represented in the House of Commons of to-day than they were in the eighteenth century. Also during the last thirty years of the nineteenth century there was always a little group of labour representatives in the House. But in spite of the presence of these men, and of the larger representation of industry, commerce and the learned professions, the House of Commons Its Effect on the House of Commons.

to-day is as much composed of men of means as it was when the statute of Queen Anne was in operation, and the landed interest embodied the bulk of the wealth of the country. The House owes this abiding characteristic to the fact that, although a certain measure of assured wealth has for nearly half a century ceased to be a statutory qualification, a man who has not means at his command cannot meet the election expenses thrown on him by law, nor comply with the usage that, if elected to the House, he must attend there for six or seven months out of the year without pay or any kind of allowance from public funds.

Election Expenses originally small.

Election expenses, which were thrown by usage or custom on candidates, date from a comparatively late period in the history of the representative system. So long as members were compelled to find sureties for their attendance in the House of Commons, and received wages from their constituents, elections cost little or nothing. The machinery of election was of the simplest character, and it was then to everybody's interest that elections should cost as little as possible: for all election expenses, like the wages and the travelling allowances of knights and burgesses, were a common local charge. Official election expenses must have continued small, so long as elections were made in the county court. Then the sheriff was the returning-officer for a county, no matter how many cities and boroughs it might contain. When, however, after 1444, the sheriffs were compelled by law to direct their precepts to returning-officers in the cities and boroughs, and all these elections had to take place within the constituencies, there would be, as seats in the House of Commons became in demand, and as popular interest in elections increased, a gradual increase in the number of officials, all ready to demand some compensation for their services from Parliamentary candidates.

No Expenditures authorised.

Until 1712 a returning-officer could point to no statute authorising him to charge Parliamentary candidates with a single item of the expense attending an election. Prior to the reign of William III, by common law the returning-officer was not expected to put himself to any expense to accommodate candidates or voters. It was sufficient that he was personally present at the time and place appointed, and ready to take and count the votes of such electors as tendered themselves. He was not required to erect hustings or booths, or to appoint poll-clerks for the more convenient taking of the poll[1].

[1] Cf. Heywood, *Borough Elections*, 164.

It is improbable that the charges of returning-officers formed any considerable item in the expenses of candidates until the end of the seventeenth century. But from the middle years of the seventeenth century it is possible to trace the establishment of a system of fees and charges which increased in amount with the generally changing relations between candidates, members, and constituencies. As candidates who would serve without wages were succeeded in the seventeenth century by candidates who, in addition, were willing to buy votes individually and in the aggregate, it was natural that returning-officers and their official associates should desire that some of the spoils should fall to them, and that candidates so eager for election should meet all the official outlays necessary for conducting an election with order and expedition. Furthermore, it is not difficult to conceive that these officials soon began to insist on fees proportional, not to the actual value of the services rendered, not to the calls on their time and labour, but to the ability and willingness of candidates to spend[1]. On no other assumption is it possible to account for the abnormally large fee charged in the last decade of the old representative system by the returning-officer at Winchelsea. Here there were only thirteen voters in 1811; yet—according to Oldfield, who, as a borough broker of long standing, was well acquainted with many of the boroughs usually in the market—the mayor's fee as returning-officer was two hundred pounds[2].

Returning-Officers begin to charge Fees.

It is certain that before the Revolution, official election expenses were being charged, and were already engaging the attention of Parliamentary reformers. In the abortive bill of 1679 for repealing the laws directing the payment of wages, there was a clause fixing the sheriff's fee at half-a-crown, in order "to prevent exactions, extortions, and briberies, under the pretence of gratuities, presents or recompense[3]." Again, about 1688, when Shaftesbury drew up his elaborate scheme of Parliamentary reform, in which he advocated property qualifications for members, the ballot, and an advance from twenty-one to forty in the age at which a man could be of the House of Commons, he anticipated the demand of the Radicals of the latter half of the nineteenth century that official election expenses should be a public charge. He suggested that parishes and counties should bear the cost of elections, thus reverting

Efforts to check Official Charges.

[1] Cf. *Select Committee on Election Expenses*, 1834, Rep. xxii.

[2] Oldfield, v. 412.

[3] Somers, *Tracts*, viii. 396, 397.

to the practice of the early period of the representative system, when the constituencies paid members' wages and travelling expenses out of local funds. " It is also fit," wrote Shaftesbury in putting forward his suggestion that candidates should be relieved of official expenses, " that a limited allowance be made for the expense of the day, which is to be in parishes at the parish charge, and in the county town at the expense of the county[1]."

Proofs of Official Extortion.

The bill of 1679 and Shaftesbury's proposal for Parliamentary reform make it certain that soon after the Restoration returning-officers were mulcting candidates in comparatively heavy charges; and that extortions similar to that at Winchelsea in 1811, and at Woodstock, where, in the early years of the nineteenth century, the town-clerk demanded a fee of £51. 11s. 4d. for unopposed returns[2], had already begun.

Official Charges in London.

Long before these seventeenth century schemes of reform, and until as late as 1813, there were charges in London as well as in the constituencies which fell on Parliamentary candidates. With the demand for seats in the sixteenth century, there had grown up a practice of bribing clerks and messengers in the Crown Office to secure early and oftentimes irregular possession of the writs. Before seats were in demand, knights of the shire sometimes carried the writs from London to the sheriffs, this service being one of several extra-Parliamentary duties thrown on knights of the shire in the fifteenth and sixteenth centuries. But when seats in Parliament became objects of desire, this mode of conveyance was too slow and too regular for candidates who were anxious to forestall their competitors. Douceurs were accordingly given to officials in the Crown Office for possession of the writs; and for centuries these douceurs were regarded as part of the official incomes of the clerks and messengers. In 1813, when the delivery of the writs to the sheriffs was turned over to the Post Office, it was enacted that one official should receive during his lifetime five hundred pounds every time a new Parliament was called, and two guineas in respect of each by-election; while another official, in lieu of the fees he had received under the old system, received a pension of five hundred pounds a year for life[3]. These charges in London, together with those made by the returning-officers in

[1] Somers, *Tracts*, viii. 396.
[2] *Return of Electors Registered and Returning-Officers' Charges, Session Papers*, 1833, No. 189, p. 224.
[3] 53 Geo. III, c. 89.

the constituencies, were saddled by custom on candidates. Both sets of charges had their origin in the eagerness of men to be chosen, and in their readiness to buy their way into the House of Commons.

There was no statutory warrant for any local charge upon a candidate at an election prior to 1712. Between the Revolution and the first Act throwing charges upon candidates, Parliament made improvements and additions to the machinery for electing knights of the shire. These all involved expenses; but in these Acts there was not so much as a hint as to who was to pay these new charges. In 1695–96 the sheriff of the County of Southampton was empowered by statute to adjourn the polls from Winchester to Newport, Isle of Wight. He was to do this at the request of "one or more of the candidates"; after every freeholder then and there present at Winchester had polled. These adjournments across the Solent were for the convenience of the freeholders in the Isle of Wight. To carry the poll-clerks and all the paraphernalia of a county election from Winchester to Newport must have entailed expense; but the Act does not indicate by whom these charges were to be borne[1]. The inference is that they were to be paid by the candidates, for it was at the request of candidates that adjournment to Newport was to be made.

Statutory Expenditure inferentially thrown on Candidates.

Up to this time there was no general law directing at what town in a county the election of knights was to be held. The writ did not point out the place at which the election was to be made. It directed only that it should be at the next county court; and so long as the writ was the only guide to the sheriff, he exercised the power vested in him by common law, unless restrained by special Act, of holding his court wherever he thought fit within his county[2]. The simplicity of election procedure until after the Revolution is shown by Dalton's treatise on the office of sheriff. "This election of knights and burgesses," reads a paragraph in the edition of 1682, "may be by voices or holding up of hands, or by any other like way whereby it may be discovered who hath the greater number[3]." But although this is a statement of the law of election as it existed at the time Dalton wrote—a statement made for the guidance of sheriffs—in practice the procedure was not so simple as the quotation from his book would suggest.

Simplicity of early Election Procedure.

[1] 7 and 8 W. III, c. 21.
[2] Heywood, *County Election Law*, 227, 228.
[3] Dalton, *Office of Sheriff*, 333.

Develope-
ment of
Election
Machinery.

Before Dalton wrote, sheriffs and candidates had, without any direct sanction by statute, devised much machinery; and at this time it was the practice for sheriffs and candidates to meet on the eve of a contested election, and formulate the rules for taking the polls. "I never observed," wrote Sir Thomas Browne, on May 7th, 1679, after the election for the County of Norfolk, "so great a number of people who came to give their voices; but all was civilly carried at the polls; and I do not hear of any rude or unhandsome carriage, the competitors having the week before set down rules and agreed upon articles for their regular and quiet proceeding[1]." At the election for Cardiganshire in 1688 there was an agreement between the candidates that non-resident freeholders should not poll[2]. This was no doubt with a view to avoiding the expense of carrying electors long distances to poll, a practice which owed its origin to the court candidates at the general election following the dissolution of the Pensioners' Parliament[3]. Long before Dalton wrote his book for the guidance of sheriffs, candidates were being represented at elections by agents. A land steward acted as Sir Henry Slingsby's agent at Knaresborough in 1640[4]. Henry Sidney was represented by an agent when he was a candidate for Bramber in 1679[5]; and how completely the early simplicity of election machinery was becoming of the past in the seventeenth century is shown by the fact that, as early in the eighteenth century as 1701, inspectors were established at county polls in the interest of candidates[6].

More
Election
Charges on
Candidates.

In the Parliamentary session of 1695–96, which witnessed the enactment of the special law for adjournment of the poll from Winchester to Newport, there was also passed a general law directing where sheriffs were to hold the polls, and also adding to the machinery of elections. The county election henceforward was to be held " at the most public and usual place of election, and where the same has most usually been for forty years past[7] "; and for the " more due and orderly proceeding at the poll," the sheriff was directed to " appoint such number of clerks as to him shall

---

[1] Sir Thomas Browne, *Works*, Bohn edition, 1846, iii. 454.

[2] *H. of C. Journals*, x. 188.

[3] R. S. Ferguson, *Lecture on Carlisle and its Corporation*, March 7, 1882.

[4] Slingsby, *Diary*, 51.

[5] Sidney, *Diary and Correspondence*, i. 119.

[6] *Hist. MSS. Comm. 12th Rep.*, App., pt. iv., vol. ii. 443.

[7] 7 and 8 W. III, c. 25.

seem meet and convenient." The Act set forth the oath these clerks were to take, and the manner in which they were to make entries in the poll-books; but it was silent as to who was to pay their fees. These became, of course, a charge on candidates; but no statutory warrant was given to the sheriff to levy them; nor did the Act contain any safeguards against the over-charging of candidates for these clerical services.

Later than this Act adding to the machinery of elections, there was the Act of 1710[1] establishing a landed qualification for members of the House of Commons. Under its provisions candidates, at the request of opposing candidates, or of two or more electors, could be compelled to take oath as to their qualifications. For administering this oath, and for a certificate that it had been taken, a returning-officer was empowered to charge a fee of three shillings. Only inferentially, however, was the payment of the fee thrown upon the candidate called upon to take the oath; and not until 1712 was there an enactment making candidates either in boroughs or counties liable for any local charges at elections.

Fees on taking Oaths.

When at last, in 1712, there was embodied in a statute the principle that candidates were liable for election expenses, the law was not general. The principle may be said to have been foisted into a statute. The bill in which it was embodied was for another purpose. Its object was to prevent fraudulent conveyances to make forty-shilling freeholders. To it were tacked, at a late stage of the bill, clauses authorising the sheriffs of the counties of Yorkshire and Cheshire to cause a certain number of tables to be made " at the proper cost and charge of the candidates," for taking the polls in county elections[2]. These clauses did not go un-challenged. On the Chester clause the House divided. But the clause was carried by ninety-two votes to fifty-two[3]. The bill, the first enactment in a code of much constitutional import, received the royal assent on the 22nd of May, 1712[4]; and for the next thirty-three years the sheriffs of Yorkshire and Cheshire enjoyed the singular privilege of statutory powers authorising them to throw at least part of the official expenses of the election on the candidates. In this period, as before the Act of 1712, sheriffs of these two counties undoubtedly collected all their official charges; but they had statutory warrant for collecting only the charges to

The first Statutory Charge.

---

[1] 9 Anne, c. 5.   [2] 10 Anne, c. 31.

[3] *H. of C. Journals*, XVII. 189.   [4] *H. of C. Journals*, XVII. 235.

which they were put in providing tables at which the poll could be taken.

Why was the Charge made Statutory?

Why these comparatively small expenses should have been deemed worth special clauses in an Act only very slightly touching the machinery of elections, it is impossible to discover. Tables could have formed but a small item in an election bill at a time when the employment of poll-clerks was authorised by law, and inspectors were present in the interest of candidates. It is probable that a candidate had quibbled over these charges, and that the successful candidates determined that there should be no more of these quibbles at succeeding elections. Or these clauses may have been the result of the ingenuity of under-sheriffs, intent on recouping themselves for every charge arising out of an election.

A Dispute over an Election Charge.

More than a century later, the town-clerk of Woodstock was similarly anxious for statutory authority when the Marquis of Blandford refused to pay his fee of fifty-one pounds for an unopposed return. " When you shall be pleased to point out to me the Act of Parliament under the authority of which you have made your persistent demands upon me for £51. 11*s*. 4*d*. in respect of fees alleged to have been paid by the town-clerk of Woodstock on the return of a member of Parliament," wrote the Marquis of Blandford on the 20th of January, 1833, " I shall be ready, if satisfied of my liability by virtue of any Act of Parliament, to discharge the same." The town-clerk could point to no statutory authority for this charge. All he could answer was to assert that it was a customary demand, " which he believes, except in the present instance, has never been disputed here"; and to appeal, as he did, to Parliament to " come to some decision respecting similar claims, and to declare from what funds they are to be defrayed[1]." It was in all probability some dispute similar to that between the Marquis of Blandford and the town-clerk of Woodstock in 1833, which led to the Yorkshire and Cheshire clauses in the Act of 1712. They were certainly designed to meet special cases; for no other sheriffs were given statutory powers to collect any of their charges in the Act of 1712, and not until 1745 was there a general law throwing any charges on Parliamentary candidates.

The Act of 1745.

The Act of 1745[2] greatly altered in point of law the relationship between sheriffs and candidates. It made it obligatory on the

---

[1] *Return of Electors Registered and Returning-Officers' Charges, Session Papers,* 1833, No. 189, p. 223.

[2] 18 Geo. II, c. 18.

sheriff to erect " at the expense of the candidates, such a number of convenient booths or places for taking the poll as the candidates, or any of them, shall three days at least before the poll desire." Moreover the Act made it mandatory upon the sheriff to appoint " a proper clerk or clerks at each of the said booths or polling-places to take the poll, which said clerk or clerks shall be at the expense of the candidates, and be paid not exceeding one guinea a day." By the Act of 1695–96[1], the first Act in which there is a reference to poll-clerks, the sheriff was only directed to appoint such " number of clerks as to him shall seem meet and convenient." By the Act of 1745 these appointments were no longer left to his discretion; there was to be a poll-clerk for each booth. By the Act, which thus took this matter out of the discretion of the sheriff, he was further empowered to make lists " of the several towns, villages, parishes, or hamlets in the wapentake " for which each booth was designed, and to deliver copies to the candidates, " taking for the same, two shillings and no more."

For candidates the changes effected by the Act of 1745, the Candidates Act which is at the basis of the existing code, were of much made liable for Election significance. Hitherto, if a candidate had not agreed expressly or Expenses. inferentially with the opposing candidates and the sheriff as to the erection of booths, he could not be charged with any part of the expense. But after 1745 it was in the power of one candidate to insist on the erection of booths, and to make his opponents pay a *pro rata* share of the expense, whether they deemed the booths necessary or not. Moreover, poll-clerks' fees were now thrown by law upon candidates.

The principle that candidates must pay election expenses Additions to received statutory recognition in 1712, in the matter of the tables the Code. for the elections at Chester and York. In 1745 a general appli-cation was given to the principle so far as county elections were concerned; and after 1745, whenever any change was made in the detail or machinery of county elections, Parliament was consistently careful to throw the new expenses on candidates. Thus in 1794, when it was deemed expedient that, in addition to the polling-booths, there should be booths in which county electors should take the oaths of allegiance and supremacy, make the declaration of fidelity, and take also the oath of abjuration, it was enacted that the outlays of returning-officers on these booths—booths

[1] 7 and 8 W. III, c. 25.

which were to be erected on the demand of one of the candidates —" shall be repaid to them by the candidates at such elections in equal proportion[1]." The allowances and compensations to officers administering these oaths, as well as the cost of the printed blanks on which the certificates were to be written, were all to be charged upon the candidates; and it was further enacted that these costs might be recovered by returning-officers in any of the courts of record at Westminster.

The Growing Burden of Election Expenses.

Earlier than this Act of 1794, in 1781, when Parliament enacted that the certificates of the payment of land-tax should be a county elector's title to vote, it was provided in the Act that the attendance of the clerk of the peace at the election with the duplicates of the land-tax assessments should be at the expense of the candidates[2]. In short, after Parliament had once set up the tables at York and Chester at the expense of Parliamentary candidates, it seldom left in doubt, in measures affecting election procedure, who was to pay the bills. Every new expense was thrown on the candidates. It was in this period, or rather between the Revolution and the reign of George III, that elections in counties began to be extremely costly. The administration of the numerous oaths now imposed on electors, such as the oaths of allegiance and abjuration, the declaration against transubstantiation, the oaths in support of the Revolution settlement, the freeholders' oath, and the oaths against bribery, all swelled the official cost of a county election. They swelled it directly and indirectly; indirectly because they protracted the polling, and added to the charges which candidates had to meet in respect of clerks and other officials called in by the returning-officer to aid in taking the poll.

Not under the Control of Candidates.

All these were charges over which a candidate had no control when he had once entered on an election contest. He could make his own terms with his election agent. He could decide for himself how much he would spend in carrying freeholders to the poll, and in what style he would entertain them. But over official charges he was powerless. Especially was a candidate powerless in controlling these expenses when he was engaged in a contest with men with large incomes; for it was the wealthy candidate who made the pace. In 1785 the time for polling in counties was limited to fifteen days[3]. Thereafter there grew up the practice of

---

[1] 34 Geo. III, c. 73.   [2] 20 Geo. III, c. 17.
[3] 25 Geo. III, c. 84.

keeping the poll open for fifteen days by contriving to bring voters forward within the statutory limit of one an hour. This manœuvring caused great expense and infinite vexation to a candidate who was in the lead and who, it was often known, had a safe majority[1].

Men who were reckless in their expenditure thus had it in their power to penalise their opponents, and not infrequently did so in contests in boroughs as well as in counties. An example of what unscrupulous opponents might do is forthcoming in an episode in the election for the city of Norwich in 1818, when Edward Harbord, afterwards Baron Suffield, was contesting Norwich against William Smith and R. H. Gurney. At the close of the first day's poll, Harbord was left so far behind Gurney that all hope of carrying his election was abandoned. "Under these circumstances," writes Harbord's biographer, "one of the leaders of the party announced to him, that it was still desirable to keep the poll open. Mr Harbord inquired on what grounds. 'It will put Mr Gurney to a charge of one thousand pounds,' was the reply. Tears of indignation actually arose in his eyes, and he exclaimed, 'Good God, sir! What can you have seen in my conduct to lead you to infer that I would consent to put an honourable adversary, or any adversary, to such an expense for the mere purpose of aggrieving him[2]?'" Harbord, who after the melée at Peterloo in 1819 acted with the Parliamentary reformers, was the Church and State candidate at the Norwich election of 1818, and had been indemnified by the Tories of the city against any expense. But he was nearly six hundred votes behind Gurney. His idea as to what constituted an honourably fought contest prevailed, and the election was not continued a second day[3].

Only one of the measures legalising election expenses, passed in the eighteenth century, was applicable to cities and boroughs. This was the Act of 1794 for the appointment of commissioners to administer oaths, and authorising returning-officers, in constituencies with more than six hundred electors, at the instance of candidates to erect booths in which these oaths could be administered. The Act was, in practice, applicable only to a few of the larger borough constituencies; and all through the last two centuries of the unreformed Parliament, the local charges on candidates in the boroughs were generally only for services rendered by the returning-

Candidates increasing Election Expenses.

Election Expenses in the Boroughs.

[1] Cf. Hansard, 2nd Series, xvi. 1195.
[2] R. M. Bacon, *Life of Edward, Third Baron Suffield*, 60.
[3] R. M. Bacon, *Life of Edward, Third Baron Suffield*, 63.

officer and other officials engaged at the election, or in keeping
order while the poll was proceeding.   In the boroughs there were
guildhalls, market-halls and churches in which elections could be
held.   Until the Reform Act there were still a few boroughs in
which the elections were held in the churches[1].   As a general rule,
in borough constituencies, there would be no expenses for the
administration of oaths.   The Act of 1745, throwing on candidates
the expense of erecting polling-booths at county elections, was not
applicable to the boroughs, and returning-officers had no statutory
warrant for charging candidates with the payments to poll-clerks,
and the cost of erecting polling-booths, until as near the end of
the old representative system as 1828[2].

Unsuccessful   Between the reign of George II and the Reform Act of 1832
Candidates   there were at least two local or special Acts affecting the machinery
refuse to
pay at   of elections in borough constituencies.   In 1781 an Act was passed
Coventry.   regulating the admission of freemen at Coventry, which contained
a clause directing that an election booth should be " erected in the
widest and most convenient part of the open market-place, called
' Cross Cheapening,' not contiguous to any other building[3]."   But
like the Acts which were passed between 1695 and 1712 affecting
county elections, the Coventry Act of 1781 contained no provision
settling who was to pay for the election booth ; and by that
omission much trouble was caused in 1784 to the mayor and
bailiffs, who had the strongest conviction as to the persons
responsible for payment.   So in 1785 the mayor and bailiffs went
to the House of Commons with a tale of woe.   At the election in
1784, the booth had been erected in accordance with the Act of
1781, and the successful candidates paid their moiety to its cost.
One of them was Sir Sampson Gideon, notorious for his reckless
expenditure at elections, and so intent on being of the House of
Commons that one of Horace Walpole's correspondents wondered
that Gideon was alive, " considering the immense fatigue and
necessary drinking he must undergo[4]."   " But the other moiety,"
reads the Coventry petition to the House of Commons, " hath not
hitherto been reimbursed, although payment thereof has been
frequently demanded."   To prevent similar repudiations in the
future, the mayor and bailiffs conceived " that there should be

[1] Cf. Hansard, 3rd Series, v. 88, 89.
[2] 9 Geo. IV, c. 59.
[3] 21 Geo. III, c. 54.
[4] Walpole, *Correspondence*, VII. 402.

a law declaring at whose expense the election booth should be erected." They urged that "it should be erected at the joint and equal expense of the candidates[1]." Leave was given for the introduction of a bill[2]. So far as I have been able to trace, the bill made no further progress; and until 1828, when the Act of 1745 was extended to boroughs, returning-officers at Coventry, like those in all other boroughs except Westminster, had to make their bargains beforehand with candidates, or to run the risk of the charge for election booths being repudiated.

As is brought out in the correspondence between the Marquis of Blandford and the town-clerk at Woodstock in 1833, until the end of the old representative system, with the exception of the laws regulating the administration of oaths to electors, and the Act of 1828 making candidates liable for poll-clerk hire and the cost of polling-booths, there was no general statute to which returning-officers in boroughs could point when charging their expenses on candidates. The cost of the administration of oaths— only a small part of the general charges in an election—could, under the Act of 1794, be recovered in the law-courts. Later than 1828, in boroughs with more than six hundred electors, poll-clerk hire and the expense of erecting booths could be so recovered; and so could the non-statutory charges, if the candidates had expressly agreed to pay them. In the absence of these agreements, a returning-officer was in the hands of the candidate, and he had no remedy in the courts against a candidate, not a party to an agreement, who repudiated non-statutory charges. *The Position of Returning-Officers.*

At the Westminster election in May, 1807, Lord Cochrane and Sir Francis Burdett were returned. Burdett, ever ready to raise a point in constitutional law, refused to reimburse the high constable one-fourth part of the bill incurred by him as returning-officer. Burdett repudiated liability as a matter of principle, and set up the plea that a member of the House of Commons had a right to be elected free of all expense. The only statutory charge in the high constable's bill of expenses was that for administering oaths. Westminster was a large constituency—the largest scot and lot borough in the old representative system. It had 14,000 electors in 1807; and to administer oaths two commissioners had been appointed, whose fees amounted to thirty-nine pounds. The Acts authorising the erection of polling-booths and the payment *Sir Francis Burdett's Protest in 1807.*

---

[1] *H. of C. Journals*, XL. 606. [2] *H. of C. Journals*, XL. 814.

of poll-clerks were then, as until 1828, applicable only to counties. The case went to the law-courts. There it was contended, on behalf of the high constable, that " from the antiquity and notoriety of the different charges, a promise might be inferred on the part of every candidate to submit to them[1]." Lord Ellenborough, before whom the case was tried, laid down, however, that a candidate was liable to no expense except such as the statute law cast upon him, or as he took upon himself by his express or implied consent.

Burdett's Liability.

The sum for which Burdett was sued was £307. 1*s*. 10*d*. The case went against him in respect of £117. Included in this sum was one-fifth of the charge for the hustings, for which Burdett's committee had asked and received tickets from the high constable, a user of the hustings which was taken as an implied consent to their erection; and also Burdett's quota of the fees of the Commissioners who administered the oaths; and a share of the printers' bill, incurred for blanks used in the administration of oaths, and for tickets of admission to the hustings.

Returning-Officer's Bill.

The high constable's bill as made up after the election stood thus:

	£	s.	d.
Six Under-bailiffs to attend Proclamation of Election . .	6	6	0
High Constable's Attendance	1	11	6
Crier for Proclamation and Horse Hire	5	15	6
Twenty-four Poll-Clerks at £1. 1*s*. and 5*s*. a day each (15 days)	468	0	0
Twenty-four Staff Men at 7*s*. 6*d*. and 2*s*. 6*d*. a day each . .	180	0	0
Tables for High Constable and Deputies	120	0	0
Two Commissioners for Administering oaths of Allegiance at £1. 1*s*. and 5*s*. a day each	39	0	0
Bill for Erecting Hustings and Surveyor's Fee for valuing same	553	10	10
Bond of Indemnity to Church-Wardens of St Paul's Covent Garden	40	0	0
Printers' Bill	14	3	6
	1478	7	4

When the Westminster election began there were five candidates. Early in the polling, however, one of them, James Paul, dropped out and paid two hundred pounds as his quota of the high constable's expenses up to the time of his retirement. There was thus £1228. 7*s*. 4*d*. chargeable, according to the high constable's contention, to Burdett and Cochrane, and to the two defeated

---

[1] Campbell, *Reports of Cases at Nisi Prius*, I. 211.

candidates, Sheridan and Elliot, who stayed in the contest to the end.

The verdict, although it made Burdett liable for his quota of three of the charges, was really against the high constable. It was an overruling of his contention that, with or without agreements, he was entitled to recover from the candidates all his disbursements at the election. At the trial of the action in 1808, Sir Vicary Gibbs, who in the following year became Attorney-General of the Perceval Administration, had appeared for the high constable of Westminster, and the Government identified itself so closely with the high constable's case that, when the verdict made it impossible for him to recover all his charges from Burdett, it carried through Parliament an Act extending to Westminster the principle of the Act of 1745, making candidates liable for the hire of poll-clerks, and the cost of erecting polling-booths. *Westminster Act of 1811.*

This Act of 1811[1] was intended to protect the high constable, and to put a stop to such controversies as that between the high constable and Burdett, " and the ill consequences of the same." In 1813 the Westminster Act was renewed, on the ground that "it hath by experience been found useful and beneficial[2]"; and it was continued by other Acts until 1828, when at last—on the eve of the great Reform of 1832—there was passed an Act[3] extending the Act of 1745 to cities and boroughs, and making candidates in these constituencies liable for the payment of poll-clerks and for polling-booths, where these were necessary. But even this Act of 1828 was not applicable to all boroughs. It could be put in force only in boroughs in which there were more than six hundred electors, an exception which left nearly two-thirds of the borough constituencies outside its operation; and not until the Reform Act of 1832 was there a statute making liable candidates in all boroughs, as candidates in counties had been made by the Acts of 1745 and 1794, for the cost of polling-booths and for the charges in respect of returning-officers' deputies and clerks employed in taking the poll[4]. *Act of 1828.*

On two occasions subsequent to the Act of 1745 it was proposed in the House of Commons to lessen the burden thrown by usage and law on Parliamentary candidates. In 1774 it was suggested that county voters should be polled in districts, instead of at the *Efforts to lessen the Burden.*

[1] 51 Geo. III, c. 126.
[2] 53 Geo. III, c. 152.
[3] 9 Geo. IV, c. 59.
[4] 2 W. IV, c. 45.

county town, in order to save expense, chiefly the non-official expense of conveying freeholders to the poll[1]. On the eve of the Reform Act there was an ineffectual attempt to relieve members of the House of Commons of the payment of all official expenses. It was made in 1828, and is the only movement for complete relief from these charges that I have been able to trace between Shaftesbury's proposals of 1688 for throwing election expenses on parishes and counties and the end of the old representative system in 1832.

A Proposal to relieve successful Candidates.

If the attempt of 1828 had succeeded it would, for the time being, have affected only one constituency, since it was made in the abortive bill for transferring the franchise from the corrupt Cornish borough of Penrhyn to Manchester. Lord John Russell, who for years had been working for Parliamentary Reform by piecemeal, was in charge of the Penrhyn bill. His proposal was that the deposit for defraying the expenses for the hustings and other official charges should be returned to the successful but not to the unsuccessful candidates[2]. The author of the bill realized that such a discrimination between successful and unsuccessful candidates needed defence. He accordingly insisted that, if all the candidates were treated alike, " a person possessed neither of property nor of a chance of success might, by setting himself up as a candidate, throw the town into an uproar." Sir Robert Peel, who was at this time Home Secretary in the short-lived Wellington Administration of 1828–30, and government leader in the House of Commons, opposed Lord John Russell's proposal, on the ground that no man should be considered qualified as a candidate unless he were prepared to defray his proportion of the necessary expense of the election. Another argument against the bill was that it was objectionable to vary the general law and the existing usages in the case of Manchester. In view of the opposition, Lord John Russell withdrew the clause, and although he had a large share in drafting the Reform bill, and in piloting it through the House of Commons, he did not in 1831 and 1832 renew his efforts to relieve successful Parliamentary candidates. In the Reform Act there was embodied an amendment to the Act of 1828, by which in all constituencies, large or small, candidates were made liable for the erection of polling-booths, and for the payment of returning-officers' deputies and polling-clerks.

[1] Cf. Hansard, 2nd Series, xvi. 1189.
[2] Hansard, 3rd Series, xviii. 1328.

At the first election after the Reform Act, as at all general elections later than 1712, two sets of charges were paid by Parliamentary candidates. There were those thrown on them by statute, chiefly payments for booths and booth-clerks, and the general and much larger charges for which returning-officers had no warrant other than usage and custom. The Parliamentary Return which was compiled in 1833 covers a general election which is outside the scope of these volumes, which are concerned only with the representative system between 1295 and 1832. But as this return of 1833 was the first ever made of expenses at Parliamentary elections, and as the usages and customs of the old system survived the Reform Act of 1832, I quote a few of the figures from the Return for the light they throw on official charges during the last years of the unreformed Parliament.

At Banbury, where there was no contest, and consequently no occasion for polling-booths or poll-clerks, the town-clerk's bill was £109. 10s. 6d. His "usual fee" for receipt of precept from the sheriff, attendance on returning-officer, fixing time of proclamation, and making proclamation was £5. 5s. For swearing in twenty-one special constables, the charge was £3. 16s. 6d.; attending to discharge these constables, 13s. 6d.; attending to deliver check-books, 13s. 6d.; usual fee for attending election, £10. 10s.; for indentures of return and stamps, £10. 10s.; for journey to deliver return to under-sheriff and get counterparts signed by sheriff, including travelling eighty-eight miles, £8. 8s.; under-sheriff's usual fee, £15. 15s.[1] This bill at Banbury may be taken as typical of charges thrown on candidates by usage and not by law; for, excepting perhaps the charge for inland revenue stamps, the exact amount of which is not specified, there is not a single item for which the town-clerk had statutory warrant. Again, excepting the charge for stamps, every one of these charges, and in particular the several fees to the town-clerk and the fee to the under-sheriff of Oxfordshire, were of the class which owed its origin exclusively to the eagerness of men to be of the House of Commons and their willingness to pay without question to all who had any part in helping them on their way to Westminster.

Banbury was a single-member borough, so that in the unopposed election of 1833 this charge of £109. 10s. 6d. fell entirely on the member elected. Bedford, before and after the Reform Act of

---

[1] *Return of Electors Registered and Returning-Officers' Charges, Session Papers,* 1833, No. 189, p. 95.

1832, returned two members. The town-clerk's bill there in 1833 was £30. 9*s.*; and he also collected £10. 10*s.* each from the successful candidates, the "usual fee for the return[1]." The difference in the bills at Banbury and Bedford illustrates the utter lack of any uniformity in official charges under the old system; for while £59. 9*s.* represented the entire cost of returning two members at Bedford after a contest, the single member returned unopposed at Banbury had to pay £109. 10*s.* 6*d.*

Inequality of Charges.   At Birmingham the under-sheriff of the County of Warwick charged each of the successful candidates a fee of £12. 12*s.* This was Birmingham's first Parliamentary election. "The low bailiff and myself," writes the under-sheriff, who acted as returning-officer, "proposed to drive into the midst of the electors in a barouche," and take the poll in the simplest and least costly way. But one of the candidates, availing himself of the law of 1828, insisted on the erection of hustings which cost £27[2]. At Bodmin, which survived as a two-member borough, the official bill was £33. The under-sheriff's clerk for delivering the precept collected £2. 2*s.*; the under-sheriff's fee was £10. 10*s.*; the town-clerk's charge for drawing up and engrossing the indenture was £10. 10*s.*; and the other expenses attendant on an election at which 252 electors had the right to poll, were £10. 6*s.*[3] At Bridgwater there was no contest and no charge, except for the hustings[4]. At Calne there was no poll, and the only item in the Return was £10. 10*s.* for the under-sheriff's fee[5]. Each candidate at Cambridge paid the town-clerk's fee of £10. 10*s.*[6] A similar fee, and £10. 10*s.* for stamps and indenture, was charged at Carlisle[7]; where in 1754, when Sir Charles Howard and John Stanwix were returned unopposed, they paid only £2. 2*s.* as fee to the town-clerk, and £5. 5*s.* as the recorder's fee[8].

Charges in Dispute.   There was quite a series of official fees at Cirencester—£10. 10*s.* for the sheriff's precept; £4. 4*s.* for the messenger who carried the precept to Cirencester; £21 as the steward's fee; and £21 as the bailiff's fee[9]. At Cricklade all the fees paid were to the under-sheriff and his messengers—£10. 10*s.* to the under-sheriff; £2. 8*s.*

[1] *Return*, 1833, No. 189, p. 98.   [2] *Return*, 1833, No. 189, p. 99.
[3] *Return*, 1833, No. 189, p. 101.   [4] *Return*, 1833, No. 189, p. 105.
[5] *Return*, 1833, No. 189, p. 111.   [6] *Return*, 1833, No. 189, p. 111.
[7] *Return*, 1833, No. 189, p. 115.
[8] *Official List*, pt. ii. 111 ; Ferguson, *Cumberland and Westmorland Members of Parliament*, 123–125.
[9] *Return*, 1833, No. 189, p. 122.

to the messenger with the precept; and £2. 10s. to the messenger who carried it back to the under-sheriff[1]. At Devizes the town-clerk's fee was £21, and the under-sheriff's fee £10[2]. At Hertford, as at Woodstock, these fees, for which there was not statutory warrant, were in dispute. The town-clerk claimed "the usual fee" of £21; the under-sheriff here was content with £5. 5s.; while the sergeant-at-mace put in a claim for £4. 4s. The members returned from Hertford refused to honour any of these demands[3]. To get the precept for Malmesbury it cost £13. 13s.—£11. 11s. to the under-sheriff, and £2. 2s. for the messenger with the precept[4].

From Lewes, where there was no contest in 1833, there was a bill much on the lines of that from Banbury, except that the official blackmail on candidates was on a slightly less extortionate scale. The total charge was £65. 9s., made up thus:—usual gratuity to town-clerk, £21; preparing indenture, £5. 5s.; clerk's journey to London to deposit return in sheriff's office, £5; usual fee for under-sheriff for bringing down the precept, £15. 15s.; town-crier, £2. 10s.; to the band, £3. 2s.; two constables, 5s.; erecting hustings, £12. 12s.[5] At Ipswich, out of a total expenditure of £48. 12s. 3d., £28. 7s. 6d. went to the town-clerk[6]. At Warrington, which like Birmingham had its first election in 1833, the official charges were only £2[7]—the smallest in any borough from which a detailed schedule of charges was received. Windsor came very near to Warrington in this respect; for £4. 15s.—£1. 11s. 8d. for each of the three candidates—represented the total official cost of the election there[8]. Weymouth was another borough in which a candidate refused to pay the non-statutory fees, amounting to £15. 15s., claimed by the town-clerk[9]; and at Great Yarmouth the town-clerk was in dispute with the candidates over fees and charges aggregating £42. 1s. 4d., and in the Official Return he reported a loss of £10. 9s. 7d.[10] Candidates in two or three places were charged and paid such expenses as the cost of shoring up the town-hall, widening the entrance to a court-house, and repairs to buildings[11];—charges insignificant in amount as set down in the Parliamentary Return, but which mark again the

Other Examples of Election Charges.

---

[1] *Return*, 1833, No. 189, p. 124.
[2] *Return*, 1833, No. 189, p. 126.
[3] *Return*, 1833, No. 189, p. 139.
[4] *Return*, 1833, No. 189, p. 158.
[5] *Return*, 1833, No. 189, p. 151.
[6] *Return*, 1833, No. 189, p. 142.
[7] *Return*, 1833, No. 189, p. 213.
[8] *Return*, 1833, No. 189, p. 221.
[9] *Return*, 1833, No. 189, p. 217.
[10] *Return*, 1833, No. 189, p. 228.
[11] *Return*, 1833, No. 189, p. 150.

changes which five centuries of the working of the old electoral system had brought about in the relationship of candidates and constituencies.

The town-clerk of Tamworth realized that the Reform Act had made some changes, and rearranged his scale of charges. "The town-clerk's fee," reads a memorandum accompanying the Tamworth schedule, "includes all his trouble in preparing notices, oaths, proclamations, drawing and engrossing return. The anciently accustomed fee was £25; but as there was a little less trouble at the late election, in consequence of there being but one precept to be returned, the town-clerk voluntarily reduced his fee to £21[1]." At Westminster—where the contest of 1807 resulted in a high constable's bill of £1428—the total expense of the contested election of 1833 was only £362. 5s., of which £250 represented the cost of the hustings, and £48 payments to poll-clerks[2].

The Parliamentary Return from which I have taken these statements is not complete. Particulars are lacking from many of the old boroughs, and from many of those which elected members for the first time. Nor have I gone into detail concerning all the boroughs included in the Return. Incomplete as it is, the Return is valuable for two or three reasons. It shows how largely the official charges made at elections in the boroughs were matters of custom; and how comparatively small were the official charges which came within the statutes in force in 1833. Moreover the reports from Woodstock, Weymouth, Great Yarmouth, and Hertford, and other statements in the Return, show that the town-clerks and under-sheriffs realized that they were on uncertain ground when they claimed from candidates fees as distinct from charges sanctioned by Act of Parliament. This uncertainty dated from the verdict adverse to the high constable of Westminster, and it had been aggravated by the agitation for the Reform Act, of the two years preceding the election of 1833, and by the great changes brought about by that Act. Launceston had returned members to the House of Commons as early as the reign of Edward I. But at the election following the Reform Act, the town-clerk was in much doubt concerning his fee. "I have not as yet," he wrote, "made any charges on the candidates, having waited to ascertain what was done generally by other clerks[3]." "The person who brought the sheriff's precept," reads the report

---

[1] *Return*, 1833, No. 189, p. 205.   [2] *Return*, 1833, No. 189, p. 216.
[3] *Return*, 1833, No. 189, p. 147.

from Lancaster, which had returned members to Parliament from as early a period as Launceston, "demanded the usual compliment; but the returning-officer declined to pay[1]."

At Woodstock, as has been stated earlier in this chapter, the town-clerk could get no satisfaction from the Marquis of Blandford in respect to his fees and charges. Had he looked back into the electoral history of his own borough, he would have learned that the precedents for his excessive fees were, comparatively speaking, not of long standing; for Woodstock is a borough whose electoral history well illustrates the developement of the fee system, and the way in which the official practice of preying on Parliamentary candidates grew when once it had been established. In 1705 Charles Bertie and Sir John Walter were returned for the borough. Their total expenses were £15. 3*s.*; and this sum included outlays on ale, bread, cheese, pipes, and victuals for the freemen. The bill is a detailed one; but it contains no mention of any payments to the town-clerk or any official charges[2]. Again, in 1706, there was a by-election at Woodstock, when Walter, who had been returned in 1705, became member for Oxford[3]. There was then "the usual fee to the town-clerk for preparing the indenture," £2. 2*s.*; and there was also paid "to the sergeant, half-a-guinea; to the cryer who cleans the hall, 5*s.*; to the ringers, a guinea, and those who carried you (evidently William Cadogan[4]) in the chair, a guinea[5]."

The Growth of Election Charges.

The Act of 1832 made all candidates, in boroughs as well as in counties, liable for the cost of erecting polling-booths and for the payment of poll-clerks. New charges were thrown on candidates by the Ballot Act of 1872[6]; but not until 1875 was there legislation for England authorising returning-officers to collect "their reasonable charges" from candidates[7]. A statutory warrant was thus given to many charges hitherto collected only by force of custom or agreement; and England at last obtained a law on the lines of that suggested by the town-clerk of Woodstock in 1833.

Acts affecting Election Charges.

The legislation for England between 1832 and 1875 directed from what source returning-officer's election expenses were to come. They were to be paid—as had been all statutory and non-statutory charges long before 1833—out of the pockets of candidates; but

The Act of 1875.

---

[1] *Return*, 1833, No. 189, p. 147.
[2] Ballard, *Chronicles of Woodstock*, 117.
[3] *Official List*, pt. II. p. 4. [4] *Official List*, pt. II. p. 4.
[5] Ballard, *Chronicles of Woodstock*, 118.
[6] 35 and 36 Vict., c. 33. [7] 38 and 39 Vict., c. 84.

Parliamentary candidates had to wait until 1875 before they were protected by a law which limited these official charges, and gave candidates the right to have such charges taxed, as costs in a lawsuit may be taxed.   When it came, this Act—the Act still regulating returning-officers' charges—had a two-fold purpose.   It was intended to protect candidates and establish uniformity in election charges; and also, what was equally important, to check lavish expenses at elections, which often covered evasions of the Acts against bribery.

Charges formerly met by Candidates.

This Act of 1875, although it dates half a century later than the beginning of the end of the old electoral system, continued a restriction on the choice of constituencies, which, as I have shown, had gradually begun in the sixteenth century.   Until 1710 there were no laws compelling constituencies to concern themselves with the financial status of candidates.   Long before 1710, however, their financial position had not been a matter of indifference.   For a century and a half earlier than the reign of Queen Anne, it had been the custom of constituencies to ask of candidates: "Are you prepared to serve as our representative in the House of Commons without pay?"   Both county and borough constituencies had so interrogated Parliamentary candidates.   From the reign of James I borough constituencies in effect had also asked, "Are you prepared to treat and bribe electors?" while many boroughs demanded from candidates whether they were prepared to lend money to the town without interest; or to improve the navigation of the river; or to build a new town-hall; or to pave the streets; or to build bridges, or pay the charges of carrying through Parliament improvement Acts.

Charges since 1875.

These questions are no longer asked of candidates.   But the first question now put to a Parliamentary candidate, and put by or for the returning-officer acting for the constituency, is, "Can you make the deposit to cover the official expenses of the election?"   These deposits vary in amount according to the character of the constituency, borough or county, and the number of electors.   In a constituency with less than a thousand voters, the returning-officer demands a deposit of one hundred pounds from each candidate; and the sum so demanded increases in proportion to the number of the electors, until it reaches seven hundred pounds for a borough constituency with 30,000 voters, and a thousand pounds in the case of a county constituency with an equally large electorate.   Unless a man can promptly meet this demand he must stand aside, and group himself with civil servants and clergymen, government contractors and army agents, minors, aliens, and bankrupts, and persons guilty of corrupt or illegal practices at elections; in short with the men from whom constituencies are forbidden by law to choose their representatives to the House of Commons.

The deposits must be in the hands of returning-officers as soon as the nominations of candidates are made. Men could and did evade the eighteenth and early nineteenth century statutory test of financial standing. The new test comes at about the same stage in a Parliamentary election as did the first of the two tests under the Acts of 1710 and 1760. The old oath as to property qualification, when put at the election, was at the instance of a candidate or of electors; while the test under the Act of 1875 is put by the returning-officer, and without the intervention of either candidates or electors. In putting the oath as to possession of qualifying property to a candidate, a returning-officer discharged only an executive duty, and had only an official interest in it; for it was no concern of his that a candidate swore to the possession of property that he had not. The modern test, the ability of a candidate to deposit the sum of money determined according to the schedule, is one in which returning-officers, or rather the under-sheriffs and town-clerks acting with them, have a direct personal interest. Their fees and charges ultimately come out of these deposits, and no evasion of the test is practicable. As a means of restricting the choice of constituencies to men commanding some means, the laws passed at long intervals from 1712, and for the present culminating in the Act of 1875, are much more effective than the landed qualification Act of 1710 ever was. In the larger boroughs and in the industrial divisions of counties the modern test becomes increasingly effective; because in these constituencies every year sees additions to the number of electors, and as the register totals mount upwards, there are corresponding increases in the sums demanded as deposits from candidates before their names find a place on the ballot-papers at Parliamentary elections.

Men without Means still effectually excluded.

CHAPTER X.

OFFICE-HOLDERS, PENSIONERS, AND CONTRACTORS EXCLUDED.

Early
Objections
to Office-
holders.
ALTHOUGH the presence of office-holders in the House of Commons was a grievance nearly as old as the representative system, and had been complained of as early as 1348, when the Commons petitioned Edward III " that no person summoned to Parliament should be either a taxer, collector or receiver of the fifteenth then granted[1]," it was not until after the Revolution that office-holders were first placed by law on the list of persons from whom constituents could not make choice of representatives. There were two petitions to Edward III for the exclusion of collectors of revenue, one in 1348 and another in 1351[2]; but between the reign of Edward III and the Restoration the question of the exclusion of office-holders seems to have been at rest. So far as the Journals show, the grievance of which the Commons had complained in 1348 and 1351 was not again agitated within the House of Commons until 1675. In that year, in the second Parliament of Charles II, there was a bill in the House of Commons to prevent any member from taking upon himself any public office[3]; and there was then begun the agitation for the exclusion of office-holders, pensioners and government contractors which went on almost continuously until 1782,

[1] Hatsell, *Precedents of Proceedings in the House of Commons*, II. 33, 2nd Ed.

[2] Hatsell, *Precedents of Proceedings in the House of Commons*, II. 33, 2nd Ed.

[3] *H. of C. Journals*, IX. 321.

when, after many office-holders as well as pensioners had been disqualified, there was passed the Act[1] by which contractors were also excluded.

The bill of 1675 was read a first time by eighty-eight votes to seventy-four[2]; but a week later it was defeated on the motion to send it to committee[3], and there was an interval of four years between the defeat of this bill of 1675 and the next movement against office-holders. In this interval the second Parliament of Charles II had been dissolved, and the third Parliament, that of 1679, had come into being. When the agitation was renewed in 1679, it was on a bill to enact that whenever a member of the House was preferred by the King to any office or place of profit, a new writ should immediately issue for electing a member to serve in his stead[4]. Leave was given to bring in this bill; but it was not further advanced. Agitation begun in 1675.

In the fourth Parliament of Charles II, that which assembled in October, 1679, the agitation against office-holders was again renewed; and on the 30th of December, 1680, a resolution was carried, none voting to the contrary, "That no member of this House shall accept of any office or place of profit from the Crown without the leave of this House, or any promise of any such office or place during such time as he shall continue a member of this House[5]." At this time the House was intent on investigating the allowances paid to members of the Pensioner Parliament out of the secret service money. It had ordered the production of writings, papers, and proceedings relating to these payments immediately before it passed the foregoing resolution, and was in a mood for drastic measures. It accordingly further resolved that any member who acted contrary to the resolution as to the acceptance of office should be expelled[6]. This Parliament, however, did not long survive the resolution of December 30th, 1680. It was dissolved on the 18th of January, 1681, and there is no record of this far-reaching resolution ever having gone into effect. In the two Parliaments which sat between the dissolution in 1681 and the Revolution—the Parliament which met at Oxford, and the first and only Parliament of James II—there was no renewal of the agitation. Attitude of the House in 1679.

---

[1] 22 Geo. III, c. 45.
[2] *H. of C. Journals,* ix. 321.
[3] *H. of C. Journals,* ix. 326.
[4] *H. of C. Journals,* ix. 608.
[5] *H. of C. Journals,* ix. 695.
[6] *H. of C. Journals,* ix. 696.

In 1693 the movement was renewed. From that time it proceeded on two lines. There was the general movement for the exclusion of all place-men, and there was the movement for the exclusion of specific office-holders. These movements went on side by side from 1693 until the Act of 6 Anne was passed, which compels members accepting office to seek re-election, and thereafter the second movement was long continued with much of its old persistence whenever opportunity offered.

The first success attending the general movement—that dating from 1675—was not realized until 1700-1, when there was embodied in the Act settling the Crown on the House of Hanover, the clause, which however never went into effect, "That no person who has an office or place of profit under the Crown, or receives a pension from the Crown, shall be capable of serving as a member of the House of Commons[1]." Success was thus somewhat slow in coming to the agitation for the general exclusion of office-holders; while the movement for excluding certain specific office-holders was attended with success almost from the first. In 1693 members of the House of Commons, other than commissioners of the treasury and of customs and excise, were prohibited from being concerned directly or indirectly in the farming, collecting, or managing the salt and beer and ale duties, or in any new duties to be laid by subsequent Acts of Parliament[2]; and in 1694 stamp commissioners were placed on the new exclusion list, which had thus been established. Nor were these Acts permitted to be inoperative; for under them, in 1698, four office-holding members were excluded[3], and in the years intervening between the first of these enactments and the reign of George III, no opportunity was lost of adding to the exclusion list which had had its beginnings in 1693.

By the Customs Act of 1700-1[4], no member of the House could be a commissioner, or farmer of customs, or be concerned in his own name, or in the name of any other person, in any office, place or employment, touching or concerning the farming, managing or collecting the customs. In the reign of Anne, Parliament was so intent on this policy of exclusion, that when, in 1703 and 1707, the offices of registers of deeds for Yorkshire were

[1] 12 W. III, c. 2.   [2] 5 W. and M., c. 7.
[3] *H. of C. Journals,* xii. 496, 502, 512, 519.
[4] 12 and 13 W. III, c. 10.

created by Act of Parliament, clauses were inserted which enacted "that no member of Parliament, for the time being, shall be capable of being chose register, or of executing by himself or any other person the said office, or have, take, or receive any fee or other profit whatsoever; nor shall any register, or his deputy for the time being, be capable of being chose to serve in Parliament[1]." In 1708 a similar office was created for the County of Middlesex; and in the Middlesex Act there was inserted an exclusion clause, similar to that in the Yorkshire Acts of 1703 and 1710[2]. These Acts have another interest to students of the English representative system, besides that attaching to them as proofs of the alertness of Parliament in keeping down the number of offices which might be held by members of the House of Commons. The freeholders of Yorkshire and Middlesex were to elect the registers by ballot, and the Acts creating these offices were the first by which Parliament sanctioned the use of the ballot at elections.

While, between 1693 and 1708, Parliament was thus attacking The Bill by piecemeal the system of permitting office-holders to sit in the of 1693. House of Commons, and gradually limiting the number of offices which could be bestowed on members or held by them, it was also waging a continuous contest for the general exclusion of office-holders and pensioners. This general contest began again in 1693, the year which witnessed the first success of what may be described as the subsidiary movement to exclude the holders of specified offices, and in particular those concerned in the collection of the revenue. Burnet, from the standpoint of a partisan of William III, has described the conditions under which the movement of 1693 was begun. "When the party that was set against the Court," he writes, "saw they could carry nothing in either House of Parliament, then they turned their whole strength against the present Parliament to force a dissolution, and in order to that, they first loaded it with a name of ill-sound; and whereas King Charles's long Parliament was called the Pensioners' Parliament they called this the Officers' Parliament, because many that had commands in the army were of it; and the word that they gave out among the people was that we were to be governed by a standing army and a standing Parliament. They tried to carry a bill that rendered all members of the House of Commons incapable of

[1] 2 and 3 Anne, c. 4; 6 Anne, c. 62.   [2] 7 Anne, c. 20.

places of trust or profit; so that every member who accepted a
place should be expelled the House and be incapable of being
chosen again to sit in the current Parliament. The truth was,
it came to be observed, that some got credit by the opposing the
Government, and that to silence them, they were preferred, and
then they changed their note, and were ready to flatter as to
find fault. This gave a specious colour to those who charged
the Court with the design of corrupting members, or at least of
stopping their mouths by places and pensions. When this bill
was set on, it went through the House of Commons with little
or no difficulty; those who were in places had not strength and
credit to make great opposition to it, they being the persons concerned, and looked on as parties; and those who had no places
had not the courage to oppose it, for in them it would have
looked as an art to recommend themselves to one; so the bill
passed in the House of Commons; but was rejected by the Lords,
since it seemed to establish an opposition between the Crown and
the people, as if those who were employed by the one could not
be trusted by the other[1]."

Its Rejection by the Lords.   The bill whose fortunes Burnet thus describes would have
been applicable to all members elected to the House after the
1st of February, 1693. It was defeated in the House of Lords
by only a small majority. When the question was put that the
bill do pass, eighty-two peers were present. Of these forty-two
were for the bill, and forty against. Proxies were then called.
There were only two proxies for the bill, there were seven against;
but of the seven, three were questioned, and were with difficulty
admitted. The result was that the bill was lost by three votes[2].

The Failures of 1694 and 1695.   In 1694 there was another place bill, which would have disabled
all who should take office after that year. The House of Lords
amended this bill, so as to provide that a member who had taken
office could be chosen again. The Commons agreed to the amendment, notwithstanding the great change it wrought in the bill.
But William III, who had quickly grasped the possibilities of
House of Commons management, and who with the exception of
George III was the most active Parliamentary manager of any
of the sovereigns of the eighteenth century, refused the royal
assent[3]. In the next session there was a third place bill. This

[1] Burnet, *Hist. of His Own Times*, IV. 189, 190.
[2] Macaulay, *Hist. of England*, II. 406, Ed. 1877.
[3] Torrens, *Hist. of Cabinets*, I. 16, 17.

time it failed in the House of Commons, where it was rejected by 142 votes to 75[1]; and after this failure in 1695 the question was allowed to rest until 1700.

In the session of 1700 a place bill was again before the House of Commons. On the 15th of February the House went into committee upon it. "It was at first drawn," writes Vernon, "that nobody should be capable of being elected a member of Parliament, who had any office whatsoever without any exception. But Sir Edward Hussey, who had formerly brought in two bills declaring that no man should accept of an office after he was chosen, stuck to his old notion, and proposed it as an amendment, instead of the utter incapacity; which Sir Christopher Musgrave joined in; and the whole frame of the bill was altered accordingly, to the amazement of those who were for turning all men in places out of the House[2]." This bill of 1700 also failed. So did another on the original sweeping lines described by Vernon. It was introduced by Sir John Holland on the 23rd of December, 1702. Had this bill become law it would have provided "that no person whatsoever, in any office or employment, shall be capable of sitting in Parliament." It was, however, negatived by 138 votes to 77[3].

Further Attempts in 1700 and 1702.

In 1704 there was a bill to exclude "all persons in any offices or employments erected since 6th February, 1684, or to be erected." This bill was advanced through more of its Parliamentary stages than any bill since that of 1695 to which William III refused the royal assent. It was introduced in the House of Commons on the 16th of January, and by February 12th, 1704, it had come back from the House of Lords with some amendments[4]. To these the Commons refused to agree[5]. The bill went back to the Lords; and on the 24th of February their lordships were reminded of it by a message from the Commons, in which the measure was described "as a bill highly tending to impartial proceedings in Parliament[6]." Parliament, however, was prorogued before the Lords took action[7]; and in 1705 the movement assumed another form, a form in which it was continued until the time

The End of the Attempt to exclude all Office-holders.

---

[1] Torrens, *Hist. of Cabinets*, I. 17.

[2] Vernon to Duke of Shrewsbury, Feb. 16th, 1700, *Vernon Correspondence*, II. 434.

[3] *H. of C. Journals*, XIV. 95.   [4] *H. of C. Journals*, XIV. 524.

[5] *H. of C. Journals*, XIV. 529.   [6] *H. of C. Journals*, XIV. 549.

[7] *H. of C. Journals*, XIV. 578.

of Walpole, and even until the reign of George III. This year there was introduced a bill " for the more free and impartial proceedings in Parliament, by preventing too great a number of officers from sitting in Parliament[1]." After it had been read a first time no further progress was made. This bill of 1705 is none the less of significance; for it marks the time at which proposals for excluding all office-holders disappeared.

The Clause in the Act of Settlement.

From the time these eighteenth century exclusion bills were before Parliament, there was on the statute book the clause in the Act of Settlement of 1700–1 which provided that no person who had an office or place of profit under the King, or received a pension from the Crown, should be capable of serving as a member of the House of Commons. This clause—which was in the Act providing that the Princess Sophia should succeed to the Crown after William III and Princess Anne, "in default of issue of the said Princess and His Majesty respectively"—was not intended to go into effect until after the "said limitation shall take place." It never went into effect; and the abortive bill of 1705 for preventing too great a number of officers from sitting in Parliament, which was introduced on January 11th, seemingly pioneered the way for the repeal of the clause.

The Act of 1705.

The bill of 1705 was in itself an admission that it was impracticable to exclude all office-holders without recasting the organisation of the House of Commons. Its purpose was to limit the number. In the session which witnessed the adoption of this new policy there was carried the memorable Act[2] which abrogated the revolutionary exclusion clause of 1700–1; added many offices to the statutory exclusion list first established in 1693; and, most important of all, established the principle as to offices held by members of the House of Commons, which has survived until the present time. The clause excluding all office-holders was abrogated, because it appeared " reasonable " that it should not go into effect; and from the repeal of this clause in 1705 nothing more was heard in Parliament of the proposals of the period between the Restoration and the reign of Queen Anne, that the House of Commons should be denuded of all office-holders, great and small. But by this Act of 1705 there were added to the exclusion list holders of offices created subsequent to the Act, commissioners or sub-commissioners of prizes, the secretary or receiver of prizes,

---

[1] *H. of C. Journals*, xv. 84.   [2] 4 and 5 Anne, c. 20.

controllers of the accounts of the army, commissioners of transport and of the sick and wounded, agents of regiments, commissioners for wine licenses, governors or deputy-governors of plantations, commissioners of the navy employed in any of the outports, and " any person having any pension from the Crown during pleasure." All these persons were made incapable of sitting or voting in the House of Commons.

The principle that office-holders who could be of the House must take office openly, and give their constituents an opportunity of passing judgment on their acceptance of office—the great principle which in later and better times was to safeguard the independence of the House, so far as office-holding was concerned, and which from the first was to admit of the British constitution being continued indefinitely on the plan which had been slowly developed in the preceding four centuries of the existence of Parliament—was embodied in a proviso of this Act of 1705. "Provided always," it reads, " that if any person being chosen a member of the House of Commons shall at any time after the dissolution or determination of this present Parliament accept of any office of profit from the Crown during such time as he shall continue a member, his election shall be and is hereby declared to be void, and a new writ shall issue for a new election, as if such person so accepting was naturally dead ; provided nevertheless that such person shall be capable of being again elected as if his place had not become void as aforesaid." *Re-election after taking Office.*

The Journals and contemporary records show that these Acts excluding office-holders were enforced in two ways. Exceptions were taken in the House to the presence there of members who were appointed to offices which specifically disqualified, or to offices the acceptance of which necessitated re-election ; and the Acts were occasionally put into force when election petitions came up for determination. Between the Act of 1693 and the Act of 1705, in which period only the holders of specified offices were excluded, the first of these methods was adopted. Thus on the 10th of February, 1698–99, Sir John Bolles " acquainted the House that there was a clause in the Act, made in 5 and 6 William and Mary for granting a million of money by way of lottery, which would reach several members of the House, particularly James Isaacson, member for Banbury, a commissioner of the stamp office and warehouse keeper of customs." Isaacson admitted that he was commissioner of the stamp office, and a new writ was ordered. *Operation of the Acts.*

Two other members were also ascertained to be commissioners, and both their seats were vacated[1].

Interpretation of the Acts.

In 1707 the Act of 1705 was re-enacted[2], and in 1708 a committee was appointed by the House " to consider of the methods for the effectual execution of the several laws now in force for excluding from the House of Commons officers and such as receive pensions during pleasure[3]," and thereafter there grew up the usage, when an office was in question, of reading at the table the enactments concerning office-holders, and, on the motion for a new writ, taking the opinion of the House as to whether the particular office came within the provisions of the Acts.

Their Application to Military Appointments.

At first, the Act of Queen Anne, and subsequently that of George I[4] which amended the Act of 1705 with regard to pensions, were strictly interpreted; and between 1708 and 1733 the seats of several officers of the army were declared vacated, and these officers were compelled to seek re-election, because they had been appointed to the command of garrisons and forts[5]. But in 1733 a change was made in the procedure as to these appointments. General Wade, who at this time represented Bath, was in January, 1733, appointed Governor of Berwick-on-Tweed; and, following the precedents since 1708, a new writ was issued for Bath. General Wade was again returned. In the same year he was appointed Governor of Fort William in Scotland; and the opinion of the House being taken as to whether by the acceptance of this office his seat became vacant, the House first rejected the motion that a committee should be appointed to search for precedents, and then after the entries in the Journals had been read, recording previous votes on similar military appointments—votes which had led to the vacation of seats—it negatived a motion that such appointments did vacate seats. The motion was general in its terms. It read, " That the accepting of a commission as governor or lieutenant of a fort, citadel, or garrison, upon the military establishment of His Majesty's guards and garrisons in Great Britain, by any member of the House, being an officer in the army, does vacate the seat of such member in this House[6]." For the motion the ayes were eighteen, and the noes ninety-six; so that General

---

[1] Luttrell, IV. 482, 483, 485.   [2] 6 Anne, c. 41.
[3] *H. of C. Journals*, XVI. 93.   [4] 1 Geo. I, st. 2, c. 56.
[5] Cf. Beatson, I. 29, 128, 151, 207, 285.   [6] Beatson, I. 151.

Wade was not put to the trouble of a second re-election at Bath within six months, and a new precedent in these cases favourable to military officers was thereby established[1]. In 1742, when General Wade was appointed lieutenant-general of His Majesty's ordnance, the question of 1733 was raised anew; but was again decided in his favour[2].

The offices specifically named gave the House little trouble. Contro-The controversies subsequent to 1733 were chiefly concerned with versies newly-created offices. A typical case of this kind was before the concerning House in 1739. It arose out of the appointment of Thomas Offices. Corbett, member for Saltash, as secretary to the Court of Assistants for Relief of Poor Widows of Commission and Warrant Officers of the Royal Navy. The office, which was worth two hundred pounds a year, had been established by virtue of a commission under the Great Seal, dated August 30th, 1732. The question as to whether it disqualified its holder was raised on the motion of a new writ for Saltash. Before the vote the enactments of Anne and George I were read at the table. For the motion for a new writ there were one hundred and thirty-two votes, against it two hundred and twenty-three; and "so," in the phraseology of the Journals, "it passed in the negative," and Corbett retained his seat[3]. A vote like this in 1739 would almost necessarily be partisan. It would be similar to the votes which at this time determined contro-verted elections, the result of a division in which the government influence would be on the side of the member who was of its ranks, with little regard to the right or wrong of the case.

As early as 1728 the Exclusion Acts were put in force to Office-disqualify a petitioner against a return. In this year Samuel holding Ongley petitioned against the return of William Orlebar, for the Petitioners. borough of Bedford. At the time of the election, however, Ongley held an office in the customs; and when the petition reached the House, it was promptly resolved that he was incapable of claiming to sit in Parliament[4].

The most typical case that I have discovered in which a candi- An Instance date, unsuccessful at the polls, secured the seat by objecting that the of Exclusion. candidate returned held a newly-created office, did not occur until 1780, by which time petitions were being determined by Grenville

---

[1] Cf. *H. of C. Journals*, XXII. 201.   [2] *H. of C. Journals*, XXIV. 284.
[3] *H. of C. Journals*, XXIII. 473; Beatson, I. 28.
[4] Beatson, I. 2.

committees, and were no longer dependent upon partisan votes of the House. At a by-election for Fifeshire, in July, 1779, Major-General Robert Skene and John Henderson were the candidates. Skene was returned ; but Henderson, before an election committee, objected that he was disqualified by reason of his holding the offices of baggage-master to the forces and inspector of roads. There had been no House of Commons decision up to this time as to whether these offices came within the Act of Queen Anne covering newly-created offices. For Skene it was contended that they did not. But the committee was of opinion "that the novel creation of one of these offices was notorious, and that it was within the statute of Queen Anne," and Henderson obtained the seat[1].

Inefficacy of Law against Pensioners.

I can find no evidence that the laws of 1705 and 1715 against pensioners ever resulted in the exclusion of a pensioner from the House. "Had these laws been enforced," writes Mr Lecky concerning the Exclusion Acts passed from the Revolution to Walpole's time, "they would have done much to purify Parliament. But the pension bills at least were treated with complete contempt. The pensions were secret. The Government refused all information concerning them." "A bill was three times brought forward," continues Mr Lecky, "compelling every member to swear that he was not in receipt of such pension, and that if he accepted one, he would within fourteen days disclose it to the House; but by the influence of Walpole it was three times defeated[2]." The pension system, which chiefly affected Scotch members between the Union and the end of Walpole's rule, seems to have been less of an evil after the beginning of the reign of George III. Other means, such as shares in loans and lotteries, patronage judiciously distributed, and government contracts, were now used for purchasing support; and with the Civil List Act of the Rockingham Administration in 1782, it may be said that pensions ceased to be used as golden hooks for tying members of the House of Commons to the administration. This Act, a monument to Burke's untiring and well-directed agitation for economy in the sessions of 1780, 1781 and 1782, greatly limited the power of granting pensions ; put an end to secret pensions, by making all pensions payable at the Treasury ; and established the principle,

[1] Luder, *Election Cases*, i. 455; Peckwell, *Election Cases*, i. 497; *Official List*, pt. ii. 160.

[2] Lecky, *England in the Eighteenth Century*, i. 485, Ed. 1882, N.Y.

since adhered to, that pensions ought to be granted on two grounds only—as a royal bounty for persons in distress, or as a reward for merit[1]. Thus the arousing of a better public sentiment, which came with the popular agitation growing out of the American war, rather than the Exclusion Acts aimed against pensioners, ended an evil, which, in the eighteenth century, was at its worst during the forty or fifty years following the Union of 1707.

The exclusion of specific office-holders, brought about by Acts like those of 1693 and 1705, did not very materially reduce the number of office-holding members of the House of Commons. In spite of these Acts, there were in the first Parliament of George I two hundred and seventy-one members who held office under the Crown[2]. The movement for exclusion consequently still went on after the Act of 1705. In almost every session for the next seventy or eighty years there were bills for adding to the number of men who, by reason of their financial relations with the Government as office-holders, as pensioners, or as contractors, it was deemed for the public good ought not to be of Parliament. Luttrell's remarks on the bill of 1714 are particularly interesting ; for they show that soon after the Act of 1705—the great landmark in the legislation of the eighteenth century affecting office-holders—the principle then established, that a certain number must of necessity be of the House, was accepted even by members who were most zealous for the exclusion of office-holders. Luttrell notes that the chief design of the bill of 1714 was "to prevent sea and land officers who take pay from laying taxes on the subject," but that it provided for seats in the House for the Secretaries of State, the Chancellor of the Exchequer, two commissioners of the Treasury, two of the Admiralty, and for the Attorney-General and Solicitor-General[3].

Agitation modified by the Act of 1705.

During Walpole's administration the contests over place bills were almost as keen as in the days of William III. The spirit in which they were waged from 1734 is described in a contemporary letter, written by a member of the House. "We have," wrote Colonel Charles Howard to Lord Carlisle, on the 26th of February, 1734, "had a very warm debate whether we should commit a place bill Mr Sandys brought in seven or eight days ago. The House debated it till seven o'clock. For the commitment one hundred

A Place Bill in 1734.

---

[1] May, i. 259.   [2] Cf. Hansard, 2nd Series, ii. 1118.
[3] Luttrell, vi. 726.

and ninety-one; against it two hundred and thirty. This bill was to have restrained great number of employments that now sit in the House. The minority thought the influence of the Crown too great, and that a Parliament composed of such a number of officers was no true representative of the people[1]."

Public Opinion begins to tell.

To save appearances in the House of Commons, and to prevent members unnecessarily coming into conflict with their constituents, Walpole subsequently devised the plan of permitting these place bills to pass in the House of Commons; and, as the peers had no constituents to fear, bringing about their rejection in the House of Lords. "One," writes Horace Walpole, regarding a series of motions in the House of Commons in 1742, "was for a motion for leave to bring in the place bill to limit the number of placemen in the House. This was not opposed, because out of decency it is generally suffered to pass the Commons, and is thrown out by the Lords[2]." But by 1742 persistent agitation was beginning to tell. In the year in which Horace Walpole thus described the policy of the Government towards these bills, there was passed the most comprehensive place Act since 1705. It disqualified commissioners of the revenue in Ireland; commissioners of the navy and of the victualling offices; and deputies and clerks in nearly a score of the government departments, as well as persons holding civil and military offices other than commissioners in regiments within the Island of Minorca and at Gibraltar. All these office-holders were debarred from sitting or voting in the House of Commons. If they sat or voted they were to forfeit twenty pounds for every day they so acted; and moreover, after suit for penalty, they were to be incapable of holding any office of honour or profit under the Crown[3]. At the time this bill became law, two hundred office-holders were of the House of Commons[4].

Scotch Judges excluded.

Between the Act of Queen Anne and this comprehensive place Act of 1742, the most notable success of the movement for the exclusion of men whose financial relations with the Government were likely to make them subservient members of the House of Commons, was the Act of 1714, excluding from the House any man having any pension from the Crown for any term or number of years[5].

---

[1] *Hist. MSS. Comm. 13th Rep.*, App., pt. vi. 132.
[2] Walpole, *Letters to Mann*, i. 118.
[3] 15 Geo. II, c. 22.
[4] Rogers, *Protests of the Lords*, ii. 15.
[5] 1 Geo. I, st. 2, c. 56.

The Act of 1705 had excluded only pensioners during pleasure. In 1733 judges in Scotland were added to the exclusion list[1]. But this addition cannot be credited to the movement which had been going on in Parliament since 1675; for the Act of 1733, consistent as it was with the legislation against office-holders passed since 1693, was pushed through Parliament by Walpole, and was vainly intended to keep Islay's political enemy, Grange, then of the Court of Session, out of the House of Commons[2].

The Act of 1742 did not long stay the agitation for the further Contractors exclusion of office-holders, and of other men dependent on the excluded. Government. Between 1742 and the Reform Act of 1832 there were fifteen or twenty Acts disqualifying these men. The most important was the Act of 1782[3], by which government contractors were excluded. In the reign of George III, prior to 1782, the political ends served by the bestowal of government contracts must have largely neutralised the value of the Acts passed since 1693, excluding office-holders and pensioners. Government contracts, especially when the country was at war, were fully as valuable as many of the offices which could no longer be held by members of Parliament; and all these contracts went to men who, either in the House of Commons or in the constituencies, would aid and support the administration.

During this period a contract to supply rum or beef for the Contracts navy was as great a prize for a member of the House of Commons as Political Rewards. as a share in a government loan or lottery. This species of reward was particularly acceptable to the commercial members of the House; nor were its attractions confined to the members who obtained the contract. Constituents were allowed to participate in the profits, and were consequently zealous in supporting government candidates[4]. A ship worth four or five thousand pounds, and owned by a man with political influence, was in war-time a certain fortune to him. He cleared the purchase money in the first year by hiring his vessel to the Government as a transport at the rate of four hundred pounds a month. " In this," writes one of the early nineteenth century historians of the Royal Navy, and biographer of Lord St Vincent, in describing the system of

[1] 7 Geo. II, c. 16.
[2] Grange, Letters, *Spalding Club Miscellany*, III. 45, 46; *Dict. Nat. Bio.*, XVII. 414.
[3] 22 Geo. III, c. 45.   [4] Cf. May, I. 387.

hiring transports and the political jobbery which was associated with it, " borough influence reigned paramount; and the most solid information was disregarded, when the perpetrator of the greatest fraud was denounced, provided the principal was a supporter of Government. The energetic and quick-sighted St Vincent was unequal to this stronghold of corruption, and the abuse remained uncured for years after he went out of office[1]."

Culmination of the Abuse.
In the reign of George III the King's Printers held their patent subject to the condition that one member of the firm should find a seat in the House of Commons, where of course he voted as he was directed by ministers[2]. Corn factors, who were active at elections in support of the Government, were rewarded by valuable contracts[3]; while the fact that a man had a contract with the Government laid him under the necessity of receiving orders from the Treasury as to his political conduct[4]. No sovereign who ever sought and secured the control of the House of Commons was quicker or more resourceful than George III in turning all government expenditures to political account. He practised close personal economy in order that he might have ready money at his command to maintain a corps of subservient members in the House of Commons; and in the years when North was prime minister, and the King was most exerting himself in the management of the House, offices in every department of the public service, civil, military, and ecclesiastical, were turned to this account. So were also the vast sums which, between 1770 and 1782, were disbursed among contractors for the army and the navy. "At no other period in our annals," writes Mahon, in summing up the debate in the House of Commons on the motion of 1780, for the exclusion of contractors, "did the abuses of the contract system flourish in such rank luxuriance. At no other period were they so detrimental to the public service[5]."

American Revolution and the Reform Movement.
Political reform, at the time that this movement for the exclusion of contractors was going on in the House of Commons, had received an impetus from the American Revolution. In and out of Parliament there was much force behind the demand for the

[1] E. C. Brenton, *Life and Correspondence of John, Earl St Vincent, G.C.B., Admiral of the Fleet*, II. 166, 167.
[2] Cf. Hansard, 3rd Series, I. 241.
[3] *Parl. Hist.*, II. 128.
[4] Cf. *Hist. MSS. Comm. 10th Rep.*, App., pt. VI. 45.
[5] Mahon, *Hist. of England*, VII. 17.

reform of the House of Commons, the first great political movement
since the Revolution in which the electorate had seriously interested
itself. In these years, when the war in America was going against
Great Britain, concessions had to be made to popular movements
both in England and Ireland. Bills for the exclusion of contractors
date from 1779. In that year the bill was rejected in the House
of Commons. The next year it was passed by the Commons, and
thrown out by the House of Lords. In 1781 it was again rejected
in the Commons[1]. But in 1782 political conditions in England
and Ireland and in the revolted colonies were so adverse, that
concessions had to be made to popular agitation. Ireland got free
from Poyning's Law. In England the Act excluding contractors
from the House of Commons was a concession to the widespread
movement for economy and constitutional reform which had developed out of the war in America.

The bill of 1782 excluding contractors had reached committee *The Act*
stage in the House of Commons, and had there been made more *of 1782.*
far-reaching, when the North Administration came to an end in
March. With the Rockingham Ministry in power, the bill, which
the Whigs had supported when they were in opposition, soon
passed its remaining stages in the House of Commons and the
House of Lords. The Act went into effect at the end of the
session of 1782[2]. It was so comprehensive in its provisions that it
put on the exclusion list every person who had a contract with the
commissioners of the treasury, the navy, the victualling office, the
master-general or the board of ordnance, "or with any other
person or persons whatsoever for or on account of the public
service." The Act was, however, not to extend to "trading
companies now existing or established, and consisting of more than
ten persons, where such contracts shall be made for the general
benefit of such incorporation or company"; a provision which
became of much importance in the nineteenth century, when
individual enterprises so largely gave way to industrial and commercial enterprises in the hands of joint-stock undertakings.

After the Union of Great Britain and Ireland there were more *Exclusion*
of these exclusion Acts. Clergymen of the established churches of *of Clergy-*
men and
England, Ireland, and Scotland, were put on the exclusion list in *Judges.*
1801[3], for a reason which has been given in a preceding chapter;

---

[1] May, i. 338. [2] 22 Geo. III, c. 45.
[3] 41 Geo. III, c. 63.

a reason, it may be here reiterated, much the same as those which had led to office-holders being put on the exclusion list, namely that many clergymen of the established churches received their benefices from the Crown. English judges, who had long been held disqualified at common law, were excluded by resolution of the House in 1605, "they being attendants, as judges, in the Upper House[1]." The exclusion of Scotch judges by Act of Parliament was delayed for more than a quarter of a century after the Union in 1707, and was then hurriedly brought about to meet a political emergency growing out of the Earl of Islay's management of Scotland for Walpole. The exclusion of Irish judges was not brought about at the Union. It did not come until 1821[2]; although in the first session of the United Parliament there was passed a law[3], made necessary by the Union, reciting and re-enacting the exclusions established since 1693.

The last Exclusion Act before 1832.   Until the eve of the Reform Act additions continued to be made to the code disqualifying office-holders. The last addition of significance prior to 1832 was the Act of 1829, which disqualified governors and deputy-governors in the service of the East India Company[4]. This Act, however, was due not so much to an apprehension that these East India governors would not be independent members of the House of Commons, as to the changing relations between constituents and their representatives. It was expedient that it should no longer be in the power of a man to secure election to the House of Commons, and then betake himself to the other side of the world and for years utterly ignore his duty to the House and to the constituency which had sent him there.

The Present Code.   This code, the building up of which from 1693 to 1829 I have endeavoured to trace, unlike the codes which brought about exclusions from the House on religious grounds, or for the special protection of the Crown, survived the Reform Act of 1832, and those of 1867 and 1884. It exists almost in its entirety to-day. With its history after 1832 I am not here concerned. But it may be stated, as indicating the extent to which the reformed House of Commons has now safeguarded itself against an evil first seriously

[1] Anson, *Law and Custom of the Constitution,* i. 71–78; cf. Pike, *House of Lords,* 248.
[2] 1 and 2 Geo. IV, c. 44.   [3] 41 Geo. III, c. 52.
[4] 10 Geo. IV, c. 62.

combated in the reign of Charles II, that a recent student of the present-day code has traced in the statute books, from the Revolution to the Reform Act of 1884, over one hundred Acts specifying whom electors must put on one side when choosing men to represent them in Parliament. Moreover, he has divided the exclusions established by this voluminous code into four groups. These are (1) persons connected with the administration of justice, such as judges, recorders, registrars, and stipendiary magistrates; (2) persons representing the Crown as colonial governors, court officials, or subordinate members of the civil service; (3) persons connected with the collection of revenue or audit of public accounts; and (4) persons connected with the administration of property for public purposes, such as charity and Crown land commissioners, and commissioners of woods and forests[1].

With the enactment of these laws, control of the House of Commons such as was exercised by George III at the time of the American Revolution, ceased to be possible. Many influences were working from 1782—when the pension laws were amended, and contractors were put on the exclusion list—to the end of the reign of George III, to lessen the influence which the Crown could exercise over the House of Commons. Reform, economic and Parliamentary, was being agitated. Political thought was more active and more diffused than at any previous time. These were factors which gradually worked against Crown control. The growth of the newspaper press worked to some extent to the same end. But control by the Crown after 1782 was less possible than formerly, chiefly for the reason that the Crown had fewer means of rewarding members of the House of Commons who rendered it subservient service there. Its power of purchasing support was less than at any time in the eighteenth century. In the first Parliament of George I, that of 1714–15, there were two hundred and fifty-seven members of Parliament who held places under the Crown[2]. In the second Parliament of George II there were two hundred office-holders in the House of Commons alone[3]. In 1770 there were one hundred and ninety-two office-holders of the House[4]. But by 1800 the number of civil office-holders had been reduced to fifty-two[5]; while

Thinning out the Office-holders in the House.

---

[1] Medley, *Manual of English Constitutional Hist.*, 163.
[2] Hansard, 3rd Series, II. 1118.
[3] Rogers, *Protests of the Lords*, II. 15.
[4] *Annual Register*, 1770, p. 72.   [5] *Parl. Hist.*, xxxv. 122.

in the first Parliament of George IV, that of 1820–26, " the utmost number was one hundred and nine, including every member of the House who was of the army or the navy[1]."

Effect of the Reform.

Excepting the reform of the franchise and the sweeping away of the small and politically squalid boroughs by the Act of 1832, and the further extensions of the franchise by the Acts of 1867 and 1884, and also possibly the Grenville Acts, no reform in the representative system, due to Parliamentary enactment, equals in importance the reform brought about by the slowly and toilsomely enacted code excluding from the House of Commons men whose financial relations with the Government, either as office-holders, pensioners or contractors, put them out of the category of independent members.

Slow Progress of the Reform.

The men who began the movement for this reform are entitled to almost as much credit as the men who in and out of Parliament, from the American Revolution until 1832, worked for the reform of the franchise. Nor is it to the discredit of these men, whose names are unrecorded except in the pages of the Journals of the Parliaments of Charles II, that they went to extremes, and demanded that the House of Commons should be denuded of all office-holders, and that the Treasury Bench, as we now know it, should disappear. The evil against which they were then contending was great and apparent. Up to this time, political reform by Parliamentary enactment was unknown. These seventeenth century reformers had no precedents. They began the movement, and success was denied them. But they soon gave place to another generation of reformers; to men who realized that the evil could be dealt with only one step at a time, with long intervals between the steps. By this newer method, the method of the men who were of the movement after the Revolution, one success after another was achieved. First came the Act of 1693, establishing the principle; then the Act of 1705; next the Act of 1742; and then the equally important Act of 1782, excluding contractors—all converging towards the code of to-day, with its hundred or more enactments, limiting the choice of constituencies, but all to the gain and advantage of English Parliamentary and political life.

[1] Hansard, 3rd Series, II. 1118.

CHAPTER XI.

MINORS AND ALIENS ON THE EXCLUSION LIST.

FROM the beginning of the representative system minors were Minors of the House of Commons. of the list of persons from whom constituencies could not choose their members of the House of Commons. Until shortly after the Revolution minors were excluded by the law of Parliament[1]. After the Revolution they were excluded by statute[2]. But from the sixteenth century until the middle years of the reign of George III, neither the law of Parliament nor the statute against minors was uniformly enforced, and there are numerous instances of minors being of the House of Commons. The non-observance of the custom of Parliament went back to the period of many irregular departures from the original constitution of the House. It went back to the time when seats in the House became objects of ambition; and the presence of minors in the House coincides with the non-observance of the statutes which directed that electors should be resident; that members should be of the constituencies they represented; and that they should be paid by their constituencies.

Gatton, remarkable in the history of the representative system An instance in 1533. as being one of the earliest boroughs to come under the control of a patron, as well as being among the first to be controlled by a woman, and memorable also to-day from the notoriety which accrued to it during the long agitation for Parliamentary reform, is also remarkable as being one of the earliest boroughs to be represented by a minor. Sir Thomas Copley, who was returned

---

[1] Anson, *Law and Custom of the Constitution*, pt. I. 71.
[2] 7 and 8 W. III, c. 25.

for Gatton by his mother, Dame Elizabeth Copley, in 1533, was born in 1514; so that he was only nineteen when he was of the House of Commons[1].

Protests
against the
Presence of
Minors in
1613 and
1621.

Between the reign of Henry VIII and that of James I the non-observance of the custom of Parliament must have been frequent; for about 1613 it was complained that there were forty members of the House " not above twenty years of age, and some not exceeding sixteen[2]." A protest was made by Richard Martin, afterwards Recorder of London, who at this time sat in the House of Commons for Christchurch[3]. "It was the ancient custom," reads a report of his speech, "for old men to make laws for young ones; but that then he saw the case altered, and that there were children elected into the great council of the nation, who came to invade and invert nature, and to enact laws to govern their fathers[4]." In 1621 another member objected that " their meeting was pestered with the admission of so many young men; and that it was not fit they should make laws for the kingdom, who were not in their own persons liable to the law, and who could not themselves be bound by contracts except for necessaries[5]." This objection was made on the occasion of an election bill, in which an unsuccessful effort was made to insert a clause providing that members of the House should be twenty-one years of age[6]. The non-observance of the law was again noticed in 1623 by Coke. "Many under the age of twenty-one," he wrote, "sit here by connivance, but if the question would be put, one under the age of twenty-one is not eligible[7]."

From the Restoration to the Revolution, and especially in the Pensioner Parliament, the law of Parliament excluding minors was as little observed as it had been at the time of Martin's complaint. The Earl of Torrington, who in 1670 succeeded his father as Duke of Albemarle, was only eighteen at the time of his accession to the dukedom; yet he had been for three years of the House of Commons as knight of the shire for Devonshire[8]. James Herbert, who was

[1] *Dict. Nat. Bio.*, xii. 189.

[2] Extract from Naunton, *Fragmenta Regalia, Wellwood Memoirs*, Ed. 1700, App., 261.

[3] *Dict. Nat. Bio.*, xxxvi. 291, 292.

[4] *Wellwood Memoirs*, App., 1.

[5] Grey, *Parliamentary Debates*, ii. 227.

[6] Hatsell, ii. 5.

[7] Coke, *Institutes*, pt. iii. and iv. 1648, p. 47.

[8] *Official List*, pt. i. 521; Doyle, i. 31.

but fifteen years of age, was of the same Parliament, as member for the borough of Queenborough[1]. There is further testimony to the presence of minors in the Pensioner Parliament in a contemporary letter from Sir John Lowther to Sir George Fletcher. "I will," wrote Lowther in 1673, "dissuade my kinsman from coming forward. I had supposed that his minority would have been no objection, since the common practice, as well in that as those not qualified in estates in the same county, is to the contrary; and I myself served in this place when in a minority[2]."

Only when objection was taken at the election, or prior to the election, as was apparently the case with Lowther's kinsman, was a minor in any danger of being disqualified. A minor who had a borough patron behind him, a patron who could return whom he chose without any local opposition, could in the seventeenth century easily obtain election to the House. Once of the House it was nobody's business to call attention to the fact that he was under age, and to bring about his expulsion. In a House of Commons so largely composed of courtiers and dilettante politicians as was the Pensioner Parliament, and with political and social conditions as they were in the twenty years following the Restoration, the inducements for youths of aristocratic family to obtrude themselves into the House were greater than at any time in its previous history; for the House at this period was taking on the social characteristics which continued to mark it during the eighteenth century. It was pre-eminently composed of men of fashion; of men who lightly regarded their duties to their constituents and to the House. *[Little Objection to Presence of Minors.]*

Prynne, who was of the Pensioner Parliament, has left a vivid picture of the easy way in which these men of fashion took their Parliamentary duties. He complains that they wasted their time in taverns, playhouses, dicing-houses, cockpits, tennis courts, and at bowling alleys; or in visits and compliments; and "rambling abroad to such places at unseasonable hours in the night in antique unparliamentary robes, vestments fitter for a mask or a stage, than the gravity of a Parliament House." He complains also that these men of fashion "only come and peep into the Parliament House once or twice a week, to show themselves in such disguise, or ask the news, and what they are doing; or to talk with some other *[Character of the Pensioner Parliament.]*

---

[1] *Official List*, pt. I. 524; Townsend, *Hist. of the House of Commons*, II. 400.
[2] *Hist. MSS. Comm. 12th Rep.*, App., pt. VII. 104.

members; or to promote some private business for themselves or their relations; or to dine at committee dinners, or ordinaries; or to wait upon some lady mistress friend to a private committee, to solicit or to promote their business," with the result that committees on public bills were forced to be adjourned from day to day, "against their trusts and duties[1]."

Shaftesbury urges the Exclusion of Minors.

The presence of minors in the House was one of the many evils in the representative system which Shaftesbury, in 1688, urged were in need of a touch of the supreme authority to set them right. Although Shaftesbury had been elected for Tewkesbury in 1640, when he was under age[2], in his scheme of reform he insisted that " he who sits at the helm of government ought not only to be a graduate in fortune, but in prudence and experience also." " To me," he continued, "it seems extremely irregular to see the unfledged youth make his first advances into the world in the quality of a burgess for Parliament, chosen upon no other account, but because it was his fortune by his father's early death to become the landlord of a neighbouring borough, or is perhaps its best customer, deriving from thence the necessaries of a numerous family. Forty years, whereof twenty-five are generally spent in childhood and vanity, seem to be few enough to entitle anyone to the grandeur and gravity of an English senator; and why so many, who seem by their greenness to be as yet but a novelty to the world, should be admitted to a place in this great council; whilst those of greater age, wisdom and experience, must be excluded, I do not understand[3]."

The Act of 1695–96 excluding Minors.

After the Revolution, the House of Commons was not at once disposed to check the evil which had been complained of all through the seventeenth century. It had an opportunity of reaffirming the old law of Parliament in 1690. At an election for Dorchester in 1689 Sir Robert Napier and Thomas Trenchard were the candidates. Napier polled one hundred and forty-six votes, and Trenchard one hundred and sixty-nine. It was, thereupon, objected that Trenchard was a minor, and consequently disqualified. Napier embodied his objection in a petition. Counsel for Trenchard admitted that the candidate returned was under age at the time of the election, and the election committee upheld Napier's objection, and reported in favour of seating him. But the House rejected the report, and Trenchard was seated[4]. At this time, and until

---

[1] Prynne, *Brevia Parliamentaria*, 672.   [2] *Dict. Nat. Bio.*, xii. 111.
[3] Somers, *Tracts*, viii. 396.   [4] *H. of C. Journals*, x. 505.

after 1770, when controverted election cases were sent to Grenville committees, personal and partisan reasons usually determined these cases. Such reasons in all probability led to the seating of Trenchard. But his case was not long a precedent; as in 1695–96 the first statute against the election of minors was enacted. "No person hereafter," it reads[1], "shall be capable of being elected a member to serve in this or any future Parliament, who is not of the age of one and twenty; and every election or return of any person under that age is hereby declared to be null and void; and if any such minor hereafter shall presume to sit or vote in Parliament, he shall incur such penalties and forfeitures, as if he had presumed to sit and vote in Parliament without being chosen or returned."

After this enactment of 1695 minors continued to find their way into the House, but not in the numbers common in the seventeenth century. The reports of controverted elections between the Revolution and the Grenville Act show that objection was taken more frequently than in the seventeenth century to the return of minors; and it may be assumed that from the reign of William III, minors found their way into Parliament only from boroughs where the patrons were absolutely safe from local attack, or in cases where patrons knew that they would have the majority of the House of Commons with them, if the return of a minor were petitioned against. Subsequent to the Grenville Act, when the lodging of a well-grounded objection that a member returned was a minor must inevitably have led to the issue of a new writ, and the mulcting of the friends of the minor in the costs of the petition case, there grew up a system of nominating a locum tenens, a system under which duly qualified men were returned for boroughs with the distinct understanding that they should apply for the Chiltern Hundreds as soon as the minor should come of age for whom the patron intended the seat.

Gradual Disappearance of Minors from the House.

Before and after the determination of election cases by Grenville committees, there was a number of well authenticated instances in which, in spite of the Act of 1695, minors sat and spoke in the House of Commons; although they did not vote. Party lines were becoming well marked after the Act of 1695, and increasingly well marked from the time of Walpole; and while it was nobody's business to object to the presence or even to the speaking of a minor, it would promptly have become somebody's concern had

Minors cease to vote in the House.

[1] 7 and 8 W. III, c. 25, s. 8.

a minor voted in a critical division, or, prior to 1770, given a vote in the House for or against a resolution affecting the determination of a controverted election.

Later
Instances.

As soon after the Act of 1695 as 1715, Philip Dormer Stanhope, then known as Lord Stanhope, and later as Earl of Chesterfield, was returned for the Cornish borough of St Germains[1]. He spoke in the House shortly after his election, a month before he was of age. He declaimed against the Oxford Ministry, and made a strong speech against the Duke of Ormond. " As soon as he had done speaking, one of the opposite party took him aside and, having complimented him upon his *coup d'essai*, added that he was exactly well acquainted with the day of his birth, and could prove that when he was chosen, he was not of age nor was yet; but he would take no advantage of this, unless his friends were pushed, in which case, if he offered to vote, he would immediately acquaint the House with it. Lord Stanhope, who knew the consequences of this discovery, a penalty of five hundred pounds, made no reply; but making a low bow, quitted the House directly, and went to Paris[2]." The Marquis of Granby, afterwards Duke of Rutland, lacked six months of the statutory age when he was chosen one of the members for the University of Cambridge in October, 1774[3]. In the same Parliament Newcastle-under-Lyme was represented by Viscount Trentham, who was the eldest son of the first Marquis of Stafford, and was afterwards the first Duke of Sutherland. Trentham was chosen at a by-election in 1779[4], when he was still under age[5].

Fox elected
before his
Majority.

More memorable than any of these instances is the case of Fox. " Though the lad had barely turned nineteen when Parliament was dissolved," writes Sir George O. Trevelyan, in describing the election of Fox for the burgage borough of Midhurst, on the 22nd of March, 1768, " a family arrangement was made for introducing him into public life as soon as he cared to enter it. Lord Ilchester was anxious to find some serious occupation for his son, Lord Stavordale, who was very little older than Charles, and had plunged almost as deep in the pleasures of the town; so the two brothers (Lord Holland, father of Fox, and Lord Ilchester)

---

[1] *Official List*, pt. ii. 38.

[2] Maty, *Misc. Works of Earl of Chesterfield*, i. 21, 22, Ed. 1778.

[3] *Official List*, pt. ii. 149; Doyle, iii. 202; Trevelyan, *American Revolution*, pt. i. 1766–76, p. 272.

[4] *Official List*, pt. ii. 155.   [5] *Nat. Dict. Bio.*, xxx. 146.

clubbed together to hire their boys a borough, as they might have rented them a manor to shoot over in the vacation. They selected Midhurst, the most comfortable of constituencies from the point of view of a representative; for the right of election rested in a few small holdings, on which no human being resided, distinguished among the pastures and the stubble that surrounded them by a large stone set up on end in the middle of each portion. These burgage tenures, as they were called, had all been bought up by a single proprietor, Viscount Montagu, who, when an election was in prospect, assigned a few of them to his servants, with instructions to nominate the members and then make back the property to their employer. This ceremony was performed in March, 1768; and the steward of the estate who acted as the returning-officer declared that Charles James Fox had been duly chosen as one of the burgesses from Midhurst, at a time when that young gentleman was still amusing himself in Italy. He remained on the Continent during the opening session of the new Parliament, which met in May in order to choose a Speaker and transact some routine business; and it was not until the following winter that he made his first appearance upon a stage where, almost from the moment of his entry, he became the observed of all observers[1]."

Fox, although he soon became prominent in the House, and was described by Horace Walpole a week after he attained his majority as "already one of our best speakers[2]," never ventured to vote until he was of age[3]. To have voted would at once have endangered his seat, notwithstanding the peculiarly easy conditions under which it was held. A patron of a borough could help a candidate to whom he had given his interest easily through the election. If the patron were of the government forces, and his nominee also proposed to act with the Government, the patron could also, until the Grenville Act was passed, count on seeing his nominee safely through a controverted election. But the law of 1695 was explicit; and a minor who ventured to vote might at once have put his seat in danger, and placed himself even beyond the aid of the Government and its majority in the House of Commons. I have discovered no instance in which a minor not objected to on petition was excluded from the House between 1695 and 1832. Minors, as has been shown, were of the House in this period, but

Unsafe for Minors to vote after 1695.

---

[1] Trevelyan, *Life of Fox*, 145, 146.
[2] Walpole, *Letters to Mann*, v. 226.
[3] May, *Parl. Practice*, 32.

they all seem to have followed the precedent of Lord Stanhope in 1715, and to have absented themselves when the House formally divided.

Await their Majority before taking their Seats.   Much later than the election of Fox for Midhurst, Jenkinson, afterwards Lord Liverpool, and prime minister from 1812 to 1827, was chosen for Rye while he was still a minor. He was elected on the 18th of June, 1790. He was not of age until June 7th, 1791; but, unlike Fox, Jenkinson did not enter the House while a minor. He travelled on the Continent during the intervening year, acquiring knowledge of continental politics with a view to his Parliamentary career[1]. Lord John Russell was returned for his father's, the Duke of Bedford's, borough of Tavistock on the 4th of May, 1813. He was then under age, and did not attain his majority until the 18th of August, 1813. Like Fox he was making a tour of the Continent when he was elected; but unlike Fox he did not make his appearance in the House before he was of age[2].

Fox the last Minor to speak.   Fox was the last member of the House who, while well under age, sat and spoke and attained prominence there. Brougham in the debate on Burdett's motion for universal suffrage in the House of Commons on June 2nd, 1818, stated that "a noble friend of his, Lord Milton, made an admirable speech in that House on the slave trade" before he was of age[3]. But this statement cannot have been correct. The Viscount Milton referred to by Brougham was born on the 4th of May, 1786, and was chosen a knight of the shire for York on the 20th of May, 1807[4]; so that he could not have taken part in a debate on the slave trade in the House of Commons before he was of age. Jenkinson's action after his election for Rye in 1790 marks, in fact, the beginning of a new order. It marks the time when the Act of 1695 became generally observed.

Influence of Public Opinion.   Several influences were now at work to make the law at last operative, and to bring about a reform which had been advocated as far back as the reign of James I. Among these was the certainty of something like honest and equitable determinations in election petition cases, due to the working of the Grenville Act. By this

[1] *Official List*, pt. II. 197; Doyle, II. 404, 405; *New Univ. Dict. Bio.*, 357, Ed. 1882.

[2] *Official List*, pt. II. 259; Walpole, *Life of Lord John Russell*, 3, 73, 76.

[3] Hansard, XXXVIII. 1163.

[4] *Official List*, pt. II. 251; Doyle, I. 756.

time also London had several excellent daily newspapers, not all under the control of the Treasury. Reporters had now a recognized place in the gallery of the House of Commons; and, moreover, the agitation for Parliamentary reform was now in responsible hands, and through its literature was being greatly influenced by men such as Horne Tooke, well versed in constitutional usages, and the laws regulating Parliamentary elections. The House of Commons, in short, was now becoming more and more amenable to public opinion; and while, for forty years after Jenkinson's election for Rye, borough owners and borough patrons continued to do what they liked with their own, and returned to Parliament whom they pleased, they could no longer affront public opinion as they had done until the end of the first twenty years of the reign of George III, by continuing to treat well-known enactments as though they were non-existent.

Patrons of boroughs, when they were desirous that their sons should be their nominees, began about this time to exercise more caution in electioneering; and in the last half of the eighteenth century there are several instances in which patrons nominated men to act as locum tenens, until their sons or nephews came of age. The historian of the Devonshire borough of Tiverton, a borough for nearly a century under the partial or full control of the Ryder family[1], reports two such instances of the putting in of a locum tenens, one as early as 1755, and the other in 1776[2]. *Election of Locum Tenens.*

In the last decade of the eighteenth century, and in the first thirty years of the nineteenth, these instances seem to have become more frequent, and men were elected on the understanding that their seats were to be vacated when sons of their patrons were of age to be of the House of Commons. A new use was found for the London attorneys of the borough-owning families. If a borough seat fell vacant at a time when a son of the patron was nearing his majority, the London lawyer of the family was occasionally returned, and applied for the Chiltern Hundreds as soon as his client's son was of statutory age. From 1789 to 1795 Francis Gregg, solicitor in London to the Earl of Carlisle, thus sat for the borough of Morpeth. On the 17th of September, 1794, Viscount Howard, eldest son of the Earl of Carlisle, came of age, and as soon after his majority as a new writ could be obtained, he took the place of *Keeping Seats for Minors.*

---

[1] Oldfield, III. 336.   [2] Dunsford, *Hist. of Tiverton*, 455, 456.

Gregg[1]. Charles Abbot, who was subsequently Speaker of the House, and in 1817, at the end of his term in the chair, was called to the House of Lords as Lord Colchester, first entered the House of Commons in 1795 for the Duke of Leeds's borough of Helston. From the time of his election he was uneasy in his seat from a fear that it would be wanted for his patron's son, who would shortly come of age[2].

Offer of a Seat for Part of a Parliament.

In 1802 Lord Lowther was willing to elect a locum tenens for Cockermouth during the minority of his nephew Lord Burghersh, and offered the nomination to Pitt. "I wrote to Lord Mulgrave on Friday from Walmer Castle," reads a letter from Pitt to Robert Plumer Ward, dated January 28th, 1802, "to mention to him that Lord Lowther had had the goodness to offer to name a member at my recommendation for the borough of Cockermouth for the first three years of the Parliament, after which he wishes to reserve it for his nephew Lord Burghersh. The election will, I understand, be free from trouble and from anything but a very trifling expense; and though less satisfactory than one for the whole Parliament, I am in hopes it will appear to you too eligible to decline[3]." The seat offered on these terms, and which was thus the subject of correspondence between Pitt, Lord Mulgrave, and Ward, was intended by Pitt for Ward. He accepted it, and although Lord Burghersh attained his majority on the 2nd of February, 1805, Ward was not disturbed, and sat for Cockermouth throughout the Parliament of 1802–6. Burghersh seems to have been abroad when he attained his majority. But in March, 1806, he was elected for Lyme Regis[4], a Dorsetshire borough, which for more than a century had been under the control of his ancestors, the Earls of Westmorland[5].

A similar Offer objected to.

Lord Grosvenor, in 1820, offered to make Edward Harbord member for Shaftesbury. He made this offer through his appreciation of the stand which Harbord had taken against the Government at the time of the affair of Peterloo in 1819. No pledges were asked from Harbord; but Lord Grosvenor reserved the right to call upon him to resign at the end of two years.

[1] Cf. *Hist. MSS. Comm. 15th Rep.*, App., pt. vi. 15; *Official List,* pt. ii. 180, 192; Doyle, i. 333.

[2] *Colchester Diary,* i. p. xix.

[3] Phipps, *Memoirs of Robert Plumer Ward,* i. 57.

[4] *Official List,* pt. ii. 217.

[5] Oldfield, iii. 375.

Harbord hesitated to accept the seat subject to this condition, and some correspondence passed on the subject. " My letter of yesterday," wrote Lord Grosvenor on February 10th, 1820, " will have set you at ease about everything but the retiring part of the question ; and I think with you so entirely on the cruelty, as I must call it, of interrupting you in the heyday of your Parliamentary labours, that I would put myself to any inconvenience sooner than you should be thus situated. The truth is, I only looked to the possibility of wanting a seat for Robert, and to that even as by no means a probable contingency, as I have other views for him, but as a possible one I thought it right to mention it. I feel the case you state, however, so forcibly that you shall not be disturbed in your seat from any motives of conveniency[1]." Harbord was duly chosen for Shaftesbury—for " a place where no questions are asked as to political principles, and no money required[2] "—and he continued to represent the borough until he was called to the House of Lords as Baron Suffield in 1821. Abraham Moore, Harbord's colleague in the representation of Shaftesbury, occupied his seat for what was practically the length of time which Lord Grosvenor had first specified to Harbord. He resigned in April, 1822 ; and Robert Grosvenor, a younger son of Lord Grosvenor, who in the meantime had come of age, succeeded to the seat[3].

In the same Parliament Lord John Russell, who had himself been elected to the House before he was of age, was a beneficiary under this system of holding seats for young men until they attained their majority, rather than electing them, while they were minors, and trusting to their discretion to avoid the penalties of the Act of 1695. At the election of 1820 Lord Mandeville, the eldest son of the Duke of Manchester, was short of his majority by only four months. The County of Huntingdon was at this time as much under the control of the Montagu family as many boroughs were under the control of patrons ; and as Lord E. Montagu, uncle to the Duke of Manchester, did not desire re-election, Lord John Russell, who was related to the Montagu family, was chosen in 1820 without opposition : and, booted and spurred in the full dignity of a knight of the shire, he returned to the House of Commons to battle again for the disfranchisement of Grampound

Lord John Russell sits as Locum Tenens.

[1] Bacon, *Memoir of Edward, Lord Suffield,* 102.
[2] Bacon, *Memoir of Edward, Lord Suffield,* 103.
[3] *Official List,* pt. ii. 287.

and the transfer of its representation to the borough of Leeds[1]. At the next election, in 1826, Lord Mandeville succeeded to the seat for Huntingdonshire ; and it was as member for the Irish borough of Bandon, for which he was nominated by the Duke of Devonshire[2], that Lord John Russell, in the Parliament of 1826–30, continued his exertions for the movement that culminated in the Act of 1832.

The End of the Old Order.

Under the older order of things, the fact that Lord Mandeville was only four months short of his majority in 1820 would not have kept him out of the House of Commons; nor is it probable that, under it, Lord Grosvenor would have taken the trouble that he did in 1820, in negotiating with two men in order to secure a locum tenens during Robert Grosvenor's minority. But the instances which I have cited, and the correspondence I have quoted, seem to warrant the statement that the action of Jenkinson after his election for Rye in 1790—when he went abroad for a year until he was of statutory age—marks the beginning of the period when the Act of 1695, excluding minors, began to be really operative, and to exclude youths whose relatives or friends had it in their power to nominate them to the House of Commons.

Futility of Laws without Public Opinion.

Both the old law of Parliament and the Act of 1695 were eminently reasonable and just. Neither worked the least hardship to constituencies ; and their history, particularly that of the Act of 1695, is chiefly interesting as showing how futile were such enactments as these—or as the law of Queen Anne excluding pensioners, or the numerous bribery Acts of the eighteenth century—with the electoral system in the chaotic condition in which it was from the reign of Elizabeth to that of George III, when there was, and could be, no public opinion capable of making itself felt in Parliament, or of giving permanent effect to enactments intended to improve, or purify, or safeguard the working of the representative system. It is because of the light which the working of the old law of Parliament and of the statute of William III throws on the representative system as it existed in the sixteenth, seventeenth and eighteenth centuries, that I have thought it well to devote a chapter to the exclusion of minors from the House, and to the circumstances under which, in the last forty years of the unreformed Parliament, the law of 1695 at last became operative and may be said to have become uniformly observed.

[1] Walpole, *Life of Lord John Russell*, I. 125; Pryme, *Recollections*, 156 ; Doyle, II. 455.

[2] Walpole, *Life of Lord John Russell*, I. 139.

The new attitude of borough owners and borough patrons towards the law of 1695 was indeed only one of several reforms in the representative system gradually brought about by a more enlightened public opinion, which may be dated from the popular agitations of the period of the American Revolution. These reforms—such as the partial repeal of the Last Determinations Act of 1729; the partial or complete disfranchisement of hopelessly corrupt boroughs; the non-partisan bestowal of the stewardship of the Chiltern Hundreds; and the revival of the feeling, almost completely dormant for two centuries, that members had some responsibility towards their constituents and some duties in the House—all suggest that had there been no sweeping measure in 1832, the touch of supreme authority, required to remedy the grosser and more obvious abuses of the electoral system, would from time to time have been applied. During the last half century of the old electoral system the House of Commons was gradually being reformed. It was by no means at its worst when Grey, Russell, and Althorp extended the county franchise to leaseholders; swept out of existence the smaller boroughs; enfranchised the large industrial towns of the Midlands and the North of England hitherto not directly represented, and made the borough franchise uniform throughout the kingdom.

ALIENS AND NATURALISED SUBJECTS.

All through the history of the House of Commons aliens were excluded by common law; and so far as the Journals and other contemporary literature bearing on the representative system show, aliens never gave the House any such trouble as resulted from the non-observance of the law of Parliament excluding minors. After the Revolution, Parliament adopted a more definite policy towards aliens; and by the Act of Settlement of 1700–1 it expressly declared that when aliens were naturalised they should not be capable of being of the Privy Council, nor of the House of Commons[1]. From the reign of William III to that of George II this principle of excluding naturalised British subjects was embodied in several Acts varying or amending the naturalisation laws. During this period, naturalisation was possible only by Act of Parliament, a process attended with the payment of fees to the Speaker and to numerous other Parliamentary officers, and

[1] 12 and 13 W. III, c. 2.

with the taking of the oath at the table of the House by the person naturalised.

In 1740, and again in 1747[1], the Naturalisation Act of 1698–99, as amended by the Act of Settlement, was further amended. In 1740 it was amended in the interest of aliens residing in British colonies; and in 1747 in the interest of Protestants born out of allegiance to the British Crown. While both these Acts were intended to ease the conditions of naturalisation, in each there was reiterated the clause in the Act of Settlement stating that persons naturalised should not be capable of being of the Privy Council or of being elected to Parliament. In the Act passed by Parliament in 1754 for the relief of Jews applying for naturalisation—the Act repealed in response to popular clamour in the session of 1755— there was a stipulation that in every bill for the naturalisation of Jews there should be a clause excluding these newly-made British subjects from the Privy Council and the House of Commons. The enactments from the reign of William III, placing naturalised British subjects on the list of persons from whom constituencies could not choose their representatives, survived the Reform Act for forty years; and not until after the Act of 1870[2], making naturalised British subjects entitled to "all the political rights and powers and privileges of natural born British subjects," was an alien when naturalised capable of representing a constituency in the House of Commons.

---

[1] 13 Geo. II, c. 5; 20 Geo. II, c. 14.
[2] 33 and 34 Vict., c. 13.

CHAPTER XII.

THE TIE BETWEEN ELECTORS AND ELECTED.

IN the history of the changing relations which existed between electors and elected from 1295 to 1832, one fact stands out with singular prominence. Not until within half a century of the Reform Act, not until after George III had ceased to regard the stewardship of the Chiltern Hundreds as an office to be bestowed on political friends, and withheld, whenever expedient, from political opponents, did there exist any recognized and uniform method by which, during the lifetime of a Parliament, an end could be made to the tie between a constituency and its representatives. The relations between electors and elected are further remarkable from the fact that during the life of a Parliament only one party to the connection, the elected, has ever had it in his power to determine the connection. From the closing decades of the sixteenth century until the middle of the eighteenth, a member could, if the House were willing, and from about 1715 if the Crown alone were willing, resign his seat, and his constituents could have an opportunity of electing another representative. But neither before nor since 1832 has it ever been possible for a constituency between one general election and the next to rid itself of its representatives. *Character of the Tie.*

Until the reign of Henry VIII the life of a Parliament was usually comprised within a single session ; and these sessions were short. Elections were frequent ; and while short sessions and frequent elections were the rule, the occasions must have been few when members found it necessary formally to determine their connection with the House before the Parliament to which they had been elected came to an end in the ordinary course of events. So *No Need for Means of ending the Tie.*

long as wages were paid and Parliaments were elected frequently members were not likely to seek formal release.

No Means for securing Attendance.   At no time in the history of the House of Commons was it practicable for the House to secure the continuous services of members who were either unwilling or unable to render them. By calls of the House, enforced through the sheriffs, and as a last resort through the sergeant-at-arms, it was possible to secure a full attendance on a stated day; and it was within the power of the House after a call to order that members should not leave town for a certain number of days. It was also possible for the House to order that the doors be locked, and that no member leave the Chamber without leave until the business before the House was discharged. But calls and orders to members and locking of the doors were only expedients for infrequent and special occasions; and there never was devised any method which kept all the members of the House in attendance from day to day throughout the whole of a Parliament or session of a Parliament.

Expedients for securing Attendance.   The deprivation of wages was the only punishment for absence which ever had the sanction of an Act of Parliament[1]. After wages ceased to be paid no other penalty was enacted. There were other penalties. These were, however, imposed only by resolution of the House. A resolution was passed in 1581 imposing fines on members absent a whole session without excuse allowed by the House[2]. But the only effective means of reaching absentees ever devised was applicable in cases of failure to respond to calls, and not in cases of continuous or persistent neglect on the part of members to attend the House. In the seventeenth century, when the lifetime of Parliaments had become longer, the House sometimes refused to liberate a member from its service. It would refuse a new writ, and so prevent the election of a successor to an absentee, or to a member who wished to retire. Occasionally at an even earlier period, as for instance in 1585, in the case of Hall of Grantham, it would make a special order that an individual member should attend[3]. But the Journals may be searched in vain for a trace of any machinery by which a member could be compelled to be in his place on the opening day of a Parliament, and to continue in attendance day after day until the Parliament was dissolved, or, after the life of Parliaments began to extend over more than a single session, until Parliament was prorogued. There seems never

[1] 6 Henry VIII, c. 16.   [2] Parry, 226.
[3] D'Ewes, *Journals*, 338, 339.

to have been any daily calling of the roll. There certainly was none from the time when the printed Journals begin, which was in Edward VI's reign; and the only occasions when the roll of the House was called in the seventeenth, eighteenth and nineteenth centuries were after special summons, issued by the Speaker on the order of the House, had been sent out through the sheriffs, commanding the attendance of members on a particular day.

After the payment of wages had broken down, and before seats had become so much in demand that, when a member wished to resign, men eager to take his place were anxious for the issue of a new writ, it must have been practicable for a man to retain his membership and yet not attend the House. If from any cause he found himself unable or indisposed to attend he could absent himself until the Parliament was dissolved, and then decline re-election. When once the payment of wages had fallen into desuetude, and non-residents began to be elected from the boroughs, constituencies had no means of disciplining their members; and the probabilities are that those which elected non-residents were indifferent as to the attendance of their representatives.

Absenteeism.

In the seventeenth and eighteenth centuries the determination of a member's connection with the House came up on the issue of a new writ, and not in connection with any efforts on the part of the House to compel a member to give service. There was an attempt at disciplining absentee members in the reign of Philip and Mary. It was not made by the House but by the Crown, which moved in the courts to secure the attendance of a group of seceders. In the Parliament of 1554 thirty-three members of the House of Commons withdrew, "when they saw the majority was inclined to sacrifice everything to the Ministry." The Court resented this withdrawal, and ordered the Queen's Attorney-General to indict the seceders in the King's Bench. On an information being there preferred against them for departing from the House without license, contrary to the King and Queen's inhibition at the beginning of the Parliament, six of the seceders " were so timorous as to submit to the mercy of the Court, and paid fines. All the rest, among whom was that famous lawyer Plowden, traversed; but judgment against them was prevented by the Queen's death[1]."

An Attempt by the Crown to enforce Attendance.

The attitude of the House in the opening years of the seventeenth century towards motions for new writs, moved with a view

Surrendering a Seat in 1605.

---

[1] *Parl. Hist.*, i. 625; Parry, 212.

to liberating members and admitting of new elections, is described in a letter written in 1605 by the Earl of Salisbury to Sir Thomas Edmondes, who was then of the House of Commons, but who had accepted an office which he evidently conceived necessitated the resignation of his seat.   Salisbury reminded Edmondes that there must be a new election.   "And yet," his letter continues, " there can be no writ go forth, except you were dead, but by order from the Parliament.   I understand the manner is for them to look for some certificate from the party, if he be living, whereby they may be assured that his absence is not by an excursion, but by his Majesty's employment.   You do write some certificate showing you are employed in his Majesty's service, and that you do willingly surrender your place, and desire that it may be supplied."   Salisbury added that this certificate was "rather to observe formalities, wherein the Lower House is curious, than otherwise[1]."

A Request for Libera-tion refused.
    In the first forty years of the seventeenth century, the request to be allowed to vacate a seat was ordinarily more than a formality. At no time during the seventeenth century had the House any rule applicable to all cases.   It judged applications on their merits ; and not infrequently it refused them.   In 1605 Sir George Somers, one of the members for Lyme Regis, reported to the House that John Hassard, his colleague in the representation of the borough, was suffering from " sickness by the joint "; and desired that he might resign his seat.   It was resolved, "That he shall still serve, and that he shall not be removed[2]."   This was in the first Parliament of James I.   The Parliament lasted from 1604 to 1611.   In 1609 another application was made in behalf of Hassard.   This time it was in the form of a petition from the borough.   The petition was referred to a committee, which reported that Hassard was bedridden and incurable ; and on this report a new writ was at last ordered by the House[3].

Men not allowed to refuse to serve.
    Between the reign of James I and the Commonwealth, in the period when some abuses in the representative system were being remedied, the House was most insistent in its claims on the atten-dance and service of men who had willingly or unwillingly been elected to it.   In 1614 Hackwell laid down that a man who had been elected could not waive his election, "unless chosen in another shire than where resident[4]."   And Sir R. Maunsell, in the same debate, enunciated the dictum that if a man who had a freehold in

[1] Stowe MSS. CLXVIII. Folio 181.   [2] Oldfield, III. 372.
[3] Oldfield, III. 372.   [4] Parry, 266.

a shire were elected, he could not refuse to serve[1]. Again in 1624 it was determined by a vote of the House "that a man after being duly chosen cannot refuse to serve[2]." This determination was in the case of Sir Thomas Escourt, who, against his consent and desire, had been elected a knight from Gloucestershire. It was in reference to this determination that Glanville declared, "that no man being lawfully chosen can refuse the place": "for," he continued, "the county and commonwealth have such an interest in every man, that when by lawful election he is appointed to this public service, he cannot by any unwillingness and refusal of his own make himself incapable, for that were to prefer the will or contentment of a private man before the desire and satisfaction of the whole country, and a ready way to put by the sufficientest men, who are commonly those who least endeavour to obtain the place[3]."

In 1629 a new writ was refused in the case of Mr Lynn, who had been elected mayor of Exeter. As mayor he was disqualified from sitting in the House as member for Exeter. But he was of the House when he was chosen mayor; and it was determined that he ought to continue, because the House had the first call on his services[4]. *Service in the House takes Precedence.*

The need of a certain and uniform method by which members could cut the tie which held them to their constituencies was felt in 1641; for in that year a motion was made "that a member at his own request may decline his election, and a new burgess be chosen in his seat." It was, however, negatived by the House[5]. After the Restoration, when Parliamentary life was less strenuous than at any previous time during the seventeenth century, and when the House was more than ever before crowded with men of fashion and dilettante politicians, members were allowed to renounce their elections. "Mr Leveson-Gower," reads an entry in the Journals, under date of March 19, 1676[6], "did this day disclaim and renounce his election and return to serve for the borough of New Malton, and the House allowed thereof." But this was practically only a variation on the old method of moving for a new writ, since the House had to sanction it, as it did the issue of a writ. *Hold of the House on its Members.*

The motion which was made in 1641 is a proof that the tie between members and constituencies was at times irksome and *No Direct Resignation of Seats.*

[1] Parry, 266.
[2] Parry, 293.
[3] Cited, Hansard, 3rd Series, xxxvi. 528.
[4] Parry, 327.
[5] Parry, 359.
[6] *H. of C. Journals,* ix. 402.

inconvenient to members, and no doubt often equally inconvenient to borough patrons: and that the need was felt of some method which should make it possible for members to resign without having to appeal to the House for discharge, and run the risk of refusal. But all through the sixteenth and seventeenth centuries the House was tenacious of its hold on its members; and even after the Septennial Act of 1715, when the connection between members and constituencies might be of longer duration than it had ordinarily been in the two preceding centuries, no such easy and certain method as that proposed in 1641 was ever devised. Appointment to the Stewardship of the Chiltern Hundreds, or to that of the Manor of East Hendred, nominally offices under the Crown, to-day, as in the last eighty years of the unreformed representative system, constitutes the only method by which between one Parliament and the next a member who has not accepted an actual office of profit under the Crown can vacate his seat.

Stewardship of the Chiltern Hundreds. Search is made in vain in the statutes and Journals for any clue to the circumstances under which appointment to these stewardships—offices never more than nominally held—came to be substituted, as a means of enabling members to discharge themselves, for the means in use between the Restoration and the Revolution, when, as the Journals show, a member might with leave of the House renounce his election. The new method was made possible by the enactment of 1705, which specifically excluded certain office-holders, and regulated the conditions under which members appointed to office could continue of the House. The stewardship of the Chiltern Hundreds was revived as an office, solely to enable members to vacate their seats, in compliance with the section of the Act which declares that, if any member "shall accept of any office of profit from the Crown during such time as he shall continue a member, his election shall be, and is hereby declared to be, void, and a new writ shall issue for a new election, as if such person so accepting was naturally dead."

An Ingenious Use of the Act of 1705. The original intention of this section was to enable members to accept certain offices and still retain their seats in the House of Commons. It was a compromise measure, adopted at the time that Parliament repealed the radical and far-reaching clause in the Act of Settlement which decreed that " No person who has an office or place of profit under the king, or receives a pension from the Crown, shall be capable of serving as a member of the House of Commons."

The ingenious Parliamentarian who first conceived the idea that the Act of Queen Anne could be turned to account as a means of enabling members to resign, I have not been able to discover. The first instance that I have been able to trace of the Act of 1705 being used for this purpose was in 1715, when Thomas Onslow was given the office of Outranger of Windsor Forest to enable him to vacate his seat for Bletchingly, in order to succeed Sir Richard Onslow, appointed a teller of the Exchequer, as knight of the shire for Surrey. This office was similarly used in 1717, when Denzil Onslow vacated Guildford to succeed Thomas Onslow for Surrey[1].

The revival of the office of Steward of the Chiltern Hundreds appears, as far as the Journals show, to have taken place in 1750. In that year the stewardship was bestowed by the Crown on a member of the House as a means of enabling him to sever the tie between himself and his constituency. According to Hatsell and Beatson[2], the first holder of the revived office of Steward and Bailiff of the three Chiltern Hundreds of Stoke, Desborough, and Boneham in the County of Buckingham was John Pitt, who in 1747 had been elected for the borough of Wareham[3]. The office was not bestowed on Pitt that he might end his connection with the House, but that he might sever his relationship with Wareham in order to be returned for Dorchester, a borough in the same county as Wareham. The vacancy at Dorchester was due to the promotion of Nathaniel Gundry to a justiceship in the Court of Common Pleas[4]. John Pitt was a borough master, and the granting of the stewardship to him suggests a shuffle in borough patronage; such as demanded an easy and quick method by which a member could liberate himself from one constituency, and quietly betake himself to another without encountering opposition.

Two years later another of these stewardships of Crown lands was revived, and bestowed on Henry Lascelles, who from 1745 had represented the borough of Northallerton. He was made Chief Steward and Keeper of the Courts of the Honour of Berkhampstead and of the Manor, Lordship and Town of Berkhampstead, in the counties of Hertford, Buckingham and Northampton, "parcel of

The First Steward of the Chiltern Hundreds.

Another Stewardship revived.

---

[1] *Hist. MSS. Comm. 14th Rep.*, App., pt. IX. 497; *Official List*, pt. II. 44.

[2] Hatsell, II. 41; Beatson, I. 69.   [3] *Official List*, pt. II. 100.

[4] *Official List*, pt. II. 100.

the lands and possessions of the Duchy of Cornwall." A new writ was ordered on March 17th, 1752, and Daniel Lascelles was returned as member for Northallerton[1].

The House loses its Hold on Members.

In this way, and by means not yet fully disclosed by any student of Parliamentary usages and procedure whose work I have been able to discover, there was transferred from the House, nominally to the Crown but in reality to the Administration, the power of releasing a member from his constituency. " This practice of issuing a new writ in the room of members accepting these nominal offices, which began, I believe, about the year 1750," writes Hatsell, "has been now (1781) so long acquiesced in, from its convenience to all parties, that it would be ridiculous to state any doubt about the legality of the proceeding. Otherwise I believe it would be found very difficult, from the form of these appointments, to show that these were offices of profit granted by the Crown[2]."

Government acquires Power to release.

In 1750, when the Stewardship of the Chiltern Hundreds was first deemed an office of profit, it would have been within the power of any member to have taken the sense of the House as to whether these stewardships came within the provisions of the Act of Queen Anne. Such questions on the interpretation of the various laws excluding office-holders were raised with some frequency during the early years of this legislation, before the precedents were well established. But the Government must have been a party to the revival of the stewardships of Crown lands, and to the bringing of these offices within the scope of the Act of 1705. Had it not been so, Pitt and Lascelles could not have been appointed ; and with the Government as a party to the arrangement the House of Commons in all probability would have voted that these stewardships did come within the Place Act, and would also have voted down motions to withhold new writs from Wareham and Northallerton. There is no trace of any opposition to the new method of freeing a member from his constituency ; and it thus came about that the House lost the hold over its members, which it had claimed and asserted from the time when annual elections came to an end. After the Administration, by means of appointment to one of these stewardships of Crown lands, had released a member, it remained possible, as it is at the present day, for the House to withhold a new writ. But after a man had been appointed to a stewardship it was not within the power of the House to call him

---

[1] *Official List*, pt. ii. 106 ; Beatson, i. 250.   [2] Hatsell, ii. 41.

back to its service. When this appointment had been made he passed beyond the reach of the House; and to withhold a writ would only have inconvenienced or punished a constituency for a matter over which it had no control.

The circumstances under which the method was devised probably account for the fact, that for thirty years after the revival of these stewardships the gift of them was regarded as a favour of the Crown. In the last half of the period from 1750 to 1780, these offices were viewed in the same light as other civil appointments. They were regarded, like other patronage, as something to which the opponents of the Government had no claim. They were to go to the men who supported the ministers, and were to be withheld from those who acted with the opposition. This was pre-eminently the light in which all these stewardships were regarded by George III, during the period of the American Revolution, when the House of Commons was more directly under the control of the Crown than at any other time in its modern history. At this time the Administration, on two or three occasions, withheld the Chiltern Hundreds in order to harass a political opponent, or to gain an advantage in a Parliamentary by-election. *Steward-ships withheld from Members in Opposition.*

There was no concealment of the spirit in which George III and North regarded an appointment to one of these nominal offices under the Crown. In 1774 Nathaniel Bayly was elected for Westbury in Wiltshire. Bayly was a native of Abingdon in Berkshire; and in 1775 he applied for the Chiltern Hundreds in order that he might contest Abingdon at a by-election due to the unseating of Mr Mayor, who had been chosen at the general election in 1774. But Bayly had acted with the opposition on questions affecting the troubles with the American colonies. North refused to grant him a stewardship, and justified his refusal on the ground that " there was all the reason to think that if he had set Mr Bayly at liberty " there would have been a vexatious opposition at Abingdon. North assured the House that Mr Mayor, whom Bayly would have opposed, was not personally known to him; but had entitled himself to North's friendship " by showing himself a strenuous supporter of the honour and dignity of the country, in concurring with the present American measures[1]." *Lord North treats them as Patronage*

---

[1] *Parl. Hist.*, xviii. 418.

Grenville's
Bill of 1775.

The by-election at Abingdon took place on the 11th of March, when North's friend was again returned[1]. On the 15th George Grenville, son of the author of the Grenville Act of 1770, moved for leave to bring in a bill to enable the Speaker, under certain regulations, " to issue his warrants to make out new writs for the choice of members to serve in Parliament, in the room of such members as shall signify to him their desire of vacating their seats[2]." Grenville urged the need of a better and more certain method for dissolving what he described as "the great reciprocal tie between members and constituents[3]," and recalled the partisan spirit in which the Place Act was at this time being used to enable some members to vacate their seats. "The Place bill," he said, "was originally meant as a great security to independence in this House, by giving to the electors the power of rejecting those who might appear to them to have accepted employment on dependent principles. By the abuse of the times this has long been perverted to very different and unconstitutional purposes ; for it is under that bill that members wishing to vacate their seats solicit the favour of the minister[4]."

Opposition
to the Bill.

North, in opposing Grenville's bill, frankly stated that he made it a rule to refuse the stewardships "where any gentleman entitled to my friendship would be prejudiced by my compliance[5]." The most forcible speech in opposition to the bill came from Rigby, then paymaster of the land forces, an adept in borough management, and a prominent figure in political society of the period of the American Revolution. The argument he advanced—and it is admittedly an argument of great weight, and one that holds good to-day—was that it might be inconvenient to government, if members were to have the power, whenever they liked, of deserting the House of Commons in a body. He instanced the secession in Walpole's time[6], and observed that, if it had been in the power of the members who then withdrew to have vacated their seats, the secession might have been attended with the inconvenience of an almost general election[7]. Rigby's practical argument is good to-day, because if it were possible for fifty or a hundred members to

[1] *Official List*, pt. ii. 149.   [2] *H. of C. Journals*, xxxv. 119.
[3] *Parl. Hist.*, xviii. 415.   [4] *Parl. Hist.*, xviii. 414.
[5] *Parl. Hist.*, xviii. 418.
[6] In 1739 Pulteney and the Tories, together with malcontent Whigs, withdrew in a body. Cf. Cooke, *Hist. of Party*, ii. 264.
[7] *Parl. Hist.*, xviii. 419.

retire at one time it might throw it into the power of the opposition to determine when a Parliament should come to an end. Leave to introduce Grenville's bill was refused by a vote of one hundred and seventy-three to one hundred and twenty-six[1]. On a later occasion, when the Administration refused the stewardship to a member who desired to vacate his seat, the opposition resorted to new tactics, and were able to make the Act of Queen Anne serve their turn as adequately as the revived stewardships had served the purposes of the Government.

Before the new plan of vacating seats was devised by the opposition there was another contest over the Chiltern Hundreds. It arose out of the Middlesex election of 1779. At the general election in 1774 Wilkes regained the seat of which he had been deprived by his expulsion from the House in 1769, and with him was elected Serjeant Glynn. In 1779 Glynn died; and at the election for Middlesex, consequent upon his death, two men already of the House desired to contest the constituency. Colonel Tufnell, member for Beverley, was the Government candidate; George Byng, who represented Wigan, was anxious to be the candidate of the opposition. Colonel Tufnell was promptly granted a stewardship. North refused to grant the Chiltern Hundreds to Byng, and his candidature for Middlesex thus became impracticable; for while he was still of the House, votes given in his favour would have been votes thrown away. *The Chiltern Hundreds refused in 1779.*

The action of the Government in the Middlesex election led to a petition from the freeholders of the county, and to a second attempt to carry a bill taking it out of the power of the Administration to prevent a member from vacating his seat. " We presume not to dispute any prerogative which the Crown may justly exercise," reads the Middlesex petition, " but we cannot without the highest indignation see a minister avowedly assume to himself a right of discharging from the services of his constituents any member whom he may please to favour, and of deciding who shall offer themselves to the electors for their choice. It is unnecessary to observe that the Act of 6 Queen Anne was passed by men jealous of the power of the Crown, to preserve the fidelity of the representative to his constituents, and that it is from an abuse and a perversion of that Act that the power claimed by the Minister to vacate seats in Parliament is derived. The invasion of our rights is direct. The consequences arising from it plain and indisputable. *A Petition from the Middlesex Freeholders.*

[1] *H. of C. Journals,* xxxv. 199.

If any power on earth can dictate our choice, and prescribe who shall and who shall not become candidates to represent us in Parliament, we may talk of our rights, and take a pride in our freedom, but in fact we have none[1]." The petitioners appealed for justice; and prayed that some law might be provided for the perpetual security of the rights of electors; and that some known, certain and equal rule might be established for vacating the seats of members chosen to represent the people in Parliament.

The Bill of 1779. The second bill, arising from North's avowedly partisan use of the stewardships, differed materially from the Grenville bill of 1775. Grenville's bill was intended to establish a method of release open to all members; to set up a method not unlike that in use in the Parliament of Canada at the present time, where nominal offices, like the stewardship of the Chiltern Hundreds, have no place in the machinery of the constitution, and where, when a member of the House of Commons wishes to resign, he communicates his wish by letter to the Speaker, and is at once set free. The bill of 1779 was introduced in the House of Commons by Wood who had defeated Tufnell, late of Beverley, at the Middlesex by-election, Wilkes, Thomas Townsend who had been teller with Grenville when the bill of 1775 was rejected, and Byng who was to have been the opposition candidate against Tufnell. It was intended "to enable members of the House of Commons to be eligible to serve in Parliament for any other county, city, borough, or place[2]." It did not alter the then existing method of release, so far as it affected members who desired to vacate their seats for the purpose of retiring altogether from the House. Its aim was to put it out of the power of a minister to act as North had done at the Abingdon and Middlesex elections. Leave was given for the introduction of the bill; but at second reading it was rejected by sixty-six to twenty-nine[3].

Break-down of the Partisan Method. The failure of the bill of 1779 could have been a matter of little practical consequence; for between its introduction, following the Middlesex petition, in December, 1779, and its rejection in February, 1780, the opposition had discovered in the Place Act a method of vacating seats which served all the purposes of the bill; a method, moreover, which was soon to break down the partisan and obstructive practices which had grown up in connection with appointments to the Chiltern Hundreds during the

---

[1] *H. of C. Journals,* xxxvii. 506.   [2] *H. of C. Journals,* xxxvii. 507.
[3] *H. of C. Journals,* xxxvii. 507, 676.

reign of George III. The new method contrived by the ingenuity of the opposition to prevent such checkmates as that at Abingdon in 1775, and at the Middlesex by-election, was first used to enable Jervoise Clarke Jervoise to contest Hampshire in 1779. At the time of the vacancy in the county representation Jervoise was member for the borough of Yarmouth, in the Isle of Wight. When the Hampshire vacancy occurred he was desirous of contesting the county. Again, as in the cases of Bayly and Byng, North refused the Chiltern Hundreds. But in this instance Jervoise surmounted the difficulty, and ended a long-drawn-out and disturbing constitutional wrangle, by securing his appointment to the agency of the Sussex militia[1]. Two years later Thomas Thoroton vacated his seat for Bramber by becoming agent for a regiment of Leicestershire militia[2]. As these military appointments came easily within the meaning of that section of the Act of Queen Anne which excluded agents of regiments from the House, and were at once seen to offer unlimited possibilities to members who could not, under the old conditions, obtain a grant of the Chiltern Hundreds, the partisan method of appointing to the stewardships was abandoned by the Government, and there came into existence the method, in use to-day, under which a member who desires an honourable discharge from the House, and is entitled to it, can rely on a grant of a stewardship.

For the breaking down of the partisan system of bestowing the Chiltern Hundreds which existed until 1780, it is possible to cite an authority which may be regarded as official. Subsequent to 1793, when Ireland at last, after many years of agitation, had a Place Act[3], escheatorships of the Provinces of Ulster, Munster, Leinster, and Connaught were revived to serve the same purpose in the Irish Parliament as, since 1750, the stewardship of the Chiltern Hundreds had served in connection with the House of Commons at Westminster. At the time of the Union, when there were many re-elections to the Irish House of Commons, and the Government was much embarrassed by the Anti-Unionists, Cornwallis, the Lord Lieutenant, was disposed to act as North had done in 1775 and 1779, and withhold escheatorships from members of the House who were opposed to the Union. He was, however, a little uncertain of his power, and of the contemporary usage at Westminster, and wrote to Portland, Secretary of State for the Southern Department

An Irish Parallel.

---

[1] Hatsell, ii. 41 ; *Official List,* pt. ii. 155.   [2] *Official List,* pt. ii. 169.
[3] 33 Geo. III, c. 41, Statutes of Ireland.

—the Department then in charge of Irish affairs—for English precedents as to the granting of the Chiltern Hundreds.

Lord Portland's Story of the Break-down.   " What may have been the practice in ancient times," wrote Portland to the Lord Lieutenant, " I am not sufficiently informed to say; but I strongly incline to believe that the nomination to the Chiltern Hundreds, which was the model for your escheatorships of Munster, was considered very much as a matter of favour; and so much so that I should doubt whether a person in opposition to the ministry would have thought himself entitled to ask it. I rather think that instances of its being refused might be met with in Lord North's Administration, previously to the case of Mr Clarke Jervoise, who applied for it that he might be a candidate for the County of Hants, which set the ingenuity of Parliamentary and professional men to look for other expedients by which a seat could be vacated; and so many presented themselves when the Civil List Act came to be looked into with that view, that it was no longer thought expedient or worth while to refuse the specific means of vacating by an appointment to the Chiltern Hundreds whenever it was applied for. Ever since that time, it has become quite a matter of course to give it as often as it is asked for, without any consideration whatever of the political opinions or connections or views of the persons who apply for it [1]."

No Means of Liberation for Constituencies.   While since 1780 the acceptance of the stewardship of the Chiltern Hundreds has served as a certain and uniform method by which members can honourably discharge themselves from the service of the House, there has never been devised a method for constituencies to sever the tie between themselves and their representatives. In the days of the unreformed Parliament it was not uncommon for a man to be elected and seldom to go near the House. Members who had so small a conception of the responsibilities and duties attaching to a seat in the House were in fact so numerous until the end of the old representative system, that in the first Reform bill, introduced on the 1st of March, 1831, it was proposed to reduce the number of members from 658 to 596. "When Parliament is reformed," said Lord John Russell, in justifying this provision of the bill, " there will not be so many members who enter Parliament merely for the sake of the name, and as a matter of style and fashion." He reminded the House that there were some members who did not attend for two or three years at

---

[1] Portland to Cornwallis, Whitehall, May 25th, 1799, *Castlereagh Correspondence*, II. 321.

a time, and he added, " at the end of a Parliament I believe there is generally found an instance or two of individuals who, having been elected, have never appeared at the table even to take the oaths[1]." It was a common occurrence for civilians and military men to go on service abroad, and still retain their seats in the House of Commons.

The men who thus disregarded their duties both to the House and to their constituents usually represented the small boroughs in the hands of patrons. County members seldom so neglected their Parliamentary obligations; for a knight of the shire was usually amenable to the public opinion of his county, and at quarter-sessions and elsewhere came much into contact with the men who were chiefly instrumental in electing him to Parliament. Nor would such neglect have been possible on the part of members representing large commercial centres, such as London, Bristol and Liverpool. From the last half of the eighteenth century, when commercial interests were extending so enormously, the representatives of the great commercial cities were the hardest worked of the unofficial members of the House. The claims of legitimate local interests on these men were so incessant and so imperative that no member who had any thought of seeking re-election dared have gone abroad for a long period, and left his constituency only partially represented in the House of Commons. With the smaller boroughs the case was different. Many of these boroughs were never visited by their members from the election of a Parliament to its conclusion. In some of them it was not even necessary that a candidate should attend the election; while in others, as at Weymouth and Melcombe Regis, when Dodington was in control[2], and at Newport, Isle of Wight, when Lord Palmerston represented the borough[3], it was stipulated by patrons that members should not go near their constituencies.

Assiduous and Negligent Members.

Under these circumstances it is not surprising that, until towards the end of the old representative system, the Journals of the House contain no records of complaints from constituencies of neglect of Parliamentary duty. After the Restoration boroughs had become indifferent as to the doings of their representatives. Successive generations of electors had come to regard their members in the House of Commons only as men who at election times spent money freely, opened the taps at all the alehouses, and paid for

Indifference of Constituencies.

[1] Hansard, 3rd Series, II. 106, 107. [2] Dodington, *Diary*, 85.
[3] Lorne, *Viscount Palmerston*, 10.

votes at current market rates. News-letters recorded briefly the proceedings in Parliament from the opening years of the seventeenth century to the middle years of the eighteenth. Then the London newspapers superseded the news-letter writers; and as the eighteenth century advanced, Parliamentary reporting was done with increasing care and at greater fulness. But neither news-letters nor the London newspapers which displaced them were read by the electors in the smaller boroughs; and until after the French Revolution, only the larger provincial towns had weekly newspapers. Of political life and thought, as we understand them to-day, there was little in provincial England until the closing years of the eighteenth century; and in the smaller boroughs, as well as in some of the larger ones, the local political life which centred about electioneering, municipal and Parliamentary, as distinct from the ends which electioneering is supposed to serve, made it easy for the Parliamentary representatives of these boroughs to do as they pleased, after they had once been chosen to the House of Commons, with only a spasmodic fear of being called to account by their constituents.

An Isolated Complaint. In going over the Journals of the House subsequent to the Restoration, and over the records of its proceedings embodied in the Parliamentary History and the earlier Hansard Series, I have discovered only one instance in which electors formally complained to the House of Commons of the prolonged absence of a member, and this isolated instance does not occur until the eve of the Reform Act of 1832. It was from Canterbury, the city which in 1532 had made a present to one of its representatives for curtailing his attendance on Parliament[1]. The complaint was made in 1829, at a time when modern party lines were well marked in the House and in the larger constituencies, when the newspaper press was established, and when political life was being much quickened by the agitation for reform, and was beginning to take on something of the colour it assumed between the Reform Act of 1832 and the end of the nineteenth century.

A Member in India. At the general election of 1826 the representation of Canterbury became politically divided. Lord Clifton, a Whig, was chosen in company with Mr S. R. Lushington, who was a Tory. Soon after his election, Mr Lushington was appointed to the governorship of Madras, then still under the East India Company, and not covered by the Place Acts. He did not resign his seat; and in

[1] *Hist. MSS. Comm. 9th Rep.*, p. 152.

1829 Lord Clifton presented a petition from the electors of Canterbury in which it was complained that the city was partially unrepresented owing to Mr Lushington's absence. In behalf of the absentee member it was stated that the petition was signed by inhabitants of Canterbury who were politically opposed to him; and Sir Edward Knatchbull, who at this time was one of the knights of the shire from Kent, assured the House that Mr Lushington would have resigned his seat before he left for India if the request to do so had not been conveyed to him in an offensive manner. No other defence for Mr Lushington was forthcoming. Political conditions had by this time so much changed that no one contended that he was justified in retaining his seat for Canterbury while holding a governorship in a distant part of the Empire. But no way of ending the deadlock was suggested other than by a bill intended to deal specially with the case. Leave was given to Mr Baring to introduce a bill to vacate the seats of members who accepted offices in India. It was to be retroactive in order to grant relief to Canterbury; but it did not get beyond its preliminary stages in this form, and Mr Lushington retained his seat for Canterbury until the dissolution of the Parliament of 1826–30[1]. Although the Canterbury petition resulted in no relief for that constituency, the discussion to which the petition gave rise in and out of Parliament had a good effect; for in the same session the Act of Queen Anne was extended so as to bring within the list of office-holders excluded from the House of Commons governors and deputy-governors of any settlements, presidencies, territories or plantations of the East India Company[2].

There is to-day no law to prevent a member, who has not accepted an official appointment, from going to India or to any other distant part of the world, and remaining there so long as it suits his convenience. A constituency represented by a member who should so neglect his Parliamentary duties would by statute have no more effective means of compelling the vacation of his seat than had the electors of Canterbury of severing the connection between them and the governor of Madras in 1829. But with the Reform Act of 1832, and more especially with the Acts of 1867 and 1884, there came a great change in the relations of members to constituencies. The easy-going relations which existed

Still no Law to prevent Absenteeism.

---

[1] Hansard, 2nd Series, xx. 1328, 1329; xxi. 1105, 1110; *Official List*, pt. ii. 304.

[2] 10 Geo. IV, c. 62.

in connection with so many boroughs from the Restoration to the Reform Act, was one of many evils of the old representative system, which could not long have survived the immensely growing work of Parliament, the system of party government—in a period when the life of Administrations became dependent on narrow majorities in the House of Commons—a cheap and effective newspaper press and quick railway travel. All these nineteenth century political and material conditions, developing as they did concurrently with the extensions of the franchise, have in practice made unnecessary any law concerning prolonged absence of members. The organisations of the government and opposition whips, the metropolitan and provincial press, the volume of municipal legislation which now demands the attention of Parliament, and the demands of a representative system in which every man of settled abode can exercise the Parliamentary franchise have now so revolutionised the relations between members and constituents that calls of the House are to-day as much of the past as the eighteenth century distinctions and special privileges of knights of the shire; and now, in the opening years of the twentieth century, no member of the House, in the least amenable to local and national public opinion or desirous of re-election, would dream of absenting himself from Westminster for two or three Parliamentary sessions.

Modern Relations between Electors and Elected.
How great has been the change from the order under which it was possible for a man to secure election and immediately afterwards go to India to serve for a term as governor, is shown by the fact that in 1899 a member of the House of national fame, on undertaking a great biography—a work for which the whole English-speaking world may be said to have been waiting—deemed it his duty, in accordance with his conceptions of the relations between electors and elected, to place himself in the hands of his constituents, to tell them that his great task necessitated "a certain withdrawal from constant daily activity," and to give them an informal opportunity, but still an adequate one, of declaring whether they regarded this withdrawal as militating too seriously against the efficient discharge of his duties as their representative in the House of Commons[1]. It was not so regarded. The electors in this instance declared their continued confidence in their member. But the incident was none the less significant of the

[1] Mr John Morley's address to his constituents at Brechin, *Manchester Guardian*, January 17th, 1899.

change wrought in the nineteenth century in the relations of members and constituents, and in particular in the nature of the tie between the electors and elected.

So far as the machinery of the representative system goes it is still possible for the elected only to determine the connection. Public opinion, however, has long since made the tie between members and constituents reciprocal. A member, during the lifetime of a Parliament to which he has been elected, may continue to represent a constituency when he is no longer in agreement with those who elected him, or rather with the party organisation which assumes to speak for the majority of the electorate; but no member can retain his seat and continuously neglect all his duties to the House and to his constituency, and at the same time preserve his own self-respect or the good opinion of the political and social world in which he moves.

Public Opinion and the Duties of Members.

CHAPTER XIII.

POLITICAL RELATIONS BETWEEN MEMBERS AND CONSTITUENTS.

Early Close Relations. THE political relations between members and constituencies underwent great changes in the five centuries of the old representative system. These changes were due, first to the break-down of the early laws which required members to be of the constituency they represented ; and then, during the last two centuries, in a lesser degree to the longer duration of Parliaments. How close the relationship was in the middle years of the fourteenth century is shown by the action of the House of Commons which met on the 13th of October, 1339. Edward III was then absent in Flanders. Archbishop Stratford, who had just returned from Flanders, and who, with the Bishop of Durham and William de la Pole, was of the Commission which opened the Parliament, reported that the King, to carry on the war, needed a large subsidy. The Commons, however, acting for themselves as a separate and distinct body, declared that they could not grant an aid "without consulting the commons of their countries." To this end they desired that another Parliament be summoned, and they undertook that, in the meantime, they would return to their constituencies, and " would do their utmost to obtain for the King a proper aid[1]." This seems to have been the first occasion on which members of the House of Commons openly declared themselves to be the representatives of their electors. Parliament met again at the end of January, 1340. The Commons then promised to state their intentions concerning the aid on the

[1] Parry, 108.

19th of February, and on that day they intimated that they were willing to grant it[1].

So long as residents only were elected to the House of Commons; so long as wages were paid by constituents, and elections were frequent, the political relations between members and constituencies apparently continued close. "Wages," as Prynne has observed, "begat a greater confidence, correspondence, and dependence between knights, citizens and burgesses and those who elected and defrayed their expenses, than when or where no wages or expenses were demanded and received, as due by law; and gave the electors who paid just occasion to check them or detain their wages in case of absence, neglect, or unnecessary protraction of their sessions[2]." The Bond of Wages.

Some of the early borough records show that, while wages were paid, it was customary for members, on returning from a Parliament, to address their electors when they presented their bills for wages and travelling-expenses. Thus at Lyme Regis, on August 14th, 1449, Thomas Salisbury and Richard Frank " ingeniously related ye transaction of Parliament[3]." At King's Lynn, on the 8th of January, 1496, " John Gryndall, alderman, and William Horwode, chosen burgesses of the last Parliament, came in and showed what Acts were made in the said Parliament, which Acts the said John Gryndall, alderman, declared and read them openly afore all the congregation here[4]." "The mayor who is come from the Parliament," reads an entry in the corporation records of the City of Lincoln for 1523, "showeth what he and the recorder have done in the Parliament, and that there is now owing to them for their expenses twelve pounds[5]." In 1535 Vincent Grantham, " out of his zeal and love for the city," remitted part of his Parliamentary wages. He was paid four pounds three shillings and fourpence. His colleague received forty-one pounds and eightpence[6]. Very soon after this remittance of the larger part of his wages by Grantham, wages ceased to be paid at Lincoln[7], and there are no more entries in its municipal Members address Constituents.

---

[1] Cf. Parry, 108; Longman, *Hist. of the Life and Times of Edward III*, I. 163.

[2] Prynne, *Survey of Parl. Writs*, pt. IV. 7.

[3] *Archæologia*, XXIV. 324.

[4] *Hist. MSS. Comm. 11th Rep.*, App., pt. III. 171.

[5] *Hist. MSS. Comm. 14th Rep.*, App., pt. VIII. 31.

[6] *Hist. MSS. Comm. 14th Rep.*, App., pt. VIII. 34.

[7] *Hist. MSS. Comm. 14th Rep.*, App., pt. VIII. 38.

records of addresses from members who had represented the city in Parliament. A record similar to that at Lincoln in 1523 has been preserved at Coventry; it is of the year 1524. "Mr Recorder," it reads, "related the Acts and manner of the last Parliament as a burgess of the city, and had hearty thanks therefore; likewise Mr Marber[1]."

A Modern
Parallel.

These records of the old municipalities concerning the reviews of the work of the Parliaments, with the votes of thanks to members, suggest that, in the first three centuries of the representative system, the political relations between members and constituencies were in some respects not unlike those of the present day, when members of the House of Commons are expected to review the work of each session, and to give their constituents an informal opportunity of passing judgment on their Parliamentary conduct. The records which I have quoted are the only ones I have found. While they are few they afford proof that in some constituencies, representatives and electors were accustomed to meet at the end of a Parliament; and it is reasonable to believe that these meetings were more frequent and more general than the surviving records show.

Members and
Petitions.

The character of the legislation of the first two centuries of the representative system was such as would call for somewhat close relations between electors and elected. "If we glance at the rolls of the English Parliament," writes Professor Jenks, in describing the work of Parliament in this period, "we shall find that the great bulk of the petitions which are presented during the first two hundred years of its existence are complaints of the breach of old customs, or requests for the confirmation of new customs, which evil-disposed persons will not observe. These petitions, as we know, were the basis of the Parliamentary legislation of that period[2]." Petitions suggest some conference or correspondence between members and constituents, and also something in the nature of instructions.

Extra-
Parlia-
mentary
Duties for
Members.

In the period while legislation was of this character, while members were mostly resident, and while Parliaments seldom sat more than a single session, and in fact long after non-resident members for boroughs had become common and the mode of legislation had changed, sometimes the House of Commons, some-

---

[1] *Letters and Papers, Henry VIII, 1529–30*, App., 3078.

[2] Jenks, *Law and Politics in the Middle Ages*, 63, 64; cf. Hallam, *Europe during the Middle Ages*, 586; Pike, *Hist. of the House of Lords*, 326.

times Parliament, imposed extra-Parliamentary duties on members which must have tended to bring them into direct relationship with some of their constituents.

In 1495, for example, extra-Parliamentary duties were imposed on members of the House of Commons with a view to establishing a uniform system of weights and measures. An Act was passed in which it was recited that divers statutes and ordinances had been made in times past, "that one measure and one weight should be used throughout this noble realm." "These statutes," it was further recited, "had not been observed and kept"; and to secure their observance it was enacted "that unto the knights and citizens of every shire and city assembled in this Parliament, barons of the five ports, and certain burgesses of burgh towns," when they should depart from the present Parliament there should be delivered "one of every weight and measure which now our Sovereign Lord hath caused to be made of brass, for the common weal of all his subjects and lieges according to the King our Sovereign Lord's standard of his Exchequer, of weight and measure as they be in the Exchequer of our said Sovereign Lord." The knights, citizens and burgesses to whom these weights and measures were to be delivered, were directed surely to convey, or to "cause the same to be conveyed in this half the feast of Easter next coming," the citizens to their cities, and the knights "unto such burgh or town corporate or market town within the shire for which they be elected, as is specified and contained in a cedule unto this present bill annexed[1]." To this day the House of Commons, through its Speaker, has some duties in connection with weights and measures. At certain infrequent intervals the receptacle in the wall of Westminster Hall, in which the standards are incased, is unsealed and the standards compared in the presence of the Speaker and other officials of the House.

The extra-Parliamentary duty thus thrown on members of the House by the Act of 1495 was agreeable compared with some imposed on them in the seventeenth century. In 1624 members of the House of Commons were charged to report recusants in their constituencies; and on the 27th of April the counties from Bedford to Warwick were called over in the House in order that these reports might be made. From most counties no recusants were reported by the knights. In other cases the knights pleaded that they had not prepared their lists. From no county was any

Weights and Measures.

Reporting Recusants.

[1] 11 Henry VII, c. 4.

large number reported. Lancashire, then as now well known for
its landed families who adhere to the old faith, had seven. Sir
James Perrot, who represented Pembrokeshire, reported his wife
as a recusant; and Sir William Herbert, who was knight of the
shire for Montgomery, also reported his wife as "an obstinate
Papist[1]." The order in accordance with which these reports were
made was dated April 3rd, 1624, and it directed members to
report popish persons "as are in places of charge or trust in their
several counties and boroughs[2]." Similar duties were again thrown
on members of the House in 1641[3].

**Keeping
Order in
Counties.**   Duties of an entirely different character but no more agreeable
were imposed on knights of the shire for Essex in 1648, when
they were directed "to take care to prevent a meeting of the
grand jury, freeholders and inhabitants of the said county at
Stratford-Langthorne on the 4th of May." They were to undertake
this duty, ordinarily a duty which lay with the sheriff, because
the House regarded "such meetings, in so great numbers," as
"very prejudicial to the peace of the kingdom[4]." Earlier in the
same Parliament, in 1644, knights of the shire were required "to
present, with speed, three names of each several county, of persons
out of whom they think fit to have one elected sheriff[5]."

**Other
Duties.**   In 1660 members of the House of Commons were required
by resolution to concern themselves by means of letters in the
collection of the newly-imposed poll-tax[6]; and again in 1678, at
the time of the Popish Plot and, so far as I can learn, for the
last time, they were required to aid in the discovery of recusants.
"That the knights of the shire do on Tuesday next come sevennight," reads the order of 23rd November, 1678, "bring a list of
all persons of note, being Popish recusants or so reputed, resident
or having considerable estate within their respective counties ; and
that the knights, citizens and burgesses, who serve for each county,
do meet together and agree and prepare such lists and sign the
same[7]." In the next century knights of the shire were occasionally
excused service in the House, that they might go back to their
counties, when popular disturbances were apprehended ; but I can
discover in the Journals of the eighteenth century no such orders
of the House, throwing local and extra-Parliamentary duties on

[1] *H. of C. Journals,* i. 776.   [2] Parry, 295.
[3] Parry, 353.   [4] Parry, 491.
[5] Parry, 439.   [6] *H. of C. Journals,* viii. 145.
[7] *H. of C. Journals,* ix. 545.

members generally, as those which have been cited. Knights of the shire all through the history of the old representative system were resident in the counties for which they were elected, or were prominently identified with the counties they served. But non-resident members for boroughs were numerous even in the seventeenth century, and as such they could be of little service in such local extra-Parliamentary work as was contemplated by the orders to report Popish recusants of 1624, 1641, and 1678.

Soon after legislation assumed its modern form, and the procedure in the House of Commons began to approximate to Parliamentary procedure as we know it to-day, it is possible to discover a recognized connection between members and the special legislation which concerned their constituencies. In 1572 there was an order that the House should sit from three to six o'clock in the afternoon to proceed only with private bills, and that it was "not to go to the question of any such bill, if it concerned a town or shire, unless the knights of such shire or shires, or the burgesses of such town or towns be then present[1]."

Two centuries later than this order of 1572 Burke told his constituents at Bristol that, when they had chosen their member, he was not member for Bristol, but was a member of Parliament[2]. To some extent this was true; but all through the last three centuries of the unreformed Parliament it was recognized, as it is to-day, that members had special duties and responsibilities to the constituencies that elected them. The order of 1572 is proof of this; and there is evidence of the survival of this principle that local business had a first claim on the time and attention of members, in an order of the House as late as 1793, governing the service of members on Grenville committees. It directed that such members as might be engaged in the urgent business of their constituents, in committees on contested bills, should be "excused from their attendance in this House on the appointment of any select committee for the trial of contested elections on the 7th and 12th days of this instant March[3]." On the days when Grenville committees were to be drawn, every member, not over sixty years of age, and not holding ministerial office, was subject to call. Only the most adequate excuses for non-attendance were accepted; but, as this order of 1793 shows, attendance on local contested bills was deemed a sufficient

Marginal notes:

Members and Local Bills.

Local Business First Claim on Members.

---

[1] Parry, 223.   [2] Jephson, *Hist. of Platform*, I. 193.
[3] *H. of C. Journals*, XLVIII. 347.

reason to put a member beyond the liability of being balloted on to a Grenville committee.

The Business of Large Cities.   These local claims on the time and services of members at Westminster were the most demanding of all claims, and they were especially imperative and onerous on members for the larger commercial cities and boroughs. In 1830 General Gascoyne, then a Tory member for Liverpool, supported the movement for the enfranchisement of Leeds and Manchester on the ground that the local business of such large cities coming before Parliament made it essential that they should have representatives of their own, and not be dependent as they were at this time, and until after 1832, on the members for the counties of Yorkshire and Lancashire. General Gascoyne cited his own experiences in support of his argument that the great unenfranchised towns must have direct representation; and informed the House that, since he became member for Liverpool in 1796, he had brought in and carried more than two hundred local ·bills[1].

Liverpool's Representatives.   Gascoyne represented Liverpool for thirty-five years, and in nine successive Parliaments. The historian of Liverpool describes him as a man of no special ability, and as taking no prominent part in public affairs. "He was doubtless," it is added, "zealous and active in promoting the town's interest in Parliament, and he had the uniform support of the town council, 'Gascoyne and Townside' being his favourite electioneering motto[2]." One of Gascoyne's eighteenth century predecessors, Sir Thomas Johnson, rendered the town almost equally important local service in Parliament. Johnson was first elected in 1701, and was of the House until 1723. He especially watched Liverpool's interest in the Virginia tobacco trade[3]; and in the days when the latent possibilities of Liverpool as a port were being discovered, to no one more than to Sir Thomas Johnson was the town indebted for its early developement[4].

Needs of Manchester and Birmingham.   Liverpool, in the eighteenth century, had particular need of members of the type of Johnson and Gascoyne; men who were energetic and watchful in its behalf in Parliament. But its history in this respect does not differ much from that of other large towns; for in this period, in addition to Acts of Parliament directly affecting the local economy of towns, there was much general legislation, commercial and fiscal, in which the industrial and

[1] Hansard, xxii. 886. [2] Picton, *Memorials of Liverpool*, i. 275.
[3] *Dict. Nat. Bio.*, xxx. 49. [4] Picton, i. 148, 149.

trading towns and cities had a direct interest. Manchester in 1774 stood so much in need of a member like Johnson or Gascoyne, that the merchants and manufacturers contemplated going into the borough market and buying a seat, in which they could instal a Manchester man whose special duty should be to attend to Manchester's industrial and commercial interests in the House of Commons[1]. In 1780 Birmingham felt the same need. Its manufacturers appealed to the Earl of Dartmouth, then Lord Keeper of the Privy Seal, and long connected with the County of Warwick[2], to help them in electing Sir Robert Lawley as one of the knights of the shire, because he was familiar with the industrial and commercial interests of Birmingham. "The various commercial regulations, so frequently made by the Legislature, affect the trade and manufacturers of this place very much," reads the appeal to Dartmouth, "and render it an object of great importance to its inhabitants that gentlemen may, if possible, be chosen for the county who are connected with the people, and not entirely uninformed of the particulars in which their interests consist[3]."

Despite Burke's dictum that a member elected for Bristol was not member for Bristol, but was a member of Parliament, special services at Westminster in behalf of constituencies, services which associated and identified a member with his constituency, and all quite legitimate in their character, were from the earliest time demanded from members; and the existence and urgency of these demands, for at least two centuries and a half before the electoral system was reformed, were formally recognized by the House. *Local Claims fully recognized.*

Instructions from constituents to members were common in the seventeenth and eighteenth centuries. They can be traced back to the reign of James I; and in at least one instance of instructions to members in that reign, the circumstances suggest that they had been usual from an earlier period. In 1624 Sir Edward Conway and John Angell were, in their absence, elected for Rye. In apprising them of their election the mayor requested them " to come down to be sworn in as freemen, and to receive the requisite information on what is to be done in Parliament[4]." James Howell, a non-resident, was chosen with Sir Talbot Bowes for the Yorkshire borough of Richmond in 1627; and his letter of acceptance indicates *Instructions to Members.*

---

[1] Lecky, *England in the Eighteenth Century*, I. 208.
[2] Doyle, I. 517.
[3] *Hist. MSS. Comm. 13th Rep.*, App., pt. I. 253.
[4] *Cal. of State Papers*, 1623–25, 152.

that it was customary for members to receive instructions. " As I account this election an honour to me," he wrote from London, " so I esteem it a greater advantage that so worthy and well experienced a knight as Sir Talbot Bowes is to be my colleague and fellow burgess. I shall steer by his compass, and follow his directions in anything that may concern the welfare of your town and the precincts thereof, either for the redress of any grievance, or by proposing some new thing that may conduce to the further benefit and advantage thereof ; and this I take to be the true duty of a Parliamentary burgess, without roving at random to generals. I hope to learn of Sir Talbot what is fitting to be done, and I shall apply myself accordingly to join with him to serve you with my best abilities." The subscription to Howell's letter reads, " So I rest your most assured and ready friend, to do you service, James Howell[1]."

A Request for Instructions. Andrew Marvell, who has so often to be cited in these matters affecting relations of members and constituents, in 1669 asked for instructions from his constituents at Hull. "The Parliament being now shortly to sit," he wrote to the mayor on October 7th, 1669, " tho' I know you want no remembrancer in those things which concern you, yet I thought it proper to give you notice of it ; and that I shall, God willing, be present at the opening of the session. Therefore, if there be any particular that may more nearly relate to your affairs, you will be pleased to consider thereof and advertise me timely, that so I may be instrumental to serve you therein as far as my capacity will carry and my obligation binds me[2]." Again, in October, 1670, Marvell similarly put himself in communication with his constituents at the opening of the session ; and when the session was advanced, he asked, " What is your opinion at home of the bill from the Lords for general naturalisation of all foreigners that shall take the oaths of allegiance and supremacy?" "We," he adds, speaking for the Commons, "have not yet given it a hearing[3]." This inquiry shows that Marvell consulted his constituents, not only on matters affecting Hull, but on the larger and more general questions which came before Parliament.

Pressure from Constituencies. At the elections in 1678–79 to the third Parliament of Charles II, " candidates came under engagements to gratify the sanguinary wishes of the people, by a diligent investigation of the plot and a zealous prosecution of its authors[4]." The Noncon-

[1] Clarkson, *Hist. of Richmond*, App., xlix.   [2] Marvell, *Works*, II. 276.
[3] Marvell, *Works*, II. 334, 357.   [4] Somerville, *Transactions*, 78.

formists were active at this time in exacting pledges from members of the House[1]; and their hand seems visible in the advice given to George Treby, who represented Plympton Earle, and who was afterwards Lord Chief Justice. The memorandum was dated November 2nd, 1680, and in it Treby was counselled to "pass no bill sent down by the House of Lords which the Court desires, until the succession and the Protestant religion are secured"; to "pass a bill to exclude the bishops' votes, as they show themselves enemies to the Commons"; to "let the House of Commons hold a strict correspondence with the city," and "to endeavour to secure good Protestant officers for the militia[2]." "In many places" in 1681, when the Parliament which met at Oxford was being chosen, "it was given as an instruction to the members to stick to the bill of exclusion[3]." James II, when he was busy with the movement for the repeal of the penal laws and the test, availed himself of the practice of constituents instructing their members. His western progress in September, 1687, was really an electioneering tour; and his visits to the boroughs returning members so mollified the hearts of the electors, "that in most places they promised to send such members to the ensuing Parliament as would be for taking off the penal laws and the test[4]."

After the Revolution John Hervey, afterwards Earl of Bristol, who was member for Bury St Edmunds from 1694 to 1703, maintained relations with the corporation there very similar to those existing between Marvell and the corporation of Hull. Hervey wrote full and frequent letters to the corporation, explaining measures before Parliament; and he prided himself, as regarded his Parliamentary work, on acting "with such integrity and those tender regards to ye true interests of England in general, and those of my second mother, if I may so call Bury, in particular, as ye expected from me when ye reposed it in me[5]." In thanking the corporation for his election in 1701 Hervey wrote: "But as nothing can make me more your servant than I justly was before, so I can only renew the promise of employing most of my time and thoughts for ye advancement of your interests * * * I intend

Tender Regard for a Constituency.

---

[1] Somerville, *Transactions*, 78.

[2] Heads of a Paper of Advice to G. Treby, M.P., November 2nd, 1680, *Hist. MSS. Comm. 13th Rep.*, App., pt. vi. 23.

[3] Burnet, *Hist. of His Own Time*, ii. 127.

[4] Clarke, *Life of James II*, ii. 140; Luttrell, i. 427.

[5] *Letter-Books of John Hervey, First Earl of Bristol*, i. 155.

to wait on you, before ye Parliament sitts, to receive your commands and instructions[1]."

Instructions in 1701. The practice of instructing members was continued in the eighteenth century until its closing decades. At the general election of 1701—that due to the dissolution of Parliament which immediately followed the French King's acknowledgment of the Pretender—the City of Westminster instructed its members that "they endeavour to support His Majesty's title, and defend the nation against the French King, who threatens to give a King to England as he has done to Spain[2]." After Colonel Wharton and Mr Dormer had been chosen knights of the shire for Buckingham, they were instructed to the same effect as the members chosen for the City of Westminster. "We exhort, charge and require you," read the Buckinghamshire instructions as recorded by Luttrell, "to support the King with the most effectual and equal supplies, to restore and keep the credit of the nation; heartily to concur in such alliances as His Majesty has, or shall make, for pulling down the exorbitant power of France; maintain the succession as by law established; discover if possible such who are for that new Pretender, the French King would impose on us; take care the soldiers and seamen be well paid and commanded; avoid all such disputes and animosities as had lately like to have undone us; and to take care to punish all real crimes and misgovernments in the public affairs[3]." The freeholders of Cornwall called on their knights of the shire "to take care of the preservation of the established religion," and they were generally instructed to the same effect as the knights of Buckinghamshire[4]. The Administration apparently had a hand in these instructions; for the address to the King in reply to the speech from the Throne at the opening of Parliament embodied much of the sentiment expressed in the instructions[5].

And in 1715. In 1715 the electors of the City of London instructed their members rigorously to inquire into the conduct of the late Tory Ministry, and as to who had advised the Peace of Utrecht, "throwing away," as these instructions declared, "the fruits so dearly bought of a long and exhausting war[6]."

At the time of the excise agitation in 1733 instructions to

---

[1] *Letter-Books of John Hervey, First Earl of Bristol, 1651–1750*, I. 157.

[2] Luttrell, v. 115.   [3] Luttrell, v. 119.
Luttrell, v. 121.   [5] Cf. Luttrell, v. 166.

[6] Torrens, *Hist. of Cabinets*, I. 91.

members seem to have been as general as they were after Louis XIV had proclaimed the Pretender. "Most of the boroughs in England, and the City of London itself," wrote Lord Hervey, "sent formal instructions by way of memorials to their representatives, absolutely to oppose new excises and all extensions of excise laws, if proposed in Parliament, though introduced or modelled in any manner whatsoever[1]." Lady A. Irwin, writing on the 9th of January, informed Lord Carlisle that " the affair of the excise makes a noise, and I fancy will meet with great opposition, should it be attempted in Parliament." " Bristol and Leicester," Lady Irwin added, "have already sent instructions to their members to oppose it, and 'tis said all the great towns in England will do the same[2]." At Rye, long one of the most corrupt of the Cinque Ports, the electors were ready to support the Pelham candidates; but it was insisted that their members must give pledges against the excise. Colonel Pelham, who was in charge of the election for the Duke of Newcastle, the foremost of eighteenth century electioneering managers, "made no scruple of engaging that they should have that satisfaction[3]."

One of the most significant letters of the period of the excise agitation which I have found is from Colonel Charles Howard to his father, Lord Carlisle. Colonel Howard was member for Carlisle, and it was his custom to write at length to his father as to what was doing in the House of Commons. " I shall conclude this subject," he wrote on March 5th, 1733, after describing the debate on the excise bill, " with acquainting you that as the gentlemen at Carlisle, by answer to my letter, left me entirely at liberty to act for them as I thought right, nothing ever appeared to me clearer than it would raise a considerable sum[4]." In other words Colonel Howard voted with Walpole; but his letter seems to indicate that even in the case of members who held their seats largely by family influence, it was still usual for them to communicate with their constituents when this was practicable, before voting on any questions which were arousing keen popular interest. Even in the most easily controlled of patron boroughs, such for example as Rye, some appearance of conciliating the electors on these questions had to be conceded.

[1] Hervey, *Memoirs*, i. 163.
[2] *Hist. MSS. Comm. 15th Rep.*, App., pt. vi. 104.
[3] Torrens, *Hist. of Cabinets*, i. 435.
[4] *Hist. MSS. Comm. 15th Rep.*, App., pt. vi. 104.

Another
Period of
Political
Excitement.

After the resignation of Walpole in 1742 more than forty constituencies, mostly counties and cities, with here and there a borough, such as Bishop's Castle and Newcastle-under-Lyme, adopted instructions to their members recommending a strict inquiry into Walpole's Administration; urging the restoration of triennial Parliaments, and the passing of a pension and place bill on the lines of those which Walpole had caused to be rejected, the earlier ones in the House of Commons, and the later in the House of Lords[1].

Instructions
effective.

During and immediately following Walpole's administration these means of popular political agitation were undoubtedly effective. They had their part in bringing about the abandonment of the excise bill of 1733, and, after Walpole's downfall, they were to some extent instrumental in procuring the enactment of the Place Act of 1742. Until the later years of the eighteenth century there were no political meetings in which both electors and non-electors took part. Such meetings might have evoked the interference of the sheriff; but it was always possible, and had been so from the earliest days of the representative system, for electors to petition the House of Commons, and, at elections and other times, to adopt instructions to their representatives.

Instructions
and Loyal
Addresses.

In the reign of George III instructions to members have a new historical interest. In the first twenty years of the reign they led to a counter-movement on the part of the Crown, which resorted to the securing of loyal addresses as an offset to instructions to members; and after 1780 instructions began to fall into desuetude and give place to other methods of expressing popular opinion on political questions. In the first twenty years of the reign, however, instructions to members were still frequent. In 1768 the freemen of Norwich transmitted, through the mayor, a set of twelve instructions to their members, Harbord and Bacon. The freemen desired another Place bill, triennial Parliaments, and the exclusion of the sons of peers from seats in the House of Commons. The preamble to these instructions indicates the spirit in which in the early years of the reign of George III electors approached their representatives. " As it is the undoubted right of all constituents to instruct their representatives in Parliament from time to time, as they shall see occasion," it reads, " we, a considerable part of your electors, as yet your free and independent electors, take this opportunity to claim and exercise that right, and to transmit to

[1] Cf. *Parl. Hist.*, xii. 417.

you our sentiments upon some points which we look upon to be of the utmost importance at this juncture to the whole kingdom[1]."

At the time when George III was engaged in his contest with Wilkes a few constituencies instructed their members to support Wilkes's case in the House of Commons; and it was at this juncture that, to offset these instructions and the effect they might have on public opinion, the Administration—which at this time and for ten years to come meant the King—revived, or at any rate brought into more frequent use, the custom of presenting loyal addresses to the Crown at crises in public affairs. The Wilkes Crisis.

The mode of expressing public opinion by addresses, almost invariably of popular approval of the action of the Government, dated from the time of Cromwell. "'Twas in his time," says Defoe, "they came into fashion." The earliest of these seventeenth century addresses was from Durham. It was sent after the Rump Parliament had been turned out, and it engaged its promoters to "stand by Cromwell and his council of officers[2]." There were many of these addresses to King Charles at the Restoration, addresses which, again to quote Defoe, "certainly came from the hearts of the people, tired out with the oppression and corruption of the late usurpations[3]." Again in the reign of Charles II, after the dissolution of the Oxford Parliament, when the King made a declaration "that nothing should ever alter his affection to the Protestant religion, as established by law, nor his love to Parliaments," there were addresses from all parts of the Kingdom in response to the King's declaration. "The grand juries and the benches of justices in the counties, the cities and the boroughs, the franchises and the corporations, many manors, the companies in towns, and at last the very apprentices sent up addresses[4]." In 1688 also there were addresses to James II on the birth of the Prince of Wales[5]. There were more loyal addresses at the Union of Scotland with England[6]; and they were usual, until the early years of George III, on all great occasions in national life. Origin of Loyal Addresses.

From the peace of 1763, after the war with France, and especially from the time of the Wilkes agitation, loyal addresses Loyal Addresses bought by Government.

---

[1] Bacon, *Hist. of Norwich*, II. 2; cf. Stacy, *Hist. of Norwich*, 9.

[2] Defoe, *Hist. of Addresses*, pt. I. 2.

[3] Defoe, *Hist. of Addresses*, pt. I. 12.

[4] Burnet, *Hist. of His Own Time*, II. 132, 133.

[5] Defoe, *Hist. of Addresses*, pt. II. 83.

[6] Defoe, *Hist. of Addresses*, pt. II. 15.

were much more frequent and more numerous than they had hitherto been. They were now used by the Government for influencing public opinion in its favour in the contests in Parliament with the opposition. The addresses approving of the peace of 1763 were practically bought by the Government[1]. In 1769, apparently for the first time, loyal addresses were resorted to by the Government to offset instructions from constituents to members of the House of Commons[2]; and for some years after the Wilkes agitation addresses were part of the machinery by which popular enthusiasm in favour of the Government was worked up and expressed. They were much resorted to by George III during his long and unavailing struggle with the American colonies. The King often suggested them[3]. The cost of obtaining them was sometimes paid for by the King or his ministers[4]; and to carry an address from a large town to the King was to set out on the way to a knighthood or other royal recognition.

Addresses expressive of Public Opinion.

Addresses were obtained from the universities; from deans and chapters of cathedral cities; from municipal corporations; from magistrates in petty sessions, and from grand juries at quarter sessions and assizes. Their use, subsequent to the Wilkes agitation, became so general in both England and Scotland, that Cockburn, in describing public opinion in the last twenty years of the eighteenth century, states that it was "recognized only when expressed through what were acknowledged to be its legitimate organs," which meant its formal or official outlets. "Public bodies," he adds, "might speak each for itself; but the general community, as such, had no admitted claim to be consulted or cared for[5]."

Passing of Instructions.

The Wilkes agitation, the agitation for triennial Parliaments which was contemporaneous with it, and the agitation for economy and reform which was so widespread during the later years of the war with the American colonies, were the last occasions on which instructions to members were frequent or general. As late as 1780 the old idea as to the constitutional place of instructions was expressed by Horace Walpole, when he asked, "Has not every individual some member for a county or borough to whom he can give remonstrance, petition and instruction[6]?" From about 1774,

---

[1] Massey, *Hist. of England*, I. 132.   [2] Cf. Walpole, *Letters*, v. 148.
[3] Cf. Donne, *George III's Letters to North*, I. 267, 272.
[4] Cf. Walpole, *Last Journals*, I. 501, 502.
[5] Cockburn, *Memorials of His Time*, 90.
[6] Walpole, *Last Journals*, II. 381.

however, when Burke told the freemen of Bristol that electors were competent to elect a man of judgment and knowledge, but that they were not competent to determine the details of legislation— and an attempt to usurp this function would inevitably lower the character of Parliament—the practice of instructing members gradually disappeared. Burke's views on the question " were generally adopted by the Whig party, and it appears to have been mainly due to the influence of Burke that the fashion of authoritative instructions, which after the Middlesex election threatened to become universal in popular constituencies, in a few years almost passed away[1]."

The idea expressed by Burke in his speech at Bristol was not Members new. It had been put forward in Parliament as early as 1745 by represent Sir William Yonge, in a speech in opposition to annual Parliaments. the Whole "The word attorney," said Yonge, "has been artfully brought into Country. the debate, as if the members of this House were nothing more than the attorneys of the particular county, city, or borough they respectively represent. But everyone knows that, by our constitution, after a gentleman is chosen, he is the representative, or if you please the attorney, of the people of England, and as such is at full freedom to act as he thinks best for the people of England in general. He may receive, he may ask, he may even follow the advice of his particular constituents; but he is not obliged, nor ought he to follow their advice, if he thinks it inconsistent with the general interests of his country[2]." This was the theory of the constitution, as to instructions, expressed by Blackstone in his dictum that while constituents had the right to offer advice, such advice was not binding upon the votes and actions of members in Parliament[3].

About the time when instructions to members were falling into Pledges desuetude there was begun the practice of demanding pledges from to Con- candidates at elections. At Lewes, in 1780, Thomas Kemp pledged stituencies. himself that he would accept of neither place, pension, gratuity, nor reward of any kind from any administration, while he should represent the borough in the House of Commons[4]. Alderman Bull, chosen at the same general election one of the four members for the City of London, gave a similar pledge[5]. In 1784, when Fox

[1] Lecky, *England in the Eighteenth Century*, III. 221.
[2] *Parl. Hist.*, XIII. 1078.
[3] Blackstone, I. 159, Ed. Portland, U.S., 1807.
[4] Oldfield, v. 15.   [5] Oldfield, v. 15.

and Wray were candidates for Westminster, Jebb, one of the London Unitarians long associated with the movement for Parliamentary reform, called for pledges that the candidates, if elected, would act in conformity with instructions from the electors or resign their seats. " By the present unconstitutional practice," said Jebb, in a speech to the Westminster electors in support of this demand for pledges, " you are called upon to delegate this trust for seven years. It is therefore your duty, until the ancient salutary custom of annual Parliaments shall by the exertions of the people be restored, to guard with special care a delegation so important, and to use every precaution which can secure you against the consequences of its abuse ; and it is more particularly incumbent upon you at this particular crisis, when the attention of the people is so strongly called to that Parliamentary reform which can alone preserve this country from destruction[1]." Jebb carried the Radicals of Westminster with him, and Wray expressed his readiness to give the pledge which was thus demanded.

Pledges rare before 1832.   There were, however, few constituencies in which political life was so active and so dominated by the Radicals as Westminster and the City of London between the American and the French Revolutions ; and in the half century which intervened between the general election of 1784 and the reform of 1832, such pledges as those sought from Fox and Wray were, so far as I can ascertain, but infrequently demanded. They were called for in some constituencies at the dissolution which followed the failure of the Reform bill of 1831 ; and after the Reform Act of 1832 pledges, less general in their character, began to be demanded. To-day in many constituencies, particularly in boroughs and in industrial county divisions, as soon as a candidate appears on the scene he is waited upon by deputations representing groups of electors, demanding pledges for or against legislation which is expected to come before the Parliament to which he is seeking election. As recently as July 4th, 1900, Mr T. W. Russell, then member for South Tyrone, when again seeking support in view of the approaching general election, pledged himself that in the next Parliament " he would abstain from voting on the question of a Roman Catholic University for Ireland," a proposal to which he had previously given his support[2].

---

[1] Jebb, *Memoirs,* I. 197, 198.
[2] *Manchester Guardian,* July 6th, 1900.

The foregoing account of the political relations between electors and elected will naturally give rise to the question, " Did members of the unreformed House of Commons fear to incur the displeasure and the consequent opposition of their constituents ? " For the eighteenth century the answer is in the affirmative. From the time of Walpole to the American Revolution the House of Commons was at its worst as a freely chosen representation of the country. In this period borough corruption was more rampant than at any other time in the history of the representative system. It was the heyday of official election managers such as the Duke of Newcastle in the reign of George II and Robinson who was so closely associated with North and George III in the control of the House of Commons. It was the heyday also of non-official borough-mongers, soldiers of fortune or adventurers in political life, such as Dodington and Lowther. More than at any other time the House was thronged with men who in one way or another were in the pay of the Government—men who were tied to its fortunes by pensions or allowances; by patronage, civil, military or ecclesiastical; by shares in loans; by contracts; or by the expectation of peerages or other honours which it was in the power of the Crown to bestow. During the greater part of these seventy years, moreover, the administration could invariably count, through the management of Argyle, Mackenzie, or Dundas, on the unwavering support of nearly all the forty-five members from Scotland. Yet at no time in the eighteenth century was the House of Commons or the Government unmindful of public opinion.

Public Opinion never entirely ignored.

The Government was not continuously apprehensive of public opinion as is an administration at the present day. It was not nearly so sensitive to expressions of popular opinion; but neither the House nor the Government was ever long indifferent to them. From the Revolution, from the time when party government began, it was the policy of men at the head of administrations to bring over public opinion to their side. Until the newspaper press was established pamphleteers were in the government service to this end. After the newspaper press came into importance in the middle of the eighteenth century, newspaper writers took the place of pamphleteers; and scarcely at any time between the coming of the daily newspaper and the end of the old representative system was the Government without writers, directly or indirectly in its pay, whose mission it was to influence public feeling in its favour. English journalism took on its modern form in the reign

Influencing Public Opinion.

of George III; and the King, as his correspondence with North makes evident, realized the importance of this new power, and drew on his financial resources to bring as much newspaper support to his side as possible. The use of loyal addresses was to the same end—to keep the electors in sympathy with the administration, and to induce them to return administration candidates at the recurring elections.

Power of Public Opinion over Members. The Parliamentary history of the eighteenth century, and the memoirs and correspondence of men who were of the House, furnish abundant proof that representatives in Parliament did fear to incur the distrust and opposition of their constituents. County members throughout the century formed the most independent element of the House. These men usually wanted little from the Government for themselves. Their contact with constituents was frequent and wholesome; and their conduct in the House was generally such as to commend them to their neighbours and the electors whose goodwill was necessary to the long tenure of their seats. Nor were all the borough members indifferent to the goodwill of their constituents. To many borough members, it is true, it mattered little how they voted in the House. They had no constituents whose votes at elections were in the least degree influenced by the political conduct of the men for whom these votes were given. Other considerations, mostly of a sordid character, ruled elections in these places. But members for the larger boroughs had usually to keep the next general election in mind and shape their actions in the House accordingly. Why otherwise should Walpole have found it so difficult to vote down place bills, and have adopted the expedient of permitting these bills to pass in the Commons, relying on the House of Lords to reject them?

Illustrated by the Place Bills. Walpole's earliest biographer gives an explanation. "Such was the unpopularity of the rejection," writes Coxe concerning the bill of 1730–31, which Walpole defeated in the House, "that many members suspected of having pensions or places held in trust, voted for it, lest their opposition might disoblige their constituents[1]." Horace Walpole asserted that the later place bills were "out of decency" suffered to pass in the House of Commons, with an understanding that they were to be rejected in the House of Lords[2]. But nowhere are Walpole's tactics on these bills more clearly explained than in the correspondence of Colonel Howard with Lord Carlisle, a correspondence from which I have already

[1] Coxe, *Life of Walpole*, II. 95, 96.   [2] Walpole, *Letters*, I. 118.

quoted in describing the relations between elected and electors at the time of the excise bill. "Last week," wrote Howard on February 23rd, 1731, "was taken up with the pension bill, which Mr Sandys brought in. It passed through committee of the whole House without debate. It was debated on third reading. I thought they would have divided the House ; but the ministry let it go up to the Lords without a division. I believe they were sensible it would have put a great many gentlemen under difficulties that must have * * * hurt their own interests very much at the places they serve for[1]." In 1740, when Walpole reverted to the earlier plan of rejecting the place bill in the House of Commons, "all his efforts could procure only a small majority of sixteen, two hundred and twenty-two against two hundred and six. The cause of this numerous minority was practically owing to the approach of a general election which influenced many, who favoured administration, to vote for the question[2]."

The excise bill is another proof that members of the House of Commons dreaded to be on the wrong side in a popular agitation. A general election was approaching at the time the bill was before Parliament in 1733, and in consequence many members, "without being enemies to Sir Robert Walpole, were against it from prudential views to their elections[3]." Charles Ford, for whom Swift had procured the office of gazetteer—described by Swift as "one of the prettiest offices of its value"—in a letter to his patron, said that the member of the House who was to oppose Henley at the approaching election at Southampton, having voted for the excise, would not dare to show himself in the corporation, and that Henley, "after the division, thanked him for having by that vote bestowed on him fifteen hundred pounds[4]," apparently the value of a seat in the House during Walpole's rule. It was in response to popular agitation that the place bill at last became law in 1742 ; and it was equally in response to popular clamour that the Act of 1754, easing the conditions under which Jews could naturalise, was repealed in 1755. Again in the reign of George III the County Voters' Registration Act was repealed in the session following its enactment, because of the outburst of feeling against it in the counties.

Other Instances of Public Opinion.

---

[1] *Hist. MSS. Comm. 15th Rep.*, App., pt. vi. 81, 82.
[2] Coxe, *Life of Walpole*, iii. 132.
[3] Hervey, *Memoirs*, i. 208.
[4] Swift, *Works*, xviii. 172, Ed. Edinburgh, 1814.

A Case of
Divided
Allegiance.

These are general instances.   In the first half of the eighteenth
century there are not lacking instances in which members evaded
divisions apparently from fear of the disfavour of their constituents,
or were punished by loss of their seats for votes in the House to
which the electors took exception.   Letters of excuse of two
members for not voting in 1719 with the Stanhope-Sunderland
Administration of 1717–21 are among the Stowe manuscripts.
One of them was from Bryan Broughton, member for Newcastle-
under-Lyme, who at this time was looking forward to being a
knight of the shire from Stafford.   " So violent is the prejudice of
the people here against the bill," he wrote on January 2nd, 1719,
" that should I venture to appear in favour of it, I must from that
time disclaim all hopes of ever serving His Majesty in Parliamentary
station again, in this county at least.   My heart is along with the
bill, and nobody wishes it better success.   But, at the same time,
as my appearing for it must utterly clash with and quite blow up
an interest which, at no light expense for above these twelve years
I have been bringing to bear in this wretched county, this one
failure, if it will deserve so hard a name, I have confessed will be
overlooked, and that notwithstanding I may still have the pleasure
of subscribing myself, which I really am, with highest respect and
esteem, Sir, your most devoted and obedient servant, B. Broughton[1]."
There was a good reason for Broughton's subserviency to the Government, as at the time this letter was written he was a gentleman of
the Privy Chamber[2].

Avoiding a
Division.

The other excuse for non-appearance at this critical division of
1719 was from Daniel Wilson, who in this and in six of the
Parliaments between 1708 and 1747 was one of the knights of the
shire from Westmorland[3].   Wilson's excuse was that he had a "very
sick spouse."   But other reasons seem to lie behind his expression
of the hope that his failure to attend will be overlooked, in view
of " his long service since the Union in the most perilous times[4]."

Constitu-
encies show
Displeasure.

Coming to instances in which men were compelled to seek other
seats in consequence of votes which their constituents did not
approve, there is the case of Viscount Perceval who was elected for
Westminster in 1741.   In 1744 he supported the war with France,
and his unpopularity was so great in Westminster, owing to his
desertion of the independents to whom he owed his return, that he

---

[1] Stowe MSS., Folio 162.　　　　[2] Beatson, i. 179.
[3] Beatson, i. 212.　　　　　　　　[4] Stowe MSS., Folio 156.

had to seek another constituency at the general election of 1747[1].
At a later period, in 1818, William Hanbury, who had been one
of the members for Northampton in the two preceding Parliaments,
was compelled to retire at the general election because he had
not supported a Northampton petition against the Corn Bill[2].
Politically docile as were the electors of Scotland and the members
from Scotland, and stagnant as was political life in that country
during the greater part of the period between the Union and 1832,
Scotch electors and Scotch members of the House of Commons
put their mark on the one Scotchman who voted with Walpole in
favour of the legislation for the government and policing of
Edinburgh which followed the Porteous riots.

Walpole's plan of using the House of Lords as a shield between
members of the House of Commons and their constituents was
reverted to on at least one occasion in the reign of George III,
when there is much testimony, specific and general, that members of the House were at times greatly in fear of their
constituents. In 1772, when Sir Henry Hoghton, one of the
members for Preston, and long an advocate of the cause of the
dissenters in the House, introduced his bill to relieve Protestant
dissenters from obligation on certain occasions to subscribe to the
Thirty-nine Articles, Lord North and his colleagues on the Treasury
Bench offered no opposition. "The ministers," wrote Horace
Walpole in following the bill through its later stages, "afraid of
disobliging the dissenters before the general election, suffered the
bill to pass the House of Commons, hoping the loss would be
imputed to the Lords only, and not to members of Parliament[3]."
This treatment of Hoghton's bill was suggested by George III.
"As I understand the petition of the dissenters is to be presented to-morrow," he wrote to North on April 2nd, 1772,
"I take this method of acquainting you that I think you ought
not to press those gentlemen, who are brought on that interest into
Parliament, to oppose this measure, as thus you will be driving
them out of those seats on a new Parliament. But I think you
ought to oppose it personally through every stage, which will gain
you the applause of the Established Church, and every real friend
of the constitution. If you should be beat, it will be in doing
your duty, and the House of Lords will prevent any evil. Indeed
it is the duty of ministers, as much as possible, to prevent any

Government afraid to disoblige Dissenters.

---

[1] *Dict. Nat. Bio.*, xliv. 370.   [2] *Northampton Borough Records*, ii. 509.
[3] Walpole, *Last Journals*, i. 80, 81; cf. 92, 93.

alterations in so essential a part of the constitution, as everything that relates to religion; and there is no shadow for this petition, as the Crown regularly grants a *nolle prosequi* if any over-nice justice of the peace encourages prosecutions[1]." North did not keep quite to the lines of the King's plan. He relied more on the House of Lords than the King had suggested, as is shown by Walpole's account of the progress of the bill through the Commons, and also by the fact that, on a division on the bill in the Commons, only nine members voted in the minority in opposition to it[2]. When the bill reached the Lords, it was made known that the King had declared himself much against it[3], and the Lords, understanding why it had been allowed to reach them, threw it out as the King and North had expected.

Taking Refuge behind the House of Lords.   A century later, when the utility of the House of Lords was much discussed, the occasional services rendered to members of the House of Commons in the days of Walpole and North had been forgotten or were ignored. But even in the nineteenth century the House of Lords did not entirely lose its place as a shield between members of the House of Commons and their constituents. Had many members of the House of Commons not realized in 1893 that the House of Lords stood ready for once to resume its almost forgotten eighteenth century function, it is extremely improbable that Gladstone's second Home Rule bill would have obtained a majority in the Lower House.

Members and Local Trade Interests.   A convincing proof that on occasions members of the House of Commons felt themselves obliged to act in accordance with the wishes of their constituents is to be found in the correspondence of 1778 between North and Buckinghamshire, when Buckinghamshire was Lord Lieutenant of Ireland. The Irish Octennial Act had been passed; and, growing out of the new political life, Ireland was at this time demanding freer trade laws. Writing to the Lord Lieutenant on the 18th of August, 1778, North expressed a hope that Ireland would make no more demands affecting trade. "The representatives of the trading towns and manufacturing counties," he continued, in describing the situation which confronted him in the House of Commons at Westminster, "are fully apprised of the sentiments and wishes of their constituents. The members of both Houses, after the trouble and

[1] Donne, *Letters of George III to North*, I. 101.
[2] Donne, *Letters of George III to North*, I. 101.
[3] Chatham, *Correspondence*, IV. 218.

disputes caused last year by these questions, will receive with disgust any proposal for renewing the subject in the next session[1]."

Earlier than this, in 1775, North and George III had had some experience of the sensitiveness of members of the House of Commons to the feelings of their constituents, on the question of rescinding the order of the House for the expulsion of Wilkes. The fears of the court arose at this time "from the obligation members for counties and popular boroughs were under of humouring their constituents by voting for Wilkes, the idol of the people[2]." Popular Admiration of Wilkes.

All through the later years of the American war the King and North were much disturbed by popular feeling in the large towns. Members from the small boroughs gave them little trouble in their management of the House of Commons; for it was usually possible to keep a hold on these members, as the administration could always give them some *quid pro quo* for their Parliamentary support. But the members for the large popular constituencies did not so easily come under regal and ministerial influence. Men of decided opinions were in these days the popular candidates in large constituencies; and when elected, they had to keep in view their re-election, and hold themselves in the House in such a way as to carry their constituencies with them. "My experience has taught me," North assured Buckinghamshire in 1780, "that no friends are so little to be depended upon in difficult times as those who have built upon the foundation of popularity, and have shown too great an attachment to the charms of it." This, North added, was his experience after "a very troublesome and bustling political life of ten or twelve years[3]." Much the same sentiment was expressed by the King himself to Shelburne two years later. "If Lord S. can secure the election of Westminster in favour of Mr Pitt," he wrote, "I shall think that a sufficient reason to prefer Sir George Rodney[4] being an English baron to an Irish viscount, if he can at the same time prevent his (Pitt's) becoming dipped in the wild measures that sometimes men are drawn into by representing popular cities[5]." Rodney was made an English peer. There was consequently an election at Westminster; which would not have been the case had he been made an Irish viscount. But Pitt did not succeed to Rodney's seat in the House of Commons. Power of Large Constituencies over Members.

[1] Add. MSS. 34523, Folio 310.   [2] Walpole, *Last Journals*, I. 465.
[3] Add. MSS. 34523, Folio 338.
[4] Elected member for Westminster at the general election of 1780. *Official List*, pt. II. 166.   [5] Add. MSS. 34523, Folio 367.

Influence of a Pending Election.

At the time of the agitation for economy, led in the House of Commons by Dunning and Burke, there is again proof that an immediately pending election had much influence on the votes of members. Sir Fletcher Norton, who was then Speaker, availed himself of the Speaker's privilege of addressing the House when it was in committee on the 5th of April, on Dunning's resolution. He supported it, and declared that "if honourable members should now vote the petitions of the people unfounded, he wished them joy of going down to their constituents with that opinion[1]." At this time the administration had a majority in the House, and it was only the fear of the approaching general election that induced many members to desert Lord North[2]. "It is acknowledged," wrote Lord Shelburne to Lord Mahon on the 2nd of April, 1780, "that the approaching election has a very great influence on the divisions now taking place in the House of Commons in favour of reform and redress of grievances. The county members have very generally voted on the public side, except a few who are likely to lose their seats for not doing so[3]." Mahon also concedes that many members "were swayed by the argument at which the Speaker had so unscrupulously glanced, that the Parliament was now near closing the sixth year of its existence, and must at no distant period be dissolved[4]."

Apathy of Members after an Election.

One of the bills before the House in the stirring and eventful session which preceded the dissolution of 1780, was the measure for disfranchising revenue officers, a bill which was carried by Mr Crewe in the next Parliament. On April 12th, 1780, however, it was rejected by two hundred and twenty-six votes to one hundred and ninety-five; and Walpole states that some of the opposition Whigs voted against the bill, as many of their electors were officers of the revenue[5]. The election of 1780 was at an end by the autumn; and when the new House of Commons assembled on the 31st of October Walpole, in noting the decline of enthusiasm for the reforms which had so stirred the House in the early months of 1780, gives as his reason for this apathy "that the greater number of those who had joined the associations had concurred for fear of their elections, of which they were now secure[6]."

[1] Mahon, vii. 19.
[2] Cf. Fitzmaurice, *Life of Shelburne*, iii. 81; Walpole, *Last Journals*, ii. 376.
[3] Fitzmaurice, *Life of Shelburne*, iii. 74, 75.
[4] Mahon, vii. 21.   [5] Walpole, *Last Journals*, ii. 376.
[6] Walpole, *Last Journals*, ii. 429.

All through the first eighty years of the eighteenth century An Old and apprehension and uneasiness on the part of members as to how a New House their constituents would regard their votes in Parliament depended of Commons. on the nearness of the next general election. How the moods of the House were affected by the fact that it was just at the outset of its term or near the end of it was remarked by Vernon as far back as 1700. "Is it not obvious," he asked in a letter to Shrewsbury, " that there may be different expectations from the last year of an old Parliament or the first sitting down of a new one? In a concluding session do people consider anything so much as the securing their next elections, and does not that naturally run them into an opposition against the court, and setting up pretences for the good of the country; whereas a new Parliament have not that so much in their thought[1]?" Horace Walpole expressed the same truth in another way when, at the opening of the Parliament of 1780–84, he recalled the agitation for economy and reform in the closing session of the Parliament of 1774–80, and the active interest of members in and out of Parliament in the movement, and expressed his conviction that only with a view to their elections had members of the late Parliament been of the county associations, organised by Wyvill, the foremost Parliamentary reformer of this period not of the House[2].

In the period between Vernon's characterisation of the House Effect and that of Horace Walpole, the influences described by both were of Public more or less continuously at work. All through these years county Opinion. members were to some degree amenable to public opinion in their constituencies, and they formed the most independent element in the House. In by far the majority of the boroughs local public opinion had little or no weight. But in the larger boroughs public opinion at times made itself felt, and the representatives from these constituencies could not go heedlessly through a Parliament without keeping their re-election in mind. The influence thus exercised on the House may have been fitful; but, as the instances which have been quoted show, it told on many occasions both against legislation which was proposed by government, and in favour of legislation for which there was a popular demand. This influence defeated the excise bill of 1733, and brought about the repeal of the Act for the naturalisation of Jews of 1754. It carried the Place Act of 1742, as well as several of the measures in the interest of economy

[1] Vernon, *Correspondence,* III. 113.
[2] Cf. Walpole, *Last Journals,* II. 429.

and of a purer electoral system, which were passed in the years immediately following the downfall of North. Thenceforward the House of Commons became by degrees more continuously amenable to public opinion. Even in the reactionary period between the French Revolution and the peace after Waterloo, public opinion was generally with Parliament and with the repressive legislation which marked those years. After 1817 popular opinion gradually worked back into the mood of the period between the downfall of North and the French Revolution. Again, as immediately before and after the general election of 1780, there were popular demands for reform. From 1780 to 1782 the demand was summed up in the phrase " Economy and Reform." After Waterloo there was once more a popular cry for economy ; parliamentary reform was again agitated, and the cause now began to make converts. From this time may be dated the origin of the cry " Peace, Retrenchment, and Reform," which survived as the campaign slogan of the Liberals until after the Reform Act of 1867. The movement for reform gradually made headway, and in 1832 public opinion achieved its last and greatest triumph in the history of the old representative system.

CHAPTER XIV.

LETTERS BETWEEN MEMBERS AND CONSTITUENTS.

It was always a theory of the representative system that there Intercourse was frequent intercourse between members and constituents, and between Members this theory survived long after the early laws requiring that and Con- members should be resident in the constituencies they represented stituencies. had fallen into desuetude; and after the Septennial Act had lengthened the duration of Parliaments, and it had become usual, at least with many borough members, not to visit their constituencies between one general election and the next.

The privilege of sending and receiving letters post-free, which Privilege of members of the House of Commons enjoyed from the Common- Franking. wealth to the early years of the reign of Queen Victoria, arose out of the theory as to the frequency of communication with constituents. In the eighteenth century this theory was accepted as accounting for the origin and as warranting the continuance of the privilege. "Supposing it true," said Sir William Yonge, in opposing in 1745 a motion in the House of Commons for annual Parliaments, "that some members never see their constituents from the time they are chosen until they return to solicit their votes at a new election, which I believe is very rarely the case, is there not, or may there not be, a constant intercourse by letter? Are not all letters from or to members of Parliament made free of postage for this very purpose[1]?" That this was also the official eighteenth century view of the origin and use of franks is proved by a letter of 1784 from Lord Sydney, secretary of state for the southern department, to the Duke of Rutland, Lord Lieutenant of

[1] *Parl. Hist.*, xiii. 1077.

Ireland. It was written at a time when members of the Irish Parliament were agitating for the privilege of franking letters during their sojourn in England. Lord Sydney informed the Duke of Rutland that the request of the Irish members could not be granted. "Privilege of franking," he wrote, "had its original foundation in the necessary communication between the representative and the constituent. That principle cannot with any reason be extended to English members franking in Ireland, or the Irish members franking in England[1]."

Establishment of the Franking Privilege. The earliest record of the enjoyment by members of the House of Commons of the privilege of sending and receiving letters free by post is in 1658. The Commonwealth Parliament then ordered that "the post letters directed to the several members of this House be brought to the door of this House, and that they be free from postage as formerly"; and "that the letters of the several members of this House that go to the several parts of England, Scotland and Ireland, be also free from postage[2]." At the Restoration, when there was an Act for the settlement of the post-office revenues, the privilege which members of Parliament had enjoyed during the Commonwealth was continued. A proviso was inserted which directed "that all letters which at any time hereafter shall be sent by or unto any of the knights, citizens, and burgesses, chosen and continuing to be members of the Parliament of England, shall be freely and without any charge unto them safely carried and conveyed by every letter post established by this Act, according to the directions of the said letter, anything in the said Act notwithstanding[3]."

Marvell's Letters to Hull. After the privilege of franking had thus been established by statute it is possible, in respect to a few borough constituencies, to trace more frequent communications by letter than hitherto between members and their constituents. Marvell's famous letters to the corporation of Hull began in 1660 and were continued until 1678. When Parliament was in session Marvell wrote by every post, and no London correspondent of the present day could possibly serve his paper better or more loyally than Marvell served the corporation of Hull, when acting as its London and Parliamentary correspondent. He did not confine himself to political matters, local or general. He sent commercial and shipping news of interest and value to Hull. He told what was doing in London;

---

[1] *Hist. MSS. Comm. 14th Rep.*, pt. i. 79.   [2] Parry, 517, 518.
[3] *H. of C. Journals*, ii. 212.

and he also forwarded for the information of the corporation reports of Parliamentary committees, copies of resolutions, proclamations, and speeches from the throne.

Municipal corporations apparently appreciated extra-Parliamentary services such as Marvell rendered to Hull. The corporation there made many presents to its member. It sent him Hull-brewed ale and salmon from the Humber, in addition to regularly paying him his Parliamentary wages[1]. In 1677, when Henry Savile became member for Newark, his brother, Viscount Halifax, advised him to write often to the corporation and to send it speeches from the throne, addresses from the House, and other Parliamentary papers[2]. During the nine years, from 1694 to 1703, in which Henry Hervey was one of the members for Bury St Edmunds he kept up nearly as close a correspondence with the corporation there as Marvell had done with that of Hull[3]; and from 1697 to 1716 Peter Shakerley, one of the members for Chester, wrote frequently to the mayor and aldermen, and occasionally to the merchants of Chester, informing them of business before Parliament[4].

Letters from Members appreciated.

Henry Savile's correspondence with the corporation of Newark was of a spasmodic character ; and Marvell, Hervey, and Shakerley are the only members, so far as I can trace from municipal records and from letters, memoirs and biographies, who long maintained a close and regular correspondence with the corporations. Such correspondence as that of these members appears to have come to an end early in the eighteenth century. News-letter writing had become a profession in London in the last half of the seventeenth century, and the news-letter writers frequented the lobby of the House of Commons much as journalists do to-day. Their services of news were subscribed for by men of importance in the constituencies, and with the establishment of the news-letter, there was less need for letters, such as Marvell, Hervey and Shakerley wrote to their constituents. The need became still less as, in the middle years of the eighteenth century, news-letter writers were gradually superseded by the London newspapers. With individual electors members of the House of Commons must always have been in more or less frequent correspondence, especially members representing counties and larger commercial towns.

News-letters supersede Members' Letters.

[1] Marvell, *Works*, II. 585.   [2] Savile, *Correspondence*, 57.
[3] Hervey, *Letter-Books*.
[4] *Hist. MSS. Comm. 8th Rep.*, 394–396.

Franking Privilege early abused.

While the privilege of franking was of advantage to members in enabling them to keep in touch with their constituents, it was from the first greatly abused. As early as 1711 complaint was made by the postmaster-general that the system had led to fraud by booksellers and other tradesmen, who endorsed letters and newspapers with the names of members of Parliament to the prejudice of the revenue[1]. There was a similar complaint in 1717, when the postmaster-general reported to the treasury that the franks of the state departments amounted to about £8,270, and "the members' letters to £17,470[2]."

Franks in the Eighteenth Century.

In the first eighty or eighty-five years of the eighteenth century, for one frank which was used in accordance with the theory on which the privilege had been established, it would appear that a hundred were used for social purposes, or in connection with the professional or business interests of members. In reading eighteenth and early nineteenth century memoirs and letters one wonders who then paid postage, and from what sources the revenue of the post-office was derived. Apparently nobody paid postage who was within reach of a member of Parliament on whom he could establish a claim for a frank. News-writers, who frequented the lobby, counterfeited franks when they could not obtain them from members[3]. Wealthy squires wrote to correspondents in London asking them to get their Parliamentary friends to frank covers wholesale for their booksellers, in order that Parliamentary papers, gazettes and new books might be regularly forwarded to them[4]. Fashionable ladies demanded franks by the score. "I have been so silly," wrote Mrs Delaney to one of her friends in 1749, "as to forget franks. I must beg the favour of you to get a dozen or two for me from Sir Charles Mordaunt. You will find paper in the middle drawer of the walnut table in my closet. A dozen will do if I am to see you soon[5]." Members who were sick in bed were worried with requests for franks[6]; and it was a common occurrence for them to receive letters from their friends with enclosures to be transmitted under franks[7].

---

[1] *Cal. Treasury Papers, 1708–14*, 332.

[2] *Cal. Treasury Papers, 1714–19*, 287.

[3] Cf. *H. of C. Journals*, x. 801.

[4] Cf. *Hist. MSS. Comm. 12th Rep.*, App., pt. ii. 418.

[5] Mrs Delaney, *Correspondence*, ii. 511.

[6] Walpole, *Letters*, vii. 402.

[7] Walpole, *Letters*, iv. 99; Wilberforce, *Correspondence*, i. 195, 196.

A new member of the House often used his first frank to convey to his wife or his mother the news of his election. Scott, afterwards Lord Eldon, after his election for Weobly in 1783, delayed sending news of his success to his mother and sisters until he had taken his seat, " lest there should be a difficulty about the postage[1]." " I write to you forthwith," reads Bulwer Lytton's letter to his mother, after his election for St Ives in 1831 ; " I am returned to Parliament this day and hour. Post waits. This is my first frank[2]." These first franks were frequently much cherished by their recipients. " How kind and flattering was it of you," wrote Sir J. E. Smith to Roscoe, who was elected in 1806 for Liverpool, " to write to me the very day, when you must have been so busy, so agitated, and so fatigued. Your letter and especially your first frank will be kept by me as relics[3]."

The right of a member to frank began as soon as the returning- officer's writ or precept was made out in his favour ; and when once members had enjoyed what Bulwer Lytton described as the " right divine to post-office immunities," they and their families and friends were loath to part with the privilege. Cave, who will always have a place in eighteenth century literary history as the owner of the *Gentleman's Magazine,* and as the employer of Johnson, was for many years supervisor of franks. In 1735, when he was before a Parliamentary committee, which was inquiring into the abuse of the franking privilege, he stated that his experience, which went back to 1721, was that franks increased in number with every new Parliament. " Those who were in the last Parliament, but not of the new one," he stated, " did not willingly part with the privilege of franking, and by the acquaintance they still had in the House of Commons, they obtained blank franks[4]." After the general election in 1784, at which Lord Sheffield, who was an Irish peer, failed of election at Coventry, Maria Holroyd, his daughter, confided to one of her correspondents that she was not reconciled to a loss of franks. " I love the liberty," she wrote, " of enclosing letters, and of scribbling as much as I please." When in 1796 this same young lady became engaged to Mr Stanley, afterwards Lord Stanley of Alderley, who at this time represented Wootton Bassett,

---

[1] Twiss, *Life of Lord Eldon,* i. 104, 105.

[2] Lytton, *Life, Letters, and Literary Remains of Edward Bulwer, Lord Lytton,* i. 603.

[3] Sir J. E. Smith, *Memoirs and Correspondence,* ii. 303.

[4] *Parl. Hist.,* ix. 846.

a relative at Bath asked was Mr Stanley of the House of Commons?
Maria Holroyd answered the question with another.   " How could
he frank if he was not in Parliament[1] ? "

Business
and Social
Advantages.

The privilege of franking added much to the social consideration of a member of the House of Commons.   To men who were
in business it was of material advantage.   In the eighteenth century, when posts were slower, and when the world of commerce
moved at a more leisurely pace, it was the custom with many
business men who were of the Commons to have all their correspondence addressed to the House ; and it was stated in 1784,
when the franking privilege was about to be curtailed, that mercantile firms whose members were of the House saved from three
hundred to eight hundred pounds a year by the privilege which
they thus secured of having all their correspondence within the
kingdom carried postage free[2].   At this time the most exaggerated
estimates were popularly current as to the annual cost to the
country of the privilege which members of Parliament enjoyed.
The figures were put as high as £300,000 or £400,000 ; but
Mr Pulteney stated, in the discussion which preceded the revision
in 1784, that the abolition of franking would not save the country
more than £40,000 a year[3].

Curtailments
of the
Privilege.

On two or three occasions during the last seventy years of the
unreformed Parliament the franking system was revised with a view
to checking its abuses.   In 1760 the House of Lords deleted the
franking proviso which had stood in the post-office Acts since the
Restoration.   The Commons accepted the bill as thus amended on
the understanding, however, with the ministers of the crown, that
the privilege should be continued by royal warrant.   It was so
continued, but a two-ounce limit was then imposed on letters sent
under Parliamentary franks[4].   In 1784 there was another revision
of the privilege, by which it was made obligatory on members to
write on a frank the place, day, month, and year, of its issue[5]   In
1795 a member of the House, who was too infirm to write, was
reprimanded for having permitted his wife and son to frank in
his name.   At this time Lord Sheffield, who was then prominent
as a political economist, urged on Pitt the desirability of abolishing

[1] Adeane, *Girlhood of Maria Joseph Holroyd*, 386.
[2] *Parl. Hist.*, xxiv. 1331.
[3] *Parl. Hist.*, xxiv. 1331.
[4] Townsend, *Hist. House of Commons*, i. 330.
[5] Wraxall, *Posthumous Reminiscences*, 140.

the privilege[1]. No other change was made, however, than the
establishment of a list of the members who, in consequence of
bodily infirmity, had appointed some other person to frank in
their name[2].

Abuses still continued; and in 1802 the system was again The Abuses
revised by Act of Parliament. The number of letters that a member abated.
might send within the United Kingdom was now restricted to ten
a day, and the number that he might receive to fifteen. None of
these letters was to exceed one ounce in weight; and, in the
case of letters franked by a member, none was to be exempt from
postage unless the whole superscription were in his handwriting[3].
All letters over ten which were franked by a member were
charged to the recipients, and it became the rule of the post-
office to select the heaviest letters for payment[4]. Members were
still worried for franks by their friends. Men with great fortunes
still delayed writing, even to their wives, until they could obtain
"the palliative of a frank," and members of Parliament who were
of country-house parties were still expected to frank the correspondence of their fellow-guests[5]. But the abuse, so far as
letters were concerned, was greatly checked by the Act of 1802;
for, while not refusing franks, it was always possible for a member
to hint that the frank he was bestowing was the nineteenth or
twentieth he had given that day[6], and thereby to put the recipient
of the favour in a dilemma as to whether it was safe to make use
of it.

From 1763, in addition to franking letters, members of Par- Franking of
liament had enjoyed the privilege of receiving and sending news- Newspapers.
papers through the post without charge, provided the newspapers
were signed on the outside by the hand of the member, or directed
to any member at any place whereof he should have given notice in
writing to the postmaster-general. The requirement as to giving
notice to the post-office of the place to which newspapers might be
addressed gradually fell into desuetude, and if a member's name
appeared on the cover newspapers were sent free to all parts of the
kingdom. This provision of the franking system was for many
years grossly abused, as it enabled printers and booksellers to send

---

[1] Adeane, *Girlhood of Maria J. Holroyd*, 318.
[2] *H. of C. Journals*, L. 384. [3] 42 Geo. III, c. 63.
[4] Hall, *Retrospect of a Long Life*, 80.
[5] Trevelyan, *Life and Letters of Macaulay*, I. 141.
[6] Cf. Hall, *Retrospect of a Long Life*, 80.

newspapers free by post merely by directing them to some member of the House of Lords or the House of Commons, at the address of the person who subscribed for the newspaper[1]. This mode of securing free transmission of newspapers was widely advertised, intended subscribers being informed by publishers that they could receive a newspaper, postage free, by having it directed to some member of Parliament, to quote from one of these advertisements, "at the person's residence for whom it is intended, in the usual manner of franked newspapers[2]." Much reform literature in the shape of newspapers was circulated in this way, the papers being ostensibly addressed to Earl Grey and other reformers in Parliament at the homes of the persons for whom the papers were intended.

Abolition of the Franking Privilege.　　The privilege enjoyed by members of Parliament of sending and receiving letters and newspapers free survived the Reform Act of 1832; and in 1837 it was computed by Sir Roland Hill that the number of franked communications was about seven million four hundred thousand, and those on which postage was collected eighty-six million six hundred thousand[3]. With the franked letters were included, of course, the correspondence of the various state departments. In 1840, after the establishment of the penny post, and the introduction of adhesive stamps as a means of prepaying postage, the "right divine to post-office immunities," enjoyed for nearly two centuries by members of Parliament, was abolished by Act of Parliament[4]; and since then members of the House of Commons, in communicating with their constituents, or in other correspondence on public or private business, have had to prepay their letters in the ordinary way.

Franking in the United States and Canada.　　The franking privilege still survives in the United States and in several of the British colonies, where the seventeenth and eighteenth century theory as to ease and frequency of communication between elected and electors was adopted, in company with many other usages and forms of the Parliament at Westminster. At Washington and Ottawa the privilege of franking is abused in rather a different way from the abuses which characterised the system in England in the eighteenth century. In these days of universal cheap postage Congressmen at Washington and members of Parliament at Ottawa are not worried to the extent that English members of Parliament were by individual applicants for franks;

---

[1] *Notes and Queries*, September 25th, 1869, 267; October 23rd, 1869, 348.

[2] *Bell's Weekly Messenger*, May 13th, 1813.

[3] *Westminster Review*, July, 1860, 33.　　　　[4] 3 and 4 Vict., c. 96.

but from both political capitals, on the eve of elections, tons of partisan literature are distributed broadcast over the country, through the post-office, by the use of members' franks. Even in some of the Canadian provincial legislatures, which have no control over the Dominion post-office, the old theory as to communication between elected and electors still survives. In the Chamber of the Legislature of the Province of Ontario at Toronto, there is to-day a large basket which, when the House is in session, stands under the clerk's table. Into this basket members throw the letters which they write on public business. At frequent intervals during the sitting of the House the basket is emptied and the letters are stamped at the charge of the Province. This plan does not meet the case of constituents who desire to communicate with their representatives; but it relieves the representatives of postal charges in their public correspondence, and to that extent is in accordance with the constitutional theory on which the franking privilege was established and maintained in England from the time of the Protector to the reign of Queen Victoria.

CHAPTER XV.

MEMBERS, ELECTORS AND THE CIVIL SERVICE.

Members distribute Government Patronage.

BETWEEN the Revolution and the Reform Act of 1832 members of the House of Commons came into a new and extra-constitutional relation with their constituents. They became the channel through which appointments in the civil service were obtained. They nominated to many offices in the state departments in London; and they gradually asserted, and had conceded to them when they were supporting the ministry, the exclusive right to nominate to all government offices, such as customs and revenue collectorships and postmasterships within the limits of their constituencies. The relation of members to government patronage on the eve of the Reform Act is described in a letter from the Duke of Wellington to Sir Robert Peel, at the time that Wellington was premier, and Peel was secretary of state for the home department. "The whole system of patronage of the Government," wrote Wellington, "is in my opinion erroneous. Certain members claim a right to dispose of everything that falls vacant within the town or county which they represent; and this is so much a matter of right that they now claim the patronage whether they support upon every occasion, or now and then, or when not required, or entirely oppose; and in fact the only question about local patronage is whether it shall be given to the disposal of one gentleman or another[1]."

System dating from 1693.

Dorman B. Eaton, an American writer who has the distinction of being the author of the only exhaustive history of the British

[1] Parker, *Sir Robert Peel*, II. 140.

civil service, dates the time at which patronage began to pass into the hands of members of the House of Commons and of men exercising Parliamentary influence from 1693, when the Cabinet system of government was originated; and he shows that this method of appointing to public office was continued without fundamental change, though somewhat modified in detail, for one hundred and sixty years, or until 1853, when the first elements of the merit system, the system we now know as that of public competitive examination, were tentatively introduced[1]. My own research has not enabled me to discover any proof of this new relation between members and electors as existing at an earlier period than that thus fixed by the American historian of the civil service. Long before this time candidates for the House of Commons had sought to bribe constituents by promising various government favours, promises like those which I have described in a preceding chapter. They promised that townspeople should not have soldiers billeted upon them; that the men of the borough should not be pressed for the navy; and, in the case of the ports on the southern and eastern coasts, that convoys should be furnished for local shipping.

As early as 1689 electors were apparently looking to members of Parliament for aid in securing appointments in the civil service[2]. But the first instance that I have found in which a candidate sought to bribe individual electors by undertaking to obtain places for them under the Crown, occurred at Abingdon in 1698, when William Hucks contested the borough with Simeon Harcourt. Harcourt was returned. Hucks petitioned; but in the hearing of the case it was proved that a letter from Hucks had been read " at the news-house" at Abingdon, in which he promised that, if he were elected, the lords of the admiralty would protect the Abingdon watermen and bargemen from being pressed for the navy, that the people should have no soldiers quartered upon them; and in this letter, moreover, Hucks stated that if he became a member of Parliament, he would be made a commissioner of the excise, and by that means could make several of the electors officers under him[3]. Hucks was unsuccessful in his petition; and on a report being made to the House of the promises he had made to the electors, it was resolved " that the proceeding of

A Candidate's Promises in 1698.

---

[1] Cf. Eaton, *Civil Service in Great Britain*, 75.

[2] Cf. *Hist. MSS. Comm. 11th Rep.*, App., pt. vii. 35, 37.

[3] Cf. *H. of C. Journals*, xii. 543; Luttrell, iv. 489.

William Hucks, Esq., in presuming to make use of the authority of the Government in order to be elected a burgess for the said borough, is a scandalous reflection upon the Government, and tends to subvert the freedom of election of members to serve in Parliament"; and it was further ordered that Hucks "be committed to the custody of the sergeant at arms[1]."

Patronage passes into Hands of Members.
Soon after the establishment of the party system in 1693 it is possible to trace the efforts of members of Parliament to obtain official patronage for bestowal on electors, and to discern the result of this new form of bribery. "As the power of Parliament and of popular opinion increased," wrote Eaton, "the House of Commons more and more encroached upon the old prerogative of the executive, and in a similar manner, of course, upon its patronage. Members seeking patronage naturally conditioned their support of aspirants for seats in the cabinet upon pledges of such patronage, and here we have the origin of members of the legislature dictating local appointments[2]"—the system, it may be added, of distributing local patronage described by Wellington in his letter of 1828 to Peel.

Increase in Amount of Patronage.
As population increased and the old system of raising national revenues by taxes levied on the towns and collected by the municipal officers gave place in the early years of the eighteenth century to the modern form of collecting all imperial revenues through the customs houses and excise department, there were large increases in the number of civil servants in London and in the districts into which the country was divided for customs and inland revenue. Soon after the Revolution all these offices came to be regarded as political spoils, and were bestowed chiefly through members of the House of Commons or their patrons on electors, or in the interest of electors, as bribes for support which was to be given, or for votes which had already been given, at Parliamentary elections. As the eighteenth century advanced Irish, colonial, and Indian patronage, and the patronage of the Church, the law establishments, and the post-office, as well as many military and naval appointments, all came to be treated as spoils, and bartered for Parliamentary support.

Distribution of Patronage.
This patronage went chiefly to the corporation and smaller freeman boroughs. In the burgage boroughs there was usually little need for patronage for electors. Money bribes were the electioneering currency generally in use in the boroughs where

---

[1] *H. of C. Journals*, xii. 543.   [2] Eaton, 75.

the burgages remained in the hands of individual electors, and were not controlled in the aggregate by local landowners or by speculative borough-masters. In the large scot and lot boroughs voters were too numerous for elections to be much influenced by the distribution of government offices. But in the corporation and freeman boroughs there was a permanent field for local political managers, whose goodwill and active influence at elections could be secured by postmasterships, by appointments in the customs and inland revenue departments, by government clerkships in London, and by the smaller crown livings in the Church—livings which members of Parliament and favoured borough patrons were able at times to secure for bestowal on local clergymen who were helpful to them, or on the sons and nephews of men with sufficient local political influence to turn the scale at a Parliamentary election[1].

In the preceding century, before the spoils system had worked its way into the electorate, crown livings had gone chiefly to the chaplains and tutors of aristocratic families. From about 1700 parish clergymen began to come into competition with these hitherto highly favoured chaplains and tutors[2]. The keenness of the new competition and the alertness of the competitors are indicated in a letter, dated April 30th, 1702, from the Rev. Thomas Roe, of Castleton, to Thomas Coke, who was one of the members for Derbyshire. "As to my own concerns," wrote Roe, after telling Coke that he would not be remiss in any service he could render in the next election, and that he was already canvassing Edale, "I would not have been so troublesome had I a competency here, or could I be easy with what I have. I have a catalogue of some livings in the Queen's and Lord Chancellor's gifts, which I have underneath sent you. If it be feasible for you to get a promise of the first of 'em that becomes void, as I am informed is frequently done on like occasion, some of 'em cannot but fall in in a little time, most of the incumbents being aged persons[3]." There were nineteen crown livings in the list which Roe forwarded to Coke. In the same correspondence there is a letter, also written in 1702, from Walter Horton, of Derby,

[margin:] Church Patronage.

---

[1] Cf. *Municipal Corp. Comm. 1835, 1st Rep.*, App., pt. III. 1871; pt. IV. 349, 403, 407, 411, 415, 420, 2087, 2206, 2262-63, 2547; *Reports of the Civil Service Comm. 1854-55*, VI. 180.

[2] Cf. Torrens, *Hist. of Cabinets*, I. 475.

[3] *Hist. MSS. Comm. 12th Rep.*, App., pt. III. 6.

who desired Coke to procure for him the next vacancy of a canon residentiary at Gloucester. Horton recounted no political services in Coke's behalf; but his sentiments towards the sitting member were expressed in the concluding paragraph of his letter. " Permit me to pray," it reads, " that you may long continue what you really are, a support to the Church, and an ornament and defence to the state, and a patriot to all honest men[1]."

Clergy and Borough-Masters.

Every considerable eighteenth century borough-master had clergymen in his train. This was the case with the Duke of Richmond in Queen Anne's reign[2]; with Lord Townshend[3] and Dodington[4] in the reign of George II; and Lowther[5] in the reign of George III.

Bishops and Electioneering.

In political conduct the clergy only followed the example of the bishops, who with an eye more to the fleece than the flock, paved the way to translation from one see to a better by their votes in the House of Lords, and by their direct or indirect interference in elections. Lloyd, Bishop of Worcester, was censured in 1702 by the House of Commons for conduct at the county election which was characterised as " malicious, unchristian and arbitrary," and " in high violation of the liberties and privileges of the commons of England[6]." At one time or another in his career as election manager, the Duke of Newcastle had the aid of Sherlock, whom he had raised from the deanery of Chichester to the bishopric of Bangor[7]; of Hare, Bishop of Chichester[8]; and of Peploe, Bishop of Chester[9]. Sherlock, while at Bangor, in 1733 used the influence he had obtained as Dean of Chichester in behalf of the Duke's candidate for the County of Sussex; and in the following year he was promoted to the bishopric of Salisbury[10]. At the same election Hare was writing electioneering literature in defence of the excise bill[11]; while at the general election of 1739 Peploe of Chester, " who did not forget to whom he owed his first mitre, and believing in the possibility of advancement to a richer one," furnished Newcastle " with copious details of how

---

[1] *Hist. MSS. Comm. 12th Rep.*, App., pt. III. 15.

[2] Cf. *H. of C. Journals*, XVII. 214.

[3] *Hist. MSS. Comm. 11th Rep.*, App., pt. I. 356.

[4] Dodington, *Diary*, 256, 260, 307.

[5] Henry Lonsdale, *Life of John Heysham, M.D.*, 99.

[6] *H. of C. Journals*, XIV. 37.

[7] Torrens, *Hist. of Cabinets*, I. 434.   [8] Torrens, *Hist. of Cabinets*, I. 436.

[9] Torrens, *Hist. of Cabinets*, I. 504.   [10] Torrens, *Hist. of Cabinets*, I. 434.

[11] Torrens, *Hist. of Cabinets*, I. 436.

he had managed to secure a majority of the chapter and choir"
at Chester, and how "Sir Watkin Wynn might best be baffled
in Cheshire, and even in Denbighshire[1]."

Sherlock of Bangor was so obviously the tool of Newcastle
in and out of Parliament that, following his speech from the
bishop's bench in the Lords against the pension bill, there was
a motion in the House of Commons on March 4th, 1731, for
leave to bring in a bill to prevent the translation of bishops.
The argument in support of the motion was that such a bill
was necessary to prevent a too great dependence of the bishops
on the Crown[2]. But the bill was aimed in particular at the
Bishop of Bangor[3]. No such bill was ever passed; and political
influence and political services in and out of Parliament, so long
as the old representative system survived, had much to do with
appointments to bishoprics and with translations from one see to
another.

A Bill to prevent the Translation of Bishops.

The Newcastle letters indicate the nature of the political services which the bishops could and did render to the Government
at election times; and there is more of the same kind of testimony,
but going back a little nearer to the Revolution, in the Le
Fleming manuscripts. Among these is a circular, issued by the
Bishop of Carlisle to the clergy in 1695, in behalf of Sir John
Lowther and Sir Christopher Mulgrave, calling on them to urge
their parishioners to support the re-election of these gentlemen
as knights of the shire for Westmorland[4]. In 1701 Compton,
Bishop of London, issued an appeal to the clergy to support
Sir Charles Barrington and Mr Bullock as knights of the shire
for Essex. "It will," the Bishop wrote, "be for the reputation
of the Church and for its service, if we be unanimous[5]." In 1710
Nicholson, Bishop of Carlisle, was declared by the House of
Commons to have "highly infringed the liberties and privileges of
Great Britain" by concerning himself in an election at his cathedral city[6]; and in 1711 it was stated in an election petition case
from Carlisle that the bishop had written a letter to all the
singing men at the cathedral, threatening their dismissal if they
voted at the election contrary to his wishes[7].

Earlier Activity of the Clergy.

---

[1] Torrens, *Hist. of Cabinets*, I. 504.   [2] *Parl. Hist.*, VIII. 858.

[3] *Parl. Hist.*, VIII. 858, footnote.

[4] *Hist. MSS. Comm. 12th Rep.*, App., pt. VII. 337.

[5] Ellis, *Original Letters of Eminent Literary Men of the Sixteenth, Seventeenth
and Eighteenth Centuries*, 192.

[6] *H. of C. Journals*, XVI. 548.   [7] Cf. *H. of C. Journals*, XVII. 106.

Bishops
and the
Treasury.

There were other methods by which the bishops could aid the fortunes of the Government. They could, and apparently sometimes did, turn over some of their patronage to the treasury, which never had sufficient spoils to go round. This way of accommodating the treasury is suggested by a letter of 1809 from Tomline, Bishop of Lincoln, to Rose, who at this time was treasurer of the navy, and who since 1784 had been active in electioneering in behalf of the Government[1]. "As this vacancy (the perpetual curacy of Stony Stratford) was not expected," wrote the bishop, "the preferment is of course at liberty, and allow me to say that, if you have any friend suited to the situation for whom you wish to make provision, I shall have great pleasure in accepting your recommendation[2]."

Evil Effect
on the
Church.

Bishops and clergy were so actively concerned in politics in the closing half of the eighteenth century that friends of the Church wished that it were modelled in some particulars after the Church in Scotland. "The Scotch clergy," reads a letter of 1770, which is among the Round manuscripts, "are models to ours for residence and watchfulness. Not because they are better men naturally, but because their stipends are nearly equal. They are above want, but cannot have pluralities, and cannot expect to be translated. If our bishoprics were of nearly equal value, it would answer the purpose here[3]." Such an equalisation of bishoprics would have rendered unnecessary the bill of 1731 for the prevention of the translation of bishops. Men of the world like George Selwyn took a less sympathetic view of all this obviously interested electioneering activity of the bishops and clergy. "The clergy," wrote Selwyn in one of his letters to Lord Carlisle, "are as so many turnspits, ready to be put into the wheel, and to turn it around as the minister pleases[4]"; while Pitt, in the first year of his premiership, described ecclesiastical preferments as the greatest plague of his official life[5].

Dodington
and Crown
Livings.

Bubb Dodington, who in the reign of George II, when the Duke of Newcastle was electioneering agent-in-chief for the administration, controlled the boroughs of Bridgwater, Weymouth

---

[1] *Nat. Dict. Bio.*, xlix. 226, 227; Colchester, *Diary*, i. 49.

[2] Rose, *Diaries*, ii. 341.

[3] T. Falconer to Charles Gray, Chester, February 10th, 1770, *Hist. MSS. Comm. 14th Rep.*, App., pt. ix. 304.

[4] *Hist. MSS. Comm. 15th Rep.*, App., pt. vi. 441.

[5] Cf. Pitt to Rutland, April 21st, 1784, *Pitt and Rutland Correspondence*, 12.

and Melcombe Regis, has left a picture of the part played by crown livings at this time in borough management. "I saw the Duke of Newcastle," reads an entry in his diary on December 11th, 1753, "and convinced him that my trouble and expense at Bridgwater was only to keep out a man (the Earl of Egmont) who opposed those to whom I attached myself; that my own seat was not concerned in it; that the maintaining the interest there was to me nothing, having nobody to bequeathe it to. I then told him that in these matters those who would take money I would pay, and not bring him a bill. Those that would not take, he must pay; and I recommended my two parsons of Bridgwater and Weymouth, Burroughs and Franklin. He entered into it very cordially, and assured me that they should have the first crown livings that should be vacant in their parts, if we would look out and send him the first intelligence[1]." Dodington was too alert a borough-master to miss an opportunity of obtaining patronage through lack of vigilance, or for want of persistency at the treasury. Only six weeks later there occurs an entry of another call on the Duke. "Went to the Duke of Newcastle," it reads, "and got the living of Broadway for Mr Burroughs[2]." Burroughs must have been active in Bridgwater politics, or he would never have had Dodington's interest at the treasury; and a later entry in the diary shows that soon after Dodington's successful efforts there in his behalf, Burroughs was in London, and in correspondence with Newcastle regarding electioneering at Bridgwater, where the fortunes of Dodington were still threatened by Lord Egmont[3].

Nowhere was the civil and naval patronage of the Government more generally and continuously turned to account for electioneering purposes than in the ports on the eastern and southern coasts, especially in those ports, such as Queenborough, Harwich, and Sandwich, which were naval depots, post-office stations, or government dockyards, and were known, so long as the old electoral system survived, as treasury or admiralty boroughs. At these ports useless vessels were retained of the establishment, solely that they might afford sinecure places as masters and mates for freemen who controlled the elections[4]. In 1788 it was stated by Alderman Sawbridge in the House of Commons that the Government paid out at Queenborough, a freeman constituency with four hundred electors, eighteen thousand pounds a year for

Patronage in the Admiralty Boroughs.

---

[1] Dodington, *Diary*, 256.   [2] Dodington, *Diary*, 260.
[3] Dodington, *Diary*, 307.   [4] Cf. *Parl. Hist.*, xxvi. 1310.

services that could have been obtained for six hundred pounds[1]. In eight Parliaments subsequent to 1768, covering a period of more than forty years, Sandwich was represented by Sir Philip Stephens, secretary to the admiralty. "The voters were bound to this gentleman by every tie of gratitude," wrote Oldfield, "as there is scarcely a single family connected with Sandwich, which has not been provided for by him in the admiralty, navy or marines[2]."

Disfranchise-
ment of
Revenue
Officers.

In the reign of Queen Anne postmasters were excluded from the franchise by Act of Parliament[3]. In 1782 customs and revenue officers were similarly disfranchised[4]. There had been an agitation for their exclusion from the electorate in 1768. Then it was proposed to extend the scope of a bribery bill so as to bring about the disfranchisement of these officers. George III, who knew the value of civil servants at election times, and how many boroughs were swayed by their votes, opposed the extension of the bribery bill, as for some years to come he opposed every movement for the purification or reform of the electoral system. "The instruction moved for the committee on the bribery bill relative to the votes of customs house and other officers having places under the Crown," wrote the King, "seems very extraordinary, and can have been proposed solely from a motive of showing an inclination to be impertinent, and to run after that empty shadow of popularity[5]."

Use of
Patronage
unchecked.

On the eve of the Act of 1782 Lord Nugent, who opposed the bill, stated that there were forty thousand revenue officers; and another opponent put the number at sixty thousand[6]. The exclusion of these office-holders from the franchise, an exclusion which was continued until 1868, although the most serious blow that had, up to this time, been administered to government interest in elections[7], did not prevent the use of the offices as patronage by members of the House of Commons. Nor did the Act of 1782 put an end to the interested activity of civil servants at Parliamentary elections. The bestowal of patronage continued as before to be a form of electoral bribery. Offices still went to those who had electoral influence; and not until 1809[8] was it declared by statute to be an

[1] Cf. *Parl. Hist.*, xxvii. 412.   [2] Oldfield, v. 394.
[3] 10 Anne, c. 31.   [4] 22 Geo. III, c. 41.
[5] George III to Lieutenant-General Conway, Ellis, *Original Letters Illustrative of English History*, 3rd Series, iv. 385.
[6] Cf. *Parl. Hist.*, xxii. 1337–42.
[7] Cf. Lecky, *England in the Eighteenth Century*, iv. 235.
[8] 49 Geo. III, c. 118.

act of bribery for a Parliamentary candidate to promise an office or employment under the Crown in order to influence an election.

The extent and nature of the work which in the early years of the nineteenth century was thrown upon members by the then prevailing system of distributing patronage, is indicated in letters from Wilberforce and Roscoe. While Wilberforce was member for the undivided county of Yorkshire, then the largest constituency in England, Yorkshiremen had always free access to him[1]; and he was so conscientious in the discharge of his Parliamentary duties that he refused all social invitations for days on which the House sat. He regularly stayed through each sitting of the House, snatching a hasty meal between the end of private and the beginning of public business; saw nothing of his family during the session; and stayed until the last day of it, every year for twenty-three or twenty-four years[2]. But while Wilberforce thus regarded his duties to his constituents and to the House, he declined any responsibilities or duties in connection with the seeking or bestowal of government patronage. "Unless I had laid down to myself the rule of declining to ask favours for my constituents," he wrote to Pitt in 1805, "there never would have been a week in which I should not have had to pester you with some solicitation or other[3]." *Wilberforce and Patronage.*

Roscoe, who had long been a Parliamentary reformer, who was elected for Liverpool in 1806, and who supported the Coalition Ministry, "the Ministry of all the Talents," took another view of a member's responsibility in connection with patronage. "You are right," he wrote to a correspondent soon after his election, "in supposing that the applications from Liverpool for places are very numerous. I divide them, however, into two classes—first such as relate to places already vacant, for which the applicant brings good recommendation; and secondly, such as require a good place, a tolerable place, an easy place, a place in the customs, or in short any place that may happen to offer. To the first of these I think myself bound to pay attention, and have not hesitated, where I thought the persons proper, to recommend them to His Majesty's ministers. But in the latter cases it is impossible for me to do anything, as I could scarcely expect that they would promise me the reversion of a place not yet vacant; but on which *Roscoe and Applicants for Office.*

[1] Wilberforce, *Correspondence*, ii. 80.
[2] Wilberforce, *Correspondence*, ii. 81, 82.
[3] Wilberforce, *Correspondence*, i. 292.

some provident expectant might have set his eye[1]." Of another Lancashire member, John Blackburne, who represented the county from 1784 to 1830, it is recorded that during these forty-six years he "asked and received only two favours of the Governments which he supported, viz., the wardenship of Manchester for his second, and the office of distributor of stamps for his third brother[2]."

Scramble for Patronage.   Comparatively few members of the House of Commons seem to have stood aside, as Wilberforce, Blackburne and Roscoe did, from the scramble for patronage which increasingly characterised Parliamentary life throughout the eighteenth century, and in fact until an end was made in 1853 to the system of treating offices as spoils which had been developed in the preceding one hundred and fifty years. When candidates promised electors in small boroughs —as was done at Malmesbury in 1722—that they would obtain for one member of the corporation " a place under Government of one hundred pounds, which might in a little time be five hundred pounds a year," and that another should have bestowed upon him " the first crown living worth one hundred and fifty pounds a year[3]," the promises could not go unfulfilled ; and as soon as members who had obtained their seats by this form of bribery threw in their lot with the Government, they were compelled to dance attendance on the treasury in order to obtain offices with which to make good their promises.

Patronage Secretary.   The pressure on the treasury soon became so great that a broker-general in offices, who subsequently became officially known as the patronage secretary of the treasury, had to be installed, whose duty it was to stand between members and borough-masters appealing for places for electors on the one side, and the heads of the state departments who had offices in their bestowal on the other. " This secretary," according to Eaton's history of the office created to meet the exigencies of the spoils system, " measured the force of threats and took the weight of influence. He computed the political value of a member's support, and deducted from it the official appraisement of the patronage before awarded to him. It is said that actual accounts, debtor and creditor, were kept with members by the patronage secretary. Degrading as such an arrangement was, it was better than to have members of Parliament going from department to department and from office to office, now

[1] Henry Roscoe, *Life of William Roscoe*, i. 387.
[2] Axon, *Annals of Manchester*, 166.
[3] Cf. *H. of C. Journals*, xx. 78.

suggesting favours and then assaults in Parliament, here using threats and there persuasion in aid of their purpose of foisting a dependent or an electioneering agent upon the public treasury. This comptroller-general of patronage continued in full sway until competitive examinations, upon the introduction of the merit system, had made an end to patronage. He still (1880) feebly survives; but only as a withered skeleton of the great political potentate which he once was, in whose presence members took off their hats, and their dependents fell to their knees[1]."

With the civil service as it existed under these conditions, and with its reform in the middle of the nineteenth century, I am not here concerned. My concern in this chapter has been with the relations between elected and electors which grew out of the practical workings of the spoils theory of government patronage. But it need hardly be said that, during the era of the spoils system, appointments were made without regard to the ability or physical or mental fitness of the persons appointed. It could not be otherwise, when there was neither age limit nor any test of fitness, mental or physical; when a government clerkship was popularly regarded as a pension, as a sinecure in which little or no work was to be done[2]; when the men appointed well understood that office came to them as a direct or indirect political bribe; when men not infrequently told their official chiefs that they were not put into the service by their patrons to work[3]; when offices were sought chiefly for the unambitious, the indolent, or the incapable[4]; when it could happen that " out of eighty clerks supplied by the patronage secretary, there were not more than twelve who were worth their salt for the performance of services requiring only a sound common education[5]"; and when a third more clerks and messengers were carried on the pay-rolls than were required to do the work[6]. *Civil Service under the Spoils System.*

Appointments in government offices, while the civil service was thus in politics, were made in two ways. In a department which was under a political head appointments were in general made by the head of the department. Where a department was *Appointment to the Civil Service.*

---

[1] Eaton, *Civil Service in Great Britain*, 154.

[2] *Reports of the Civil Service Comm.* 1854–55, vi. 278.

[3] *Reports of the Civil Service Comm.* 1854–55, vi. 53–54.

[4] *Reports of the Civil Service Comm.* 1854–55, vi. 21, 22.

[5] *Reports of the Civil Service Comm.* 1854–55, vi. 181.

[6] *Reports of the Civil Service Comm.* 1854–55, vi. 236.

not under a political head the appointments were made nominally by the prime minister, but actually by the patronage secretary of the treasury. Appointments to offices in the inland revenue and customs departments were all made by the patronage secretary. The post-office had a political head; but, notwithstanding that fact, some of the appointments were of the spoils of which the patronage secretary had the distribution[1]. The relations of the treasury and the non-political departments with respect to appointments were like those of the patron of a living and the bishop. The treasury presented a candidate, and the department, if it thought fit, as it mostly did, instituted him into the office[2].

Civil Service from the Treasury Point of View.

The spirit in which patronage secretaries presented candidates, and the point of view from which the secretaries, as government whips in the House of Commons, regarded the civil service, are described in the Report from which the foregoing quotations have been taken. "Their own tenure of office, and that of their colleagues, high and low, and the political interests of the Government to which they belonged," reads the Report, "depend in no small degree upon their exertions. It is their province and their practice to endeavour to keep their own political party together, and to secure a majority in the House of Commons; to serve their own political friends; to grant them any little favours they may require; and to look upon any change of administration as involving far more important considerations to themselves and to the country than all the drudgery of the civil service put together. It is their duty to prevent, as far as it may be in their power to do so, a great catastrophe. No means, however trivial, are to be neglected for this object; and if it should happen that some treasury rule interferes with the prospects of some relative of an important political supporter, is there not some danger that the rule will be set aside, and the interest of the latter preferred[3]?"

The Army of Civil Servants.

At the time the civil service commissioners made their investigations, there were sixteen thousand civil appointments[4], not including stipendiary magistrates, consuls, metropolitan police, and appointments in the mint and in the office of the chief secretary for Ireland[5]. About seven hundred new appointments were made

[1] *Reports of the Civil Service Comm. 1854–55,* vi. 112, 113.
[2] *Reports of the Civil Service Comm. 1854–55,* vi. 114.
[3] *Reports of the Civil Service Comm. 1854–55,* vi. 270, 271.
[4] *Reports of the Civil Service Comm. 1854–55,* vi. 8.
[5] *Reports of the Civil Service Comm. 1854–55,* vi. 57.

each year[1]. The war office and the foreign office clerkships were chiefly held by younger sons of aristocratic families, appointed under much the same political conditions as clerks in the other government departments. Only a small proportion of the whole mass of patronage was obtained by the representatives of the county constituencies, or by aristocratic families. The larger and ever increasing portion was distributed by the members of Parliament from the smaller boroughs[2].

The kind of material which was passed into the departments was described in 1854 by a retired civil servant. "Many instances could be given," he wrote, "of young men, the sons of respectable parents who were found unable to read or write, and utterly ignorant of accounts. Two brothers, one almost imbecile, the other much below the average of intellect, long retained appointments, though never equal to higher work than the lowest description of copying. Another young man was found unable on entering to number the pages of a volume of official papers beyond ten. It used to be by no means uncommon to have a fine, fashionably dressed young man introduced as a junior clerk. On trial he turns out fit for nothing. The head of the department knows from old experience that a representation of this fact to higher quarters would merely draw down ill-will upon himself. The first official duty with which the young man is charged is therefore to take a month's leave of absence that he may endeavour to learn to write. Besides the imbecile who is below work, and the coxcomb who is above it, there are other kinds of unprofitable officers, including a large class who have ability enough if they would apply it. The public offices have been a resource for many an idle, dissipated youth with whom other occupations have been tried in vain. Such a person can be made of little use, whatever be his abilities, because he cannot be trusted. No one can tell to-day where he will be to-morrow. The ice is in fine condition, and he skates for a couple of days; a review tempts him; a water-party cannot be resisted; and after dancing all night he is not seen at the office next morning. In fact causes of absence are endless. Incessant altercation takes place with his superiors, with little effect, for he knows they cannot degrade him or dismiss him, as a merchant or banker would do, and he is proof against fines and minor punishments[3]."

Unprofitable Servants.

---

[1] *Reports of the Civil Service Comm.* 1854–55, VI. 15.

[2] *Reports of the Civil Service Comm.* 1854–55, VI. 180.

[3] *Reports of the Civil Service Comm.* 1854–55, VI. 181.

Abuses
regarded as
Inevitable.

The civil service had been so long in politics when its reform was agitated in 1854–55, that some civilians, who viewed the question from inside government departments, looked on the then existing conditions as inevitable, and were nervous lest any reform of the system of patronage would "disturb the working of our multiform constitution[1]." "I fear that the tendency to favouritism and what is vulgarly termed jobbing," wrote an under secretary of state for the foreign department, "must be looked upon as inherent in every system of government; as in truth the ineradicable vice of all governments, and that, if the former is the blot of despotic, the latter is the blot of constitutional governments. Jobbing is a part, though an ugly part, of the price which a free people pay for their constitutional liberty. So long as there are Parliamentary constituents they will ask favours of members of Parliament, and members of Parliament of ministers, and ministers will on their part have a tendency to satisfy such solicitants, if in their power[2]."

Effect of
the Spoils
System on
Parliament.

The effect of the spoils system on the representation, and the character of the relations which it established between the elected and electors, are also described in these reports of 1854–55. "Let anyone who has had experience," wrote the chairman of the board of inland revenue, "reflect on the operation of patronage on elections, Parliament, and the Government. Over each it exercises an evil influence. In the electors it interferes with the honest exercise of the franchise. In Parliament it encourages subservience to the administration; it impedes the free action of a Government desirous of pursuing an honest and economical course; and it occasions the employment of persons without regard to their peculiar fitness. It is a more pernicious system than the mere giving of money to electors or members of Parliament to secure their votes. It is bribery in its worst form[3]."

Effect on
Members.

On members personally the spoils system threw work which was more disagreeable and more wearing than any of their other duties[4]; and it was, as the American historian of our civil service has insisted, "inconsistent with that independence, dignity, and disinterestedness, which the people require in a legislator, as well as a bad use of valuable time and talents for a member of Parlia-

---

[1] *Reports of the Civil Service Comm.* 1854–55, VI. 70.

[2] *Reports of the Civil Service Comm.* 1854–55, VI. 357.

[3] *Reports of the Civil Service Comm.* 1854–55, VI. 302.

[4] Cf. *Reports of the Civil Service Comm.* 1854–55, VI. 229.

ment to act as an office or patronage broker, and to go about from department to department, and office to office, begging or bullying, to-day this and to-morrow that officer in order to make a place for perhaps a needy dependent or perhaps an unscrupulous and un-rewarded supporter at an election[1]."

The condition of the Church in the period when political sup- Effect on the port of the Government in Parliament or in the constituencies was Church. the surest way to promotion or preferment for bishops as well as clergy, when church patronage was treated as spoils, has been described by many historians, and by none perhaps more fairly or more sympathetically than by May. " For many years after the accession of George III," he writes, in treating of the period in the last half of the eighteenth century when industry in England was being enormously developed, and when the dissenters, Congre-gationalists, Baptists, Methodists, and Unitarians were becoming an increasing power in political and social as well as in religious life, " the Church continued her even course with little change of condition or circumstances. She was enjoying a tranquil and apparently prosperous existence. Favoured by the State and society ; threatened by no visible dangers ; dominant over Catholics and dissenters, and fearing no assaults upon her power or privileges, she was contented with the dignified security of the national estab-lishment. The more learned churchmen devoted themselves to classical erudition and scholastic theology ; the parochial clergy to an easy but generally decorous performance of their accustomed duties. The discipline of the church was facile and indulgent. Pluralities and non-residents were freely permitted, the ease of the clergy being more regarded than the spiritual welfare of the people. The parson farmed, hunted, shot the squire's partridges, drank his port wine, joined in the friendly rubber, and frankly entered into all the enjoyments of a country life. He was a kind and hearty man ; and if he had the means, his charity was open-handed. Ready at the call of those who sought spiritual consolation, he was not earnest in seeking out the spiritual needs of his flock. Zeal was not expected of him. Society was not prepared to exact it[2]."
" A benefice was regarded," May states elsewhere, " as an estate to which was attached the performance of certain ecclesiastical duties. These once performed—the service read, the weekly sermon preached, the child christened, the parishioner buried—and the parson differed

---

[1] Eaton, 173. [2] May, III. 208, 209.

little from the squire. He was generally...moral and well educated,
according to the standard of the age, in all but theology. But his
spiritual calling sat lightly upon him: zealous for Church and King,
and honestly hating dissenters, he was unconscious of a mission to
spread a knowledge of the Gospel among the people, to solve their
doubts, to satisfy their spiritual longings, and to attach their
spiritual sympathies to the Church[1]."

Effect of the
Reform of
the Civil
Service.

Even before the Reform Act of 1832, as has been shown in
preceding chapters, there were visible signs of a change for the
better in the relations between elected and electors. As a result of
successive Reform Acts and of public opinion, these relations are
now on a higher plane than ever before. Excepting only the drastic
bribery law of 1883, no change helped more to establish the existing
wholesome relations between constituents and their representatives
than the reforms in the civil service made subsequent to 1853.
They relieved the patronage secretary of the treasury of the larger
part of his most disagreeable duties; made it impossible for members of the House of Commons to act as office brokers for their
constituents; and in short lifted the civil service out of politics,
and ended what was obviously one of the most serious evils growing
out of the system of government by party.

[1] May, III. 64.

CHAPTER XVI

RELATIONS BETWEEN MEMBERS AND PATRONS.

THE political relations between members and constituents, Seats owed described in the preceding chapters, were neither uniform nor to Patrons. general. They could not be general, for in the last century of the unreformed Parliament nearly one half of the members had no constituents to whom they had any responsibilities. These men owed their seats, not to constituents who were politically in agreement with them, but to patrons. Their political relations accordingly were with these patrons, and not with the electors who nominally chose them. It is impossible to state exactly the number of members so returned. It is beyond doubt that the number was growing all through the eighteenth century. Nominations by patrons can be traced back to the time of the Tudors[1]; and there is proof that in the closing year of the reign of James II, the Duke of Newcastle was regarded by the Court as in a position to influence the election of sixteen members; the Earl of Aylesbury, eight; Lord Teynham, eight; the Earl of Huntingdon, six; Lord Preston, six; Sir Robert Holmes, six; and a number of heads of landed families, known to be in sympathy with the Court, a lesser number each[2].

How these territorial families had become possessed of the Increase in power which Sunderland in September, 1688, appealed to them Power of Patrons. to exert in the interest of James II, has been described in that part of this volume concerned with the representative history of the boroughs. After the Revolution nominations by patrons

---

[1] Cf. *Hist. MSS. Comm. 14th Rep.*, App., pt. VIII. 47, 49, 52.
[2] Cf. *Sunderland Correspondence*, Add. MSS. 34516, Folios 50–54.

became much more common than before; for the system of government by party, dating from 1693, made it increasingly worth the
while of the territorial families to possess themselves of Parliamentary influence; while at the same time the party system,
combined with the spoils system, added to the resources at their
command, by which electoral influence, especially in the boroughs,
could be secured and maintained.

Number of Members returned by Patrons. Grey, Mackintosh and the other Parliamentary reformers
computed, in 1793, that three hundred and seven members of
the House of Commons were returned by patrons, and offered
proof in respect to one hundred and fifty-seven members, returned
by eighty-four patrons[1]. Thirty-five years later Croker, in a
memorandum intended to convince Canning that the aristocracy,
powerful as it was, did not in 1827 " enjoy any great share of
political office in the House of Commons," put the number of
members returned by patrons at two hundred and seventy-six.
Of these, two hundred and three nominations were " in the hands
of what may be called the Tory aristocracy," and seventy-three in
the hands of territorial families or patrons politically allied with
the Whigs[2].

Nearly Half the Members owe Seats to Patrons. The divergence between the numbers in the statements of
1793 and 1827 becomes more obvious when it is remembered that,
subsequent to the petition of the Friends of the People, the
number of members in the House of Commons had been increased
from 558 to 658, by the addition of one hundred representatives
from Ireland, with an increase of from seventeen to twenty in
the number of borough seats controlled by patrons. At the Union
Lord Castlereagh put the close boroughs in Ireland at thirteen[3].
In 1830 O'Connell estimated the number of nomination seats at
nineteen or twenty[4]; and in 1831 Lord Plunket stated that
seventeen Irish boroughs were in the hands of patrons[5]. The
petition of 1793 was part of the propaganda for Parliamentary
reform, and consequently, in spite of the caution with which Grey
and Mackintosh embarked in that movement, it must be considered
liable to some exaggeration. But taking Croker's enumeration as

---

[1] Petition of the Society of Friends of the People, *H. of C. Journals*, XLVIII.
740.

[2] Jennings, *Croker Papers*, I. 341, 342.

[3] Castlereagh, *Correspondence*, III. 306.

[4] Hansard, 2nd Series, XXIV. 1209.

[5] *Mirror of Parl.*, 1831, IV. 3298.

a basis, and no man knew the House of Commons from the Union with Ireland until the Reform Act more intimately than Croker, it is reasonable to conclude that from about 1760 to 1832 nearly one half of the members of the House of Commons owed their seats to patrons.

These were the members of the House to whom Fox referred when, in 1795, he spoke in support of Grey's second motion for reform. "There is," he said, "one class of constituents whose instructions it is considered the implicit duty of members to obey. When gentlemen represent populous towns and cities, then it is a disputed point whether they ought to obey their voice, or follow the dictates of their own conscience. But if they represent a noble lord or a noble duke, then it becomes no longer a question of doubt, and he is not considered a man of honour who does not implicitly obey the orders of a single constituent. He is to have no conscience, no liberty, no discretion of his own. He is sent here by my Lord This, or the Duke of That; and if he does not obey the instructions he receives, he is not to be considered as a man of honour and a gentleman. Such is the mode of reasoning which prevails in this House. If he dares to disagree with the duke or lord or baronet whose representative he is, then he must be considered as unfit for the society of men of honour[1]."

Duty of Members to Patrons.

From the seventeenth, eighteenth and early nineteenth century correspondence which has come within my reach, Fox's description of the relations between members and patrons would seem to have applied to only one, though much the largest, of the classes into which members for nomination boroughs were divided. These members may be grouped into three classes: (1) those who held seats on the understanding that they were to vote with their patrons; (2) those who held them from friends, who imposed few or no restrictions on their Parliamentary actions; and (3) those who were free to speak and vote in the House as they thought best, because they had purchased their seats and had covenanted that they should have this freedom.

Three Classes of Nomination Members.

Another fact is plain from this correspondence. From the early days of the nomination system some discredit attached to the representation of boroughs of the Gatton and Sarum type. Among the FitzHerbert manuscripts there is a letter dated August 19th, 1679, narrating the fortunes of Sir E. Mildmay, who had represented the County of Essex in the Pensioner Parliament.

Discredit attaching to Representation of Rotten Boroughs.

[1] *Parl. Hist.*, xxxiii. 728, 729.

"Sir E. Mildmay," it reads, "must now go to little Old Sarum. He will hardly recover the good reputation he formerly had in that county[1]." Old Sarum continued thus in ill-repute until it was disfranchised. Stratford Canning, afterwards Viscount Stratford de Redcliffe, was returned as one of its members at a by-election in 1828. "I cannot say," he wrote, in describing his entry into the House, "that I was much attracted by the honour of representing the rottenest borough on the list." But Canning was returned by his father-in-law who was one of the owners of Old Sarum; and several considerations "pleaded in its favour." "The seat," he wrote, "was free of expense; it had been occupied by the best of patriots, Lord Chatham; it bound me to no party; and whether I was a member or not, it would still be a close borough[2]."

Large Towns preferred. At the general election of 1714, when Edward Wortley Montagu was running all over England in search of a borough, and his prospects of success were at their worst, his wife, Lady Mary Wortley Montagu, counselled him that the readiest way to a seat would be "to deposit a certain sum in some friend's hands, and buy some little Cornish borough." "It would," she added, "indeed look better to be chose for a considerable town; but I take it to be now too late[3]."

Preference for County Seats. A member from a close borough, or a member known to owe his seat to a patron, at no time in the eighteenth century stood as high in the estimation of the House as a member for a county or for a large open borough constituency. In contrasting the early careers of Pitt and Grey, Wraxall writes that in the Parliament of 1780–84 Grey, considered as a member of the House, stood upon much higher ground than Pitt, because Grey represented a great county, while Pitt was brought in by Sir James Lowther, and sat during nearly three years for a borough[4].

Patrons' Members. It was well known in the House that most of the members who held nomination seats were subject to the orders of their patrons; that when the support of these members was needed application was usually made to the patron; and that the nomination members were whipped up by their patrons[5]. When,

---

[1] *Hist. MSS. Comm. 13th Rep.*, App., pt. vi. 19.

[2] Lane-Poole, *Life of Stratford Canning, Viscount Stratford de Redcliffe*, ii. 3.

[3] Lady Mary Wortley Montagu, *Letters*, ii. 212, Bohn Ed.

[4] Wraxall, *Posthumous Memoirs*, 222.

[5] Cf. *Pitt and Rutland Correspondence*, 1781–87, pp. 3, 4; Hansard, 3rd Series, v. 373.

as in the case of Pitt, a nominated member made his mark in the House of Commons by a great speech, congratulations were offered to his patron[1]. On the other hand when nominated members took a line not in harmony with the views which their patrons were known to hold, complaints as to their conduct were made to the patrons[2]. In Parliament, and in society also, nominated members were commonly spoken of as this or that lord's member. Sir James Lowther frequently returned nine of his nominees to the House of Commons where they were known as his "ninepins[3]." "Adam Hay, Lord March's member for Peebles, died yesterday," reads a letter dated November 16th, 1775[4]. And in the correspondence and memoirs of the eighteenth century, one can discern a well-marked dividing line at Westminster and in society between members who were free of patrons and those who were under patron control.

Although young men eager to enter on Parliamentary life were willing to pass into the House through nomination boroughs, as soon as they attained prominence they sought to shake themselves free and to secure election for larger towns or for counties. The discredit, or lack of consideration, due to the representation of a nomination borough, and the eagerness to get free from patrons, are contrary to some of the ideas which have prevailed since 1832 as to the working of this part of the old electoral system. Lord Mahon asserted "that a man brought into Parliament from his talents felt no humiliating dependence on him by whose interest he was elected[5]." Nearly thirty years after the House of Commons was first reformed, but while many of the old nomination boroughs still survived, Gladstone eulogised a representative system which had rendered easy the election to the House of such men as Pelham, Chatham, Fox, Pitt, Canning, and Peel, and defended the existence of small boroughs—of those boroughs "where, from kindly interest and from ancient and affectionate recollections; from local and traditional respect; from the memory of services received; from the admiration of great men and great qualities, the constituencies are willing to take upon trust the recommendation of candidates for Parliament from noblemen or gentlemen

Eulogy of Patronage.

---

[1] Cf. *Hist. MSS. Comm. 13th Rep.*, App., pt. VII. 139, 141.

[2] Cornewall Lewis, *Administrations of Great Britain*, 172.

[3] Ferguson, *Cumberland and Westmorland Members of Parliament*, 408.

[4] *Hist. MSS. Comm. 15th Rep.*, App., pt. VI. 302.

[5] Mahon, *Hist. of England*, II. 335, 336.

who may stand in immediate connection with them[1]." The statesmen thus mentioned by Gladstone did not represent nomination boroughs longer than circumstances compelled them, and their Parliamentary careers afford additional proof that, with a few exceptions, men who attained front rank in Parliament did not remain for long members for such boroughs.

Walpole's Preference for a Close Borough.

Walpole is perhaps the most notable of these exceptions. But two Norfolk boroughs were under his own control; and he had reasons for adhering to them which have been left on record. "What! will you take a county upon you?" Walpole exclaimed in 1727 to Onslow, who was afterwards Speaker of the House. "Consider what this is with regard to re-election, and should any accident happen to prevent your being chosen Speaker you will, I suppose, be not unwilling to come into other offices and trusts. Perhaps frequent elections may not be so practicable in a county as in a borough. I once, upon a sudden and very extraordinary occasion, was prevailed with to stand for the County of Norfolk. I lost it indeed then; but might perhaps have carried it at another time, which however I would not attempt, and kept to the boroughs, Lynn and Castle Rising, for either of which I knew I could always be re-chosen[2]."

Taking Refuge in Small Boroughs.

Office-holding members of the second rank in the House were, it is true, content to represent treasury boroughs, or other nomination boroughs placed by patrons at their disposal or at the disposal of the Government. Occasionally men of the first rank, after defeat in more important constituencies, took refuge in small boroughs, and accepted seats from patrons. Lord Howick, better known in the history of the House of Commons as Mr Grey, took refuge at Appleby after his defeat in Northumberland in 1807. At the same general election Wyndham was returned for Romney after he had been defeated at Norwich[3], and Sheridan for Ilchester after his defeat at Westminster[4]. In 1829 Peel found a seat at Westbury after his failure to secure re-election for the University of Oxford[5]. Sometimes also men who had represented large constituencies were compelled by pressure of official work to seek boroughs from which local calls for Parliamentary service were

[1] Hansard, 3rd Series, CLIII. 1056, 1057.

[2] *Hist. MSS. Comm. 14th Rep.*, App., pt. IX. 518.

[3] Earl Russell, *Recollections and Suggestions*, 283.

[4] Rea, *Life of Sheridan*, II. 258.

[5] Parker, *Sir Robert Peel*, II. 104.

less frequent and less exacting, as was the case with Canning in 1822, when he exchanged his seat for Liverpool for one for Harwich[1]. But in the last century of the unreformed electoral system, and especially as the newspaper press developed and public opinion began to have its influence on Parliamentary life, the tendency of men who were attaining position in the House was to free themselves from the control of patrons, and from the dependence and uncertainty which usually went with a seat for a nomination borough.

There is no lack of evidence as to the dependence and un-certainty of tenure of those members for nomination boroughs whom I have grouped in the first and largest class—those who held their seats subject to the call and instructions of their patrons. The seats of these men were bestowed on them by patrons who had assured themselves of the political views of their nominees; but usually the patrons were careful to make clear that any divergence from their own political line on the part of the member nominated must be followed by the resignation of the seat. *Politics of Nominated Members*

Such relations as these commonly existed between patrons of the type of the Duke of Newcastle and Sir James Lowther and the members they returned to the House of Commons. New-castle's attitude towards the members who owed their election to him is shown by his correspondence with Colonel Pelham, who from 1741 to 1761 represented Hastings. In 1755 Newcastle was interested in a controverted election case from St Michael, and he summoned Pelham to the division. Pelham failed to respond to the whip from his patron. " You will not be surprised," reads the Duke's letter of the following day, " that after the letter I wrote you, I should be much disappointed and concerned that you did not attend the Michael's election. I am convinced that it was not your age or infirmities that occasioned your absence; but some attachment separate from and independent of me. Since that is the case I should advise you for your own sake as well as mine, to quit your seat in Parliament, that I may choose one at Hastings upon whom I may entirely depend[2]." Newcastle had adopted a similar tone towards Sir William Ashburnham, Colonel Pelham's predecessor at Hastings. Ashburnham, like many other members of the House of Commons, was apparently indisposed to vote against the place bills which were so frequently before Parliament *Newcastle as a Patron.*

[1] Hill, *Life of Canning*, 162.   [2] Torrens, *Hist. of Cabinets*, II. 207.

in the last years of Walpole's rule; and in 1740, after his failure to attend the division on the bill, Newcastle told him that no man could be a friend to the administration who would not come to town for a division of that importance[1]. At the general election of 1741 Ashburnham dropped out of the representation of Hastings.

Pitt the Nominee of Lowther.

Pitt's indebtedness to Sir James Lowther for his seat in the House of Commons is one of the familiar facts in the history of the old representative system, and has often been cited as proof of the opportunities opened to young men of ability by nomination boroughs. Lowther's conditions with Pitt were those usually made by borough patrons who used their power to secure their own personal ends. They are described in a letter from Pitt to his mother, written in November, 1780. "I can now inform you," he wrote, "that I have seen Sir James Lowther, who has repeated to me the offer he had before made, and in the handsomest manner. Judging from my father's principles he concludes that mine would be agreeable to his own, and on that ground—to me of all others the most agreeable—to bring me in. No kind of condition was mentioned, but that if ever our lines of conduct should become opposite I should give him an opportunity of choosing another person. Appleby is the place I am to represent; and the election will be made probably in a week or ten days, without my having any trouble, or even visiting my constituents[2]."

Lowther as a Patron.

While Pitt thus obtained his entry to the House by the patronage system, and at the hands of one of the most notorious of eighteenth century borough-masters, it cannot be said that Lowther was a patron who was on the look-out for young men of ability and eager to give them a start on a Parliamentary career. He did not discover Pitt. Pitt owed his introduction to Lowther to his friend, the Duke of Rutland, with whom he had been at Cambridge[3]. Lowther needed for the nine or eleven seats in his gift men who would do his bidding in the House, and resign their seats when it suited his convenience[4]. Ability and independence usually go together. This was a combination which was ill-suited to Lowther's Parliamentary campaigning, and of the

[1] Torrens, *Hist. of Cabinets*, i. 496.

[2] Stanhope, *Life of Pitt*, i. 47.

[3] Cf. *Hist. MSS. Comm. 13th Rep.*, App., pt. vii. 139.

[4] Cf. Ferguson, *Cumberland and Westmorland Members of Parliament*, 169; *Political Memoranda of Francis, Fifth Duke of Leeds*, 70.

many men whom he returned to Parliament during the forty years he was in political control of Westmorland and Cumberland and of boroughs elsewhere, Pitt was the only one who achieved national fame. Robinson, who was associated with North in the management of the House of Commons, owed his first seat to Lowther. But Robinson achieved notoriety rather than fame; and after he had become secretary of the treasury in 1770 Lowther quarrelled with him, and in 1774 he was compelled to retire from the representation of Westmorland, for which county he had been chosen in 1764, through Lowther's influence[1].

Pitt was indebted to Lowther for a seat in the House only from 1781 to 1784, when he became member for Cambridge University, which he represented until his death in 1806. A member of the House who had made his way into the front rank could never have tolerated Lowther's conditions or have continued of the squad at Westminster which had to wheel to the right or the left at Lowther's bidding. "They had," writes the historian of the representation of Cumberland and Westmorland, in describing Lowther's remarkable career and the position of members who accepted his nomination, " to obey their patron's behest on pain of having to seek a fresh constituency. To take one instance. In 1788 Sir James, then Lord Lonsdale, on the personal solicitation of the Prince of Wales, made all his people declare themselves against Mr Pitt's Government. They had to obey; but were most unwilling[2]." "One borough proprietor," said Brougham, in speaking in support of the Reform bill in the House of Lords, on October 7th, 1831, and alluding obviously to the first Earl of Lonsdale, " is well remembered, who would deploy his forces; command them in person; carry them over from one flank to the other, or draw them off altogether, and send them to take the field against the larks at Dunstable, that he might testify his displeasure. Accordingly the leader of that Parliamentary force raised himself to an earldom and two lord lieutenancies, and obtained titles and blue ribbons for others of his family[3]." Brougham had personal reasons for strong feeling as to the Lowthers; for in 1806 the second Earl of Lonsdale refused overtures made through Wilberforce, that

Lowther's Squad of Members.

---

[1] *Dict. Nat. Bio.*, XLIX. 27.

[2] Ferguson, *Cumberland and Westmorland Members of Parliament*, 408, 409.

[3] Hansard, 3rd Series, VIII. 261.

he should include Henry Brougham in his Parliamentary force. " The subject he has thought proper to introduce to me through your intervention," wrote Lonsdale to Wilberforce, May 21st, 1806, " is one which under no circumstances, either from the respect due to the County of Westmorland or with regard to my own interests in it, can I presume to discuss in the way he proposes[1]."

A Nomination to Huntingdon.

Robinson, when he broke with Lowther in 1770, engaged in electioneering and borough-mongering on even a larger scale than his late patron. He became election manager for George III and North ; and among the correspondence in the Abergavenny Manuscripts there is a letter to him from the Earl of Sandwich, which throws much light on the relations between borough-masters who supported the Government and their nominees. " When a vacancy happens at Huntingdon," wrote Sandwich to Robinson on the 6th of September, 1775, " I could wish to have a candidate ready to start immediately. I should not like a merchant or a mere moneyed man for reasons which I have already told you ; and yet a sum of money will be necessary ; though upon such terms as no one would refuse. The terms in short that I must have are two thousand pounds, to be lent me for five years on my bond, and to pay the expenses of the election, which in all probability would not amount to three hundred pounds." The election at Huntingdon which Sandwich was thus expecting in September, 1775, occurred in January, 1776, when Lord Mulgrave, an Irish peer, and a captain in the navy, succeeded the Honourable W. A. Montagu, second son of the Earl of Sandwich, whose death had caused the vacancy. The political conditions on which Lord Mulgrave was elected were stated in Sandwich's letter to Robinson— " the thinking and acting as I do on all American points, and supporting the present administration in their whole system[2]."

Code governing Relations of Members to Patrons.

The political conditions thus insisted upon by Sandwich may be taken as typical of those usual between patrons and the members whom they nominated ; and instances are not wanting in which the connection between member and patron was terminated when a member took a line in opposition to that to which his patron was committed. Members who accepted seats from patrons were aware of the expressed or implied conditions on which they were returned ; and while they knew that, when once they were in possession of a seat, it was constitutionally impossible to disturb them

---

[1] *Hist. MSS. Comm. 13th Rep.*, App., pt. VII. 184.

[2] *Hist. MSS. Comm. 10th Rep.*, App., pt. VI. 11 ; Beatson, II. 124.

between one general election and the next, they nevertheless regarded themselves as in honour compelled to resign when they could no longer act as their patrons directed. This, as Fox stated in his speech of 1795, was in accordance with the code which had grown up in the eighteenth century governing the relations of patrons and members. The beginnings of this code can be traced back to a period at least as early as the reign of William III. At that time nominated members knew that if they did not act in accordance with the policy of their patrons they must at once look out for other constituencies. " I hear," wrote Lord Stanhope in 1702, to Thomas Coke, " Sir Michael Biddulph does not vote along with you in the House; and if it be so he must expect to lose my interest for the future[1]." As the nomination system became more widespread, patrons evidently became less disposed to wait until the next election to depose a recalcitrant member; and after the Chiltern Hundreds came into use as a means of securing a discharge from the House of Commons, it became an article of this peculiar code that if a member parted political company with his patron, he must at once give the patron an opportunity of naming another member to take his place.

How the code worked in the early years of the reign of George III is illustrated by a passage in a letter from Horace Walpole to the Earl of Hertford, dated December 2nd, 1763. " Walsh," Walpole wrote concerning the member for Worcester, " has behaved nobly. He said he could not in conscience vote with the administration and would not vote against Lord Clive who chose him. He has therefore offered to resign his seat[2]." Another instance of this kind may be quoted from the Abergavenny Papers, papers which throw more light on electioneering and Parliamentary management during the period of the American Revolution than any correspondence yet in print, except the letters of George III to North. In November, 1781, Sir Walter Rawlinson, who in 1780 had been returned for Queenborough by the Earl of Sandwich, who was then at the admiralty, informed his patron that as he was by this time convinced that the American war must end in ruin for the mother country he could no longer vote with the ministry. As however he was unwilling to vote against the Government, he was ready to absent himself from

Members offer to resign.

---

[1] *Hist. MSS. Comm. 12th Rep.,* App., pt. II. vol. II. 451.
[2] Walpole, *Letters,* IV. 139.

the House or to resign his seat[1]. Sandwich's answer to Rawlinson is not preserved. An arrangement agreeable to both must, however, have been arrived at—helped doubtless by the change which soon took place in the administration—for Rawlinson continued as member for Queenborough until the dissolution in 1784[2], when he was returned for Huntingdon, a borough long under the private control of the Earl of Sandwich[3].

Seats lost for Wilkes.

A memorable instance in which a member was compelled to resign for voting in opposition to his patron was that of Wedderburn—an instance which was marked by an opposition dinner at the Thatched House Tavern, at which the toast was the "Steward of the Chiltern Hundreds." Wedderburn, who had been nominated at Richmond by Sir Lawrence Dundas at the general election of 1768, as a supporter of the Government, voted in 1769 with the opposition in the Middlesex election controversy, and was compelled at once to resign his seat[4]. The Middlesex election case also ended the Parliamentary career of John Hope, the author of *Thoughts in Prose and Verse.* At the election in 1768 he had been nominated for Linlithgow, by the Earl of Hopetoun; but in 1770 he lost his seat and an allowance of two hundred pounds a year, by giving offence to his patron in voting against the expulsion of Wilkes[5].

Gibbon offends his Patron.

Gibbon, who in 1774 owed his election at Liskeard to his cousin Edward Eliot, afterwards Earl of St Germains, was refused re-election in 1780 because he had offended his patron by taking office; and his letter to Eliot, who was at this time in opposition to North, affords another proof of the exacting conditions and precarious tenure under which nominated members held their seats. "I am asked," Gibbon wrote, "why Mr Eliot, who re-elected a placeman last year[6], has maintained to the last moment an ambiguous silence, without condescending to inform me that I must not depend on his friendship at the general election. I confess that I am at a loss for an answer. I am equally at a loss how to answer that part of your letter which represents, in

---

[1] *Hist. MSS. Comm. 10th Rep.*, App., pt. vi. 46.

[2] *Official List*, pt. ii. 165.

[3] *Official List*, pt. ii. 178.

[4] Donne, *Letters of George III to North*, i. 49.

[5] Andrews, *Hist. of British Journalism*, i. 187.

[6] July 12th, 1779, when Gibbon was re-elected at Liskeard after appointment as one of the Commissioners for Trade and Plantations. *Official List*, pt. ii. 150.

polite language, my Parliamentary conduct as the cause of your displeasure. You will not expect that I should justify the grounds of every silent vote which I have given, or that I should write a political pamphlet on the eventful history of the last six years. But I may fairly rest my apology on the truth of a single assertion, that I have never renounced any principle, deserted any connection, or violated any promise. The mere acceptance of a seat at the Board of Trade does not surely convey any reproach or disgrace, since you yourself, my dear Sir, have held the same disqualifying place under several successive administrations, without any of those domestic reasons which, if an excuse were necessary, might be alleged in my favour[1]."

In 1789 General Cunninghame, who in October, 1788, had A Matter of been returned by the Duke of Dorset for the burgage borough Conscience. of East Grinstead, failed to vote on Pitt's motion for limiting the continuance of the Regency. On the following day Lord Bulkeley, a peer of Ireland, who controlled several Welsh seats, and who expected a strict compliance with his wishes from his own members, even from his father-in-law[2], wrote a letter to the Marquis of Buckingham which affords another proof of the little real independence which was permitted to members who owed their elections to patrons. " General Cunninghame," wrote Bulkeley from London, " has been blowing hot and cold in his language here; but has not voted, not even last night, when he appeared for the first time in the House. I have a letter from the Duke of Dorset, complaining of his conduct in not resigning his seat, as his conscience troubled him[3]." Bulkeley's letter to Buckingham was dated January 20th, 1789. Exactly a month later Cunninghame was given the stewardship of the Chiltern Hundreds[4], and on the 27th of February he was succeeded at East Grinstead by a barrister from the Temple[5].

In the closing decades of the old electoral system, when Catholic Questions Emancipation and Parliamentary Reform were the great questions dividing which divided political parties, there are several instances of Members. members being dropped by patrons, because the members were not at one with their patrons on these questions. From 1818 to 1826 Sir George T. Staunton, a distinguished Orientalist, sat

---

[1] Gibbon, *Autobiographic Memoirs*, 96; cf. Mahon, vii., App. xi., xii., xiii.

[2] Cf. Buckingham, *Courts and Cabinets of George III*, i. 155; ii. 82.

[3] Buckingham, *Courts and Cabinets of George III*, ii. 99.

[4] Beatson, ii. 270.   [5] *Official List*, pt. ii. 182; Beatson, ii. 270.

for St Michael; and during these eight years he was not in any way tied by his patron. But in 1826 there was a difference of opinion between them on the Catholic question, and in consequence Staunton was refused re-election at St Michael[1]. Lord Brudenell, afterwards Earl of Cardigan of Balaklava fame, who at the general elections of 1820 and 1826 was nominated by the Marquis of Aylesbury, his father's cousin, as one of the members for Marlborough, was compelled in March, 1829, to resign his seat, because he differed from the Marquis on Catholic Emancipation—a question which had divided Cabinets and stirred up partisan feeling in the House of Commons ever since the agitation had been transferred at the Union from College Green to Westminster[2]. Brudenell was anxious to be of the House at this time, and although the Parliament was nearing its end he bought a seat for Fowey, and was back in the House for the final session of the Parliament of 1826–30[3]. In 1830 Scarlett, afterwards Lord Abinger, who had been Attorney-General in the Duke of *Wellington's* Administration, was returned by Earl Fitzwilliam as member for Malton. Fitzwilliam supported Parliamentary reform. Scarlett was of the anti-reformers. He spoke against the bill at second reading stage on the 22nd of March, 1831[4]; and on the 6th of April he was succeeded at Malton[5] by Francis Jeffrey, of the *Edinburgh Review*.

Patrons pledge Members to Reform.

To this period belong the few instances I have discovered in which patrons, in returning members for their boroughs, stipulated for the support of specific measures likely to come before Parliament. Many of the nominees for the boroughs of Whig proprietors were returned to the Parliaments of 1830 and 1831 on the understanding that they were to support the measure for Parliamentary reform. The Earl of Radnor who, as Lord Folkestone, had for nearly twenty years advocated advanced Liberal principles in the House of Commons, and continued his advocacy of Parliamentary reform when of the House of Lords, made it an express condition with his members for the burgage borough of Downton that they should vote for its disfranchisement[6].

---

[1] *Memoirs of Sir George Thomas Staunton, Bart.*, 116.

[2] Colchester, *Diary*, III. 598.

[3] *Dict. Nat. Bio.*, VII. 136; *Official List*, pt. II. 300, 308.

[4] *Dict. Nat. Bio.*, L. 401.

[5] Cockburn, *Life of Lord Jeffrey*, I. 246; *Official List*, pt. II. 322.

[6] *Dict. Nat. Bio.*, VI. 37.

No patrons seem to have been more exacting in their relations A Brother
with their members than were some of the peers whose sons or as Patron.
brothers represented in the House of Commons family boroughs,
or counties controlled by family influence. The nature of the
relations between the Marquis of Buckingham, who was intensely
sensitive regarding the maintenance of his own dignity[1], and his
brother Thomas Grenville, is shown in a letter of July 2nd,
1800, from Grenville, when he communicated to his brother his
appointment as Chief Justice of Eyre, and asked that he might be
re-elected at Buckingham. " I ought to ask how far it will suit
your convenience," wrote Grenville, " to re-elect me at Buckingham,
but I know your kind and warm heart so well in all that regards
me, that I will not allow myself to ask more than whether one
day will be more agreeable to you than any other for my writ
being moved[2]." Again in 1807, when Thomas Grenville was
seeking re-election, he wrote to the Marquis : " whenever you
will let me know your arrangements as to the day of election, I
will do my best to obey your orders if you wish me to be
present[3]."

Yarmouth, in the early years of the nineteenth century, was An Inde-
a borough over which the Suffield family exercised influence. pendent Son.
During the life of the first Baron Suffield it was represented by
Edward Harbord, Lord Suffield's second son ; and in the same
Parliament, that of 1807–12, William Assheton Harbord, the
heir to the peerage, was member for the Devonshire borough of
Plympton Earl's. Edward Harbord was disposed to act with the
opposition, and at a later period of his life was an advocate of
Parliamentary reform. He and his brother took opposite sides
in the House ; so much so that in 1807 Lord Suffield remonstrated
with his son Edward, and counselled a " general though not a
blindfold support of His Majesty's ministers," otherwise the Harbord interest at Yarmouth would not be of long duration. " That
town," Lord Suffield continued, " has been, ever since I knew it,
in the enjoyment of many favours which it was in the power of
ministers to bestow. A general support of ministers, I believe,
will content them. But a systematic opposition would not, I think,
be long or twice endured[4]."

[1] Cf. Buckingham, *Courts and Cabinets,* iii. 118, note.
[2] Buckingham, *Courts and Cabinets,* iii. 80.
[3] Buckingham, *Courts and Cabinets,* iv. 176.
[4] Bacon, *Memoir of Edward, Lord Suffield,* 31.

Brothers at
issue.

In 1810 the first Lord Suffield died, and Edward Harbord
soon began to experience the hard lot of " a younger brother whose
fortunes were afloat." The second Lord Suffield succeeded to the
peerage in March ; and early in April he made it plain to his
brother, who sat for Yarmouth, what were his ideas as to the
political relations which should exist between member and patron.
" Having just read over the newspaper list of the names of the
members of the House of Commons who voted on Lord Por-
chester's motion of censure, and not finding yours amongst them,"
he wrote, " I cannot rest till I hear from you on that subject,
conceiving it impossible, all circumstances considered, that you
should not have attended. Till I receive your answer, I shall
consider the omission of your name to be a mistake[1]." Edward
Harbord resented this dictation, and threatened to resign his seat.
" Candidly ask yourself," wrote Lord Suffield, on receiving this
intimation, " whether considering all the money that has been
expended to bring you in for Yarmouth, * * * you can think yourself justified in thus abandoning the interests of your family. * * *
I beg to hear from you immediately, and that you will not write
any letters expressive of your intentions to withdraw till you have
my answer ; as I must have time to consider what steps must be
taken to support my friends[2]."

A Brother's
Seat as an
Investment.

Edward Harbord's reply is significant, for it makes clear the
end which borough owners intended their nominees to serve in
the House of Commons. Their first consideration, and the one
they were always to keep in mind, was not the interests of the
country, nor what they thought best for the interests of the
constituency, but the aggrandisement of the family to whose head
they owed their seat in the House of Commons. " As to my
being justifiable in thus abandoning the interest of my family,
after all the money that has been spent to bring me into Parliament," Harbord wrote, " I have only to answer that the money
so spent has, I think, been well spent. Your lord lieutenancy and
Peter's receiver generalship have been the consequence. In point
of pecuniary advantage to the family the receiver generalship pays
more than the interest of the capital sunk ; and I am sure you
will not rate your desire of being lord lieutenant of the county
so low as to say the attainment of that object was worth
nothing. * * * As to withdrawing from Parliament, time will prove

---

[1] Bacon, *Memoir of Edward, Lord Suffield*, 44, 45.

[2] Bacon, *Memoir of Edward, Lord Suffield*, 45.

whether I shall do so.   But I do not choose to entail upon myself
any further trouble respecting Yarmouth; and if I should take
my seat for another place I shall do so upon terms which will not
render me amenable to anyone for my political conduct[1]."

In 1830 Lord Mount Charles, heir to the Marquis of Conyngham, A Threat to
who was knight of the shire from Donegal, threatened to resign resign.
his seat, in order to force his father " to give him a larger allowance,
unaccompanied by the condition of constant attendance in Parliament[2]."

Grantley Berkeley's Parliamentary career is not of the period A Member
with which these volumes are concerned.   He was not elected in Fetters.
until 1832, at the general election which followed the Reform Act.
But he owed his seat for the newly-created Western Division of
Gloucester to his brother, Lord Seagrave; and his experience of
the working of the patronage system, with a brother as patron,
comes sufficiently near to the Unreformed Parliament to be cited
as an illustration.   "While serving in Parliament," wrote Berkeley
in his *Recollections*, "I was a good deal fettered by the urgent
requests of Lord Seagrave as to my not taking any political line
without consulting him.   Thus, in many a debate, when a chance
of joining in it was offered, the opportunity was let slip because I
was uncertain of the view he would take.   All who are acquainted
with the business of the House are aware how very seldom a
chance to make a hit occurs unless a member gives up his whole
time and attention to look for it.   Fettered thus I turned my
thoughts to sport and pleasure, and merely attended to affairs of
state when put on committees, or called on to record a vote on
some great public measure[3]."

The reasons for Grantley Berkeley being so tied down by his Loyal Family
brother are also explained in his *Recollections*.   They are similar Support.
to those for which scores of patrons, from 1760 to 1832, had
kept the whip-hand on their nominees in the House of Commons.
But they have an additional interest because they show that the
relations between patrons and members, which I have been here
tracing, long survived the Reform Act of 1832 ; and also that
the Whigs rewarded patrons who kept their members in line in
much the same way as the Tories had done throughout the long
reign of George III.   "Another general election," writes Berkeley,

[1] Bacon, *Memoir of Edward, Lord Suffield,* 46.
[2] Ellenborough, *Diary,* ii. 180.
[3] Hon. Grantley Berkeley, *My Life and Recollections,* i. 359.

of the dissolution of July, 1837, "was not far off; and before it
took place I found that Lord Seagrave had made a bargain with
the Whig Government that, if he returned four of his brothers
to Parliament instead of three, all in support of what were termed
Liberal opinions, they would promote him again, creating him an
earl.   It was as much a matter of engagement or a case of barter
as any mercantile transaction could be[1]."   Three Berkeleys were
again returned at the general election of 1837 from Gloucestershire
constituencies.   A fourth failed of election at Gloucester City[2].
It was often remarked in the House "how the Berkeleys stood
together[3]"; and they apparently did so with good results to their
patron brother; for in 1841, shortly before the Melbourne Administration came to an end, Lord Seagrave, who owed the barony to
which he was raised in 1831 to the Whigs, skipped the intermediate
stage of viscount, and was advanced to the dignity of an earldom[4].

Limits of Patron Control.
While it is possible to divide members who were of the House
by the nomination of patrons into three groups, it is not feasible
even to attempt to estimate the number who, at any given time,
were of a particular group.   It is obvious, however, from a study
of the conditions of the representative system and of the House
of Commons between the Revolution and 1832, that an over-
whelming majority of nominated members were of the first group.
They were of those who held their seats on the understanding,
expressed or implied, that they should act as their patrons directed.
Not that a nominated member looked to his patron for instructions
as to every vote.   That would have been impracticable.   But while
a patron was not constantly on hand to direct his corps, and
while few patrons wheeled their members to the right or to the
left as arbitrarily as did Lowther, every nominated member knew
the general lines his patron was taking in politics, and knew that
if he deviated from these lines his connection with the constituency
by which he was returned might soon come to an end.

Patronage System fully developed.
It is certain also that the great majority of borough owners
from the reign of George II to the end of that of George IV
were generally supporters of the Government.   Croker's enumeration of the members returned by patrons and his statement

[1] Hon. Grantley Berkeley, *My Life and Recollections*, i. 370.
[2] McCalmont, *Parliamentary Poll-Book*, 34, 54, 122, 123.   Ed. 1895.
[3] Hon. Grantley Berkeley, *My Life and Recollections*, ii. 349.
[4] Hon. Grantley Berkeley, *My Life and Recollections*, ii. 345; *Dict. Nat. Bio.*
iv. 365.

of the political affiliations of these patrons—two hundred and three members returned by Tories, and seventy-three by Whigs—are of the year 1827. There are grounds for believing that this proportion would have been approximately correct in almost any year between 1760 and 1827. The nomination system had apparently reached its height by the early years of the reign of George III. By that time there were few boroughs capable of control which were without patrons,—few boroughs still awaiting capture by borough-managers. In the next sixty or seventy years many boroughs changed hands, and the power of the greater borough owners was augmented by these changes. But before the American Revolution the patronage system in the House of Commons had reached its fullest developement. All through the long reign of George III, during most part of which the Tories were in power, it was obviously to the advantage of men who possessed Parliamentary influence to throw in their lot with the Government; for it was only from the Government that borough patrons could obtain the official patronage which helped them to secure control of boroughs, and also the varied and ample rewards which compensated for the expense and trouble which borough-owning and borough-management necessarily entailed.

The more powerful and politically ambitious of these borough patrons secured places in the administration as their reward. Others like Lord Darlington, who was in control of the Cornish boroughs of Camelford, St Michael, and Truro, by means of his Parliamentary influence " passed from one rank of the peerage to another, until the glories of a dukedom were his[1]." Lowther, by virtue of the many nominations to Parliament which he was so long in a position to control, in 1784 jumped two stages in the peerage, and at one bound became Baron Lowther of Lowther, Kendal, and Burgh, Viscount Lonsdale and Lowther, and Earl of Lonsdale[2]; and before he was of the peerage he held the lieutenancy or deputy lieutenancy of Cumberland, Westmorland, and Yorkshire[3]. *Rewards of Borough Patrons.*

From 1760 to 1821, the period in which the nomination system was at its height, there were two hundred and nine creations or promotions in the peerage[4]; and of these no fewer than one *Additions to the Peerage.*

[1] Courtney, *Parl. Representation of Cornwall*, Intro., xx.

[2] Doyle, II. 412, 413.

[3] Doyle, II. 412, 413.

[4] Lord Folkestone's speech on Russell's motion for reform, April 25th, 1822, Hansard, 2nd Series, VII. 95.

hundred and forty were of the seventeen years, from 1784 to 1801, in which Pitt was prime minister[1]. By Pitt's use of his power, " he created a plebeian aristocracy and blended it with the patrician oligarchy." " He made peers," again to quote Lord Beaconsfield, " of second-rate squires and fat graziers. He caught them in the alleys of Lombard Street, and clutched them from the counting-houses of Cornhill[2]." Creations and promotions were thus unprecedently numerous notwithstanding that, as early as 1780, the King had laid down the rule not to grant more than one step at a time in the peerage[3].

Service that earned Peerages.

The reasons which led to the recruiting of the peerage, and to the advancement in rank of men already of the peerage, were described by Brougham when speaking in the House of Lords in 1831 in support of the Reform bill. " Service without a scar in the political campaign—constant presence in the field of battle at St Stephen's—absence from all other fights, from Blenheim down to Waterloo; but above all steady discipline, right votes in right places—these," said the Lord Chancellor of the administration that carried the Reform Act, " are the precious but happily not rare qualities which have generally raised men to the peerage. For these qualities the gratitude of Mr Pitt showered down his baronies by the score; and I do not suppose he ever once so much as dreamt of ennobling a man who had ever been known to give a vote against him[4]." In other words, in the last seventy years of the old representative system the votes which owners of boroughs could command were placed at the disposal of ministers, in return for peerages or advancement of rank in the peerage[5]; and of the peerages which were created between the Revolution and the beginning of the reign of Queen Victoria, peerages of Ireland as well as peerages of the United Kingdom, at least two-thirds were bestowed as the rewards of borough-mongering. They were earned by the services of those members of the House of Commons to whom Fox referred in his speech of 1795; and they stand to-day as a monument of the system of Parliamentary patronage, of which the beginnings can be traced back to the reigns of the Tudors, and which did not wholly

---

[1] Anson, *Law and Custom of the Constitution*, pt. I. 294, 295.

[2] Disraeli, *Sybil*, 22. Ed. 1871.

[3] North to Buckinghamshire, November 15th, 1780, Add. MSS. 34523, Folio 340.

[4] Hansard, 3rd Series, VIII. 224.   [5] Cf. Anson, pt. I. 294, 295.

disappear until after the redistribution of seats which followed the last extension of the franchise in 1884.

Borough owners in this period had also first claim on official patronage, English, Irish, Indian, and colonial. The best Irish preferments, treasurerships, vice-treasurerships and commissionerships, were conferred by prime ministers upon their supporters in England, who received the salaries and left the duties to be discharged by deputy. Irish patronage was used to purchase Parliamentary support at Westminster, and favourites whom English ministers dared not recommend for pension or office at home were quartered on the Irish Establishment. "The English statesmen of the eighteenth century—the Graftons, the Weymouths, the Norths, and the Shelburnes," writes Froude in describing the use made of Irish offices before and during the reign of George III, " had learned in official routine to regard these resources as indispensable for the public service[1]." This was so much the case, and so pressing were the needs of the treasury to satisfy the borough patrons at Westminster, that in 1774—although Ireland had then a Parliament controlled much like that of Great Britain—when Flood was an applicant for the vice-treasurership, a sinecure of £3,500 a year, North informed Lord Harcourt, then Irish Viceroy, that " he had England to care for as well as Ireland." " My objection to Mr Flood's having a vice-treasurership is that I fear much blame here ; and no small difficulty in carrying the King's business, if I consent to part with the disposal of these offices, which have been so long and uniformly bestowed on members of the British Parliament[2]."

Patronage for Borough Owners.

" When Britain had been drained dry and there was nothing more to be squeezed from Ireland," writes Sir George Trevelyan, " ministers, in an evil hour for themselves, remembered that there were two millions of Englishmen in America, who had struggled through the difficulties and hardships which beset the pioneers of civilisation and who, now that their daily bread was assured to them, could afford the luxury of maintaining an army of sinecurists[3]." As early as the reign of George II civil appointments in the American colonies were given out as spoils to borough-mongers ; and in the reign of George III " the measures of oppression against the colonies were," to quote the American historian of the British civil service, " so ingeniously contrived

Patronage in the American Colonies.

[1] Froude, *English in Ireland,* II. 90.
[2] Froude, *English in Ireland,* II. 170, 171.
[3] Trevelyan, *Charles James Fox,* 110.

as to take away their liberties at the same time that they made more places to be filled.   Under this voracious spoils system, for example, in 1774, the elective council of Massachusetts was made appointable by the Crown, and the selection of judges, magistrates, and sheriffs was also added to the royal patronage[1]."

Shares in Loans.

To this period also, and growing out of the necessity of paying for Parliamentary support, belongs the system of loan-mongering. Bute, Grafton and North assigned to their friends and supporters shares in government loans and lotteries.   In this way the country was made to borrow money on terms considerably above the market price, and in the case of a loan negotiated by Lord North, it sustained a loss of nearly a million sterling upon the transaction[2]. Offices and titles were currency in which borough owners were paid so long as the old representative system survived and for many years subsequent to 1832.   Loan-mongering came to an end as soon as Pitt became prime minister in 1784[3].

To whom the Offices went.

The more important offices, as the Suffield correspondence quoted in this chapter indicates, went to the borough owners themselves, and to their sons and sons-in-law.   The less important offices and appointments, places in the civil service at home, Crown livings, naval and Indian cadetships, and appointments in the colonial service went to their near dependents : and, after their needs had been met, to the men who aided the patrons in borough management.   George Selwyn controlled the election of the two members for Ludgershall, and at times had sufficient influence at Gloucester to secure the election of one member there.   Owing to this influence and to the discretion with which he used it for securing favours, he was, " at one and the same time, Surveyor-General of Crown Lands, which he never surveyed ; Registrar of Chancery at Barbadoes, which he never visited ; and Surveyor of the Meltings and Clerk of the Irons in the Mint, where he showed himself once a week, in order to eat a dinner which he ordered; but for which the nation paid[4]."

Speculating in Parliamentary Influence.

" Courtiers," wrote Peregrine Bertie in 1694 to his brother, the Earl of Lindsay, who was spending freely to secure the return of his nephew as his nominee at Stamford, " must venture their fortunes, and they can have no better lottery than our House

[1] Eaton, *Civil Service in Great Britain,* 117.
[2] Cf. Anson, pt. I. 290.   [3] Cf. Anson, pt. I. 292.
[4] Trevelyan, *Charles James Fox,* 108, 109.

to push their fortunes in[1]." Prizes in this lottery were never more numerous, more varied or more valuable than from 1760 to 1820. Borough owners ventured their fortunes in acquiring and maintaining Parliamentary influence, and systematically carried their influence to market at the treasury.

These bargains were on a perfectly business-like footing. The A Bargain borough owner pledged himself that his nominees in the House of for a Peerage. Commons should support the Government, and was assured of his reward when he had fulfilled his part of the bargain. In 1763 Lord Clive was at issue with the Government; and Lord Powis, then comptroller of the household, had an interview with him at which a settlement was arranged. Its terms were embodied in official minutes, which set out that Lord Clive wished to put a stop to a contest at Bishop's Castle, and that if ministers would call off the candidate who was opposing his nominee, he would defray the expenses of the contest, and would engage that, when Mr George Clive was elected, he and Lord Clive, then an Irish peer and of the House of Commons, " and all his friends" in Parliament, would support the measures of the Government. " That under these circumstances," read the minutes of the conference, " as opportunities will offer for his giving the strongest proof of his attachment to His Majesty's service, he desires the favour of being advanced to a peerage of England at a convenient time, when the like favour shall be granted to others." " If these propositions be complied with," continue the minutes, " Lord Powis in Lord Clive's absence, if occasion shall require, is to let Mr Walsh and others know it is Lord Clive's request that they will assist and concur with the ministry in Parliament[2]." The consideration in this case was to be a seat for Clive in the House of Lords at Westminster, a distinction much more coveted by borough owners than an Irish peerage, which was so often a borough owner's half-way house to the higher distinction of a peerage of Great Britain.

The Powis minutes of the transaction with Clive of 15th and A Proposal 16th November, 1763, made whilst the by-election was proceeding to buy out Borough at Bishop's Castle which resulted in the return of George Clive[3], Owners with may be taken as typical of the bargains for peerages of the period Peerages. from 1760 to 1820. Peerages were so well known to be the rewards of borough owners that in 1782 Horne Tooke proposed a plan of reform under which all the borough owners were to be bought out

---

[1] *Hist. MSS. Comm. 13th Rep.,* App., pt. vi. 250.

[2] *Grenville Papers,* iv. 14.   [3] *Official List,* pt. ii. 129.

with peerages. " Let every man who has a borough," he urged on the Duke of Richmond, who was then the foremost Parliamentary reformer in the House of Lords, " be made a peer, and if he has more than one, let him nominate a friend or friends. He would be glad of the exchange, and the people would be equally so ; because they would care but little how many peers were made ; but would care very much for the money to be taken out of their pockets ; and there could be no injustice in the case, even considering the seats in the view of private property ; because those who did not choose to be lords of Parliament, might be permitted to sell their seats to such as did[1]."

Horace Walpole's Testimony.

Horace Walpole, who did not fail to hear of the settlement of the Government with Clive at the time of the Bishop's Castle election[2], has also recorded some typical instances of borough-mongers' bargains for offices in the reigns of George II and George III. " Lord Cowper," he wrote to Mann, on the 5th of May, 1747, " has resigned the Bedchamber[3] on the Beefeater's being given to Lord Falmouth[4]. The latter, who is powerful in elections, insisted on having it[5]." " Lord Sandwich," Walpole writes in his *Last Journals*, under date of May 9–14th, 1783, at the time of the Fox and North Coalition, " who had threatened the new ministry with the number of votes at his command, was made Ranger of the Parks[6] in room of Lord Orford, and his son, Hitchinbroke[7], got a place likewise[8]."

Disaffection through Refusal of Patronage.

High-handed demands for official patronage on the part of borough owners, such as those described by Walpole, provoked some of the bitterest personal conflicts in eighteenth century political life. In 1783 Mr Rose and Lord Shelburne were sharply at issue over a collectorship at St Christopher's—to be held, of course, by deputy—which Rose wanted for his brother-in-law. Rose was worsted, and declared that he never would be in a room with Shelburne again[9], to whom henceforward he was bitterly hostile[10]. Shelburne's Administration was one of the shortest-lived of the reign of George III. He was First Lord of the Treasury

[1] Stephens, *Life of Horne Tooke*, ii. 376; cf. Howell, *State Trials*, xxv. 377.

[2] Cf. Walpole, *Letters*, iv. 134.

[3] Doyle, i. 479.

[4] Doyle, i. 732.

[5] Walpole, *Letters*, ii. 82.

[6] Doyle, iii. 261.

[7] Master of the Buckhounds, May 30th, 1783. Doyle, iii. 262.

[8] Walpole, *Last Journals*, ii. 621.

[9] Rose, *Diaries*, i. 30.

[10] Cf. Fitzmaurice, *Life of Shelburne*, iii. 410.

only from July, 1782, to February, 1783[1]—from the fall of North to the Fox and North Coalition—and the biographer of Shelburne gives as one of the contributing causes of the weakness of his administration the refusal of some small pieces of private patronage which the Duke of Grafton had solicited for his friends[2]. Later, Rose was at issue with Lord Percy, as before with Shelburne, on a question of patronage[3]. Lord Percy, who in 1786 became Duke of Northumberland, had returned Rose for his borough of Launceston in 1784. In 1788, when Rose was appointed Clerk of the Parliaments, his trouble with Northumberland over patronage resulted in his election, after taking office, not again for Launceston, but for Lymington, a borough which subsequently came under his control. From 1784 to 1806 Rose was to Pitt what Robinson was to North. He was active from the treasury in the management of elections for the Government, and distributed government patronage[4]; and although he came into conflict with Shelburne and Northumberland, Wraxall credits him with successfully dispensing patronage " so as to offend as few disappointed claimants as possible[5]."

In the expressive vocabulary of present-day American politics An American there is a phrase which is often applied to a man who is bent Parallel. on turning his political influence, or any office he may hold, to pecuniary account. It is said of such a man that " he is not in politics for his health." Translated into English it means that he is not disinterestedly concerned in politics, not so engaged in order to forward any political principles, but to make all he can for himself. An American would apply this phrase to the English borough-masters of the eighteenth century, the prototypes of the " bosses " who to-day hold the municipal fortunes of so many American cities in their hands.

The eighteenth century English borough-masters did not thrust Personal themselves into the beery atmosphere of elections in potwalloper Interests of Borough and freeman boroughs, bribe conscienceless and grasping aldermen Owners. in corporation boroughs, or marshal burgage-holders to the polls, either to safeguard the Hanoverian succession, or to uphold the cause of England in the quarrel with the American colonies, or to sustain Pitt in his long struggle with Napoleon. Nor did they concern themselves with borough-mongering merely that they might

---

[1] Doyle, II. 319. [2] Cf. Fitzmaurice, *Life of Shelburne*, III. 343.
[3] Cf. Rose, *Diaries*, I. 51, 52. [4] Cf. *Dict. Nat. Bio.*, XLIX. 227, 228.
[5] Wraxall, *Memoirs*, III. 457, 458.

have the pleasure and satisfaction of discovering a Chatham or a
Pitt, and giving him an easy start on the highroad to Parliamentary fame. They looked first to " my own interest "—as the
Earl of Lonsdale described it, when in 1806 he declined Wilberforce's overtures for a seat for Brougham—to their own reward,
to the gains material, social, and political, which the power
to nominate members of the House of Commons gave them.
Borough owners of the type of Clive, Falmouth, Sandwich and
Lowther, and in fact all borough owners who were busy in politics
for their own gain and advancement, as the majority of them
undoubtedly were, had necessarily to have as their nominees in
the House men who could be implicitly relied upon to keep in
mind the aims of their patrons, men who could be trusted on no
occasion in their House of Commons life to forget or ignore the
relations of their patrons with the treasury.

Personal
Interests of
Members.
It was consequently useless for a candidate for the House to
open negotiations with a borough-master whose eye was always
on the treasury, on a place in the ministry, on a peerage or a
step upwards in the peerage, or on offices for himself and his
dependents, unless the candidate were prepared to hold himself in
the House always ready to advance his patron's interests. That
was his chief mission in the House. In most cases it would
appear to have been the only reason why his patron put him
there. The next mission of many of the members who were of
the House by the good-will of patrons was to make their seats
in Parliament a stepping-stone to official preferment. Thus in
many instances the line of advancement for the member ran in
the same direction as the line of advancement for the patron;
and in cases in which the interest of both patron and member
was to be served by the same line of conduct, there was little
likelihood of friction or antagonism. The patron was usually in
pursuit of larger game than his member; and when the member
was about to reach his prize, all that the patron asked from him
was that he should not accept office without the patron's permission. He naturally desired that there should be no bargaining
without his knowledge between his nominee and the treasury;
and the exigencies of borough control, especially in boroughs
where the patron was not in easy and undisputed possession and
might have opposition at any time, made it necessary that he
should have due notice of an appointment which would necessi-
tate an election.

It was, moreover, part of the unwritten code regulating the Asking relations of members and patrons that, when a member desired Leave of to absent himself for any long period from the House, he should Absence obtain his patron's consent. When Anthony Storer, who was one from of Lord Carlisle's members for Morpeth, was appointed Secretary Patrons. to the Embassy at Paris in 1783 he promptly acquainted Carlisle with his good fortune. He thought it right to do so lest Carlisle should imagine that it might make him neglect that attendance in Parliament which might be material to Carlisle's interest. " I shall," wrote Storer, " be ready at all times to return to England upon the shortest notice that I may receive that my attendance is wanted[1]." In 1790, when Sir Gilbert Eliot was returned for Helston by Lord Malmesbury, " the conditions under which he accepted the seat offered him were that he should not be required to attend regularly or constantly in his place, but while residing habitually in Scotland, should hold himself in readiness to be summoned up to London whenever it was judged necessary or advisable that he should act in Parliament with his party[2]." Minto, where Eliot lived, was fifty miles beyond Carlisle, and was a post-chaise journey of fifty-four hours from London.

In 1808, when Sir Robert Adair, then member for Camelford, A Patron was sent by Canning on a special diplomatic mission to Constanti- permits a nople, he felt it incumbent on him to explain to his patron, the go abroad. Duke of Bedford, that there was nothing in his mission to Constantinople which need alter his political connections; " but," he added, " it is no less clear that I ought not to retain a situation which my absence will for a time necessarily render inefficient." To this the Duke of Bedford replied, requesting Adair to retain his seat in Parliament. " The length of your stay abroad," he wrote, " is of course very uncertain from the nature of the mission; and as I should at all events restore you on your return to that seat which you had temporarily vacated, it would subject me to frequent elections at Camelford, an inconvenience which I must at all times wish to avoid[3]." Throughout the eighteenth century members of the House of Commons did not regard it as inconsistent with their duties to their constituents or to the House to go abroad for years at a time, and utterly ignore their

---

[1] *Hist. MSS. Comm. 15th Rep.*, App., pt. VI. 638.

[2] Minto, *Life and Letters*, I. 347.

[3] Albemarle, *Fifty Years of My Life*, 10, 12; cf. Sir Robert Adair's *Mission to Constantinople*, XXI.

Parliamentary service. But when they were of the House by the grace of a patron it was the usage to obtain his sanction to any long absence.

The Elder Pitt's Relations with his Patron. As far as can be traced from memoirs and correspondence it would seem that comparatively few members who were of the House by the grace of patrons felt no humiliating dependence on those by whose interest they were returned. After allowing for the formal courtesy which characterised eighteenth century correspondence it must be conceded that there is a lack of independence, and frequently a tinge of subserviency, in the letters from members to their patrons. Take for example the elder Pitt's letter to Newcastle after his return, on the nomination of the Duke, for Aldborough in Yorkshire in 1754. "Among the many who will be proud of the honour done them by their constituents," wrote Pitt from Bath in April, 1754, "none be with more reason vain of their election than myself, and of the goodness to which they owe it. My satisfaction is abated by one only consideration, that your Grace has been so good to nominate a very useless person, and who, I fear, fills the place of a better man. I consider my political life as some way or other drawing to a conclusion, or rather as arrived at a period. If my private life should by any of the chances of this world still afford me an opportunity of marking my attachment to your Grace, in anything personal to you, you will find a man not very ungrateful however insignificant[1]." But obsequiously grateful as Pitt was in 1754 for his return by Newcastle, he did not remain longer than he could help as the nominee of a patron[2]. He owed his seat to the Duke only from April 17th, 1754, to December 11th, 1756. When he became secretary of state in 1756, and had to be re-elected, he was returned for Okehampton, a seat which he relinquished in July, 1757, in favour of the City of Bath[3], which had recently got free from the patronage of Sir Robert Henley. Pitt thus emerged from a condition of Parliamentary nomineeship into that of representing a free constituency[4].

Adopting a Patron's Opinions. Not much change had come over the attitude of members towards their patrons, even by the time the end of the old representative system was in sight. Robert Plumer Ward, who by the grace of the second Earl of Lonsdale was chosen for Cockermouth in 1802, assured his patron in 1806, after he had learned that he was to be of the next House of Commons for one of the

[1] Torrens, *Hist. of Cabinets*, II. 180.   [2] Cf. Green, *William Pitt*, 57.
[3] *Official List*, pt. II. 119, 111, 115.   [4] Torrens, *Hist. of Cabinets*, II. 400.

Lowther boroughs, that he considered himself "now as entirely belonging to the Lowther party"; and asked for some instructions as to how he was to hold himself politically in the future. "I trust," his letter continues, "you will not think me very pragmatical in bringing a subject of such magnitude before the person in the world whose sentiments upon it are to me of the utmost importance. It is with the greatest truth that I repeat that a seat in Parliament is nothing in comparison with the thought that I have enjoyed your confidence, and shared, as well as acted upon, your opinions[1]."

Neither of these letters, written at an interval of half a century, depicts the state of mind of nominated members described by Lord Mahon[2]. Nor is it shown in the writings and utterances of such men as Abbot, who was Speaker of the House; as Denman, who was Solicitor-General in the Grey Administration, and afterwards Lord Chief Justice; or as Sir George Staunton, the Orientalist—all of whom were at one time or another in the House of Commons by nomination. Their experience does not leave the impression that in their Parliamentary careers as nominated members there was "a sort of romantic element," such as Bagehot conceived characterised Parliamentary life in the days of the nomination system, when a young man of promise, a Gibbon or a Macaulay, opened a letter "which looked like any other letter, and found it contained an offer of a seat in Parliament"; and when "there was a regular connection between the unions, the great debating societies of Oxford and Cambridge, and Parliament," and "young men who seemed promising, had even a chance of being competed for by both parties[3]."

Glamour of the Old System.

Abbot, who was Speaker from 1802 to 1817, was nominated for Helston in 1795, by the Duke of Leeds, under conditions which warrant his being grouped in the second class of patron-returned members—among those who held seats from friends who imposed few or no restrictions on their Parliamentary action. The Duke of Leeds had known him at Westminster School, and in later years Abbot had seen him "accidentally, but very seldom, at the Westminster plays and meetings." Politically there had been no intercourse between them; and no terms were made when the Duke returned Abbot for Helston. All that the Duke intimated to

Abbot's Discomfort as a Nominee.

---

[1] *Hist. MSS. Comm. 13th Rep.*, App., pt. VII. 222.   [2] Cf. *supra*, 313.
[3] Bagehot, "Lord Althorp and the Reform Act of 1832," *Fortnightly Review*, November, 1876, 596, 597.

Abbot concerning the borough was that "Mr Fox had moved for the writ." Yet Abbot was not easy as the Duke's nominee. "It is very possible," he wrote to a colleague at the bar, "that you may see mine very shortlived, and me in possession of the Chiltern Hundreds during this very winter. Not that I have anything like certain grounds for such a supposition; but I cannot be any man's blackamoor, and if I should think it right to give a current support to one side, while our friend should take a line decidedly opposite; although I should not conclude unnecessarily that he meant me to follow in his train, yet I should not be unprepared to quit upon notice[1]."

Denman finds Dependence painful.

Denman, at the time the Reform bill was under discussion in 1831, took the House into his confidence as to his feelings when he sat in the Parliament of 1818–20 by the grace of patrons; for he owed his election in 1818 to the joint influence of the Duke of Devonshire and the Marquis of Lansdowne, two Whig potentates who, after Denman's defence of the Luddites at Nottingham, "were desirous of securing so able and efficient a recruit for the ranks of the Liberal party[2]." "A seat was found for him," Denman told the House, in recalling his experience of the nomination system, "for the borough of Wareham, and though averse to the system, he confessed with some sense of shame that he had not the virtue to resist it." On the dissolution of 1820 he was not re-elected for a close borough[3], "but sought and obtained the suffrages of one of the most enlightened towns of England." "There was something about it," Denman continued, in describing the tenure of the borough of Wareham, "that an independent spirit could but ill bear; for though he was bound to feelings of gratitude for treatment the most kind and liberal, the sense of uncertainty and dependence upon others was fraught with painful feelings. From the very nature of the case, when the point was to be determined, a secret council must sit, canvassing a nominee's claims and merits in comparison with others, and disposing of his hopes of public usefulness without hearing or consulting him[4]." Although Denman,

---

[1] Colchester, *Diary and Correspondence*, I. xviii., xix.

[2] Arnould, *Memoir of Lord Denman*, I. 118.

[3] Tierney, then the leader of the Whig opposition, in anticipation of the death of George III, intimated to Denman that he would have to find another seat, and he accordingly went to Nottingham where he was returned. Arnould, I. 129.

[4] Hansard, 3rd Series, II. 1246, 1247.

as he told the House in 1831, was unequal to resisting the offer of
a nomination seat in 1818, he declined one offered him in 1826 by
the Duke of Norfolk[1]; and he was out of the House of Commons
until 1830, when he was re-elected for Nottingham, and continued
to represent that borough until 1832.

Sir George Staunton has recorded his impressions of the lot of
a nominated member in his *Memoirs.* The position to him was
unsatisfactory for the reason " that a pocket borough afforded no
stimulus, because a member so placed had no constituents." " I
had," he states, " no constituents for whom it might have been
both my right and my duty to plead. I had literally nothing
to do; and therefore I hope it will not be a very serious charge
against me that I did nothing[2]." Sir George Staunton belonged to
the third group of members, those who had obtained their seats
by purchase. His position was unsatisfactory from a feeling
that he was of the House under false pretences. "There is," he
writes, "another defect in the position of a member for a close
borough of which I soon became sensible, and which it appears
to me impossible for any ingenuous mind to contemplate without
some degree of humiliation and pain, and which consequently
appears to me very much to strengthen the argument for the
abolition of these boroughs. I felt that I entered the House
under false colours. I felt that I was not what I professed to
be, really the representative of the borough for which I was
nominally returned. I came into Parliament by means, which,
under the circumstances of the case[3], I conceived to be perfectly
justifiable; but which, being illegal[4], I could not rise up in my
place and avow. It may have been useful and right that a certain
number of seats in Parliament should be obtainable by purchase,
or through the influence of certain wealthy commoners or peers;
but I consider the false position in which members for close
boroughs were placed in the House under the old system wholly
indefensible, and that these boroughs were therefore very properly
abolished[5]."

[margin note: False Position of a Member for a Close Borough.]

[1] Arnould, I. 204.

[2] Staunton, *Memoirs*, 118, 119.

[3] Elsewhere he writes: "My first eight years in Parliament was an affair
of money." *Memoirs*, 192.

[4] An Act which made illegal the sale of seats was passed in 1809,
49 Geo. III, c. 118.

[5] Staunton, *Memoirs*, 120.

TREASURY BOROUGHS.

Members
nominated
by the
Treasury.

Comprised within the first of the groups into which members who were of the House by nomination have been here divided were those members who sat for what were known as treasury boroughs. The number of these members varied in different Parliaments, and was increased after the Union with Ireland. During the last hundred years of the old electoral system there were certain boroughs, such as Hastings, Harwich, Queenborough, Rye, Sandwich and Winchelsea, in which the Government was in control of the elections by virtue of the money expended in these places by the post-office, the customs department, and the admiralty. In these boroughs there were local managers, men who controlled the corporations or the freemen for the Government, whether Tory or Whig. But the managers had not the power of Dodington or Lowther. They could not nominate whom they pleased as members for the boroughs, or give them instructions as to their conduct in Parliament. They were the agents of the Government; and it was their business to secure the election of the nominees of the Government. The boroughs which were directly and almost absolutely under the control of the Government seldom varied in number. The variation in the number of members of the House nominated by the treasury was due to the fact that in some Parliaments borough owners turned over their nominations to the treasury in return for offices or titles, or sold outright to the Government their right or power to nominate.

Purchase of
Seats by the
Treasury.

In the reign of George III, and until the Reform Act of 1832 cut so many nomination boroughs out of the electoral system, it was usual for administrations, Tory or Whig, to go into the market and purchase the right to nominate members for a Parliament. George III and North's transactions in boroughs at the general election of 1774, illustrate the business-like way in which these purchases were made. " Lord Falmouth," wrote North to Cooper, " must be told in as polite terms as possible that I hope he will permit me to recommend to three of his six seats in Cornwall. The terms he expects are two thousand five hundred pounds a seat, to which I readily agree[1]." The boroughs for which

---

[1] Donne, *Letters of George III to North,* i. 6.

North was negotiating were Tregony, East Looe, and Lostwithiel. "Sir Charles Whitworth," continued North's letter, "must for the present be sent to East Looe, and Mr Henry Conway to Lostwithiel." It was in this transaction of 1774 that Lord Falmouth earned notoriety by insisting on guineas, not pounds, in his bargaining with the treasury. "My noble friend," wrote North, "is rather shabby in desiring guineas instead of pounds. If he persists I would not have the bargain go off upon so slight a difference[1]." In another letter concerning the purchase of five more seats North wrote to Robinson: "Let Cooper know whether you promised Masterman two thousand five hundred pounds, or three thousand pounds for each of Lord Edgcumbe's seats. I was going to pay him twelve thousand five hundred pounds; but he demanded fifteen thousand pounds[2]."

After the Union the treasury made purchases of seats in Ireland in the same business-like way as characterised North's transactions in boroughs in 1774. In 1807 Cashel, Tralee, Enniskillen, Athlone, Dundalk and Carlow were each the subject of negotiation by the treasury[3]. Cashel, Tralee and Athlone were in 1807 at the command of the highest bidder[4]; and although the market for Irish seats in England was at this time but newly established, Irish borough proprietors had quickly learned how to make the most of their properties, and were as much disposed to drive hard bargains with the treasury as were the English borough owners who dealt with George III and North. In England at this time the more wary purchasers of seats bought them for a term of years, and not for the lifetime of a Parliament. But when the treasury was in the Irish market in 1807 the Irish proprietors realized the advantage of selling their seats for a Parliament only, and when approached by the treasury agents, "not a man would engage for a term of years[5]." *Irish Seats in the Market.*

The boroughs in which the treasury had permanent control, those placed at the disposal of the Government by patrons and those for which the nominations were purchased were represented (1) by official members; (2) by men who, while outside Parliament, had rendered some partisan services to the Government, and whom *Members for Treasury Boroughs.*

---

[1] Donne, *Letters of George III to North*, i. 6.

[2] Donne, *Letters of George III to North*, i. 7.

[3] *Civil Correspondence of the Duke of Wellington*, v. 23.

[4] *Civil Correspondence of the Duke of Wellington*, v. 22.

[5] *Civil Correspondence of the Duke of Wellington*, v. 66.

the Government deemed it wise to have among its supporters in the House of Commons; and (3) by men who, while able to raise part of the purchase money of a seat, were not able to raise the whole, and who were willing, if the Government would seat them at one-third or one-half the sum usually demanded by borough owners, to give a uniform and unquestioning support in return.

The Treasury and Patrons of Boroughs.   To the treasury boroughs of the first and third classes the treasury nominated absolutely, and merely sent to its agents the names of the men who were to be returned[1]. In nominating to boroughs of the second class, to those placed at the disposal of the treasury for other considerations than money, it was usual to show some deference to the patrons and to submit to them the names of the men to be nominated. In 1790 Pitt had at his disposal the nomination of a member for Old Sarum, which at this time was in the control of Lord Camelford; and a letter from Pitt to Camelford, preserved in the Fortescue Manuscripts, illustrates the relations of the treasury to patrons who put seats at its disposal. " I called this morning," wrote Pitt from Downing Street, March 11th, 1790, " to mention to you the result of my researches, with a view to the object we talked of. There are three persons that occur, any one of whom would, I believe, readily close with the proposal. But before I determine which to apply to first, I wish to know whether you prefer a Scotchman, an Irishman, or an East Indian, as my friends divide themselves into these three descriptions. The first is Mr Grant, a lawyer rising into eminence, and very eager for Parliament. The second, Mr Coote, nephew and heir to Sir Eyre Coote, and as I am told a very respectable man. The third, Mr J. Sullivan, who was a considerable time in India, and returned both with a good fortune and a good character. I have little doubt that any one of the three would close. But I should add that Mr Coote is at present in Ireland, and I imagine that whoever is fixed on will be expected to pay his respects on the spot[2]."

Office Holders from the Treasury Boroughs.   The boroughs in which the treasury was permanently in control were almost uniformly reserved for the placemen in the House. They were constituencies from which were returned, at election after election, commissioners of the treasury, of the admiralty, of the ordnance, and of trade and plantations; and the Parliamentary secretaries to these boards[3], who had no borough influence of their

---

[1] Cf. *Civil Correspondence of the Duke of Wellington*, v. 22.

[2] *Hist. MSS. Comm. 13th Rep.*, App., pt. III. 567.

[3] Cf. Beatson, I. 76, 94, 242 ; II. 107, 130, 329.

own; with an occasional variation in favour of a lawyer whom the Government desired to enlist in its corps, or a pamphleteer or writer, whose services were deemed sufficiéntly meritorious to warrant their retention by the bestowal of a seat in the House. These boroughs admirably met the needs of office-holders. Their elections cost them little, because the electors, the members of the corporation or the freemen, received their bribes, not from the men whom they returned, nor from patrons in the ordinary sense of the term, but from the Government, chiefly in the form of local offices, many of them sinecures, in the customs department or in the admiralty. Re-election, a contingency office-holders had constantly to keep in. mind, was much easier in the treasury-controlled boroughs than in any others, except those in which the office-holders themselves, as was the case with Rose at Christchurch, happened to be in control. If a member representing a treasury borough were appointed to a new office, the notice in the *London Gazette* was almost a sufficient intimation to the local agent of the Government to arrange for a re-election. In these cases the member had no need to obtain the sanction of a patron or to consult a patron's convenience as to when his re-election should take place.

In other respects the Government was an exacting patron. A seat for a borough such as Harwich or Hastings never went to a man on whom the Government could not absolutely rely. It was moreover the rule with the treasury never to " let a natural interest arise between the representative of one of their boroughs and the represented ; but to move the member by the time his constituents became acquainted with him[1]." The object of thus moving a member from one treasury borough to another was to prevent a member from establishing an interest personal to himself in any one.of them, which might become antagonistic to the Government. In this the treasury only acted as many private patrons did, who when they had nominated a member prohibited him from visiting his constituency between one general election and the next. Nor in the case of the treasury boroughs was reason for this caution lacking. Up to 1754 Winchelsea was a treasury borough. In that year an Irish gentleman named Nesbit was nominated by the Duke of Newcastle, who was then managing the treasury boroughs. To make his seat secure Nesbit began at once to purchase houses in Winchelsea in order to control

The Treasury as Patron.

---

[1] *Parl. Hist.*, xxi. 412.

the borough, where the right of election was in the freemen, and he so far succeeded as to establish fully the command over one of the seats, and occasionally, when he stood well with the treasury, he was able to nominate for both; and much effort and a correspondingly large expenditure of money were necessary to bring the borough back under the control of the treasury[1].

Representing successively Five Boroughs.

The Parliamentary career in the House of Commons of Vansittart, afterwards Lord Bexley, illustrates this custom of the treasury in the management of its boroughs. Vansittart, who was Chancellor of the Exchequer from 1812 to 1822, first attracted Pitt's notice by pamphlets in support of the war with France, and of Pitt's financial policy. Having thus shown himself likely to be useful to the Government in the House of Commons, he was returned for Hastings in 1796; and continued to sit in the House for the next twenty-six years, being returned for Old Sarum, Helston, East Grinstead and Harwich, and he represented Harwich until shortly before he was made a peer in 1823[2]. Vansittart had thus an experience of all three classes of boroughs in the nomination of the treasury; the boroughs in which by virtue of its local patronage the treasury was in easy control, and those which were turned over to the treasury by patrons in return for offices or titles, or came into its possession or use by the purchase of the right to nominate.

Part-Payment by Candidates.

It was chiefly from boroughs controlled by the treasury through purchase that treasury nominees of the third class, those who paid part of the cost of their elections, were brought into Parliament. This kind of treasury jobbery in boroughs can be traced back at least to the early years of the reign of George III. Extracts from the correspondence of George III and North, which have been cited earlier in this chapter, show how these boroughs were acquired. How their representation was parcelled out to treasury nominees is made clear in the same correspondence. "'Mr Legge," wrote North in 1774 to Robinson, " can afford only four hundred pounds. If he comes in for Lostwithiel, he will cost the public two thousand guineas. Gascoyne should have the refusal of Tregony if he will pay one thousand pounds; but I do not see why we should bring him in cheaper than any other servant of the Crown. If he will not pay he must give way to Mr Best or Mr Peachy[3]."

[1] Cf. Oldfield, v. 413, 417 ; Beatson, II. 336.
[2] *Dict. Nat. Bio.,* LVIII. 141.
[3] Donne, *Letters of George III to North,* II. 7.

After the Irish members were at Westminster it is also possible to trace another method in treasury borough management, a method by which the treasury financed or partly financed contested elections in the interest of candidates who had given proof that they had good chances of success, and who pledged themselves in return to support the Government. John Wilson Croker, long secretary to the admiralty, whose career was that of a treasury member of the type of Robinson and Vansittart, first came into Parliament in 1807 for the Irish potwalloper borough of Downpatrick, under an arrangement by which his election was partly financed by the treasury. The circumstances of Croker's entry into the House are detailed in the *Civil Correspondence of the Duke of Wellington*, who at this time, as Sir Arthur Wellesley, was secretary for Ireland[1], and was busy in Dublin, managing for the Government the elections which followed the dissolution of 1807. "I have," wrote Wellesley to Lord Hawkesbury from Dublin, May 9th, 1807, "made an arrangement respecting the borough of Downpatrick. This borough formerly belonged to Lord de Clifford, whose interest in it has lately fallen into the hands of Mr Rowley, a commissioner of the revenue here, and of Mr Croker, a gentleman who lately contested it against Lady Downshire. If Mr Croker will now stand he is to have the de Clifford interest, and he has proved to me that he can carry the election. * * * Under these circumstances, I have thought it advisable to encourage Mr Croker to persevere at Downpatrick. He has promised allegiance; and all that was required was a sum of fifteen hundred, or two thousand pounds, to enable him to carry on the contest, and I have by the Duke's (of Portland) advice promised to supply it[2]." This money for Croker's contest, according to Wellesley's letter, was to come out of the Irish secret service fund; or failing that fund, as the sum then in hand was small, "out of any fund applicable to election purposes existing in England." Wellesley's suggestion was that it should come out of the electioneering fund, as the process was a long one by which money could be obtained for electioneering from the civil list fund[3].

At the preceding general election in 1806, which took place whilst the Whigs were in office, the Whigs engaged in borough-mongering in an even more business-like way than that which had

[1] Doyle, III. 617.
[2] *Civil Correspondence of the Duke of Wellington*, v. 42.
[3] *Civil Correspondence of the Duke of Wellington*, v. 42.

characterised their predecessors at the treasury since the days when
North and Robinson were in charge of elections in the interest of
George III. The Tory plan—that pursued by North and Robinson,
and that in which the Wellington correspondence shows the
Canning Administration to have been engaged—entailed heavy
charges on the treasury. The Whigs improved on these older
methods of borough-broking, and made their transactions in nomination boroughs carry the burden of some of their contests in
the open constituencies. This plan has been described by Lord
Palmerston. "The method adopted by ministers with regard to
their borough seats," he writes, "was very politic and ingenious.
They purchased seats from their friends at a low price, making
up the deficiency probably by appointments and promotions.
These seats were afterwards sold out at the average market
price to men who promised their support, and with the difference
they carried on their contested elections. The sum raised in this
manner was stated by a person who was in the secret to be in-
conceivably great, and accounts for an assertion afterwards made
by Lord Grenville in the Lords that 'not one guinea of the
public money had been spent in elections.' It may be imagined
that if seats were bought for two thousand five hundred pounds,
or even two thousand, and sold again for five thousand, a comparatively small number of such transactions would furnish a
considerable fund ; and the Government had so many seats passing
through its hands that, at least in one or two instances, it sold
them to people who only professed themselves in general well-
disposed towards it, without exacting a pledge of unconditional
support[1]."

Carrying
Reform by
Means of
Purchased
Boroughs.

In 1809 an Act was passed against the sale of seats in Parliament. It was abortive, and treasury borough-mongering survived
as long as the old representative system, even if it did not outlive
it. At the general elections of 1830 and 1831, when the Whigs
were again in power, they repeated the borough-jobbing tactics of
1806, which Lord Palmerston has described. At these elections the
treasury transactions in boroughs were on a larger scale than in
1806. Edward Ellice was secretary of the treasury in Lord Grey's
Administration, and he "beat the enemy with their own weapon."
He collected large sums of money from the leading Whigs with
which he purchased nomination boroughs previously represented by
Tories, and secured the nomination for them of men pledged to

[1] Bulwer, *Life of Lord Palmerston,* i. 52.

support Parliamentary reform[1]. Had it not been for this borough-mongering by the treasury, and for the pledges which Whig borough owners such as Earl Radnor and Earl Fitzwilliam exacted from the nominees they returned, the Reform Act could not have been carried in 1832.

Eighteenth and early nineteenth century correspondence and memoirs, as well as the Parliamentary reports of this period, record few instances in which the treasury was at issue with its nominees in Parliament. Men who accepted nominations from the treasury were already in office under the Government, or were anxious for seats in Parliament in the expectation of being appointed to office. Men of independence, who were determined on a line of their own in the House, were not likely to lay themselves under obligations such as obviously went with the representation of a borough, directly or indirectly controlled by the treasury. I have found only two instances in which representatives of treasury boroughs failed to keep the pledges, implied or expressed, which went with their election. In 1781 Rawlinson, who then represented Queenborough, found himself unable to act with the North Administration on the American war, and accordingly he placed his resignation in the hands of Lord Sandwich[2]. In 1809 Quinton Dick, who at the general election of 1807 had made a bargain with the Government for the nomination at Cashel—one of the instances in which the member paid part of the cost of his election—found himself unable to support the Government on all occasions in the House of Commons, and it was intimated to him by Castlereagh that he must either vote with the Government or at once resign his seat[3]. He accordingly applied for the Escheatorship of Munster, the Irish equivalent of the Chiltern Hundreds; and by this resignation there occurred the vacancy at Cashel which gave Sir Robert Peel his first entry into the House of Commons[4].

No nominated members were more loyal to the code which Fox outlined in his speech of 1795 than were those in every House of Commons, from the early years of the eighteenth century to 1832, who owed their seats to the treasury. Every condition impelled these members to loyalty—the offices they held, or were in hopes of holding, as well as their pledges at the time of election—and of them successive secretaries of the treasury must usually

[marginal note: Treasury Nominees who failed to support the Government.]

[marginal note: Steady Allegiance of Treasury Nominees.]

---

[1] *Dict. Nat. Bio.*, xvii. 246.
[2] *Hist. MSS. Comm. 10th Rep.*, App., pt. vi. 46.
[3] Cf. Hansard, 1st Series, xiv. 402.   [4] *Official List*, pt. ii. 256.

have been able to say, as George III said in 1782 of the members
whom he and North had helped to seats in the House in 1780,
"they all behaved with very steady attachment to the end[1]."
Social ostracism would have been the lot of a member had he dared
to ignore his express or implied pledges to a private patron. An
end to an official career, if not complete political extinction,
would have been the lot of the member returned for a treasury
borough who was wanting when the Government called for his
support in the House of Commons.

MEMBERS NOMINATED ON EASY CONDITIONS.

Borough
Owners in
Opposition
and their
Nominees.

In the second group of nominated members I have placed
those who held seats from patrons or friends who imposed few
restrictions on their Parliamentary actions. These members could
never have been as numerous as those who held their seats on
the understanding with their patrons that they were to support the Government. Usually members of the second group
owed their seats to borough owners who were in opposition. But
before these patrons made their nominations they assured themselves that the men they were about to return held political
opinions in harmony with their own. This was certainly the
case with the heads of the great Whig territorial families; with
the Duke of Devonshire, the Marquis of Lansdowne, and Earl
Fitzwilliam, in the period between the American Revolution and
the incoming of the Grey Administration in 1830. A Tory of
the days of North, Pitt, Perceval, or Wellington, would never
have been returned for a borough in the control of any of
these great landed proprietors. Having nominated members whose
political opinions were in general harmony with their own, it was
easy for these Whig borough owners to give their members a
free hand. It was scarcely necessary for them to make conditions
with their nominees, as there was only one line of action open
to those whose patrons were in opposition. But had a member,
nominated by one of these Whig borough proprietors, gone over
to the Government, or taken office under the Government, he
would soon have been compelled to find another seat.

Nominees
in Political
Sympathy
with Patrons.

Mackintosh and Macaulay are sometimes cited as members
who held their seats subject to no conditions; but the freedom
these members enjoyed was not unrestricted, for they could not

---

[1] Donne, *Letters of George III to North*, II. 425.

have permitted themselves to be returned for boroughs with Whig proprietors, and then have failed to act with the Whigs in Parliament. Mackintosh admitted this condition in his speech in the House of Commons on the second reading of the Reform bill. "I know one nomination borough," he said, in describing his own relations with the Duke of Devonshire's borough of Knaresborough, for which he had sat from 1819, "where no seat was ever sold; where no member ever heard a whisper of the wishes of a patron; where a member was under no restraint beyond the ties of political opinion and friendship which he voluntarily imposed upon himself[1]." The Marquis of Lansdowne, before he returned Macaulay for Calne in 1830, knew that his political sympathies were with the Whigs; and while he disclaimed any desire or intention of influencing Macaulay's votes in the House of Commons, and intimated to him that he was quite at liberty to act according to his conscience[2], there was none the less a tie or understanding between patron and member, like that described by Mackintosh as existing between himself and the Duke of Devonshire during Mackintosh's long tenure of the seat for Knaresborough. Mackintosh and Macaulay, in short, would no more have thought it consistent with the conditions under which they held their seats to have voted frequently in support of the Wellington Administration, than a member sitting for Harwich or Hastings, or any other treasury borough, would have regarded it as consistent with the conditions of the tenure of his seat to have supported the Whigs in opposition to the Government. The unwritten code which so long regulated the relations of members and patrons did not touch members returned by patrons who were in opposition so often or so closely as it touched members whose patrons had pledged them to the support of the Government. But members returned by patrons in opposition none the less came within its provisions; and its existence and its application to these men were recognized in Mackintosh's statement of his relations with the Duke of Devonshire.

Scott, afterwards Lord Eldon, is also cited as a member who sat for a nomination borough free from conditions. "I was then," said Lord Eldon in recalling, in the debate on the Reform bill in the House of Lords, the circumstances in which he came into Parliament, "what is called a nomination borough member. But

Eldon's Case.

[1] Hansard, 3rd Series, iv. 697.
[2] Cf. Trevelyan, *Life of Macaulay*, i. 135, 136.

I would not have sat one moment in that House if I had not
been at liberty to act upon my own opinions. No man would
have dared to ask me to sit in Parliament otherwise than upon
that understanding[1]." Eldon owed his election for Weobly in
1783 to Lord Thurlow ; but, as is shown by a letter in the Kenyon
Manuscripts, Thurlow had assured himself of how Eldon stood
politically before he offered him the nomination. He had made
sure that the young lawyer was not likely to embark " in any of
these confederacies by which knots of men struggle in a body for
places[2]."   Thurlow, in other words, had satisfied himself of Eldon's
political principles much as the Whig borough proprietors who
seated the Barres, the Mackintoshes, and the Macaulays made sure
that their nominees were not likely to take a line in Parliament
out of harmony with the one they themselves were pursuing.

Nominees left Free.
    Instances can be quoted in which patrons returned their sons,
their sons-in-law, brothers, nephews or friends, and were indifferent
whether they threw in their lot with the Tories or the Whigs,
whether they allied themselves with the Government or with the
opposition.   In 1705 the Earl of Shaftesbury returned his brother,
Maurice Ashley, for Weymouth and Melcombe Regis " without," as
the Earl afterwards stated, " taking from him the condition of a
free man[3]."   In 1770, when Wedderburn by reason of his vote
on the Middlesex election had been compelled to resign the seat
at Richmond held by the grace of Sir Lawrence Dundas, a
supporter of the Government, Lord Clive returned him for
Bishop's Castle, and gave him an assurance " in writing that he
left him altogether free and uncontrolled as to his future course
in politics[4]."   When Burgoyne entered the House in 1768 as
member for Preston, where he had been elected through the influence of the Earl of Derby, whose daughter, Lady Charlotte
Stanley, he had married, he had " free leave to say what he liked,
and began as a candid friend of the ministry[5]."   Wraxall has also
left on record the statement that when, in 1784, Lord Sackville
returned him as one of the members for Ludgershall, his patron
left him as free in his Parliamentary capacity as he did his
son-in-law, Mr Herbert, who was returned at the same election

---

[1] Twiss, *Life of Lord Eldon*, ii. 278.

[2] *Hist. MSS. Comm. 14th Rep.*, App., pt. iv. 516.

[3] Rand, *Life of Anthony, Earl of Shaftesbury*, 324 ; cf. *Official List*,
pt. ii. 2.

[4] Mahon, v. 448, 449.   [5] *Dict. Nat. Bio.*, vii. 340.

for the borough of East Grinstead[1]. The return of Stratford Canning for Old Sarum in 1828 by his father-in-law is another instance of a nominated member who was bound by his patron to no party[2].

These instances, however, are isolated. They can never have been numerous; and, excepting such cases as these, it may be asserted that the only nominated members who did not come under the code regulating the relations of members and patrons were those who purchased their seats from borough owners who found it more profitable to sell their nominations outright and without political conditions than to go to market directly or indirectly at the treasury. Freedom the Exception.

Members who held seats from even the easiest of patrons were often in much uncertainty as to their tenure. The Whig borough owners of the last seventy years of the old representative system, who had many seats at their disposal, were constant to the men whom they took under their patronage. General Fitzpatrick, who, at the desire of Fox, was returned for Tavistock in 1774 by the Duke of Bedford, represented the borough for thirty-three years[3]. Barre represented the Lansdowne boroughs of Chipping Wycombe and Calne from 1768 to 1790[4]; and Mackintosh was undisturbed in the representation of the Duke of Devonshire's borough of Knaresborough from 1819 until the end of the old Parliamentary system[5]. This permanence in the relations between patrons and members was easily possible in the case of patrons who had half-a-dozen nominations in their gift, and who were too wealthy to desire to sell. But in the case of the smaller proprietors, the men who controlled only a single borough, even when personal relations between patrons and members were at their best, the member's tenure was often insecure for reasons other than political. If a patron had a son whom he was desirous of seating in the House, the nominated member had to betake himself to another constituency when the son came of age. In 1723, when Lord Hervey required for his son the seat at Bury St Edmunds, then held by Serjeant Reynolds, he suggested that Reynolds make an application for a judgeship, and promised to use his influence to that Insecurity of Tenure from Patrons.

---

[1] Wraxall, *Posthumous Memoirs*, i. 418, 419.
[2] Lane-Poole, *Life of Stratford Canning*, ii. 3.
[3] *Dict. Nat. Bio.*, xix. 192.
[4] *Official List*, pt. ii. 123, 137, 157, 170, 183.
[5] Mackintosh, *Life of Sir James Mackintosh*, ii. 371.

end with Walpole. " Your advantage alone," wrote Hervey to Reynolds, " would be sufficient to engage my utmost endeavours ; but I shall have a double satisfaction in bringing this matter to a head, as your promotion to an attendance in the Upper House will make room for my son to supply your place in the Lower[1]."

Prior Claims on Patrons.

A member who owed his seat to the friendship of a patron was liable at any time to a gentle hint, such as Lord Hervey thus conveyed to Reynolds, that his place was needed for someone who had stronger personal claims than himself.   The marriage of a patron's daughter and the need of seating a son-in-law in the House might thus be a cause of disturbance.   From 1807 to 1812 Francis Horner was of the House as member for Wendover.   At the general election in 1812 he was not returned.   " As to Parliament," he wrote, in explaining why for the time being his House of Commons career was at an end, " I have no seat ; because Lord Carrington, to whom I owed my last, has to provide for a nephew who has come of age since the last election, as well as for his son-in-law (Lord Mahon), who, being abroad, loses his seat for Hull ; and because I have not money or popularity of my own to obtain a seat in a more regular and desirable way[2]."   Horner's career aptly illustrates the ups and downs of a member who was dependent on the goodwill of friends for his seat in the House. Family claims on Lord Carrington led to an end of Horner's connection with Wendover in 1812.   After the general election there was a vacancy at St Mawes, a borough controlled by the Duke of Buckinghamshire.   It was offered to Horner " without stipulation or pledge of any sort or kind, saving that which, of course, you will feel it just to admit, namely, to resign whenever your politics should differ from the person who is the means of recommending you to the seat[3]."   Horner accepted it ; but in 1815 he differed from the Duke of Buckinghamshire on the war, and so seriously that in accordance with the conditions of his election, he offered to resign his seat[4].

Financial Stress of Patrons.

Even the financial vicissitudes of a borough-owning family might affect the tenure of a nominated member.   Burke owed his first seat to the second Earl of Verney.   Verney early recognized Burke's ability, and in 1761 returned him for Wendover,

---

[1] Hervey, *Letter-Books*, II. 339.
[2] Francis Horner, *Memoirs*, II. 114, 115.
[3] Francis Horner, *Memoirs*, II. 130.
[4] Francis Horner, *Memoirs*, II. 265.

which was then controlled by the Verney family. Burke represented this borough until 1774, when the condition of Earl Verney's affairs obliged the Earl to ask Burke to find another seat. This he did at Bristol; but the termination of Burke's tenure at Wendover made no break in his friendship with his first Parliamentary patron. "His private circumstances," wrote Burke in 1774, in explaining why Verney and he were soon to end the relation of patron and member, "are very indifferent. Indeed, I am infinitely far from having any sort of reason to complain of the step which he is going to take. He will, indeed he must, have those to stand for Wendover who can bear the charge that borough is to him[1]."

Under the most easy and pleasant conditions—conditions similar to those which existed between Mackintosh and the Duke of Devonshire, between Macaulay and the Marquis of Lansdowne, between Burke and Earl Verney, and between Horner and Lord Carrington—there was always some measure of dependence, and some degree of uncertainty for members who were of the House by the grace of patrons; and an examination of the relations existing between members and patrons affords good ground for Sir Erskine May's statement—made thirty years ago, when much of the correspondence on which this chapter is founded had not yet come to light—that if a member "accepted a seat from a patron, his independence was compromised; but if he acquired a seat by purchase he was free to vote according to his own opinion and conscience[2]." Of the two hundred and fifty or three hundred members who were of the old House of Commons by the goodwill of men possessed of Parliamentary influence, only those were really independent and entirely uncontrolled who owed their places to the money they had paid for them, and not to the favour, interested or disinterested, of patrons.

Patronage and Independence Incongruous.

SEATS ACQUIRED BY PURCHASE.

Boroughs were treated as property, and the right to elect members of Parliament regarded as an appanage of an estate, as early as the reign of Elizabeth, when in 1594 the Lancashire

Early Sale of Boroughs.

---

[1] *Dict. Nat. Bio.*, LVIII. 265.
[2] May, *Constitutional Hist. of England*, I. 343.

borough of Newton was transferred by purchase from the Langton to the Fleetwood family[1]. Such transfers were not uncommon in the seventeenth century[2]. In 1669, when Sir William Drake bought Shardeloes from the Earl of Bedford, the transfer carried with it the right to nominate two members for the borough of Agmondesham[3]. I have not, however, been able to trace back the sale of nominations to seats in Parliament, as distinct from the sale of the right to make these nominations, to a period earlier than the Revolution.

Sale of a Nomination in 1698. The earliest instance which I have found of a nomination being offered for sale is recorded in the *Vernon Correspondence*, in which there is a letter describing Colonel Mordaunt's election experiences at Malmesbury in 1698. Lord Wharton's steward had " at this time the leading interest" there; and he told Colonel Mordaunt " in plain terms that whoever expected to be chosen there should pay him four hundred pounds down." " What reasons were given him to make this demand," adds Vernon, " I know not[4]." The tone of surprise and indignation which marks this letter suggests that the sale of seats was not yet open and frequent. But there is proof that as soon as the eighteenth century began borough-broking became more common. " It is said," wrote Davenant in reference to the general election of 1701, " there were known brokers who have tried to stock-job elections upon the exchange, and that for many boroughs there was a stated price[5]."

Purchase of Seats in the Eighteenth Century. By 1714 the purchase of seats had become a matter of notoriety; for at the general election in that year, when her husband was hunting for a borough, Lady Mary Wortley Montagu suggested that the most certain and expeditious way of entering the House of Commons would be for him " to deposit a certain sum of money in some friend's hands, and buy some little Cornish borough." As the century progressed the sale of nominations to seats in the House became increasingly common. Boroughs, as in the case of Stockbridge in 1756[6], were sometimes leased for a term of years, like country houses; and between 1790 and 1830 it was a practice with men who desired to be of the House, unfettered by any conditions, to hire their seats at the rate of so much a year. The

---

[1] Earwaker, *Local Gleanings relating to Lancashire and Cheshire*, ii. 184.

[2] Cf. *Surrey Archaeological Collections*, v. 211, 213; Torrens, *Hist. of Cabinets*, i. 454.

[3] Oldfield, iii. 98.

[4] *Vernon Correspondence*, ii. 148.

[5] Davenant, *Works*, iii. 326.

[6] Torrens, *Hist. of Cabinets*, ii. 337.

earlier plan had been to hire boroughs for the lifetime of a Parliament; but as prices for seats mounted upwards—and subsequent to the Union five or six thousand pounds came to be regarded as the market value of a nomination—a man who went into the borough market became more chary about taking the risk of a short-lived Parliament, and substituted for payment down the system of paying borough patrons one thousand pounds and later twelve or eighteen hundred pounds[1], for each year during which he occupied a seat.

Davenant in describing borough-broking at the election of 1701 gives no hint as to the prices which then prevailed. Nor does Lady Mary Wortley Montagu in her letter of 1714 furnish any information as to the sum for which a little Cornish borough could be secured. In 1727 Richard Hampden, a great-grandson of the Hampden of the Long Parliament, who had lost eighty thousand pounds in South Sea speculations, and was at this time pressed for money, offered the reversion of his seat at Wendover to the Government[2]. But again in this early instance of taking a seat to market to the treasury there is no hint as to the sum that Hampden expected as the price. In 1734 Sir William Wyndham, when supporting in the House of Commons the repeal of the Septennial Act, made an allusive reference to members who had purchased their seats " at the rate of perhaps fifteen hundred pounds, besides travelling expenses and other little expenses[3]." But the earliest eighteenth century quotation which I have found for a nomination for a borough, made in a business-like way, is of the year 1747. James Tilson, of Hampton Court, was in that year offered a nomination at Cricklade, for fourteen hundred pounds; and it was a condition in a regularly drawn up contract of sale that the fourteen hundred pounds were not to be paid over " until Mr Tilson had sat fourteen days in the House of Commons without a petition being presented against him, or been confirmed in his seat in the case of a hostile petition." It was a further condition that Mr Tilson " must come to the borough, or some proper person with the money," and that the out-of-pocket expenses of the election, not exceeding fifty pounds, must be advanced by the candidate[4].

Price of Seats.

[1] Hansard, 2nd Series, xxv. 1253. [2] Torrens, *Hist. of Cabinets*, I. 374.
[3] Coxe, *Life of Walpole*, II. 260.
[4] *Hist. MSS. Comm. 13th Rep.*, App., pt. III. 118.

Consti-
tutional
Changes
enhance
the Value
of Seats.

Between the time of Lord Wharton's steward's demand for four hundred pounds for a return at Malmesbury in 1698, and this agreement for fourteen hundred pounds as the price of a seat at Cricklade in 1747, there had been two constitutional changes, both of which had enhanced the value of a nomination to a seat in the House of Commons. The Act of Queen Anne's reign which compelled a member who took office to be re-elected if he desired to continue of the House had put a premium on close boroughs; and the Septennial Act of 1715 by lengthening the tenure of Parliaments had also given a greater value to a seat in the House. The Last Determinations Act of 1729, which gave a quasi-Parliamentary title to many borough owners, had made borough property much more secure than it had been before; and consequently made it easier for borough patrons to find purchasers for their nominations. An applicant for a seat was prepared to pay a higher price for a nomination when he knew that there was little likelihood of a successful petition against his return; for although purchasers of nominations protected themselves against loss of seats on petition, a seat for which there was no likelihood of a petition was more valuable than one which was obviously open to attack.

Price of a
Seat in 1747.

The agreement for the sale of the nomination for Cricklade in 1747, which did not, however, result in the return of Mr Tilson for the borough, was made by Dr Ayscough, who in that year was organising a party in the House of Commons in the interest of Frederick, Prince of Wales. It was one of several agreements drawn up by Dr Ayscough between 1747 and 1749 for the purchase of nominations to seats in the House of Commons. Another of these agreements in 1747 was with Lord Edgcumbe for the nominations at Grampound[1]. A third was of the year 1749; and by its terms the Prince of Wales was to pay three thousand pounds down to Mr Thomas Pitt, and "to put Mr Pitt in the receipt of his allowance and salary of fifteen hundred pounds a year," in return for conceding to the Prince "the nomination of each and every member of Parliament that shall be elected at the borough of Old Sarum for the term of — years, without expense to his Royal Highness, except the sum of forty pounds to pay usual fees of each election[2]." Dr Ayscough, in his own field, which was confined to the counties of Cornwall and Wiltshire, was an

[1] *Hist. MSS. Comm. 13th Rep.*, App., pt. III. 119.
[2] *Hist. MSS. Comm. 13th Rep.*, App., pt. III. 134.

expert in borough-mongering. Few men could have been more familiar than he with the current quotations for nominations to the House in the last half of the reign of George II. It may therefore be concluded that fourteen hundred pounds, the sum proposed for the nomination for Cricklade in 1747, represented the market price of a seat in the House in the middle of the eighteenth century.

Between the reign of George II and that of William IV prices for nominations advanced from fourteen or fifteen hundred pounds to as high as seven thousand pounds, when bought for a Parliament, and to twelve hundred or even eighteen hundred when seats were rented by the year[1]. In this period several forces were at work which influenced the upward movement in the value of seats. By the end of the reign of George II returned Anglo-Indians were making their way into Parliament. They were in the market for seats[2], with the result that, at the first general election in the reign of George III, two thousand pounds was considered a fair price for a nomination[3]. During the reign of George III, especially from 1760 to about 1783, members who steadily voted with the administration were rewarded with un-exampled prodigality; and in consequence of the titles, offices, pensions, shares in loans, and government contracts which votes in the House commanded, seats were increasingly in demand, and nominations continuously advanced in price.

[marginal note: Reasons for the Advance in Value of Seats.]

It was in this period when, as the North correspondence shows, a nomination to a seat fetched from two thousand five hundred to three thousand pounds, that seats were first advertised for sale in the London newspapers. Nominations at Honiton, Milborne-Port, and Reading, were offered in the *London Chronicle* of December 26th and 29th, 1767, and in the *Gazetteer* and *New Daily Advertiser* of February 4th, 1768. The boroughs were not named. It was merely stated that there were for sale "some boroughs which would come reasonable," and that inquiries respecting them could be addressed to the printers. These advertisements of 1767 and 1768 brought the printers into conflict with the House of Commons on a question of privilege[4]. But advertisements offering boroughs for sale, and advertisements of men seeking nominations

[marginal note: Seats Advertised for Sale.]

---

[1] Hansard, 2nd Series, xxv. 1253.
[2] Cf. Walpole, *Letters*, iii. 379.
[3] Cf. Chesterfield, *Letters to His Son*, iv. 218.
[4] *H. of C. Journals*, xxxi. 603, 617.

for boroughs continued to appear at general elections until as late as 1807, the last general election preceding the Act of 1809, which made the sale of seats illegal[1].

From 1784 to 1800 the growing wealth of the country and the great fortunes made in the industrial and commercial world tended to force up the value of seats. The Union of Ireland with Great Britain had also its effect in the same direction. In 1799, when the bill for the Union was about to be introduced in the Irish Parliament, Lord Castlereagh estimated the value of a seat in the Parliament at Westminster at four thousand pounds[2]. Values, however, did not long remain at these figures. In 1807 fourteen hundred guineas a year were offered by advertisement in the *Morning Chronicle* of May 21st for a seat in the Parliament of 1807–12. Between then and 1832 from five to six thousand pounds was the ordinary price of a seat purchased for the lifetime of a Parliament[3]; while for a seat rented by the year the price had advanced to eighteen hundred pounds before the old electoral system came to an end. Borough brokers continued in business long after the Act of 1809 was supposed to have put an end to the sale of seats. Oldfield, the most notorious of them, was so engaged in 1812[4]; and he is credited with having negotiated the sale at some general elections of as many as fifteen or twenty nominations[5].

While the sale of nominations is traceable back to within a decade of the Revolution, the purchase of them by men who desired to be of the House, unfettered by conditions made either by patrons or by the Government, was one of the most modern developements of the old representative system. There are no traces of it, none at least that I have been able to discover, earlier than 1796, when Sir Francis Burdett bought, free from any political conditions, the nomination of Boroughbridge from the Duke of Newcastle[6]. At the same general election Sir John Aubrey made an agreement with Sir Claude de Crespigny, the proprietor of the Suffolk borough of Aldborough, by which he was to pay one thousand pounds a year for his seat there, on

---

[1] *Morning Chronicle*, May 4th and 21st, 1807, and *Morning Post*, May 21st, 1807.

[2] *Castlereagh Correspondence*, II. 150.

[3] Cf. Bacon, *Memoir of Edward, Lord Suffield*, 43; Romilly, *Memoirs*, II. 56; *Paget Papers*, I. 138; Pryme, *Autobiographic Recollections*, 179.

[4] Hansard, 2nd Series, XVII. 1210.

[5] Cf. Hansard, 2nd Series, XVII. 693.

[6] Cf. Hansard, 2nd Series, XXII. 707.

the understanding that he was to vote as he pleased[1]. Prior to this time borough owners with nominations for sale would appear to have disposed of them to the treasury, where there was usually a market; or to have bestowed them free of expense or on easy terms to men who were eager to be of the House, and were willing to pledge allegiance to their patrons, and to push the fortunes of their patrons as well as their own in Parliament.

Occasionally it may have happened, as it did in 1774, when Lord George Gordon was pressing General Fraser hard in the election for Inverness-shire[2], that a man possessed himself of a borough nomination and transferred it unconditionally to a rival candidate, as a means of buying off opposition in a more desirable constituency. Gordon owed his seat at Ludgershall from 1774 to 1780 to the fact that General Fraser was alarmed at his popularity in Inverness-shire, and in order to remove him from the field he purchased for him, from Lord Melbourne, a nomination for the Wiltshire borough.

Buying off a Rival.

It sometimes happened that men procured nominations either by gift or purchase, in order that they might enjoy the privilege of Parliament, and elude their creditors[3]. All through the eighteenth century men sought nomination for a variety of reasons. But not until the stirring period ushered in by the French Revolution do men appear to have bought seats in the House in order to advance political reforms in which they were interested. To these men the relation of member and patron would have been irksome in the extreme. Men like Burdett and Hume could no more have worn the collars of patrons like the Duke of Devonshire and the Marquis of Lansdowne—the collars which sat so lightly and pleasantly on Mackintosh and Macaulay, and to the outward eye were invisible—than they could have worn the close-fitting collars of the treasury, or of patrons like the Duke of Newcastle or Sir James Lowther. The code which regulated relations between members and patrons, even in its easiest and most elastic form, would have been intolerable to the members who in the last forty years of the old House of Commons bought their way into it, and covenanted with the borough owners from whom they purchased

Seats Purchased by Reformers.

---

[1] Cf. Pryme, *Autobiographic Recollections*, 179.

[2] Cf. Watson, *Life of Lord George Gordon*, 6, 7; *Dict. Nat. Bio.*, XXII. 197; and for another instance, *Caldwell Papers*, II. 135–37.

[3] Cf. *Hist. MSS. Comm. 15th Rep.*, App., pt. VI. 457; and *10th Rep.*, App., pt. VI. 38, 39; Hansard, 3rd Series, III. 1061.

that they should be absolutely free. The pace these men were bent on making in constitutional, legal, and economic reforms, was not the pace which the great Whig borough proprietors usually desired to go ; and accordingly these reformers went into the open market and purchased nominations on terms which put them beyond any man's call in the House of Commons.

Reformers detest the System.
Nearly all the men who, between 1790 and 1832, thus bought their seats were opposed to the, system of which they availed themselves. Burdett, Romilly, Hume, Warburton, and Ricardo were all Parliamentary reformers. They all worked for the great movement which culminated in the peaceful revolution of 1832. "This buying of seats," wrote Sir Samuel Romilly in 1807, "is detestable." "And yet," he continued, "it is almost the only way in which one in my situation, who is resolved to be an independent man, can get into Parliament. To come in by popular election in the present state of the representation is quite impossible. To be placed there by some great lord, and to vote as he shall direct, is to be in a state of complete dependence ; and nothing hardly remains but to owe a seat to a sacrifice of a part of one's fortune[1]." Joseph Hume disliked the old nomination system as heartily as Romilly. He was, however, anxious to work for its overthrow ; and to that end in 1812 he purchased a nomination for the borough of Weymouth[2].

Political Conditions accompanying Purchase of Seats.
Sir Erskine May in his presentation of borough-mongering from the accession of George III to 1832 states that "it was the sole redeeming quality of this traffic that boroughs were generally disposed of to persons professing the same political opinions as the proprietors[3]." This was undoubtedly true of the traffic until the last decade of the eighteenth century ; and this attitude of borough proprietors towards their boroughs partly accounts for the fact that, during the long reign of George III, the great majority of nominated members of the House supported the Government. May's statement is also partly true of the sale of nominations between the Union and 1832. Sir George Staunton, who had bought the nomination for St Michael in 1818 and 1820 at the current market rates, was refused the nomination in 1828 on the old terms, because the owner of the seat differed from him on the Catholic question[4]. For one thousand pounds Praed, in

[1] Romilly, *Memoirs*, II. 56.   [2] *Dict. Nat. Bio.*, XXVIII. 230.
[3] May, *Constitutional Hist. of England*, I. 235.
[4] Staunton, *Memoirs*, 116.

December, 1830, bought a seat for St Germains for two years, subject to the condition that he should support the Tory Government[1]; and in 1830, when Gatton was in the hands of a borough broker, and a seat there was sold for twelve hundred pounds, it was made a condition that the purchaser should support the Wellington Administration[2]. But while the sale of nominations to men in political sympathy with the borough owners continued to the last, there were, between the coming of the Irish members to Westminster in 1801 and the Reform Act, and, as is proved by the cases of Burdett and Aubrey, at an even earlier period, sales of nominations in which the patrons were indifferent as to the political opinions of the men to whom they sold.

In the last forty years of the old House of Commons seats for both English and Irish boroughs were sold to the highest bidder without any political conditions, and without any care on the part of patrons whether their nominees were of their political party or not. Burdett, in speaking on Lord Blandford's Reform bill of 1830, told the House that "early in life he came into that House in order to defend the Constitution of England. He purchased his seat of a borough-monger. He purchased it of the Duke of Newcastle. He (the Duke) was no patron of his. He took his money, and by purchase he obtained a right to speak in the most public place in England[3]." In 1822 Edward Stanley, afterwards Earl of Derby, was elected for Stockbridge under circumstances which afford further proof that there were borough owners at this time who had no compunction about returning men whose political principles were not those which they themselves professed. "This borough," reads the account of the beginning of Stanley's Parliamentary career, "had been in the hands of a Tory, a West Indian proprietor, named Joseph Foster Barham, who being in difficulties sold it to a Whig peer, Earl Grosvenor[4], and on a successor being found by the purchaser, in the person of young Stanley, at once vacated the seat, and introduced him to the electors[5]."

Romilly, Hume, Warburton and Ricardo, all of whom were of the House subsequent to Burdett's election in 1796, held their seats under conditions similar to those on which the Duke of Newcastle sold to Burdett the nomination for Boroughbridge.

Margin notes: Seats sold without Political Conditions.

A new Avenue into the House.

[1] *Dict. Nat. Bio.*, XLVI. 282.   [2] Hansard, 3rd Series, v. 123.
[3] Hansard, 2nd Series, XXII. 707.
[4] Cf. Bacon, *Memoir of Edward, Lord Suffield*, 101.
[5] *Dict. Nat. Bio.*, LIV. 54; *Official List*, pt. II. 291.

Their relations with the borough owners were at an end when they had paid the purchase money, and they were of the House free from any vestige of patron control. This developement coincided with the beginnings of a more active and stirring political life, with the dawn of Radicalism in England; and it opened a new avenue into the House to men who were strongly in opposition to the existing order of things, to the Toryism of the period, and who were too independent and too Radical in thought and speech to obtain nominations at the hands of the great landed proprietors, such as the Lansdownes, the Devonshires, and the Fitzwilliams, who were at this period the mainstay of the formal Liberalism of the Whigs.

Few Independent Members in the House.

The developement in the old electoral system, or rather the new departure in the corruption of the old system, which opened a way into the House for the Burdetts and the Humes, was late in coming. The number of men who were of the House between 1790 and 1832, under conditions such as have been described, members who had no constituents to whom they were answerable and no patrons whose wishes they were in honour bound to respect, was never large. It could never have been large, because to the last the treasury was in the market for boroughs, and in most cases in which boroughs were not sold outright to the treasury it was still possible for the treasury to make it worth the while of borough owners to return members pledged to support the Government. Nominated members, free from patron control because they had paid full value for their seats, had not begun to make their appearance in the House when Fox depicted the working of the patron and member code. Burdett was not of the House until a year after Fox's memorable speech in favour of Parliamentary reform in 1795. Excepting these members there can have been, at any time between the Revolution and 1832, exceedingly few nominated members who were really and in all respects in the position of the patron-returned member of whom Lord Mahon affirms that "he felt no humiliating dependence on him by whose interest he was elected." Even these few members whose bargains with borough owners left them absolutely free were not easy in their positions. Romilly apologises for his presence in the House by virtue of a purchased nomination; and Sir George Staunton in his *Memoirs* offers a similar apology.

For the nomination boroughs it has been claimed that they served to keep up the intellectual level of the House of Commons.

"They were," wrote Bagehot in 1876, "an organ for what may be
called specialised political thought; for trained intelligence busy
with public affairs.   Not only did they bring into Parliament men
of genius and ability; but they kept together a higher political
world, capable of appreciating that genius and ability when young,
and learning from it when old[1]."   The representative history of
Cornwall, with its twenty-one boroughs, most of them for nearly
one hundred and fifty years absolutely in the hands of patrons,
should, more than that of any other county of England, furnish
instances to substantiate this claim.   There, if anywhere, the
nomination system must have been seen at its best, as in the
last century of the unreformed Parliament its boroughs were
mostly in the hands of large landed proprietors, whose wealth
might have put them above sordid considerations when making
nominations.   When examined, however, the representative history
of this county of many boroughs affords the smallest possible
ground for the claim made for the nomination system.   "During
the reign of George III," writes Mr W. P. Courtney, who has
traced the history of these twenty-one Cornish constituencies, and
followed with scholarly care and detail the careers of the men who
represented them at Westminster, "nearly six hundred members
were returned to Parliament by the boroughs of Cornwall, and of
this large total the representatives eminent in literary or political
life can be counted on the fingers of the hands[2]."

Pelham, the two Pitts, Fox, Canning, and Peel, none of whom
ever represented a Cornish borough, would seem to have been the
accidents of the old nomination system rather than the results of
it.   These men would have found their way into the House and
made themselves famous there in a representative system as uniformly democratic as that of England to-day.   It is probably
true that men are as closely held within party lines by the whips
and the party organisations of to-day, local and national, as they
were under the system of patronage.   It may be that there are
fewer really independent members to-day, men who say what
they think, and vote as conscience dictates, than there were in
the period between 1790 and 1832, when it was possible for men
like Burdett, Romilly, and Hume to buy their way into the House

Marginal notes:
Nomination Boroughs and the Encouragement of Genius.

Independent Members before and since Reform.

---

[1] Bagehot, "Lord Althorp and the Reform Act," *Fortnightly Review*,
November, 1876, 595.

[2] Courtney, *Parliamentary Representation of Cornwall to 1832*, Intro., xxi.

of Commons. But these are questions which do not come within the scope of this chapter, or even of these volumes. My purpose is to trace how the House of Commons came to stand in need of the sweeping reform of 1832, and to describe the representative system and its workings in and out of Parliament, while it was slowly taking on the form and character it presented in the opening years of the nineteenth century.

PART III

THE CROWN AND THE FRANCHISE

CHAPTER XVII.

THE CROWN AND THE FRANCHISE—TO THE END OF THE SIXTEENTH CENTURY.

It is not my purpose in these chapters to write of the contests of the Crown with the House of Commons. My concern is only with the attitude of the Crown to the franchise and its exercise by the electorate, and to bring forward such evidence as I have found to warrant the statement made in these pages that, from the earliest days of the representative system until the eve of the reform of 1832, there were few sovereigns who stood aside when the House of Commons was being chosen and did not seek to influence elections.

During the era of personal government sovereigns almost in- *Effects of* variably worked for the control of the House of Commons. It *Crown Inter-* was the desire of the Crown for this control which caused seats *ference.* in the House to become valued; for it was from the Crown that the courtiers and the lawyers who were the earliest non-resident members from the boroughs received their rewards in offices and other royal favours. It was chiefly owing to the same desire of the Crown that, between the reigns of Henry VI and James I, so many boroughs were enfranchised and the number of members of the House of Commons so largely increased.

The evidence of Crown interference in the elections before *Early Inter-* the reign of Henry VIII is scanty and fragmentary. Of the *ference.* reign of Edward I there is a record that in the writs for the Parliament of 1300-1 there was a request for the attendance of knights, citizens and burgesses who had been of the Parliament which had met in 1300 at York. If living and able to attend these men were to be chosen of the new Parliament; if not then others were to be elected in their room[1]. In the reign of Edward III, when the Duke of Lancaster was in control, the Duke so contrived to influence the elections to the Parliament of 1376–77 that those who had opposed him in the Parliament of 1375–76 were not re-elected, with the exception of twelve men who could not be removed, "for that the countries where they were would not elect any other[2]." The Parliament of 1375–76 had been independent. The House of Commons had elected a Speaker hostile to the Duke of Lancaster, and demanded the correction of abuses and the punishment of "certain persons who had seemed to have impoverished the King and the realm and greatly blemished their fame[3]."

Richard II and the Sheriffs.

Richard II packed the House of Commons; and moreover, "by prorogation and adjournment, substantially an innovation on popular rights, he was enabled to continue his packed Parliaments[4]." Of Richard II it is also recorded that in 1386 he called the sheriffs and justices of the County of Nottingham to Nottingham, where it was proposed to the sheriffs that they should not permit any knights of the county to be chosen to the Parliament, but such as the King and his council should appoint; unto which the sheriffs answered "that the commons would keep their old customs, which will that the knights be elected by the commons[5]." Further it was objected against Richard II that although, by the statutes and customs of the kingdom, in the calling of every Parliament "the people in every county ought to be free to choose and depute knights to be in the Parliament, yet the King, to the end he might the more freely gain in Parliament the effect of his rash will, did often direct mandates to the sheriffs that they should cause to come to the Parliament as knights of the shire certain persons named by the King; whereof things prejudicial to the kingdom and burdensome to the people were ordained[6]." Among the articles for the King's deposition was one which asserted that to serve his purpose he would suffer the sheriffs of shires to remain above one year or two in their office; and another in which it was complained that at the summons of the Parliament, when knights and burgesses were elected and the

---

[1] *Rep. on the Dignity of a Peer*, 215. [2] Longman, *Edward III*, II. 276.
[3] Longman, *Edward III*, II. 248. [4] Ferrall, *The Law of Parliament*, 16.
[5] Whitelocke, *Notes on the King's Writ*, I. 383.
[6] Whitelocke, *Notes on the King's Writ*, I. 384.

election had fully proceeded, " he put out divers persons elected, and put others in their place to serve his will and appetite[1]."

Besides originating prorogations as a means of enabling him to continue the life of a subservient House of Commons, Richard II is credited with bringing into existence a committee corresponding closely to the Committee of Articles of the Parliament of Scotland. It came into being in the Parliament which met at Westminster on the 17th of September, 1397, and which was adjourned to Shrewsbury, where it met on the 28th of January, 1398. Sir John Bussy, a servile supporter of Richard's arbitrary and unconstitutional action, was Speaker of the House of Commons of 1397–98. The Parliament sat only three days at Shrewsbury, and by its last act delegated its authority to a committee of eighteen members. Twelve were of the House of Lords; six, of whom Bussy was one, were of the Commons. Thus Richard contrived to become an absolute King; as every man of the committee was believed to be devoted to his interest[2]. *The Shrewsbury Parliament.*

Of Richard's successor, Henry IV, it was complained about the time of his fourth Parliament that no justice could be expected at his hands, because, contrary to the oath which he took at his coronation, he had by letters written and sent into sundry shires procured certain burgess-ships for the Parliament, all of which he bestowed upon such as would not fail to serve his turn[3]. *Henry IV.*

The reign of Henry VI was marked by the protest of Jack Cade and his followers against the interference of the Crown in elections. Towards the close of the reign, in 1459, there was a Parliament at Coventry to which " a great part of the knights, citizens and burgesses for divers cities and boroughs " were returned by virtue of the King's letters without any other election. In the next Parliament this irregularity was the subject of a petition to the King, who was besought " to consider the premises, and to ordain that the Parliament at Coventry be void and taken for no Parliament, and all Acts and ordinances there made be repealed," which the King granted[4]. *The Parliament at Coventry.*

The most remarkable fact in representative history in this reign is that there was then begun the enfranchisement of new boroughs by charters granted by the Crown, or the revival of the Parliamentary franchise in boroughs which had allowed their *Enfranchisement by Royal Charter.*

---

[1] Hayward, *Life of Henry IV*, 91.   [2] Cf. *Dict. Nat. Bio.*, VIII. 40.

[3] Whitelocke, *Notes on the King's Writ*, I. 384.

[4] Whitelocke, I. 385; Parry, 188, 189.

privilege of returning members to lapse.   Thirteen boroughs came
into the electoral system in the reign of Henry VI.   Some of
them, such as Plymouth, Coventry, Westbury, Poole, and Chippenham, were then undoubtedly considerable places, and of importance as centres of commerce or industry.   But only the
exigencies of House of Commons control, or the ingenuity of
courtiers eager to be of the House, can account for the enfranchisement of what were then miserably small places, such as
Bramber, Steyning, and Gatton.   Bramber and Steyning are only
half a mile apart; and in the days before they allowed their
privilege of returning members to lapse, they were often represented by the same burgesses.   When they were re-enfranchised
the two places could together have made little more than a village;
but by the charters of Henry VI each was given the privilege of
returning two members to Parliament[1].   Gatton, only a century
later than Henry VI's reign, was without inhabitants, and the right
to elect had become an appanage to a manor.

Courtiers and Borough Charters.   In the reign of Edward IV the desire of the Crown to exercise
control over the Commons is reflected in the eagerness of courtiers
to be of the House.   In the *Paston Letters* there is a passage which
throws light on the enfranchisement of such boroughs as Gatton
and Bramber in the reign of Henry VI, and on similar enfranchisements in subsequent reigns, especially in those of Edward VI and
Elizabeth.   In 1472 Sir John Paston was anxious to be of the
House of Commons.   He had unsuccessfully sought to become a
candidate for the County of Norfolk, and in his behalf his brother
had written to the bailiff of Maldon asking that Sir John might be
chosen as one of the burgesses of that borough.   "If ye miss to be
burgess of Maldon, and my Lord Chancellor will," John Paston
wrote to his brother Sir John, " ye may be in another place.   There
be a dozen towns in England that choose no burgesses which ought
to do, and ye may be set in for one of those towns and ye be
friended[2]."   Gatton, Steyning, and Bramber were of the kind of
boroughs indicated in the Paston letter of 1472, and in all probability they owed their charters to the foresight of borough-
hunting courtiers, who saw in their enfranchisement an easy way
into the House of Commons.   In later reigns petitions to the
Crown for enfranchisement were often at the instance of men

[1] Lewis, i. 211, iv. 178; *Official List*, pt. i. 356.
[2] Gairdner, *Paston Letters*, iii. 55.

who were aiming at the control of the boroughs for which representation was sought[1].

Henry VII was a dictator rather than a constitutional sovereign. The times required a strong will and high-handed determination on the part of the King, and the first of the Tudors seems to have succeeded in effectually bringing the House of Commons under his influence and control, and in continuing this control during his entire reign. Some of the King's power has been attributed to the charters of incorporation which gave the select bodies in many cities and boroughs the exclusive right to elect to the House of Commons[2]; but the political and social conditions of the period were also favourable both to the King's independence of Parliament, and to Crown control when it was necessary that Parliament should be convened. In the civil wars of the preceding reigns a great part of the nobility had been cut off. Those who remained and had contrived to preserve their estates were restrained by the policy of the Tudors from regaining their influence. Many were deeply in debt to the Crown. "It will at once be perceived," writes Brewer, "that such a state of things greatly increased the influence of the Crown. It proved a powerful check upon the nobility and gentry, who at any time were liable, if they showed signs of insubordination, to be brought to their account and suffer the extreme rigour of the law. The fact is that in the reign of Henry VII, as is often the case at the close of a civil war, money more than arms had become the great power of the State, and no one understood this power more perfectly than did the founder of the Tudor dynasty[3]."

Although Henry VIII in his communications to the Pope laid much stress on the independence of Parliament, there is proof in the state papers that the King at times personally interested himself in elections to the House of Commons, and also abundant proof that Cromwell managed elections for the Crown. "A little before the receipt of your letter," reads a letter from Sir Ralph Sadleir, in the state papers for 1529–30, "I spoke with Mr Gage at the court, and as you commanded, moved him to speak to the Duke of Norfolk for the burgess-room (at Oxford) of the Parliament on your behalf. The Duke said he had spoken with the

[1] Cf. *Hist. MSS. Comm. 12th Rep.*, App., pt. IV. 117.
[2] Merewether and Stephens, II. 1043.
[3] Brewer, *Reign of Henry VIII*, II. 392.

King, who was well-contented that you should be a burgess if you would follow the Duke's instructions[1]." To the City of Colchester the King himself wrote a letter requesting the corporation to return to the House of Commons a candidate whom he nominated[2].

Cromwell's Activity in Elections. Cromwell in 1533 was managing the by-elections to the Parliament of 1529–36—attending in behalf of the Crown to "new elections of such knights and citizens as are lacking in Parliament[3]." It would also seem that Cromwell was whip to the nominees of the Crown in the House of Commons, for among the correspondence of this year there is a letter from Thomas Hall, one of the members for the borough of Huntingdon, asking leave of absence from attendance in Parliament, because he had taken the office of receiver to the Bishop of Lincoln[4].

Subserviency of Henry VIII's Parliaments. A considerable part of the Commons of the Parliament of 1523—that which met at Blackfriars, and from which Wolsey asked a grant of eight hundred thousand pounds for the prosecution of the war with France—consisted of the King's household officers[5]. Of the Parliament of 1529–36—the Parliament which it has been supposed differed greatly in its character, independence, and aims, from all its predecessors, and was animated with a spirit of liberty never manifested before—Brewer affirms that only a very lively imagination indeed can find in its dry records and authenticated proceedings any support for such captivating notions. "There is," he continues, "no ground for imagining that it differed much from other Parliaments assembled by the Tudors, in the mode of its election, in the choice of its members, in the measures it passed, or its exemption from the dictation and interference of the Crown. The choice of the electors was still determined by the King or his powerful ministers, with as much certainty and assurance as that of the sheriffs. * * * The evidence that the King throughout his reign interfered with the elections for Parliament, determined its measures, regulated its debates, is too clear and too abundant to be disputed[6]."

During the reign of Henry VIII the number of members of the

[1] *Letters and Papers of Henry VIII*, 1529–30, 3180.
[2] Merewether and Stephens, ii. 93.
[3] *Letters and Papers of Henry VIII*, 1533, vi. 551.
[4] *Letters and Papers of Henry VIII*, 1533, vi. 505 ; *Official List*, pt. i. 396.
[5] Hallam, *Hist. of England*, 1855, i. 17.
[6] Brewer, ii. 466, 467.

House of Commons was increased from 296 to 334[1].　The larger Additions to the House of Commons. part of this increase was due to the inclusion of Wales in the representative system by Act of Parliament.　The County of Chester and the City of Chester were similarly included.　The boroughs of Buckingham, Berwick-on-Tweed, and Oxford, as well as Calais, were enfranchised by charter.　Henry VIII in his management of the House of Commons did not resort to the expedients of Henry VI or to those subsequently adopted in the reigns of Edward VI, Mary, and Elizabeth.　No decayed boroughs were revived to add to the strength of the King's supporters in the House of Commons.　No Gattons or Grampounds dated their charters from his reign; and the additions made by Henry VIII to the representation were free from the suspicion of any sinister motive[2].

In the short reign of Edward VI the interference of the Crown Open Interference by Edward VI. in elections was more open, if not more general, than in the preceding reign.　There is, at least, more trace of its being general; for at the election of 1553 letters were addressed to every sheriff informing him that the royal pleasure was "that where our Privy Council, or any of them within their jurisdictions in our behalf, shall recommend men of learning and wisdom, in such case their directions shall be regarded and followed, as tending to the same which we desire, that is to have this assembly of the most chiefest men of our realm for advice and good counsel[3]."　Several persons accordingly were recommended by letters to the sheriffs, and elected as knights for different shires, all of whom belonged to the court or were in places about the King[4].　Sir William Drury and Sir Henry Bedingfield were recommended to Suffolk as being "well furnished with all good qualities to be knights of that shire[5]."　To Hampshire was recommended "our right trusty and well-beloved counsellor Sir Richard Cotton, knight, comptroller of our house, one who we need not to commend, being for his place with us of no less knowledge than authority[6]."

Twenty-two boroughs electing forty-four members were created Incoming of Cornish Boroughs. or restored in the reign of Edward VI.　Several of them, such as Westminster, Maidstone, St Albans, Lichfield, and Preston,

---

[1] Hatsell, ii. App. iii. 386, Ed. 1796.

[2] Cf. Anson, *Law and Custom of the Constitution*, pt. i. 284.

[3] Parry, 209.　　　　　　　　[4] Hallam, i. 46.

[5] Merewether and Stephens, ii. 1170, 1171; cf. *Official List*, pt. i. 380.

[6] Merewether and Stephens, ii. 1173; cf. *Official List*, pt. i. 379.

were as worthy of inclusion in the representative system as Oxford, Berwick, or Buckingham in the reign of Henry VIII. But nothing except the desire of the Crown, or of ministers acting for the Crown, to control the House of Commons, or the eagerness of courtiers to serve the Crown there, could account for the enfranchisement of such Cornish boroughs as Newport, Saltash, Camelford, West Looe, Grampound, Bossiney and St Michael. Until the reign of Edward VI Cornwall had not been over-represented. Only six of its boroughs had continuously sent members to Parliament; and it was in the reign of Edward VI that Cornwall first began to attain notoriety as a county of many boroughs. It owed this notoriety to the fact that it was a royal duchy, a county over which the Crown exercised more direct control than over most of the other counties of England.

Mary's Letters to the Sheriffs.   With the writs for the election of the third Parliament of Mary's reign, called in 1554, there went letters addressed by the Queen to all the sheriffs, commanding them to admonish such "our good loving subjects as by order of our writs" choose knights, citizens and burgesses that such should be "of their inhabitants, as the laws require, and of the wise, grave and Catholic sort; such as indeed mean the true honour of God, with the prosperity of the Commonwealth[1]."

Boroughs Enfranchised by Mary.   Fourteen additional boroughs, electing twenty-five members, came into the representative system during Mary's short reign. Most of them were places of some importance, and all but four of them, Aldborough, Boroughbridge, Castle Rising, and Higham Ferrers, survived the Reform Act as Parliamentary boroughs. St Ives and Penryn were the only Cornish boroughs added in Mary's reign. Both survived the Reform Act; and had the Crown been as intent on influencing the House through the enfranchisement of boroughs as it was in the reign of Edward VI, it is inconceivable that Higham Ferrers, Banbury and Abingdon, should have been brought in as single-member constituencies. Except for the letters to the sheriffs at the election to the Parliament of 1554, and for the interference of the Earl of Sussex, one of the Queen's most active counsellors, in the elections for the County of Norfolk and the borough of Yarmouth[2], there seems little evidence that in the reign of Mary there was any such interference with the electorate on the part of the Crown

---

[1] Parry, 211.   [2] Hallam, I. 46.

as there was in the reign of Edward VI. Unlike the reigns of Edward VI and Elizabeth the reign of Mary left few permanently adverse effects on the representative system. The borough creations of the reigns of Edward and Elizabeth set up plague-spots which grew increasingly troublesome in the next two centuries, and with the exception of Grampound survived as long as the old representative system lasted.

One interference with the representative system by the Crown in Mary's reign was of a peculiar character. Maidstone forfeited its charter, and with the loss of its charter, the privilege of returning members to the House of Commons, as a punishment for its part in Wyatt's rebellion[1]. This was the only instance in which a borough, as a punishment, was deprived of its right to elect, until the disfranchisement of Grampound. Except for the cases in which writs were temporarily withheld by the House of Commons, Maidstone and Grampound stand out in representative history up to 1832 as the only boroughs which were ever deprived of their right to elect. Disfranchisement of Maidstone.

Elizabeth began the creation of boroughs in 1562 to secure ascendancy in her second Parliament. Cornwall was again turned to, and Tregony, St Germains and St Mawes were of the six boroughs created or revived at this time. Minehead in Somerset, as insignificant as any of the Cornish hamlets, and Tamworth and Stockbridge were the other boroughs brought into the representative system for the Parliament of 1562-63. At later dates in Elizabeth's reign twenty-five other boroughs, including Callington, Fowey and East Looe, all in Cornwall, were added. A few of Elizabeth's creations, such as Tamworth, Cirencester, and Andover, were market towns and places of local importance, and well entitled to be of the representative system. But most of the thirty-one boroughs returning sixty-two members, enfranchised between 1588 and 1603, were rotten boroughs from the beginning of their Parliamentary history. They came at once under the control of the Crown, or under that of territorial families. An example of territorial control is seen in the case of the Lancashire borough of Newton. It was enfranchised in 1558. On the return to the first writ it was described as "the borough of Sir Thomas Langton, knight, Baron of Newton, within his Fee of Markerfylde[2]"; and Elizabeth's Rotten Boroughs.

---

[1] Hatsell, II. 387.   [2] *Official List*, pt. I. 400.

in 1594 the manor was sold, and with it the right of returning two burgesses to Parliament[1].

Members from the New Boroughs.

The boroughs of Elizabeth's reign of this type, like many of those created in the reigns of Henry VI and Edward VI, were not long, if ever, free from patron control; and when the end came, these boroughs of themselves almost filled the disfranchising schedule of the first Reform Act. " The elevation of these petty villages into Parliamentary boroughs," writes the historian of the representative system of Cornwall, " brought about at once the result which the royal advisers expected. The newly-born constituencies were immediately seized upon by a swarm of greedy courtiers or expectant lawyers. From the eastern counties and from the northern shires they rushed to fill the seats which had been made for them. Every hanger-on in the chambers of the royal palace, who could contrive to obtain a mandate of election from one of the Queen's ministers, and every student at Gray's Inn who could ingratiate himself with the legal advisers of the State, sought election from these subservient constituencies, and then repaired to Westminster to render that support which had been stipulated for[2]."

Burleigh and the Borough of Gatton.

The zeal of the Council in electioneering, its acquaintance with the actual conditions in some of the rotten boroughs and with the nature of the territorial control over them, is seen in several letters of Elizabeth's reign concerning the borough of Gatton. Two of these were written by Burleigh in 1584, and addressed to the sheriff of Surrey. Burleigh recalled the fact that hitherto the members for Gatton had been nominated by Mr Copley, " for that there are no burgesses in the borough there to nominate them." He informed the sheriff that by the death of Mr Copley and the minority of his son, the son with his lands was within the survey and rule of the court of wards, whereof Burleigh was Her Majesty's chief officer. " You shall therefore," was Burleigh's command to the sheriff, " forbear to make return of and for the said town without direction first had from me therein, whereof I pray you not to fail." Francis Bacon and Thomas Byshopp were at this election returned for Gatton. They were chosen on the 21st of November. On the 24th Burleigh again wrote the

---

[1] Earwaker, *Local Gleanings*, II. 184.

[2] Courtney, *Parliamentary Representation of Cornwall to 1832*, VII. ; cf. Hallam, I. 266.

sheriff that, "forasmuch as Mr Francis Bacon is returned also for another borough and so certified and sworn, you shall appoint in his room and place Edward Brown, Esq., and so to certify him with Mr Byshopp[1]."

The third letter, dated September 27th, 1586, is from Walsingham, when he was one of the secretaries of state. "Whereas my lords of the Council do understand," it reads, "that Mrs Copley hath the nomination of the two burgesses for the town of Gatton, being a parcel of her jointure, it is not thought convenient, for that she is known to be evil affected, that she should bear sway in the choice of the said burgesses, Her Majesty's pleasure being such as by our letters hath been signified unto you, that a special choice should be had for this present Parliament of fit persons, known to be well-affected in religion and towards the State. Their lordships have thought good therefore you should recommend unto the said burgesses William Wood and Nicholas Fuller, a counsellor-at-law, whom if they shall not be willing to make choice of for their burgesses, at the least you must see that care be had that discreet persons be chosen[2]." At the same election Walsingham was interesting himself at Colchester, where the bailiffs, aldermen and common council, " to serve the Queen's peace and get rid of all trouble," made an order that Walsingham should have " the nomination of both the burgesses of the town for the Parliament for time to come, according to his honour's letter[3]."

Walsingham's Electioneering.

More general in its bearing is a letter addressed from Windsor Castle on the 19th of September, 1586, at the time the election of the Parliament of 1586–87 was pending. " Her Majesty," it reads, " has for special and urgent causes hastened the High Court of Parliament with a new summons to begin on the 15th of October. In the last election of knights and burgesses very good and discreet choice was made of sundry wise and well-affected gentlemen and others. We require you, having called together three or four of the well-affected gentlemen of the county, to send for or to the principals of the cities and boroughs, and to let them understand that we think that they will do very well to nominate in their free elections those whom they elected before, unless they be dead or otherwise employed in Her Majesty's service beyond the seas. The like course may be followed in the election of knights of

Royal Directions to Sheriffs.

---

[1] Harleian MSS. 703, 9, 10; *Official List*, pt. i. 415.

[2] Losely MSS., 242, 243.

[3] Merewether and Stephens, ii. 1346.

the shire[1]." This letter apparently was sent to all the sheriffs; for from the court at Windsor Sir H. Bagnall wrote to the Earl of Rutland, asking the Earl to nominate him for one of his boroughs. "Perhaps," Bagnall added, "I shall be elected a knight for a shire in Wales; unless hindered by the directions sent to all the sheriffs for preferring such as served in the last Parliament[2]." Rutland elected Bagnall for his borough of Grantham. Bagnall, however, was also elected for Anglesea, and chose to sit for that county[3].

[1] *Hist. MSS. Comm. 12th Rep.*, App., pt. IV. 207.
[2] *Hist. MSS. Comm. 12th Rep.*, App., pt. IV. 207.
[3] *Official List*, pt. I. 418, 421.

CHAPTER XVIII.

THE CROWN AND THE FRANCHISE—FROM JAMES I
TO THE REVOLUTION.

JAMES I called his first Parliament by a remarkable proclama- A Procla-
tion in which he lectured the freeholders and burgesses as to the mation to Electors.
men they were to choose, and the sheriffs as to their manner of
conducting the elections. It called God to witness that, in the
coming Parliament, " we have nothing to propound for satisfaction
of any private desire or particular profit of our own, but merely
and only to consult and resolve with our loving subjects of all
those things which may best establish the public good, with the
general safety and tranquility of this realm." " All those that will
be accounted lovers of their country," were counselled to take great
heed " that both knights and burgesses may be chosen accordingly,
without desire in any particular men to please parents or friends,
that often speak for their children or kin." Great care was also to
be taken by the electors " to avoid the choice of any persons either
noted for their superstitious blindness one way, or for their turbulent humours other ways." Bankrupts or outlaws were not to be
chosen; " but men of known good behaviour, and sufficient live-
lihood, and such as are not only taxed to the payment of subsidies
and other like charges; but also have ordinarily paid and satisfied
the same; nothing being more absurd in any commonwealth than
to permit those to have free voices for law-making by whose own
acts they are exempt from the law's protection."

As to sheriffs they were charged not to direct any precept to Reform by
any ancient borough town within their counties " being so utterly Procla-
ruined and decayed that there are not sufficient residents to make mation.

such choice, and of whom lawful election may be made." Sheriffs
were further to charge all cities and boroughs and the inhabitants
of the same, "that none of them seal any blanks, referring or
leaving to any other to insert the names of any citizens or burgesses to serve for any such city or borough; but do make open
and free election, according to the law, and set down the names of
the persons whom they choose before they seal the certificates[1]."
An election in accordance with this proclamation would have
wrought sweeping changes in the representative system. It would
have disfranchised the Gattons and the Sarums, and made elections
from many of the other rotten boroughs less easy for their patrons.
But there is no reason to believe that James was sincere in his
attempt at reform. Precepts went as usual to all the decayed
boroughs. Blank indentures continued to be common in James's
reign[2]. It was complained of the Parliament of 1603–4 that it
was packed with courtiers[3]; and in the short-lived Parliament of
1614, through the exertions of Bacon and Sir Henry Neville, there
was a court party in the House, not merely of placemen or
nominated members, but of aspirants for court favours answering
to the King's Friends of George III[4].

A Protest
against
Under-
taking.

The King's Friends were not in a majority in 1614; and there
was a strong protest in the House of Commons against the methods
by which the court had sought to control the House. It was at
this time that the word "undertaker," as applied to a manager of
elections, came into vogue. The House was put in a flame by
a rumour that "some one great man had, by letters, procured
sixty voices." The Chancellor of the Duchy of Lancaster, who was
of the House, by reason of his interference in an election at Stockbridge was charged with being an undertaker; and by order of the
House was sequestered[5]. It was even proposed that he should be
excluded, and disabled from sitting in that or any other Parliament. It was recalled that undertaking was one of the causes of
the deposition of Richard II, and of the downfall of Cromwell in
the reign of Henry VIII. One member expressed the wish that all
those who came in by letters should be made incapable of sitting
in the House, for by these means the House was brought to

[1] *Parl. Hist.,* I. 969.   [2] Cf. Parry, 289.
[3] Dixon, *Personal History of Lord Bacon,* 249.
[4] Cf. Hallam, I. 338; Forster's *Life of Eliot,* I. 21; Anson, *Law and
Custom of the Constitution,* pt. I. 287.
[5] *H. of C. Journals,* I. 477.

servitude; and it was urged that proceedings against the Chancellor of the Duchy would have three good effects: "It will be a caution to great ones hereafter how to write; an encouragement to freeholders to use their own right in elections; and a good precedent for future ages that this shall be punished in any how great soever[1]."

Other grievances against the Crown, particularly the imposition of customs at the outports, occupied the attention of the Commons, and supply was delayed. The King at length sent a message requesting that supply might be granted, with a threat of dissolving Parliament unless it were done. But the days of intimidation were gone by. The House voted that they would first proceed to the business of the impositions, and postpone supply until their grievances should be redressed. Aware of the impossibility of conquering their resolution, the King dissolved the Parliament. It had sat only from April 5th to June 7th, 1614, and had not passed a single bill. *Parliament dissolved.*

Six years elapsed before there was another Parliament. Like that of 1603–4 it was convoked by a remarkable proclamation. The electors were this time admonished that choice be made of persons approved for their sincerity in religion. They were counselled that for knights of the shire they cast their eyes on the worthiest men, those that were guides and lights of their country, and that they choose no bankrupts or discontented persons that could not fish but in troubled water. As for burgesses, in the choice of these the electors were admonished not to send young and inexperienced men " that are not ripe and mature for so grave a council," nor yet " curious and wrangling lawyers, who may seek reputation by stirring needless questions[2]." *Calling of James I's Third Parliament.*

James did not look idly on while the elections were proceeding. At the opening of the Parliament of 1614 he disavowed from the throne that he ever " directly or indirectly did prompt or hinder any man in the free election[3]." The state papers of 1620 make it clear that the Crown was recommending candidates to many of the boroughs[4]; and they also show that the Duke of Buckingham had by this time become electioneering manager for the King, a work on which he was engaged until 1628. At the calling of the Parliament of 1624 the King again busied himself with elections; *James I's part in Elections.*

[1] *H. of C. Journals,* i. 478.   [2] Parry, 269.
[3] Parry, 163.   [4] *Cal. State Papers,* 1619–23, 200.

for in the state papers of this year there is a letter in which it is asserted that "the Prince's letters disappointed many, for few towns were left unsolicited by him[1]." Williams, the Lord Keeper, was associated with Buckingham in the management of the elections for the last of the Parliaments of James[2]; and when Charles I came to the throne in 1625, the Lord Keeper was at hand to advise the new King that it had been usual in the preceding reign to take certain precautionary measures to allow the King's trusted friends "to deal with the counties, cities, and boroughs where they were known to procure or promise for their elections[3]."

Borough Creations of the Reign of James I.   Eight charters of enfranchisement were granted by James I. Two of these were to the Universities of Oxford and Cambridge. The others were to Bury St Edmunds, Tewkesbury, Tiverton, Bewdley, Evesham, and Harwich, all towns of some importance. Six other boroughs, Ilchester, Hertford, Wendover, Amersham, Marlow, and Pontefract had their ancient right to send members revived by resolutions of the House. There were no enfranchisements by charter of obviously decayed boroughs to add to the influence of the Crown. Wendover, Amersham, and Ilchester in 1832 were in schedule A, and were deprived of their members. But these places, as has been stated, were enfranchised by the House and not by royal charter. The eight boroughs enfranchised by charter all survived the reform of 1832. James in his admonition to the freeholders and burgesses encroached on the freedom of elections. Undertaking was more open, or perhaps its existence became better known than in the reigns of the Tudors. Still it has to be credited to the first of the Stuarts that by his borough creations he made no additions to the plague-spots of the electoral system.

Charles I and Elections.   Charles I in his conflicts with the House of Commons was more open and daring in his direct interference with elections than any of his predecessors. Unlike James I he issued no proclamations; and he did not follow the precedents of Edward VI and Elizabeth and enfranchise rotten boroughs to add to his influence in the House of Commons. Nine boroughs, whose rights had long lapsed, came back into the representative system during this reign, but by resolution of the House, not by royal charter[4]. The most open

---

[1] *Cal. State Papers,* 1623–25, 152.

[2] *Cal. State Papers,* 1623–25, 148.

[3] D'Israeli, *Commentaries on the Life and Reign of Charles I,* i. 246.

[4] Cf. Hatsell, ii. 388.

interference of the Crown was directed to keeping out of the House men who were obnoxious to the King, rather than to adding to the number of his partisans.   In the recommendation of members to constituencies, to counties as well as to boroughs, the Crown was as active in this as in the preceding reigns.   But the innovation for which Charles I was responsible was introduced at the election of the Parliament of 1625–26.

None of the grievances of the reign of James I had been redressed when the Parliament of 1625 assembled.   It was insisted by the opposition, which was in a majority, that supplies must be voted slowly and conditionally, if there was to be any reform.   The House accordingly granted tonnage and poundage for a year only, instead of for the King's life, and by reason of this innovation the bill failed.   Added to this the House was slow and disposed to be niggard in voting supplies for the war with Spain.   Moreover it was threatening the impeachment of Buckingham ; and in consequence of all this friction the King brought the Parliament to what Clarendon has described as an abrupt and ungracious close. Clarendon has further characterised it as an " unseasonable, unskilful and precipitate dissolution[1] " ; and Eliot left a memoir in which he affirms that reasons of state and all considerations of good policy were so strongly against the step thus taken by the Court, that it was supposed that even Buckingham's influence might have failed finally to carry it, but for a notable project which had then been conceived.   This new scheme of Crown interference in elections was to make ineligible for seats in Parliament the most active of the Commons, " by charging them with employments that might make them incapable of the Parliament, presuming thereby others would be deterred, and the whole ability of that House extracted with those persons[2]."

An Innovation in Electioneering.

The new Parliament was not convened until February, 1626. But in November, 1625, Sir Edward Coke, Sir Thomas Wentworth, Sir Miles Fleetwood, Sir Francis Seymour, Sir Robert Philips, Sir Guy Palmes and Mr Edward Alford, who had been in opposition, were all pricked for sheriffs.   This was to prevent their being of the new House of Commons ; for, as Wentworth wrote when he heard of his appointment as high sheriff of Yorkshire, a sheriff " according to the received rule of our forefathers is tied to his county, as a snail to his shell[3]."   The spirit in which Charles and

Unwilling Sheriffs.

---

[1] Clarendon, *Hist. of the Rebellion*, i. 61.   [2] Forster, *Life of Eliot*, i. 443.
[3] *Strafford Despatches*, iii. 31.

Buckingham made these appointments is brought out in a letter which Sir Arthur Ingram, who had been high sheriff of York in 1620, wrote from London to Wentworth, giving him the news of his appointment. " God give you joy," Ingram wrote, " you are now the great officer of Yorkshire; but you had the endeavours of your poor friend to have prevented it.   But I think if all the council that was at court had joined together in a request for you, it would not have prevailed.   For it was set and resolved what should be done, before the great Duke's going over; and from that the King would not change a little.   The judges proceeded in their old course; and so it went to the King.   But when the names went to the King the King declared himself that he had the names of seven that he would have sheriffs, and so named them himself, and my Lord Keeper set them down.   There is now no more to say but to undergo it cheerfully[1]."

The Sheriffs excluded from the House.   Other of Wentworth's friends advised him to pursue " a private and husbandly course."   He was assured by his father-in-law, the Earl of Clare, that he " could not quit the King's service for that of his subjects[2]"; and so when the Parliament of 1625–26 met, Wentworth stayed in Yorkshire, and attended to " justices, escheators, juries, bankrupts, thieves and such kind of cattle." Alford, Palmes, and Fleetwood all took the same course; they did not seek election.   Philips, Seymour, and Coke were returned for their counties.   They intended at first to have abandoned those seats, and tried the question with the court by obtaining seats in other shires.   But on Seymour offering Wentworth a borough in the West in exchange for one in the North, the backwardness of Wentworth, who had no taste for a conflict with the prerogative out of Parliament, broke down the scheme[3].   Coke persisted in his claim to be of the House, and obtained his writ for the county which he had to serve as sheriff.   But the law was against his right to take his seat.   His election was objected to; and although there was not time in the Parliament of 1625–26 for a decision, Coke was treated by the House as merely a member *de facto*, and he abstained from attending[4].

Charles I's Second Parliament dissolved.   The foremost opponents of the Crown were thus excluded from the new Parliament; but for the most part the House of Commons

[1] *Strafford Despatches*, i. 29.   [2] *Strafford Despatches*, i. 29, 31.
[3] *Strafford Despatches*, i. 30.
[4] Cf. Douglas, *Controverted Election Cases*, iv. 100–3; Forster, *Life of Eliot*, i. 476.

was made up of former members, more irritated and desperate of reconciliation with the sovereign than before.   The prosecution of Buckingham, to avert which Charles had dissolved his first Parliament, was commenced with redoubled vigour.   The Commons also delayed to pass a bill for subsidies which they had voted until they should obtain some satisfaction for their complaints; and to end the contest the King, contrary to the advice of the House of Lords and the Privy Council, dissolved the Parliament on the 15th of June, 1626.

The need of money for the war with Spain compelled Charles in 1628 to call another Parliament.   Then extraordinary efforts were made by the Crown to influence the election of knights of the shire.   Orders were sent to the magistrates to command the high constables of the hundreds to bring in the freeholders to the county towns, where the freeholders were to learn the king's pleasure touching the election.   The high constables, reads the order, " are to entreat the freeholders to attend, and to give their voices for such gentlemen as shall be agreed upon by the more part of the magistrates[1]."   The magistrates were to act as a county caucus; and the high constables were to use their influence with freeholders to elect the nominees of the magistrates.   These methods were used, or tried, in the shires of Essex, Bedford, Dorset, Hertford, Kent, Lincoln, Northampton, Hants, Suffolk, Worcester, Cornwall, Nottingham, York, and Glamorgan[2].   In some of the counties changes had been made in the commissions of the peace and new justices appointed with a view to carrying out this policy of the Crown of influencing elections of knights of the shire[3].

Influencing County Elections.

Forster in tracing the fortunes of Eliot at this election describes the working of the caucus of magistrates in Cornwall. " Mr Richard Trevanion and Mr Walter Langdon," he writes, " constituted themselves a kind of royal commission.   They declared that the care of the County of Cornwall had been entrusted to them by His Majesty's Council; announced it to be their duty to secure a free election for knights of the county, by naming beforehand those who should be presented to be chosen by the freeholders; and, in compliance with such ancient and laudable custom as they termed it, now named accordingly as most fit to be so elected, Mr John Mohun and Sir Richard Edgcombe, communicating their

The Election for Cornwall.

[1] *Cal. State Papers,* 1627–28, 592.
[2] Forster, *Life of Eliot,* ii. 102; *Cal. State Papers,* 1628–29, 5, 13.
[3] Forster, ii. 102.

decision to all parts of the county—to the high sheriff and other gentlemen and freeholders—by means of official posts, appointed and provided for His Majesty's special service, and summoning the train-bands to be present and assist at the election. That was a strong proceeding, but it was not all. At the same time they sent letters subscribed with all their names to Eliot and Coryton, warning them against persisting in their attempt to present themselves to the electors; and to the freeholders generally, in letters similarly under-written, they made appeal that they should not, by electing Eliot and Coryton, give their voices to men having perverse ends, and respecting not the common good; but likely to breed mischief in the State, and whom they further branded as unquiet spirits, who were under His Majesty's ill-opinion[1]."

An Election Manager for the Crown.　Much of this activity on behalf of the Crown in Cornwall was organised and directed by James Bagg, who had sat for various Cornish boroughs in the Parliaments of James and Charles. He had become associated with the Duke of Buckingham in 1623; and his letters to the Duke preserved in the state papers from 1623 to 1629 show him to have been one of the boldest and shrewdest managers of elections in the service of the Crown in the seventeenth century. Bagg was to Buckingham in Devon and Cornwall in the reign of Charles I what Dundas in Scotland was to Pitt in the reign of George III. In Cornwall Bagg kept watch on the movements of Eliot and the other men prominent in the west in opposition to Charles I, and apprised Buckingham of their doings. The boroughs of Plympton and Saltash were partly under his control. He distributed naval, civil and ecclesiastical patronage in the west. Admiralty contracts were in his disposition. For his partisans he was also instrumental in procuring letters of marque. He had the oversight of the billeting of soldiers and the pressing of seamen in Devon and Cornwall. Men in gaol obtained pardons through his good offices. Gentlemen were put in and out of the commission of the peace at his suggestion, and baronetcies and peerages were bestowed on his recommendation.

His Quali-fications.　Bagg is a typical electioneering manager. He is the earliest whose career can be traced from official records; and these show that he would have been accounted an acceptable leader in an organisation like Tammany Hall. He was loyal to Buckingham, and constant and zealous in his service. He was equally true to

[1] Forster, ii. 109.

his followers. The favours of the Crown, of which he was the channel, went to his adherents; and when any of these were in trouble Bagg was quick to use his good offices with Buckingham for their relief. A month after the election of 1628 the mayor of Saltash was summoned to London to answer a complaint of inattention to a press warrant. Bagg was at once in communication with Nicholas, the secretary to the admiralty, and with Buckingham, in the mayor's behalf. Buckingham was informed that the mayor was a friend of Bagg's, and that at the late election, in opposition to Sir Richard Buller, the recorder of Saltash, and other members of the corporation, the mayor had given him the burgess-ship of Saltash, then held by Sir Francis Cottingham[1].

When Parliament met, Mohun and other of the Cornish magistrates were summoned by the House of Commons to answer for the undue practices to which they had unsuccessfully resorted to prevent the election of Eliot and Coryton. Bagg immediately wrote to Buckingham expressing his sorrow that "those gentlemen, truest and best affecting His Majesty's honour and service, should be so troubled[2]"; and by the manœuvring of Buckingham and Bagg the arrest of the offending magistrates by the messenger of the sergeant-at-arms of the House of Commons was delayed for two weeks. In the meantime, through the exertions of Bagg, Mohun was created a peer, and in consequence his name was struck out of the warrant for the arrest of the magistrates who, by their violent interference in the election, had come into serious conflict with the House of Commons. Bagg had news on the 4th of April that Mohun was to be made a peer, and on the 8th he wrote to Buckingham expressing his satisfaction. Mohun had long desired a peerage. Coming when it did, it cleared him of his trouble with the Commons. Bagg was also elated at this proof of his ability to obtain favours from the court. It strengthened his position in the west as Buckingham's lieutenant[3].

He obtains a Peerage for a Friend.

A few days after Mohun was made a peer the messenger of the sergeant-at-arms was again in Cornwall, and this time took back as prisoners Edward Trelawney, Walter Langdon, Sir William Wray, and John Trelawney, who with Mohun had signed the letter against Eliot and Coryton. Counsel were heard in their defence at the bar of the House of Commons; and at the close of the arguments Langdon and John Trelawney were ordered

His Care for his Partisans.

[1] *Cal. State Papers,* 1628–29, 65. [2] *Cal. State Papers,* 1628–29, 45.
[3] Cf. *Cal. State Papers,* 1628–29, 67.

to the Tower, there to be kept until they made full acknowledgment not only of their offence against the liberty of free election, but also of their contempt of the House in failing to answer the first summons to the bar. Wray and Edward Trelawney were retained in the custody of the sergeant-at-arms. All the Cornishmen refused to make submission to the House, and remained in custody until the prorogation on the 26th of June. The two prisoners in the Tower had petitioned the King for their release on the 3rd of June. But while the House still sat the King did not interpose. An hour, however, had not passed after the dissolution of the Parliament, when the King signed a warrant to the governor of the Tower, for the release of Langdon and Trelawney, and apprised the governor that he would pay all the charges of their imprisonment. While they were still in the Tower, Bagg had asked as a special favour that Trelawney should be made a baronet. Four days after the release a baronetcy was bestowed on Trelawney, with the remission of the ordinary fees[1]; so that Bagg's active partisans in the opposition to Eliot and Coryton came out of their conflict with the House of Commons with flying colours.

Ill-success of Crown Electioneering.

All this extraordinary activity on the part of the Crown in the election of 1628 counted for little. Except in the boroughs where members of the Council and peers could nominate, not an adherent of the court was returned[2]. In the boroughs generally, usually its strongholds, the Crown was less successful than in previous reigns. Buckingham at this time was steward of Westminster. By the influence of that office, he had at the election of 1625 forced his agent, Sir Robert Pye, on the City as one of its representatives. Pye was a moderate man and not unpopular; but at the election of 1628 his connection with Buckingham was fatal to him, and two Westminster tradesmen were elected[3]. Conway, secretary of state, was much pushed to find a borough for his son. At Evesham the corporation would not promise until they had conferred with their recorder[4]. From Yarmouth, Isle of Wight, the answer to Conway was that the electors would choose someone of their own county; and from Newport that they were resolved not to elect the son of Lord Conway. Finally a seat was found for Ralph Conway at Andover, where the

[1] Cf. Forster, ii. 280.   [2] Cf. Forster, ii. 92.
[3] Cf. Forster, ii. 101; *Official List*, pt. i. 470, 476.
[4] *Cal. State Papers*, 1627–28, 562.

nomination was in the gift of Sir Thomas Jervoise[1].   At Southampton, where Conway sought a seat for Sir Francis Annersley,
the response was so repellent that Conway marvelled to find so cold
an answer; for "in all things which concern their town or the
commonweal, he has endeavoured to act for the good of both."
After his first repulse Conway wrote expressing the hope that the
corporation would consider better of his request[2].   The second
letter had no more favourable effect; and in the Parliament of
1628–29 Southampton was represented by two of its aldermen[3].

Again the Crown was in a minority in the House of Commons. Charles I
The question of tonnage and poundage, which had been standing dissolves his
over since the first Parliament of the reign, once more occupied Third Parlia-
attention.   To prevent a remonstrance against these impositions ment.
being levied without the sanction of Parliament, Charles had resort
to a prorogation.   Next session the question came up again in a
new form—this time as one of privilege arising out of the seizure
of the goods of Rolle, a member of the House, for non-payment
of the imposition.   This new turn was given to the question by
Eliot; and on March 2nd, 1629, his three resolutions led to the
memorable scene in which Finch, the Speaker, and Holles and
Valentine had their part, and to the dissolution on March 10th.
For eleven years thereafter England was without a Parliament.

Two other Parliaments were convened by Charles, the short- Elections of
lived Parliament which assembled on April 13th and was dissolved 1640.
on May 5th, 1640, and the Parliament which met on the 3rd of
November, 1640, and is known in history as the Long Parliament.
So far as can be traced in the state papers and in memoirs, only
the usual methods of Crown interference were practised at these
elections.   There was apparently no resort to such unusual expedients as had marked the elections of 1625 and 1628.   Courtiers
were as busy as at preceding elections in endeavouring to get
themselves and their friends chosen[4]; and among the state papers
for the year there is a list of burgesses to be nominated in the
interest of the Crown, and by whom they were to be nominated,
as well as a list of the borough towns in Cornwall and elsewhere the
nomination to which lay with the attorney of the Prince of Wales[5].

Charles had become a man of business and affairs since the The King
death of Buckingham in 1628.   Under Buckingham the favourite and Buckingham.

[1] *Cal. State Papers,* 1627–28, 566; *Official List,* pt. i. 477.
[2] *Cal. State Papers,* 1627–28, 577.   [3] *Official List,* pt. i. 477.
[4] Cf. Whitelocke, *Memorials,* i. 94.   [5] *Cal. State Papers,* 1640, 4.

was everything. He governed alone. The King scarcely intermeddled with business; he was seldom heard of in such affairs,
and still more seldom seen. After Buckingham's death Charles
had become well versed in business; was informed of whatever
was going on; attended meetings, even of committees, and when
not present was consulted on all important matters. The
Government was thus really and truly his, not by a compli-
mentary official figment but by actual interference with its
management and direction[1].

Charles I's Personal Part in Elections.

This is a characterisation of Charles in the long period in
which there was no Parliament. It is borne out by the part taken by
the King in the elections to the last of his Parliaments. He was
then in command, and gave directions as to which of the servants
of the Crown were to be provided with seats in the House of
Commons. " I enclose by His Majesty's command," wrote Secretary
Vane to Secretary Windebank, on September 27th, 1640, " a note
of the names of such of his servants as he thinks should be
provided with burgess-seats to attend this Parliament, and it is
his pleasure that you speak with the Lord Chamberlain concerning
it; His Majesty expecting some help from him for the others. You
are to see them provided out of such places as are in His Majesty's
and the Prince's gift." In the same letter there was an intimation
that the King, the better to facilitate the matter he had in hand,
" and sweeten his proceedings therein," had commanded Vane to
let Windebank know that he was pleased to release all those
committed to the Fleet or other prison for refusing to pay coat
and conduct money, and that other prisoners were to be discharged
" the discharging of whom would help to His Majesty's service[2]."
By Attorney-General Bankes, Windebank was informed that His
Majesty had given directions at York, where the King was when
the council of peers advised him to call a Parliament, that his
learned counsel, the counsel in the Marches, the judges in Wales,
the Queen's counsel, the Prince's counsel, and Mr Surveyor-General
were to have notice to do their best endeavours to be of the
Parliament[3].

Buckingham's Election Management.

Buckingham managed the elections for the first three Parliaments of the reign. Eliot attributed to Buckingham the device
of ridding the House of Commons of men who had been obnoxious

---

[1] Bruce, *Introduction to Cal. State Papers*, 1646–47, vii., viii., ix.

[2] *Cal. State Papers*, 1640–41, 104, 105.

[3] *Cal. State Papers*, 1640–41, 166.

to the Crown by pricking them for sheriffs. It is extremely probable that the idea of inducing county magistrates, favourable to the court, to take upon themselves the nomination of knights of the shire and to use their influence to secure their election, also originated with Buckingham ; for at this time his word gave the impulse to the whole machine of government. Every act was submitted to his approval, and every office was filled by personal followers, who had learned that their fortunes could be made or marred by his nod[1]. No such expedients, no such inroads on the freedom of election are traceable at the second general election of 1640, when Charles was personally directing affairs. It would seem therefore that the innovations in Crown methods of election management, for which the reign is chiefly remarkable, must be credited to the ingenuity and daring of Buckingham rather than to the King, to the favourite who had the audacity to tell the House of Commons leaders in the early years of Charles's reign, that "if a Parliament was to continue to sit in England, it must act with him and follow only where he was ready to lead[2]."

In tracing the relations of the Crown to the franchise—and it is, I may repeat, exclusively with its relations to the franchise that I am now concerned—it is possible to note some distinctive features in nearly every reign. The reigns of Henry VI, Edward VI, Mary, and Elizabeth are remarkable for the additions made by the Crown to the number of members of the House of Commons and for the enfranchisement of rotten boroughs. James I is distinguished by his proclamations to the electorate. The reign of Charles I is marked by the expedients adopted to restrict the choice of the constituencies. The reign of Charles II acquires distinction as the last in which the Crown granted a charter of enfranchisement, and, pre-eminently, from the attack on the corporations. *Crown Methods of the Several Reigns.*

From the reign of Henry VI there had been frequent additions to the House of Commons. The earliest of them, and in fact most of them, as has been shown, were made by the Crown by charter. Enfranchisement by Act of Parliament was begun in the reign of Henry VIII, with the admission of Wales and the County and City of Chester. Until the reign of James I charters and Acts of Parliament were the only means by which additions were made. *Three Modes of Enfranchisement.*

[1] Cf. Gardiner, *Personal Government of Charles I,* i. 1, 2.
[2] Forster, i. 398.

In the reign of James the House assumed the right of reviving by resolution the privileges of boroughs, and in the Long Parliament of Charles I this method was again resorted to. In the reign of Charles II there were admissions by charter and by Act of Parliament. The County and City of Durham then came in by Act of Parliament, and Newark was enfranchised by the last charter of the Crown by which the Parliamentary franchise was conferred on a borough.

Additions to the House of Commons.   At the beginning of the reign of Henry VIII the number of the members of the House of Commons stood at 296. The additions during the reigns from Henry VIII to Charles II were as follows :—

Henry VIII,	32	counties and boroughs,	38	members[1].
Edward VI,	22	„	44	„
Mary,	14	„	25	„
Elizabeth,	31	„	62	„
James I,	14	„	27	„
Charles I,	9	„	18	„
Charles II,	3	„	6	„

Calais, which first sent a burgess to Parliament in the reign of Henry VIII[2], ceased to be represented after the Parliament of 1555[3]. One of Elizabeth's thirty-one charters was for the re-enfranchisement of Maidstone, which had lost its charter in Mary's reign; so that three must be deducted from the number of additions made to the roll of members of the House from the beginning of the reign of Henry VIII to the end of that of Charles II. Consequently after the enfranchisement of Newark the number of members was 513; and so long as the old representative system survived there were no additions to the English and Welsh members. The power of the Crown to add members to the House fell into desuetude after the grant of the Newark charter. After the Revolution, petitions for enfranchisement were addressed to Parliament[4], petitions which went unheeded until the Reform Act.

Opposition to the Crown in the Boroughs.   In the reign of Charles I, as is shown by Buckingham's ill-success in carrying elections, the popular and nonconforming interests gained an ascendancy in the corporations of most of the boroughs, and this ascendancy was strengthened and extended during the Commonwealth. At the Restoration an Act was passed to regulate the corporations. The Act imposed oaths and a test

[1] Hatsell, ii. 388.
[3] *Official List*, pt. i. 395, 399.
[2] Hatsell, ii. 389.
[4] Cf. *H. of C. Journals*, xi. 85.

which it was thought that the nonconformists would not take, and it was expected that the nonconformists would be ejected from the corporations. Some of them were excluded, but most of them found pretexts for qualifying themselves; and in the reign of Charles II the corporations continued to be the Parliamentary strongholds of the nonconforming interests; and, although the King dissolved four Parliaments between 1679 and 1681, he was not able to bring the House of Commons into compliance with his will. If the King could not govern without Parliament, it had now become necessary to devise some plan to change the complexion of the House of Commons, and this change must be brought about in the boroughs.

From this necessity, after the dissolution of the Oxford Parliament, and while the country was still agitated over the Exclusion bill, arose the audacious policy of wresting charters from corporations in order to new model them, by introducing such restrictions as might render the members from the boroughs in future Parliaments entirely devoted to the interests of the Crown. Some interference with municipal corporations with a view to the control of elections seems to have been contemplated as early as 1661 ; for in the state papers of that year there is a warrant " that in drawing up all future charters for boroughs or corporations there be express reservation to the Crown of the first nomination of aldermen, recorders and town clerks; and also that there be a proviso for elections to Parliament to be made by the common council only[1]." Such a policy could be embodied only in new charters, or in charters voluntarily surrendered for revision. There were no reasons to justify their forfeiture. It was, however, possible to enquire into the validity of charters by writ of *quo warranto* ; and Jeffreys suggested to the King that most of them might be annulled in consequence of such enquiries, and that a beginning could be made with the City of London, which had long been hostile to the court. *Quo warranto* proceedings were accordingly begun in the court of King's Bench in 1682 against the corporation of London. Two acts of the common council were alleged as sufficient misdemeanours to warrant judgment of forfeiture ; one the imposition, by an ordinance or by-law made by the council, of certain tolls on goods brought into the city market ; the other a petition of the council to the King in

Charles II's Attack on the Corporations.

---

[1] *Cal. State Papers,* 1660–61, 582.

December, 1679, for the sitting of Parliament and the publication of this petition throughout the country.

The court of King's Bench pronounced judgment of forfeiture against the corporation; but this judgment, at the request of the Attorney-General, was only recorded. The city continued in appearance to possess its corporate franchises, but upon submission to certain regulations. These were, that no mayor, sheriff, recorder or other chief officer should be admitted until approved by the King; that in the event of the King twice disapproving the choice of a mayor he should nominate a fit person, and the same in the case of sheriffs without waiting for a second election; that the court of aldermen, with the King's permission, might remove any of their body; that they should have a negative on the elections of common councilmen, and in case of disapproving a second choice, have themselves the nomination. The corporation thus submitted to purchase the continued enjoyment of its estates at the expense of its municipal independence, and did not recover its old liberty until the Revolution[1].

At the time that these proceedings against the City of London were pending, Lord Halifax, who was eager for the calling of a Parliament, wrote to Reresby, governor of York, that "they were in a very fair way," and that if the case in the King's Bench succeeded, "every other corporation would be obliged to truckle[2]." The prediction of Halifax was justified. The King named a committee to receive information against corporations. Judgments of forfeiture fell on many boroughs; and many more, conscious of the inequality of a contest between them and the Crown, made voluntary surrender of their charters. Jeffreys when on circuit in July, 1684, induced the surrender of the charters of Lincoln and of other corporations in the eastern and north-eastern counties. Lincoln made its formal surrender on Sunday, November 2nd, 1684, when a deputation of four of its citizens waited on the King with the charter. They were introduced by Jeffreys, and on surrendering the old charter petitioned for a new one. The King, according to the report which the deputation made to the common council on their return, received them very kindly and promised them a new charter. In the formal surrender stress was laid on the importance to the Crown "to have men of known loyalty

The Submission of London.

Surrender of Charters.

---

[1] Cf. Hallam, iii. 454; Evelyn, *Diary,* Ed. 1879, ii. 407, 408, 419.
[2] Reresby, *Memoirs,* 266.

and approved integrity to bear offices of magistracy and places of trust." A desire was also expressed for a re-grant of all privileges " in such manner and form as His Majesty shall judge most conducive to the good government of the city, and with such reservations, restrictions and qualifications as he shall appoint[1]."

In the west of England the Earl of Bath was as successful in inducing surrenders as Jeffreys had been in the eastern and north-eastern counties. He obtained no less than fifteen charters from Cornwall[2]. The Cornish Charters.

The attack on the corporations was the most open and audacious expedient to which a Stuart sovereign had resorted in order to influence elections to the House of Commons. It availed Charles nothing. The work of securing forfeitures or surrenders and the remodelling of charters was necessarily slow. It spread over nearly three years. Charles died while writs of *quo warranto* were still issuing, while charters were still coming in, and before the remodelling of the corporations had gone sufficiently far to warrant him in calling another Parliament. Charles II leaves the Work unfinished.

During the Parliament of 1661–79, when an opposition to the court had been developed in the House of Commons, Charles II personally concerned himself in the by-elections. At an election at Liverpool in 1670 he commanded a would-be candidate to desist, as he had resolved " that one, Sir William Bucknall, shall if possible be the man." This interference on behalf of Bucknall was successful; but it led to a protest from Liverpool that, " if these were suffered, the King might as well call burgesses into the House of Commons by special writ, and then good-night to the liberty of the subject[3]." " In places of members who died," writes Clarendon of this Parliament, " great pains were taken to have some of the King's menial servants chosen ; so that there was a very great number of men in all situations in the court, as well below stairs as above, who were members of the House of Commons[4]." His Direct Interference in Elections.

Concerning the three Parliaments which followed the Pensioner Parliament there is evidence from a variety of contemporary sources

[1] *Hist. MSS. Comm. 14th Rep.*, App., pt. viii. 110.

[2] Evelyn, ii. 466.

[3] *Hist. MSS. Comm. 10th Rep.*, App., pt. iv. 118; cf. *Official List*, pt. i. 524.

[4] *Life of Clarendon*, i. 495; cf. Somerville, *Political Transactions*, 47.

His Distinctive Place in Electioneering.

that Charles II busied himself in elections[1]. He owes his distinctive place in the history of the representative system, however, not to such methods as he adopted at the elections to the four Parliaments of his reign, methods not peculiar to himself, but to the preparations which he set on foot in more than a hundred boroughs[2] for a Parliament which he did not live to call.

James II.

When James II convened his first and only Parliament he took every advantage of the changes which had been made in the corporations in the reign of Charles II, or which were still pending at the time of Charles's death[3]; and when he contemplated calling his second Parliament, the regulation of the corporations was resumed and pushed with even more vigour and less scruple than in the preceding reign.

His Active Part in Elections.

James may not inaptly be described as having been engaged in electioneering from the beginning to the end of his ill-starred reign. In the elections to the House of Commons of 1684–85 he threw himself with great zeal and energy into securing a majority favourable to his policy towards the Roman Catholics. In the Rutland correspondence there is a letter which shows that, in the counties as well as in the boroughs, the King actively concerned himself with the choice of the constituencies. The letter is dated Whitehall, February 17th, 1684–85. It is from the Earl of Sunderland to the Earl of Rutland. " His Majesty, being well satisfied with your lordship's zeal for his service and not doubting but you will use your utmost endeavours and employ all your interests that good members may be chosen for the approaching Parliament, commands me," Sunderland wrote, " to tell you that he would have you take care of the Leicestershire elections, so as to prevent all intrigues and disorders which ill-affected persons may endeavour to set on foot; and therefore His Majesty thinks it necessary you should be present at the county election, and at as many of the borough elections as you can, and to take all possible care that persons of approved loyalty and affection to Government be chosen[4]." Three days later the Earl of Aylesbury wrote to Rutland, who was his son-in-law, suggesting that he should come to London for some days to attend His Majesty, " and congratulate this beginning

---

[1] Cf. Sidney, *Diary of the Times of Charles II,* i. 16, 98; *Letters of Humphrey Prideaux,* 1674–1722, 82; *Clarendon Correspondence,* i. 66; Reresby, *Memoirs,* 217.

[2] Cf. Macaulay, i. 482.   [3] Evelyn, ii. 451, 465.

[4] *Hist. MSS. Comm. 12th Rep.,* App., pt. v. 86.

of his reign, as most persons of your quality have done." "He said he knew, when I spoke to him," added Aylesbury, "that you had been employed about the ceremony of proclaiming him, or about choosing the Parliament men[1]."

In Lincolnshire, particularly at Stamford and Grantham, the Earl of Lindsey was similarly occupied in electioneering by the direct command of the King.   In respect to Grantham, Lindsey had "received His Majesty's positive commands to be assisting with all the interest he had in the election of one, Mr Graham." "I never saw the gentleman in my life," Lindsey wrote to Rutland who controlled Grantham, in asking for his influence in favour of Graham, "but since the King judges him fit for that service, I acquiesce in His Majesty's commands[2]."   At Clitheroe the Duke of Albemarle, by the King's direction, laboured for the return of Colonel Ashton[3].   To Winchester, Ken, the Bishop of Bath and Wells, carried a message from the King to Mr Morley, who was contesting the borough with good hopes of success, that it was the King's pleasure that Mr Lestrange and Mr Hanses should be chosen[4].   At Berwick-on-Tweed the King interfered in a three-cornered contest, in order to secure the election of a member whom he desired to be of the House[5]; and a letter in the Sutherland papers shows the King's concern in the election at Newcastle-under-Lyme, from which borough an erroneous rumour had reached Whitehall that Sir W. Leveson-Gower was promoting the choice of such burgesses as were "not principled to contribute to the supporting of His Majesty and Crown[6]."

His Majesty's Commands.

Of Lord Keeper Guilford's zeal at the election there is an enlightening account in the *Lives of the Norths.*   "His lordship," it reads, "got as many of his friends and relations to be chosen as he could, in which, besides his own influences, he had the nomination to some of the King's boroughs.   Those who came in by his recommendation were for the most part gentlemen of honour and estates, as well as credit in their countries ; and to make the attendance easy to these gentlemen, whose concerns were in the country, he took divers of them to rack and manger in

The Lord Keeper's Friends as Members.

---

[1] *Hist. MSS. Comm. 12th Rep.,* App., pt. v. 87.
[2] *Hist. MSS. Comm. 12th Rep.,* App., pt. v. 86, 87.
[3] *Hist. MSS. Comm. 13th Rep.,* App., pt. iv. 179.
[4] Cf. *Hist. MSS. Comm. 11th Rep.,* App., pt. v. 123; *Official List,* pt. i. 555.
[5] *Hist. MSS. Comm. 11th Rep.,* App., pt. v. 124.
[6] *Hist. MSS. Comm. 5th Rep.,* App., 186.

his family, where they were entertained while the Parliament sat[1]."

Not all the corporations were as yet amenable to the royal will. Lord Langdale, the governor of Hull, informed that corporation that Sir James Bradshaw was recommended by James as one of the members for the borough; and further wrote that he would give them notice of the other member whom the King recommended. The reply of the corporation was that they could not assure the King or the governor who should be chosen, but that they would take care that the election, when the King commanded it, should be fair and free, according to the laws of the land. This answer so enraged the King that he quartered twelve hundred soldiers on the town, to have free quarters on the inhabitants; "who accordingly came and conducted themselves in the most disgraceful and infamous manner[2]."

The King and the courtiers who were electioneering on his behalf in 1685 met with few rebuffs like this at Hull; for when the lists of the new House of Commons were presented to him he remarked with satisfaction that there were not above forty names which he could wish to expunge[3]. Large as was the majority secured by these exertions, and dependent as were most of the members on the court, the King could obtain from the House of Commons none of the legislation on which he had set his heart. The Commons opposed the King in his design to set up a standing army, and also on the question of tests. Accordingly on the 2nd of July, 1687, after six prorogations, the most obsequious Parliament of the Stuart régime was dissolved; and by the middle of August the King had launched on an electioneering campaign with more vigour and more openness in making direct personal appeals to the electorate than had been displayed by any sovereign who had preceded him. The attack on the corporations was recommenced. There were endeavours to influence the elections of knights of the shire even more audacious and more flagrantly interfering with the freedom of elections than those of Buckingham in 1628; and, as a preliminary to all these efforts to secure a subservient House of Commons, the King made a royal progress, in which he personally appealed to the electors

---

[1] *Lives of the Norths,* II. 115.

[2] Bean, *Parliamentary Representation of the Six Northern Counties,* 845, 846.

[3] Somerville, *Political Transactions,* 177.

to choose representatives pledged to the repeal of the penal laws and the Test Act.

The King left Windsor on his electioneering tour on the 16th of August. He visited Portsmouth, Salisbury, Bath, Bristol, Gloucester, Ludlow, Shrewsbury, Whitchurch, Chester, Newport, Lichfield, Coventry, Banbury, and Oxford, and arrived at Windsor again on the 17th of September[1]. " His kind and affable reception of the gentry where he passed," writes Clarke in estimating the success of this tour, " had gained in some measure upon their stubborn temper, and they seemed at last to be convinced how just and reasonable it was to give ease to others so long as it did not prejudice themselves, it being represented to them that the freedom of conscience was dearer to men than all the freedoms and immunities Magna Charta could possibly procure. 'Tis certain the King had no reason to be dissatisfied with his own endeavours therein ; for the benignity of his carriage and the awful presence of a sovereign imposed such veneration upon the generalty of the people where he passed, that their joyful acclamations and dutiful acknowledgments seemed to be pledges of their compliance, and appeared as unfeigned as they were universal. Portsmouth, Salisbury, Bath, Bristol, Worcester, Chester, Shrewsbury, Ludlow, Newport, Lichfield, Coventry, and Banbury seemed to vie with each other in demonstrations of duty and respect. Nay, Oxford itself, though the dispute was then pending about Magdalen College, was not behindhand with assurances of the like nature. In fine, this kind visit from their Prince so mollified their hearts that in most of those places they promised to send such members to the ensuing Parliament as would be for taking off the penal laws and tests, he having dissipated their main prepossession by assuring all who had the honour to approach him, that, though he had admitted Catholics into civil as well as military employments, yet he had no intention to introduce them into the House of Commons, whereby all imaginable innovation in religion would be rendered impossible[2]."

The King's Electioneering Tour.

In the preceding reign the corporations had been remodelled to uproot the influence of the nonconformists, and in all the remodelled corporations Churchmen had taken the places of the ousted members. But in 1687 Churchmen were no longer devoted

The Regulation of the Corporations.

[1] Cf. Luttrell, i. 411, 412, 414; Clarke, *Life of James II*, ii. 140.
[2] Clarke, *Life of James II*, ii. 140.

to the sovereign. They were as hostile to James II and the purpose for which he designed the Parliament as the old corporations had been to Charles II; and a remodelling was now determined upon by which nonconformists, supposed to have been placated by the Declaration of Indulgence, and Roman Catholics, assumed as a matter of course to be favourable to James and his schemes, were to be put in the places in the municipal bodies from which Churchmen were to be ousted. This second attack on the corporations was in the charge of a committee of seven Privy Councillors, of whom Jeffreys was one, and Petre the Jesuit another. Associated with this board was a sub-committee entrusted with the management of details, and there were local sub-committees of regulators all over the country. On the lord lieutenants there was thrown the duty of examining into the state of the boroughs in their counties, and making reports to the board of regulators. Many of the lord lieutenants resigned their commissions rather than undertake this duty and other unconstitutional services demanded of them by the Crown in the management of elections.

Extent of the New Modelling.

From the records of the Privy Council it appears that the number of regulations made in the reign of James exceeded two hundred[1]. Some of the corporations were remodelled twice or three times, when it was seen that the nonconformists or the Roman Catholics who had taken the places of the ousted Churchmen were not to be relied upon for subserviency to the court.

Bury St Edmunds.

The municipal records of Bury St Edmunds furnish a succinct narrative of the steps by which that corporation was remodelled, a narrative which may be taken as typical of the regulation of many of the other municipalities, in order, as Reresby expresses it, that the King might " draw the majority of Parliament unto his own way of thinking as to the test and penal laws[2]." " On March 16th, 1688, one of his Majesty's messengers," reads the Bury St Edmunds record, " brought two instruments, removing Richard Pryme, mayor and alderman, five other aldermen, and ten common councilmen; and for forthwith electing and admitting John Stafford to be mayor and alderman, and others into the other places, without administering to them any oath or oaths, but the usual oath for the execution of their respective places. The orders are obeyed; and immediately afterwards Richard Pryme,

[1] Macaulay, ii. 493.   [2] Reresby, *Memoirs*, 332.

the late mayor, delivered to Stafford, the new mayor, the sword and seals of office." On May 14th, 1688, four more aldermen and eight common councillors were removed. Three days later an address to the King was agreed upon; and on June 11th the remodelled corporation wrote to Lord Dover "promising to elect such members for Parliament as shall comply with His Majesty in all his gracious intentions[1]."

An instance showing the part that James personally had in the work of the regulators is to be found in the Reresby *Memoirs*. Reresby was commanded by the King to stand again as a candidate for York, for which city he had been returned to the Parliament of 1685. "I sent notice to the mayor and others of York," Reresby writes, "that I intended to stand for one of their representatives at the ensuing election, and found the magistracy would be for the most part against me, though I had good encouragement from the other citizens. The truth is, I was at some loss to know how to act in this matter. I was not desirous to be of this Parliament, not only because I was grown infirm and almost unfit to attend the duty of the House, but also because I was afraid the King would expect more from me than my conscience would extend to; for as I was determined not to violate this on the one side, I could hardly resolve to offend so good a master on the other. In these straits I went to the King at Windsor, and showed him the letters I had sent to York, and the answers I had received thereto, desiring His Majesty to indulge me with replies to three queries I had to make: (1) Whether seeing the contest was likely to be both chargeable and difficult, and the success extremely doubtful, it was his pleasure that I should stand. He replied positively I should. (2) Whether as the opposition was very strong against me, he would impute it to my remissness if I miscarried. He promised he would not. (3) Whether he would assist me all he could to prevent my being baffled, and particularly by such means as I should propose to him. His answer was 'yes'; and he gave immediate orders to the Lords for the Purging of Corporations to make whatever change or alteration I desired in the City of York, and to put in or out— which the King it seems had reserved to himself by the last charter—just as I pleased. But I was careful of what I did in this regard. I considered that if I put out none, it would look

The King's Candidate at York.

---

[1] *Hist. MSS. Comm. 14th Rep.*, App., pt. VIII. 151.

as if I had not power, and debase me into contempt; and that
if I displaced too many, it might exasperate the city against me,
making them believe I was too deep in the court interest, and
prevent my success on the other hand. I therefore only desired
that the Lord Mayor might be dismissed his office and Sir
— Thompson appointed in his stead, which would prevent his
being a member of Parliament; and that too Mr Edward Thompson
and Mr Ramsden, who were my principal friends in the former
election of me for York and were afterwards turned out, partly
on my account, might be restored as aldermen. Then taking
leave of the King, he again charged me to do what I could
to be chosen. I afterwards desired Mr Brent, the agent for
corporation matters, that if he had the power, I might, with some
others I should name, be added to the bench of justices in that
city by writ of assistance, which he promised me should be done[1]."

Opposition
in Spite of
the Regu-
lation.

Resuming his story under date of 10th September, 1688,
Reresby writes, "Sir Walter Vavasor and Mr Middleton came up
to make report to the King of the answers they had received
from the West Riding and the corporations to the queries they
had put to them, in which I found the Lord Mayor and aldermen
of York were so faulty that they would be out of course, and that
I need not give myself the trouble of getting them removed.* * *
So I left them to their stars, and only insisted on the commission
of assistance for myself and friends I should name. ·But every
post brought me new fears that I should not be chosen at York,
though several alterations and restrictions from popular elections
to a mayor and twelve aldermen, whom the King appointed as
he pleased, were now made by new charters for the more certain
election of such members as might be to the King's good liking[2]."

The King's
Failure and
Unpopu-
larity.

The account thus given by Reresby is a clear demonstration
of the failure of the regulations of the corporation of York. The
King's scheme was similarly a failure all over the country, as is
acknowledged by Clarke, the royalist biographer of King James,
who describes the work of the regulators. "In this, as in most
other cases," he writes, "the King had the fortune to choose
persons not too well qualified for such employment, and extremely
disagreeable to the people. It was a sort of motley council, made
up of Catholics and Presbyterians, a composition which was sure
never to hold long together, or that could probably unite in any

---

[1] Reresby, *Memoirs*, 350–52.   [2] Reresby, *Memoirs*, 353.

method suitable to both their interests. It served therefore only to increase the public odium by their too arbitrary ways of turning out and putting in; and yet those who were thus intruded, as it were by force, being of the Presbyterian party, were by this time become as little inclinable to favour the King's intentions as the excluded members, which gained the King a great deal of ill-will from the people, and no advantage in the business he aimed at[1]."

The King's plan of campaign in the counties was much more open, more daring and more comprehensive than that which had been adopted by Buckingham in the reign of Charles I. Buckingham's plan was to use the magistrates in each county as a caucus to name candidates favourable to the Crown. James's plan brought the lord lieutenants and the judges who went on circuit into his service as electioneering agents. They were to bring pressure to bear on electors, as well as on Parliamentary candidates, to answer in the affirmative three questions: " (1) In case you shall be chosen knight of a shire or burgess of a town, when the King shall think fit to call a Parliament, whether you will be for taking off the penal laws and tests; (2) Whether you will assist and contribute to the election of such members as shall be for taking off the penal laws and tests; (3) Whether you will support the King's declaration of liberty of conscience by being friendly with those of all persuasions as subjects of the same Prince and good Christians ought to do[2]." *The Plan of Campaign in the Counties.*

Lord lieutenants were instructed to put these questions to deputy lieutenants and to all justices of the peace in their counties; and as a preliminary to these interrogatories, it was proclaimed in the *London Gazette* on the 12th of December, 1687, that the King had determined to revise the commissions of the peace and lieutenancy, and to retain in public employment only such gentlemen as should be disposed to support his policy. Judges on circuit had orders from the King " to feel the pulses " of probable candidates for the House of Commons[3]; and moreover in addressing the grand juries on the summer circuit of 1688 the judges stated that they had it in command from His Majesty to announce that there would be a Parliament in November at the farthest, and exhorted the juries and all who were in court *Duties laid on Lord Lieutenants and Judges.*

[1] Clarke, *Life of James II*, ii. 139, 140.
[2] Nicholson and Burn, *Hist. of Cumberland and Westmorland*, i. 167.
[3] Reresby, *Memoirs*, 331.

to behave themselves like honest men and loyal subjects, and give their support to the policy of the King, embodied in the Declaration of Indulgence[1].

Disaffection in the Counties. These appeals to the freeholders were of no avail. In most counties, according to Burnet, the lord lieutenants put the questions in so careless a manner that it was plain that they did not desire answers in the affirmative. Some went further and declared themselves against the questions; and a few of the more resolute refused to put them. They said this was a prelimiting and the packing of a Parliament which in its nature was to be free, and under no previous engagement. Many counties answered very boldly in the negative; others refused to give an answer, which was understood to be equivalent to a negative[2]. " When His Majesty thought fit to ask many people of distinction," writes Clarke of James's failure to bring freeholders in the counties to his way of thinking, " he found a much greater reluctancy than could well have been imagined, and indeed that method was no ways relished by the people, who looked upon it as a forestalling the liberty of debates, and set many in opposition to the thing because it seemed to be extorted, who probably would have yielded to the reason of it had it been proposed in the usual forms[3]."

Popular Demands for a Parliament. James began this electioneering in August, 1687. A year elapsed before he was ready to announce the calling of a Parliament. On August 24th, 1688, the King declared in council his intention of convening Parliament on the 27th of November, and the Chancellor was ordered to issue the writs on the 5th of September. But by this time the invasion of William of Orange was threatening, and the writs were stopped, because, as the King's sympathetic biographer explains, it was impossible for him to be present at the opening of Parliament and be at the head of his army, where his presence would be no less necessary[4]. After the Prince of Orange had established himself at Exeter, and before James set out for Salisbury, a number of peers and bishops, with Sancroft at their head, petitioned the King for the calling of a free and legal Parliament, and for negotiation with the Prince. The King assured them that he passionately desired the meeting of a free Parliament, and that he would call one as soon as the

---

[1] Cf. Ellis, *Correspondence*, 370, 371.

[2] Burnet, *History of His Own Time*, III. 183; cf. Macaulay, II. 489; Clarke, II. 185.

[3] Clarke, II. 143. [4] Clarke, II. 185.

Prince should have left the island.   On his return to London, after his retreat from Salisbury, "seeing the people still longing after a Parliament, though present circumstances were very unseasonable[1]," the King ordered writs to go out for its meeting on the 15th of January.   These writs, however, met a fate similar to that of the writs for the Parliament which was to assemble on the 27th of November.   They never reached the sheriffs.   This time they were recalled to add to the civil difficulties and perplexities of the Prince of Orange and those who had been chiefly associated with him in the Revolution.   Clarke asserts that the King himself burnt the writs on the night of his flight from Whitehall, when he dropped the Great Seal into the Thames in order to embarrass the Prince in the calling of a Parliament.

One of the charges against James II in the Act of Settlement was that by the assistance of divers evil counsellors, judges and ministers employed by him, he endeavoured to subvert and extirpate the Protestant religion and the laws and liberties of the kingdom, by violating the freedom of elections to serve in Parliament.   Few sovereigns who had preceded him had not violated the freedom of elections.   None had done this so outrageously and so flagrantly, or taken so large a direct and personal part in the violations, as the last of the Stuarts.   One of James's successors zealously and persistently concerned himself in electioneering.   George III, however, only availed himself of existing conditions in the representative system ; and after the Revolution flagrant expedients for influencing elections, such as had been resorted to and widely applied by the Crown in the reigns of Charles I, Charles II and James II, were of the past.

Passing of the Stuart Methods of Electioneering.

[1] Clarke, ii. 238.

CHAPTER XIX.

THE CROWN AND THE FRANCHISE—FROM THE REVOLUTION
TO THE REFORM ACT.

William III.   Soon after the Revolution government by the sovereign gave place to government by administrations dependent for their continuance in power on majorities in the House of Commons ; and with this great constitutional change, until George III came to the throne, sovereigns ceased to have any direct, active, and personal concern in the management of elections.   William III relied more on the purchase of votes in the House than on any continuous and systematic exertion to bring about the election of a House of Commons which would do his bidding.   Bribery in the House of Commons antedated the Revolution.   Money bribes, as distinct from bribery by office, were as old as the Parliament of 1661-79 ; and when William sought to manage the House of Commons he had resort to means already to hand.   " I took the liberty once," writes Burnet, " to complain to the King of this method. He said he hated it as much as any man could do ; but he saw it was not possible, considering the corruption of the age, to avoid it unless he would endanger the whole[1]."

Election of 1695.   I have been able to trace little or no direct interference on the part of William III in the actual choice of constituencies.   I have found no such letters as those of James II on the eve of the Parliament of 1685, in which he insisted on men whom he named being chosen for particular boroughs.   It would therefore seem that

[1] Burnet, ii. 76; cf. "The Danger of Mercenary Parliaments," Harleian Miscellany, ix. 395; "Some Reasons for an Annual Parliament," Harleian Miscellany, xii. 239.

Burnet was correct in his statement, when he avers that "the elections were managed fairly all England over," and that "the Prince did in no sort interpose any recommendations directly or indirectly." William III made a careful choice of the season for the dissolution of the Parliament of 1690–95. The Triennial Act had made an election in 1695 or 1696 inevitable. He appealed to the constituencies in November, 1695, while his brilliant military campaign and the surrender of Namur were still fresh in the public mind. At this general election he followed one precedent of James II's. He made a royal progress to influence the choice of the constituencies. Cambridge, Huntingdon, Suffolk, Northampton, Lincoln, Nottingham, Warwick, Gloucester, and Oxford—all these shires were visited by the King while the elections to the Parliament of 1695–98 were in progress, and the election resulted in the return of a House of Commons which promptly pledged itself to the prosecution of the war with France. James II and William III were the only sovereigns who in this way sought to exercise an influence over the electorate; and after the Revolution, with the exception of George III, William III was the only sovereign who selected the time of a general election with a view to a House of Commons which would support his policy.

While Queen Anne did not disguise with which political party Anne. her sympathies lay, I have found no evidence of her personal interference in elections, and I am inclined to regard her reign as the first in which the sovereign stood aside when the House of Commons was being chosen.

There were attempts to instruct George I in the intricacies George I. of English politics, to convince him that his safety lay in the ascendancy of the Whigs. He was told soon after he arrived in England that in numbers, wealth and social influence the Whigs and Tories were so nearly equal that it was necessary that a decided preference should be shown by the Crown for the Whigs before the first general election of the new reign[1]. In this as in other matters George I acted on the advice of his ministers. He had no part in elections, and no determining share in the transactions of Parliament[2]. The Whigs kept in their own hands the actual authority of the State, and the sovereign was merely the motionless representative of the monarchical principle[3]. In the history of the

---

[1] Cf. Torrens, *Hist. of Cabinets*, I. 84.   [2] Cf. *Dict. Nat. Bio.*, xxi. 150.
[3] Cf. Buckingham, *Courts and Cabinets*, I. 8, 9.

representative system the reign of George I is memorable chiefly for the Septennial Act. Until after the Revolution, there was no law limiting the life of a Parliament, although the Triennial Act passed in 1640 by the Long Parliament was repealed in 1664, because the House of Commons conceived that it might determine the existence of the Pensioner Parliament. In 1694 came the Triennial Act; and this was superseded in 1716 by the Septennial Act, passed after the rising of 1715 to safeguard the Hanoverian succession.

George II.   George II took infinitely more interest in Parliament than George I. At court the contests and divisions in the House of Commons of the Walpole era were followed with close attention. Occasionally George II evinced concern in a particular election. In 1737 he claimed Windsor as his borough, and was insistent that it must re-elect Lord Vere Beauclerk, who had resigned his seat on his appointment as one of the lords commissioners of the admiralty[1]. In 1754 the King took some interest in the fortunes of Lord Egmont at Bridgwater, and showed some knowledge of Bubb Dodington's position as a borough patron there and at Weymouth[2]. At times also the court, Queen Caroline as well as George II, concerned itself in controverted election cases[3]. But traces of the King's actual interference in elections are few; so few in fact as hardly to warrant the statement that the King concerned himself in electioneering. George II's reign was the era of great election managers, such as the Duke of Newcastle in England, and the Earl of Islay in Scotland. Majorities in the House of Commons were now the concern of the administration, in whose behalf the election managers conducted their campaigns. Elections were left by the King to the ministry[4]; and so little was it the custom of George II to take any personal part in elections, that after the dissolution of 1741, and while the elections were still going on, the King betook himself to Hanover[5]. Parliament was dissolved on the 27th of April; on the 7th of May the King left London for his German dominions.

George III.   With the accession of George III elections and the management of the House of Commons were no longer left entirely to the

---

[1] Torrens, *Hist. of Cabinets*, i. 483; *Official List*, pt. ii. 72.
[2] Dodington, *Diary*, 276.
[3] Cf. Thomson, *Memoirs of Viscountess Sundon*, i. 383.
[4] Cf. Hervey, *Memoirs*, i. 88.
[5] Coxe, *Life of Walpole*, iii. 223.

administration. George III was intent on having ministers of his own choosing, and it was long his steadfast purpose to maintain a party in the House of Commons which would support his ministers without question. To the House of Commons—to its management and the details of its business—he gave closer and more continuous personal attention than any sovereign who had preceded him, and concerned himself more than any except James II in the actual business of electioneering.

There were in this reign no such extraordinary expedients to influence elections as were devised in the reigns of Charles I, Charles II and James II; nor was George III's interference in elections so open as that of the Stuart kings. The day for such methods had now gone by. But in the first thirty years of the reign of George III, the electoral system was at its worst. The smaller boroughs were more under the control of patrons than at any previous time. Seats in the House were openly sold. Bribery was rampant in the larger boroughs. It was by turning these conditions to account that George III secured and maintained his control over the House of Commons. The King came to the throne with the intention to be his own master. He was determined that if Parliament was to be corrupted, and he had no objection to its corruption, it should be corrupted to serve his purpose; and it was "an unconstitutional habit of George III to regard every minister as a mere instrument[1]." *Parlia-mentary Corruption.*

Much of the control which George III exercised over the House of Commons—most of it in fact—was obtained by the purchase of votes, by money bribes, and by the lavish bestowal of official patronage and regal honours. Part of his control—that with which I am here alone concerned—was due to the activity of the King in electioneering, and to the support of members whose seats had been purchased for them by the King, or whom the King had assisted in meeting the expense of their election. *The King's Control over the House of Commons.*

At the death of George II the Duke of Newcastle was still in charge of the management of elections in England. At the general election in 1761, the first of the reign, the management of the boroughs under the control of the Duchy of Cornwall was taken out of the hands of Newcastle, and George III began his long career as an election manager by nominating the members for these *His Part in Elections.*

---

[1] Anson, *Autobiography and Political Correspondence of the Duke of Grafton,* xiii.

Cornish boroughs[1]. The King devoted himself to electioneering with all the application and perseverance which were characteristic of him; and between the election of 1761 and that of 1780 he became as adept in election procedure as the most expert patronage secretary to the treasury. His interest in elections was continuous. He watched the by-elections, followed the proceedings in petition cases and threw himself into a general election with all the zeal and energy of a party manager. The *Letters to North* and the Abergavenny Manuscripts contain the fullest evidence of the part which the King had in elections and in the management of the House of Commons between 1770 and 1782. These not only show the great efforts and the personal pecuniary sacrifices which George III made at the general elections of 1774 and 1780; but they also show the King's intimate acquaintance with the prevailing conditions of the representative system. He was familiar with the character of most of the nomination boroughs, with the conditions under which the patrons were in control, and was constantly alert to turn this knowledge to account.

His Care for his Supporters.

There was a vacancy in the court of King's Bench in 1770. Serjeant Burland and Serjeant Nares were candidates. Nares was of the House of Commons as member for the City of Oxford. The judgeship went to him; but the King's preference was first of all for Burland, who was not of the House, because the appointment of Nares "would be very detrimental to the interest of the Duke of Marlborough, as his influence in Oxford would be much shook by opening that borough for so many months[2]." The Duke of Marlborough's nominees supported the North Administration, and the King was anxious to take no step which would jeopardise the Duke's control in the City of Oxford. He was equally careful that his supporters in the House should not be pressed to give votes which might unnecessarily endanger their seats. In 1772 the dissenters were petitioning for a bill to relieve them from subscription to the Thirty-Nine Articles. The King was opposed to the bill; but he urged North "not to press those gentlemen who are brought on that interest into Parliament to oppose this measure," as by doing so he might drive them out of their seats on the election of a new Parliament[3].

[1] Dodington, *Diary*, 433; Courtney, *Parliamentary Representation of Cornwall*, xviii.

[2] Donne, *Letters of George III to North*, i. 30; cf. *Official List*, pt. ii. 141.

[3] Donne, *Letters of George III to North*, i. 101.

John Calcraft, one of the members for the City of Rochester, His Watch-
died on the 23rd of August, 1772.   He was a man of great wealth, fulness
and had taken an independent line in the House of Commons. Elections.
of By-
The King was a constant reader of the newspapers, and on the
24th of August he wrote to North expressing his hope that the
death of Calcraft would bring the City of Rochester into " its
ancient hands[1]," in other words that henceforward both its members would be supporters of the North Administration.   Sir Robert
Ladbroke, one of the members for the City of London, died on the
31st of October, 1773.   The same day, at " 42 minutes past 6 p.m.,"
the King wrote to North about the Parliamentary vacancy.   " The
hearing of Sir Robert Ladbroke's death," reads the letter, " gives
me infinite concern, as it opens a seat in Parliament for the city.
If Alderman Bull can be with success opposed, I should think it
eligible.   But if that is not pretty certain it is best not to interfere[2]."
Bull's election was unsuccessfully opposed by Roberts, formerly a
director of the East India Company, and the state of the poll was
daily sent to the King[3].   In 1774 there was a by-election at Worcester.   The opposition candidate was Sir Watkin Lewes, who had
been invited to contest the borough by a committee of independent
electors[4].   The election was on the 1st of March.   North was in
consultation with George III as to the ministerial candidate.   " The
changing the candidate for Worcester from Mr George Rous to
Captain Lechmere," wrote the King, on February 9th, " seems very
proper, and I trust that the valiant Welsh knight will come back
without any other advantage than the huzzas of the Worcester
mob[5]."

The Parliament of 1768 was unexpectedly dissolved on the 30th Precipitating
of September, 1774; not however until the King had made pre- a Disso-
parations for the general election, and had balanced in his own
lution.
mind the advantages of a premature dissolution.   " I think it not
unlikely," he wrote to North, on the 27th of September, " but that
a premature dissolution may in some places be disadvantageous;
yet upon the whole, even in that view, it will not be of much consequence; and considering the chapter of accidents it will, I trust,

---

[1] Donne, *Letters of George III to North*, i. 109.
[2] Donne, *Letters of George III to North*, i. 153.
[3] Cf. Donne, *Letters of George III to North*, i. 214.
[4] Cf. Oldfield, v. 242.
[5] Donne, *Letters of George III to North*, i. 165; *Official List*, pt. ii.
144.

prove a very salutary measure, and when that is the case I do not grudge a little additional trouble[1]."

The Westminster Election of 1774.
Two elections in particular engaged the personal attention of the King—Westminster and the County of Middlesex. For Westminster the King was anxious that Lord Percy should be nominated by the Duke of Northumberland. Lord Percy at first was unwilling to enter on the contest; "and this," wrote the King, "from no nobler idea than the fear of some scurrilous abuse in the newspapers." But when the King received the news of Lord Percy's hesitation, he urged North to press the Duke of Northumberland, as "a meritorious conduct" towards himself, to nominate his son. "And you may easily add," continued the King, "that Lord Mahon cannot be a very formidable opposer, as he will not open any houses," a touch which shows that George III understood the use of beer in elections, and had gauged the ability of Lord Mahon to spend money. The Duke of Northumberland's idea was that if Lord Percy became a candidate he should join his interest with that of Lord Mahon; but after Mahon had issued his election address, the King did not regard him as in the least preferable to Humphrey Coates, another of the Westminster candidates, who was an intimate friend of Wilkes[2]. The appeal from the King had its effect; Lord Percy and Lord Thomas Pelham Clinton became the ministerial candidates, in opposition to Lord Mahon, Lord Mountmorres and Humphrey Coates.

The King's Efforts in the Election.
The election began on the 4th of October, and was watched with the keenest interest by the King. On the 10th the King informed North that he had apprised Lord Delawarr, colonel of the first troop of horse guards, " to have the horse and grenadier guards privately spoke to for their votes in favour of Lord Percy and Lord Thomas Pelham Clinton." " They have," he added, " a large number of votes[3]." Two days later the King was disturbed by a rumour that efforts were being made to secure the votes of the soldiers for one of the opposition candidates. " I can scarcely credit," he wrote to North, " the report of Lord Harrington having solicited his troops in favour of Lord Mahon; for his house are so zealous for the success of the other candidate, that Lady Harrington has sent me word that she can prove Lord Mahon not of age till next May; which she will do, if he obtains a victory; as

---

[1] Donne, *Letters of George III to North*, i. 205, 206.

[2] Donne, *Letters of George III to North*, i. 204, 205.

[3] Donne, *Letters of George III to North*, i. 210.

that laid before the committee must incapacitate him." For the present, however, the King thought it best to be silent about Lord Mahon's incapacity for a seat in the House of Commons, as otherwise another candidate might be set up by the opposition to the court in Westminster[1].

The Westminster poll went on from the 4th to the 27th of October, when it ended in the return of the ministerial candidates. At this time the King was at Kew; and from thence wrote frequent letters to North commenting on the progress of the elections. On the 14th he congratulated him that the poll at Westminster continued more prosperous. "The poll," he wrote again on the 18th, "could not be more favourable than this day. I have heard it pretty positively reported that Lords Mahon and Mountmorres polled yesterday many bad votes." *His Interest in the Polling.*

The election for the County of Middlesex, where Wilkes and Serjeant Glynn were the opposition candidates, engaged the attention of the King as closely as that at Westminster. Robinson, the secretary to the treasury, who had begun his career as an election manager as an agent of Sir James Lowther[2], was managing the Middlesex election, and was engaged in what proved to be the impossible task of finding ministerial candidates willing to lead a forlorn hope against Wilkes and Glynn. Robinson hoped that Sir Charles Raymond and Mr Clitherow would come forward; and he kept the King informed as to the likelihood of success in inducing these two supporters of the Government to stand. The election was fixed for the 20th of October. On the 10th the King had news that Raymond refused to become a candidate. "The trying every means to get him to step forth," he wrote to North on that day, "is certainly quite right; but if he could withstand the very able letter Mr Robinson wrote him I do not think a conversation will have much effect." Clitherow was more inclined for a fight than Raymond. The King was elated at this "manly and sensible conduct," and was hopeful that Clitherow's standing alone as ministerial candidate might keep out Glynn, although he could not defeat Wilkes. Later in the day the news reached Kew that Raymond was still wavering and might yet become a candidate. "Nothing," wrote the King on the receipt of this news, "could give me more satisfaction than Sir Charles Raymond having consented to stand for the county. If the plan for managing the *The Election for Middlesex.*

---

[1] Donne, *Letters of George III to North,* i. 211.
[2] Cf. *Hist. MSS. Comm. 13th Rep.,* App., pt. viii. 129.

elections proposed by Mr Robinson be exactly followed, it will undoubtedly be crowned with success[1]." Still later on the 10th of October the King had tidings that Robinson's efforts with Raymond and Clitherow had failed. "I am much disappointed," he wrote at 33 minutes past 10 p.m., "at the seeming end of the Middlesex contest but still hope Mr Robinson may set it again on float." Robinson's efforts were unavailing. "I am sorry to see by the papers," wrote the King to North on the 12th, "Mr Clitherow has openly declined standing for the county." On the 20th, no other candidates appearing to oppose Wilkes and Serjeant Glynn, the sheriff declared them duly elected[2].

The King's Success.

Elsewhere the elections in 1774 generally went as the King desired. The opposition could muster only seventy-three votes in the House of Commons[3]; and on the 14th of November the King assured North that he was "much pleased at the state of the supposed numbers of the new Parliament."

His Share in the Purchase of Cornish Boroughs.

The transactions in Cornish boroughs, the bargains with Lord Falmouth and Lord Edgcumbe which have become part of the general history of the eighteenth century, occurred at the election of 1774. These transactions were arranged by North and Robinson. It was North who wrote the often quoted letter in which Lord Falmouth is described as "rather shabby in desiring guineas rather than pounds" for his six seats in Cornwall, seats which were purchased at two thousand five hundred guineas each; and George III's principal part in these transactions was that he was responsible for the fund with which North and Robinson went into the borough market[4].

The General Election of 1780.

At the general election of 1780 George III exerted himself even more strenuously than in 1774 to keep up the number of the King's friends in the House of Commons. For months before the dissolution the King had systematically laid by one thousand pounds a month to form an election fund. Parliament was dissolved on the 1st of September. On the 21st of August, at a time when much secrecy was being exercised to prevent its becoming known that a dissolution was immediately pending, the King transmitted fourteen thousand pounds in bank-notes to Robinson,

---

1 Donne, *Letters of George III to North*, I. 210.

2 *Annual Register*, XVII. 157.

3 Mahon, *Hist. of England*, VI. 20.

4 Cf. *Hist. MSS. Comm. 10th Rep.*, App., pt. VI. 6, 7; Donne, *Letters of George III to North*, II. 421.

and a few days later added another six thousand pounds "to be placed to the same account as that sent on the 21st of August." With the first of these remittances there was an intimation to Robinson that Thurlow, the Lord Chancellor, while at Bath, had been making inquiries as to the likelihood of success for ministerial candidates at Bath, Bridgwater and Taunton. "If you have been attentive to Bridgwater and Taunton," the King added, "you can have them both. If not they are sadly lost[1]."

As far back as April, 1780, the King while at Windsor for Easter had been canvassing the royal borough. "I made it my business," he wrote to Robinson on April 10th, "privately to sound the inhabitants of that borough. The corporation has ever been adverse to the Government; and whilst Mr Fox, when secretary at war, represented that borough, he was chosen by the inhabitants at large. Now the corporation is desirous of having a candidate recommended by administration, and the inhabitants will warmly espouse such a person. Admiral Keppel can be thrown without any difficulty[2]." Windsor was an inhabitant householder borough; and on the 3rd of May Robinson, with a view to the coming election, suggested to the King that six houses there rented by the King should be entered in the names of six different members of the royal household[3]. The King was always prompt and systematic in his correspondence. He replied the same day to Robinson, telling him that at North's suggestion Mr Powney was to be a candidate at Windsor. "I shall in consequence," continued the King, "get my tradesmen encouraged to appear for him. I shall order, in consequence of Mr Robinson's hint, the houses I rent at Windsor to stand in the parish rate in different names of my servants, so that it will create six votes[4]." *The King's Management of Windsor.*

In addition to this direct personal aid from the King, Powney received fifteen hundred or two thousand pounds[5] from the fund chiefly raised by George III, out of which North and Robinson financed ministerial candidates. This fund was kept open until the downfall of the North Administration in 1782. Then it was unexpectedly realized by the King that the expenditures to which he had been committed were much in excess of what he had *The King's Election Debts.*

[1] *Hist. MSS. Comm. 10th Rep.,* App., pt. vi. 35.

[2] *Hist. MSS. Comm. 10th Rep.,* App., pt. vi. 29.

[3] *Hist. MSS. Comm. 10th Rep.,* App., pt. vi. 30.

[4] *Hist. MSS. Comm. 10th Rep.,* App., pt. vi. 30.

[5] *Hist. MSS. Comm. 10th Rep.,* App., pt. vi. 41.

contemplated; and in the correspondence between the King and North at the final settlement much additional light is thrown on the King's part in elections, and the uses to which the fund had been put. "As to the immense expense of the general election," the King wrote to North on the 18th of April, 1782, "it has quite surprised me. The sum is at least double of what was expended at any other general election since I came to the throne, and, by the fate of the last month, proves most uselessly. Certainly the thirteen thousand pounds due to Mr Drummond I shall by degrees pay off; but I cannot bind myself further. I think it is most likely that on the reduction of the expenses of the civil list, I shall be obliged to see my privy purse diminished by twelve thousand per annum. If that should happen I have no means of satisfying the remainder you unexpectedly put to my account of £19,754. 18s. 2d. Had Lord North thought it necessary, he ought, during the arrangements, to have had secret service money to have defrayed that sum. Now that is impossible I cannot conclude without saying that I am sorry to see that there has been such a strange waste of money[1]."

Lord North's Statement of Account. In answer to the King's letter North, "with a heart full of the deepest affliction at having incurred His Majesty's displeasure," explained that although he had repeatedly pressed Robinson for a statement of the election account he had not received it until the 27th of March, when it was sent to the King. "If Lord North had thought that the expense attending elections and re-elections in the years 1779, 1780, and 1781 would have amounted to £72,000," his letter continues, "he certainly would not have advised His Majesty to have embarked in any such expense. He begs, however, a few moments of His Majesty's attention to state some circumstances which may in a degree account for the largeness of the sum in the election account. That account contains, besides the expenses attending the general election, the expenses of the Hampshire contest in 1779, and of the elections of Bristol, Coventry, and Gloucestershire, together with about two thousand pounds for sundry small elections. The two thousand, sent to the Duke of Chandos and Sir R. Worsley in Hampshire, bore, as Lord North fears, a very small part of the expense. Mr Chester in the great contest for Gloucestershire has, it is said, spent from twenty thousand to thirty thousand; but nevertheless left at his death from three to four thousand pounds unpaid. This debt was a great

---

[1] Donne, *Letters of George III to North,* II. 423.

prejudice to the friends of the Government in the contest[1] which followed upon Mr Chester's death.   To assist in removing it two thousand pounds were paid.   The sitting members for Coventry had stood three contested elections, two trials before the committee, and a long examination at the bar of the House in the course of a year and a half before they made any application.   They then received two thousand pounds.   The general election at Bristol cost but one thousand pounds to the Government ; but Mr H. Lippincott's death bringing on a fresh contest on the back of the former, the merchants of Bristol, who had contributed largely to the first contest, as well as to many loyal subscriptions, thought they might without impropriety apply for assistance.   They received at different times five thousand pounds.   Lord North encloses an abstract of their expenses and of the assistance they received. Lord North was very unwillingly drawn into the contests for Westminster, Surrey, and the City of London ; but the necessity of strengthening the Government at that time and weakening the opposition, and the importance of a victory, with the fair prospect of success, prevailed on him to advise the beginning, which drew on the subsequent expense.   The expense of the Westminster amounted to more than eight thousand pounds[2] ; Surrey to four thousand ; the City of London to four thousand ; the amount of all three to more than sixteen thousand pounds.   These three contests were unhappily not successful, and therefore the expense is the greater grievance.   But Lord North must, in justice to the members who were assisted to come into Parliament, say that they all behaved with very steady attachment to the end[3]."

In further justification of the bill of seventy-two thousand pounds, Lord North reminded the King that the general election *Economies in Electioneering.*

---

[1] January 24th, 1781, when James Dutton succeeded to the seat, held from September 16th, 1780, by William Bromley Chester. *Official List,* pt. ii. 165.

[2] Fox was the opposition candidate at Westminster.   Lord Lincoln and Sir George Rodney were the ministerial candidates.   "If Mr Fox stands," wrote North to Robinson on August 13th, 1780, " we shall have much trouble and more expense, which will all fall upon us.   Neither Lincoln nor Rodney will contribute."   Next day Robinson informed North that the Duke of Newcastle had written to Lord Lincoln to prevail on him to stand for Westminster.   "But you are right," he added, "that it must be all at your expense.   In that case it may be well to fight for both seats." *Hist. MSS. Comm. 10th Rep.,* App., pt. vi. 33.

[3] Donne, *Letters of George III to North,* ii. 423–26.

in 1774 had " cost near fifty thousand pounds to the Crown, beyond which there was a pension of one thousand pounds a year to Lord Montacute, and five hundred pounds a year to Mr Selwyn, for their interest at Midhurst and Ludgershall." " The elections in 1779, 1780, and 1781," he continued, " will cost fifty-three thousand pounds ; but then there has been no additional pensions promised. Nay Lord Montacute's pension is struck off ; because two friends of the Government, Mr Samson Gideon and Mr Drummond, purchased with their own money, at Lord North's recommendation, the two seats at Midhurst ; so that all things considered this election will not in the end be as burdensome to His Majesty as the last[1]."

Selwyn's Pension.

The bargain with George Selwyn as to Ludgershall, here alluded to by North, was continued until 1782. Then with the downfall of North a rearrangement of the pension list was necessary. " Sir James Cockburn's pension," wrote George III, when he was making this rearrangement, " I will set down in the name of his wife, and Mr Bowlby's[2] in that of Lady Mary. As to Mr Selwyn, I do not see a possibility of its continuance. He must view it like the loss of a place, and must look to better days[3]."

Lord North's Excuses.

As a final appeal to the King Lord North justified his conduct of the election of 1780 on the ground of policy. " Lord North begs leave to submit to His Majesty," he wrote, " that at the time of the election it was thought of the highest importance to secure a number of friends in the House of Commons—the opposition was eager, numerous and powerful ; that the times were distressing upon gentlemen, very few of whom were able to assist themselves so well as in former times ; that in fact till after the calamity of Yorktown, the Parliament appeared very friendly to the last administration ; and that, as Lord North mentioned above, he was not able to stop the expense in some cases, nor to know its extent until very lately. Lord North states all these circumstances only in hopes of reinstating himself in some degree in His Majesty's good opinion. He has no other wish or desire. He has endeavoured through the course of his life to promote His Majesty's service to the best of his judgment. He hopes His Majesty will not embitter the remainder of his days by withdrawing from him that good opinion which he has long, and often by the sacrifice of his

---

[1] Donne, *Letters of George III to North*, ii. 426.

[2] Member for Launceston.

[3] Donne, *Letters of George III to North*, ii. 421.

inclinations and private comfort, endeavoured to deserve[1]."   " Lord
North cannot be surprised," wrote the King in answer to this appeal,
" that a mind truly torn to pieces should make me less attentive to
my expressions.   I certainly did and do still think the accounts
ought to have been regularly given in ; but I did not mean by
that to express any intention of withdrawing my good opinion of
him[2]."

It is no part of my plan to follow George III in his manage- The King
ment of the House of Commons, or to concern myself with the and Reform.
general history of the reign.   My purpose has been to show his
interference with elections, and the methods which he used in the
constituencies to swell the number of his supporters in Parliament.
While he was thus busy in elections the King opposed every movement to purify the electoral system.   In 1768, when Dowdeswell
moved to disfranchise officers in the customs, the King wrote of the
proposal as " very extraordinary " ; as one which could have been
proposed " solely from a motive of showing an inclination to be
impertinent, and to run after that empty shadow of popularity[3]."   In
1770 Dowdeswell again asked leave to introduce a bill to disqualify
revenue officers.   Leave was refused by a majority of seventy-five.
" As the question proposed by Mr Dowdeswell was well calculated
to catch many persons," the King wrote to North, " I think it has
been rejected by a handsome majority[4]."

In 1770, when Grenville brought forward his bill for transfer- His Oppo-
ring the trial of election cases from the House to select committees, sition to all
the King was hostile to the reform, and was still opposed to it in Movement.
1774 when the Grenville Act was made permanent[5].   The defeat of
Sawbridge's motion of 1774 for shortening the duration of Parliament gave him great satisfaction[6], as did the rejection of the bill
of 1779 to exclude government contractors from the House of
Commons.   " I could not restrain," he then wrote to North, " the
pleasure of expressing my satisfaction at the rejection, by so good
a majority, considering the strange scruples many of the country
gentlemen have harboured on that subject[7]."   His attitude towards

---

[1] Donne, *Letters of George III to North*, ii. 426.
[2] Donne, *Letters of George III to North*, ii. 427.
[3] Ellis, *Original Letters Illustrative of English History*, 3rd Series, iv. 385.
[4] Donne, *Letters of George III to North*, i. 14.
[5] Donne, *Letters of George III to North*, i. 169.
[6] Donne, *Letters of George III to North*, i. 169.
[7] Donne, *Letters of George III to North*, i. 240.

Parliamentary reform is expressed in his letter to Pitt, after Pitt, as Prime Minister, had introduced his bill of 1785 to the House of Commons. " Mr Pitt must recollect," the King then wrote, " that though I have thought it unfortunate that he had early engaged himself in this measure; yet that I have ever said that, as he was clear on the propriety of the measure, he ought to lay his thoughts before the House; that out of personal regard to him, I should avoid giving any opinion to anyone on the opening of the door to Parliamentary reform except to him. Therefore I am certain Mr Pitt cannot suspect my having influenced anyone on the occasion. If others choose for base ends to impute such conduct to me, I must bear it as former false suggestions[1]." All corruption of the electoral system was turned to account by George III in his long continued efforts to control the House of Commons. Much of the corruption was aggravated by him; and any reform, no matter how slight or how obvious its need, encountered his opposition.

The Later Elections of George III's Reign. After the end of the North Administration, traces of the actual interference of the King in elections become fewer, although they do not disappear altogether from the memoirs and letters of the period. In 1782 the King was in correspondence with Lord Shelburne concerning a pending by-election at Westminster, due to the bestowal of a peerage on Rodney[2]. In 1794 he personally interested himself in the election of a successor to Mr Powney at Windsor, and sent notice to the " principal persons who look up to the Castle " to support Mr Grant[3]; and as near the end of the reign as 1807, it was believed that the King advanced " a very large sum out of his privy purse " to enable Portland and Perceval to go into the borough market, as North and Robinson had done in 1774 and 1780[4].

The Last of Royal Interference. George III was the last sovereign to concern himself systematically in elections. George IV exercised no personal influence on the House of Commons[5]. In his reign and in that of William IV elections were again managed from the treasury without interference from the Crown; and after the Reform Act their management devolved on the party organisations which the enlarged electorate and the new political life brought into existence.

[1] Stanhope, *Life of Pitt,* i., App. xvi.   [2] Add. MSS. 34523, f. 367.
[3] Cf. *Harcourt Papers,* vi. 42, 43.   [4] Cf. *Romilly Memoirs,* ii. 206.
[5] Cf. Lewis, *Administrations of Great Britain,* 421.

PART IV

THE HOUSE AND ITS USAGES.

CHAPTER XX.

THE PLACE OF MEETING.

UNLIKE the Parliaments of Scotland and Ireland the Unreformed An Accidental Home. Parliament never met in a building specially designed for its accommodation. The Parliament of Scotland, by threats to meet elsewhere, compelled the City of Edinburgh to build a Parliament House. The Parliament of Ireland raised for itself a building which is to-day an ornament to the City of Dublin. But it was the lot of the English House of Commons to occupy, for nearly three centuries prior to the reform of 1832, a part of "the most ancient palace in England, applied accidentally in the lapse of ages to a purpose for which it was not originally intended[1]." Of the House of Lords it may be said that when Parliament assembled at Westminster it never met elsewhere than in the great palace, of which S. Stephen's Chapel, so long the legislative chamber of the Commons, formed a part.

The first meeting-places of the representatives of the Commons, Meetings in Westminster Abbey. deliberating apart from the House of Lords, were the Chapter House and the Refectory of Westminster Abbey[2]. From the reign of Edward I—from 1295, when the Commons began to be continuously represented in Parliament—until the reign of Edward VI, the elected body assembled occasionally in other chambers at Westminster than those in the Abbey. Sometimes also Parliament met elsewhere than at Westminster. Occasionally it met no further away than the Priory Church of the monastery

---

[1] *Mirror of Parl.*, 1833, III. 2699.   [2] Cf. Stubbs, III. 443, 444.

of Blackfriars[1], well within sight of the towers of the palace and the spires of the neighbouring Abbey. Occasionally Parliament met as far from Westminster as Coventry or York; once as far away as Carlisle[2]. But in the period extending from 1332—the first year in which there is a record of the Commons sitting apart from the Lords[3]—to the reign of Edward VI, the assembling of the Commons elsewhere than in the Abbey, when Parliament was in session at Westminster, was exceptional. It is believed that in the two centuries which intervened between 1332 and the setting apart of the Chapel of S. Stephen's as the meeting-place of the Commons about 1547, the sessions of the House of Lords were ordinarily held in the Chamber of Parliament or White Chamber, lying south of the Painted Chamber in the Palace of Westminster, and the Chapter House or the Refectory was the chamber of the Commons[4].

S. Stephen's Chapel.

The stately and noble Chapel of S. Stephen's, dating back to the reign of Edward I, the chapel of a rich ecclesiastical foundation planted in the middle of the Palace, became the chamber of the Commons when the collegiate foundation was vested in the Crown in pursuance of the statute for the suppression of free chapels[5]. Within this Chapel, which, after it was diverted to its new purpose by Edward VI, was first ceiled and much later lined with galleries, the House of Commons met for the next three centuries. Except on two occasions—the first in the reign of Charles I, and the second in the reign of Charles II, when Parliament convened at Oxford—and again in the session which followed the Union of Great Britain and Ireland in 1800, the Commons during these centuries never sat elsewhere than in S. Stephen's Chapel, until the Houses of Parliament were destroyed by fire in 1834.

A Royal Palace.

At no time, however, had the Commons absolute control over the building in which they met. With the House of Lords the House of Commons occupied a palace only lent to Parliament by the Crown, and never alienated from the Crown. The relations between the Crown and the House of Commons, in regard to the use of the royal palace, were not materially altered from the time of Edward VI to the reign of William IV. All through these

[1] Cf. Heckethorn, *London Memories; Social, Historical and Topographical,* 123.
[2] Cf. *Official List,* pt. I. vii., xix., xxiv.; Parry, 69.
[3] Stubbs, III. 445.   [4] Cf. Stubbs, III. 444.
[5] Cf. Stanley, *Hist. Memorials of Westminster Abbey,* 426, 2nd Ed.

centuries the relations were so well recognized, that it was to the Crown surveyor of works that the Commons appealed in 1604 when structural alterations within the chamber were deemed necessary[1]; and it was to the Crown that the House appealed when, in 1691, a new chamber was felt to be needed, owing to what was then described, in an address to William III, as the "ruinous and dangerous condition" of S. Stephen's Chapel[2]; and again, in 1732, when a new Parliament House was urged[3].

It was due to these relations of the Crown to the Palace, moreover, that, apparently from the time when the Speaker began to occupy chambers within the Palace, it was the custom on the dissolution of a Parliament for the late Speaker to ask at a private audience the permission of the sovereign to continue in occupation of his chambers, until the assembling of a new House of Commons, and the election of a Speaker. As recently before the disappearance of the old Palace as 1831, Sir Charles Manners Sutton, who was then Speaker, received an intimation that the sovereign would resume possession of the Palace, and that George IV would occupy the Speaker's chambers on the night before the coronation[4]. *The Crown and the Speaker's Chambers.*

The House of Commons began its tenure of S. Stephen's Chapel in the reign of Edward VI, when the counties, cities and boroughs of England and Wales were represented by three hundred and thirty-four members[5]. When the Chapter House of the Abbey was exchanged by the Commons for S. Stephen's, except for the enfranchisement of the County of Durham and the addition of one hundred and eighty members from the boroughs which took place between the beginning of the reign of Edward VI and the end of that of Charles II, the House of Commons was organically complete. Its relations to the Crown were not those of to-day, but it was organised and doing its work much as at the present time; and of the officers of the House who now have their place within the Chamber only the chaplain seems to have been wanting. *From the Chapter House to S. Stephen's.*

Of the internal arrangement of the House in the reign of Elizabeth, when S. Stephen's Chapel was still newly in the possession of the Commons, and when the members had increased *S. Stephen's in the Reign of Elizabeth.*

---

[1] Cf. *H. of C. Journals*, i. 141.   [2] *H. of C. Journals*, x. 618.

[3] Cf. *H. of C. Journals*, xxxi. 24.

[4] Cf. *Select Committee on the Losses of the Late Speaker and other Officers of the House of Commons by the Fire at the Houses of Parliament*, 1837, 3, 4; Hansard, 3rd Series, xxvi. 19.

[5] Cf. Hatsell, ii. 386.

in number to four hundred and sixty-five, there is a contemporary description of value, written by Hooker, who was of the Commons as one of the members for Tiverton. In the carefully prepared statement of procedure and usages at Westminster, submitted by him for the guidance of the House of Commons of the Irish Parliament, of which he was also a member, Hooker wrote : " The Lower House is a place distinct from the others. It is more length than breadth. It is made like a theatre, having four rows of seats, one above the other, round about the same. At the higher end, in the middle of the lower row, is a seat made for the Speaker, in which he always sitteth. Before is a table board at which sitteth the Clerk of the House, and thereupon layeth his books and writeth his records. Upon the lower row, on both sides the Speaker, sit such personages as be of the King's Privy Council, or of his chief officers ; but as for any other, none claimeth nor can claim any place but sitteth as he cometh, save that on the right hand of the Speaker next beneath the said Counsels, the Londoners and the citizens of York do sit, and so in order should sit all the citizens accordingly. Without this House is one other in which the under clerks do sit, as also such as be suitors and attendants to that House[1]."

The Ceiling.   Hooker in his description of S. Stephen's makes no mention of galleries in the Chamber. Nor does his description enable one to ascertain whether up to this time the beautiful pointed arches of the famous old chapel had been hidden by the flat ceiling, the ventilator through which, during the last twenty years of the eighteenth century, was made to serve as a ladies' gallery, and was then the only place, until after the old representative system had come to an end, to which ladies had access while the House was sitting[2]. All that seems to be ascertainable as to the date of this alteration of S. Stephen's Chapel is that after the Reformation, which may mean as soon as the House of Commons migrated from the Chapter House, the upper part of the Chapel—its vaulted roof and its upper lights—was cut off by the ceiling. The only mention of the ceiling in the Journals—which, it is significant to note, begin from the time of the migration from the Abbey to the Palace—is of the date of 1691. Then Sir Christopher Wren reported to the House

[1] Hooker, " Order of Parliament," Mountmorres, *Ancient Parliaments of Ireland*, I. 113, 114.

[2] Cf. *Memoirs of the Verney Family during the Civil War*, I. 329; Pryme, *Autobiographic Recollections*, 209, 210.

that the ceiling could not be "presumed to last many years longer"; and that therefore "it seemed most reasonable that ere long a new room be thought of, where the important affairs of the nation may be transacted without suspicion of this sort[1]."

By the time James I came to the throne the number of members had increased from three hundred and thirty-four, the number when Edward VI assigned S. Stephen's to the Commons, to four hundred and sixty-five. Of these additional members, forty-four came in during the reign of Edward VI; twenty-five in that of Mary; and sixty-two in that of Elizabeth[2]. In the first session of the Parliament of 1604 there is an authentic record that the House was inconvenienced by the lack of seating accommodation for its members. At this time it would seem that the arrangements and furniture of the House were similar to those described by Hooker, and also that the seats were still without backs; for backs to the seats in the Chamber were an innovation for which the Rump Parliament was responsible[3].

Many charters of enfranchisement, it was recited in a resolution passed by the House in 1604, had been granted in recent years; members were attending "in greater multitudes than heretofore had been usual"; hence they "do want convenient room to sit in the place accustomed for their meeting; and by reason of this lack of room, many were forced to stand in the entrance and midst of the House, contrary to order." "It is required in behalf of said House," further reads the entry in the Journals, "that the officers of His Majesty's works do immediately give order for erecting and fitting such and so many rooms and seats as the whole House may sit, and attend the service with more ease and conveniency[4]." No considerable alterations within the Chapel of S. Stephen's can have followed this order of 1604; for in the Pensioner Parliament, in which the number of members stood at five hundred and thirteen, there were again complaints of lack of room, and when the House was full members had to sit on the steps of the gangways[5].

In no session of the House of Commons does it appear to have been more difficult to keep a full attendance of members than during the Pensioner Parliament[6]. At one time, as a means of securing better attendance, calls of the House were ordered to be

Seating Accommodation in 1604.

Lack of Room in the House.

Irregular Attendance and Lack of Seats.

[1] *H. of C. Journals*, x. 605.
[2] Cf. Hatsell, ii. 386.
[3] Cf. Grey, *Debates*, iii. 403.
[4] *H. of C. Journals*, i. 141.
[5] Grey, *Debates*, iii. 403.
[6] Cf. *Pepys' Diary*, vi. 88. Wheatley Ed.

published in the *London Gazette*[1], the government journal which had been started by Sir Joseph Williamson in November, 1665[2]. At other times bills were introduced to impose penalties on defaulters[3]. On one occasion a committee was appointed to examine the Journals to ascertain what punishments in days gone by had been imposed on " members who absent the service of the House," and to report " what ways they think fit for filling up of the House[4]." From this committee, appointed in 1670, there was a recommendation that persistent absentees should be doubly assessed in the bill of subsidies[5]. Nothing came of any of these proposals; but when one of them was under discussion, a member ridiculed resort to such expedients so long as the Chamber was not sufficiently large to seat all who were of the House[6].

Undignified Over-crowding in 1832.   At no time after wages had disappeared, and there had come about the great change in the personnel of the House due to the election of non-residents from the boroughs, was there any efficacious and uniform obligation on members for even a single day's attendance on Parliament. All through the last two centuries of the unreformed House of Commons want of room in S. Stephen's Chapel was chronic; so much so that after the membership of the House had been increased in the nineteenth century to six hundred and fifty-eight, by the additions at the Union with Ireland, and at the reform of 1832, it was complained by Cobbett, newly of the House as one of the members for the recently enfranchised borough of Oldham, that the seating accommodation of the Chamber afforded members only half a foot square each. " Why," Cobbett asked, " are six hundred and fifty-eight of us crammed into a space that allows to us no more than half a foot square? There we are, crammed into this little hole; squeezing one another, treading upon each other's toes, running about to get a seat, going to the House at seven o'clock in the morning, as I do, to stick a bit of paper with my name on it on a bench to indicate that I mean to sit there for that day; then routed out of those places again after a division has taken place, and running and scrambling for a seat in just the

[1] Cf. *H. of C. Journals*, VIII. 670.
[2] Cf. Millington, *Sir Joseph Williamson, Knight*, 1630–1701, 8.
[3] Cf. *H. of C. Journals*, VIII. 670, IX. 616.
[4] *H. of C. Journals*, IX. 175.
[5] *H. of C. Journals*, IX. 191.
    Cf. Grey, *Debates*, I. 393.

same manner as people do when they are let into a dining room at a public dinner at the Crown and Anchor or elsewhere[1]."

Lack of any efficient means of compelling full and constant attendance doubtless led to the assumption that occasions when there would be a full House would be few and far apart. However this may be, it is possible to trace internal alterations in the Chamber intended to provide more seating accommodation only after the Union of Scotland with England in 1707, and again after the Union of Great Britain and Ireland in 1800.

Additions to Seating Accommodation.

When galleries were first built about the walls of the Chapel I have not been able to discover. But one of the payments to officers of the House sanctioned in the closing days of the Restoration Parliament suggests that there was a gallery in 1660[2]; and there is proof in the Journals that it was in existence in 1662, and that by this time strangers were finding their way into it. Smoking in the House was practised during the Commonwealth, when the "tobacconists" sat apart from the non-smoking members[3]; and in 1693 the House made an order that "no member do presume to take tobacco in the gallery[4]." At the Union of England and Scotland, but before provision had been made for the accommodation of the forty-five members from Scotland, the Chamber was described as "a commodious building, accommodated with several ranks of seats, covered with green, and matted underfoot, for five hundred and thirteen gentlemen." "On three sides of the House," continues this description, "are beautiful wainscot galleries, sustained by cantilevers, enriched with fruit and other carved curiosities[5]."

The Galleries of the House.

The structural alterations designed by Wren, intended to make room for the additional forty-five members from Scotland, did not for long quiet the agitation for a new Parliament House. In 1732 the House of Commons petitioned George II that he would be graciously pleased to give directions for the building of a more "spacious and convenient edifice, that may be made use of for the reception of the Parliament," and at the same time assured His Majesty "that this House will make good the expenses of the same[6]."

Proposed New Buildings.

[1] Townsend, *Hist. of the House of Commons*, II. 463.

[2] Cf. *H. of C. Journals*, VIII. 229.

[3] Cf. Burton, *Cromwellian Diary*, I. 320.

[4] *H. of C. Journals*, XI. 137.

[5] Brayley and Britton, *Hist. of the Ancient Palace and Late Houses of Parliament at Westminster*, 361, 362.

[6] *H. of C. Journals*, XXII. 89.

By 1739 the movement for larger accommodation had progressed so far that Kent, who built the Horse Guards, the old Law Courts at Westminster, and Devonshire House, Piccadilly, and who altered and decorated Kensington Palace[1], was directed by the treasury to prepare designs and estimates for a new Parliament House. Kent made a series of designs, which received the approbation of the treasury and of Speaker Onslow. The estimated cost was £157,000. Old Palace Yard was to be greatly enlarged; the new buildings were to present a grand façade to the river, and the Chapel of S. Stephen's was to be retained[2]. With the completion of Kent's elaborate designs progress came to an end in the scheme of 1739; and, so far as the Journals and the extra-official Parliamentary records show, Parliament remained content with its accommodations until 1794.

The Last Proposal before Reform. In 1794 the House of Lords moved for a better Chamber[3]. In 1831 the House of Commons again urged a new Parliament House[4]. But a much larger and more pressing question was at this time engaging Parliament and the country. This was the reform of the constitution of the House itself—a reform which had been conceded as necessary not many years after the migration of the Commons from the Abbey to S. Stephen's—and the proceedings of 1831, with respect to a new building, a subject which the House first debated as early as 1691, are now of interest chiefly from the fact that in 1831 one member was daring enough to suggest that the site consecrated to Parliament since the days of Edward I should be abandoned, and a new Parliament House be built near S. James's Palace[5].

The Old and the New Era. S. Stephen's Chapel outlasted the Unreformed Parliament, though altered internally and built about externally, during the three centuries that the Commons met within its walls, to such an extent as to have brought down to the nineteenth century but few traces of its original thirteenth century grandeur, little to recall the fact that, when the Commons took possession, its carved work and decorations were perhaps more finished than those of any other chapel in the country[6]. It survived just long enough to permit the short-lived House of Commons chosen by the new electorate to meet,

---

[1] *Dict. Nat. Bio.*, xxxi. 24.   [2] Cf. Brayley and Britton, 395.
[3] Cf. *Mirror of Parl.*, 1833, iii. 2698.
[4] Cf. *Mirror of Parl.*, 1833, iii. 2698.
[5] Cf. *Mirror of Parl.*, 1833, iii. 2698, 2699.
[6] Cf. Fergusson, *Handbook to Architecture*, 871, Ed. 1859.

for its first two sessions, under, though not in sight of, the vaulted roof which had been raised nearly five centuries before in the reign of the great sovereign whom history has credited with the idea that " that which touches all shall be discussed by all," and who " created the most effective law-declaring machine in the Teutonic world of his day," and " gave to England her unique place in the History of Law[1]."

[1] Jenks, *Law and Politics in the Middle Ages,* 44.

CHAPTER XXI.

THE SPEAKER.

TURNING now from S. Stephen's Chapel to the House, its internal organisation and mode of work, its procedure, its usages, and its attitude towards the world outside, first to demand attention are the officers, and first among these the Speaker, around whom, since Sir Thomas Hungerford was chosen to the Chair in 1377, the organisation of the House of Commons has centred. Some presiding officer, some spokesman also to communicate with the Crown, the House must have needed from the time when its members sat apart from the Lords. There is evidence that the Houses were sitting apart as early as 1332[1]. It is probable that they may have deliberated apart at an earlier period. But there is no record of the existence of an officer of the House of Commons to whom the title of Speaker was applied earlier than 1377, the last year of the reign of Edward III, when Hungerford, knight of the shire for Wilts, is described as acting as Speaker[2].

In reviewing the history of the office of Speaker from the reign of Edward III to that of William IV, in which the House of Commons was reformed, two facts stand out with prominence. The first is that from the earliest days of the office, from soon after the time when the House became possessed of a presiding officer to whom the title of Speaker was applied, until the reign of Charles II, the Commons were never in a position to elect whom they pleased of their members to the Chair, and to put aside the nominee of the Crown.

---

[1] Cf. Stubbs, III. 445.   [2] Hatsell, II. 153.

During these three centuries, as at the present time, on the assembling of a new Parliament the Commons were commanded or requested to attend its ceremonial opening in the Chamber of the Lords. They were then directed by the sovereign, or by the Lord Chancellor acting for him, to return to their own Chamber, and choose their Speaker, and to present him for the approval of the sovereign. It is doubtful whether at any time during this long period the Commons were free to choose whom they pleased, and to disregard the wishes of the sovereign as conveyed to them by a member of the King's Council or an officer of the royal household; and in the case of most Speakers there is good reason to believe that their choice by the House was brought about by the Crown. In this period the Speaker was a link between the Crown and the House[1]; and the representative system had existed for nearly four centuries, from 1295 to 1679, before he ceased to serve in this capacity—before it ceased to be possible to say of him, as was said of Speaker Finch by Bagg, the electioneering manager for Buckingham in the West of England, that he must endure the frowns of his fellow-members and "hazard his credit with them for His Majesty's service[2]."

The second fact, which stands out in the survey of the changes which took place in the office of Speaker between the reign of Edward III and the years immediately following the Reform Act of 1832, is that even after the Commons in the reign of Charles II had successfully asserted the right to elect the Speaker without the intervention of the Crown, another century and a half was to elapse, and the representative system was to undergo its first great reform, before the Speakership was to become a non-partisan office, and the occupant of the Chair was to assume and maintain the attitude which he now holds towards political parties and towards measures submitted to the House.

The history of the Chair in respect to the relations of its occu- pants to the Crown and to the House thus divides itself into two periods. In the first of these, from the reign of Edward III to that of Charles II, the Speaker, as has been said, was a link between the Crown and the House. On one memorable occasion, in the eventful period when the double relation was becoming impossible, a Speaker admitted his relation to the Crown before the assembled

---

[1] Cf. Gardiner, *Personal Government of Charles I*, i. 94.
[2] Bagg to Buckingham, March 17th, 1628, *State Papers*, 1628–29, 24.

Commons. "I am not the less the King's servant," Finch declared when Eliot pressed his resolution, "for being yours[1]."

Second Period of the Speakership. The second of these periods began with the contest of the Commons with Charles II over his rejection of Seymour as Speaker in the Parliament of 1679, and ended with the Speakership of Shaw Lefevre, which lasted from 1839 to 1857. In these one hundred and fifty years the Speakership was slowly evolving from a partisan to a non-partisan office; to an office the holder of which must, if he acts in accordance with the later traditions of the Chair, completely dissociate himself from all partisan ties and connections, and eschew all appearance of interest and concern in party politics[2].

Speakers of the First Period. It is not possible, and it would be tedious if it were, to go over the long list of Speakers from Hungerford to Seymour, over the roll of Speakers from the reign of Edward III to that of Charles II, and to attempt to prove that each one owed his election to the Crown. The roll of Speakers is not complete. In the early days of the Chair it is so defective that the names of more than one Speaker may have been altogether lost. But there is an agreement among historians versed in the period which lies between the reign of Edward III and the Great Rebellion, and also some contemporary evidence, that Speakers were usually nominated by the Crown and subservient to it.

Evidence of Regal Influence in the Choice of Speaker. Of the choice of Catesby, who was elected Speaker in 1483, Gairdner writes: "the Commons elected as their Speaker, William Catesby, and presented him to the King on the following Monday. The appointment was approved, as it had in all probability been suggested by the King himself, for Catesby was one of Richard's principal councillors[3]." "Finch's position," writes S. R. Gardiner of the Speaker who figures so prominently in the contest between the House of Commons and Charles I, "was indeed a hard one. Elected by the Commons, but with a tacit regard to a previous selection by the King, the Speaker had hitherto served as a link between the King and the House over which he presided. In Elizabeth's day it had been easy for a Speaker to serve two masters. It was no longer possible now. The strain of the breaking constitution fell upon him. 'I am not the less the King's servant,' he said piteously, 'for being yours. I will not say I will not put

---

[1] Gardiner, *Personal Government of Charles I*, I. 94.

[2] Cf. Speaker Gully, "Address to the Electors of Carlisle," *Manchester Guardian*, July 5th, 1895.

[3] Gairdner, *Hist. of Richard III*, 199, 200.

the reading of the paper to the question; but I must say I dare not[1]."' Eliot, even a more central figure in the scene of March 2nd, 1629, than Finch, writing in 1625 of the Speakership as then regarded by members of the House of Commons, described it as "an office heretofore frequently filled by nullities, men selected for mere court convenience[2]."

In the *Harleian Miscellany* there is a contemporary tract which bears out Eliot's description of the office, and of the relations of the Crown to the Speaker. It was published in 1641. "The first day," wrote the author, in detailing the mode of procedure in the House of Commons on the assembling of a new Parliament, "each member is called by name, every one answering for what place he serveth. That done, they are willed to choose their Speaker, who, though nominated by His Majesty, is to be a member of that House[3]." In another tract in the same collection, published about the same time, additional light is thrown on the election of the Speaker, and the part which it was usual for the Crown to have in it. "He that shall be Speaker," it reads, "must be a knight or burgess returned, and cometh to the House and taketh the ordinary oath as others. One of His Majesty's Council doth use to propound that it is His Majesty's pleasure that they shall freely choose a Speaker for them, and yet commendeth in his opinion some person by name[4]." *[margin: Speakers Nominated by the Crown.]*

Presumptive evidence is not lacking to warrant acceptance of the belief that during this long period the Speaker was serving two masters, the House and the Crown, and was oftentimes more zealous for the Crown than loyal to the House. From the time when the House of Commons began to gain power, approximately from the reign of Henry VI, there was scarcely a sovereign who did not interfere in Parliamentary elections with a view to control of the House of Commons; and it was inevitable in the case of sovereigns who thus interfered in the election of members, that they should also seek to strengthen their position in the House by bringing about the choice of a Speaker on whom they could depend. During this period Speakers were proposed by members in the service of the Crown. The Crown sent orders to the Speaker[5]. It was also usual when a Speaker wished to retire to give notice of *[margin: Dependence of Speakers on the Crown.]*

---

[1] Gardiner, *Personal Government of Charles I,* I. 94.
[2] Forster, *Life of Eliot,* I. 225.   [3] *Harleian Miscellany,* IV. 369.
[4] *Harleian Miscellany,* IV. 561.   [5] Cf. *Parl. Hist.,* II. 190.

his intention to the sovereign[1]. What is equally significant is that in those days Speakers received their pay directly and indirectly from the Crown, and were often rewarded according to the measure of their service to it. At this period they were as much in the pay of the Crown as the sergeant-at-arms,—an officer who was from the first always appointed by the Crown, removable only by the Crown, and merely assigned to the service of the House by the sovereign.

Speakers receive Pay from the Crown.

In the sixteenth century Hooker, in enumerating the emoluments of the Speaker, wrote: " he hath allowances for his diet, one hundred pounds of the King for every session of Parliament ; also he hath for every private bill passed both Houses and enacted, five pounds[2]." In the early years of the seventeenth century, according to the writer of one of the tracts in the *Harleian Miscellany* already cited from, the Speaker was "wont to have one hundred pounds of the prince for the Parliament ; of the subject, for every private bill for assurance five pounds before he deliver it out of his hand; for every name in any bill for denizens five pounds, unless he do agree for less[3]." This hundred pounds was seemingly a regular time-honoured payment. But from as early as the reign of Henry IV, much ampler rewards were bestowed on the Speakers by the Crown. Sir John Tiptoft, who was Speaker in the Parliament of 1406, received from the King as marks of royal generosity and gratitude, large gifts of forfeited land in Carmarthen and Cardigan, and elsewhere in Wales; chattels and goods of a felon, of the value of one hundred and fifty pounds; and also the office of keeper of the forests of Waybridge and Sapley, in the County of Huntingdon, without fee or out-payment[4]. The Parliament in which Tiptoft earned these rewards was the longest on record up to the reign of Henry IV. It was three times prorogued, and continued for nearly a year[5].

Offices bestowed on the Speaker.

As time went on much more valuable offices than keeperships of forests were bestowed on Speakers. Sir Robert Bell, who was Speaker of Elizabeth's fourth Parliament, was lord chief baron of the exchequer[6]. Sir Edward Coke, who was Speaker in the Parliament of 1593, was Solicitor-General to Queen Elizabeth[7]. In the reign of James I Sir Edward Phelips, who was Speaker from

[1] Cf. *Parl. Hist.*, I. 704, 705; IV. 970; V. 907.

[2] Mountmorres, I. 121.   [3] *Harleian Miscellany*, IV. 561.

[4] *Parl. Hist.*, I. 306.   [5] *Parl. Hist.*, I. 306.

[6] Cf. *Parl. Hist.*, I. 810.   [7] Hatsell, II. 157.

1604 to 1611, was King's Sergeant[1]. Sir Edward Seymour, over whose re-election to the Chair in 1679 the House of Commons successfully asserted itself, was, while Speaker in the preceding Parliament, treasurer of the navy[2]. This was an office held by a Speaker as late as 1741[3], when it was resigned by Onslow at the end of the second of his five terms in the Chair; because he conceived it incompatible with the dignity of the Speaker, and the necessary independence of the Chair, that he should hold an office during pleasure, which the Crown bestowed[4].

The strain to which the Speaker's office, as a link between the Crown and the House, was subjected in 1629, when Finch so profitably hazarded his credit with the House for His Majesty's service[5], did not end the relations hitherto existing between the Crown and the Speaker, or give the House independence in its choice. Independence did not come even during the Commonwealth; for it was on Cromwell's recommendation that Lenthall was chosen Speaker in 1654[6]; and at the Restoration the old relations between the Crown and the Speaker were revived. *The Speaker-ship in Charles I's Reign.*

The link was finally broken at the instance and by the persistence of the House of Commons of Charles II's third Parliament—that which followed the dissolution of the Pensioner Parliament by the King, in order to save Danby from impeachment. The third Parliament of Charles II was convened on March 6th, 1679[7], when, as was customary, the Commons, on being requested to attend in the Chamber of the Lords, were directed by the Lord Chancellor to proceed to the choice of a Speaker, and to present him on the following day. Seymour was Speaker when the Parliament of 1661–79 came to an end. On March 6th, when the newly chosen House of Commons was assembled to elect its Speaker, " Colonel Birch," in the language of a contemporary record, " did nominate and recommend the Right Honourable Edward Seymour, knight of the shire for the County of Devon, treasurer of the navy, one of His Majesty's most honourable Privy Council, and Speaker of the last Parliament, being a person acceptable to the *Contest of 1679 over the Election of Seymour.*

---

[1] *Parl. Hist.*, I. 159.

[2] Chandler, *Hist. of the House of Commons from the Restoration to the Present Time*, 1742, I. 230.

[3] Beatson, *Pol. Index*, II. 79.   [4] Cf. *Parl. Hist.*, XXVIII. 514.

[5] Cf. Forster, *Life of Eliot*, II. 116, 117.

[6] Cf. "Three Letters Illustrative of English History," *Archæologia*, XXIV. 138.

[7] Cf. Parry, 585.

King, and one who, from his great integrity, ability, and being experienced, was the fittest for so great a trust[1]." Seymour was accepted by the House. The same day he waited privately on Charles II at Whitehall, and acquainted him that the House had again chosen him to the Chair, "and then His Majesty was very well pleased with the choice[2]." But the next day, when the Commons presented Seymour to the Lord Chancellor in the House of Lords, the Chancellor made a speech quite out of the line of Chancellors' speeches on these occasions. " If His Majesty should always accept a person pitched upon by the House of Commons," he said, " then it would be no great favour to be chosen Speaker; and therefore His Majesty, being the best judge of persons and things, thought fit to except against Mr Speaker, as being fitly qualified for other services and employments, without giving any reason to the persons choosing or the person chosen[3]."

Ceremonial Excuses by the Speaker-elect.   It had long been the usage of Speakers, when presented to the Crown for approval, to implore the sovereign " to command his Commoners to do what they can very easily perform, to make choice of another person more proper for them to present on such an occasion[4]." These excuses to the Crown, and the excuses to the Commons which preceded a Speaker's installation in the Chair, can be traced at least as far back as the reign of Henry IV, when Tiptoft " excused himself on account of his youth and other causes[5]." " Your Speaker ought," said Christopher Yelverton, who was chosen to the Chair in 1597, in excusing himself to the House, " to be a man big and comely, stately and well-spoken; his voice great, his carriage majestical, his nature haughty, and his purse plentiful. But contrarily, the stature of my body is small, myself not so well spoken, my voice low, my carriage of the common fashion, my nature soft and bashful, my purse thin, light, and never plentiful[6]." These excuses were " anciently both hearty and real[7]"; but by the reign of Elizabeth they had long been theatrical and insincere, and long so understood[8]. When Crewe was chosen to the Chair in 1625 Eliot wrote of the " pretended unwillingness in him and importunity in us, with much art and rhetoric on both sides," all " usual more than necessary[9]."

[1] Chandler, i. 330.	[2] Chandler, i. 331.
[3] Chandler, i. 330.	[4] Hatsell, ii. 159.
[5] *Parl. Hist.*, i. 239.	[6] D'Ewes, *Journals*, 549.
[7] D'Ewes, *Journals*, 41.	[8] D'Ewes, *Journals*, 41.
[9] Forster, i. 235.	

When Seymour was chosen in 1679 there was a departure from the long established usage. The Speaker-elect knew that it had been determined at a Council the night before to accept his excuse, on account of some dispute he had at that time with Danby; and when presented on March 7th to the Lord Chancellor he made only the time-honoured request that his own mistakes might be excused[1], and purposely avoided making the traditional appeal that the Commons should be directed to choose a worthier man. Seymour took this course designedly, in order to throw the greater difficulty on Chancellor Finch in refusing him[2]. But although not afforded the opportunity which ordinarily came, and in the past had never been taken advantage of, the Lord Chancellor delivered his peremptory speech to the Commons, directing another election to the Chair[3].

As soon as the Commons were back in S. Stephen's Chapel Sir John Ernley stood up and acquainted them "that he had orders from His Majesty to recommend Sir Thomas Meres to be their Speaker, as a person well known in the method and practice of Parliament, and a person that he thought would be very acceptable and serviceable to them[4]." "But the House in a great heat cried 'No, no, no,' and fell into a warm debate." This is the description of the scene by a contemporary reporter; but the speeches which followed Ernley's motion, a motion which found no seconder, cannot accurately be described as a debate. All the speeches were in the same strain; all were marked by temper; and all were in opposition to accepting a Speaker who was to be thrust on the House in this fashion.

Sacheverel, who set the opposition ball rolling, declared that Seymour in the last Parliament had performed the service of the Chair without complaint, and that his rejection had been brought about to gratify some particular person[5]. Williams, then comparatively a newcomer in the House, and seemingly not yet familiar with the history of the Chair which he was later to occupy, and not realizing, or perhaps choosing to ignore, its long use as a link, conceived that the presentation of the Speaker by the Commons to the sovereign was "but a bare compliment," a mere matter of form. "If we suffer this," he protested, "we shall be

---

[1] Cf. Onslow Narrative, *Hist. MSS. Comm. 14th Rep.*, App., pt. IX. 474.
[2] Cf. Hatsell, II. 109.   [3] Chandler, I. 330.
[4] Chandler, I. 330.   [5] Chandler, I. 330.

put upon daily.   Let us adjourn for the present[1]."   "If you admit
of this," Garraway warned the House, "you would admit of
anything."   "If Mr Seymour be rejected from being Speaker, and
no reason given," he continued, "pray who must choose the
Speaker, the King or us?   It is plain not us."   Sir Thomas Lee,
having in mind the dissolution of 1679 to save Danby, "conceived
that the same person who advised the dissolution gave this also."
Lee was a county member[2], and full of the independence and
fearlessness long characteristic of the knights of the shire.   "I shall
not consent," he declared, "to part with the least right that
belongs to my country, for which I am chosen a representative[3]."

Upholding the Rights of the Commons.   All this time the House was without a Speaker, with the clerk
at the table ready to put the vote for the choice of Speaker.   Sir
Thomas Clarges recalled the attention of the House to its situation,
in view of the suggestion from Williams that there should be an
adjournment.   "There were Parliaments," he said, "long before
there were Speakers chosen," and he insisted that the clerk could
put a motion to adjourn.   "All our lives and liberties," he
continued, "are to be preserved by this House, and therefore we
are to preserve the liberties of it[4]."   "He that advises this,"
declared Colonel Birch, who followed with his protest against the
action of the King, "will readily advise more, I'll warrant you.
This is only a bone cast among us.   I will not touch upon the
prerogative.   But let us think of adjournment for the present[5]."
To Mr Powle, who was subsequently Speaker of the Convention
Parliament, it was an ominous thing to stumble thus at the
threshold before they were in the House; "but this ill advice,"
he went on, "must proceed from some who are too near the King,
and fearful we should agree.   But I hope there is no man here,
a representative of his country, fearful of speaking his mind freely
in favour of those whom he represents, nor yet afraid of being
dissolved, if it should be to-morrow, for maintaining the right of
those who choose them to sit here for them.   I will not invade
the prerogative, neither will I give consent to the infringement of
the least liberty of my country."   "But let us," Powle counselled,
"do nothing hastily, but consider precedents, and adjourn ourselves
till to-morrow at nine[6]."

"These heats were so much the greater," the chronicler of the

---

[1] Chandler, I. 331.   [2] Cf. *Official List*, pt. I. 162.
[3] Chandler, I. 331.   [4] Chandler, I. 331.
[5] Chandler, I. 331, 332.   [6] Chandler, I. 332.

events of March 7th records, "because they reasonably supposed that it was all occasioned by the Earl of Danby, whose power was not wholly at an end, and between whom and Mr Seymour there was a particular resentment[1]." Danby and Seymour.

With or without a formal putting of the motion by the clerk— and the Journals do not enable one to determine beyond all doubt what course was followed[2]—the House adjourned until Saturday, March 8th, when, with the Chair still vacant, members agreed upon a message to the King. In this it was set forth "that the matter yesterday delivered by the Lord Chancellor relating to the Speaker is of so great importance that this House cannot immediately come to a resolution thereon, and therefore do humbly desire His Majesty that he will be graciously pleased to grant some farther time for this House to take it into consideration." Lord Cavendish, Lord Russel, and Sir Henry Capel carried this message to Whitehall. The King was in Council when the members arrived. But he "immediately came out and received them with great cheerfulness and kindness," and bid them tell the Commons that they could have until Tuesday to determine the matter, "unless you shall find," reads the royal message as delivered to the assembled members, "some expedient in the meantime; for, as I would not have my prerogative entrenched upon, so I would not do anything against the privileges of the House[3]." A Representation to the King.

Members met again on Tuesday, March 11th, still in no mood to make any concession. On the contrary a representation was sent to the King justifying the stand they were making in the matter of the Speakership. It was asserted in this representation that "it is the undoubted right of the Commons to have the free election of one of their members to be their Speaker, to perform the service of the House"; and the King was reminded that "the Speaker so elected, and presented according to custom, hath by the constant practice of all former ages, been continued Speaker and executed that employment, unless such persons have been excused for some corporal disease, which has been allowed by themselves, or some others in their behalf in full Parliament." "According to this usage," the representation of March 11th continued, "Mr Edward Seymour was unanimously chosen, upon the consideration of his The Claim of the Commons.

---

[1] Chandler, i. 333.
[2] Cf. *Report of the Select Committee on the Office of Speaker,* 1853, 9.
[3] Chandler, 332.

great ability and sufficiency for that place of which he had large experience in the last Parliament, and was presented by us to your Majesty, as a person we conceived would be most acceptable to your Majesty's royal judgment. This being the true state of the case, we do in all humility lay it before your Majesty's views, hoping that your Majesty upon due consideration of former precedents, will rest satisfied with our proceedings, and will not think fit to deprive us of so necessary a member by employing him in any other service[1]."

The King insists.

"All this is but loss of time," answered the King, when this representation was laid before him. "Therefore I desire you to go back again, and do as I have directed you[2]." On the receipt of this answer, the Commons adjourned; and meeting again on March 12th, after a warm debate, drew up an address beseeching the King to take the representation of March 11th into his further consideration, "and give us," it continued, "such a gracious answer that we may be put into a capacity to manifest our readiness to enter into those consultations which necessarily tend to the preservation and welfare of your Majesty and your kingdom[3]." When the deputation from the Commons read this address to the King, he immediately gave this quick and sharp reply: "Gentlemen, I will send you an answer to-morrow." "Accordingly, as he had often done before upon great difficulty," continues the narrative of these exciting days at the beginning of the Parliament of 1679, " he resolved to put an end to the dispute, and the next day being Thursday, the 13th of March, he came to the House of Peers, and sending for the Commons he immediately prorogued the Parliament till the Saturday following, after the Commons had sat without a Speaker for but six days; and thus the King found a way to gain his point; but with very little advantage to his own business and affairs[4]."

A Compromise effected.

Saturday was March 15th. On that day the King attended in the House of Peers. The Commons were again commanded to attend in the Peers' Chamber, and after the King " was pleased to put both Houses in mind of what he said to them at the opening of the Parliament," Finch, the Lord Chancellor, directed the Commons, for the third time within ten days, to return to their House

---

[1] Chandler, I. 333.
[2] Chandler, I. 334.
[3] Chandler, I. 334.
[4] Chandler, I. 334.

and proceed to the choice of a Speaker. Back once more in their own Chamber Lord Russel put the House in mind of the King's command, and immediately recommended William Gregory, ser-geant-at-law, member for Weobly, "as a person, for his great learning and integrity, fit for the employment; and Mr Sergeant Gregory being unanimously called upon to the Chair, he in a short speech modestly excused himself, and desired the House that another might be nominated. But no excuse being admitted he was formally conducted to the Chair by his two intimate friends, Lord Russel and Lord Cavendish, and there confirmed in the place. On the Monday following he was presented by the Commons to the King in the House of Lords, who without hesitation approved of the choice[1]."

Both sides to this memorable constitutional contest of 1679 made some concession. The Commons did not insist that Seymour should be Speaker. Charles II did not persist in his order, as conveyed to the House by Sir John Ernley, that the Commons should choose Meres. The King gained his end in so far as he prevented the enemy of Danby from being again installed in the Chair. But the permanent gain lay with the House of Commons. In the next Parliament Charles had to accept as Speaker, Williams, recorder of Chester, who had so strongly opposed him in the contest over Seymour, a lawyer whom even the offer of the chief-justiceship of Chester could not buy; and who, when approached, declared that "he would not be thought to do anything that might seem to incline against the interest of the Commons in that trust[2]." *The Advantage with the Commons.*

In Sir John Trevor, afterwards dismissed from the Chair and expelled the House for bribery, James II in his only Parliament obtained a Speaker who was highly acceptable to him. In 1701, and again in 1705, court influence was exercised in the election of Speakers[3]; and as late as the Parliament of 1722–27 Walpole was wont to tell Onslow, then ambitious to be Speaker, that "the road to that station lay through the gates of S. James's[4]." As long after the contest of 1679 as 1780 George III took an active part in bringing about the election of Charles Wolfran Cornewall to the Chair[5]. But subsequent to the short-lived Parliament of 1679, *The House Free to choose its Speaker.*

[1] Chandler, i. 335.
[2] Cf. *Dict. Nat. Bio.,* lxi. 458.
[3] Cf. *Parl. Hist.,* v. 1330; vi. 450.
[4] *Hist. MSS. Comm. 14th Rep.,* App., pt. ix. 516.
[5] Cf. Donne, *Letters of George III to North,* ii. 337.

and to the stand which the Commons made in its opening days for freedom of choice in the election of Speaker, it was never again of any avail for the sovereign openly to send to the Commons an order like that which Ernley conveyed to them on the 7th of March, 1679, after Chancellor Finch had, for Charles II, refused to approve of the election of Seymour.

An Attempt to reassert Regal Influence.   In 1679 Ernley had told the House that he "had orders from His Majesty to recommend Sir Thomas Meres to be their Speaker[1]." Fifteen years later, Wharton, comptroller of the household, set out to perform a service for William III similar to that attempted by Ernley for Charles II. After the venal Trevor had been deposed, Wharton attempted to impose a nominee of the Crown on the House[2]. Exception, however, was promptly taken, "that it was contrary to the undoubted right of the House of choosing their Speaker, to have any person who brought any message from the King to nominate one of them." Wharton was not easily frustrated. Notwithstanding the objection, "the comptroller," to quote from the Journals of the House, "stood up again, and named Sir Thomas Lyttleton, who was seconded by Sir Henry Goodrich." "Whereupon," continues the official record, "arose a debate, and another person, viz. Paul Foley, Esq., was proposed by Sir Christopher Musgrave, and seconded by the Lord Digby." Wharton and Goodrich pressed their motion. On a division, it was rejected, and Foley, whom Burnet characterised as "a learned lawyer, and a man of virtue and good principles," was chosen to the Chair[3].

An Independent Speaker in 1695.   There was no compromise nor anything of the spirit of compromise about this election of Speaker midway in the Parliament of 1690–98. The new Speaker was as little a courtier as Speaker Williams had been in the last two brief Parliaments of Charles II. Only a year before Foley was chosen to the Chair he had, in grand committee on the state of the nation, used remarkably plain language in speaking of the King's veto of the Place bill. "I believe," Foley then said, "the King hath a negative voice, and it is necessary that it should be so. But if this be made use of to turn by all bills and things the court likes not, it is misused; for such a prerogative is committed to him for the good of us all[4]."

---

[1] Chandler, I. 330.
[2] Parl. Hist., v. 908.
[3] Cf. H. of C. Journals, XI. 272 ; Dict. Nat. Bio., XIX. 354, 355 ; LVII. 222.
[4] Parl. Hist., v. 829.

CHAPTER XXII.

THE EVOLUTION OF THE NON-PARTISAN SPEAKER.

FROM Foley's election in 1695, if not from that of Sergeant The Sovereign and the Gregory in 1679, may be dated the beginning of the evolution of the Speakership from the semi-courtier to the strictly non-partisan Chair. office which we know to-day ; and from about this time it is possible to watch its slow developement into an office like that pictured by Hooker, when in the reign of Elizabeth he was giving his counsel of perfection to the ill-organised and disorderly House of Commons of the Irish Parliament. "During the time of the Parliament," Hooker wrote of the Speaker, "he ought to sequester himself from dealing or intermeddling in any public or private affairs, and dedicate and bend himself wholly to serve his office and function[1]." After the attempt made by William III in 1695 there is ground for the belief that no sovereign, except George III, interested himself to bring about the election of a particular member to the Chair, or the defeat of a candidate who had incurred the displeasure of the Crown.

While sovereigns with one exception thus concerned themselves The Speaker in Com- little with the Speakership, the evolution of the non-partisan mittee. Speaker was exceedingly slow. As far back as the Journals and the unofficial records go, it would seem to have been the rule of the Commons to do much of their work in committee. "It was the way," said Eliot, in urging the House to go into committee on the Bill of Rights in 1628, "that led most to truth. It was the more open way. It admitted of every man's having his reason and making answer upon the hearing of the reasons and arguments

[1] Mountmorres, I. 120, 121.

of other men[1]." From this usage of the House of going into committee and of appointing a member other than the Speaker to act as chairman, the Speaker never lost his right as a private member of having a voice for or against a measure at committee stage.

Foley.

Foley, who throughout his Parliamentary career was so independent that the greatest fault that could be imputed to him was that he paraded his independence too ostentatiously[2], frequently exercised his right as a private member when the House was in committee. He spoke against the employment of Dutch and French officers in the English army and navy; and he also took a prominent part in the debate on the abortive scheme of 1696 for a land bank[3].

Foley's Successors.

Lyttleton, who succeeded Foley in 1698, was not an efficient Speaker and added nothing to the traditions of the office[4]. Harley, who was elected to the Chair in 1701, took part in debates both in the House and in committee in 1704; but the debates were on the famous constitutional case of Ashley *versus* White, and it was only natural that in matters of this kind, involving Parliamentary law, the Speaker should intervene[5]. John Smith, who was in the Chair from 1705 to 1708, left no mark on the office. Richard Onslow, Smith's successor, was of a family which has given the House three Speakers and two clerks at the table, a family with more traditions of the Chair attaching to it than any other family in England[6]. Onslow was Speaker only from 1708 to 1710; and his term was in no way remarkable. But the fact that he had to fight a hotly contested election for the County of Surrey, and failed of re-election there at the dissolution of 1710, is proof that as yet one term in the Chair was not regarded as implying re-election as Speaker, and that as yet it had not become the usage to return the Speaker unopposed when he sought re-election from his constituency. Onslow was a Whig; and his defeat in Surrey was the occasion of much exultation by the Tories " who thought there could not be a greater mark of an universal disaffection to the Whig cause[7]." In the new

[1] Forster, *Life of Eliot*, II. 188.
[2] Cf. Macaulay, *Hist. of England*, Ed. 1877, II. 467.
[3] Cf. *Dict. Nat. Bio.*, xix. 355.
[4] Cf. *Dict. Nat. Bio.*, xxxiii. 376.
[5] Cf. Chandler, *Debates*, v. 308, 310, 360.
[6] Cf. *Hist. MSS. Comm. 14th Rep.*, App., pt. ix.
[7] *Hist. MSS. Comm. 14th Rep.*, App., pt. ix. 492.

Parliament Onslow was back in the House as member for the little Cornish borough of St Mawes, where he was nominated by Godolphin, without his knowledge, a few days after his defeat in Surrey[1].

The immediate successor of Richard Onslow was William Bromley; and he was succeeded in 1714 by Sir Thomas Hanmer. On at least one occasion Hanmer addressed the House in committee. He spoke on April 15th, 1714, when the House was in committee on the state of the nation, an occasion which gave the Speaker much more latitude than in committee on a bill, when general principles cannot be discussed, and by the rules of the House the discussion is of details. The danger to the Protestant succession was the theme of Hanmer's speech and a contemporary reporter describes it as a speech which had " a great influence on all unbiassed and unprejudiced minds[2]." Judged by the division its effect on the committee was not far-reaching. But however little influence Hanmer's speech may have had on the House, it is of some historical significance, because for the next fifty or sixty years speeches in committee by Speakers disappear from the Parliamentary reports.

Hanmer's Speech in Committee.

Hanmer's successor, Compton, who was Speaker from 1715 to 1727, like Richard Onslow left no impress on the office. But like Harley he was of the Administration after he was in the Chair[3]. He had been treasurer to George II while the King was Prince of Wales, and in the early days of the new reign George II strongly desired that Compton should be prime minister. " It went so far," wrote Arthur Onslow, " as to be almost a formal appointment, the King for two or three days directing everybody to go to him on business." But by the Queen's management all this was over-ruled and Walpole continued as minister[4].

A Speaker becomes Minister.

Compton's Speakership is also memorable from the fact that he was the last Speaker who was confronted in the House by two ex-Speakers. Bromley and Hanmer were both of the Commons during the Parliament of which Compton was Speaker. Bromley was still of the House during part of Arthur Onslow's long term. Cornewall, who was Speaker from 1780 to 1789, had to confront

Ex-Speakers in the House.

---

[1] *Hist. MSS. Comm. 14th Rep.*, App., pt. ix. 490; *Official List*, pt. ii. 19, 24.

[2] Cf. Chandler, v. 125.

[3] Cf. Doyle, iii. 66.

[4] *Hist. MSS. Comm. 14th Rep.*, App., pt. ix. 516.

for nearly two years, Fletcher Norton, his predecessor in the Chair. Abbot, who was Speaker from 1802 to 1817, for some years had to confront Addington, one of his immediate predecessors in the Chair, both as leader of the House and as private member. Abbot was the last Speaker so placed with respect to a predecessor in the Chair.

Slow Developement of the Speakership.   Richard Onslow's unsuccessful fight for re-election as knight of the shire from Surrey in 1710, and the jubilation of the Tories at his defeat; Bromley's and Hanmer's part in the Tory opposition in the Parliaments when Compton was in the Chair; Compton's close connection with George II; and Walpole's hint to Arthur Onslow that the way to the Chair was through S. James's Palace— all suggest how different was the position of the Speaker in the first forty years of the eighteenth century from the office as it exists to-day.

Seeking Help from the Speaker to promote Legislation.   As late as 1695 aldermen of the City of London, when it was reported to them that a bill in which they were interested " would not go on, if there were not some guineas given," did not hesitate to enter into a bond for the payment of one thousand guineas to Speaker Trevor contingent on the bill becoming an Act.   Later still, in 1732, Arthur Onslow—than whom there never was a more impartial Speaker, or, until the reign of Queen Victoria, one who did more to make the office what we regard it to-day—was waited upon by a committee representing the dissenters of London, who were then agitating for a repeal of the Test Act, to ask for his aid in the promotion of a bill to that end[1].   There is a wide difference between a bond secretly given to a Speaker to push forward a bill and an open deputation to a Speaker to ask his interest in legislation.   But so much conceded, the dissenting deputation of 1732 is proof that out of doors the Speaker was still regarded as a man whom it was well to have on one's side when agitating for legislation.

Speaker Onslow.   Arthur Onslow was Speaker from 1727 to 1761; and during these thirty-three years, during the five Parliaments when he was in the Chair—in spite of the opinion of the Scotch members who, in 1734, were hostile to Walpole and Islay, that Onslow had of late " showed great complaisance to men in power[2]," and despite the fact that at that time it was not considered improper

---

[1] Cf. Hervey, *Memoirs*, I. 157.

[2] Graham, *Annals and Correspondence of Viscount and First and Second Earls of Stair*, II. 207.

for people agitating for constitutional reform to appeal to the Speaker for aid—it is possible to trace distinct steps forward towards the Speakership of to-day. It is doubtful whether any man ever went into the Chair with a fairer and higher conception of what the Speakership should be than Onslow. He understood the attitude of eighteenth century ministers towards the House. "Ministers," he wrote in 1770, in reviewing his career up to his first election to the Chair, "seldom love Parliament, never bring business there for counsel, but to carry points that must have the authority of the Legislature; and in order to carry such points must previously strengthen themselves there by collecting all the force they can get for it[1]."

Throughout his long career as Speaker Onslow showed that he realized that other members besides those acting with the adminis- tration had rights in the House which the Chair was bound to respect and safeguard. Onslow's working theory of life was that men should not act for the sake of popularity. "Fame after a man's death," he wrote, " is never but for real virtue. Be there- fore of the first Duke of Ormonde's opinion, who used to say, 'however ill I may stand at court I am resolved to lye well in the chronicle[2].'" Onslow realized this ambition. He lies well in the chronicles of the House of Commons. His attitude towards administrations during his tenure of the Chair is illustrated by two incidents: his resignation of the lucrative office of treasurer of the navy in 1742, and his answer to the overtures of Pelham when, in 1747, he was asked to take another term in the Chair.

Onslow's Principle of Action.

It was a House of Commons tradition as late as 1790 that Onslow resigned the treasurership because, during a heated contest in the House, he had the place which he held under the Crown thrown in his teeth after a division in which, as Speaker, he had to give the casting vote[3]. It is more than a tradition that he resigned the treasurership, and for the next eighteen years received as his emolument only the fees assigned to the office, because he regarded it as incompatible with the dignity of the Speaker and the necessary independence of the Chair that he should, during the royal pleasure, hold a place which the Crown

His Resig- nation of the Treasurer- ship of the Navy.

---

[1] *Hist. MSS. Comm. 14th Rep.*, App., pt. IX. 460.
[2] *Hist. MSS. Comm. 14th Rep.*, App., pt. IX. 462.
[3] Cf. *Parl. Hist.*, XXVIII. 515; Hatsell, II. 157.

bestowed[1]. Onslow's Speakership thus marks a break in the usage under which Speakers held lucrative offices at the pleasure of the Crown. The period had not yet begun, however, when Speakers ceased to hold any paid office except the Speakership; for during the whole of the time Abbot was in the Chair, and in receipt of six thousand pounds a year, the sum fixed as the Speaker's salary by the Act of 1790, he was in possession of a valuable sinecure held for life on the Irish establishment[2].

His Attitude towards Administrations. The circumstances under which Onslow resigned the treasurership of the navy have to be gleaned from speeches by men who were his contemporaries in the House of Commons[3]. His interview with Pelham is told in his autobiographical memoir. When Pelham suggested still another term in the Chair for Onslow, he was told that he must not expect that Onslow would act otherwise than he had hitherto done, "and which he knew," added Onslow, "was not always pleasing to ministers[4]." "I shall as little like as any one in my station," Pelham replied, "to have a Speaker in set opposition to me, and to measures I may carry on; but I shall as little like to have a Speaker over complaisant, either to me or them[5]."

His Conduct in the Chair. These incidents of 1742 and 1747 show Onslow's attitude toward administrations. His relations with the House and his fairness as Speaker are shown by his constant watchfulness for the rights of the minority. He enforced the rules with greater strictness than any Speaker of the eighteenth century; and according to Hatsell, clerk of the House from 1768 to 1797, who for some years sat below Onslow at the table as clerk assistant[6], one of Onslow's reasons for this strict adherence was that "nothing tended more to throw power into the hands of administration and of those who acted with the majority in the House of Commons than a neglect of or departure from these rules[7]." Onslow firmly held " that the forms of proceedings, as instituted by our ancestors, operated as a check and control on the action of ministers, and that they were in many instances a shelter and a protection to

---

[1] *Parl. Hist.*, xxviii. 514; Walpole, *Memoirs of the Reign of George II,* i. 129.

[2] Cf. Hansard, 3rd Series, xiv. 995.

[3] Cf. *Parl. Hist.*, xxviii. 514.

[4] *Hist. MSS. Comm. 14th Rep.*, App., pt. ix. 517.

[5] *Hist. MSS. Comm. 14th Rep.*, App., pt. ix. 517.

[6] Cf. *Dict. Nat. Bio.*, xxv. 15.   [7] Hatsell, ii. 171.

the minority against the attempts of power[1]." His principle of conduct in this matter, as enunciated by Hatsell, was that only by a strict adherence to these forms of the House could the weaker party "be protected from those irregularities and abuses which these forms are intended to check, and which the wantonness of power is but too often apt to suggest to large and successful majorities[2]."

There is corroborative contemporary evidence that this was Onslow's guiding principle. Horace Walpole concedes Onslow's impartiality; but as is characteristic of Walpole, he attributes it to the desire to conciliate public opinion, and he complains— thus fully bearing out what Hatsell has recorded—that Onslow "was so minutely attached to forms, that it often made him troublesome in matters of higher moment[3]." This is a testimony to Onslow's independence of administrations, and to the impartiality with which, no matter what the question involved, he held himself in the Chair.

His Impartiality.

The long Speakership of Onslow, the longest in the history of the House, marks many significant reforms and developements in the office. In 1741 Onslow abandoned the long-standing usage in accordance with which, when Speakers were presented to the Crown, they besought the sovereign to direct the Commons to choose a worthier and more capable man[4]. "To the Crown," wrote Horace Walpole, in his estimate of Onslow's career as Speaker, "he behaved with all decorum of respect without sacrificing his freedom of speech[5]." To a man of Onslow's intellectual character the meaningless pleas hitherto made by Speakers to the Crown must have been distasteful, and have seemed out of keeping with the growing power and dignity of the House and its post-Revolution relations with the sovereign.

Changes effected by Onslow.

In 1727, when Onslow began his thirty-three years' tenure of the Speakership, it had long been customary with members who had been nominated to the Chair to make three separate pleas to the House that they be excused from service. First came the excuse which the Speaker-elect made while still in his place on the benches of the House. When this had been shouted down, and the proposer and seconder of the Speaker-elect had escorted

Excuses of Speakers-elect.

---

[1] Hatsell, ii. 172. [2] Hatsell, ii. 172.
[3] Cf. Walpole, *Memoirs of George III*, i. 51, 52.
[4] Cf. *Parl. Hist.*, xii. 219.
[5] Walpole, *Memoirs of George III*, i. 51, 52.

him from his seat to the vicinity of the Chair, it was usual for him to stand on the steps and make a second appeal. Hanmer's speech in 1714 at this stage will serve as a specimen of the oratory to which the House was wont to listen, and which it was wont to expect from Speakers-elect in the early days of the eighteenth century. "It was not too late," Hanmer then said, "for gentlemen to alter their resolution, and he begged leave to repeat his first excuses, and to assure them that no one ever came so near the Chair who was so little qualified to do the duty of it, and therefore he hoped they would consult their honour by turning their thoughts to a better choice[1]." "But," continues the report, "the House cried ' no, no,' whereupon he took the Chair, and said that though the House would not allow of his excuse, he hoped they would be pleased to permit him to intercede with Her Majesty to command them to proceed to another election. The members cried ' no, no,' and then the mace was laid on the table[2]."

Onslow establishes a New Usage.

Compton, who was Onslow's immediate predecessor, went through these meaningless and hollow forms in 1715, and again when he was re-elected Speaker in 1722[3]. Onslow early in his Parliamentary career had been ambitious for the Speakership, and had made known his ambition to Walpole[4]; and when he was elected in 1727 he made the three excuses demanded by long usage, and at the bar of the House of Lords made the equally time-honoured plea to the Crown that the Commons might be directed to make a better choice[5]. But in 1741 he abandoned the appeal to the House that he might be permitted to make a plea to the sovereign to direct the Commons to choose a worthier member as Speaker, and instead he thanked the House for his re-election. "Since gentlemen have commanded me to this eminence," he said, while still on the steps of the Chair, and before the sergeant-at-arms had put the mace on the table, "I have now only to return them my humblest thanks for this particular instance of their favour to me, the sense of which I hope I shall always retain, with that respect and gratitude to the House this mark of their esteem will ever claim from me[6]." Cust, who succeeded Onslow in 1761, and who added little to the dignity of the office and nothing to its developement, returned ·to the

[1] *Parl. Hist.*, vi. 1254.
[2] *Parl. Hist.*, vi. 1254.
[3] *Parl. Hist.*, vii. 40, 41; viii. 28.
[4] *Hist. MSS. Comm. 14th Rep.*, App., pt. ix. 56.
[5] *Parl. Hist.*, viii. 632.
[6] *Parl. Hist.*, xii. 219.

old usage, and made the meaningless plea at the bar of the Lords[1]. Grenville followed the precedent set by Onslow in 1741, and made no plea to the King[2]. Addington, courtier-like, reverted, as Cust had done, to all the former usages associated with the election of Speaker[3]. He was, however, the last Speaker to make the mock modesty plea; and before the Reform Act the ceremonies connected with the Commons' choice of their Speaker were well established on the basis on which Onslow had first placed them.

From Onslow's time must be dated the beginning of liberal pensions for Speakers. Onslow died a commoner. Cust died within a week after he had vacated the Chair. Norton, his successor, became Baron Grantley in 1782, but his peerage was not bestowed directly and immediately in acknowledgment of services in the Chair. Cornewall died in office in 1789. Grenville was created a baron in 1790, but for other services than his single session as Speaker[4]. Thus while pensions for Speakers date from Onslow's retirement from the Chair in 1761, peerages along with pensions date only from Abbot's retirement in 1817. Addington had other claims to the viscountcy conferred on him in 1805 than his services in the Chair from 1789 to 1801[5]. Abbot's peerage was earned exclusively by service to the House of Commons. Since Addington resigned as chancellor of the exchequer in 1804, no Speaker has gone back to the benches of the House of Commons; and every Speaker from Abbot to Peel, from 1817 to 1895, has, at the end of his term, been rewarded by Parliament with a pension, and by the sovereign with a peerage.

Pension and Peerage for Ex-Speakers.

Another dignity has gone with the Speakership since Onslow's memorable occupancy of the Chair. Onslow was appointed a trustee of the British Museum. His trusteeship began a few months after the end of his last term as Speaker[6]; and since then election to the Chair has carried with it a seat at the board of trustees of the Museum.

Trusteeship of the British Museum.

Onslow was indisputably the 'greatest Speaker of the period between the Revolution and the Reform Act. His conception of the office was larger and broader than that of any of his predecessors or successors in that period. " When I began my duties here," he said, in his farewell speech to the House on March 18th,

Onslow's Services and Rewards.

[1] *Parl. Hist.,* xv. 1104–6.
[2] *Parl. Hist.,* xxvii. 907.
[3] *Parl. Hist.,* xxviii. 157.
[4] Cf. *Dict. Nat. Bio.,* xxiii. 134.
[5] Hansard, 3rd Series, xiv. 993.
[6] *Dict. Nat. Bio.,* xlii. 617.

1761, " I set out with a resolution and promise to the House to be
impartial in every thing, and to show respect to everybody.   The
first I know I have done ; it is the only merit I can assume.   If I
have failed in the other, it was unwillingly.   It was inadvertently ;
and I ask their pardon most sincerely to whomsoever it may have
happened.   I can truly say the giving satisfaction to all has been
my constant aim, my study and my pride[1]."   Parliament recognized Onslow's merit by awarding him a pension, the first that had
been bestowed on a Speaker.   Out of doors, recognition was also
given to Onslow's great services to the House and to the country.
The City of London, for the first time in the modern history of the
Chair, conferred its freedom on a Speaker.   This honour was bestowed on Onslow as a testimony to the city's appreciation of his
impartiality and his judicious conduct as Speaker, and as a recognition of " that exemplary zeal which upon all proper occasions he
exerted with so much dignity and success in support of the rights,
privileges, and constitutional independence of the Commons of
Great Britain[2]."

His Impress
on the
Speakership.
These compliments from the House and from the city, these
new honours for an occupant of the Chair, Onslow had well
deserved.   He did more than any other Speaker between the
Revolution and the Reform Act to rid the office of its remaining
semi-courtier associations ; and more than any other Speaker of the
unreformed Parliament did he assist in raising the Speakership to
that high and dignified level of non-partisanship on which it
stands to-day, to the pride of Englishmen who love their country,
and care to understand the working of its political institutions—
institutions which have moulded the form of government and
affected the well-being of the Anglo-Saxon race the world over.

Political Life
during
Onslow's
Speakership.
Why there came a halt in the evolution of the Speakership,
why progress towards the Speakership as it is to-day lagged after
Onslow was no longer in the Chair, is not difficult of explanation.
It has to be borne in mind that Onslow's thirty-three years in the
Chair formed what in American political history would be described
as an era of good feeling.   Party lines there were at this time in the
House of Commons ; for it was during Onslow's rule that members
began generally to seat themselves on different sides of the Chamber,
to the right of the Speaker if they were supporting the Government, to the left if they were in opposition.   But from 1727 to

<hr/>

[1] *Parl. Hist.,* xv. 1014.   [2] *Annual Register,* 1761, 106.

1761 was a period of comparative quiet in the House of Commons. Party lines at this time were determined according to principles that were traditional rather than alive and active. In the constituencies there was little of the political thought and activity that came after the American Revolution, through the developement of the London and provincial press, and with the supersession of the news-letter in manuscript by the newspaper, which reported the proceedings of the House and discussed political questions by the eighteenth century method of letters to the editor.

In the period between the Revolution of 1688 and the revolt of the American colonies the nation as a whole was contented with its institutions. There was as yet no large class which had political aspirations, and was unable to gain a hearing. England was still mainly an agricultural country, and the agricultural labourer was fairly prosperous; while his ignorance and isolation made him indifferent to politics. The farmer or yeoman was not much less stolid. His politics meant at most a choice between allegiance to one or other of the county families. To possess a vote at this time was to have a claim to an occasional bonus rather than a right to influence legislation. Anything that deserved to be called public opinion was limited to the gentry and the more intelligent part of the middle classes[1]. The dissenters agitated for relief from tests in the early years of Onslow's tenure of the Chair; but the only questions coming before Parliament during his thirty-three years as Speaker which deeply stirred the popular mind, were the excise in 1733 and the naturalisation of Jews in 1758. Political life away from Westminster was fitful and spasmodic. While general elections gave rise to much popular movement of a noisy character, and diffused a beery atmosphere over the larger borough constituencies, elections prior to the American Revolution were popularly regarded as an end not as a means to an end, and after a general election little interest was taken in proceedings in the House of Commons. In a word, during Onslow's long Speakership there were no political questions which deeply and for any long time touched the life and thought of the country or came close home to the people.

In examining the reasons for the slow progress of the Speakership towards a non-partisan office after the end of Onslow's tenure of the Chair, prominence must be given to the attitude of George III towards the representative system and the House of Commons. It was unlike that of the two preceding Hanoverians—

Indifference in the Country.

Influences retarding the Developement of the Speakership.

[1] Cf. Leslie Stephen, *English Utilitarians*, I. 17.

for it was marked by a dogged determination on the part of the King, early asserted and long maintained, that at any personal cost to himself, and by any means, unconstitutional or corrupt—for methods mattered little to George III if the end in view was achieved—he would control the House of Commons. Until well on towards the middle of his sixty years' reign George III was in fact his own prime minister. He was at once prime minister, election manager, and chief distributor of government patronage. In these years government by Cabinet was practically suspended; and never during the reign of George III did the Cabinet system exist as we know it to-day, when the Crown has been dissevered from all active connection with the electorate, never exercises the veto on the action of Parliament which it still possesses, and never forces a prime minister on Parliament as George III did in the case of Addington, and as William IV did in that of Peel.

American and French Revolutions.
Next in importance to the influence on the House of Commons, on its personnel and its life, which George III so long exercised, must be placed the long and unsuccessful conflict with the American colonies; for from this conflict—and growing out of the influence which it had on political thought and popular political movement in England and Ireland—soon followed, as it was, by the French Revolution, must be dated the activity, intensity, and bitterness which characterised political life in Parliament and in the constituencies during the period between Yorktown and the first Reform Act. Out of the unsuccessful struggle with the American colonies there came the movements for economic and Parliamentary reform; and subsequently, as a result of the influence which the American revolt had on both sides of St George's Channel, the movements in both countries for Catholic enfranchisement and for the relief of Protestant dissenters. Later came the long and terribly costly struggle with Napoleon; and before this was well at an end the questions of Catholic emancipation and Parliamentary reform, partially at rest while the country was locked in its life-and-death struggle with France, again pressed for settlement.

Party Feeling in the Country.
These political contests divided England as it had not been divided since the Great Rebellion; divided it even more than did the Revolution. Ireland at one time was verging on rebellion; and even Scotland was aroused from its long political lethargy. These controversies, now kept at white heat by the press, concerned the religious life of the country, or rather that part of it which was interwoven with the nation's political and institutional life. They

threatened the enormous power which, through corrupting influences at work since the days of the Tudors, had accrued to the
landed aristocracy over the representative system and over the
House of Commons. The Church, then more than now regarded
as a religious department of the State, as part of the garrison
distributed through the country to support the cause of property
and order, a section of the ruling class told off to perform divine
service, to maintain order and respectability, and to uphold traditional morality[1]; the legal profession, then closely allied with the
landed aristocracy and largely recruited from it; the municipal
oligarchies; the official class in both the national and the municipal
service; the landed and farming classes, who derived advantage
from the protective system; all who profited from things as they
were and who dreaded any change were deeply stirred by this
political awakening. Everything that Toryism held dear, nearly
everything, the Crown alone excepted, that cemented Toryism
together and made it the dominant force in English life, was
threatened and was in danger in the eventful and stormy half-
century which intervened between the Declaration of Independence
and the downfall of Wellington's last Administration in 1830.
Family and social life was riven and embittered in these years,
especially after the French Revolution, as it had never been
before by political controversy; and all over the country people
ranged themselves on the one side for reform, and on the other in
defence of the old political institutions, with which, in their conviction, the national life was bound up.

From Pitt's first term as prime minister, which began in 1783,
to the end of Wellington's political career, the Tories, except for a
brief interval in 1806, were continuously in a majority in the House
of Commons. They were more fully and easily in control of Parliament during this long period than ever again in the history of
the party until the general election of 1895. During these years it
followed as a matter of course that Speakers were of the party
dominant in the House and country. It was natural also that
they should be men stirred by feelings and motives like those
which so strongly moved the leaders and the rank and file of the
political party from which they were drawn; and there is not
much evidence that the House and the country as yet demanded or
even expected that the Speaker should be non-partisan, in the
comprehensive sense in which to-day that word is applied to the

*Tories and
Tory
Speakers.*

[1] Cf. Stephen, *English Utilitarians*, I. 41, 48.

Speakership. In this period Onslow, with his ideas of independence towards administrations, and his watchfulness that minorities should not be overridden by government forces, might have been regarded as in advance of the times.

Cust as Speaker.   Cust, who succeeded Onslow, and was Speaker until 1770, was what Eliot would have described as a nullity. The House got much out of hand during his tenure of the Chair; and Cust, early in his career as Speaker, received a rebuke from Rigby, which, both by the occasion of it and by Cust's demeanour during Rigby's lecture, marked the difference in strength and character between the Speaker of the last Parliament of George II and the Speaker of the first Parliament of George III. The incident occurred in 1762. It arose out of the hearing of an election petition, and in particular out of the latitude which Cust had permitted to counsel; for as yet Grenville Committees were non-existent and it was the usage for counsel in election cases to address the House at the bar. "I am very sorry," said Rigby, in calling the Speaker's attention to a transgression of the rules by counsel, "to address you in this manner, and put you in mind of your duty, which you should know much better than I. Give me leave to tell you that you are seated in that Chair to enforce order and support the dignity of the House, and not to suffer our orders to be transgressed by that long-winded pleader. Permit me to say you are but young in that Chair. I wish to see you many years in it. But I have been long enough in the House to know what is and what is not disobedience to orders." The Speaker answered mildly that he endeavoured to do his duty; that if he failed he hoped it would be imputed to the cause which Rigby had mentioned, his being young in the Chair; but on this occasion he maintained that the learned counsel had not transgressed the orders of the House[1]. The trouble with Wilkes began while Cust was in the Chair, and it has been said that a single session of Wilkes killed the Speaker[2].

Sir Fletcher Norton.   By the time that Sir Fletcher Norton succeeded Cust in 1770 party lines were being more sharply drawn in the House than heretofore. Before Norton was defeated when a candidate for re-election to the Chair in 1780 the party conflicts, which were waged with increasing vigour and asperity and with but few intervals of calm until 1832, were well begun. Norton later in his career in the Chair was a partisan whose sympathies were openly and actively with the opposition, with the opponents of the war

[1] Massey, *Hist. of Eng.*, I. 548.   [2] Cf. Trevelyan, *Life of Fox*, 146.

with America, and with the party in the House which was contending for such reforms in the representative system as were
embodied, for instance, in the Grenville Act, and also for economic
reforms.

In the long reign of George III Speakers reverted to the usage
of addressing the House when it was in committee. Norton, who
was Speaker from 1770 to 1780, in 1772 incurred the displeasure
of the court by his attitude towards the Royal Marriage bill, and
by his speech when the bill was in committee[1]. He also incurred
the ill-will of George III by the support he gave to the Grenville
bill[2], a measure to which the King had a strong dislike, as he had
to every bill for the reform of the representative system which was
in the least likely to interfere with his management of the House
of Commons and his command of a majority there. Nor did
Norton confine himself to committee in expressing his opinions.
It came within the province of the Speaker to address the Crown
at the close of the session when money bills were presented.
Fulsome addresses were usual on these occasions; but in 1777,
when a bill had been passed making better provision for the
support of His Majesty's household, Norton bluntly told the King
that the grant was "great beyond example, great beyond His
Majesty's highest expense"; "but all this, Sir, they have done,"
Norton added, "in a well grounded confidence that you will apply
wisely what they have granted willingly[3]."

Norton was again a candidate for the Chair in the Parliament
of 1780–84. It was now a usage of the House, dating from
Compton's tenure of the Chair, to re-elect the Speaker unless he
felt himself physically unable to continue in the office. But in
view of Norton's attitude on the Royal Marriage bill and on the
Grenville bill, and of his patronising speech to George III on
presenting the money bill of 1777[4], it is not surprising that on
the 25th of October, 1780, six days before the assembling of the
new Parliament, the King was moving in behalf of another candidate for the Chair, and making the most of an ill-founded rumour
that Norton's health would not permit him to accept another
term. "Mr Cornewall," the King wrote to North, "is a very
respectable person for the office of Speaker, and ought to be
assured of the support of the Government on this occasion, and

Marginal notes:
Speaker Norton and George III.

George III's Active Hostility.

---

[1] Cf. *Harcourt Papers*, III. 108.   [2] Cf. *Parl. Hist.*, xxi. 797.
[3] *Parl. Hist.*, xix. 213.
[4] Cf. Donne, *Letters of George III to North*, II. 72, 73.

called on to attend the first meeting, and to take all the pains he can to show his willingness to accept that honourable office[1]."

Norton's Successor.

Cornewall had not always been in royal favour. He had incurred the displeasure of George III by his objections in 1771 to the raising of public funds by lotteries; and in 1772 by his action on the Royal Marriage Act[2]. But in 1773 he did the Government good service on an East India bill, and in 1774 he became a junior lord of the treasury; and when he was about to join the ministry he was welcomed as a " very valuable and accredited instrument of public business[3]." When the House of Commons met on the 31st of October Norton was willing to resume the Chair, and there was a contest over the election, the last until the election of Manners-Sutton in 1817. The administration supported Cornewall, for whom there were two hundred and three votes, as against one hundred and thirty-four for Norton[4].

Charles Wolfran Cornewall.

Like Cust, Cornewall was a man of no peculiar merit or ability. He may be said to have left no impress on the office. He spoke at least once in committee in 1785; but this speech was not of the partisan character of the speeches of his successors, Addington, Abbot and Manners-Sutton. He merely bore testimony as Speaker to the successful working of the Grenville method of trying controverted election cases, which at this time was about to undergo further improvement[5]. He was distinguished by a fine voice and a commanding figure. In these respects he realized the ideal of the Speaker-elect of the Elizabethan House of Commons, whose speech is recorded by D'Ewes, and who told the House: " your Speaker ought to be a man big and comely, stately and well-spoken, his voice great and his carriage majestical[6]." Cornewall, whom George III commanded to the Chair, was such a man. But his voice and figure did not impress the House as they might have done because of Cornewall's habit, when in the Chair, of having a porter pot at hand from which he drank largely. The porter produced somnolence, which on more than one occasion, as, well it might, is said to have caused inconvenience to the House[7].

---

[1] Donne, *Letters of George III to North,* ii. 337.

[2] Donne, *Letters of George III to North,* i. 71, 146.

[3] *Chatham Correspondence,* iv. 333.

[4] Donne, *Letters of George III to North,* ii. 340.

[5] Cf. *Parl. Hist.,* xxv. 406, 407.

[6] D'Ewes, *Journals,* 549.

[7] Cf. Jesse, *Letters of George A. Selwyn,* iv. 379; *Dict. Nat. Bio.,* xii. 233.

Grenville, who, on Cornewall's death, succeeded to the Chair, *Grenville's* held office only from January until June, 1789. Within a few *Speakership.* days after his election he spoke in committee on the Regency bill[1].

In 1797 Addington, who was Speaker from 1789 to 1801, made *Addington's* a short but memorable speech on Pitt's proposition for trebling the *Influence on Legislation.* assessed taxes. It is a speech from which has been dated the origin of the income tax; for Addington suggested, when the House was in committee of ways and means, that a clause should be added to the bill to give persons who did not consider themselves adequately reached by Pitt's new taxation, an opportunity of making voluntary contributions to the revenue. A sum amounting to two million pounds was thereby raised; and by the budget of 1798 an income tax was imposed[2]. In 1799 Addington spoke at length in favour of the resolutions for the Union of Ireland with Great Britain[3]. His Speakership, moreover, is remarkable as showing at what a comparatively late period the idea was evolved that a member on being chosen to the Chair should entirely dissever himself from all party ties and connection, and regard the Speakership as the last great office to which he could aspire.

Addington's failure, or inability, or refusal to conceive of the *Addington* office as Onslow had done, or as Speakers of the post-Reform period *and Party Ties.* have subsequently done, is emphasised less by his interventions in debate in committee than by his permitting Pitt to set at naught the authority of the Chair; and by his migration from the Chair to the treasury bench. He retired from the Chair in 1801, after Pitt had been dismissed by George III, to head an Anti-Catholic administration[4].

The episode of 1798 was the most memorable in Addington's *His Inability* tenure of the Chair. Pitt made a proposal that a bill for the *to maintain Discipline.* increase of the navy should be carried through all its stages at one sitting. Tierney, who was then the leader of the opposition, objected. Pitt angrily charged him with a desire to obstruct the defence of the country. Tierney complained that Pitt's language was unparliamentary, and appealed to the Speaker to protect him. The Speaker called upon Pitt to explain his meaning and intimated that the House would wait to hear Pitt's explanation.

---

[1] *Parl. Hist.*, xxviii. 994; Pellew, *Life of Sidmouth*, i. 59.

[2] *Parl. Hist.*, xxxiii. 1089; Pellew, *Life of Sidmouth*, i. 98; 37 Geo. III, c. 15.

[3] *Parl. Hist.*, xxxiv. 448–467.

[4] Cf. Croker, *Papers*, ii. 136.

Pitt answered that he was afraid the House must wait a long while before it heard such an explanation as was demanded of him, and intimated that he adhered to what he had said concerning Tierney. The Speaker made no further attempt to press for an explanation from Pitt.   As the outcome of the episode, which proved Addington to have been either partisan or so weak a Speaker as to be incapable of preserving order, there was a duel on Putney Heath on the ensuing Sunday between Pitt and Tierney[1].   If further proof were wanted of the difference between Addington's conception of the Speakership and the conception of to-day, it is forthcoming in the statement he made, that he was not conscious of having committed any error in the Pitt-Tierney episode of May 25th, 1798[2].

Influence of the Speaker on the House.
    Every House of Commons, it has been said by Sir John Mowbray, who was of eleven Parliaments after the Reform Act, has its own special characteristics, which depend to some extent on the circumstances under which the House came into existence, the authority of the Speaker, and the personal influence of the leaders of the House[3].   This is as true of the unreformed House of Commons as it was of the House when the ten-pound householder was supreme in the electorate, or later still, when it was chosen chiefly by the artisans of the industrial centres and the rural labourers of the county divisions.   The authority of the Speaker, or his lack of authority, and his personal weight told on the House of the eighteenth century as it did on the many Parliaments of which Sir John Mowbray was a member ; for it was of the House of Commons over which Cust, Fletcher Norton, and Cornewall presided, that Hatsell wrote, when he attributed a much less close adherence to the rules than had marked Onslow's Speakership, and a resulting lengthening out of the sessions, to the lack of the exercise by Speakers of the full authority which the rules of the House vested in them[4].

Objections to Ex-Speakers in the House.
    Addington was the last Speaker to be again of the House as a private member.   But his first migration was from the Speaker's Chair to the treasury bench, where, on the 23rd of March, 1801,

---

[1] Cf. *Parl. Hist.*, xxxiii. 1460, 1462; Pellew, *Life of Sidmouth*, i. 204, 206; Ashbourne, *Pitt*, 167, 168.

[2] Cf. Pellew, *Life of Sidmouth*, i. 206.

[3] Cf. Mowbray, "Seventy Years at Westminster," *Blackwood's Magazine*, July, 1898, 20.

[4] Cf. Hatsell, ii. ix. 168.

he took his seat as chancellor of the exchequer, succeeding Pitt in this office and also as prime minister. He was in office until June, 1804. Then he gave place to Pitt, and like Norton continued of the House as a private member. By this time it was regarded as not seemly to have an ex-Speaker in the House as a private member; which shows that the House had now a different conception of the office of Speaker from that of the days of Bromley and Hanmer. Addington regarded his position as unsatisfactory, and told Pitt that his continuance in the House without being connected with the ministry was open to strong and most serious objection. This communication with Pitt was on the 28th of December, 1804. On January 9th, 1805, Addington bade farewell to his constituents at Devizes; and a few days later he was of the House of Lords as Baron Sidmouth[1].

Abbot, who was Speaker from 1802 to 1817, was as promi- Abbot's nent in committee as Fletcher Norton, and on one question was Partisanship. a strenuous partisan. Abbot was much in earnest in behalf of measures for the purification of the House of Commons; and in 1809 opened the debate in committee on Curwen's bill for the prevention of the sale of seats in the House[2]. But his greatest effort was against Grattan's bill of 1813 for Catholic Relief. The bill was in committee on the 24th of May. Abbot then made a speech to which an opponent of Catholic claims has, and with sufficient reason, credited the failure of the bill. According to Pellew the speech brought about the rejection of the clause to enable Catholics to sit and vote in either House of Parliament; and with this clause defeated by two hundred and fifty-one votes to two hundred and forty-seven Grattan and his friends moved the chairman of committees out of the Chair, and thereby hung up the bill[3]. Sir Robert Heron, a Lincolnshire baronet, who was of the House at this time, acting with the reformers, and who left some useful memoirs of House of Commons life in the twenty years preceding the Reform Act, describes the opposition as led by the Speaker; and characterises Abbot's speech as " violent, inflammatory, and injudicious[4]."

It was a personal and partisan triumph for Abbot, such as

[1] Cf. Pellew, *Life of Sidmouth*, II. 316, 336, 345.
[2] Cf. Hansard, 1st Series, XIV. 837–843.
[3] Cf. Hansard, 1st Series, XXVII. 361, 495; Pellew, *Life of Sidmouth*, III. 99.
[4] Heron, *Notes of Public Life*, 18.

His Address at the Bar of the House of Lords. no Speaker had ever before achieved; and not content with his signal success in committee, Abbot took a course for which he ultimately failed to find precedents. In his address as Speaker to the Prince Regent, when he presented the money bill at the bar of the House of Lords at the close of the session, he returned to the temporary triumph of the opponents of concessions to Catholics. In this address, on the 22nd of July, 1813, Abbot named the finance bill and the bill for the government of the British possessions in India among the measures of the session, and then referred to the bill for the relief of Roman Catholics which had not passed. " But, Sir," he said, " these are not the only subjects to which our attention has been called. Other momentous changes have been proposed for our consideration. Adhering, however, to those laws by which the Throne, Parliament, and the government of this country are made fundamentally Protestant, we have not consented to allow that those who acknowledge a foreign jurisdiction should be authorised to administer the powers and jurisdictions of this realm, willing as we are nevertheless, and willing as I trust we ever shall be, to allow the largest scope to religious toleration[1]."

The Feeling aroused. Abbot's extraordinary speech caused much consternation among those members of the House, two hundred and forty-seven in all, who had supported Grattan's bill. But no action could be taken on the speech in that session; for the session came to an end with the speech from the Prince Regent, which immediately followed Abbot's address at the bar of the House of Lords.

Popular Support for the Speaker. The new session began on November 4th, 1813; and on that day Lord Morpeth gave notice that he intended to submit a motion to the House upon certain passages in the Speaker's speech[2]. Outside the House of Commons, and in particular among the opponents of Catholic relief, it was realized that an effort was to be made to call the Speaker to account. The Anti-Catholic Committee, which had organised the petitions of the previous session against Catholic enfranchisement, promptly called a meeting in London at which resolutions were passed thanking the Speaker for his efforts in committee on May 24th, and more particularly thanking him for having, in his address to the Prince Regent, given due effect to the vote of that date by proclaiming it at the bar of the House of Lords. These resolutions were engrossed on vellum, and presented to the Speaker[3].

[1] Hansard, 1st Series, xxvi. 1223; cf. Colchester, *Diary*, ii. 452–8.
[2] Hansard, 1st Series, xxvii. 42.   [3] Hansard, 1st Series, xxvii. 519.

Although Lord Morpeth gave notice of his motion on the 4th of November, 1813, it was April 22nd, 1814, before it was submitted to the House and debated. Morpeth then moved "that it is contrary to Parliamentary usage and to the spirit of Parliamentary proceedings for the Speaker, unless by specific instruction of this House, to inform His Majesty, either at the bar of the House of Lords or elsewhere, of any proposals made to the House by any of its members, either in the way of bill or motion, or to acquaint the Throne with any proceeding relative to such proposals, until they shall be consented to by the House[1]." Morpeth's contention was that there was absolutely no precedent for utterances such as those given expression to by the Speaker; that they were of a nature of which the Roman Catholics had good reason to complain; and that, if such speeches were allowable, a future Speaker might feel justified in availing himself of the occasion of a rejected measure to make it the vehicle of censorious remarks, perhaps of sarcastic animadversion[2].

Abbot in his defence went back to the reign of Henry VIII, to show that it had been usual for Speakers to address the Crown on the proceedings of the House, when presenting money bills at the end of the session. As to the nature and scope of these speeches, he quoted Hatsell to prove that it had been customary for the Speaker on these occasions to recapitulate the principal subjects which had engaged the attention of the Commons during their sittings. Moreover, Abbot claimed that an examination of these speeches showed that, during the eighteenth century, they had referred not only to bills offered for the royal assent, and to matters on which the House had expressed its opinion by addresses; but that they had also entered at large into various other public occurrences at home and abroad, upon which Parliament had employed its time and deliberations. "It has also," said Abbot, "been within the province of these speeches to advert to proceedings within the walls of Parliament, some of which, although of a legislative character, were not in progress or preparation for the royal assent, and others exclusively concerned the privileges of this House[3]."

In brief, Abbot took the ground that, by the usage of Parliament, the Speaker was authorised, in presenting money bills

---

[1] Hansard, 1st Series, xxvii. 467. [2] Hansard, 1st Series, xxvii. 472.
[3] Hansard, 1st Series, xxvii. 478.

His Con-
ception of a
Speaker's
Functions.

at the close of the session, to address the sovereign upon the result of any of the proceedings which had principally employed the attention of the House during the course of the session, and that the political importance of those proceedings and the length of time and attention which they had occupied were to be the just criterion of the Speaker's selection. "In considering the duty which I had to discharge at the close of the last session of Parliament," he said, "I saw the proceedings upon the Roman Catholic claims amongst the most important in character and the longest under discussion. I conceived it therefore to be incumbent upon me to state the result, and that statement I made[1]." To make good his defence Abbot had ransacked the Journals of the Irish Parliament as well as the Journals and extra-official records of the two Houses at Westminster. He had had access also to the private papers of Onslow, who was Speaker from 1727 to 1761. Among these he discovered a speech which Onslow had intended to make to the Crown, but did not make. Abbot laid some stress upon this speech; but with all his research he was unable to cite a precedent for a partisan speech from a Speaker, such as he had made at the end of the previous session.

His Ordeal.

For two or three hours after Abbot had made his defence he had to undergo an ordeal more prolonged, more public, and scarcely less trying, than that which preceded Trevor's dismissal from the Speakership in 1695. He had to sit in the Chair and listen to the scathing condemnation of his conduct by Whitbread, Plunket, and Tierney, all men in the front rank of Parliamentary life; while the only serious effort in his defence was from Canning, and even he did not deny that Abbot had been indiscreet. Whitbread, who addressed the House after the Speaker had sought to vindicate himself, moved as an amendment to Morpeth's re-solution, that by reason of his speech the Speaker "was guilty of a violation of the trust reposed . in him and of a breach of the privileges of this House, of which he is the chosen guardian and protector[2]." He conceded that the Speaker, as a private member, had a right to speak in committee; but, as Speaker, he had no right afterwards to mention to the Crown what had passed in committee. He had acted contrary to the example of Lenthall, who, when Charles I demanded the five members, answered: "I have neither eyes to see, ears to hear, nor tongue to speak, but as the

[1] Hansard, 1st Series, xxvii. 484, 485.
[2] Hansard, 1st Series, xxvii. 492.

House directs." Abbot, Whitbread complained, had used his ears to hear and his eyes to see as a private member, and had used his tongue as Speaker to give utterance to that which he had no right to state[1].

As an amendment to Morpeth's motion Bankes moved a re- A Defence solution which declared "that it has been customary for the of Abbot. Speaker of this House, on presenting the bills of supply at the close of the session (the King being present on the throne), to make a speech at the bar of the House of Lords, recapitulating the principal objects which have employed the attention of. the Commons during their sittings, without receiving any instructions from the House as to the particular topics, or in what manner he should express himself, and that nothing has occurred which calls for any interference on the part of this House for the regulation of the conduct of the Speaker, either at the bar of the House of Lords or elsewhere[2]." Vansittart, who was then chancellor of the exchequer, supported Bankes's resolution in a speech which was little more than a reiteration of its phraseology, a speech which may be summed up by saying that the chancellor of the exchequer saw no breach of privilege in Abbot's conduct.

The strongest denunciation of the Speaker came from Plunket. Plunket's "Sir," he said, in addressing himself to the Chair, "I am free to Attack on the say that the speech was one of the most formidable attacks on the Speaker. constitution of Parliament since the Revolution. After all the inquiries made by yourself, Sir, so capable of deep research, and after all the inquiries made by your numerous friends, has a single precedent been found of a Speaker having referred, in his speech to the Throne, to any measure which has been rejected by the House[3]?" He charged the Speaker with having failed to tell the Throne that, notwithstanding all the efforts made· to whip up the opposition to Grattan's bill, there were still two hundred and forty-seven members in favour of the clause which was rejected on May 24th, 1813; and asked, "Will any man lay his hand on his breast, and declare upon his honour that he thinks you were authorised, upon a decision of a majority of four, to represent to the Crown that the question was finally at rest[4]?" "This speech, which in my opinion was a violation of the privileges of Parliament, and which misrepresented the conduct and sentiments of all parties,"

---

[1] Hansard, 1st Series, xxvii. 491.   [2] Hansard, 1st Series, xxvii. 495.
[3] Hansard, 1st Series, xxvii. 506.   [4] Hansard, 1st Series, xxvii. 506.

continued Plunket, one of the orators whom Ireland had given to the Parliament at Westminster by the Union, "appears to me to have been wholly uncalled for. There was nothing, Sir, in the bill which you held in your hand at the time you uttered it, or in any other bill which passed during the last session, that required such an exposition. When you adverted to the splendid victories of our illustrious commander, who has just gained such transcendent fame—when you spoke of the passage of the Douro, of the battles of Rolica, of Vimiera, of Talavera, of Salamanca, of Vittoria, the feelings of all who heard you vibrated in unison with your own. Every heart exulted, and every Irish heart peculiarly exulted, that Ireland had given birth to such a hero. Was that a well-chosen moment, Sir, to pronounce the irrevocable doom of those who, under their immortal commander, had opened the sluices of their heart's blood in the service of the Empire ? * * * While you were binding the wreath round the brow of the conqueror, you assured him that his victorious followers must never expect to participate in the fruits of his valour, but that they who had shed their blood in achieving conquests were to be the only persons who were not to share by the profits of success in the rights of citizens[1]."

A Lukewarm Defence.
 Canning, who was of the minority when the clause in Grattan's bill was defeated in committee[2], pleaded that the Speaker, in delivering his speech on July 22nd, was exercising a discretion which he believed to be vested in him[3]. If the Speaker were vested with a discretion the word implied that that discretion might be exercised either judiciously or not, but still that the exercise could not draw down censure on him[4]. He might, Canning continued, think the Speaker had committed an error of judgment; but he could never think it a criminal abuse of authority[5]. He wished the speech had not been such as it was; but he did not therefore mean to deny to the Speaker the right of exercising the same discretion which he would have claimed for himself. In the constant usage of Parliament there would be found such expositions as those which the present Speaker had used; and Canning thought it peculiarly hard to visit on Abbot all the inconvenience of such a practice. It was impossible to separate the individual honour and character of the Speaker from the consideration of the question; and to Canning's mind Abbot's speech contained nothing which,

[1] Hansard, 1st Series, xxvii. 510.   [2] Cf. Hansard, 1st Series, xxvi. 364.
[3] Hansard, 1st Series, xxvii. 511.   [4] Hansard, 1st Series, xxvii. 511.
[5] Hansard, 1st Series, xxvii. 512.

looking to the established practices and privileges of the House, called for its interference[1].

Tierney, like Plunket, was intensely personal in his arraignment of the Speaker. "I, for my part," he declared, after expressing his surprise that Canning, the embodiment of all the eloquence of the two hundred and forty-seven members whose motives the Speaker had misrepresented, should have vindicated the Speaker's action, "have no objection, Sir, to your being an orator; but I have a strong objection to your being an historian. I have an objection to your taking upon you to give a narrative of the opinions of the House, and betraying that which the House did not want to communicate[2]." He, and all of the two hundred and forty-six gentlemen who voted with him, necessarily felt that they were held up to public notice by the Speaker in a way which was not correct and on an occasion when he had no right to refer to them. When a bill was passed, continued Tierney, it spoke for itself. But if the discretion were to be considered as vested in the Speaker of adverting to the proceedings of the House, the Speaker must be a party man: and there would be an end to a Speaker by whose experience in the manner of conducting the business of the House, the House could derive advice and instruction[3].

An Infringement of the Rights of the Minority.

Whitbread's amendment had been seconded by Creevey[4]; and as the debate proceeded General Mathew had intimated that he intended to vote for it[5]. But when the debate had exhausted itself Whitbread told the House that he had moved the amendment only for the purpose of recording his own opinion in the Journals, and that he had no intention to press it to a division. When at last the House divided Morpeth's motion was negatived by two hundred and seventy-four to one hundred and six, and Bankes's amendment was carried. Abbot thus escaped formal censure by the House.

Outcome of the Debate.

Great interest was taken in the controversy beyond the walls of the House of Commons—an interest which is significant as showing that by 1814 public opinion was coming to regard the Speakership as a non-partisan office. "The great majority in favour of the Speaker," wrote a chronicler of the debate of April 22nd, and of the attitude of the world outside the House of Commons towards

Public Opinion on the Speaker's Action.

[1] Hansard, 1st Series, xxvii. 514. [2] Hansard, 1st Series, xxvii. 516.
[3] Hansard, 1st Series, xxvii. 517. [4] Hansard, 1st Series, xxvii. 492.
[5] Hansard, 1st Series, xxvii. 520.

the Speaker, " seems to denote either that the House in general regarded him as blameless, or that the weight of his character, and the connection of his honour and reputation with those of the body over which he presided, rendered, in the opinion of the greater number, a public censure inexpedient or indecorous. Yet upon perusing the speeches made on the occasion, few, it is imagined, will be insensible of a great superiority in point of argument as well as of eloquence on the side of reproof; and were the question referred to the public at large, it can scarcely be doubted that the decision would be that the Speaker had been betrayed by party zeal—for his honourable character will not admit a more unfavourable interpretation—into a step at least improper and of dangerous example, if not unconstitutional. The discussion of the subject will have a good effect if it prevent the recurrence of anything similar[1]." A recent biographer freely concedes that Abbot was in the wrong. He quotes Sir Erskine May to prove the correctness of the doctrine upheld by Morpeth, Whitbread, Plunket, and Tierney in the debate of April 22nd; and adds that this doctrine has since been recognized in practice, and that the Speaker in addressing the Crown now adverts only to the most important measures which have received the sanction of Parliament during the session[2].

Popular Interest in Proceedings in the House.

A variety of causes in and out of the House combined gradually to create the modern conception of the Speakership. Chief among the causes at work in the constituencies was the increase in intelligent and sustained interest in politics and in the proceedings of the House of Commons, due partly to the domestic questions which had been pressing for settlement since the American Revolution and also largely to the newspaper press and its wide diffusion of Parliamentary debates. When Fletcher Norton was in the Chair, the circulation of newspapers reporting debates was limited, not amounting in the aggregate to that of a single daily newspaper of to-day. Further, popular interest in politics, as distinct from mere electioneering, was then only just beginning. By the time Abbot was in the Chair, the circulations of the London newspapers had greatly increased; and Manchester, Leeds, Liverpool and many other large provincial towns had their weekly newspapers. In the more prosperous of the London daily journals Parliament was reported as well and almost as fully as at the

[1] *Annual Register*, 1814, 117.   [2] Cf. *Dict. Nat. Bio.*, i. 5.

present time. These reports were reproduced by the provincial press; so that in 1813, when Abbot displayed his partisan zeal in committee, and misused at the bar of the House of Lords his opportunity as Speaker, the world was looking on. In 1814, when Abbot's conduct was challenged, public opinion was against him, and against his conception of the functions of the Chair, and disposed to declare for a Speaker whose duty it should be to hold the balance fairly between contending political parties in the Commons.

In Parliament greater emoluments and added dignity were accruing to the Speakership. The office was gradually becoming one which a man of commanding ability might reasonably regard as his greatest and final prize. In 1761 the precedent was established of granting a large annuity to the retiring Speaker[1]. In Onslow's case the annuity was three thousand pounds a year, " to be held, received, and enjoyed by the said Arthur Onslow during his natural life and that of his son George Onslow, for and during the natural life of the longest liver of them." The long-standing usage of remunerating the Speaker principally by fees on private bills, which went back at least as far as the reign of Elizabeth, was abandoned in 1790, and a fixed and liberal salary was granted by Act of Parliament in its stead. *Emoluments and Dignity of the Chair.*

At the time this change was made the Speaker was empowered by the rules of the House to collect five guineas for every private bill, five guineas for every private enacting clause, and ten guineas for every bill which concerned a county or a corporation[2]. For some years prior to the abandonment of this system, the fees collected by the Speaker had averaged twelve hundred and thirty-two pounds a session. He was then also in receipt of an allowance of five pounds a day from the exchequer. This payment after 1695[3] had seemingly taken the place of the hundred pounds a session paid by the sovereign to the Speaker in the sixteenth and seventeenth centuries. In addition to fees and this payment from the exchequer, at the opening of a new Parliament the Speaker was paid one thousand pounds as equipment money. He also received a service of plate of two thousand ounces, estimated in 1790 as worth a thousand pounds; and there was a payment of one hundred pounds a session for stationery. As a perquisite *Old System of remunerating the Speaker.*

[1] Cf. *H. of C. Journals*, xxix. 244; 2 Geo. III. c. 33.
[2] Cf. *Parl. Hist.*, xxviii. 1003.   [3] Cf. *Parl. Hist.*, v. 889.

there were two hogsheads of claret annually[1], which, with the
service of plate, was apparently a recognition of the fact that, as
Speaker, it was incumbent on him to entertain.

Social Duties of the Speaker.   When these social obligations were first thrown on the Speaker
can be only a matter of conjecture. They could scarcely have
existed until the reign of Edward VI, when the Commons crossed
the road from the chapter-house of Westminster Abbey to
S. Stephen's Chapel, nor, in fact, until an official residence was
assigned to the Speaker in Westminster Palace. The earliest
mention of the social functions of the Speaker which I have traced
is in the year 1688, when Powle, Speaker of the Convention
Parliament, gave dinners at his house[2]. In the last half of the
eighteenth century the Speaker, according to Lord Bexley, gave
evening parties, misnamed levees, on Saturday[3], and official dinners
on Sunday[4]. By this time the order of these official dinners had
become well established, and was as closely adhered to as the rules
of the House. The Speaker's first dinner of the session was for all
privy councillors in the House of Commons holding office, and for
the lords and secretaries of the treasury and the attorney-general.
The next was for privy councillors and leading men in opposition;
and the third for official members, not privy councillors, or only
privy councillors in Ireland, and a few leading men of the government side[5].

The Chair as a Perquisite.   In the unreformed House of Commons it was also the Speaker's
privilege—as it is to this day the privilege of the Speaker of the
House of Commons at Ottawa—at the end of a Parliament to
carry off the great chair as a memento of his service to the House[6].
In many English country homes there must still be found these
chairs, of lumbering size and gaunt, inconvenient form, richer in
historic associations than in beauty; for, like many House of
Commons usages, this one was of long standing, and there was
no break in it while the Commons met in the ancient Chapel of
S. Stephen's. Onslow carried away five chairs to his seat in Surrey.
Three fell to the lot of Sidmouth, and were long in use in the
dining-room at White Lodge, Richmond Park, a residence assigned,
as a mark of George III's appreciation of his services to the

---

[1] Cf. *Parl. Hist.*, xxviii. 515, 518.   [2] Cf. Addit. MSS. 34516, Folio 55, 4.
[3] Cf. Pellew, *Life of Sidmouth*, i. 368.
[4] *Hist. MSS. Comm. 14th Rep.*, App., pt. i. 194.
[5] Cf. Croker, *Papers*, i. 409.
[6] Cf. Pellew, *Life of Sidmouth*, i. 67, 68.

Crown[1], to Sidmouth when he was chancellor of the exchequer— "my chancellor of the exchequer," as the King styled him[2].

In 1790 the attention of the House was called by Montague, knight of the shire for Huntingdon, to the fluctuating and objectionable manner in which Speakers had hitherto been paid, and as a safeguard to the independence of Speakers an annual salary was proposed. Montague moved that it should be five thousand pounds. Sir James Johnstone, as an amendment, proposed six thousand pounds. Pitt, on behalf of the Government, intimated its willingness to support this reform in the method of remuneration. Montague's amended resolution was assented to by acclamation[3]; and on it was founded a bill, which quickly went through its several stages, "for better supporting the dignity of the Speaker of the House of Commons." It directed the treasury to issue at the exchequer an allowance to the Speaker "which, with fees and allowances of five pounds per day, now payable on account of his office," should amount to the clear yearly sum of six thousand pounds. A clause in this Act directed that thereafter the Speaker was not to hold any place of profit under the Crown during pleasure[4]. In 1832 the Act of 1790 was repealed, and there was substituted for it another Act which cut the Speakership entirely clear of the fee system; made the salary, still kept at six thousand pounds a year, payable out of the Consolidated Fund; and directed that it should be clear "of all taxes, impositions, fees, and other charges whatsoever." It further directed that on a dissolution of Parliament the payments to the late Speaker should run "until a Speaker shall be chosen by the new Parliament[5]."

The Speaker's Salary.

A service of plate was given to each Speaker at the opening of a new Parliament until 1839, when, on the suggestion of Hume, the most persistent advocate of economy who was ever of the House of Commons, the service of plate was attached to the office[6].

The Speaker's Service of Plate.

Long before these changes were made in the emoluments of the office, and before the beginning of the custom of conferring a peerage on the retiring Speaker, the Speaker's precedence had been determined by Act of Parliament[7]; and from the Revolution, when this Act was passed, the Speaker, as the First Commoner, ranked next to the peers of Great Britain both in and out of

Rank of the Speaker.

[1] Pellew, *Life of Sidmouth*, i. 68.   [2] Cf. *Dict. Nat. Bio.*, i. 119.
[3] *Parl. Hist.*, xxviii. 518.   [4] Cf. 30 Geo. III, c. 10.
[5] 2 and 3 W. IV, c. 105.   [6] Cf. Hansard, 3rd Series, xxvi. 603.
[7] 1 W. and M., c. 21.

Parliament.   In all public commissions he was so ranked, and had the precedence at the council table among the privy councillors[1]. Since 1761 Speakers have been *ex-officio* trustees of the British Museum; commissioners for the reduction of the national debt; for the building of new churches; and commissioners of the Caledonian Canal[2].   Since 1769 the Speaker has had power to issue warrants to the clerk of the Crown to make out new writs for the election of members to fill vacancies in the House caused by death during a Parliamentary recess[3].

Contact of
Parliament
with the
People.

While new power and dignity were thus accruing to the Speakership by the action of Parliament and of the Crown, increasing importance and added esteem were being attached to it outside the walls of S. Stephen's.   This more exalted popular conception of the office grew out of the fact that after the American Revolution, the House of Commons and its work began to touch the life of the people much more closely than hitherto. The House now ceased to be regarded as a mere machine for levying taxes and voting supplies.   The contact of the House with life outside was becoming very real even before the representative system was reformed.   Between the French Revolution and the Reform Act the criminal code was humanised; a beginning was made with the factory code; railway legislation was begun; and, more than all, the power of the House of Commons was brought home to every family in the land by the heavily increased taxation due to the long struggle with France.   People with incomes of more than sixty pounds a year felt the weight of direct taxation. So did every family dwelling in a house with seven or more windows.   No self-sustaining family, however poor, escaped the comprehensive indirect taxation of this period, when it was easier to enumerate the articles in daily use by all classes which were not taxed than to catalogue those on which the tax-collector demanded his due.   There were at this period many popular grievances to be remedied, constitutional, religious, and fiscal; and from the platform and the press people were counselled to look to Parliament for relief.

Manners-
Sutton inter-
venes in
Committee.

Only twice between 1813, when Abbot led the attack on the enfranchisement clause in Grattan's relief bill, and 1832 did a Speaker intervene in debate in committee.   Sir Charles Manners-

---

[1] Cf. Hatsell, ii. 179.

[2] Cf. *Report of Select Committee on Office of Speaker*, 1853, xiii.

[3] Cf. 10 Geo. III, c. 41; 15 Geo. III, c. 36; 24 Geo. III, c. 26.

Sutton, Abbot's successor in the Chair, shared Abbot's dread of Catholic enfranchisement; and in 1821, and again in 1825, spoke in committee in opposition to Catholic relief bills. One drawback to these interventions of the Speaker was that from the nature of the situation Speakers so intervening were compelled to make second reading speeches at committee stage. Manners-Sutton was conscious of this when he interposed in committee in 1825, on the Catholic relief bill which Brougham was endeavouring to carry through the House of Commons. He knew that he was about to make a second reading speech, a speech affecting the principle of the bill. He was perfectly well aware, he said, that, according to the strict rules and forms of the House, the committee stage of a bill was neither the most convenient nor the most regular occasion for any member to state his opinions on the measure. But as his opinion on the question of Catholic enfranchisement remained unchanged, unchanged from the opinion he had held in 1821, and as that was the first opportunity, and perhaps would be the last, which he would have of addressing the House on the measure, he trusted he might be permitted to say a few words[1]. As if to give more point to this apology the Speaker recalled the fact that it was the only time he had interposed in committee since 1821, and frankly conceded that the course he was pursuing was inconvenient, and was to be justified only by the necessities of the case. Still, feeling that the question of Catholic enfranchisement admitted of no compromise, and retaining as he did his conscientious objection to Catholic emancipation, he should, he said, have been ashamed if he had not declared what his opinions were.

On this occasion the Speaker was the first member to address the committee. Under ordinary circumstances a member would have to propose a motion, usually an amendment, in order to put some question before the committee. When Abbot interposed at the same stage on Grattan's bill in 1813 he proposed the amendment which, when accepted by the committee, deprived the bill of all its vitality[2]. When Manners-Sutton addressed the committee in 1825 he intimated early in his speech that he did not intend to propose any amendment to the clause under consideration; and in short he admitted that he had intervened in committee to make a second reading speech[3].

A Second Reading Speech in Committee.

---

[1] Hansard, 2nd Series, xiii. 434.   [2] Hansard, 1st Series, xxvi. 332.
[3] Cf. Hansard, 2nd Series, xiii. 434, 435.

Another In-
tervention in
Committee.

Nine years later Manners-Sutton again for a brief while divested himself of his character as Speaker, and in committee spoke as member for the University of Cambridge in opposition to the bill for admitting dissenters to the Universities. Again, as in 1821 and 1825, he made a second reading speech, and was as apologetic as he had been on the previous occasions. He objected on principle to the bill. Though members might think him committing an act of imprudence by his intervention in committee, yet he thought it more manly to declare the sentiments he entertained. As in 1825, he moved no amendment to any clause in the bill. The House had gone into committee on it *pro formâ*; and Manners-Sutton was the only member who spoke at this stage of the bill[1].

The Place of
the Speaker
during
Committee.

This was in 1834, in the first Parliament after the Reform Act; and it was nearly the last occasion on which a Speaker intervened in committee. Since that time Speakers have been wont to act on Onslow's dictum that the place for the Speaker, when the House is in committee, is his private room, whence he cannot be fetched except to restore order in the House, or to resume the Chair when progress in committee is reported[2]. From two points of view the modern practice of Speakers, as to committee, is of advantage. It enables Speakers to preserve the strict impartiality which now for sixty years the House and the country have demanded of the Chair. Moreover, it conduces to the upholding of the rules of the House as to the character of debate and discussion at the various stages of a bill; saves the Speaker from temptations like that to which Manners-Sutton at Westminster, and Foster, the last Speaker of the Irish House of Commons, both succumbed; and obviates any necessity of the chairman of committee being called upon to enforce the rules against the Speaker, the one member of the House who of all others should be most jealous and most careful of their preservation.

Manners-
Sutton's Im-
partiality in
the House.

Although a zealous and even a bitter Tory, Radical critics of the Toryism of the period from the Union to the Reform Act of 1832 have conceded that in his management of the House Manners-Sutton was an impartial Speaker[3]. Even Radical agitators like Hunt eulogised his "riding the House with a snaffle rein, and not with a curb[4]." Adequate proof of his understanding of the changing

---

[1] Cf. Hansard, 3rd Series, xxiv. 1088, 1092, 1093.   [2] Hatsell, ii. 177.
[3] Cf. Verax (Dr Dunckley), "The Speakership," *Manchester Guardian*, April 16th, 1895.
[4] Hansard, 3rd Series, xiv. 996.

relations of the Chair to the House is forthcoming in the apologies for intervention in committee contained in his speeches on the Catholic relief bill of 1825 and the University bill of 1834.

While Manners-Sutton was thus an impartial Speaker, and, except during the debates on the Reform bills, gave even the advanced Liberals of that exciting period of Parliamentary history no cause of complaint, he cannot be said to have dissevered himself from party ties and connections. In this respect he had scarcely advanced beyond Addington, who vacated the Chair for the treasury bench. Twice during the fifteen years that Manners-Sutton was in the Chair he was pressed to take office in Tory administrations. On Canning's accession to power in 1827 he was offered the secretaryship of state for the home department. He declined the offer, "from his feelings on the Catholic question," the question which perturbed every administration from the Union until 1829. When in 1831–32 the Grey Administration was trembling in the balance in the crises over the Reform bill, at a time when even William IV admitted that the ultra-Tories of the opposition "had become one of the most virulent factions that differences in political or constitutional questions had ever produced in this country[1]," Manners-Sutton took part in the confidential consultations of the Tory leaders. Early in 1831 the opponents of reform, at a party at the Speaker's house, discussed a plan of assault, and "looked with confidence to its affording them the means of striking an effectual blow at the administration on the question of reform[2]." Afterwards, in May, 1832, Manners-Sutton refused, after some hesitation, to undertake the formation of a Tory administration[3]. The evolution of the Speakership into a non-partisan office was long in coming; and the unreformed House of Commons did not survive to be presided over by a Speaker who, on assuming the Chair, severed himself from all party connections, and regarded the Speakership as his final prize in the House of Commons.

Catholic emancipation and the repeal of the Corporation and Test Acts preceded Parliamentary reform. After the Reform Act Ireland, and municipal, poor law and economic reform occupied

Speakers still Party Men.

Manners-Sutton's Connection with Party.

---

[1] Sir H. Taylor to Earl Grey, Feb. 4th, 1832; *Correspondence of Earl Grey with William IV and with Sir Herbert Taylor*, II. 189.

[2] Earl Grey to Sir H. Taylor, Jan. 19th, 1831; *Correspondence of Earl Grey, &c.*, I. 73, 74.

[3] Cf. *Dict. Nat. Bio.*, XXXVI. 48.

the attention of Parliament and of the new electorate.   Much of
the intense acerbity which had marked political life in the years
when Catholic emancipation, relief of dissenters from tests, and
the reform of the representative system were in agitation, disappeared after the stress of the preceding twenty years.   Political
life entered on a new phase.   But the standard of strict impartiality
demanded nowadays of the Speaker in and out of the House was
not reached until the third Parliament after the Reform Act.
Manners-Sutton was in the Chair during the Parliament of 1832–34;
for the Whig leaders were nervous at the prospect of meeting the
first Parliament chosen by the new electorate with a new Speaker,
and besought him to accept still another election to the Chair[1].   It
was in this House of Commons that Manners-Sutton, now member
for the University of Cambridge, spoke in committee against the
bill for the admission of dissenters to the universities; and it is
still not a settled question whether he had a part in bringing about
the downfall of the Melbourne Administration.   His biographer,
in the volume of the *Dictionary of National Biography* published
in 1893, asserts that Manners-Sutton effectually disproved the
charges brought against him, namely, (1) that, being Speaker, he had
busied himself in the subversion of the Melbourne Administration;
(2) that he had assisted in the formation of the Peel Administration;
and (3) that he had counselled the dissolution of 1835[2].   He
may have disproved the first and third of these charges.   He did
not clear himself of the second; for he admitted that he was at the
Privy Council after Melbourne's dismissal by William IV; that he
was in consultation with Wellington, who was in charge of affairs
pending Peel's return from the continent to assume the office from
which Melbourne had been thrust by the King, and that he was in
consultation with Peel[3].   As Lord John Russell said in the House,
of Manners-Sutton's conduct at this juncture, " the political bias of
the right honourable gentleman had not remained entirely inert,
but had got the better of him, and induced him to concur in acts
which, as Speaker, he had much better have avoided[4]."

The House
demands a
Non-partisan
Speaker.
Manners-Sutton was willing to enter on an eighth term in the
Chair; and the Tories—now beginning to style themselves Con-
servatives[5]—who were in office, but did not, as the result of the
general election of 1835, command a majority in the House, were

[1] Cf. Walpole, *Life of Lord John Russell*, I. 224.

[2] Cf. *Dict. Nat. Bio.*, xxvi. 59.   [3] Cf. Hansard, 3rd Series, xxvi. 22–39.

[4] Hansard, 3rd Series, xxvi. 41.   [5] Cf. Croker, *Papers*, II. 2.

anxious to re-elect him[1]. They were, however, outnumbered by
the Whigs and Radicals, and the Irish members led by O'Connell, by one hundred and twelve[2], and the Radicals, who had
divided the House on Manners-Sutton's re-election in 1832, would
not hear of his re-election in 1835. They were convinced that he
had, by his conduct during the ministerial crisis of 1834, greatly
aggravated his earlier failures to maintain, while Speaker, a non-
partisan attitude in and out of Parliament. Lord John Russell,
who led the opposition, realized that a change in the Speakership
was necessary. Manners-Sutton's vindication did not fully satisfy
him. He did not regard the ex-Speaker as having cleared himself
of the charge that he was in consultation with the Tory ministers
after the dismissal of Melbourne. Moreover, in Russell's opinion
recent changes in the constituencies demanded a change in the
Speakership. What was now wanted was " a man who was zealous
in behalf of the liberties of the people, zealous in behalf of the
popular prerogatives; to be the organ of the House in its communication with the Crown; to represent their feelings firmly,
zealously and openly, without fear of offending, or a wish to conciliate those who might have the dispensing of favours[3]." In brief,
the House had now need of an Onslow, although several years were
to elapse before such a Speaker was forthcoming. The Liberals
nominated Abercromby, in opposition to Manners-Sutton, and on
a division Abercromby was elected by a majority of only ten votes[4].

Abercromby sat for Edinburgh, and he has the distinction of Abercromb
being the only member for a Scotch constituency and the only as Speaker.
Scotchman, who has ever been of the Chair. He was also the first
Speaker for nearly half a century who did not intervene in committee. More than this, he was the first Speaker who had been of
the Cabinet before he was elected to the Chair. He was master of
the mint in the Grey and Melbourne Administrations[5]; and he
did not, it would seem, completely dissever himself from his former
political associations. He has been credited with being " probably
the last of those Speakers who maintained a close connection with
their party during their tenure of the Chair[6]." Abercromby, who
had most unwillingly permitted the Liberals to make him their

[1] Croker, *Papers*, ii. 63 ; Walpole, *Life of Russell*, i. 224.
[2] Cf. "Election Statistics," *The Times*, July 31st, 1895.
[3] Hansard, 3rd Series, xxvi. 43.
[4] Hansard, 3rd Series, xxvi. 43.
[5] Walpole, *Life of Russell*, i. 215 ; *Dict. Nat. Bio.*, i. 41.
[6] Dunckley, "The Speakership," *Manchester Guardian*, April 16th, 1895.

candidate for the Chair in 1835[1], and who did not make an efficient Speaker[2], resigned in 1839. Again, as in 1835, there was a contest for the Speakership, and Shaw Lefevre was chosen by the action of the independent members[3].

The First of the Modern Speakers. "Shaw Lefevre," wrote the late Sir John Mowbray, "was a strong Speaker. We owe to him greatly the continuance of the authority which still surrounds his successors. When he came to the Chair the discipline of the House was relaxed, and there was a great want of decorum. Cock-crowing and other disorderly interruptions had not been uncommon. Lefevre changed all that[4]." This restoration of order does not constitute Shaw Lefevre's chief claim to an honourable place in the history of the Speakership. He was the first of the modern Speakers. As Lenthall, Williams, and Foley stand out in the period when the Speakership was ceasing to be a courtier office—the period when it ceased to be a link between the Crown and the House; and as Onslow was pre-eminent among the Speakers of the eighteenth century; so Shaw Lefevre stands out among the First Commoners of the nineteenth, during the evolution of the non-partisan Speaker. To him we owe the establishment of the principle—since his Speakership jealously guarded and well maintained by his four successors—that the Speaker must not only be impartial in action and utterance but must abstain from everything in and out of the House of Commons which could expose his impartiality to the slightest suspicion. Denison, who succeeded Shaw Lefevre, once during his fifteen years' tenure of the Chair spoke in committee, and helped to defeat a budget proposal which he regarded as foolish and unjust[5]. But this was thirty years ago; and to-day the Speaker may be said to have disappeared from committee[6], and is never seen in a division lobby.

The Speaker and Party Ties. To-day the Speaker never enters a political club. Unlike every other member of the House of Commons he makes no political address when he seeks re-election from his constituents. Unlike most members he never publicly discusses politics with his constituents. He is outside the arena of party politics. When he represents a single-member constituency, as was the case with the

---

[1] Walpole, *Life of Russell,* I. 225.

[2] Walpole, *Life of Russell,* I. 335; Mowbray, "Seventy Years at Westminster," *Blackwood's Magazine,* July, 1898, 22.

[3] Walpole, *Life of Russell,* I. 224.

[4] *Blackwood's Magazine,* July, 1898, 22; cf. Walpole, *Life of Russell,* I. 337.

[5] Denison, *Notes from my Journal,* 257.

[6] Cf. Speaker Gully at the Mansion House, *The Standard,* April 17th, 1902.

last two Speakers of the nineteenth century, and, as seems most
convenient under the newer but unwritten code governing the
relations of the Speaker to political parties and political controversies, it is not too much to say that the Speaker's constituency is
practically disfranchised. Even in the days when double-member
constituencies were almost uniform, a Speaker seeking re-election
from his constituency was not opposed; and since the Reform Act
of 1832 there is only one instance in which the electors in a
Speaker's constituency were called upon to go to the polls after
their member had been chosen to the Chair[1]. This was in 1885,
when Peel, Speaker from 1884 to 1895, was opposed in the newly-
created constituency of Warwick and Leamington[2].

The Speaker's constituents not only do not go to the poll; The
they cannot, according to present-day usages, call on their repre- Speaker's
sentative to vote either for or against any measure which may be Con-
before Parliament. As the Speaker never meets his constituents to stituency.
discuss politics, one of the chief means of present-day political
education is lost to them. Political organisation is suspended in
a Speaker's constituency; for a present-day Speaker has no need of
any local party organisation to secure his return, even if he deemed
it proper to contribute to party funds. The newspapers in the
constituency have necessarily to refrain from criticism or comment
on the Parliamentary conduct of its representative; and in nearly
all the essentials which go to make representation the constituency
is unrepresented. In the constituency represented by the Speaker
of to-day political life is dormant; for all its outward activities, as
they concern both political education and local political organisation, are suspended. But no constituency complains or frets under
its temporary and peculiar political disabilities. It is honoured in
the honour done by the House of Commons and the country to its
representative. It realizes that its member is rendering to the
State services as honourable and as necessary as those performed
by any member of the House of Commons; and when these services
have been recalled in the brief and politically colourless addresses
of Speakers seeking re-election from their constituencies, only in
the one instance which has been cited, and which arose out of the
confusion in political parties following the new distribution of
political power, has a Speaker been opposed at an election.

---

[1] Cf. Gully, *Address to the Electors of Carlisle*, 1895; McCalmont, *Parl.
Poll Book*, 4th Ed., 42, 102, 131, 223, 41.   [2] McCalmont, 114.

CHAPTER XXIII.

THE ATTITUDE OF THE HOUSE TOWARDS THE CHAIR.

The attitude of the House of Commons towards the Chair, the way in which it showed its deference to the Speaker and gradually clothed him with the powers which he has come to exercise, can be learned from the printed Journals. In these, for the first thirty or forty years following their commencement in 1547, the entries are so brief, so much in mere catalogue form, that not until the middle years of the reign of Elizabeth is it practicable to follow the House in the process of conferring power on the Chair, and, in general, of organising itself for its work. In the earlier centuries of the representative system, when Parliaments were short, and when there was little legislation beyond that necessary for the raising of supplies, there would be need for comparatively few rules; and that in this period there were few rules is suggested by the character of those of which the adoption can be traced onwards from the reign of Elizabeth, when entries in the Journals become fuller and more detailed.

One of the earliest of the more detailed entries affords a good picture of the relations of the Speaker to the House, and illustrates the deference which the House in the middle years of the reign of Elizabeth was paying to the Chair. "The litany being read by the clerk, and the old prayer that was used in former sessions being read also by the Speaker," runs the entry, "Mr Speaker made a short oration to the House, partly touching himself and partly touching them; for his part acknowledging his infirmities, and praying both their patience and assistance; and for them, he advised them to use reverent and discreet speeches, to leave curiosities of form; to speak to the matter; and for that the Parliament was likely to be very short, willed them further to forbear speaking to bills at first reading, and not to spend too much time in unnecessary motions or superfluous argument[1]." This was in 1581; and immediately after the address from the Chair there was established a rule which still exists, and which to-day, three centuries after its first adoption, attracts the attention of even the most casual visitor to the House of Commons. In the earlier Parliaments of Elizabeth's reign it had become a usage that members on entering the Chamber should courtesy to the Speaker. By the rule of 1581 it was made imperative on members at the end of a sitting to "depart and go forth in comely and civil sort, for the reverence of the House"; and members were directed, when they left the Chamber, to make a low courtesy to the Speaker, "like as they do at their coming into the House[2]."

In the reign of James I entries of the adoption of rules New Rules of vesting power and authority in the Speaker to insist on decent the House in 1604. and orderly procedure are much more frequent than in the Journals of the three preceding reigns. In the first session of the Parliament of 1604–11 they are so frequent as to suggest that the House must have spent some time in overhauling its methods of work and in making new rules. Of these rules of 1604 affecting the Speaker one reads: "if any man speak impertinently or besides the question in hand, it stands within the orders of the House for Mr Speaker to interrupt him, and to know the pleasure of the House, whether they will hear him further[3]." "Agreed," reads another of these rules, "that if any superfluous motion or tedious speech be offered in the House, the party is to be directed and ordered by the Speaker[4]." "If any doubt arise upon a bill," reads a third, "the Speaker is to explain but not to sway the House with argument or dispute[5]"; and by still another of these orders of 1604 hissing was to be regarded and treated by the Speaker as disorderly[6].

Some such rules must have been imperatively needed; for in Bad Manners the reign of Elizabeth there was at times much disorder in the in 1601. House, and long-winded members were treated with little patience and less courtesy. How such bores then fared is shown by a

[1] *H. of C. Journals,* I. 118.   [2] *H. of C. Journals,* I. 118.
[3] *H. of C. Journals,* I. 172.   [4] *H. of C. Journals,* I. 175.
[5] *H. of C. Journals,* I. 187.   [6] *H. of C. Journals,* I. 152.

report of a debate in the House in 1601 given by D'Ewes. "After this speech," writes the contemporary reporter quoted by D'Ewes, " an old doctor of civil law spake; but because he was too long and spake too low, the House hawked and spat, and kept a great coil to make him make an end[1]."

Order in Debate.   By the time Charles I was on the throne the code governing the duties of the Speaker had been further extended. "If two persons shall rise to speak," reads a contemporary statement in the reign of Charles I, " the Speaker must appoint him to speak first that first arose, and offered to speak. One man may not speak twice to one bill in one day, although he will change his opinion, except it be only for the moving of some order. Every man that will speak must direct his speech to the Speaker, and not to any other but only by circumlocution, as by saying, ' he which spoke with the bill, or he which made this or that reason.' If any touch another by nipping or irreverent speech the Speaker may admonish him. If any shall speak dishonourably of the King or his Council he is not only to be interrupted; but may be also sent by the House unto the Tower. If any man speak too long and speak within the matter he may not be cut off; but if he be long and out of the matter, then may the Speaker gently admonish him of the shortness of the time, or the business of the House, and pray him to make it as short as he may. But if he range in evil words then to interrupt him, saying, ' I pray you to spare these words; they become not this place of state and council. It hath not been the order here so to do. I pray you take care of us all, considering what danger the report hereof may breathe unto us[2].' "

Equal Rights in the House.   This contemporary statement of the duties of the Speaker and of the attitude of the House towards the Chair in the period just before the Great Rebellion, is corroborated in many of its details by the description which Eliot has left of the House of Commons at this time. He enumerates the rules and orders then governing procedure, emphasising a little more strongly than the writer just quoted some of the rules which he regarded as worthy of commendation. "The meanest burgess," Eliot wrote, in commenting on the rule that " he that does first stand up has the first liberty to be heard," "has as much favour as the best knight or councillor; all sitting in one capacity of commoners, and in like relations to their countries." "I name these," added

[1] D'Ewes, *Journals*, 640.   [2] *Harleian Miscellany*, IV. 561, 562.

Eliot, "for the honour of that House. Nowhere more gravity can be found than is represented in that Senate. No court has more civility in itself, nor a face of more dignity towards strangers[1]."

Before the Great Rebellion, as these two contemporary state- Ceremony in speaking of Members. ments show, the main lines of procedure in the House were well established, and the Speaker was in possession of nearly all the powers which he was exercising within the House when the representative system was reformed in 1832. After the Restoration it is possible to trace developements in the ceremonial of the House, and to note an increasingly formal deference to the Chair. Greater ceremonial is apparent in the phraseology which members used towards one another in debate. The circumlocution in vogue in the reign of Charles I is described in the Harleian tracts from which quotation has been made. In 1670 another extra-official memorial of the method and manner of proceeding in Parliament was published. "No member," wrote the author, in describing the phraseology of the House when one member was addressing or referring to another, "may mention the name of any other member then present, but to describe him by his title or addition, as that noble lord, worthy knight, or by his office, as judge, serjeant, gentleman of the long robe, or short robe; or by his place, as the gentleman near the Chair, near the bar, on the other side, or thus, the gentleman that spoke last, or last save one, or the like[2]"; and the phraseology which thus became customary in the seventeenth century survived well on into the nineteenth; for it was not until the eve of the Reform Act that the simple usage of present-day debate of identifying a member with his constituency came generally into vogue.

Another rule established the custom which holds good to-day, Precedence of the Speaker. that when the Speaker stands up the member in possession of the floor shall sit down; and at this time there also existed a rule which decreed that when members were leaving the Chamber at the end of the sitting, "no man should stir until Mr Speaker do arise and go before, and then all the rest to follow after him[3]." In a period when members were employing more ceremony one towards another, and when the House was more thronged with

---

[1] Forster, *Life of Eliot*, i. 238.

[2] *Memorials of the Method and Manner of Proceedings in Parliament.* By H. S. E., C. P., 1670, 9.

[3] *Memorials of the Method and Manner of Proceedings in Parliament.* By H. S. E., C. P., 1670, 8.

courtiers and more aristocratic in its characteristics and tendencies than at any time in its history, it was only natural that there should be an increase in the ceremonial usages towards the Chair.

The Speaker reconciles Quarrels. In 1661 authority was vested in the Speaker to reconcile disputes and quarrels which had arisen between members in consequence of anything that had passed within the House, disputes and quarrels which were likely, as the House was then constituted, to lead to hostile meetings elsewhere. The Speaker had been vested with this power only a few days when an opportunity of exercising it occurred in a dispute between Mr Marvell and Mr Clifford. The Speaker intervened, and reported the result of this intervention to the House. He had, he said, examined the matter of difference between Mr Marvell and Mr Clifford, and found that Mr Marvell " had given the first provocation that begot the difference; and that his opinion was that Mr Marvell should declare his sorrow for being the first occasion of this difference, and then Mr Clifford should declare that he was sorry for the consequence of it; and that Mr Clifford was willing to yield to this determination but that Mr Marvell refused." " And the House," continues the report in the Journals, "thereupon directing the said Mr Marvell and Mr Clifford to withdraw, and taking the matter into debate, resolved that the said Mr Marvell and Mr Clifford be called in to their places, and that each of these shall have a reprehension from Mr Speaker for breach of the peace and privilege of this House, and according to Mr Speaker's report be enjoined to declare their sorrow for it, and to crave the pardon of the House ; and the said Mr Marvell and Mr Clifford being accordingly called to their places, and having received a grave reprehension from Mr Speaker, and Mr Marvell declaring that he was sorry that he should give the first provocation of the difference, and Mr Clifford acknowledging that he was sorry for what ensued, and both of them engaging to keep the peace and privilege of the House for the future, and not renew this difference, but have the same correspondence they had before it did happen, with which the House was well satisfied, and did remit the breach of privilege[1]."

The Speaker's Relation to the House. From time to time, as altering conditions begat new exigencies in the proceedings of the House, additional authority was vested in the Speaker. But at no time has the Speaker become above or independent of the House. His rulings have usually been based

[1] *H. of C. Journals*, viii. 319.

on some order in the Journals, or some accepted interpretation of an order, or on some precedent which can be cited from the Journals. " It is the Speaker's duty," wrote Speaker Denison in his journal for 1860, " to preserve order in the House, and when any breach of order or supposed breach of order arises, it is his duty to inform the House what the rules of the House are on the point, subject to the correction of the House[1] "; and as far back as the Journals go this appears to have been the position which the House consistently assigned to the Speaker.

The Speaker has been described as a link between the Crown and the House. This term was applied to Speakers of the courtier class, who owed their election to the Crown, and often used their position to advance the interests of the Crown in the House. The Speaker has always been the spokesman of the House to the Crown; and in this respect he has never ceased to be the link between the House and the Crown. As early as any records go it was usual for the Speaker, on being approved by the Crown, to ask that " the proceedings of the Commons may receive the most favourable construction, and that whatever he should speak which might be taken in evil part, might be imputed to his ignorance and not unto the Commons[2]." In the first Parliament of Henry IV Sir John Cheney, who was then Speaker, made a general request to the King that the Commons might enjoy their ancient privileges and liberties, not naming any liberty in particular[3]; and of Sir Thomas Moyle, who was Speaker of the eighth Parliament of Henry VIII, it is recorded that he began a new usage by making a petition for freedom of speech for the House[4]. But whatever the form may have been, it seems agreed that after the Speaker had been approved by the King, it was always customary for him to claim the several privileges of freedom of speech and freedom from arrest. These claims were considered as of right; and were not regarded as an appeal to the Crown for favours but rather as a public assertion and notification to the King and the people of the privileges of the House of Commons, in order that no man might plead ignorance[5]. These claims were made only on the assembling of a new Parliament. They were not in order from a Speaker who had been chosen midway in a Parliament.

The Speaker and the Crown.

---

[1] Denison, *Notes from My Journals*, 431; cf. Mr A. J. Balfour's Speech on Mr Mooney's motion, *The Times*, May 8th, 1902. [2] Hatsell, II. 163.
[3] Atkins, *Parliament and Parliamentary and Political Tracts*, 1734, 64.
[4] Atkins, 64. [5] Hatsell, II. 153.

The
Speaker's
Contact
with the
Sovereign.
When addresses are presented to the Crown in person, such as those in answer to the speech from the Throne at the opening of a session, on presentation of bills of supply, or any special occasion, the Speaker is now, as in the past, the spokesman of the House. Until the time of Queen Victoria these occasions were much more frequent than during her long reign. The rule is that, when the sovereign opens Parliament in person, each House shall present its address to him if he remains in London. When Parliament is opened by commission, the House of Commons presents its address in answer to the speech from the Throne by commissioners, viz. by Privy Councillors. Such was the usage, with only one exception, all through the nineteenth century[1]; and from the reign of William IV to the beginning of the twentieth century, the Speaker, as the spokesman of the House of Commons, was brought into the presence of the sovereign much less frequently than in the seventeenth and eighteenth centuries.

[1] Denison, *Notes from My Journals*, 239.

CHAPTER XXIV.

THE OFFICERS OF THE HOUSE.

Two officers of the House of Commons, the Clerk and the The Clerk, Sergeant-at-Arms, are presumably as old as the Speaker. The the Sergeant-at-Arms office of Clerk has been traced back at least as far as 1388[1]; and and the there are good and practical reasons for believing that both offices Chaplain. have existed from the time when the House of Lords and the House of Commons first sat apart. The Chaplain, the third officer who has his place on the floor of the House and his part in its proceedings, is the most modern in the organisation of the House. In its present form this office dates no further back than the Cromwellian Parliaments; and it differs from the offices of Clerk and of Sergeant-at-Arms in that it is not a patent office, not an office held for life. The Chaplain's tenure corresponds with that of the Speaker, for it is by the Speaker that the Chaplain is appointed.

From the first the Clerk of the House of Commons, or the The Clerk of Underclerk of the Parliaments attending upon the Commons, has the House. been appointed by the Crown[2]. It has been suggested that before the Houses sat continuously apart there were two clerks of the Parliament, a clerk and an assistant clerk; and that when the separation came in 1332 the underclerk went with the Commons. He has accordingly, from soon after that time, in his patent and in several public instruments, been styled, "Underclerk of the Parliaments attending upon the Commons[3]." By his oath on entering office, administered by the Clerk of the Crown, and taken on his knees before the Lord Chancellor, the Clerk binds himself to

---

[1] Stubbs, III. 469.   [2] Cf. Hatsell, II. 207.
[3] Hatsell, II. 207; cf. Stubbs, III. 459.

attend upon the Commons, " making true' entries, remembrances and journals of the things done and passed in the same"; and also to "keep secret all such matters as shall be treated in his (the King's) said Parliament, and not disclose the same before they shall be published; but to such as it ought to be disclosed to[1]."

His Emolument.

The office of Clerk has grown in importance with the increasing volume of legislation. Nowadays its holder receives his emolument in the form of a salary, not, as until the end of the eighteenth century, partly by salary payable at the exchequer, and partly by fees on bills coming before the House. As late as the reign of Elizabeth the larger part of the emoluments of the Clerk accrued from gratuities from members. Every member at his departure at the end of a Parliament was expected to bestow a few shillings on the clerk[2]. But this was at a time when the exchequer defrayed few of the charges incidental to the meeting of Parliament; and when, as in 1592, even such an obviously necessary article of furniture for the Chamber as the clock, had to be paid for by a levy on the members[3]. It is no longer the right of the Clerk to nominate the Clerk Assistant and "all the other clerks without doors," and to make the appointments to these offices yield a con- siderable part of his income, as it was until nearly the end of the unreformed House of Commons. These appointments are now in the Crown.

Duties of the Clerk.

While in these particulars there have been changes in the office, and, since 1832, some additional duties have been thrown upon the Clerk, the principal duties to-day are similar to those which the Clerk has been discharging since the title of Clerk first makes its appearance in the Journals, and the early series of Journals became identified with the names of the Clerks who had written them or supervised their writing[4]. The Clerk no longer reads the litany at the opening of each sitting of the House, as he did in the reigns of Elizabeth and James I[5]; but his principal duty to-day, as in the past, is to record the proceedings of the House, to sign its orders, to endorse the bills sent or returned to the House of Lords, and to read whatever is required to be read at the table of the House while the Speaker is in the Chair[6].

---

[1] Hatsell, ii. 183, 184.   [2] Cf. D'Ewes, *Journals*, 569.
[3] Cf. D'Ewes, *Journals*, 507.   [4] Hatsell, ii. 185.
[5] Cf. D'Ewes, *Journals*, 47; *H. of C. Journals*, i. 150.
[6] Cf. *Rules and Orders of the House of Commons*, 9th Ed., 179; cf. Anson, *Law and Custom of the Constitution*, i. 140.

To-day the table of the House testifies more obviously than The Clerk's Table. anything within the Chamber to the increase in Parliamentary work which has gone on continuously since the sixteenth century, when S. Stephen's Chapel became the permanent meeting-place of the Commons.   In the reign of Elizabeth, when Hooker wrote his detailed statement of the organisation of the House and of its procedure, there was only one Clerk at the table.   "Before is a table board, at which sitteth the Clerk of the House, and thereupon layeth his books and writeth his records," wrote Hooker, after describing the great seat made for the Speaker[1].   In the reign of James I prints of the House of Commons show two Clerks at the table; and from 1640, when Rushworth was appointed Clerk Assistant[2], an officer with that title has always had his place at the table[3]; while at least as early as the middle years of the eighteenth century, if not earlier, it was the practice for the Clerk Assistant alone, and not the Clerk, to take his place at the table when the House resolved itself into committee of the whole[4].   The presence of the Clerk synchronises with that of the Speaker and with the display of the mace on the table; for the Clerk has properly nothing to do with the House, except when it is sitting with the Speaker in the Chair[5].

Except for the added dignity which has accrued to it, the office The Sergeant-at-Arms. in which time has wrought the fewest changes is that of Sergeant-at-Arms.   The Sergeant is to-day what he has been since there existed a House in which his services were required, an officer of the Crown, lent to the Commons to assist in the preservation of order, and in the last resort to enforce the orders of the Chair. He is the attendant of the Speaker when Parliament is sitting. He also attends him on ceremonial occasions beyond the walls of the House; and when Parliament is not sitting, sometimes even when it is assembled, he may be called upon to attend on the person of the sovereign.   When Edward VII opened Parliament on February 14th, 1901, the Sergeant-at-Arms was in attendance on the King as Groom of the Robes; and the Deputy Sergeant-at-Arms attended the Speaker when the Commons were summoned to the Lords to hear the reading of the King's speech[6].

Like the Clerk of the House the Sergeant is appointed by the His Appoint-ment. Crown.   He is removable only on an address from the House to

---

[1] Mountmorres, i. 113, 114.
[2] Parry, 338.
[3] Cf. Hatsell, ii. 191.
[4] Hatsell, ii. 200.
[5] Hatsell, ii. 200.
[6] Cf. *Morning Post*, Feb. 15th, 1901.

the Crown; and there is at least one instance, as remote however as 1675, in which a Sergeant who had been false to his trust, and had permitted the escape of prisoners held by the House for breach of privilege, was dismissed by this method of appeal to the sovereign[1].

His Duties.   Inside the House the place of the Sergeant-at-Arms is at the bar. He attends the Speaker when he enters and leaves the House. He usually accompanies him when he goes to the House of Lords; keeps order within the precincts of the House; brings to the bar persons who are summoned to attend there; and introduces at the bar persons who are entitled to make communications to the House. Outside the House he is charged with the execution of warrants issued by the Speaker for bringing persons in custody to the bar; for retaining these persons in charge, or committing them to such place of detention as the House may order[2].

Duties now Obsolete.   I have described the office of Sergeant-at-Arms as the one that has been least affected by modern conditions. On its ceremonial side, and theoretically as regards its functions, this is true. But in practice the office has not been unaffected by changed conditions; for to-day the number of duties thrown upon the Sergeant is less than it was in the unreformed House of Commons. From the Restoration until the reign of George III, one of the duties of the Sergeant-at-Arms, acting through his deputies, was to bring to the bar members of the House who had failed to answer calls issued by the Speaker to the sheriffs on the order of the House. On some occasions the Sergeant-at-Arms received as many as twenty orders at a time for the arrest of delinquent members[3]. Calls of the House were occasionally issued after the Reform Act; but Hatsell, when reviewing in 1781 his twenty years' service at the table, first as Clerk Assistant and from 1768 as Clerk, could not recall a single instance in which a defaulting member had been in the custody of the Sergeant[4].

Summoning of Lawyer Members.   From the reign of Elizabeth the House imposed on the Sergeant-at-Arms another duty which has long ago ceased to fall to his lot. Lawyers, from the time when seats were objects of ambition, were most anxious to be of the House, and usually they were disposed

---

[1] Cf. *H. of C. Journals*, x. 351.

[2] Cf. *Rules and Orders of the House of Commons*, 205.

[3] Cf. *H. of C. Journals*, ix. 203, 205.

[4] Hatsell, ii. 94, Ed. 1796.

to shirk its duties when these clashed with their professional engagements. In the reign of Elizabeth it began to be the duty of the Sergeant to go with the mace into Westminster Hall to summon the sergeants-at-law and gentlemen of the long robe who were of the House to give their attendance at its sittings[1]. In the reign of James I there were many orders calling upon the lawyers to attend upon their Parliamentary duties, and the Sergeant-at-Arms was frequently directed to make a round of the law-courts and bring with him into the House those lawyers who persisted in making Parliamentary service subservient to their professional engagements[2]. These orders to the Sergeant-at-Arms were frequent until the reign of George I; and they were issued as late as 1764[3]. But with the developement of government by party new influences began to be at work which ensured for the administration a full attendance of its supporters on all critical occasions. Opposition as well as government had its whips from the early years of the eighteenth century; and gradually the Sergeant-at-Arms was relieved of the duties which in the sixteenth and seventeenth centuries had been thrown upon him by the remissness of lawyers who put their business in the courts before their duties in the House, and of knights of the shire and burgesses who failed to respond to calls for their attendance at Westminster.

As the custodian of the mace the Sergeant-at-Arms must The Mace. always have been a picturesque figure in the House. When the mace was first introduced I have not been able to discover. The probability is that it is as old as the office of Sergeant-at-Arms. Its use apparently antedates the beginning of the Journals in 1547; and as the entries in the Journals become fuller in the reign of Elizabeth, it is possible to ascertain the uses to which it was put. Since the Journals were begun there have been at least three maces. The one which figured on the table in the stormy period which preceded the Great Rebellion was replaced by a new one in 1648, after the death of Charles I[4]. This mace was in use until April 19th, 1553, when, after it had been stigmatised by Cromwell as a bauble, it was removed from the House by the Lord Protector's order. In July of the same year, in the first Parliament of Cromwell's protectorate—"the Parliament of the Commonwealth of England" as it styled itself—Edward Birkhead was appointed Sergeant-at-Arms; and on the 12th of July it was resolved that the

---

[1] D'Ewes, *Journals*, 347.   [2] Cf. *H. of C. Journals*, I. 188, 650, 925; II. 9.
[3] *H. of C. Journals*, XXIX. 842.   [4] Cf. *H. of C. Journals*, VI. 166.

Sergeant-at-Arms "do repair to Lieutenant Colonel Worsley for the mace, and do bring it to this House." It was further resolved that "it be referred to the committee who brought in the report touching the Sergeant, to consider of the use of the mace, and with whom it shall remain[1]." On the same day this committee recommended "that the mace should be made use of as formerly." The House agreed to the recommendation, and ordered that the mace be brought in, which was accordingly done[2].

History of the Present Mace.

At the Restoration, when the Convention Parliament was obliterating the arms of the Commonwealth, which had been displayed in the Chamber during the Protectorate, and was establishing an anniversary of the Restoration, a new mace was ordered "with the Crown and King's Majesty's arms and such other ornaments as have been usual[3]"; and this mace, which was furnished to the House by the Council of State[4], is still in use[5], and has stood on the table before thirty-two Speakers. It escaped the fire of 1834 by reason of the fact that, when the Houses of Parliament were destroyed, Parliament stood prorogued; and when Parliament is out of session the mace is deposited for safe custody in the Tower of London.

The Place of the Mace.

A variety of usages, all of ancient standing, have grown up about the mace. When a new Parliament has been convened, and members are awaiting the summons to the Lords for the signification from the Crown to choose a Speaker, the mace is brought into the House and placed under the table. There it remains until the Speaker has been chosen, when, on his taking the Chair, it is placed upon the table. When the Speaker goes to the House of Lords for the royal approval of the choice of the Commons, the Sergeant-at-Arms, in accordance with a usage traceable at least to the reign of Elizabeth[6], heads the procession with the mace, not over his shoulder but in the arm, for the mace is not to be carried before the Speaker until the sovereign has approved of his election[7]. When the House goes into committee, as soon as the Speaker has left the Chair the mace is placed under the table, and remains there until the House resumes[8].

[1] *H. of C. Journals*, vii. 282.   [2] *H. of C. Journals*, vii. 284.
[3] *H. of C. Journals*, viii. 39, 40.   [4] *H. of C. Journals*, viii. 39.
[5] Cf. Denison, *Notes from My Journals*, 200, 201.
[6] D'Ewes, *Journals*, 17.
[7] *Report of the Select Committee on Office of Speaker*, 1853, App. 36; Denison, *Notes from My Journals*, 185.
[8] Cf. *Rules and Orders*, 1, 4, 108.

In the days before the Grenville Act of 1770, when election cases were determined by the House, and counsel and witnesses were heard at the bar, the mace was on the table[1]. In 1696, when Fenwick's bill of attainder was before the House and Fenwick was to appear at the bar, there was a discussion on the place of the mace, and much debate, marked by the citation of numerous precedents as to whether the mace ought to be on the table when Fenwick was at the bar, or whether the Sergeant ought to stand by Fenwick, with it. It was urged that if the mace were not on the table members were muzzled. " We are," said one member, " in the nature of judges; and shall we pass a vote that judges shall not ask questions[2]?" The decision of the House was that the Sergeant should stand with the mace at the bar[3]; and that with the mace off the table, no member could address the House, not even to suggest to the Speaker such questions as he might wish to ask[4]. With such usages attaching to the mace it is easy to understand how it came to be retained on the table when election petitions were heard; for with the mace at the bar, members could have had no part in the examination of witnesses called in support of or in opposition to a petition. Admonitions from the Speaker to persons not of the House who have incurred its displeasure are the rule when the offenders are not in custody. Reprimands are only possible when the offender is at the bar, and in the custody of the Sergeant-at-Arms. Then the Sergeant-at-Arms holds the mace at his side; and no member may speak except the Speaker[5].

Besides the distinction which attaches to the Sergeant-at-Arms as custodian of the mace, he has another distinction, not unworthy of notice in an endeavour to trace how the House comes to have the grouping and appearance which it presents to-day. The Sergeant alone of all the officers who are distinguished from the members by their dress can point to an authority for the use of his vesture. In the early patents from the Crown appointing the Sergeant-at-Arms it was stipulated that the office was to be held for life, and that from the Crown the holder was to have a fee of twelve pence a day, and a vesture[6]. While the payments from the Crown were so small, and they remained at this sum as late as the appointment of the last Sergeant of the reign of Charles I, the

The Mace at the Bar.

The Sergeant's Dress and Remuneration.

---

[1] Howell, *State Trials*, XIII. 544.
[2] Howell, *State Trials*, XIII. 544.
[3] Howell, *State Trials*, XIII. 546.
[4] Cf. Hatsell, II. 107.
[5] Denison, 25.
[6] Cf. *H. of C. Journals*, VII. 282.

greater part of the emoluments of the Sergeant was derived from fees and fines. Some of these fines were petty. In 1640, for instance, the House made an order that if a member "stood in the entry," or did not take his place when he came into the House, or spoke loud "when any bill or other matter is reading, as to disturb the House," he should "pay twelve pence, to be divided between the Sergeant and the poor[1]."

Origin of Distinctive Dress.

Hooker, when he wrote his description of the House of Commons, made no mention of the vesture of the Sergeant-at-Arms, nor gave the least hint that in the last half of the sixteenth century the Speaker and the Clerk at the table were in any way distinguished in dress from the members of the House. The Journals contain no orders on these matters; and it is solely from extra-official records, and usually only incidentally from these, that anything can be ascertained regarding the date of the dress of the Speaker and the Clerk. There is an incidental allusion in D'Ewes's *Journals* which shows that Speakers of Queen Elizabeth's Parliaments wore gowns. This is the earliest mention that I have found of the Speaker's gown. Nowhere have I discovered when it became customary for the Speaker to wear it. It may be conjectured that the gown was introduced by the lawyers who were of the Chair. The wig which the Speaker now wears was not permanently part of his attire until after Onslow's time; for there is a picture of the House in which both Walpole and Speaker Onslow are shown wearing high hats of the shape in vogue early in the Hanoverian dynasty[2]. A guide to London, published in the early years of the reign of George III, describes the Speaker and the Clerks as wearing gowns[3]; and this is the earliest of the few mentions of the attire of the Clerks at the table which I have been able to discover.

Prayers in the House.

As early as the reign of Richard II it was customary to open a new session with a sermon in the Abbey, and on holy days Parliament assembled at prime, in order that the members might attend service before beginning the day's work[4]. By the reign of Richard III the custom of opening a new session with a sermon at the Abbey was well established. The Parliament of 1483 was opened with a sermon preached by the Lord Chancellor, Bishop

---

[1] *H. of C. Journals*, II. 44.   [2] Denison, 47.

[3] Cf. Enticks, *London and its Environs Described*, II. 166.

[4] Cf. "Manner of Holding Parliaments in the Reign of Richard II," Somers, *Tracts*, I. 11.

Russell; and in writing of the opening of this Parliament Gairdner states that the sermon was according to custom[1]. Daily prayers were not the custom until after the Reformation. They were begun in the Parliament of 1563–67; for in 1571 it was agreed by the House, on the assembling of the third Parliament of Elizabeth's reign, "that the litany shall be read every day, as in the last Parliament, and also a prayer said by Mr Speaker as he shall think fittest for this time, to be begun every day at half-past eight a.m., and that each then making default shall forfeit for every time fourpence to the poor man's box[2]."

In 1574 Thomas Norton, "citizen and grocer," who was of the House of Commons of 1571, and again of the Parliament of 1572–83, as one of the members for London, and who at this time was city remembrancer, was called upon by the Lord Mayor to prepare a scheme of procedure for the court of aldermen and the common council. In doing so he suggested that the proceedings of these bodies should be opened with prayer. "I could gladly wish," Norton wrote in his paper of 1574, "that some form of prayer might daily be used in your court and council chamber by you and all your brethren before you enter into causes. It is so used in the Parliament, and though such use be but of late, I trust it shall be continued, and grow to be old[3]." Norton's wish was realized; and from the reign of Elizabeth to the Cromwellian Parliaments, it was the rule for the clerk to read the litany, and for the Speaker to offer a special prayer at the opening of each sitting of the House[4]. There was an alteration in this usage towards the close of Elizabeth's reign, when a minister was brought into the House to read prayers[5].

The New Usage commended in 1574.

The order of 1571 left the Speaker to make such prayer "as he shall think fittest for the time[6]." But later on in the reign of Elizabeth the extemporary prayer had given place to a liturgy. The liturgy in use in the first Parliament of James I contains the following prayer:—"Oh God most great and glorious, which dwelleth in the Heavens over all, yet humbleth thyself to behold the things that are done upon the earth, We, thy people and the sheep of thy pasture, assembled by thy providence to the performance of this high service whereupon the honour of thy Name, the

A Prayer used in James I's Reign.

---

[1] Cf. Gairdner, *Richard III*, 195, 196.   [2] Parry, 217.
[3] *Archæologia*, xxxvi. pt. i. 97–104.
[4] Cf. *H. of C. Journals*, i. 118, 150, 266, 353.
[5] D'Ewes, *Journals*, 566, 567, 661.   [6] Parry, 217.

beauty of thy Church among us, the glory of our King and the
wealth of our State doth depend, Let the good of this whole island
move our care and zeal, which consisting the safety and honour of
the King and the enacting and execution of good laws, let us be
wisely careful and faithfully zealous for the person of our King,
whom thou, the King of Kings, hath in mercy set over us. And
because no law can be good that is not agreeable to thy law, which
containeth the fundamental equity of our laws; in making laws to
govern thy people, let us always have an eye to thy law, not
digressing from the holy equity thereof; and what through thy
mercy we shall here profitably enact, we pray thee through the
whole Kingdom it may be truly executed, that our great labour
may not be disgraced with little fruit[1]."

A Chaplain appointed.   The Speaker and the Clerk were relieved of their part in the
religious service at the opening of each day's sitting in 1654, in
the first of the Cromwellian Parliaments, when the governors of
the school and almshouse of Westminster were ordered to take
care "that such of the morning lecturers as preacheth on the
respective days, do attend each morning that they preach to pray
in this House[2]." In Richard Cromwell's Parliament this plan was
abandoned; and William Cooper, at this time minister of S.
Olave's, Southwark, was on January 31st, 1659, desired by resolution "to continue to officiate and perform the duty of prayer in
this House every morning during this session of Parliament"; and
at the end of the Parliament, April 22nd, 1659, it was resolved
"that the sum of fifty pounds be given and bestowed on Mr
Cooper, the minister, for his great labour and pains in attending
the House daily[3]."

**Remune-
ration of the
Chaplain.**   After the Restoration the first reference in the Journals to the
Chaplain as one of the officers of the House is of September 8th,
1660. On that day there was an expectation that the Parliament,
which had assembled on the 25th of April, 1660, would be prorogued; and accordingly a resolution was then adopted with
respect to the Chaplain which was to be the precedent for many
similar resolutions passed in the closing days of a Parliament.
"Ordered," it reads, "that the members of the House who are of
His Majesty's Privy Council are hereby desired to attend the King,
and humbly to recommend to His Majesty from this House

---

[1] *H. of C. Journals,* i. 150.

[2] *Cromwellian Diary of Richard Burton,* i. xxvii.

[3] *Cromwellian Diary of Richard Burton,* iii. 17

Mr Edward Voyce, Master of Arts, for some mark of His Majesty's favour in regard to his constant and diligent attendance upon this House ever since the beginning of this Parliament, as Chaplain[1]." Parliament was not prorogued; it continued in session until December 29th, 1660. It was then dissolved; and on the eve of the dissolution the House voted the Chaplain one hundred and twenty-five pounds, out of the excise, as compensation for his services[2].

The payment made in 1660 to the Chaplain did not form a precedent, for during the next one hundred and eighty years the House provided no fixed and regular salary for him; none that can be traced in the payments out of the exchequer to the Speaker and the other officers of the House[3]. The usage, which had its origin in the Parliament of 1660, of recommending the Chaplain to the Crown for preferment was continued until the reign of William IV. The last of these recommendations before the Reform Act of 1832 was in 1829. It was made on behalf of the Rev. Evelyn Levett Smith[4]. *Recommending the Chaplain to the Sovereign.*

In the first Parliament of William III the House was specific in its recommendation on behalf of its Chaplain. It asked that Mr Manningham should have conferred upon him "the next prebend of Windsor or Westminster that shall fall vacant[5]"; and although this specific recommendation was peculiar to the first of the post-Revolution Parliaments, in the eighteenth century a deanery or a prebend came to be looked upon as the certain reward of the clergyman who had the good fortune to be appointed Speaker's Chaplain. Arthur Young's father, Dr Young, who was Chaplain during part of Onslow's Speakership, became a prebendary of Canterbury[6]; and in the eighteenth century Canterbury was so often the cathedral to which Speakers' Chaplains went on ending their terms of service at S. Stephen's, that Sir Egerton Brydges, in describing the metropolitan cathedral city in the early years of the nineteenth century, wrote of it as "richer in inanimate than in animate attractions." "The metropolitan church," he added, "ought to have been the reposing place of genius and learning. It was the feasting and sleeping spot of Speakers' *Preferment for the Chaplain.*

---

[1] *H. of C. Journals*, VIII. 155.   [2] *H. of C. Journals*, VIII. 229.

[3] Cf. Hansard, 3rd Series, XXVI. 602.

[4] Cf. *Mirror of Parliament*, 1829, III. 1989.

[5] *H. of C. Journals*, X. 533.

[6] Cf. Stephen, *Studies of a Biographer*, 191.

Chaplains, and powerful noblemen's tutors. Dr Wellfit, the Senior
Prebendary, lately deceased, who was Chaplain to Sir Fletcher
Norton, held his stall forty-seven years[1]."

The Last Appeal to the Crown for the Chaplain.

The usage, in accordance with which the House petitioned the
Crown for preferment for its Chaplains, came to an end in 1835,
when, at the instance of Hume, several reforms were made in
the office of Speaker. Hume objected that the appeals to the
Crown on behalf of the Chaplain were undignified; and he suggested that instead the House should vote him a salary. The
discussion took place immediately after Abercromby had succeeded
Manners-Sutton in the Chair. After Hume had made his plea
for reform the new Speaker intervened in the debate, and stated
that the appointment of the gentleman who was his Chaplain
" had been made without any inducement being held out to him of
a prospect of preferment[2]." Since 1835 addresses to the Crown on
behalf of Speakers' Chaplains have disappeared from the Journals;
but in the nineteenth century, as from the Restoration, a deanery
or a prebend continued to be the reward of the Chaplain[3].

Duty of the Chaplain.

Ever since 1660, when the Chaplain began to be recognized as
an officer of the House, he has been described as the Speaker's
Chaplain, and has been appointed by the Speaker after his own
election has been approved by the Crown. In a new Parliament
his duties begin the day after the approval of the Speaker. At
the daily sittings the doors of the press and public galleries are
not opened until after prayers have been read[4]. These usages as
to prayers, like so many of the usages at Westminster, have been
closely followed in the Parliaments of British colonies. At Ottawa
it is still the duty of the Speaker, as it was the duty of Speakers at
Westminster from the reign of Elizabeth until the Great Rebellion,
to read prayers; and at Ottawa, as at Westminster, the doors of
the House of Commons are barred against all strangers until
prayers have been read.

The Prayer for Parliament.

Almost contemporaneously with the establishment of the
Chaplain—on the passing of the Act of Uniformity of 1662[5]—
there was inserted in the Book of Common Prayer in general use
the prayer for the High Court of Parliament, which, with only one

---

[1] Brydges, *Autobiography*, i. 39, 40.
[2] Hansard, 3rd Series, xxvi. 603.
[3] Cf. Denison, *Notes from My Journals*, 250.
[4] *Rules and Orders of the House*, 17 ; Denison, 185.
[5] 13 and 14 C. II, c. 4.

verbal alteration made in 1801, has its place in the liturgy of the Church of England to-day. From the Journals it would seem that as early as the reign of Elizabeth there was a prayer for Parliament in the Book of Common Prayer[1]. Blount records that the prayer, much in the form in which it now stands, and in which he conceives it was written by Laud, when Bishop of St David's, appeared in a special fast-day service in 1625[2]. At the Restoration the Prayer-Book of 1636 was the one in general use; and it was accepted as authoritative. The Prayer for Parliament was not in this book. But in 1661, when the Convocations of Canterbury and York revised the liturgy, they made the Black Letter Prayer-Book of 1636 the basis of their revision; and, as can be seen from the facsimiles of the Prayer-Book of 1636, and of the manuscript alterations and additions to which the members of Convocations subscribed on the 20th of December, 1661, it was at this revision, which preceded the Act of Uniformity, that the Prayer for Parliament was inserted in the Prayer-Book which in 1662 came into general use[3].

[1] Cf. *H. of C. Journals*, i. 150.

[2] Blount, *Annotated Book of Common Prayer*, New York, 1844, 237.

[3] Cf. Stanley, *Introduction to Facsimile of the Black Letter Prayer-Book*, London, 1871.

CHAPTER XXV.

THE SEATING OF THE HOUSE.

Early Distinctions of Rank among Members.

THE Journals afford the student no aid concerning the seating of members. They can be gone through, page by page, from 1547 to 1832, without finding the least hint as to how members came to be seated, or grouped, as they were when the Reform bill was before the House in 1832. There are traditions that in the early days of the House knights of the shire monopolised the front benches, and that members for the boroughs were relegated to the back seats, and to the seats near the door[1]. It is more than a tradition that in the period before the Commons sat apart from the Lords, before the House was organised as it was after 1332, that, when a Parliament assembled, the names of members were called in feudal order, in accordance with the usage of the time when every man had his definite place in society. Burgesses and citizens were called on the first day; knights of the shire on the second day; and barons of the Cinque Ports and peers on the third day[2]. In the Journals there is also abundant proof that from soon after the time when the Commons met in S. Stephen's Chapel there were clearly marked distinctions between knights of the shire and burgesses. In the reigns of Elizabeth and James I, when there were collections in the House for poor prisoners in London, Westminster, and Southwark, and for other charitable purposes, and when the poor man's box was an institution in the House, larger contributions were levied on knights of the shire than on citizens and burgesses[3].

---

[1] Cf. Townsend, *Hist. of House of Commons*, II. 429.   [2] Lewis, I. 68.

[3] D'Ewes, *Journals*, 83, 497, 502, 661 ; *H. of C. Journals*, I. 250.

From 1631 to 1698, if not from an earlier period, the clerk of Knights and the Crown received a fee of four shillings on the return of a writ Burgesses. for the election of a knight; while the fee in respect of a burgess or a citizen, or a baron of the Cinque Ports, was only two shillings[1]. In 1664 the fines to be imposed on defaulters, after a call of the House, were ten pounds in the case of a knight of the shire, and five pounds in the case of a burgess[2]. In 1668 it was ordered by the House that the fees payable to the fund for distribution at the end of a session among the under-clerks and officers attending the House should be ten shillings for a knight, and five shillings for burgesses and citizens[3]. In 1700, when there was a revision of the fees payable to the sergeant-at-arms, it was ordered that knights should pay ten shillings when sworn in at the table, and burgesses five shillings[4]. In 1695, when members were required to subscribe to the association " mutually promising and engaging to stand by and assist each other to the utmost of their power in support and defence of His Majesty's most sacred person and government, against the late King James and all his adherents," knights took the oath before citizens and burgesses[5].

After the Revolution some distinctions between knights and Distinctions burgesses found their way into enactments. In 1698 the fee to by Enactment. the clerk of the Crown on the return of the writ for the election of a knight was fixed at four shillings, and that for a burgess at two shillings[6]. In 1710 there was the well-known Act establishing landed qualifications for members of the House, by which a knight was compelled to have freehold or copyhold estate of the yearly value of six hundred pounds; while the qualification for a citizen or burgess was fixed at three hundred pounds[7].

From the earliest times added dignity was bestowed on knights Privileges of at their election by girding them with sword in the county court. Knights. They were also privileged to wear boots and spurs within the Chamber; and until nearly the end of the eighteenth century they were keenly jealous of their privileges[8]. It was the privilege also of county members to attend court in leather breeches and top-boots; and although this privilege fell into desuetude in the eighteenth century, it was revived and exercised as late as 1782,

---

[1] Cf. *H. of C. Journals*, XII. 484.   [2] Cf. *H. of C. Journals*, VIII. 538.
[3] Cf. *H. of C. Journals*, IX. 88, X. 277, XI. 374.
[4] *H. of C. Journals*, XIII. 356.   [5] *H. of C. Journals*, XI. 470.
[6] Cf. 10 W. III, c. 8.   [7] Cf. 9 Anne, c. 5.
[8] Colchester, *Diary*, I. 45, 46.

when, after the opposition had been triumphant in the House, an address was carried to court, urging George III to make peace with the American colonies[1].

Their Sense of their Importance.   As early as the reign of Elizabeth men of wealth and social standing who were of the House were usually eager to exchange a seat for a borough for election as knight of the shire; and from this time, among unofficial members, knights of the shire regarded themselves as of more public and social importance than citizens and burgesses; and so esteemed themselves until conditions began to change after the first reform of the representative system. This feeling of importance on the part of knights of the shire is illustrated in an early history of the press gallery at Westminster, wherein it is stated that, in the years immediately preceding the Reform Act, one county member, typical of his class, was wont to frequent the gallery and appeal to the reporters for more liberal and careful treatment on account of his position in the House as a knight of the shire. "Now, my good fellows," was the way he phrased his appeal to the reporters of the pre-reform era, "give us a decent speech. Don't cut it short by saying only that Mr Joliffe supported the motion. Remember I am a county member, and people think what I say of consequence[2]."

No Distinction in the Seating of Knights.   While all this proof is forthcoming that there were for centuries some distinctions existing in the House between knights and burgesses, it is impossible to find evidence that at any time subsequent to the commencement of the Journals, at any time after the Reformation had produced the masterless man and a vast population had grown up outside the old feudal order, knights of the shire enjoyed any special privileges in the matter of seats in the House. On the contrary there is evidence that at as early a period in the history of the House as the reign of Elizabeth no such consideration was shown to them, and that no claims of knights of the shire to particular places in the Chamber were recognized. "Upon the lower row on both sides the Speaker," wrote Hooker, "sit such personages as be of the King's Privy Council, or of his chief officers; but as for any other, none claimeth nor can claim any place; but sitteth as he cometh, saving that on the right hand of the Speaker, next beneath the said counsels, the Londoners and the citizens of York do sit, and so in order should

[1] Pryme, *Autobiographic Recollections*, 219, 220; *Hist. MSS. Comm. 15th Rep.*, App., pt. vi. 585.

[2] *Westminster Review*, xxix. 255.

sit all citizens accordingly[1]." As early as this the four members for
the city of London had by usage a claim to particular seats in the
House. After Hooker's time there were additions to the occupants
of the benches reserved for "such personages as be of the King's
Privy Council or of his chief officers."

Until 1549 heirs-apparent of peerages were excluded from the
House by law of Parliament[2]. Then the law was abrogated;
and between 1549 and the reign of Charles I sons of peers were
accorded the privilege of sitting on the benches immediately to the
right and left of the Speaker. Denzil Holles, second son of the
first Earl of Clare, accounted in this way for his nearness to the
Chair during the eventful sitting of March 2nd, 1629, when he
and Valentine held Finch in the Chair, while Eliot's resolutions
were put to the House. "The place he had so taken," Holles
said in his explanation, "he had before frequently occupied,
being entitled to it as an earl's son[3]." This is the only evidence
which I have found that sons of peers were privileged in the seating
of the House; and in later times this usage as to peers' sons seems
to have fallen into desuetude. While the privilege was continued
it must have been based on usage and not on any order of the
House.

Place of Peers' Sons.

Even the reservation of the benches next the Speaker's Chair
for privy councillors is by usage only; for in 1833, when the first
House of Commons elected after the Reform Act met, and Cobbett
rudely crowded Peel out of the place in which he had sat in the
Parliament of 1831–32 on the front bench to the Speaker's left—
then, by custom, the bench of privy councillors in opposition[4]—
there was no order which it could be affirmed that Cobbett, then
newly of the House, had transgressed.

The Front Benches.

In the eighteenth century it became a usage that members
who had received the thanks of the House when in their place
were entitled to that place whenever they were in the House, at
least during the Parliament in which they had been so honoured.
But this was only a courtesy extended to an honoured member,
and was based on no order or resolution which can be found in the
Journals[5].

Courtesy Places.

Until after the Revolution the seating of the House was as

---

[1] Mountmorres, I. 113, 114.   [2] Hatsell, II. 18.
[3] Forster, *Life of Eliot*, II. 447, 448.
[4] Parker, *Life of Peel*, II. 211; Croker, *Papers*, II. 4.
[5] Hatsell, Ed. 1796, II. 88.

Seating
of the
Opposition.

described in Hooker's statement. The modern usage, in accordance with which the administration and their supporters sit to the right of the Speaker, and members in opposition to the left of the Chair, can date no further back than the beginning of government by party and by cabinet. And here again, in the period after government by party had become established, the Journals can be searched in vain for any reference to the existence of party lines within the House of Commons, or any indication of the time at which members of opposite political principles began to sit on different sides of the Chamber. The germ of the modern system of government by party first manifested itself in the Parliament at Oxford in 1625[1]. Between 1666 and 1671 the Whig and Tory parties had come into being[2]. By 1708 not only members of the House of Commons but mayors and members of municipal corporations were being elected on party lines, "and in every corner of the nation the two parties stand as it were listed against one another[3]."

Pairing.

Some years before political party organisation had thus extended over the country, members of the House of Commons professing Whig and Tory principles were "listed against one another" in the Chamber. They were more or less organised as distinct political parties, and were testing their strength on even such matters as the election of Speaker[4]. But the eighteenth century was nearly half-way through before there was a single entry in the Journals which directly or indirectly indicated the existence of opposing political parties in the House of Commons. There is only one entry of the kind to be found; it occurs in 1743. The terms Whig and Tory have never been entered on the Journals; and only inferentially does the entry of 1743 point to the existence of party lines. It is in the form of a resolution, and reads: "That no member of this House do presume to make any agreement with another member to absent themselves from any services of this House or any committee thereof, and that this House will proceed with the utmost severity against all such members as shall offend therein." The yeas for the resolution were one hundred and thirty-nine; the noes one hundred and seventy-one, "and so it passed in the negative[5]." Pairing, the now long-established House

---

[1] Forster, *Life of Eliot*, I. 385.   [2] Cooke, *Hist. of Party*, I. 1.
[3] Burnet, *Hist. of His Own Time*, IV. 425.
[4] Cf. *Hist. MSS. Comm. 14th Rep.*, App., pt. IX. 492.
[5] *H. of C. Journals*, XXIV. 602.

of Commons practice aimed at by this resolution of 1743, at once suggests party organisation and party whips to sanction and arrange pairs; and though the resolution, an utterly impracticable one in view of the fact that there was no means of compelling constant attendance on the House, came to naught; and although it contains no mention of political parties, it is none the less a landmark in the history of the House and its organisation; and it is all the more valuable, because it is the only indication in the Journals of the unreformed House of Commons that party lines ever existed there.

How much earlier than this movement of 1743 against pairing members of opposing political parties were sitting on opposite sides of the Chamber can, in the absence of any authentic records, be only a matter of conjecture. It seems natural that when one group of men professing one set of political principles displace, as ministers of the Crown, another group professing other principles, the ministers displaced should retire from the treasury bench, and betake themselves with their supporters to the other side of the Chamber. Natural as these movements of ex-ministers from the treasury bench to the front opposition bench seem to-day, only by inference can it be concluded that such changes of position in the House took place earlier than 1740. There is evidence—some of it, however, not very direct or positive—that in 1740 and also in 1741 the Tories, then in opposition, were grouped on the benches to the left of the Speaker, and that Walpole and the Whigs were on the benches to the Speaker's right. The evidence as to members being so seated in 1740 rests upon the often-told story of the interchange between Pulteney and Walpole as to the correctness of a Latin quotation used by Walpole. Pulteney took exception to Walpole's Latin. He made a wager that Walpole was wrong, and is described as throwing a guinea across the House to Walpole[1].

Ministry and Opposition in 1740.

There are other versions of this little pleasantry of Pulteney's in 1740. One version has been used as proof that, as late as the closing days of Walpole's career, the leading political opponents sat side by side in the House[2]. But the coalition against Walpole, at this time led by Pulteney, had been in existence since 1728[3]. After the general election of 1734—the election of the House of Commons which witnessed the interchange between the two leaders

Advantage of Party Grouping in the House.

[1] Cf. Cooke, *Hist. of Party*, II. 276.
[2] Cf. Townsend, *Hist. of House of Commons*, II. 429, 430.
[3] Morley, *Walpole*, 77.

—the opposition added so largely to its strength that, two days before Parliament met, Pulteney regarded its successes at the polls as sufficient to encourage it to attempt to elect the Speaker[1]. The opposition by this time was of considerable numerical strength. Half the advantage of an opposition would be lost if its members were scattered all over the Chamber. Similarity of opinions and identity of purpose suggest the propriety, even the necessity, of members in opposition grouping themselves together; and grouping themselves in such a way as to be able to applaud and support their leaders, and otherwise show their strength. Such a grouping would scarcely be possible unless the leaders were on what has long since come to be known as the front opposition bench; and it seems reasonable to conclude that for some time before 1740 the opposing parties were grouped on different sides of the Chamber.

Opposition Benches in 1741.

Such a grouping and seating of parties at as early a period as the time of the coalition against Walpole—a coalition composed of Tories, malcontent Whigs, and members from Scotland in conflict with Islay—seems all the more probable because it is beyond dispute that in the first session of the Parliament of 1741–47, the session which witnessed the downfall of Walpole, the opposition sat as a group apart. Walpole resigned on the 11th of February, 1741. On the 21st of January Pulteney made his arraignment of Walpole's conduct of the Spanish war; and at the opening of this memorable sitting the supporters of Walpole are described as being startled upon entering the House of Commons to find the opposition benches crowded with the whole strength of the party[2].

The Confronting of Parties.

The structure, the seating, and the furniture of the old Chapel of S. Stephen's all lent themselves to the custom under which supporters of the Government grouped themselves on one side, and opponents of the Government on the other. Until the end of the era of personal government by the Crown organised and permanent oppositions had no place in the scheme of government. With the establishment of government by party and by cabinet, and the subordination of the Crown, organised oppositions necessarily came at once into being; and what was more a matter of course than that, as soon as these conditions became settled, members of the opposition should take advantage of the structural arrangements of the Chamber, and so seat themselves as to confront the men to whom they were opposed? In the reign of George III there is no

[1] Cf. *Marchmont Papers*, ii. 34; *Official List*, pt. ii. 72.
[2] Cooke, ii. 299.

lack of evidence as to how members were seated. House of
Commons phrases, long since of every-day use, such as the "government side of the House" and the "benches below the gangway"
were then coming into vogue. Wraxall describes Rigby, paymaster
of the forces from 1768 to 1782, as "never sitting on the government side of the House"; as if he had meant to show that he
acted independently of ministers, and was above their control[1].
When Trevelyan writes of Fox as sitting with the army contractors
and retired Anglo-Indians "below the gangway[2]," it is unnecessary
for him to add that at this time Fox was still supporting the
administration of North, and was on the government side of the
House.

Some of the modern usages and phraseology of parties are of Party Whips.
much later date than grouping by parties in the House of
Commons. Whips, underscored by as many as six lines, were
sent to the King's friends in the House of Commons as early as
1621[3]. They were issued by the King's express command in the
Pensioner Parliament[4]; and in the Convention Parliament—even
before the beginning of government by cabinet—parties had their
whips[5]. The circulars issued by the administration to its supporters became known as treasury notes in the reign of George III[6],
seemingly from the fact that they were sent out by the patronage
secretary of the treasury, who by this time was installed in office as
chief government whip. In the reign of George III treasury notes
and more personal appeals by letter from ministers went exclusively
to the supporters of government[7]; for on critical occasions the
opposition whips were as busy summoning their supporters as were
the whips at the treasury. But while members were marked in the
House by the side of the Chamber on which they sat, by the
whips to which they responded, and by their inclusion in or exclusion from the distribution of patronage, not until the end of the
reign of George III were opponents of the Government excluded
from the meetings at the Cockpit on the night before the beginning

---

[1] Cf. Wraxall, *Hist. Memoirs of My Own Time*, 188.

[2] Trevelyan, *Fox*, 503.

[3] Addit. MSS. 34324, Folio 290.

[4] Townsend, *Hist. of House of Commons*, II. 368.

[5] Cf. *Dict. Nat. Bio.*, LIII. 76.

[6] Cf. Walpole, *Last Journals*, II. 299.

[7] Cf. *Hist. MSS. Comm. 14th Rep.*, App., pt. IV. 517; *Letters of Maria Joseph Holroyd*, 260.

of a session at which the forecast of the speech from the throne was informally read[1].

Later than the establishment of this last dividing line between parties in the House came the dignifying of the party in opposition by the title "His Majesty's Opposition," which has been applied to it in and out of Parliament since the years immediately preceding the Reform Act, when Canning was leader of the government forces and the Whigs were led by Tierney. The phrase originated in a half-derisive speech made by Hobhouse, afterwards Lord Broughton. Hobhouse was then in opposition, and in a discussion on April 10th, 1826, on the union of the office of president of the board of trade with that of treasurer of the navy, he remarked, "it was said to be hard on His Majesty's ministers to raise objections of this character. For his own part he thought it was more hard on His Majesty's opposition to compel them to take this course." Canning hailed the phrase as a happy one; and Tierney followed with a speech which had much to do with giving Hobhouse's phrase the permanence it has since had in the language of Westminster and of British politics. "My right honourable friend," Tierney said, "could not have invented a better phrase to designate us than that which he has adopted; for we are certainly to all intents and purposes a branch of His Majesty's Government. Its proceedings for some time past have proved that, though the gentlemen opposite are in office, we are in power. The measures are ours, but the emoluments are theirs[2]." The phrase itself, its hearty adoption, and its long and constant use, mark the change in spirit and attitude of those in power towards those in opposition which has come over political life since the days of George III's letters to North; and like so much of the usage and phraseology of Westminster, the phrase has long been in use in the Parliaments of the British colonies[3].

[1] Cf. Hansard, 2nd Series, iv. 48.

[2] Cf. Hansard, 2nd Series, xv. 135.

[3] "The duty of Her Majesty's loyal opposition is to exercise its vast influence in restraining vicious legislation, and in giving a loyal support to proposals of the Government, which commend themselves as in the interests of the country; while initiating itself such measures for the common weal as are neglected by the administration."—Sir Charles Tupper, Farewell Letter. to the Conservative Party in the Senate and the House of Commons in the Dominion Parliament, Jan. 17th, 1901.—*Montreal Witness*, Feb. 6th, 1901.

CHAPTER XXVI.

THE PERSONNEL OF THE HOUSE.

UNTIL wages began to disappear and until, in the fifteenth century, seats in the House of Commons began to be in demand, there must have been much uniformity in the two well-defined classes in the House. The counties at this time were represented by landowners who were not of the peerage. The cities and boroughs, as the municipal records show, sent men who were of the trading and craftsman classes. They sent these men because, at this period, none but such men were available. The cities and boroughs had then no leisured and wealthy class from which members of the House of Commons could be drawn; and as yet the lawyers and the courtiers, who were outsiders and who at a later period were willing to represent cities and boroughs without pay, had not appeared. *County and Borough Members.*

In respect to the counties it may be affirmed that never, while the unreformed representative system survived, was there any great change in the personnel of their representatives. As time went on and election to the House of Commons became more prized, and added to a man's local social consequence, there was more competition for election. Men were increasingly eager to be chosen; but from the time when seats began to be objects of desire there was little change in the class of men who sought the suffrages of the county electorate; and it may be said that, with here and there an exception, in the early days of the representative system the counties were represented by men of landed wealth and social standing, and that the election of men not possessing land in the counties they represented was comparatively rare. *Landed Gentry as County Members.*

Non-
Resident
Borough
Members.

The great change in the personnel of the House affected chiefly the representation of the cities and boroughs. It was directly due to the gradual disappearance of wages for Parliamentary service, and to the consequent election of non-residents. Courtiers and lawyers were the first to take advantage of these altering conditions; and this outside competition for seats was almost confined to them until the seventeenth century, when goldsmiths and scriveners, and wealthy merchants and traders, often settled in London, began to find their way into the House of Commons, as non-resident representatives of cities and boroughs.

Lawyers in
the House.

Lawyers were apparently the first non-resident members to secure election from the boroughs. Parliamentary life in the fourteenth, fifteenth, sixteenth, and seventeenth centuries, as nowadays, had obvious advantages and many prizes for those whom the Journals describe as the gentlemen of the long robe. At times the presence of lawyers was undoubtedly of advantage to the House. But after this has been conceded, and every tribute has been paid to those lawyers who helped to mould the House into the great institution which by the seventeenth century it had become, it has to be stated that if proclamations, statute books, and the Journals are to be relied upon, no class of men of the House continuously gave it more trouble. There are more entries in the Journals concerning lawyers than concerning all other classes of men combined. Most of the entries are due to the lawyers' habit of combining attendance in Parliament with the pushing of professional business in the courts; and to an equally well-marked and persistent determination to turn their membership of the House to advantage in their professional careers.

An Attempt
to exclude
them.

From the time when lawyers began to be of the House in any large numbers, there were objections to their presence. As early as 1330, long before the boroughs had become so easily open to them, there was an ineffectual attempt to exclude lawyers from the representation of counties[1]. In 1372 one of the first questions which occupied the House of Commons was a complaint that lawyers abused their privileges as members of Parliament by taking advantage of these privileges to promote the business of their clients[2]. Resulting from this complaint there was enacted the statute of 46 Edward III, which in its preamble set forth

[1] Cf. Longman, *Edward III*, i. 348.
[2] Cf. Longman, *Edward III*, ii. 216.

that "men of the law who follow divers businesses in the King's courts on behalf of private persons do procure and cause to be brought into Parliament many petitions in the name of the Commons which in no wise relate to them." To end this abuse it was enacted that henceforward "no man of the law following business in the King's court was to be returned or accepted as a member of the House of Commons[1]."

The exclusion, brought about in 1372, was not long operative. In the next century the cities and boroughs began to send their recorders to represent them in the Commons. Between 1372 and 1547, when the Journals begin, outsiders had largely possessed themselves of borough representation, and many of these outsiders were lawyers. Testimony to the presence of lawyers in the House is abundant as soon as the entries in the Journals begin to be full and detailed. In the reigns of Elizabeth and James I there were frequent orders directing the sergeant-at-arms to summon members who were of the bar to their duties in the House; and from the beginning of the reign of James I there are entries recording leave of absence granted to lawyers by the House, in order that they might go on circuit. *Failure of the Attempt.*

James I had no liking for members of the House who were of the bar; and when the Parliament of 1624–25 was about to be elected, he issued a proclamation in which constituencies were counselled "not to choose curious and wrangling lawyers, who may seek reputation by stirring needless questions[2]." That lawyers were comparatively numerous in the Parliaments of James I, and that they were alert in the House for their professional interests may be judged from a resolution which the House negatived in 1615. "Sir Edward Hobby," reads the entry in the 'Journals, "moveth that the sergeant may go to all the courts to move them from the House to hear those of the House before the others; that so they may attend their service in the House, and yet not lose their practice[3]." In the reign of Charles I it was proposed that "the judges be moved to give precedence in the motions to all such lawyers as are members of this House[4]." This motion of 1640 failed to pass, like that of 1615, which was to the same effect. *Lawyers seek Advantage from their Position as Members.*

In the Cromwellian Parliaments the persistence with which the

---

[1] Cf. 46 Ed. III.
[2] Barrington, *On the Statutes*, 337.
[3] *H. of C. Journals,* i. 479.
[4] *H. of C. Journals,* ii. 9.

Difficulty in securing Attendance of Lawyer Members.

lawyers put their business in the courts before their duties in the House was again a source of trouble.   In 1657, on the occasion of a motion that the sergeant-at-arms go with the mace into Westminster Hall to bring the lawyers into the House, it was proposed that the judges there should be required to sit at seven o'clock in the morning, and to rise at ten, to meet the convenience of members of the bar who were of the House.   " You will make yourselves very cheap," said Mr Bond, who supported the motion, " to send your mace every day out for your members.   I would rather have you to require your judges to sit at seven and rise at ten, that all may attend ; and if you take away the counsel wholly, you will undo many a poor man who has retained them from the beginning in their causes."   Against this proposal it was urged by Mr Weaver that the House ought not to put the judges " to harder task than ourselves, that are younger constitutions, to sit at seven."   "I would rather," he continued, " have you require the counsel to attend here, or stick wholly to their practice, and let others come in their places that will attend.   We have little of their help either here or below (at committees, I mean), though they are very useful, I confess, if they would apply themselves in it[1]."

Objections to Lawyers in the House.

In and out of Parliament, at the time of the Great Rebellion, there was much opposition to the presence of lawyers in the House.   In 1645, when members taking part in divisions in the House seldom exceeded one hundred and thirty-five, and when new writs were being issued by the score to replace members who had been excluded by the House[2], an anonymous pamphlet was issued to the electors counselling them against choosing lawyers.   " I have heard old men say," the author wrote, " they remembered when lawyers at the beginning of a term would stand at a pillar in Paul's, Temple Bar, the corner of Chancery Lane, and other avenues, attending the coming-in of their countrymen, with cap in hand, courteously saluting them and inquiring what business brought them to town, not much unlike watermen plying for a fare.   But now they are grown to that height of pride that a man can hardly, after long attendance, come so near a great lawyer's study door as to bid God save him, without a fee or a bribe."   " Take heed," the writer went on, after having shown that many lawyers had risen from nothing to great estates, "how you fill up elections with these

---

[1] Burton, *Cromwellian Diary*, ii. 394.   [2] Parry, 445, 446, 448.

kind of men. The recorder of every borough will, of course, look to be chosen as being the mouth of the corporation; but it is a custom not fit for the necessity of these times. Our affairs require rather statesmen than lawyers." "If the making and penning of good laws were the work of these times—as they are not—" he continued, "it were not wisdom to choose mercenary lawyers to make laws, because they are the first men to invent subtilties to evade them, and make them useless, and will pen them obscurely on purpose to make themselves work in the interpretation." "Lawyers being a bold and talkative kind of men," reads the last of these objections to lawyer-candidates, "will intrude themselves into the chairs of all committees, where, being accustomed to take fees, they will underhand protect delinquents and their cancelled estates with tricks and devices." It was also necessary that Parliament should "make a law for the limitation of exorbitant fees and prevarication amongst lawyers," and limit the number of practitioners in each court. "This blessing you will never attain unto," the pamphleteer finally declared, "unless God give you the wisdom to avoid such elections[1]."

Pride was even more outspoken against lawyers who were of the House than the unknown author of the pamphlet of 1645, whose denunciations, according to an introductory note by Sir Walter Scott, the editor of the *Somers Tracts*, "made such an impression on the public that John Cooke, of Gray's Inn, who acted after as solicitor in the trial of Charles I, set forth a long and laboured answer to them[2]." Pride declared that it would never go well with the country until the lawyers' gowns, like the Scottish colours, were hung up in Westminster Hall[3]. In the Rump Parliament there was a great pique against the lawyers, "insomuch," Whitelocke records, "as it was again said, as it had been formerly, that it was not fit for lawyers who were members of Parliament, if any lawyers ought to be of Parliament, to plead or practise as lawyers during the time they sat as members of Parliament[4]." Whitelocke championed the lawyers and their right to be chosen and to sit as members. To him it was just as reasonable to enact that merchants should forbear their trading; to forbid physicians from visiting their patients, and country gentlemen from selling

Feeling against them in the Rump Parliament.

---

[1] Some Advertisements for the New Election of Burgesses for the House of Commons, 1645, *Somers Tracts*, v. 62.

[2] *Somers Tracts*, v. 62. [3] Barrington, 337.

[4] Whitelocke, *Memorials*, III. 118.

their corn and wool while they were of the House, as to deter
lawyers who were of it from following their practice while Parliament was in session[1].

Claims for
Pre-audience
in the
Courts.

After the Restoration lawyers were again of the House in large
numbers; and at this time members of the House who were of the
bar individually claimed pre-audience from the judges as a Parliamentary privilege. Prynne asserts that lawyers who were of the
House gained clients and fees in consequence, and he urged such a
revival of the Act of Edward III—held by lawyers such as Coke
and Whitelocke to have been repealed by legislation in the reigns
of Richard II and Henry IV—as would prohibit lawyers who were
of the House from practising in the courts while Parliament was in
session[2].

Neglect
of Parlia-
mentary
Duties.

At this period also there are again frequent entries in the
Journals respecting lawyers, similar to those which first began to
make their appearance in the reign of Elizabeth. Again the
sergeant-at-arms with the mace was making his round of the
courts in Westminster Hall, summoning gentlemen of the long
robe to attendance on the duties of the House[3]. Again also the
Speaker was sending out his letters to members of the bar who had
gone on circuit, recalling them to Westminster[4]; and again, as in
the reign of James I, when a bill touching the law was referred to
a committee, after the names of members selected for the committee
there was added, " and all the gentlemen of the long robe[5]."

Gentlemen
of the Long
Robe.

Exactly whom this description " gentlemen of the long robe "
included was never authoritatively settled until some years after
the Reform Act. After 1832, as for two centuries preceding,
gentlemen of the long robe were sometimes added to committees.
They were added to a committee under this designation in 1847;
and as two Queen's counsellors, who had long ceased to practise in
the courts, regarded themselves as coming within the meaning of
the old term, their right to be of the committee came up for
settlement. As a search in the Journals afforded no explanation of
the meaning of the term, on the suggestion of Speaker Denison it
was agreed that " the best definition would be that all who were
entitled by the usage of the profession to hold a brief should be of
the committee[6]."

---

[1] Whitelocke, *Memorials*, iii. 124.

[2] Cf. Prynne, *Survey of Writs*, 618; Whitelocke, *Memorials*, iii. 117–124.

[3] *H. of C. Journals*, ix. 102, x. 421.   [4] *H. of C. Journals*, ix. 571.

[5] *H. of C. Journals*, ix. 326.   [6] Denison, *Notes from My Journals*, 6, 7.

In the eighteenth century lawyers seem to have made fewer Popular attempts than in the seventeenth to turn their membership of Distrust. the House to direct advantage in the law-courts. There are now no entries in the Journals of motions like those of 1615 and 1640, intended to establish a right of pre-audience in the courts for lawyers who were in the House of Commons. But, as in the preceding century, Parliamentary life offered many and great prizes to the gentlemen of the long robe; and the eagerness with which they manœuvred for them, especially in the last half of the century, engendered a popular distrust of lawyers in the House of Commons and in political life which survived the Reform of 1832.

" No one conversant with the political literature of the middle Trevelyan's of the eighteenth century," writes Trevelyan, in describing the Characteri- place of the lawyer in political life during the early years of the sation. reign of George III, " would deny that the members of the House who, as a class, then enjoyed the affection and confidence of their colleagues in the least ample measure, were the lawyers. Something of their unpopularity may be traced to a social prejudice against men who had worked their way from a humbler level into a sphere which, but for their intrusion, the aristocracy would have preserved almost exclusively to itself.   But the small esteem in which gentle- men of the long robe were very generally held was due to what Bubb Dodington and Henry Fox would have termed moral causes. Everybody—such would be the theory of those profound observers— was greedy, but the lawyer was selfish.   Everybody was ready to change sides with the rest of the connection to which he belonged ; but the lawyer ratted alone, and at the moment which suited his individual interest.   The Bedfords hunted in a pack ; the Pelhams ran in couples ; but the lawyer pursued his peculiar prey with solitary avidity, and with a clamour which went far to spoil the sport of the entire field.   It was bad enough that a barrister with a seat which he had bought cheap from some patron of a borough who had overstayed his market should talk of himself as ill-used if he did not secure a recordership in the course of his second session, and a judgeship before the end of his second Parliament. * * * But it was positively insufferable that a quiet supporter of the Government, who after much study and many misgivings had screwed himself up to the determination of showing his leaders that he could speak as well as vote, should find himself forestalled at every stage of the debate by the fluency of men whose trade, as Chatham told them, was words. * * * Ten words from Conway or Savile went further than an hour of Sergeant Nares or Dr Hay; and there was nothing more sure to take with the House of Commons than an allusion to the difference in quality of the attention which it paid the statesmen who were thinking of their subject, and the aspirants for legal promotion who were thinking of themselves[1]."

A Radical View.

This was the House of Commons view of its lawyer members. The outside view, the popular view as expressed by Radicals at the end of George III's long reign, is summed up in the famous *Black Book*, which was first published in 1820. "Lawyers," it is there written, "are eaten up by mutual rivalry and ambition. It is a profession into which no one enters without views of aggrandisement. If by any contrivance or claptrap the representative function be obtained, it is mostly used only as a stepping-stone to wider practice at the bar, or to government employment[2]."

Lawyers in the Modern House.

The reforms in the representation which came in 1832, and again in 1867 and 1884, have worked but little change in the lawyer element of the House of Commons. They have not made membership of the House less desirable to lawyers. In the first House elected after the Reform Act of 1832 there were seventy-one barristers[3]. In the last Parliament of Queen Victoria's reign there were one hundred and thirty-one barristers in and out of practice, and nineteen solicitors[4]. The advantages which accrue to barristers from a seat at Westminster are even greater to-day than they were in the reign of George III. The widespread publication of speeches in Parliament by the newspaper press makes it much easier than it was before the Reform Act for lawyers to add to their reputation by their activity and prominence in political life. For lay members of the House of Commons there are to-day far fewer prizes than there were when the treasury whips had commissionerships and other highly paid offices in the civil service for distribution among adherents of the Government. But for the lawyers there are more prizes than ever; more recorderships, more appointments as stipendiary magistrates, more county-court judgeships, and more judgeships in the higher courts; while in the nineteenth century, as in the eighteenth, a seat in the House was usually a makeweight in favour of a barrister who applied for the rank of Queen's Counsel[5].

[1] Trevelyan, *Life of Fox*, 378–380.   [2] *Black Book*, 61.
[3] *Black Book*, 61.   [4] Cf. *Co-operative Annual*, Manchester, 1900, 501.
[5] Cf. Selborne, *Memorials*, ii. 22.

Long before the Reform Act of 1832 the sergeant-at-arms had ceased to make his appearance in the law-courts summoning gentlemen of the long robe to their duties in the House. By this time also Speaker's letters recalling lawyers to the House from the circuits had fallen into desuetude. But in the nineteenth century the disposition of lawyers to shirk the less showy but more arduous Parliamentary duties was as marked as at any time in the history of the House. At the end of the century this abstention had come to be looked upon so much as a matter of course that the standing committee charged with the selection of committees had long maintained a distinction, by which members of the bar were exempted from committee service, a duty to which all other unofficial members were liable[1].

The reign of Elizabeth witnessed the entrance of merchants and traders into the House as the representatives of cities and boroughs of which they were not residents. Merchants and traders of London represented that city all through its Parliamentary history. There is good reason to think that this is true also of Bristol, as it is of Liverpool from the time when that borough became of some importance as a port[2]. But the earliest instance which I have found of a merchant being elected for a city or borough other than that in which he was commercially established was in 1562, when Coventry returned Richard Grafton, a London merchant and member of the Grocers' Company[3]. Grafton had twice been of the House as one of the members for the City of London before he was chosen at Coventry. In the same reign, in 1601, John Herrick, a London goldsmith and money-lender, was returned for the borough of Leicester, where he had been born in 1557[4]. In the reigns of James I and Charles I merchants and traders became more numerous. Rolle, who represented Callington in the Parliament of 1628-29, and who came into conflict with the officers of the Crown in the tonnage and poundage seizures, was a London merchant[5]; and in this Parliament Aldborough, then of importance in Suffolk as a commercial and shipbuilding town, was represented by Marmaduke Rawdon, the son of a gentleman of good family and small estate, one of the smaller

---

[1] Cf. D. A. Thomas, M.P., Letter to the Committee of Selection, *The Times* (Weekly Ed.), March 4th, 1898.

[2] Pink and Beavan, *Parl. Representation of Lancashire*, 178.

[3] *Dict. Nat. Bio.*, xxii. 312.   [4] *Dict. Nat. Bio.*, xxvi. 243.

[5] Cf. Forster, *Life of Eliot*, ii. 406.

gentry of the county, who in the sixteenth and seventeenth centuries thought it no degradation to bring up their sons to trade and commerce in London[1]. Pennington, Soame, Venn, and Vassal, all citizen merchants, represented London in the Parliament of 1640[2]; and that there were others of the merchant-class is shown by an order of the House of December 4th, 1640, " that Mr John Moore and all the merchants of the House be added to the committee for monopolies[3]."

Intrusion of the Newly Rich.   After the Restoration the courtier and the lawyer candidates had increasingly to compete with merchants. At Lynn Regis, in 1673, Francis North, who was then solicitor-general, was opposed by Sir Simon Taylor, a wealthy wine merchant who was resident there[4]; and a few years later, when Charles II's third Parliament was being elected, Evelyn, who had been an office-holding member of the Parliament of 1661–68, lamented the activity and prominence of the new men of wealth in the Parliamentary contest. He complained that "worthy persons of known integrity and ability in their respective counties," who would still serve the electors "generously and as their ancestors have done," had to stand aside because they were not able "to fling away a son's or daughter's portion to bribe the votes of a drunken multitude, more resembling a pagan bacchanalia than an assembly of Christians and sober men, met upon the most solemn occasion that can concern a people; and stand in competition with some rich scrivener, brewer, banker, or one in some gainful office whose face or name " the electors perhaps had never seen before[5].

Their Purchase of Seats.   Although merchants and traders representing cities and boroughs with which they had no permanent connection began to find their way into the House of Commons in the reign of Elizabeth, the courtiers and lawyers would seem not to have felt their competition in the boroughs until the reign of Charles II. Henceforward, however, this new competition was to become much more keen, and it accounts in part for the fact that from the beginning of the eighteenth century may be dated the system of openly selling nominations for boroughs.

Returned East Indians.   Despite the Act of Queen Anne's reign, establishing landed qualifications for members of the House of Commons, as the

---

[1] *Life of Marmaduke Rawdon*, Camden Society, 1863, Introd., ix., x.
[2] Masson, *Milton*, ii. 173.   [3] Rushworth, *Hist. Collections*, iv. 84.
[4] *Lives of the Norths*, i. 176.
[5] Evelyn, *Diary*, Bohn Ed., ii. 276, 277.

eighteenth century progressed men who had made their wealth in
the City of London, or acquired it from the enterprises of the East
India Company, found their way in larger numbers into the House.
As early as the reign of Charles I the East India Company was
established in the dominion of fourteen sovereign princes; it had
twenty-three factories .in India, at which it was represented by
ninety-two English factors or agents; and was then employing
twenty ships[1]. In the reign of Charles II returned East Indians
were buying landed property and establishing county families[2].
Soon after the Revolution men who, like Sir Bazil Firebrace, had
become rich through their connection with the East India Company,
were of the House of Commons[3]; and by this time returned East
Indians, men like Thomas Pitt, Governor of Madras, were spending
some of their enormous wealth in the acquisition of boroughs like
Old Sarum, and were being returned to Parliament[4].

With the developement of the enterprises of the East India
Company there was an increase in the number of Anglo-Indians
desirous of being of the House of Commons; and in the early years
of the reign of George III prices for nominations for boroughs had
been forced up to four thousand pounds[5]; whilst in the smaller
householder boroughs, in which East Indians tried their fortunes at
the polls, bribery was so open and profuse as occasionally, even in
that loose period, to bring a candidate into the custody of the
sergeant-at-arms[6]. At this time there were complaints against
Anglo-Indians similar to those which a century earlier Evelyn had
made against the scriveners, bankers, and brewers who had amassed
their wealth in the City of London. "Without connections," said
Lord Chatham, in speaking of them and their inroads into the
borough constituencies, "without any natural interest in the soil,
the importers of foreign gold have forced their way into Parliament
by such a torrent of corruption as no private hereditary fortune
could resist[7]."

East Indians and Corruption.

Most of these possessors of ducal incomes had one aim in view.
Like Clive, the object of their desire was ·a peerage. Almost
invariably the Anglo-Indians supported the administration. So

East Indians and Administrations.

[1] *Hist. MSS. Comm. 10th Rep.*, App., pt. VI. 156.
[2] Cf. *Hist. MSS. Comm. 14th Rep.*, App., pt. IX. 506.
[3] Cf. *H. of C. Journals*, XI. 317, 318.
[4] *Dict. Nat. Bio.*, XLV. 347; *Official List*, pt. I. 562, 577.
[5] Massey, *Hist. of England*, I. 336, 337.
[6] Oldfield, IV. 449.
[7] Trevelyan, *Life of Fox*, 143.

did their nominees when, like Clive, they had followed the example of Governor Pitt, and ventured part of their fortunes in borough property; and at the time of the American Revolution the Anglo-Indians formed a group on the benches below the gangway on the government side of the House[1].

Manu-facturers in the House.

Bankers, merchants, brewers, and traders had been long of the House before men engaged in manufacturing, or their sons, began to find their way into Parliament. The first industries to be represented there were the Worcestershire iron trade and the west of England clothing trade.

The Foleys.

Early in the seventeenth century Richard Foley embarked in the iron trade near Stourbridge. He learned the secret of the Swedish process of iron making, engaged in the manufacture of iron on a scale which ultimately brought him an income of five thousand pounds a year, and died in 1657 possessed of enormous wealth. His son, Thomas Foley, who was associated with him in the iron industry, acquired large estates in Worcestershire. He was high sheriff in 1658; and in the Convention Parliament of 1660 represented the borough of Bewdley. About this time the Foley family got control of the borough of Bewdley; later on of that of Droitwich; and in the closing years of the seventeenth century they were also politically dominant at Stafford and Weobly. Between the Revolution and the reign of Queen Anne Paul and Philip Foley, sons of Thomas Foley, were of the House of Commons, and in 1695 Paul Foley, then knight of the shire for Worcestershire, succeeded Trevor as Speaker. A grandson of Thomas Foley became Baron Foley in 1711; and during the greater part of the eighteenth century Droitwich at least was under the control of the Foley family[2].

John Methuen.

The first of the Foleys who went into the House of Commons, Thomas Foley of the Convention Parliament, may fitly be described as a manufacturer, since he was actively engaged with his father, Richard Foley, in the Stourbridge enterprise. In the case of the clothing industry it was the son of a manufacturer who first went into Parliament. In 1690 John Methuen, son of Paul Methuen, a prosperous clothier of Bradford, Wiltshire, was elected for

---

[1] Trevelyan, *Life of Fox*, 503.

[2] Cf. Oldfield, v. 253, 258, 259; *Hist. MSS. Comm. 14th Rep.*, App., pt. ii. 469, 473, 474, 475, 558; Smiles, *Self-Help*, Ed. 1877, 205, 207; Orme, *Life of Richard Baxter*, ii. 128, 129; *Official List*, pt. i. 517, 535, 539; *Dict. Nat. Bio.*, xix. 354, 355, 356.

Devizes to the House of Commons in which sat two of the grandsons of Richard Foley. Methuen had been educated at Oxford, and called to the bar before he was of the House of Commons[1]: so that he is scarcely to be classed among manufacturers, although he may be described as a representative of wealth acquired by manufacturing.

The next manufacturers to be of the House were of the cotton trade, or, as they were called in the closing years of the eighteenth century, the "cottoners[2]." But there was a long interval between Thomas Foley's election to the Convention Parliament of 1660, and the appearance in the House of Commons of a man who had come into wealth and prominence from his connection with the great Lancashire industry which had its beginnings, or rather reached the factory stage, in the opening years of the reign of George III. Sir Robert Peel, father of the more famous Robert Peel, commenced manufacturing cotton in 1764, and he ranks among the pioneers of the factory era of the industry. He entered the House as one of the members for Tamworth in 1790. While he was in Parliament, Peel is said to have had 1500 workpeople in his employ at Bury and other centres of the Lancashire trade. The first Sir Robert Peel, like the Foleys, spent part of his wealth in the acquisition of political influence. Tamworth, near which he had established himself as a landowner in 1788, soon became a Peel borough. The elder Peel sat as one of the members continuously from 1790 to 1820. Then he was succeeded by his second son, William Yates Peel, who had previously been of the House as member for Bossiney—a nomination borough like Cashel, for which the elder Peel purchased an election for Robert Peel in 1809[3].

The Yorkshire woollen industry entered on the factory stage about 1794[4]; and between the election of the elder Peel at Tamworth in 1790, and the Reform Act of 1832, the Lancashire cotton industry was enormously developed. But in this period the only other manufacturers who were of the House, so far as I can trace, were John and Samuel Horrocks. John Horrocks began cotton spinning in Preston in 1786, about the time that Sir Robert Peel

The Cottoners. The Peels

The Horrockses.

---

[1] *Dict. Nat. Bio.*, xxxvii. 310 ; *Official List*, pt. i. 570.

[2] Cf. Wallas, *Life of Francis Place*, 174.

[3] Cf. Parker, *Sir Robert Peel*, i. 5, 6, 24; *Official List*, pt. ii. ; *Civil Correspondence of the Duke of Wellington*, v. 619 ; *Dict. Nat. Bio.*, xliv. 210, 213.

[4] Cf. Webb, *Hist. Trade Unionism*, 34.

had amassed a fortune and was contemplating establishing his
family near Tamworth.   Later, his elder brother Samuel Horrocks
joined him in the mill at Preston ; and when John Horrocks died
in 1804 he had, chiefly through the manufacture of muslins for the
East India trade, amassed a fortune of seven hundred and fifty
thousand pounds.   As was the case with the Foleys and with the
elder Peel, the Horrocks brothers pushed into politics ; but unlike
the earlier manufacturers who were of the House, they did not go
afield for boroughs to control.   Preston was a householder borough
with over two thousand electors.   The Horrockses were large
employers of labour ; and about 1796 they began to dispute the
political supremacy which the Earls of Derby had long and easily
held in Preston.   In 1796 John Horrocks failed in his candidature
there, although he had the support of the Earl of Liverpool, then
chancellor of the Duchy of Lancaster, in addition to that of the
famous Church and King Club of Manchester.   At the 1796 election
he was less than a score of votes behind Sir H. P. Hoghton, a local
landowner, who was returned as junior member with Lord Stanley.
But in 1802, as a result of a coalition of the Derby and Horrocks
political interests, John Horrocks was successful, and represented
the borough at the time of his death in 1804.   The coalition of
1802 was continued, and John Horrocks was succeeded by his elder
brother Samuel, a partner in the great cotton mills, who represented Preston until 1826[1].

George III
and Men in
Trade.

Between the Revolution and the end of the eighteenth century
these new interests in the House, the bankers, merchants, Anglo-
Indians, and manufacturers, received but small recognition in the
way of office from succeeding administrations.   Peerages were
occasionally bestowed on bankers and Anglo-Indians.   Knighthoods
and baronetcies were the highest rewards that the most wealthy of
the traders and manufacturers could expect, no matter how constant
and subservient their support of the Government ; for throughout
his reign George III adopted as a fixed principle, that no man
engaged in trade, however ample might be his nominal fortune,
should be created a British peer[2]; and while the well-born politicians of the Georgian era were ready to welcome any member of
a family which they socially recognized, they knew the secret of
making public life uncomfortable to the vulgar herd[3].

[1] *Official List*, pt. ii. 219, 232, 246, 261, 275, 288 ; Oldfield, iv. 97 ; *Dict.
Nat. Bio.*, xxvii. 375.
[2] Wraxall, *Posthumous Memoirs*, ii. 66.   [3] Cf. Trevelyan, *Life of Fox*, 499.

Soon after the Revolution the Foleys and the Harleys became allied; and largely as a result of this alliance a Foley was chosen to the Chair of the House. Of the merchants who were of the House in the first half of the eighteenth century Sir John Barnard was about the only one to achieve a Parliamentary reputation. He was a debater of the first rank, whom even Walpole could not ignore[1]. But the nineteenth century was advancing and the great reform of 1832 was at hand before the son of a merchant or manufacturer was of the Cabinet. Peel became secretary of state for the home department in 1822[2]; and in 1827 Herries, the son of a London merchant, became chancellor of the exchequer[3].

Cabinet Rank for the Newly Rich.

Not until after the Reform Act did any member of these new classes in the House hold the highest political office within reach of a British subject; and when this great prize fell to Sir Robert Peel, it was soon made evident that the feeling of the well-born politicians described by the author of the *Life of Fox* had outlasted the eighteenth century, and survived unabated even the Reform Act and the changes which that measure was popularly supposed to have made in English political conditions. Peel himself alluded to this feeling in a speech at Merchant Taylors' Hall in May, 1835, a speech in which he did not hesitate to group himself with the manufacturers. " Will you allow me," he then said, " to recall to your recollection what was the grand charge against myself?—that the King had sent for the son of a cotton spinner to Rome, to make him prime minister of England. Did I feel that by any means a reflection on me? Did that make me at all discontented with the laws and institutions of the country? No; but does it not make me, and ought it not to make you, gentlemen, do all you can to reserve to other sons of other cotton spinners the same opportunities, by the same system of laws under which this country has so long flourished, of arriving by the same honourable means at the like distinction[4]? "

Sir Robert Peel.

Scotchmen domiciled in England were first of the House of Commons in the reign of James I. The new King was accompanied to England by many of his countrymen, who were advanced to honour and shared in the King's bounty. Englishmen were jealous of these new-comers, and of their good fortune; and several times

Scotchmen and English Constituencies.

[1] Cox, *Life of Walpole*, i. 344.
[2] Parker, *Sir Robert Peel*, i. 300.
[3] *Dict. Nat. Bio.*, xxvi. 256.
[4] *The Times*, May 12th, 1835.

in the reign of James I it was proposed in the House of Commons that, in the bills for naturalising Scotchmen, a clause should be inserted making them ineligible for Parliament[1]. None of these proposals was carried; but twice in the reign of James I Scotchmen who had been elected were, on proof that they had not been naturalised, disqualified from sitting in the House[2]. After the reign of James I, and after the Parliaments of the Commonwealth, it is possible to discover a Scotchman occasionally seeking election for a borough. Ross, secretary to the Duke of Monmouth, was an unsuccessful candidate at Liverpool in 1670[3]. But until after the Union few Scotchmen wooed borough constituencies, the only constituencies which either before or after 1707 were really open to them.

Irishmen in the House before the Union.

Englishmen were of the Irish Parliament as early as the reign of Elizabeth, when Hooker, who had been of the House of Commons at Westminster as one of the members for Tiverton, represented the borough of Athenry in the Irish House of Commons. To Sir John Clotworthy would appear to attach the distinction of being the first Irishman to be of the English House of Commons. He was elected for the Cornish borough of Bossiney in 1641[4]. The appearance of an Irishman in the House of Commons was then remarkable. Clarendon took note of it; and he attributes Clotworthy's election to "the contrivance and recommendation of some powerful persons," whose purpose was that the Irish knight should attack Strafford, who was then Lord Lieutenant; and he adds that, in accordance with this plan, Clotworthy made in the House of Commons a long and confused relation of Strafford's "tyrannical carriage in Ireland; of the army he had raised there to invade Scotland; and how he had threatened the Parliament[5]."

Irish Peers in the House of Commons.

After the Revolution the number of Irishmen in the House of Commons increased. Irish peers now began to bargain for nominations from borough owners; and in the reigns of the first two Georges Irish peers, in quest of government appointments or of elevation to the peerage of the United Kingdom, or desirous of becoming marriage-known, could not make a better investment

---

[1] Cf. *H. of C. Journals*, i. 493, 494.
[2] Hatsell, ii. 2.
[3] Pink and Beavan, *Representative History of Lancashire*, 139.
[4] *Official List*, pt. i. 486.
[5] Clarendon, *History of the Great Rebellion*, i. pt. i. 172, 173.

than the purchase of a seat in the House of Commons[1]. These were political adventurers from Ireland. In the reign of George III Irishmen of another and distinctly better type were of the House, men whose names stand out in Parliamentary history. Burke was returned for Wendover in 1765; and between then and the Union there were at Westminster two other Irishmen, Flood and Tierney, both of whom had achieved fame as orators in the House of Commons of the Irish Parliament.

[1] Cf. Torrens, *Hist. of Cabinets,* i. 452.

CHAPTER XXVII.

PROCEDURE OF THE HOUSE.

Modern
Procedure
identical
with that of
1547.

THE most remarkable fact in regard to the procedure of the House is the small change which has taken place since, in the reign of Henry VII[1], enactment by bill superseded enactment by petition. It is not affirming too much to say, that the last House of Commons which met in the old Chapel of S. Stephen's—that of the Parliament in existence at the time of the fire of 1834— was following in its main lines the procedure which the Journals show to have been in use when, in 1547, the House migrated from the Chapter House of Westminster Abbey to the famous Chapel which Edward VI then assigned to the Commons for their meeting-place. First reading, second reading, reference to committee, third reading, the stages of a bill in the House of Commons as we know them to-day were the steps in procedure when the House first met in S. Stephen's, and the Journals now printed were begun on the 8th of November in the first year of Edward VI.

Procedure
by Bill.

In the interval between the reign of Edward I and the reign of Henry VII, that is during the first two hundred years of the House of Commons, petitions were the basis of legislation. Most of them were complaints of the breach of old customs, or requests for confirmation of new customs which evil-disposed persons would not observe; and in these two centuries Parliament was a law-declaring rather than a law-making body[2]. Towards the close of this period the form of bill, drawn as a statute, began to take the place of petition. This custom was introduced first in the

---

[1] Cf. Stubbs, III. 480.

[2] Cf. Jenks, *Law and Politics in the Middle Ages*, 63, 64.

legislative Acts which were originated by the King—government measures as they would to-day be called—when the law proposed was laid before the two Houses in the form which it was ultimately to take. Next this procedure was adopted in private petitions. The new form was found convenient by the Commons in their money grants to the Crown, grants which they had been making " with the advice and assent " of the House of Lords since the reign of Richard II. It was found convenient also by the King in bills of attainder; and from the reign of Henry VII it became applicable to all kinds of legislation[1].

Not, however, until the reign of Edward VI is there explicit testimony as to how the House of Commons proceeded with its work. Even in the reigns of Edward VI and of Mary, and in part of that of Elizabeth, entries in the Journals are exceedingly brief. They do little more than show that the present-day form of procedure was at that time established. But it is possible to supplement the Journals by extra-official yet authentic statements, such for example as the descriptions of procedure written by Hooker, and D'Ewes's *Journals.* Hooker was of the House at this time; and D'Ewes in the next century devoted many years of his life to collecting and compiling the history of Queen Elizabeth's Parliaments[2]. From these three sources it is possible to learn how nearly the procedure of the House in the long reign of Elizabeth resembled that of the period when the first Reform Act was passed.

Evidence concerning Procedure.

The first bill entered on the Journals was intended to enact " that clothiers shall not take aliens to their apprentices," a measure which apparently failed, for no trace of it is to be found in the statutes[3]. Brief as are the entries, the early pages of the Journals show that all bills which passed the House at this period had three stages. More than that cannot be determined; and not until 1572 is there an entry which shows that after second reading it was the practice of the House to refer a bill to committee. The first bill of which there is an entry of reference to committee was for an almshouse at Plymouth—a bill which, to quote the words of the Journals, was " committed unto Mr Edward Stanhope and Mr Robert Snagge, and by them in certain points amended and returned again[4]."

Stages of a Bill in 1572.

---

[1] Stubbs, iii. 459, 480.   [2] Cf. *Dict. Nat. Bio.,* xiv. 451.
[3] Cf. *H. of C. Journals,* i. 1; *Chronological Table of the Statutes,* 9th Ed., 48.
[4] *H. of C. Journals,* i. 95.

Committee
Stage before
1572.

The practice of committing bills in this way was certainly of an earlier date than 1572. Hooker wrote his statement for the Irish Parliament of 1568–71; and he there states that "when any bill is committed, the committees have not authority to conclude, but only to order, reform, examine, and amend the thing committed unto them, and of their doing they must give report to the House again, by whom the bill is to be considered." "Every bill which is brought into the House," he continued, "must be read three several times, upon three several days; and a bill which upon any reading is committed and returned ought to have its three readings, unless the committee have not altered the bill in any substance or form; but only in certain words[1]."

Procedure
in Elizabeth's
reign.

The permanent establishment of this form of procedure did not date much further back than the time at which Hooker undertook to enlighten and guide his fellow-members of the Irish House of Commons; for D'Ewes states that "bills have been committed on first reading down to as late as Henry VIII and Edward VI," and that this procedure was sometimes followed in the reign of Elizabeth[2]. The two statements show that as early as Elizabeth's reign the present-day form of procedure—first reading, second reading, committee, report, and third reading—was in use. At this period and for a long time to come, after second reading there was, in respect to a bill which had originated in the House of Commons, a motion for engrossment, "which," to quote D'Ewes, "is no more than to transcribe the bill fairly out of the paper in which it was written into parchment[3]."

Rules of
Debate.

Hooker makes no mention of rules of debate affecting each stage of a bill. He describes what should be the behaviour of a member who was addressing the House on a bill; but gives no hint as to the stage at which the principle of a measure should be debated, and when discussion of details was in order. "If a man do speak unto a bill, and be out of his matter," he wrote, "he ought to be put in remembrance of the matter by the Speaker only and by none other, and be willed to come to the matter. Whenever any person doth speak to any bill he ought to stand up and be bare-headed, and then with all reverence, gravity, and seemly speech to declare his mind[4]."

Debate at
Second
Reading.

The modern procedure which, except in special instances, admits of no debate at first reading, and ordains that debate on

[1] Mountmorres, i. 147, 148.   [2] D'Ewes, *Journals*, 17.
[3] D'Ewes, *Journals*, 18.   [4] Mountmorres, i. 148, 149.

the principle of a bill shall be on second reading, and discussion of details in committee, had apparently not been developed to this point at the time when Hooker wrote. But it would seem to have been reached a few years later. In 1581, when Popham, who represented Bristol in the Parliament of 1581–83, was elected to the Chair, he made a speech in which he suggested that members should forbear speaking to bills at first reading[1]. This may possibly have been only a suggestion that the House should adhere to an existing order. But whether Popham's suggestion was for an amendment in the order of procedure, or for a revival of an order which had fallen into desuetude, it was apparently adopted and adhered to in the later years of Elizabeth's reign. D'Ewes makes this clear. " Most true it is," he wrote, " that usually a bill is seldom rejected until second reading; for then it is most proper to be spoken unto; and when it hath received either a longer or shorter disputation in the House, then the proceedings commonly are either to order it to be engrossed, or refer it to committees[2]."

Although the Journals and this extra-official evidence show *Committees.* that between 1570 and the beginning of the reign of James I procedure was much as it is to-day, at this period it differed in practice in one noteworthy detail from that of the House of Commons of the twentieth century. The term " committees " as used both by Hooker and D'Ewes means members of a committee; for as yet bills were seldom or never dealt with in committee of the whole House. At this time, when a bill was referred to committee the members of the committee were named, and thus a select committee was constituted; and usually there was added to the order by which the committee came into existence an instruction as to where it should meet. Committees often met elsewhere than at the House; as at Lincoln's Inn Hall, Middle Temple Hall, Sergeant's Inn Hall, and sometimes at Guildhall[3].

By the reign of James I committees of the whole House, as *Procedure in* we know them to-day, had their place in the stages of a bill. As *Committee.* early as this, distinctions were drawn between the House with its Speaker and mace, and committees of the whole House without these formalities; and also between the methods of telling in a division in the House, and in a division in committee[4]. As early

---

[1] *H. of C. Journals,* i. 118.   [2] *D'Ewes, Journals,* 17.

[3] D'Ewes, *Journals,* 231, 345, 346, 355, 410, 412.

[4] Forster, *Life of Eliot,* i. 237 ; Coke, *Fourth Part of the Institutes of the Laws of England,* Ed. 1648, 35.

as this it was an established rule that debate should be freer
in committee than in the House. "At second reading," wrote
Eliot, in describing the progress of a bill through the House,
"all objections come in. Then were particulars both of the form
and matter argued and debated; and thereupon it passed to
commitment, when, by answer and reply, the discussion might be
freer in the counterchange of reason and opinion. The latter is
not admittable in the House, where, to avoid contestation and
disorder which replies and contradictions might introduce, and
to preserve the gravity, no man may speak in one day and to
one business above once, though he would change opinion, which
in committee is allowable; and therefore, upon the second reading
of bills, they have such reference and commitment, that there
they may be the more punctually considered, and so come to
the exacter re-formation and amendment. In general all committees are for the preparation and despatch; the judgment and
conclusion is the House's. To facilitate that court in the multi-
plicity of her labours these are the Argus and the Briareus[1]."

The Speaker and Committee.

It is possible by 1640 to see the Speaker withdrawing from
the House when it goes into committee, and leaving the chairman
in charge. Onslow, the famous Speaker of the reign of George II,
held that when the House was in committee the Speaker's place
was elsewhere, ánd that he could not be summoned back to the
Chamber until the committee was ready to report and the House
to resume. Lenthall preceded Onslow in the Chair by nearly a
hundred years; and presumably it was conceded, when he was of
the Chair, that the House could not command the attendance of
the Speaker when it was in committee; for on November 11th,
1640, a resolution was passed that "Mr Speaker be entreated to
be here this afternoon to sit by at the grand committee, if there
be cause to resume the House[2]."

The Chairman of Committees.

Not until 1800 was there a permanent Chairman of Committees.
The creation of the office of Chairman of Ways and Means dates
from the same year; and that was the first year in which an
address was voted to the Crown for the payment of a salary for
this office. From the Revolution, however, it was the custom
for the chair of the committees of supply and of ways and means
to be ordinarily taken by the same member for several years in
succession; and during the last half of the eighteenth century he

---

[1] Forster, *Life of Eliot*, I. 236.   [2] Parry, 342.

became known as the Chairman of Ways and Means[1]. Until this new office was created in 1800 all members were held to be equally eligible for the office[2]. In the Long Parliament, in May, 1641, when the committee on Episcopacy was sitting, Hyde was put in the chair "that he might not give them trouble by frequent speaking, and so too much obstruct the expediting of the bill[3]," a novel but very practical way of silencing a House of Commons bore.

While until 1800 there was no permanent Chairman of Committees, much power gradually came to be vested in the member who was voted into the chair at the clerk's table. Like the Chairman of Committees and Deputy-Speaker of to-day—an office created in 1854[4]—the Chairman in the old days was not subordinate to the Speaker. The Speaker had no control over him. If he ruled wrongly there might be an appeal to the House. No appeal of an individual member lay to the Speaker from a decision of the Chairman. The only appeal was from the committee, when the Chairman was directed to report to the Speaker any question of order which might have arisen in committee[5]. None the less the minor importance of the Chairman must always have been manifest to the House; for in the unreformed Parliament, as in the Parliament of to-day, the Speaker sat in a great chair, commanding the House; while the Chairman of Committees sat beside the clerk, dressed as an ordinary member; and while he was at the table the mace, denoting the authority of the House, was out of sight. Until the office of Chairman of Committees was created in 1800 there were no emoluments for the Chairman. *The Nature of his Office.*

Not until 1854 was the Chairman of Committees vested with authority to take the Chair of the House in the temporary absence of the Speaker; although there is direct and presumptive proof that for three hundred years before the creation of the office of Deputy-Speaker in the reign of Queen Victoria, the House was at times much inconvenienced, and public business delayed, by the lack of an officer who could act for the Speaker during his *The Deputy-Speaker.*

---

[1] Cf. *Report of the Select Committee on the Office of Speaker*, 1853, 3.

[2] Cf. Hatsell, II. 147; Burton, *Cromwellian Diary*, II. 254.

[3] Parry, 354.

[4] 18 and 19 Vict., c. 84.

[5] Cf. Wemyss Reid, *Memoirs of Lord Playfair*, 291, 292; *Report of the Select Committee on the Office of Speaker*, 1853, 15; Denison, *Notes from My Journals*, 9.

unavoidable absences[1]. There were constitutional difficulties in the way of the creation of the office of Deputy-Speaker ; difficulties arising from the relation of the Speaker to the Crown, and particularly from the fact that the choice of Speaker by the House is subject to the approval of the sovereign. Another reason for the unwillingness long displayed by the House to create the office of Deputy-Speaker was advanced by the committee which, in 1853, was deputed to consider the desirability of the creation of the new office. "They cannot," the committee then reported, "overlook the hazard which would arise from the destruction or diminution of the prestige which has, for a century and a half at least, attached to the office of Speaker, as held undivided by one man, and which the willing confidence of the House has always sustained, evidenced as it has been by the implicit acquiescence in the decisions of the Chair, which, with scarcely an exception and certainly without any record to the contrary, has appeared to characterise all the proceedings of the House during that period ; and by the respect uniformly shown to the person and office of the Speaker, a respect never more due than at this day. This confidence and respect, cheerfully paid to one man selected by the House for the office, cannot be expected to attach easily to another, who may be his substitute for a few days and then sink again into the general body of the House[2]."

Instructions to Committee. Nineteenth century usage also made another change in the procedure as to committee. At an early period after the institution of committees the practice of moving instructions came into vogue, and until 1849, on every occasion on which a bill went into committee, instructions might be moved before the Speaker left the Chair. By the modern regulations all instructions must be moved on the first occasion on which a bill goes into committee, as no opportunity now presents itself for an instruction when progress is established[3].

A Modern Amendment in Procedure. It is not my purpose to follow in detail the history of the organisation of the House and the developement of its modes of procedure beyond 1832. But parenthetically it may be remarked that it was in connection with committees—select committees and committees of the whole—that the nineteenth century witnessed some of the most important changes in House of Commons

---

[1] *Report of the Select Committee on the Office of Speaker,* iii.–x., xvii.

[2] *Report of the Select Committee on the Office of Speaker,* iii.

[3] Denison, *Notes from My Journals,* 52.

procedure. When it is remembered that under eighteenth century procedure instructions could be moved on each occasion when the House went into committee on a bill, and that there could be debate and divisions on motions nominating a chairman[1], it will be realized how great is the saving of time and the elimination of opportunities of obstruction which have come from these nineteenth century amendments in procedure.

In the eighteenth century members went in and out of any private bill committee. They sat and voted as they pleased. In the early years of the nineteenth century, at the opening of the railway era, when Parliamentary counsel were making fortunes in a single session and the lobbyist was rampant at Westminster, this looseness of committee organisation became a scandal. Members of the House who had not attended a committee, and consequently had not heard the evidence for and against a bill, were beset and importuned by lobbyists to attend the committee when it was agreeing on its report, and give their votes for or against the scheme. Under the terms of the reference to committee all members of the House who attended "had voices"; and it was not unusual for scores of members, who were susceptible to this system of canvassing, and who knew nothing of the merits of the bill, to vote in committee. Committees were, on these occasions, so thronged with members that outside the House it was a widespread popular delusion, and one which survived even the second Reform Act, that members received ten guineas for attendance on committee, and that they were qualifying for this fee when they crowded in to vote. When complaint of the scandal was made in 1834 one member, Lord Granville Somerset, who had been of the House since 1816, drew on his recollections of committee procedure of an earlier day. "Bad as the conduct of committees might be," he said, "and he certainly did not defend it, the mode of conducting business before committees at present was greatly superior to the practice formerly[2]."

Division lobbies date from the occupation of the temporary chamber after the fire of 1834. Hooker, whose narrative may be accepted as describing House of Commons procedure about 1570, makes no mention of divisions. This omission, in a statement so minutely detailed, warrants the inference that at

Voting in Private Bill Committees.

Divisions.

---

[1] Hatsell, II. 147; Burton, *Cromwellian Diary*, II. 254.

[2] Cf. Hansard, 3rd Series, XXV. 1129–1131, XXXIV. 120; *Official List*, pt. II. 262.

this time divisions were so few that no machinery for telling the House had as yet been devised. But by 1593 a usage in regard to divisions was established, which was continued as long as the Commons met in the ancient Chapel of S. Stephen's. On the second reading of a bill for the better expedition of justice in the Court of Star Chamber, which came before the House in 1593, " there was," wrote D'Ewes, " much division thereupon." " Wherefore," he continued, " the Speaker propounded the question that as many as will not have the bill rejected say ' ay,' and the others say ' no.' The voice was so indifferent that it could not be discerned which were the greater. Then the question grew whether part should go out—those that said ' ay ' or those that said ' no.' Mr Speaker said the order of the House is that ' ay ' being for the bill must go out, and that ' no ' against the bill doth always sit, The reason is that the inventor, that will have a new law, is to go out and bring it in, and they that are for the law in possession, must keep the House, for they sit to continue it[1]." This explanation from the Chair, and the fact that such an explanation was needed, would seem to show that up to 1593 divisions had not been frequent ; or at any rate that as yet the order and usage of them were not well established.

Tellers.

Before the end of the reign of Charles II there is evidence that procedure as to divisions had been further developed. It was now the rule that, when a division was called, the Speaker should nominate " two of those that are in the affirmative, and two of the negative, to count the House ; which four, each of them having a staff in his hand, are to count the number of persons who remain sitting in the House, and then stand within the door, two on the one side and two on the other, and count the number of them who went forth, as they come in[2]." From this time also dates the usage, still followed, in accordance with which, when the tellers advance from the bar to the table to report a division to the Speaker, those who are of the majority advance towards the Speaker's right hand. In committee in the latter half of the seventeenth century, on a division the numbers were ascertained by the ayes going to one side of the Chamber, and the noes to the other[3].

[1] D'Ewes, *Journals*, 505.

[2] *Memorials of the Method and Manner of Proceedings in Parliament*, 1670, 26.

[3] Cf. *Memorials of the Method and Manner of Proceedings in Parliament*, 1670, 26 ; Coke, *Fourth Part of the Institutes of the Laws of England*, 1648, 35 ; *Rules and Orders of the House of Commons*, 9th Ed., 82.

Early in the eighteenth century voting by ballot was introduced Voting by in the determination of election petitions. In 1707 the House Ballot on appointed a committee to revise the mode of procedure in election Petitions. cases. The committee reported on February 18th in favour of election petitions being heard at the bar, and also made a recommendation " that all questions at a trial of elections shall, if any member insist upon it, be determined by ballot." The House agreed to the report, and instructed the committee which had presented it to consider " of the proper method for the said balloting." On February 21st the committee recommended that a ballot box and balls be prepared; that two clerks attend in the House when a division is taken, one to deliver the balls, the other to carry the box; that two members appointed by the Speaker attend the box; and that when a ballot is being taken " each member present his hand, bare and open, to receive the ball, and that he hold it up between his finger and thumb before he put his hand into the box, and that the box be immediately afterwards brought to the table, and the votes counted there by the clerk in the presence of the said two members." It was further recommended that it should be an order " that all members sit in their places till the votes are given, and the affirmative or the negative declared by the Speaker[1]."

All the recommendations of the committee were agreed to by The Plan in the House, and the resolutions in which they had been embodied Operation. by the committee were added to the orders[2]. The first petition determined in accordance with the new orders was from Ashburton. It came before the House on February 26th, 1707. A ballot was taken, after which " the box was carried to the clerk's table, and after counting the balls at the table by the clerks, in the presence of the said two members, who stood at each end of the table, the two members went to the bar, and came up to the table as usual on other occasions of reporting, and reported to the Speaker[3]."

High expectations were entertained of this new method of Expectations ascertaining the will of the House. " I don't doubt," Vernon from the Plan. wrote to Shrewsbury, on February 9th, 1707, " but you have the votes sent to you. Those of yesterday contain something remarkable as introducing the ballot on questions relative to elections. It may be hereafter carried further; and how convenient that will be to a court and a monarchy time will show. It was

[1] *H. of C. Journals*, xv. 551–559.   [2] *H. of C. Journals*, xv. 559.
[3] *H. of C. Journals*, xv. 577.

afterwards moved that the Speaker should be chose by balloting; but Mr King, who was the chairman of committee that brought in these regulations, said he had not heard before of that motion, and thought time ought to be allowed to consider it, which stopped it for the present. But it may be taken up again when the method of balloting comes to be reported from the same committee[1]."

The Plan abandoned. The new method of dealing with contested elections was originated in the closing days of the Parliament of 1705–8. When the Parliament of 1708–10 assembled in November, 1708, the orders of the previous Parliament were again adopted[2]. But the next day, by a vote of one hundred and seventy-eight to one hundred and sixty-nine, the order as to the use of the ballot was rescinded. At this period election petitions were seldom determined on their merits; and with many controverted elections pending, as was usual at the opening of a new Parliament, the administration would not be likely to give its countenance to any plan which in the least degree tended to ensure a non-partisan vote on an election petition. At this time the majority of the members of the House of Commons, nearly all those from the boroughs and from Scotland, had no constituents whom they need fear, or who were much concerned as to how they voted at Westminster. But had voting by ballot been extended to other divisions than those on election cases, as Vernon thought it might be, such a method of voting would have been extremely inconvenient to Government. It must have weakened the control of administration over the House of Commons; and with conditions as they were throughout the eighteenth century, a ballot which was really secret, to say nothing of its undesirability as affecting the constitutional relations of members and constituents, could never have had the sanction of Government.

The Hearing of Election Cases. From 1604 until 1708 election petitions were determined by committees of privileges and elections, whose reports were adopted or rejected by the House[3]. In the Pensioner Parliament there was a variation from this procedure, and the committee on elections became an open committee of the whole House[4]. After the Revolution the old plan was reverted to, and petition cases were again

[1] *Vernon Letters,* iii. 351, 352.   [2] Cf. *H. of C. Journals,* xvi. 6.

[3] Cf. Anson, pt. i. 149, 151; *H. of C. Journals,* x. 481, 482, 492, 507, 508.

[4] Anson, pt. i. 151.

heard by committees of privileges and elections[1]. In 1690 there was a movement for the trial of election cases at the bar. A bill was passed by the House of Commons to this end, but was thrown out in the House of Lords[2]. Had this bill of 1690 become law it would have been imperative on the House to have heard all these cases at the bar, and to have dealt with all election petitions presented on the assembling of a new Parliament before the House turned its attention to any other business[3]. In 1708 the House appointed a committee to consider methods for the speedy determination of controverted elections: and on the recommendation of this committee it was ordered that " all matters which shall come in question touching returns or elections shall for the future be heard at the bar of the House[4]."

A petition from Ashburton was heard on the 26th of February, 1708, in accordance with this new method of procedure; but the practice then begun was not uniformly followed. After 1708 committees of privileges and elections again heard petitions[5]; but from the time of Arthur Onslow's tenure of the Chair until 1770 petitions were, with increasing frequency, heard at the bar and determined by the House[6]. During this time committees of privileges and elections also heard petition cases, and when a petition first came up in the House it was decided by vote whether it should be heard by the House or by the committee[7]. There would seem to have been no uniform rule as to whether petitions should be heard before the committee or by the House. When they were taken in the House counsel and witnesses were heard at the bar, and a member whose election was controverted was permitted to defend his return from his seat[8]. In the eighteenth century there were sometimes as many as sixty or seventy controverted election cases at the opening of a new Parliament; and although a large part of the first session was occupied with them, some of the petitions went over to the second, occasionally even to the third, session of the Parliament[9].

Petitions heard at the Bar.

---

[1] *Cal. of State Papers,* Domestic Series, 1689–90, 169 ; *H. of C. Journals,* x. 481, 492.

[2] *H. of C. Journals,* x. 531; *House of Lords MSS., Hist. MSS. Comm. 13th Rep.,* App., pt. v. 251, 252.

[3] *H. of C. Journals,* x. 531. [4] Luttrell, vi. 269.

[5] *H. of C. Journals,* xxi. 117, xxvii. 623. [6] Cf. Anson, pt. i. 151.

[7] Cf. *H. of C. Journals,* xxiii. 5, xxv. 449.

[8] Cf. *H. of C. Journals,* xx. 621. [9] Cf. *H. of C. Journals,* xlviii. 741.

The Gren-
ville Act.

In 1770 the hearing and determining of election cases was transferred from the House to committees of fifteen members, whose determinations were final. The change was brought about by the Grenville Act, carried against the opposition of George III and the North Administration[1]. The reasons for the change are set out in the preamble. They were that the old method of procedure obstructed public business; caused much expense, trouble, and delay to the parties concerned; and was defective from want of those sanctions and solemnities which were established by law in other trials[2]. Hatsell, who was at the clerk's table during nearly the whole of the period in which election cases were heard at the bar, described the Grenville Act as "one of the noblest works for the honour of the House of Commons and the security of the constitution that was ever devised by any minister or statesman."

Balloting a
Grenville
Committee.

Under the provisions of the Act a day was appointed for taking a petition into consideration: and as soon as the sergeant-at-arms had secured the attendance of one hundred members, counsel for the petitioner and for the sitting member were called to the bar. The doors were then locked, and the names of all the members of the House were written on separate pieces of parchment or paper. These were put in equal numbers in six glasses, and the clerk drew them out in turn until the names of forty-nine members then in the House were drawn. Not every member who was drawn was liable for service. Members over sixty years of age were excused. So were members against whose returns petitions were depending. Members who were already serving on select committees, or had so served during the session, might also be excused; and a member who had voted at the election in dispute was disqualified. As many as thirty or forty members were at times thus set aside. When the names of forty-nine members, all eligible for service, had been drawn, counsel for the petitioner and for the sitting member each named a member from among those in attendance, whose names had not been drawn. The doors of the House were then unlocked. The parties to the petition withdrew and alternately struck off one member from the list of forty-nine, until the number was reduced to thirteen, after which the thirteen so remaining, together with the two nominated members, were sworn at the table to try the

---

[1] Cf. *Chatham Correspondence*, III. 439.   [2] 10 Geo. III, c. 16.

petition, and to give a true judgment according to the evidence. Next, a time was fixed for the meeting of the committee, which had to be within twenty-four hours of its appointment; and until a time of meeting was appointed none of the fifty-one members drawn or named of the committee was to leave the House. The committee was compelled to sit every day, usually from ten o'clock in the morning until three in the afternoon. It could not adjourn for longer than twenty-four hours without leave of the House. No member of the committee was to be absent without leave of the House, and it was made incumbent on the Chairman to report to the House any absentees without leave.

A petition from the county of Pembroke was the last heard at the bar[1]. The last case heard by the committee of privileges and elections was from Dover[2]. The first case reported from a Grenville committee was from New Shoreham. The corruption of the Christian Club was then exposed[3], and following this exposure there was the Act of Parliament by which New Shoreham, for electoral purposes, was thrown into the rape of Bramber.

New Shoreham.

Partisan influences were not eradicated by the transference of petitions to Grenville committees[4]. When petitions were determined by the House members were openly canvassed for their votes. After the Grenville Act the House made an order " that no person do presume to solicit the attendance of members when the matter of any petition complaining of an undue election or return is ordered to be taken into consideration[5]." But in spite of this order, members were canvassed by both parties to a petition to attend in the House when the ballot for a committee was being taken[6]. The committees at best were not ideal tribunals for the determination of the questions which came before them. Procedure was slow. The shortest cases were seldom determined in less than a fortnight. Frequently committees were occupied for from thirty to forty days; and the average expense of a committee was a hundred pounds a day[7]. But the new method was a distinct improvement on the old openly partisan method of

Working of the Act.

---

[1] *H. of C. Journals*, April 27th, 1770, xxxii. 904.

[2] *H. of C. Journals*, March 12th, 1770, xxxii. 779.

[3] *H. of C. Journals*, xxxiii. 70.

[4] Ridgway and Son, *Abuses of Election Committees*, 1837.

[5] *H. of C. Journals*, xxxviii. 273.

[6] Cf. *Mirror of Parl.*, 1835, ii. 1908; May, *Hist. of England*, i. 367.

[7] Cf. *H. of C. Journals*, xlviii. 741.

determining these cases by a vote of the House; and in 1774, again in spite of the opposition of George III and the administration[1], an Act was passed making the Grenville Act of 1770 perpetual[2].

Difficulty of Securing Attendance. Much difficulty was always experienced in securing the attendance of the hundred members when a committee was to be balloted. In 1793 the House resolved itself into a committee to consider this question; but the only outcome was a recommendation in favour of calls of the House for days on which election petitions were to come before it[3]. There was difficulty also in securing the attendance of members who had been balloted on committees, notwithstanding that the House required strict proof of the facts and circumstances which were alleged in excuse for non-attendance[4]. Petition cases were so numerous and were determined so slowly that it often happened that members whose returns were petitioned against were of the House for three years before their right to their seats was determined[5]. Between 1770 and 1832 there were many amendments to the Grenville Acts intended to simplify procedure or to give new powers to committees; and the Grenville plan survived the Reform Act, and continued in operation, with later amendments, until 1868, when the House at last relinquished the right which it had tenaciously held from the reign of Elizabeth, and an Act was passed transferring to the courts the determination of election petitions[6].

Few Changes in Procedure. The short-lived experiment with the ballot in the reign of Queen Anne, and the turning over of election petitions to Grenville committees in 1770 were the only marked innovations in procedure from the reign of James I to the Reform Act of 1832. In its organisation for work the House of Commons was complete before the Great Rebellion; and on the eve of the Reform Act there was scarcely an order or a usage which could not be traced as far back as the reign of James I or Charles I. In 1640 the quorum of the House was fixed at forty[7].

Reading of a Bill pro formâ. As early as the reign of Elizabeth there is extra-official proof of the existence of the present-day custom by which, at the opening of a new session, the House reads a bill in order to assert its right of deliberation without reference to the immediate cause of summons[8]. The first mention of this custom in the

[1] Donne, *Letters of George III to North*, i. 169. [2] 14 Geo. III, c. 15.
[3] Cf. *H. of C. Journals*, XLVIII. 221, 263. [4] *H. of C. Journals*, XLVIII. 264.
[5] Cf. *Parl. Hist.*, xxx. 468, 471. [6] 31 and 32 V., c. 125.
[7] Cf. Parry, 345. [8] Cf. D'Ewes, *Journals*, 41.

Journals is in 1603, when, under date of March 22nd, there is the statement " that the first day of every sitting in every Parliament some one bill and no more receiveth a first reading for form's sake[1]." This usage could scarcely have arisen before the supersession, in the reign of Henry VII, of legislation by petition by legislation by bill. There is evidence of the usage as early as 1558[2]; and D'Ewes, in his narrative of the opening of the session of 1563, describes in detail the reading of a bill by the House to assert its independence. " The Speaker being placed in the Chair," he wrote, " — Seymour, Esq., clerk of the aforesaid House of Commons, who sat uncovered at a table at the upper end of the House, just before the Speaker, stood up and read a bill, which had been treated of in the last Parliament, being entitled ' the bill touching the felling of wood and timber trees in forests and chases,' which done, kissing his hand, he delivered the said bill to the Speaker, who standing up uncovered (whereas he sitteth covered), and holding the bill in his hand, said the bill is entitled, and then having read the title of the bill, as is before set down, he opened to the House the substance thereof, which it is most probable he did out of the breviate, which was filed to the bill, and had been delivered unto him together with the bill by the clerk of the House aforesaid, which being done, he then said, 'This is the first reading of the bill'; and so delivered it unto the clerk again; which ended, the House arose, which hath been the constant use and custom ever since, and also divers years before, that after the presentment and allowance of the Speaker, one bill be once read after his return from the Upper House in the House of Commons[3]."

Some practices on the part of members of the House which have been regarded as modern innovations, and due chiefly to the incoming of the Irish members, were well established before the Great Rebellion. In the reigns of James I and Charles I sitting until it was dark was so exceptional with the House, that candles could not be introduced except by the express order of the House. Many a division was taken at this period and later on the question, " that candles be now brought in." A decision in the negative was necessarily followed by adjournment[4]; and the modern House of Commons, the House which is contemporaneous with the printed Journals, may be said to have first turned its attention to a

Obstruction in the 17th Century.

---

[1] Cf. *H. of C. Journals*, i. 150.   [2] Cf. *D'Ewes, Journals*, 41.

[3] *D'Ewes, Journals*, 43, 44.   [4] Cf. *H. of C. Journals*, xiii. 379.

revision of its orders to reduce opportunities for obstruction when, in 1717, it was made a standing order, "that when the House, or a committee of the whole House, shall be sitting, and daylight be shut in, the sergeant-at-arms attending the House do take care that candles be brought in without any particular order for that purpose[1]." This order of 1717, aimed at obstructive tactics which had first come into play in the reigns of James I and Charles I, may not inaptly be described as a precursor of the order of 1849, which diminished the opportunities for debate on the motion that the House go into committee, and of the orders adopted in the Parliaments of 1881–85 and 1886–92 for circumventing the obstructive tactics, then carried further than ever before in the history of the House by the Irish Nationalists led by Parnell and Biggar.

Conservatism of the House.

In a word, by the end of the reign of James I the procedure of the House of Commons had so taken the form in which it came down to the nineteenth century, that could a member of the House of Commons which passed the Reform Act of 1832 have been transported back to the days of the first of the Stuart kings, he would have been at home with the orders and usages, the written and unwritten laws which governed its procedure. He would, it is true, have found the Speaker reading prayers. He would have seen only one clerk at the table. Forty members did not as yet constitute a quorum. Had he failed to comply with the orders of the House calling for attendance on a given day, he would have found the sergeant-at-arms at hand ready to collect for his own use one half the fine of a shilling imposed for tardiness. He would have been free to seat himself on either side of the House; but when it came to the orders and usages governing debate and division, and his bearing towards the Speaker and his fellow members, all would have been as familiar to him as those of the House of Commons in which he had learned the art of Parliamentary business.

[1] *H. of C. Journals,* xviii. 718; cf. Speaker Gully, Lecture on "Some Old Parliamentary Journals," *Manchester Guardian,* Jan. 10th, 1899.

CHAPTER XXVIII.

RELATIONS OF THE HOUSE OF COMMONS TO THE HOUSE OF LORDS.

From the time when the two Houses sat apart—from 1332 until the beginning, in 1696, of the system of government by ministers dependent upon majorities in the House of Commons— the Commons gradually obtained control over the voting of sup- plies and over the right to tax. The rights of the two Houses as to the levying of taxation were not finally and conclusively settled, and the strong position of the Commons did not become absolutely safe from attack until 1678[1]. In the meantime, between 1332 and the Revolution, the Lords had been excluded from any part in the determination of election petitions, and the Commons had denied to the peers, though by no means with success, all right to interfere in the election of members to the Lower House.

Leaving for the present the rights which the Commons obtained over supplies and taxation, the earliest matter in which the Lords were shut out from any interference with the Commons was in regard to disputed elections. In the first century and a half of the representative system, and until seats in the House of Commons came to be in demand, controverted elections were rare. During the period in which manucaptors still had their place in the machinery of the representative system disputed returns, if they were not unknown, must have been infrequent. But early in the fifteenth century the records of these cases begin ; and petitions against returns were presented to the sovereign and determined by the King's Council. In 1417 there was a petition from the county of Rutland. The burden of the complaint was that the sheriff had

[1] Cf. Pike, *House of Lords,* 344.

returned William Ondeby as one of the knights of the shire, instead of Thomas Thorpe, whom it was affirmed the electors had chosen.   The Commons then prayed the King and the Lords in Parliament that the matter might be examined; and the King commanded the Lords in full Parliament to make examination and act according to their discretion.   The Lords called Ondeby and Thorpe before them, and after hearing argument they agreed that the sheriff's return was incorrect, that it must be amended, and that Thorpe must be returned[1].

Indirect Interference of the Lords.   It is doubtful whether the House of Lords ever again exercised jurisdiction in controverted elections; for in 1427 an Act was passed transferring these cases to the jurisdiction of the judges of assize[2], where they remained until the reign of Elizabeth.   The House of Commons then obtained full control over them, a control which it never relinquished until the reign of Victoria, when these cases were again put within the jurisdiction of the judges[3].   After this Act of 1427 peers could interfere only indirectly in the determination of election petition cases.   But in the period between the reign of Elizabeth and the Grenville Act of 1770, whilst partisan considerations determined most of these cases, there is evidence that peers who nominated to the House of Commons whipped up their members, and directed their votes on petitions.

Excluding Peers from Interference in Elections.   Only partially successful also were the Commons in excluding peers from any part in elections.   Letters from peers urging or directing borough constituencies to elect their nominees had long been a cause of complaint when, in 1641, the House of Commons declared " that all letters of that nature from any peers of this realm do necessarily tend to the violation of the privileges of Parliament and the freedom of election," " that notwithstanding such letters, all persons to whom election of knights and burgesses do belong ought to proceed to their election with that freedom which by the laws of the realm and of right they ought to do." Electors were warned that the House " do expect if any such letters from any peers of the realm shall be hereafter sent to them, that the parties receiving the same shall certify the contents thereof, or bring the letters themselves to the Speaker of the House of Commons[4]."

These measures of 1641 had no effect in checking the interference of peers in elections.   After the Restoration it was as

[1] Pike, *House of Lords*, 484, 485.
[2] 6 Henry VI.
[3] 31 and 32 Vict., c. 125.
[4] *H. of C. Journals*, ii. 337.

rampant as ever; and soon after the Revolution the House of Commons again addressed itself to the abuse. In 1689, by Act of Parliament, the Lord Warden of the Cinque Ports was dispossessed of the power which had long been claimed as a right, " of nominating and recommending to each of the said Cinque Ports, the two ancient towns and their respective members, one person whom they ought to elect, to serve as a baron or member of Parliament, for such respective port, ancient town, or member[1]." Dispossessing the Wardens of the Cinque Ports.

At the end of the seventeenth century the House sought, as in 1641, to deal by standing order with the interference of peers. In 1699, after the Earl of Manchester had voted at an election at Huntingdon, the House resolved " that no peer of this kingdom hath any right to give his vote at the election for any member to serve in Parliament[2]." In 1701 this order was supplemented by another which declared " that it is a high infringement of the liberties and privileges of the Commons of Great Britain for any Lord of Parliament, or any lord lieutenant of any county, to concern himself in the election of members to serve for the Commons in Parliament[3]"; and these two standing orders of the reign of William III, with some variation after the Union of Great Britain and Ireland, have been re-affirmed by every House of Commons to the present time. Two Standing Orders.

The order against peers voting at elections was continuously and uniformly effective, for the reason that the House of Commons had jurisdiction over election petitions. Only in the smaller boroughs, where a single vote was of consequence, could there have been any inducement to peers to vote, and in such instances, a peer's vote might invalidate the election. The second order of the House was entirely without effect. Peers never made even a pretence of acting in accordance with it. They never stood aloof from elections to the House of Commons. They were much more active in elections in the eighteenth century than in the seventeenth. The number of boroughs under their control from the Revolution of 1688 to the American Revolution was continually on the increase; so much so that in 1827 two hundred and seventy-six members of the House of Commons were returned by the landed aristocracy, most of them by peers[4]. Non-success of the Attempt of the Commons.

---

[1] 2 W. and M., c. 7.   [2] *H. of C. Journals*, XIII. 64.

[3] *H. of C. Journals*, XIII. 654; cf. Clarendon, *Correspondence and Diary*, II. 305.

[4] Cf. *Croker Papers*, I. 341, 342.

The Voting of Supplies.

Complete success attended the stand which the Commons took with respect to the Lords in regard to the granting of supplies to the Crown. In the early days of Parliament Lords and Commons made separate grants, not in the form of bills. By the reign of Richard II it had become the practice that all grants made by the Commons, all taxation which was to be raised from the people who returned the Commons to Parliament, should be made by the Commons, with the advice and assent of the Lords, in a documentary form which may be termed an Act of Parliament[1]. By the reign of Henry IV three points had been settled as to the constitutional method of voting supplies. They were to be granted by the Commons; to have the assent of the Lords; and to be reported, as is the usage to-day, to the King by the Speaker of the House of Commons[2].

Development of Taxation.

The mode of granting supplies at this time, however, had but little analogy to that of later days. There were long intervals between Parliaments. Grants were made for long periods; often for the life of the sovereign. Taxation did not begin to assume its present form, Parliament did not levy taxes which all classes were to pay, until after the Great Rebellion. At the Restoration, with the abolition of feudal tenures there came a complete revolution in the relations of the great landowners to the State. Their feudal obligation to provide a national army had now come to an end. The great landowners now constituted but a small proportion of the whole population. Everything that was necessary for the public service had now to be raised by taxation; and the members of the House of Commons represented nearly the whole of the persons who were to be taxed. When, therefore, the Commons claimed, as they did immediately after the Restoration, exclusive privilege in regard to money bills, not only was there historical ground for their pretension, but also a powerful argument in the interests with which they were charged[3].

The First Contest with the Lords.

The first fully recorded contest on this great question was over a bill which was of merely parochial importance. In 1661 the House of Lords was concerned at the deplorable condition of the streets of Westminster, through which the King had to pass when he went in state to Parliament. They accordingly passed and sent to the House of Commons a bill for paving and repairing the streets in the neighbourhood of Westminster Palace. When the

---

[1] Cf. Stubbs, iii. 459; Denison, *Notes from My Journals*, 57.
[2] Cf. Pike, 342.
[3] Cf. Pike, 342.

bill reached the Commons an objection was promptly raised. "This House," reads the first entry in the Commons' Journals regarding the bill, "observing that the said bill was to alter the course of law in part, and to lay a charge upon the people; and, conceiving that it is a privilege inherent in this House that bills of that nature ought to be considered here, Ordered that the said bill be laid aside, and that the House of Lords be acquainted with the reason for doing so." Moreover it was ordered that the House of Lords be "asked not to suffer any mention of the bill to remain in their Journals"; and that they be "further acquainted that this House, finding the matter of their bill to be very useful, and of public concernment, have ordered a bill of the like nature to be prepared and brought in to-morrow[1]."

This was on the 24th of July, 1661. The next day the substitute bill was introduced in the Commons. It was then read a second time; and progress on it was so much expedited that by the 27th of July it had been read a third time and sent to the Lords[2]. On the 29th of July the bill was back in the Commons, with a proviso which the Lords desired to be embodied in it[3]. The Lords objected to the quashing of their bill, and to the substitution of the bill which had originated with the Commons. They cited, in support of their contention that such a bill could properly originate in the Lords, an Act of 1562 for the relief of the poor[4]; an Act of 1588 for the improvement of Dover harbour[5]; and an Act passed about the same time for the preservation of Orford Haven[6]; all of which had originated with the Lords, although apparently not without protest from the Commons[7]. "Yet out of their tender and dutiful respect to His Majesty, who is much incommoded by the neglect of those highways and sewers mentioned in the bill, they have," reads the entry in the Lords' Journals, "for this time, in that respect alone, given way to the bill now in agitation which came from the Commons, with a proviso of their Lordships." The Lords' proviso declared that "nothing in the bill shall extend to the privileges of both or either House of

The Lords suggest a Compromise.

---

[1] *H. of C. Journals*, VIII. 311.

[2] *H. of C. Journals*, VIII. 311, 314.

[3] *H. of C. Journals*, VIII. 315.

[4] Cf. *H. of L. Journals*, I. 597, 601, 604.

[5] Cf. *H. of L. Journals*, II. 151, 152.

[6] Cf. *H. of L. Journals*, II. 157.

[7] Cf. D'Ewes, *Journals*, 70, 71, 72, 413.

Parliament," and that the Act " should not be drawn into example
to their Lordships' prejudice[1]."

The Commons insist on their Right.
The Commons would not accept this proviso; but offered one
as a substitute. It read " that nothing in this Act shall be understood, or shall extend to the admitting or creating of any right or
principle of either House of Parliament which have not formerly
and justly belonged to either of them[2]." The Commons objected
to the Lords' proviso because " it did insinuate a right which their
Lordships claimed, which they (the Commons) could not admit[3]."
With the Commons' proviso attached the bill went back to the
Lords. There it was objected that the Commons' proviso destroyed
the proviso of the Lords. The bill failed to pass; and the
Lords contented themselves with a proclamation calling upon the
justices of the peace to clean the streets of Westminster[4]. The
repairs contemplated in the bill went undone; but the Commons
successfully asserted themselves, and by their action in 1661 served
notice on the Lords that all bills involving the expenditure of
money must originate and take their final form in the Lower
House.

The Right again contested by the Lords.
The Lords were not willing to accept this notice of 1661, nor
to regard the question as settled. The question came up again on
a larger issue ten years later. In 1671 there originated with the
Commons a bill for an imposition on foreign commodities. By the
bill as it left the Commons an import duty was imposed on white
sugars at the rate of one penny a pound. The Lords substituted
a halfpenny half-farthing duty. As soon as the amendment was
read in the House of Commons it was resolved, *nemine contra*,
" that in all aids to be given to the King by the Commons, the rate
or tax ought not to be altered by the Lords[5]."

Conference on the Question.
It would seem that the Lords had made the amendment to
provoke another contest on the claim which the Commons had
asserted in 1661; and the Commons were ready to accept the
challenge. After passing the resolution which has been quoted
they proceeded to the appointment of a committee " to prepare
and draw up reasons in order to a conference to be had with the
Lords, why the Commons do not agree with their Lordships' amendment." The Lords agreed to the conference; and on returning
from it the Commons representatives reported that it had been

[1] Cf. *H. of L. Journals*, xi. 328.   [2] *H. of C. Journals*, viii. 316.
[3] Cf. *H. of L. Journals*, xi. 328.   [4] *H. of L. Journals*, xi. 328.
[5] *H. of C. Journals*, ix. 235.

communicated to the Lords "that there is fundamental right in that House alone, on bills of rates or impositions on merchandise, as to the matter, the measure, and the time." They also reported that for the Lords it was claimed that "to alter such a bill is a fundamental, inherent and undoubted right of the House of Peers, from which they cannot depart[1]"; and "that by this new maxim of the House of Commons a hard and ignoble choice is left to the Lords, either to refuse the Crown supplies when they are most necessary, or to consent to ways and proportions of aid which neither their own judgement or interest nor the good of the government and the people can admit[2]."

Nine reasons were advanced by the peers to support their claim, and they wound up their argument with a demand for evidence in support of the claims of the Commons. "If there was delay in granting this aid, at whose door," they asked, "must it lie—theirs that assume to themselves more than belongs to them, to the prejudice and diminution of the others' right; or theirs that do only exercise that just, lawful, and necessary power which, by the very nature and constant practice of Parliament, is and for many ages hath been vested in both Houses[3]?" "We find," they said in their request for documentary evidence, "no footsteps in record or history for this new claim of the House of Commons. We would see that charter or contract produced by which the Lords divested themselves of this right and appropriated it to the Commons with an exclusion of themselves. Till then we cannot consent, or shake, or renounce foundations, in the laying whereof it will not be denied that the Lords and grandees of the kingdom had the greatest hand[4]." *Argument of the Peers.*

To all of this the Commons made only one reply, a reply which was practically an elaboration of the resolution which they had passed when they first found that the Lords had amended the bill. "We rely," they said, "upon usage on our side and non-usage on your Lordships' part, as the best evidences by which your Lordships or we can claim any privilege[5]." The conference took place on the 20th of April, 1671. The Commons' conferrees made their report to the House on the 22nd; and the same day, after the Commons had thanked the Attorney-General who drew up their case, "for his vindication of the Commons' *Reply of the Commons.*

[1] *H. of C. Journals,* ix. 239.
[2] *H. of C. Journals,* ix. 239.
[3] *H. of C. Journals,* ix. 240.
[4] *H. of C. Journals,* ix. 240.
[5] *H. of C. Journals,* ix. 244.

privilege and the just and undoubted right of the Commons of England[1]," Parliament was prorogued, and the drawn battle came to an end[2].

The Contest renewed. Seven years later the contest between the Houses, which had thus abruptly ended in 1671, was renewed. On the 14th of June, 1678, the Commons sent to the Lords "an Act for granting a supply to His Majesty for enabling His Majesty to pay and disband the forces which have been raised since the 29th September, 1677[3]." On the 15th of June the bill was read a second time in the House of Lords; and on the 17th it went to committee of the whole[4]. In committee, on June 19th, a message was received by the Lords from the King "that the French Ambassadors had declared to the Dutch Ambassadors that they would not void any of the places they held in the Spanish Netherlands, until Sweden be effectually restored to the places taken from them; no, notwithstanding that the peace were already signed and ratified between them"; and "that upon this is arisen a difficulty on the side of the Spaniard, whether they will accept the French conditions." On the same day it was ordered by the Lords that this message be communicated to the House of Commons[5].

The Lords again amend a Money Bill. The Commons in the meantime were becoming impatient concerning the bill sent up on the 14th; and on the 20th of June they sent a message to the Lords to remind them of the bill[6]. On the 21st the House of Lords was again in committee on the bill; and at this sitting they introduced an amendment extending the time for the disbandment of the troops from June 30th to July 27th[7]. On June 22nd the bill was returned to the Commons for concurrence in this amendment. The same day the House rejected the amendment, and appointed a committee to search for precedents and draw up reasons to be offered at a conference, why the House would not agree to it[8].

A Deadlock in 1678. The report from the committee was presented by Sir Richard Temple on the 25th of June. As was the usage when a conference was pending, the reasons were twice read in the House. They were agreed to; and a resolution was passed, declaring that the

---

[1] *H. of C. Journals*, ix. 244.

[2] Cf. Annesley, *The Privileges of the House of Lords and Commons Stated and Argued, April 19th and 22nd, 1671*, London, 1702, pp. 2, 4.

[3] *H. of C. Journals*, ix. 495. [4] *H. of L. Journals*, xiii. 251.

[5] *H. of L. Journals*, xiii. 254. [6] *H. of C. Journals*, ix. 502.

[7] *H. of L. Journals*, xiii. 257. [8] *H. of C. Journals*, ix. 504.

Commons found themselves obliged to disagree with the Lords, "by reason of the methods and rights of their own House in a matter very tender to them[1]." They offered, however, to compromise on a proviso which read " that if by reason of the said forces lying dispersed and in remote places, or any other just and necessary impediment, the disbanding thereof cannot be effected by the day mentioned in this Act, that in such case the disbanding be proceeded with in as near the aforesaid day as that work is capable of[2]." The House of Lords would not agree to the proviso[3], and the House of Commons refused to recede from its position[4]. Then the House of Lords asked for another conference, " that His Majesty may not want the money so necessary to his service, and the kingdom's quiet[5]." The second conference, held on June 28th, did not break the deadlock; for neither House would recede[6]. On July 2nd there was a third conference[7], when the House of Commons appointed a committee to draw up a statement of the rights of the Commons in granting money, and to consider how the rights of the House might be asserted[8].

By this committee a report was made, which was approved in the usual manner by the House, in which it was declared that "all aids and supplies to His Majesty in Parliament are the sole gift of the Commons; and all bills for granting any such aids and supplies ought to begin with the Commons; and that it is the undoubted and sole right of the Commons to direct, limit, and appoint in such bills, the ends, purposes, and considerations, conditions, limitations, and qualifications, of such grants, which ought not to be changed or altered by the House of Lords[9]." At the third conference, held on July 2nd, the Commons desired the Lords to consider the condition which the nation would be in for the want of the passing of the bill, and recalled the rule that " whoever makes a proposition to adhere to their own amendments, a second adhering concludes them," " which," it was added, " the Commons say they have done, and that the whole matter lies with your Lordships now[10]." The Commons, in other words, submitted at this conference their ultimatum. The Lords must

The Commons insist on their Claim.

---

[1] *H. of C. Journals*, ix. 505.
[2] *H. of L. Journals*, xiii. 260.
[3] *H. of L. Journals*, xiii. 260.
[4] *H. of C. Journals*, ix. 508.
[5] *H. of L. Journals*, xiii. 262.
[6] *H. of L. Journals*, xiii. 266; *H. of C. Journals*, ix. 508.
[7] *H. of L. Journals*, xiii. 269.
[8] *H. of C. Journals*, ix. 509.
[9] *H. of C. Journals*, ix. 509.
[10] *H. of L. Journals*, xiii. 269.

give way or the bill would fail. When the Lords' conferrees returned to the Upper House the Lord Privy Seal reported "that the managers had done what they were directed by the House, and have left the bill with the Commons[1]." There it stayed. No further progress had been made with it when Parliament was prorogued[2].

Victory of the Commons.

Ever since the contest of 1678 the House of Commons has been governed in regard to money bills by the resolution of the 3rd of July. This resolution did not, in terms, affect the power of the Lords to reject a money bill ; though it denied them the power of initiating or altering one. The Lords could not be taxed without their consent ; but they could not direct the course of taxation[3]. Since then, in bills of supply and in appropriation Acts, the relation of the Commons to money bills has been carefully defined. "We, your Majesty's most faithful Commons," reads the preamble of bills of supply, "have given and granted to your Majesty"; while the preamble to an appropriation Act now reads ; "We, your Majesty's most dutiful and loyal subjects, the Commons of the United Kingdom of Great Britain and Ireland, in Parliament assembled, towards making good the supply which we have cheerfully granted to your Majesty in this session of Parliament, have resolved to grant to your Majesty, the sums hereinafter mentioned ; and do therefore most humbly beseech your Majesty that it may be enacted, and be it enacted by the King's most excellent Majesty, by and with the advice and assent of the Lords, Spiritual and Temporal, and the Commons in this Parliament assembled, and by the authority of the same." In modern times also the speech from the throne at the commencement of each session recognizes the peculiar privilege of the Commons to grant all supplies[4].

A Renewal of the Question in 1747.

The Lords never again assailed the position of the Commons as they did in 1661, 1671, and 1678. The Commons notwithstanding have never ceased to guard their position with the closest vigilance. The establishment of government by cabinet, with the dependence of ministers on the House of Commons which came with it, rendered the principle successfully asserted by the Commons in 1678 less liable to attack than it was in the seventeenth century. But at least on one occasion between the reign of Charles II and

[1] *H. of L. Journals*, XIII. 266.   [2] *H. of C. Journals*, IX. 515.

[3] Cf. Pike, *House of Lords*, 343.

[4] Denison, *Notes from My Journals*, 49 ; May, *Parliamentary Practice*, 534.

1832, a government bill came to grief in the House of Lords because it was in contravention of the rights of the Commons. In 1747, when measures were being pressed through Parliament for the settlement of Scotland after the rising of 1745, the Lord Chancellor introduced into the Lords a bill for the abolition of heritable jurisdictions of justiciary and for the restoration of jurisdiction to the King's court. After the bill had been read a first time a question of privilege was raised. The Lord Chancellor had inserted in the bill a compensation clause under which the court of session in Edinburgh was to ascertain the value of the jurisdictions and report to the King in Council. This gave rise to doubts whether it was or was not a money bill; and without any formal movement on the part of the Commons, the Government deemed it wiser that the bill should originate in the Lower House[1].

Later than this acknowledgment by the Government of the limited powers of the Lords, the Commons literally kicked out a corn bill which had come back from the House of Lords; because " the Lords had ventured to touch a tax, by inserting the words 'that no bounty should be paid on exported corn[2].'" *An Active Protest from the Commons.*

In 1801, at a time of special distress, a bill to empower justices of the peace for a limited time to relieve certain persons from the payment of rates and assessments for the relief of the poor, originated in the House of Lords, and was sent to the Commons. "There the title of the said bill having been stated by Mr Speaker to the House," it was " ordered, *nemine contra*, that the said bill be laid aside[3]." No demur was raised by the Lords. In 1831 another bill to amend the poor law originated in the House of Lords. It was introduced by the Duke of Richmond, and was to amend the law as to settlement by hiring and service. The bill came up for second reading in the Commons on August 31st, when it was ordered that it " be read a second time this day six months[4]." It was put aside solely because it was a measure which, in the opinion of the House of Commons, should have originated there, and not in the Lords; for later in the same session a bill was introduced in the Commons, making the *Commons guard their Right.*

---

1 Cf. Omond, *Lord Advocates of Scotland,* ii. 35, 36.
2 Denison, *Notes from My Journals,* 245.
3 *H. of C. Journals,* LVI. 88 ; *H. of L. Journals,* XLIII. 22, 24, 25.
4 *H. of C. Journals,* LXXXVI. pt. II. 84.

amendments to the poor law proposed in the Richmond bill, and was promptly carried through both Houses[1].

A Scotch Instance.
Much later than these pre-reform attempts of the House of Lords to originate amendments to the poor law which would have affected local taxation—in 1857—there originated in the House of Lords a bill for fixing the salaries of schoolmasters in Scotland. "But the preamble and everything about it," wrote Mr Speaker Denison in his Journals, "pointed it out as a bill which should have originated in the House of Commons. Objection being taken by Mr Crawford, of Ayr, I told the Lord Advocate that the bill could not properly be proceeded with. Bill withdrawn, and a new bill brought in the House of Commons[2]."

Constitutional Result of the Struggle.
The House of Commons in the reign of Charles II asserted its right to initiate and mould all bills affecting national taxation. By the stand the House took between then and the Reform Act, it also secured similar rights in respect to bills affecting local rating. By the three contests, over the Westminster bill of 1661, over the alteration in the duty on sugar in 1671, and over the military forces disbandment bill of 1678, the House of Commons of the Restoration and Pensioner Parliaments, Parliaments not ordinarily associated in the minds of historical students with constitutional advance, rendered to the country services of inestimable value. At a time when modern methods of taxation were originating; when the feudal obligations of the great landowners were at an end; when the clergy were ceasing to be taxed by convocation; and when England was settling down to the new economic and social conditions which date from the Restoration, the House of Commons boldly asserted its position in respect to the Lords, and re-asserted and made secure the right of the Commons to the control of the public purse. Any wavering or compromise on the part of the House of Commons at these crises in the reign of Charles II might have put the Lower House into some such impotent position as that now held by the House of Representatives at Washington, in respect to fiscal legislation. As it was, the House of Commons then compelled the House of Lords to stand clear when legislation imposing taxation was being formulated. The result was that when the era of personal government came to an end, and was succeeded by government by cabinet, the existence of a cabinet came to be dependent solely

---

[1] Cf. *H. of L. Journals,* LXIII. 1090.

[2] Denison, *Notes from My Journals,* 9.

on the House of Commons; and when England became a great
colonial power, and representative government was established in
Canada and Australasia and in the British colonies in Africa,
from the first the chambers elected by the people were placed,
as in England, in control of the purse, and the existence of
administrations, as in England, was made dependent on the
support of that House of Parliament in which bills for levying
taxation must originate.

To-day, a bill not affecting imperial taxation or local rating
can originate in either House. When for instance a bill has
passed all its stages in the Commons it is sent to the Lords.
There it goes through similar stages to those in the Commons.
If the Lords make no amendment the bill is ready for the royal
assent. If amendments are made the bill goes back to the
Commons, with a request from the Lords that the Commons do
concur. Procedure on some such lines as these must have been
necessary from the reign of Henry VII, when legislation by bill
became the rule. But until the Journals begin in 1547, there
are no means of ascertaining the orders and usages which governed
the relations of the two Houses in their legislative work. Communication between them there must always have been. Not,
however, earlier than the reign of Mary is it possible to trace
communication by message, and a fuller interchange by means of
conference. *Procedure on Bills not Money Bills.*

The first conference of which there is a record in the Journals
was in 1554, when in the House of Commons " the Master of the
Rolls and Mr Solicitor declared from the Lords, that they had
appointed the Lord Chancellor, four earls, four bishops, and four
barons, to confer with a number of this House, who immediately
were sent in to them[1]." Of another conference in 1604, on the
subject of wardship, more details are forthcoming in the Journals.
Then the Masters in Chancery—who at this time, and for
two centuries to come, carried messages from the Lords to the
Commons—attended in the Commons to inform them " that their
Lordships had named thirty of that House to meet such a number
of this House as should be thought fit; the place and time to
be the Painted Chamber at two o'clock in the afternoon[2]." *Conferences between the two Houses.*

By this time the orders and usages of conferences are traceable
in the Journals. Most of them had been determined by the *The Lords' Rules of Conference.*

---

[1] *H. of C. Journals*, i. 38.   [2] *H. of C. Journals*, i. 154.

House of Lords, and were inspired by a reminiscence of feudalism. "The place of our meeting with the Lower House upon conference," reads the order of the Lords governing conferences in the reign of Elizabeth and James I, "is usually the Painted Chamber, where they are commonly, before we come, and expect our leisure. We are to come thither in a whole body, and not some Lords scattering before the rest, which both takes from the gravity of the Lords, and besides may hinder the Lords from taking their proper places. We are to sit there and be covered; but they are, at no committee or conference, either to be covered or sit down in our presence, unless it be some infirm person, and that by contrivance in a corner out of sight, but not covered. None are to speak at a conference with the Lower House but those that be of the committee; and when anything from such conference is reported, all the Lords of that committee are to stand up. No man is to enter at any committee or conference (unless it be such as are commanded to attend) but such as are members of the House, or the heir-apparent of a Lord who has a right to succeed such Lord, or the eldest son of any peer who has a right to sit and vote in this House, upon pain of being punished severely with example to others[1]."

The Commons' Rules.

In the Commons the first step towards a conference was the appointment of a committee to draw up reasons to be presented to the Lords. These were reported from the committee to the House, and read a first and second time. At these stages amendments could be offered. After first and second reading the report from the committee became the Commons' presentation of their case[2]. Members were next chosen to represent the Commons; and it was a rule, dating from before 1604, that "upon any conference the number of the Commons are always double to those of the Lords, and the place and time of meeting appointed by the Lords[3]." Concerning the conference of 1554, when the Lords named as commissioners the Lord Chancellor, four earls, four bishops, and four barons, there is no record in the Journals of the number of Commons conferrees appointed[4]; but in 1604, when there was a conference on wardship, and the Lords named thirty peers, the Commons appointed sixty of their members[5].

A usage common to both Houses was that while managers

[1] May, *Parl. Practice*, 419.
[2] Cf. *H. of C. Journals*, i. 350.
[3] Cf. *H. of C. Journals*, i. 154.
[4] Cf. *H. of C. Journals*, i. 38.
[5] *H. of C. Journals*, i. 154.

were at a conference, all other proceedings should be suspended[1]. At conference members of neither House were at liberty to speak, either to enforce the resolutions or reasons communicated, or to offer objections to them. One of their number read the resolutions, and afterwards delivered the paper on which they were written, which was received by one of the managers for the other House. When the conference was at an end, the conferrees returned to their respective Houses, and reported their proceedings. In the case of a conference called by the Commons to object to an amendment made in a bill by the Lords, if the Lords should be satisfied with the reasons offered they would not desire another conference, but would send a message by the Masters in Chancery to acquaint the Commons that they did not insist upon their amendments. On the other hand if they insisted upon the whole or part of their amendments, the Lords would desire another conference and communicate the reasons of their persistence. If the Commons were still dissatisfied with the reasons of the Lords, they might desire a free conference. Procedure at a free conference was materially different from that at an ordinary conference. Then the managers, instead of being confined to the formal communication of reasons, were at liberty to urge their own arguments; offer and combat objections; and, in short, to attempt by personal persuasion to effect an agreement between the two Houses which the written reasons had failed to bring about[2].

As long as conferences were held, the Lords were punctilious in guarding the orders and usages which had originated in their House in connection with them. At the conference of 1604 the Lords protested "that sundry others of both Houses, besides the committee themselves, were present, which was conceived to be against order[3]." The Commons were equally jealous that nothing more in the way of ceremony and deference should be conceded to the Lords than usage demanded, and that the Lords should always treat them with due courtesy[4]. In 1620, when a message was received from the Lords, a member complained that the Speaker was too courteous to the Lords' messengers; that he put off his hat too often; and he reminded him that he should not move until the third congé[5].

In 1675, after a conference had been determined on concerning

---

[1] Cf. May, 413.
[2] Cf. May, 417, 418.
[3] *H. of C. Journals*, I. 156.
[4] Cf. D'Ewes, *Journals*, 558.
[5] Denison, *Notes from My Journals*, 47.

A Confer-
ence breaks
down.

the refusal of counsel who were of the Commons, to plead in the Lords against a member of the House of Commons, the House of Commons failed to send its conferrees. The Lords were affronted, and promptly asked for a conference to treat of the failure of the first conference. At this conference they declared that they had appointed the first conference " out of that constant desire and resolution they have to continue a fair correspondence between the two Houses, which is the essence of Parliamentary proceedings." " For this end," they continued, " their lordships have commanded us to tell you that they cannot but take notice of the House of Commons failing to be, on Friday last, at the conference desired by themselves, and appointed by the Lords at ten of the clock in the Painted Chamber ; that they conceive it tends to an interruption of all Parliamentary proceedings, and to evade the right of the Lords to appoint time and place for a conference[1]." The Lords moved in the matter as one of privilege[2]. The failure of the Commons to send conferrees was due to the fact that when the Lords consented to the conference, they embodied in their consent a proviso that " nothing be offered at the conference that may in any way concern the judicature of the Lords " ; a proviso which the Commons regarded as unreasonable and as adverse to the " course of proceeding betwixt the two Houses of Parliament in coming to a conference[3]."

Decline
of the Con-
ference.

In the eighteenth century conferences were much less frequent, and concerned much less important questions than in the seventeenth. Four years after the Reform Act of 1832 there was a conference between the two Houses[4]. All the machinery and old-world ceremonial for conferences is still in existence. But in 1851 the Houses by resolution agreed to receive the reasons for disagreement or for insistence on amendments in the form of messages, unless a conference should be specially demanded by one or other of the Houses[5] ; and conferences may now be regarded as of the past[6].

Messages
between the
two Houses.

In the seventeenth century joint committees of the two Houses were occasionally appointed. But between 1695 and 1832 these committees fell into desuetude[7]; although again, as in the case of conferences, all the machinery for bringing joint committees

---

[1] *H. of C. Journals*, ix. 348.
[2] *H. of L. Journals*, xii. 706.
[3] *H. of C. Journals*, ix. 350, 351.
[4] Anson, pt. i. 246.
[5] Cf. *Rules and Orders*, 146, 147.
[6] Cf. Pike, 251.
[7] May, 419.

into existence still survives. Towards the end of the eighteenth century means were devised for bringing select committees of the two Houses into communication[1]. Nowadays messages are the usual means of communication between the Commons and the Lords ; and even in the ceremonial of messages there were great changes in the direction of simpler procedure in the nineteenth century. In the unreformed House of Commons, when a bill was sent to the Lords it was usually carried thither by the chairman of the committee which had considered it, and the usage was that he should be accompanied by not less than seven other members of the House of Commons. The Lords sent their messages to the Commons by the Masters in Chancery or the judges.

The rules of the Lords governing the reception of messages dated from 1597. In that year there was a dispute as to how members from the Commons should be received by the Lords, the Commons having complained of a lack of deference. The Lords then formulated in an order of their House the code which was to govern the reception of members from the Lower House. It set out " that when any bills or messages are brought from the House of Commons to be presented in the Upper House, the Lord Keeper and the rest of the Lords are to arise from their places and go down to the bar, there to meet such as come from the House of Commons, and from them receive in that place their messages or bills. But contrariwise, when any answer is delivered by the Lord Keeper in the name and behalf of the House to such knights and burgesses as come from the House of Commons, the said knights and burgesses are to receive the same, standing towards the lower end of the House without the bar, and the Lord Keeper is to deliver the same sitting in his place with his head covered, and all the Lords to sit in their place[2]." *The Lords' Rules governing the Reception of Messages.*

Soon after the Reform Act the ceremony attending the interchanges between the Houses was curtailed. The number of members attendant on a bill to the Lords was reduced to four[3]; and since 1855 bills have been carried by clerks of either House, and received at the bar while the House was sitting or in committee without interrupting the business then proceeding[4]. Seldom, however, do the Houses entirely abandon the usages which have come down from an earlier period. In this case *Simplification of Procedure.*

[1] May, 420.

[2] D'Ewes, 585.

[3] Denison, *Notes from My Journals*, 47.

[4] Cf. *Rules and Orders*, 145.

while a simpler method of communication was adopted the newer
method was introduced without formally superseding the older
one.

Bills which
must origi-
nate in the
Lords.

It has always been the custom of Parliament that bills which
affect the rights of the peerage should originate in the House
of Lords, and that they should not be amended in the House of
Commons, though that chamber has always had the power of
rejecting them. This usage was ignored by the Commons in the
last Parliament of Charles I, when bills were introduced for
depriving the bishops of their votes in Parliament, and otherwise
affecting the House of Peers. In modern times, in 1832 and
1867, there were again departures from the usage; but in neither
instance did the bill pass the House of Commons. In 1832 a
member gave notice of his intention to move for a bill to prevent
members of the House of Lords from voting by proxy. The notice
was, however, withdrawn on an intimation that it was an interference with the privilege of the House of Lords. In 1867 a
bill was introduced to alter the mode of electing representative
peers in Scotland and Ireland. This bill did not get beyond first
reading; so it may be said that the usage has been continuously
observed[1].

Attendance
at the Bar of
the Lords.

From the time when the Houses sat apart there have always
been, as there are to-day, occasions on which members of the
House of Commons attend at the bar of the House of Lords.
At the opening of a new Parliament they attend there to receive
the direction from the sovereign to choose a Speaker; and again,
usually on the following day, that the sovereign may approve
of their choice. At the opening of each session they also attend
to hear the speech from the throne. They attend when the royal
assent is given to bills, when money bills are presented by the
Speaker to the sovereign, and when, at the end of the session,
Parliament is prorogued.

Treatment
of the
Commons by
the Peers.

From as early as the beginning of the Journals, heirs-apparent
to peerages, whether of the House of Commons or not, were
accorded special privileges in the House of Lords[2]; and, as time
went on, these privileges were extended to men allied to the peerage,
when, as members of the House of Commons, they attended in
the Lords. A line was drawn between Commoners who were
allied to the peerage and all others of inferior standing, a line
which was especially marked in the eighteenth century. "Lords'

[1] Cf. Pike, 336; Parry, 377, 379.   [2] Cf. May, 419.

brothers and Lords' cousins," said Rigby, a prominent member of the House of Commons, in tones of complaint in 1777, " might be accommodated behind the throne; but the rest of that House must be content to stand below the bar, with an intolerable crowd of other persons, and with a risk of having their pockets picked[1]." In the early years of the reign of George III the relations of the two Houses were not marked by any special cordiality; for in 1772 Burke complained that he had been kept for three hours at the door of the House of Lords, whither he had gone to carry up a bill[2].

In the Chamber of the House of Commons to-day there is The Peers' a gallery for peers. The peers' gallery dates back at least as far Gallery. as 1698. At the trial of Sir John Fenwick in that year the Speaker's chamber and the lobby were ordered to be cleared of all persons not concerned in the trial. "But it having been said that the Lords did admit the members of this House to hear their debates, there was private intimation given to the sergeant to let them remain in the Speaker's gallery when others were removed[3]."

Elsewhere reference has been made to the number of orders Lawyer in the Commons' Journals concerning members of the House who Members were of the long robe. From the reign of Elizabeth to that of the Lords. Anne many of these orders were intended to regulate the attendance as counsel in the House of Lords of members of the Commons who were of the bar. During this century and a half there was usually on the order-books an order which read " that no member of this House of the long robe during the sessions of Parliament, plead as counsel before the House of Lords in any cause without leave asked and granted by this House[4]." When the House first made an order to this effect does not seem ascertainable from the Journals; but as early as 1558 there was a complaint that the order had been infringed by a member who had gone before the Lords as counsel with the Bishop of Winchester. It was resolved that the member was at fault. He, however, pleaded ignorance, and no punishment was imposed[5]. In subsequent years there are frequent entries in the Journals which read in this wise: " Ordered that Mr Finch, a member of this House, have leave to attend the bar of the House of Lords

---

[1] *Parl. Hist.*, xix. 210. [2] Denison, *Notes from My Journals*, 245.
[3] Howell, *State Trials*, xiii. 544, 545; cf. Hatsell, ii. 128.
[4] Cf. *H. of C. Journals*, xi. 104. [5] Cf. Parry, 215.

as counsel in a case to be heard there to-morrow[1]." The last of these permissions to plead was given in 1710. The practice thereafter was for members of the House of Commons to attend without let or hindrance in their professional capacity in the House of Lords. The modern practice applied, however, only to litigation; and in 1820, when counsel to Queen Caroline were of the House, a motion had to be carried granting them permission to attend in the Lords in opposition to the divorce bill which was then pending against the Queen[2].

[1] Cf. *H. of C. Journals*, x. 62.
[2] Cf. Hansard, 2nd Series, i. 363–364, 401, 402.

CHAPTER XXIX.

RELATIONS OF THE HOUSE TO THE OUTSIDE WORLD.

FROM the earliest times Parliament demanded consideration and deference from the community in which it met. In 1332, when the Lords were sitting in Westminster Palace, and the Commons were most probably meeting in the Chapter House of the Abbey, there was a royal proclamation in which boys were forbidden to play at bars, or other games, or to amuse themselves by knocking off the hats of passers-by, in the neighbourhood of Westminster Palace; and long afterwards similar proclamations were made in whatever place Parliament was convened[1]. *(margin: Enforcing Order near Westminster Palace.)*

Nearly three centuries and a half after this proclamation of 1332, there was passed an order which, with some variation, was never off the Journals of the House until 1829, when the policing of London ceased to be a matter for the parish vestries and became the charge of the home office. In 1667 it was ordered by the House " that the constables and other officers of Middlesex and Westminster concerned do take care that from eight o'clock in the morning till two in the afternoon, being the usual time of the meeting and rising of this House, the passage through the streets between Temple Bar and Westminster Hall be kept free and open; and that no obstruction be made by cars, drays, carts or otherwise to hinder the passage of the members to and from this House[2]." *(margin: Keeping clear the Streets to the House.)*

Until the reign of Charles I, what we now know as the London season had centred, not as to-day about Parliament, but about the Inns of Court. The lawyers set the fashion in dress and *(margin: The London Season.)*

[1] Longman, *History of Edward III*, I. 52.
[2] *H. of C. Journals*, IX. 45.

amusements. They chiefly constituted the fashionable world of London; and while they were socially supreme, the eastern side of Temple Bar was the centre of fashionable society[1]. After the Restoration this supremacy of the Inns of Court passed to Parliament; for in the House of Commons of the Parliaments of Charles II there were more men of fashion, more men of the type that makes the world of Piccadilly, Pall Mall, and St James's Street of to-day, than in any preceding Parliament. With the passing of this supremacy from the Inns of Court to Parliament the fashionable world gradually moved westward of Temple Bar.

The Growth of Westminster.   In 1631 the fourth Duke of Bedford, having completed his great undertaking of the drainage of the Fens, turned his attention to the improvement of a piece of pasture land owned by him, lying to the south of Holborn which had by this time become valuable, and was known as Covent Garden. Inigo Jones was associated with the Duke in the developement of this property. The square, now occupied by Covent Garden Market, was laid out; and the plaza on the Holborn side of the square was built. Several of the adjacent streets were also laid out and lined with houses[2]. Lincoln's Inn Fields were similarly developed about this time[3]; and from even before the Restoration, until almost the close of the eighteenth century, when the world of fashion began to recede still further westward, this was the Belgravia of London. This seventeenth century Belgravia, as well as the Strand and the then fashionable region of St Martin's, were all part of the City of Westminster.

The City and the Parliament.   Westminster profited from the seventeenth century change of the social centre of London. Its citizens with houses to let, its innkeepers, its tradesmen, and its coffee-house keepers, all now reaped advantage from the sessions of Parliament, and from the London season centring about them; and though the order of the House of 1667 did not have the force of an Act of Parliament, no Act was necessary to induce the city, during the hours when the House was sitting, to keep the streets leading to Westminster Palace free from obstruction. By the order of 1667 the sergeant-at-arms was instructed to confer with the

---

[1] Cf. "The Long Vacation," *Pall Mall Gazette*, August 13th, 1896; Burton, *Cromwellian Diary*, i. 211.

[2] Cf. John Bruce, "Observations on a Lease of Two Houses in the Plaza, Covent Garden," *Archæologia*, xxxv. pt. i. 194, 195; Burton, *Cromwellian Diary*, ii. 180.

[3] Cf. Burton, *Cromwellian Diary*, ii. 258.

justices of the peace "to see the order executed and performed[1]."
The conference established good relations which were to be of
long standing; for the order of 1667, with scarcely a change in
its phraseology, continued to be renewed by successive Houses
of Commons until as late as 1800[2]; and as far as the Journals
show, there were no complaints from members of its non-
observance.

In the reign of Queen Anne the House ordered lamp-posts The Parlia-
to be set up in all the places leading to the Houses of Parliament. ment City.
The charge for this was thrown, not on the City of Westminster,
but on the treasury[3]. At this time also members became fas-
tidious about the surroundings of Westminster Palace. A bill
was introduced in 1706 "for suppressing of all new glass-houses,
brew-houses, dyeing houses, melting houses for tallow, and pot-
houses, erected since the beginning of this Parliament, within a
mile of any part of the Palaces of Whitehall and St James's,
and for preventing the setting up of such houses within the like
distance for the time to come." The bill was read a second time
by sixty-nine votes to sixty-four[4]. But such a measure would
have affected other areas than Westminster. It threatened the
pottery and glass and brewing industries across the river in
Lambeth; and when a motion was made that the House go into
committee on the bill it was negatived[5]. Nearly a century and
a half were to elapse before the narrow streets and courts and
alleys of old Westminster were to disappear, and Westminster
become a city of magnificent streets, all converging on S. Stephen's
Palace and the Abbey—pre-eminently the Parliament City.

It was in connection with the privileges of members that the Privileges of
House first demanded deference from the outside world. Through Members.
privilege people outside might come into contact with members
to whom they did not stand in the relation of constituents, but
whom, in special circumstances, they were compelled to regard
as on a different plane from other men. The privileges of the
Commons, which from the first had to be respected, were the
freedom of members and their servants from arrest during the
continuance of the session, and for forty days before its commencement and after its conclusion, and the inviolability during this
time of their lands and goods. The object of such privilege was

---

[1] *H. of C. Journals*, ix. 45. [2] *H. of C. Journals*, lv. 801.
[3] Cf. *Calendar of Treasury Papers*, 1708–14, 204.
[4] *H. of C. Journals*, xv. 230. [5] *H. of C. Journals*, xv. 238.

doubtless to secure the safe arrival and regular attendance of members in Parliament, and to save them from distraction of either body or mind during service[1]. Its origin has been traced back to the Saxon rule, when such persons as were on their way to the gemot were in the King's peace[2]. The privilege of freedom from arrest at no time in the history of the House protected members from the consequence of treason, felony, or breach of the peace[3].

Penalties for Assaulting Members or their Servants.　　One of the earliest enactments extending privilege was of the reign of Henry IV. In 1404, after an assault on "Richard Chedder, Esq., who came to this Parliament with Thomas Broke, Knight, one of the knights of the shire for Somerset," it was made a high contempt of Parliament to assault a member of either House, or his menial servant[4]; and in the reign of Henry VI "the King, willing to provide for the ease and tranquility of them that come to the Parliaments and Councils of the King by his commandment," ordained and established that the penalty for assaulting any Lord or Commoner attending Parliament should be "double damages to the party, with fine and ransom to the King[5]."

Utterances in the House Privileged.　　Up to this time members had still no statutory protection for what they might do or say in the House of Commons. But in 1512, in the reign of Henry VIII—after Richard Strode had been worsted in a conflict with the Stannary Court in Cornwall, owing to violent local opposition to a bill which he had introduced in the House of Commons to regulate the tin trade, then of much value to the county—an Act was passed giving members privilege in respect to their actions in Parliament. The judgement in the Stannary Court had led to Strode's imprisonment in the Castle of Lidford, one of the "most anoyous, contagious, and detestablest places in this realm." After three months in Lidford Castle Strode was liberated by a writ of privilege out of the King's Exchequer at Westminster. By the Act of 1512, perhaps the most important of any of the enactments passed respecting privilege, all "suits, accusements, condemnations, executions, fines, amendments, corrections, grievances, charges, and impositions, put or had, or hereafter to be put or had, unto or upon the said Richard, and to every other of the person or persons afore-specified, that now be of this present Parliament, or that of any

---

[1] Cf. D'Ewes, *Journals*, 612.　　　　[2] Anson, pt. I. 143.
[3] Cf. D'Ewes, *Journals*, 612; Beatson, *Chronological Register*, III. 216.
[4] 5 Henry IV, c. 2.　　　　[5] 11 Henry VI, c. 10.

Parliament hereafter shall be, for any bill, speaking, reasoning, or declaring of any matter or matters concerning the Parliament to be communed and treated of, utterly void and of none effect[1]."

Later in the sixteenth century the House of Commons widened the interpretations given to the enactments governing privilege; and took upon itself, without the sanction of any legal ordinance or enactment, to be the sole judge in its own causes[2]. Between the Act of 1512 and the reign of James I there were no noteworthy additions to the Acts affecting privilege. Hooker, when he furnished the Irish Parliament with his account of procedure, included a statement as to privilege which, excepting the fact that it takes no account of the Act of the reign of Henry VIII, shows the extent of the privilege enjoyed by members of Parliament in the middle of the reign of Elizabeth. "Every person of the Parliament during the time of the Parliament and at his coming and going from the same," wrote the mentor of the Parliament in Dublin, "is free from all troubles, arrests, and molestations, no action or suit taking effect which during that time is begun, entered, or commenced against him, in what court soever the same be, except in causes of treason, murder, and felony, and except all executions in law awarded and granted before the beginning of Parliament[3]." *Hooker's Account of Privilege.*

In the reign of Elizabeth, however, members were not satisfied with a protection which was dependent on the duration of Parliament. They were disposed to push their privilege much further. Evidently they were sometimes successful in stretching privilege to the extreme; for in the first year of the reign of James I an Act of Parliament was necessary to define what privileges members of Parliament enjoyed. It was stated in the preamble that doubts had arisen "if any person, being arrested in execution, and by privilege of either of the Houses of Parliament set at liberty, whether the party at whose suit such execution was pursued be forever after barred and disabled to sue forth a new writ of execution in that case"; and to end these doubts it was enacted that "executions may be renewed against persons discharged by privilege of Parliament, when they ceased to be privileged[4]." *Stretching Privilege.*

This Act doubtless corrected some of the grosser abuses of privilege; but from the reign of James I privilege began to be *Privilege for Members' Servants.*

[1] 4 Henry VIII, c. 8.
[2] Cf. Parry, xxxix. 255.
[3] Mountmorres, i. 140.
[4] 1 James I, c. 13

pushed to the verge of constitutional licence; and from 1621 the
Journals abound in complaints by members of breaches of privilege. Most of these arose in connection with the serving-men
of members—always a troublesome class so far as the precincts
of the House were concerned, and men who, by reason of their
habits, were much more liable than members themselves to be
involved in petty litigation. Between 1621 and the Long Parliament one member of the House of Commons complained that
his servant's cloak had been detained as security against a tavern
bill; and another that his servant had been committed to prison
as the father of an illegitimate child[1].

*Act of 1701,
limiting
Privilege.*

Another abuse especially rampant in the Restoration Parliaments, though more peculiar to the Lords than to the Commons,
was that orders securing privilege were obtained for men who
were neither of the House, nor menial servants to those who
were of the Parliament. Burnet described this abuse in com-
mending the Act of Parliament of William III by which another
attempt was made to check the stretching of privilege. " Another
very good Act passed this year," he wrote in reviewing the session
of 1701, " concerned the privilege of Parliament. Of late years
sessions were long and continued by intermediate prorogations;
so that the whole year round was a time of privilege. This made
great obstruction in the courts of justice; and none who were
so protected could be sued for debt. The abuse was carried
further by the protection which some Lords gave, or rather sold,
to persons who were in no way concerned in their affairs; but
when they needed this shelter they had a pretended office given
them that was a bar to all arrests. After many fruitless attempts
to regulate these abuses, a bill was brought into the House of
Commons that took away all privilege against legal prosecutions
in intermediate prorogations, and did so regulate it during the
sitting of Parliament that an effectual remedy was provided for
a grievance that had been long and much complained of[2]."

*Provisions of
the Act.*

The Act which Burnet thus eulogised was described in its
preamble as a measure " for preventing all delays the King or
his subjects may receive in any of his courts of law or equity,
and for their ease in the recovery of their rights and titles to
any lands, tenements, or hereditaments, and their debts and other
dues for which they have cause or suit." It enacted that suits

---

[1] Townsend, *Hist. of the House of Commons*, i. 256, 257.
[2] Burnet, *Hist. of His Own Time*, iii. 347.

might be brought against peers and members of Parliament and judgement given therein during the intervals of Parliament, after dissolution or after any adjournment for more than fourteen days, until both Houses should meet or reassemble, and under similar conditions also against the menials of members or other servants entitled to privilege[1]. The Act, however, continued the prescriptive freedom of members from arrest during the time of privilege.

In the eighteenth century the Commons continued to stretch privilege, and to press it against petty thieves, trespassers, and poachers on their rabbit warrens and fisheries[2]; and until well on in the last century of the unreformed House of Commons men procured election to the House in order that they might evade their creditors and keep outside the debtors' prison. In 1738 the Act of 1701 was re-enacted, and made more comprehensive[3]; and in 1764 the law of privilege was so amended as to make it possible for creditors to reach by proceedings in bankruptcy at any time, not all members of Parliament, but " any person deemed a merchant, banker, broker, factor, scrivener, or trader having privilege of Parliament," who could not or would not pay his debts. Two months were allowed a member so proceeded against in which to pay the debts. If he failed he was to be " accounted and adjudged a bankrupt" from the time of the service of the summons. Further than this, if any member, coming within the classes described in the Act, committed any act of bankruptcy, in that event his creditors might sue out a commission of bankruptcy, and might " proceed thereon in like manner as against other bankrupts, any privilege of Parliament to the contrary notwithstanding[4]."

Privilege was further restricted in 1770 by an Act which provided that any suit might be brought at any time against persons entitled to the privilege of Parliament; and though, as in the Act of 1701, immunity of members of Parliament from arrest was expressly continued, no such privilege was any longer extended to their servants[5]. Before this time, in 1767, the claim of the House to constitute itself a tribunal for the trial and punishment of private injuries done to its members had been suffered to fall into desuetude. While this claim had been

Limitations of Privilege in 1738 and 1764.

Further Restrictions.

---

[1] 12 and 13 W. III, c. 3.
[2] Mahon, *Hist. of England,* iv. 30.
[3] 11 Geo. II, c. 24.
[4] 4 Geo. III, c. 33.
[5] 10 Geo. III, c. 50.

maintained offenders had been compelled to kneel at the bar
for censure. By a standing order passed in 1772 this practice,
which involved a submission so abject that it degraded the
prisoner, was abandoned[1].

Bankrupts in Parliament.

In 1805 the Act of 1764 affecting merchants, bankers, brokers,
factors, scriveners, or traders, was so amended as to make its
operations more certain and expeditious[2]; and in 1812, with a
view to "the preservation of the dignity and independence of
Parliament," there was an Act imposing disabilities on all members
of the House of Commons who became bankrupts and did not
pay their debts in full. It provided that when a member was
declared a bankrupt, "such member shall be, and shall remain
during twelve calendar months" from the time of the issue of
the commission, "utterly incapable of sitting and voting in the
House of Commons, unless within the said period the creditors
of such member shall be paid or satisfied to the full amount
of their debts." If the commission in bankruptcy were not
suspended within twelve months, nor the debts satisfied, the
commissioners of bankruptcy were to certify the same to the
Speaker, and thereupon the delinquent member's seat was to
become vacant, and a writ for a new election was to issue[3].

The Decline of Privilege.

By the series of Acts of Parliament passed at long intervals,
and beginning as early as the reign of James I, fewer advantages
and less deference were gradually demanded by the House for its
members in their relations with the outside world. The plane on
which the House in this respect had pushed its members in the
sixteenth and seventeenth centuries was, from the beginning of
the eighteenth century, slowly brought down: and members away
from Westminster became less a class apart, with privileges and
advantages often onerous and harmful to those with whom they
came into business contact. By the time of the Reform Act of
1832 the only privileges remaining to members beyond the walls
of S. Stephen's were freedom from arrest, and inviolability, so
far as the outside world was concerned, for their utterances within
the Chamber. On the eve of the Reform Act there was a change
in the usage of the House, which, though small in itself, marked
the change which had come over the House in these relations
with the outside world. Until 1831 the Speaker included the

---

[1] May, *Constitutional Hist.*, ii. 74.   [2] 45 Geo. III, c. 124.

[3] 52 Geo. III, c. 144.

estates of members in the claim of privilege preferred to the Crown. This was last done in October, 1830, and first omitted when the new Parliament assembled in June, 1831[1].

The House of Commons had taken on its modern form before there were any orders or enactments governing the method by which it was to be approached by the outside world. Petitions are almost as old as the representative system. They long formed the basis of legislation. When legislation by bill superseded legislation by petition, petitions for legislative enactments or constitutional changes would seem to have fallen into desuetude. There is no mention of petitions in Hooker's statement of procedure nor in D'Ewes's *Journals*, which cover the whole of the Parliaments of the reign of Elizabeth. But in the seventeenth century, especially at the time of the Great Rebellion, petitions were revived, and began to take on their modern form[2]. At this period they were so numerous, and petitioners so troublesome to the House, that one of the first Acts of Parliament after the Restoration was for the regulation of petitioning.

"It hath been found by sad experience," reads the preamble of this Act, "that tumultous and other disorderly soliciting and procuring of hands by private persons to petitions, complaints, and remonstrances, and declarations, and other addresses to the King, or to both or either House of Parliament, for alteration of matters established by law, redress of pretended grievances in Church or State, or other public concernments, have been made use of to serve the end of factious and seditious persons, gotten into power to the violation of the public peace, and have been a great means of the late unhappy wars and confusion and calamities in this realm." To prevent recurrence of similar mischiefs it was enacted that no persons were to solicit, labour, or procure the getting of hands, or other consent of any persons, above the number of twenty or more, to any petition, complaint, remonstrance, declaration or other address to the King, or both or either House of Parliament, for alterations of matters established by law in Church or State, unless the matter thereof had been first consented unto and ordered by three or more justices of the county, or by the major part of the grand jury of the county, or division of the county, or in London by the lord mayor, aldermen, and commons, in common council assembled. It was

Petitions to the House.

Their Regulation in 1661.

---

[1] Cf. Anson, pt. i. 146.   [2] Cf. Parry, 459.

further enacted, that no persons were to repair to the sovereign or to Parliament, upon pretence of presenting a petition, accompanied by an excessive number of people, nor at any time with more than ten persons. It was, however, provided that nothing in the Act was " to be construed to extend to debar or hinder any person or persons, not exceeding the number of ten, to present any public or private grievance or complaint to any member of Parliament after his election and during the continuance of the Parliament[1]."

The Act enforced against the Chartists.
This Act of Charles II, arising out of the tumults of the reign of Charles I remains on the statute books to-day ; and although after the Revolution all its provisions seem never to have been insisted upon, the Act was brought into use as recently as 1848, when twenty-five thousand Chartists, who had assembled on Kennington Common to petition Parliament, were prevented from going in procession to Westminster, and were compelled to send their petition by deputation, limited in numbers in accordance with the Act of 1661[2].

Orders regulating Petitions.
Until the Revolution petitions were regulated only by this Act of 1661, and by the usage of the House. After the Revolution, when petitions affecting general policy again became common, orders were made by the House for their regulation, which form the basis of those governing the presentation of petitions to-day. Under these orders, which originated in 1689 and in 1699, petitions must be fairly written. They must be respectful, decorous, and temperate in language. Each petition must conclude with a prayer ; and except in two cases all petitions must be presented by members of the House[3].

Petitions from London and Dublin.
The exceptions are in favour of the corporations of the cities of London and Dublin. The City of London, from time out of mind, has enjoyed the privilege of presenting petitions at the bar of the House by its sheriffs. Dublin enjoyed a similar privilege in the Irish Parliament ; and from 1813 the Corporation of Dublin has enjoyed the privilege of presenting its petitions by the lord mayor at the bar at Westminster. Neither of these cities has a right to present at the bar. The messenger from the Crown only has a right to knock at the door of the House of Commons and demand admittance. When the sheriffs of the City of London

---

[1] 13 C. II, c. 65.
[2] Cf. Walpole, *Life of Russell*, II. 64 ; May, *Constitutional Hist.*, II. 411.
[3] *Rules and Orders*, 155 to 160 ; cf. Colchester, *Diary*, II. 601.

attend, and their presence is announced, the Speaker puts it to
the House, " Is it your pleasure that the sheriffs be called in ?"
On at least one occasion the request was denied. The procedure
is the same when the lord mayor of Dublin is announced with
a petition[1].

After the Union of Great Britain and Ireland Dublin claimed Dublin and
at Westminster a privilege similar to the one it had enjoyed in Edinburgh.
the Irish Parliament. When Grattan in 1813 made this claim
for Dublin Lord Cochrane moved that the same privilege be
granted to Edinburgh, which after the Union of 1707 had made
no claim for special treatment. It was objected, however, that
the Scotch were sensible people, and would never think of sending
the Provost of Edinburgh four hundred miles to present a petition.
Edinburgh, moreover, had made no request for any special favour ;
and for these reasons the motion as regards Edinburgh was
negatived. Leave was granted to the lord mayor of Dublin to
present a petition at the bar of the House. In 1868 Edinburgh
was disposed to put itself into line with London and Dublin ;
but after the lord advocate and one of the members for Edinburgh
had had a private interview with Speaker Denison, the request
from the City of Edinburgh was not further pressed[2].

In the unreformed House of Commons members were permitted Speeches on
to address the House in support of petitions. Great debates Petitions.
occasionally took place on petitions. In 1817, to cite only one
instance, Lord Cochrane occupied the House for two hours with
the presentation of petitions in favour of Parliamentary reform.
He was followed by Canning, who " made a most brilliant speech,
and declared his opposition to Parliamentary reform, not professing
to hesitate upon remedies, but denying the evil[3]." Nowadays, in
accordance with a more modern standing order, a member who
presents a petition must confine himself " to a statement of the
parties from whom it comes, of the number of signatures attached
to it, and of the material allegations contained in it, and to the
reading of the prayer of such petition[4]."

One of the greatest changes which the House underwent in the Strangers in
period between its first meeting in S. Stephen's Chapel and the the House.
Reform Act, was in its attitude towards strangers who, from

[1] Denison, *Notes from My Journals*, 218.
[2] Denison, *Notes from My Journals*, 218.
[3] Colchester, *Diary*, ii. 601.
[4] *Rules and Orders*, 160.

interest or curiosity, desired to look on at its proceedings. The Journals afford no means of ascertaining its attitude towards the outside world in this respect in the reigns of Edward VI and Mary. They are not very helpful as regards the reign of Elizabeth; but there is extra-official testimony that in this reign the House was rigid in the exclusion of all strangers from the Chamber, and severe in its punishment of all intruders. "No manner of person, being not one of the Parliament," wrote Hooker, "ought to enter or come within the House as long as the sitting is there, upon pain of imprisonment, or such other punishment as by the House shall be ordered and be adjudged[1]."

Their Exclusion in Elizabeth's Reign.

D'Ewes's *Journals* show that the House was exceedingly strict in enforcing this exclusion of strangers, and that its orders against them were frequently invoked. In 1584, for instance, Richard Robinson, a skinner, "being no member of the House," yet, "being found to have sat here this present day by the space of two hours, during the whole time of the speeches delivered by Mr Chancellor and the Vice-Chamberlain," was at the bar "stript to the shirt, and his pockets searched, and then remanded to the custody of the serjeant-at-arms," while a committee made enquiry into his antecedents and character[2]. After the committee had reported Robinson was again placed at the bar, where he was censured by the Speaker; made to take the oath of supremacy; and also sworn to keep secret what he had heard. In 1586 a chandler and a butcher, both from Shoreditch, "presumed to come into the House, being not members of the same." It was ascertained that they had committed this grave offence through "ignorance and meer simplicity"; and on their making submission and asking pardon, it was agreed by the House "that they shall be discharged and set at liberty, first taking the oath of supremacy openly in this House, which they so did, and afterwards departed[3]." Occasionally a culprit had to listen to "a grave admonition" from the Speaker[4]. If these trespassers were possessed of means they were condemned in the sergeant's fees[5]; and in the reign of Elizabeth no intruder was liberated from the custody of the sergeant until he had, at the bar, taken the oath of supremacy—a method of treating intruders which suggests that at this time the House was disposed to suspect that they were emissaries of the Church of Rome.

[1] Mountmorres, i. 143.   [2] D'Ewes, *Journals*, 334.
[3] D'Ewes, *Journals*, 394.   [4] D'Ewes, *Journals*, 491, 512.
[5] D'Ewes, *Journals*, 334.

The orders against strangers were continued in the reign of James I; for in a description of the procedure of the House of the early seventeenth century, there is a statement that persons, "for coming into the House, were brought to the bar and some committed and some sworn before they departed to keep secret what they had heard there[1]." In the Cromwellian Parliaments there was a rule that no bill could be read in the presence of a stranger[2].

An order against strangers must have been in existence in 1662; for then "upon information that several persons, not members, had come by the back door into the Speaker's chamber and into the gallery while the House was sitting," it was ordered that the back door be constantly kept shut while the House was sitting; and similar orders were made until the Revolution[3]. In 1689 the form of the order was changed. It now became the duty of the sergeant-at-arms "to take into custody such strangers who presume to come into the House of Commons, while the House or any committee of the whole House is sitting[4]." As the eighteenth century advanced the order was made more comprehensive, and so worded as to prohibit members from bringing strangers into the House. "That the sergeant-at-arms," read the orders of 1718, "do from time to time take into his custody any stranger or strangers that he shall see, or be informed of, to be in the House or gallery, while the House, or any committee of the whole House, is sitting," and that "no member of this House do presume to bring in any stranger or strangers into the House or gallery thereof, while the House is sitting[5]."

Session after session some such order as this of 1718 was continued so long as the Commons met in the old Chapel of S. Stephen's, and until the building of a gallery in the new Chamber, appropriated to strangers, brought with it a more elastic order. Occasionally in the eighteenth century, as for instance in 1734, the order of the House was read at the table, and an order was made that the sergeant-at-arms "do his duty in executing thereof[6]." In 1777, at a time when the outside world was beginning to show a more lively interest in the House and its proceedings,

---

[1] *Memorials of the Method and Manner of Proceeding in Parliament,* 1670, 86.

[2] Cf. Burton, *Cromwellian Diary,* I. 184.   [3] Hatsell, II. 128.

[4] *H. of C. Journals,* x. 291.   [5] *H. of C. Journals,* xix. 5.

[6] *H. of C. Journals,* xxII. 406.

there was a motion that the standing order should be referred for consideration to a committee of the whole House. Fox was one of the tellers in favour of the reference; but the motion was defeated by eighty-three votes to sixteen[1], and the order, much as it was first drawn in 1718, continued to be renewed as long as the un-reformed House survived.

Orders not uniformly enforced.

Notwithstanding these orders there is abundance of testimony that during the eighteenth century neither the floor of the House nor the gallery was kept free from strangers, and that but seldom did the sergeant-at-arms put the standing order of the House into force on his own initiative. Even when members called the attention of the Speaker to the presence of strangers it was not an easy matter to gain the consent of the House to their exclusion. "It very seldom happens," wrote Hatsell, in reviewing his long experience of the House as clerk at the table, "that this can be done without a violent struggle from some quarters of the House that strangers may remain. Members often move for the order to be read, endeavour to explain it, and debate upon it, and the House as often runs into great heats upon this subject. But in about half-an-hour the confusion subsides, and the dispute ends by clearing the House; for if anyone insist upon it, the Speaker must enforce the order and the House must be cleared." "The House has in many instances," Hatsell continued, "winked at the breach of it, and it has often been understood that the observance of it should be remitted with respect to peers, members of the Irish Parliament, eldest sons of members, and with other exceptions. But this has been only on sufferance[2]."

Admission to the Floor of the House.

To-day, none but members and officers of the House are per-mitted to pass beyond the bar when the House is sitting. At Washington, displayed at the doors of the Senate and the House of Representatives, there are lists of the names of men, not of Congress, to whom each House has accorded the privilege of the floor, and who, by reason of this privilege, can pass into the Chamber when the Senate or House is in Session. Distinguished soldiers and civilians and many ex-members of Congress are granted these privileges at Washington, and the privilege is sometimes extended to distinguished visitors from other countries. There is no such rule at Westminster. Places under the gallery are assigned to distinguished strangers; but they are never permitted beyond

---

[1] *H. of C. Journals*, xxxvi. 458.   [2] Hatsell, ii. 128, 129.

the bar. This rigid exclusion of strangers from the floor is, however, comparatively modern. In the eighteenth century, during the Speakerships of Onslow, Cust, Norton, and Cornewall, strangers were frequently admitted to the floor of the House[1].

How little the order of 1718, prohibiting strangers from entering the House, was heeded during Cornewall's Speakership, may be judged from the notes of travel published by Moritz, a German pastor, who was a frequent visitor to the House about 1780. Moritz notes that while members of the House sat covered, visitors in the gallery were uncovered; that some members lay stretched out on the benches; that others cracked nuts and ate oranges; that there was no end to the going in and out of members; that each member on going out placed himself before the Speaker, and made his bow, "as if, like a schoolboy, he asked his tutor's permission"; and he ends his realistic description of the House in session with the remark, "I have now and then seen some of the members bring their sons, whilst quite little boys, and carry them to their seats along with themselves[2]."

Strangers in the House in 1780.

Sons of peers and sons of members of the House of Commons were long privileged visitors at Westminster. In the opening years of the seventeenth century, by the orders of the House of Lords governing procedure at conferences, strangers, with the exception of heirs to peerages, were excluded from the Painted Chamber when a conference was in session. In the eighteenth century—how much earlier, I have not been able to ascertain—the boys of Westminster School had also some privileges in the Houses of Parliament. In the old Chapel of S. Stephen's they were privileged to seat themselves under the gallery on a level with the floor of the House[3]. After the Houses met in the new Palace of Westminster some of these privileges were continued, and Westminster boys had what may be described as a right of way into the strangers' gallery of the House of Commons until about 1887, when the privilege came to an end[4].

Privileged Visitors.

[1] Cf. *Parl. Hist.*, xix. 207; Betham Edwards, *Autobiography of Arthur Young*, 16, 17; *Report from Select Committee on Strangers and Divisions*, 1853, 3.

[2] Moritz, "Travels in Several Parts of England," Pinkerton, *Collection of Voyages and Travels*, ii. 507.

[3] Mowbray, "Seventy Years at Westminster," *Blackwood's Magazine*, 1898, clxiv. 3.

[4] Claude Greening, "Westminster School Privileges," *Morning Post*, April 25th, 1899.

Women as
Visitors in
the House.
Women would appear to have begun to attend the sittings
of the House in the reign of George II, during the long period
over which Onslow's Speakership extended. They were occasionally
present during the Pensioner Parliament[1]. At this time they
were admitted into the House of Lords[2]; but the custom of
women attending debates in the House of Commons did not
become established until the reign of George II. In the eighteenth century they were first attracted by election petitions;
contests which, as long as they were determined by the House,
always aroused deep personal interest. Grantley Berkeley, who
occupies a niche in House of Commons history by reason of his
advocacy of the admission of women to the House as spectators,
stated in a debate in 1835 that, as early as 1716, women were
admitted not only to the gallery, but to the floor of the House[3].
Women were occasionally in the lobby, lobbying in behalf of
private legislation, as early as 1698[4]. But, except during the
time of the Pensioner Parliament, the earliest evidence which I
have found of women regularly attending the House as spectators
is of the year 1755.

Ladies and
Election
Contests in
the House.
In the autobiography of Arthur Young there is a letter of
that year from Young's mother, describing her attendance in the
House from one o'clock at noon until nine o'clock at night, on the
hearing of an election petition from one of the Cornish boroughs,
"when the great ones (the Duke of Cumberland on one side, and
the Duke of Newcastle on the other) were setting themselves in
combat against each other." "It was a most hard-fought battle,"
and so famous an affair that all the town wanted to hear it, and
evidently the gallery would hold only a small part of them.
"However," the letter continues, "we had the luck to get excellent places, having a chair for one of us brought out of the
Speaker's chamber." "Tuesday last," it is elsewhere stated in this
letter, "the message was brought from the King to the House.
I should have much liked to have been there; but the ladies'
privilege extends to no further than elections[5]." Arthur Young's
father was chaplain to Speaker Onslow, a fact lending additional
value to this letter, which describes the usage of the Commons

---

[1] Cf. Grey, *Debates*, iii. 222.
[2] Hatsell, ii. 173.
[3] *Mirror of Parliament*, 1835, ii. 1928.
[4] *Hist. MSS. Comm. 12th Rep.*, App., pt. viii. 351.
[5] Betham Edwards, *Autobiography of Arthur Young*, 16, 17

in regard to women visitors in the closing years of the reign of George II.

Early in the reign of George III the Grenville Act transferred election petitions from the House to committees, and put an end to exciting sittings like that of 1755. But before this change was made in 1770, women had become privileged to attend the ordinary sittings of the House, and were permitted to occupy seats in the gallery until 1778. Then, on one of the few occasions when the standing orders excluding strangers were put into force, the officers of the House had some difficulty in clearing women from the gallery. Business was interrupted for two hours, and there was much commotion before the order could be enforced. The result of the incident was that from 1778, and as long as the House met in its old Chamber, women were rigorously excluded from the gallery[1]. The incident which led to their exclusion occurred during the Speakership of Fletcher Norton; and while it apparently resulted in no new order of the House, no order in which women were mentioned, Cornewall and Addington, who were Norton's successors in the Chair, persistently refused to admit women visitors to the floor or to the ordinary gallery[2].

Ladies excluded from the Gallery.

Women were not, however, entirely excluded from the House. Soon after the Commons first met in S. Stephen's Chapel the Chamber had been ceiled. In later times the ceiling had been pierced for a ventilator; and at some time subsequent to 1779 a chamber was built about this ventilator, and by usage of the House it became a ladies' gallery, for which tickets were issued each day by the sergeant-at-arms. "Only the lower half of S. Stephen's Chapel," writes the daughter of a member of the House in recalling her visits to the ladies' gallery in the first Parliament after the Reform Act, "had been used by the Commons. The upper part, with its vaulted roof and unglazed windows, was a large vacant chamber, and in the centre of this was a wooden lantern called the ventilator. This had eight small openings in it, just large enough to admit a head, and was surrounded by a circular bench. By this means ladies who were privileged to go there, could catch a glimpse of speakers within a certain radius. When tired of peering through these pigeonholes we roamed about our prison; and it was very refreshing to look out on a summer's evening upon the Thames. We were

The Ventilator as a Ladies' Gallery.

---

[1] May, *Constitutional Hist.*, II. 52.   [2] Cf. Hatsell, II. 172.

locked up; and every now and then our custodian came to tell us who 'was on his legs.' Sometimes members came up. * * * The present gilded cage (the ladies' gallery of the House of Commons of to-day) which is complained of is a paradise to the draughty dusty room I speak of; but we liked it nevertheless, and it was a great treat to have tea in a committee room[1]." "It was the only ladies' gallery," writes Lady Verney, in recalling the chamber under the roof of S. Stephen's, "and I can remember being taken there as a child to listen to the debates, and seeing the ministerial and opposition ladies keeping rigorously to their own sides of the hole[2]."

Strangers
allowed
in the
Galleries.

Frequently in tracing the history of usages of the House it is impracticable to fix the date at which a change occurred. The Journals in these cases often give no aid. They afford no assistance in determining when strangers ceased to be excluded from the floor and the gallery, because, as has been shown, orders excluding strangers were ever off the Journals. Yet there is extra-official testimony whi￼" proves that for nearly a century before the Commons occupied their new Chamber and set apart a gallery for strangers—except on infrequent occasions when the standing orders were enforced—strangers were freely admitted. While it is impossible to determine the exact year when the orders of the House excluding strangers ceased to be heeded, it may be taken that strangers were attending the House from the reign of George I. All through this period, and for some years after the House met in the new Palace of S. Stephen's, strangers were excluded when the House divided. As soon as a division was called the officers of the sergeant-at-arms made them withdraw from the Chamber, and until the last stranger had disappeared the House did not divide. The change in this usage came in 1853, when the old order governing divisions gave place to a new one. The sand glass which now stands on the table is a monument to this change. It is turned by the clerk directly a division is called. At the same time electric bells are rung, summoning members into the Chamber. As soon as the sand has run out, the doors are closed, and the division begins. When a division is called the Speaker still orders strangers to withdraw; but the order affects only those occupying places below the bar. Those in the

[1] Pryme, *Autobiographic Recollections,* Footnote, 209, 210.

[2] Lady Verney, *Memoirs of the Verney Family during the Civil War,* Footnote, i. 339.

press and public galleries remain; and while the orders of the House still make it possible for a single member to bring about the exclusion of all strangers, nowadays not once in the lifetime of a Parliament are the galleries cleared[1].

[1] Cf. *Report from Select Committee on Strangers and Divisions*, 1853, 3; *Rules and Orders*, 30, 80, 81.

CHAPTER XXX.

THE HOUSE OF COMMONS AND THE PRESS.

Secrecy of Proceedings. THE attitude of the House in respect to the dissemination of information concerning its proceedings underwent a change in the first half of the seventeenth century. The Journals throw little light on its usages in this regard in the sixteenth century. Again, however, Hooker and D'Ewes fill the gap; and their statements put beyond a doubt the attitude of the House towards the world outside in the reign of Elizabeth. " Every person of the Parliament," Hooker laid down, " ought to keep secret and not to disclose the secrets and things done and spoken in the Parliament House to any manner of person, unless he be one of the same House, upon pain to be sequestered out of the House, or otherwise punished as by the order of the House shall be appointed[1]." This must have been the usage from the early years of Elizabeth's reign. The later years of the reign witnessed no change. In 1589 there was a complaint from Sir Edward Hobby that matters under discussion in the House were made the subject of table-talk out of doors; and by order of the House members were admonished by the Speaker not to discuss its affairs out of doors, and to give no written note of its proceedings to " any person or persons whatsoever, not being members of this House[2]." At this time, and in the reign of James I, strangers who had found their way into the House were held in custody of the sergeant-at-arms until they had sworn at the bar not to disclose what they had heard within the Chamber.

Copies of Processes permitted. In the early days of Parliament Acts were promulgated in the county courts[3]; and the outside world must necessarily always

[1] Mountmorres, i. 143.
[2] D'Ewes, *Journals*, 432, 433.
[3] *Report of the Select Committee on Publication of Printed Papers*, 1837, 2, 3.

have had some notice of the Acts which were passed. Even before the House changed its attitude in regard to its daily proceedings, a change which was made in 1641, there had come into existence a rule that "the clerk of the Parliament shall not deny to any man a transcript or copy of his process, or processes in Parliament, if he do desire it." The rate of payment for these transcripts was fixed at a penny for each ten lines, "unless haply that he that requireth the transcript will give his faith that he is not able to give it"; in which case the clerk was to take nothing for his labour[1].

In the reign of Elizabeth some members of the House kept private journals of its proceedings, in which were included summaries of the speeches as well as orders and resolutions. Such diaries were largely drawn upon by D'Ewes, who frequently expressed his impatience with the inadequate and, at times, slovenly way in which the Journals of the House of Commons were kept. About 1640 the speeches of leading members began to be printed by order of the House, and members also began to print their own speeches, from their own notes, without the sanction of such orders[2]. In the Parliament in which these practices were begun there came the first formal recognition of the principle that the world had a right to know what the House was doing. Newspapers as yet were not. At this time the writers of news-letters, although busy at their trade, had given the House no trouble. What the House determined on in 1641, and what it contended for until far on in the eighteenth century, was that the world outside should know of its proceedings, but only through its own action and through official channels.

Private Journals of the House.

The earliest order in pursuance of this policy was made on the 30th of July, 1641, when the House adopted certain resolutions and ordered that they should be printed. From 1641 to 1680 there were various resolutions for the printing of specific votes and papers. In 1681 a general resolution was adopted for printing the votes and proceedings of the House; and from that year such general order was renewed every session, excepting in 1702, when the order was, for a very short period, suspended. It may be asked whether the papers printed in accordance with these orders were for the exclusive use of the members of the House or for general publication. " No doubt can exist," reported

Official Publication of Proceedings.

[1] Cf. Hakewel, *The Old Manner of Holding Parliaments*, 30.

[2] D'Israeli, *Commentaries on the Life and Reign of Charles I*, IV. 147.

a committee of the House which enquired into this question in 1837, "that it was with a view to the latter object." "This is shown," the report continues, "by the subsequent proceedings of the House with regard to the order for printing of 1641, and by the appointment of a committee in the subsequent year to consider the 'best way of divulging, dispersing, and publishing the orders and votes, and also the declarations of the House through the kingdom, and of the well and true printing of them.' This committee presented on the 16th of June, 1642, an order for dispersing and divulging the orders and declarations of the House through the sheriffs, under-sheriffs, constables, headboroughs, and tithing men of the several counties, with directions for the speedy publication to the inhabitants, and an order was made for the payment of the expense[1]."

A Debate on the Publication of Proceedings.

After the Restoration the publication of papers printed for the House was continued, apparently without objection, until 1681, when it was the subject of a debate in the House. The debate was on a motion for the publication of papers; and the only opposition came from Mr Secretary Jenkins, who resisted it on the ground that it was an appeal to the people, unsuited to the gravity of the House. For the motion it had been urged that the printing of the votes was for the honour of the King and the safety of the nation. "Let men think what they please," said Sir William Cowper, speaking in favour of the continuance of the rule which had been in existence since 1641, "the weight of England is the people." "I beg pardon," answered Jenkins, "if I consent not to the motion. Consider the gravity of this assembly. There is no great assembly in Christendom that does it. It is against the gravity of this assembly; and it is a sort of appeal to the people." Another member conceded that it was proper that what passed in Privy Council should be kept secret. "But," he continued, "your journal books are open, and copies of your votes in every coffee-house; and if you print them not, half votes will be dispersed to your prejudice. This printing is like plain Englishmen, who are not ashamed of what they do, and the people you represent will have a true account of what you do." "But pray," asked Sir Francis Winnington, "who sent us hither? The Privy Council is constituted by the King, but the House of Commons is by the choice of the people. I think

---

[1] *Report of the Select Committee on Publication of Printed Papers*, 1837, 3.

it not natural, nor rational, that the people who sent us hither should be not informed of our actions. In the Long Parliament it was a trade among clerks to write votes; and it was then said by a learned gentleman that 'it was no offence to inform the people of the votes of Parliament, and they ought to have notice of them.'" The speech of Jenkins is the only one recorded in opposition to the motion, which was carried, as was also a second order by which the care and oversight of the printing of the votes was committed to the Speaker[1].

From 1641 until the middle years of the following century, many of the papers so printed purported to be published by order of the House. The sale of these Parliamentary papers was open, though no express order for their sale can be found in the Journals. Nevertheless a profit was derived from them, which was accounted for by the printers to the Speaker. Later on the account was transferred to the treasury; and when the expense of printing became more than the receipts from sales, credit was given by the printer for the sums in payment for copies of votes sold by him, and the balance due to him was paid by the treasury[2]. The publicity of printed Parliamentary papers was not only sanctioned by the House of Commons from 1641, and by the House of Lords in 1690, but in 1802 it received an express sanction from Parliament by the exemption of such papers from payment of postage[3]. Moreover, until the Stockdale case came into the courts in 1836, it was held that legal proceedings could not be instituted for anything contained in the papers so printed[4]. *Official Sanction of Sale of Publications.*

The votes and orders of the House, printed in pursuance of these orders regularly made from 1641, never in the history of the unreformed House of Commons included the division lists, which to-day form part of the votes. At the dissolution of 1689 division lists were for the first time published unofficially as electioneering literature. In 1696 the Commons declared the printing of the names of a minority a breach of privilege, as destructive of the freedom and liberties of Parliament. Burke in 1770 advocated the official publication of division lists. In 1782 lists of divisions were again published unofficially as electioneering literature; but not until 1836 did the House adopt *First Publication of Division Lists.*

[1] *Report of the Select Committee on Publication of Printed Papers*, 1837, 4.
[2] *Report of the Select Committee on Publication of Printed Papers*, 1837, 4.
[3] 42 Geo. III, c. 63.
[4] *Report of the Select Committee on Publication of Printed Papers*, 1837, 5, 6.

the present-day plan of recording the votes of every member, and publishing them day by day as part of the official proceedings of the House[1].

Efforts to check Unofficial Publications.

While to the House of Commons of the Long Parliament credit has to be given for the system under which the outside world was informed of what was being done in the House, in this House of Commons there was also first exhibited a jealousy of all but official publications covering the proceedings of the House. When Rushworth became clerk-assistant—only two years before the appointment of the committee of 1642 to consider the best way of publishing the orders and votes of the House—it was ordered " that Mr Rushworth shall not take any notes here without the precedent directions and commands of the House, but only of the orders and reports made in this House[2]." In the same session Overton, a stationer, was reprimanded for printing an order of the House[3]. In 1641 there was an order that " no member of this House shall either give a copy, or publish in print, anything that he shall speak here without leave of the House[4]." A few days later members were enjoined by order " to deliver out no copy or notes of anything that is brought into the House, propounded or agitated in the House[5]." In 1642, after the Committee on Publication of Orders and Votes had been appointed, the House made an order that " whatever person soever shall print, or sell any Act or passage of this House, under the name of a diurnal, or otherwise, without the particular licence of this House, shall be reputed a high contemner and breaker of the privilege of Parliament, and so punished accordingly[6]."

News-Letters after the Restoration.

In the Cromwellian Parliaments there are indications of jealousy shown towards members who took private notes[7]; but in the Restoration Parliaments much more latitude was permitted to members. Anchitell Grey took notes in the House of Commons at great length from 1667 to 1694. Andrew Marvell wrote his detailed letters to his constituents at Hull from 1660 to 1678; and the professional news-letter writers, as the publications of the Royal Commission on Historical Manuscripts now show, flourished exceedingly between the Restoration and the Revolution, and had

[1] Cf. May, *Constitutional Hist.*, ii. 56, 57.

[2] *H. of C. Journals*, ii. 12.   [3] *H. of C. Journals*, ii. 65.

[4] *H. of C. Journals*, ii. 209.   [5] *H. of C. Journals*, ii. 220.

[6] *H. of C. Journals*, ii. 501.   [7] Cf. Burton, *Cromwellian Diary*, i. 341.

more subscribers to their letters from London than at any time in the history of the news-letter writing calling. The readers of news-letters, who were principally the county families, were eager for Parliamentary news ; and until after the Revolution the news writers were permitted to ply their business in the lobby with as little hindrance as the newspaper correspondents of to-day. Many of them were subordinate clerks in Parliament or in the government offices. Their official position gave them easy access to Westminster Palace, often secured for them franks for their news-letters, and gave them a pretext for interesting themselves in the proceedings of the Houses.

Whatever privileges in the shape of access to good sources of information, franks, and what not, fell to the pioneer news writers at Westminster—to these precursors of the London correspondents of to-day—were abundantly earned. These news-letter writers of the last half of the seventeenth century well deserved the payments of two or three guineas a year which came to hand from subscribers to their letters ; and the present-day historical value of much of their work is testified by the number of letters of this period which have found their way into the reports of the Royal Commission on Historical Manuscripts. The Parliaments of the Restoration were the heyday of the news-letter writers, and not until after William III was settled on the throne did the House of Commons come into conflict with them. Value of the News-Letters.

Dyer was the first of the news-letter writers to suffer at the hands of the House. It was complained on December 21st, 1694, that in his letters he had presumed to take notice of the proceedings of the House. On the 22nd he was at the bar in charge of the sergeant-at-arms, and after acknowledging his offence and craving pardon, he was compelled to kneel and receive a reprimand from the Speaker "for his great presumption." Then an order was made that Dyer be discharged on paying his fees to the sergeant ; and following this order came a general order "that no news-letter writers do, in their letters or other papers that they disperse, presume to intermeddle with the debates or any other proceedings of this House[1]." First Conflict with the News-Letter Writers.

Thus began the long conflict between the House and the professional Parliamentary reporters. From the Revolution until newspapers began to supersede the news-letters, there was an News-Letter Writers at the Bar.

[1] *H. of C. Journals*, xi. 193.

increasing demand for Parliamentary reports; and, in consequence, the order of 1694 was soon set at naught by the news-letter writers. Griffith Card, whose letters circulated in the London coffee-houses, was the next news writer at the bar. He was there on February 11th, 1695, to answer a charge of having, in a letter "dispersed at Garraway's coffee-house and other coffee-houses, misrepresented the votes and proceedings of this House." With Card there was also summoned to the bar Jeremiah Stokes, "who keeps Garraway's coffee-house," and who was a subscriber to Card's letters. Stokes was ordered to withdraw; but Card was brought to the bar, and upon his knees reprimanded by the Speaker. Dyer had been ordered to pay his fees to the sergeant-at-arms. In Card's case an order was made that he "be discharged without paying his fees, in respect of his poverty[1]." In 1697 there was another complaint against Dyer. One of his letters, that had been sent to Bristol, was read at the table. It proved that he had "intermeddled with the proceedings of the House"; and again he was ordered to attend at the bar. Dyer, however, defaulted[2], and presumably ceased to concern himself with Parliamentary proceedings.

First Complaints against the Newspapers.

Other news-letter writers continued to send out letters similar to those which had brought Dyer and Card to the bar; and in 1703 the Speaker acquainted the House that there had come into his hands several written papers which had been dispersed at the coffee-houses, wherein the proceedings of the House "are misrepresented, and several false things inserted, as if they had been votes of this House." Following this statement from the Chair the House re-adopted the order of 1694 against the news writers[3]. This order was renewed without much variation in phraseology until 1722. By that time, as is apparent from the Journals, the printed newspaper was beginning to displace the news-letter; for in 1722 there was a complaint that the House was misrepresented in written and printed news-letters, and, instead of the order in the old form an order against intermeddling with the proceedings of the House was made against both news-letter writers and newspaper publishers, and it was made to apply to proceedings in committee as well as in the House[4]. The news-letter had not completely disappeared as late as 1738. There

---

[1] *H. of C. Journals*, xi. 439.   [2] *H. of C. Journals*, xii. 48.
[3] *H. of C. Journals*, xiv. 270.   [4] *H. of C. Journals*, xx. 99.

were then complaints against "several written and printed news-letters"; and in consequence the order hitherto existing was made more comprehensive. It was so amended as to declare it a high indignity and a notorious breach of privilege "to presume to insert in the said letters or papers or to give therein an account of the debates, or other proceedings of the House, or any committee thereof, as well during the recess as the sitting of Parliament[1]." This order was renewed as late as 1753[2]; but the complaint of 1738 was the last against the writers of news-letters sent out in manuscript, the last against the pioneer Parliamentary reporters who began their work in the reign of Charles I.

Henceforward the contest which had been going on since 1694 was to be with the newspaper press. The first newspaper to offend was the *Flying Post*. The ground of its offence was not a report of the debates of the House, but a tart comment on speculations in exchequer bills. The offence of the *Flying Post* was taken so seriously that a bill was introduced "to prevent the writing, printing, or publishing of any news without licence[3]." *The First Newspaper to offend.*

After the news-letter writers disappeared, the business of reporting the proceedings of the House fell, not at first to the newspapers, but to the magazines; and it was these offenders that the House had chiefly in mind in 1738, when it adopted the order declaring it a breach of privilege to publish reports either during the session or in the recess. This amended order was in response to a suggestion by Speaker Onslow, who told the House that he had seen with concern that accounts of their proceedings were inserted in the newspapers and other periodical publications. Onslow feared great misrepresentations from such reporting, and appealed to the House to devise some method of preventing the abuse. The House was fully in sympathy with the Speaker. Yonge, Wyndham, and Winnington all agreed as to the impropriety of these reports. Pulteney went much further. He urged that to print speeches, even if they should not be misrepresented, tended to make members of the House accountable out of doors for what they might say within the Chamber. The new order was passed without a dissenting voice, and with little public animadversion[4]. *The House fears Misrepresentation.*

Before this time reports of the debates, thinly disguised, had

[1] *H. of C. Journals*, XXIII. 148. [2] *H. of C. Journals*, XXVI. 754.
[3] *Parl. Hist.*, v. 1164. [4] Cf. Coxe, *Life of Walpole*, III. 24–30.

The
Magazines.

regularly appeared in Boyer's *Political State*, the *London Magazine* and the *Gentleman's Magazine*; and in spite of the order of 1738, renewed in 1753, these reports were continued until the end of the reign of George II, when the modern newspaper came into existence, and gradually crowded out the magazines as reporters of the Parliamentary debates.

An Order
against
Newspaper
Reports.

At first the newspapers adopted disguises similar to those used in the magazines[1]. These did not save them; and as early in the history of the modern newspaper press as 1762 there was a complaint to the House " that the publishers of newspapers had of late taken upon them to give accounts of proceedings of this House, and of the debates pretended to have been had thereupon." Several of the offending newspapers were delivered at the table, and paragraphs in them, to which exception was taken, were read by the clerk. Then the House was moved that the entry in the Journals of the 13th of April, 1738, of " the proceedings of the House upon the complaint which was made to the House, that the publishers of several written and printed newspapers had taken upon them to give account therein of the proceedings of this House, might be read; and the same being read accordingly, it was resolved *nem. con.* that it is a high indignity to, and a notorious breach of the privileges of this House, for any news writer in letters or other papers, as minutes or under any other denomination, or for any printer, or publisher of any printed newspaper of any denomination in Great Britain, or Ireland, or any other part of His Majesty's dominions, to presume to insert in the said letters or papers, or to give therein any account of the debates or other proceedings of this House, or any committee thereof, as well during the recess as the sitting of Parliament, and that this House will proceed with the utmost severity against such offenders[2]."

The Contest
with the
Press.

The order of 1762 is reproduced in full, because it threw down the gage to the newspaper printers, and was the order on which was fought the constitutional contest of 1771, in which the House was worsted. By the beginning of the reign of George III, what may be described as the one-man political journals, which had been so largely subsidised by government in the reigns of George I and George II[3], had ceased to have any

[1] Cf. May, *Constitutional Hist.*, II. 37.

[2] *H. of C. Journals*, XXIX. 206, 207.

[3] Cf. Coxe, *Walpole*, III. 295.

usefulness, and the pamphlet was also losing its old place in the literature of politics. Both were now being superseded by the newspaper, and the term "journalist" was already in vogue[1]. The early years of the reign of George III were also the period of the *North Briton*, and of Junius. This was the period, too, of the Society of the Bill of Rights; an organisation which soon took up the cause of the printers of such popular newspapers as the *London Evening Post*, the *Public Advertiser*, and the *Middlesex Journal*, when they came into conflict with the courts, or with the House of Commons[2].

As newspapers became more firmly established and more widely supported, and as popular interest in politics was stimulated and increased by the conflict between Wilkes on the one side and the House and the Crown on the other, the printers brushed aside their earlier caution in reporting the House of Commons. By 1771, at the instigation of Wilkes[3], several of them had dropped all disguises, and boldly published reports of speeches in the House, with the names of speakers attached[4]. This was in flat contravention of the order of 1762; and on the 8th of February, 1771, the conflict between the printers and the House was begun by Colonel George Onslow. He then made a complaint. of the *Gazetteer and New Daily Advertiser*, printed for R. Thompson, and of the *Middlesex Journal*, printed by R. Wheble, as "misrepresenting the speeches, and reflecting on several of the members of this House." "The printers," writes May, "were ordered to attend; but not without serious warnings and remonstrances from those who foresaw the entanglements into which the House was likely to be drawn. They kept out of the way, and were ordered to be taken into custody. The sergeant proceeded to execute the order, and was laughed at by their servants. Thus thwarted, the House addressed the King to issue a proclamation offering a reward for their apprehension. Meanwhile the offences for which the House was pursuing Thompson and Wheble were practised by several other printers; and on the 12th of March, Colonel Onslow made a complaint against the printers of six other newspapers. All the six printers were ordered to attend at the bar; and on the day appointed four of the number appeared, and a fifth, Mr Woodfall, being already in the custody

Increasing Boldness of the Newspapers.

---

[1] Cf. Coxe, *Walpole*, iv. 114, 159. [2] Stephen, *Life of Horne Tooke*, i. 167.
[3] Cf. Walpole, *Memoirs*, iv. 278. [4] May, *Constitutional Hist.*, ii. 37.

of Black Rod by order of the Lords, was prevented from attending. Two of them, Baldwin and Wright, were reprimanded on their knees and discharged; Bladon having made a very humble submission was discharged without a reprimand. Evans, who had also attended the order of the House, went home before he was called in, in consequence, it is said, of an accident to his wife. He was ordered to attend another day; but wrote a letter to the Speaker, in which he questioned the authority of the House and declined to obey its order. Lastly, Miller did not attend, and was ordered into custody for his offence[1]."

The House and the City. Wilkes and the corporation of the City of London, headed by the lord mayor, Brass Crosby, and Alderman Oliver, now championed Wheble, Thompson, and Miller; and so manœuvred as to keep all three printers out of reach of the sergeant-at-arms, and to bring the city into open conflict with the House of Commons. Crosby and Oliver were of the House, and their actions in the case of the printers resulted in their being committed by the House to the Tower. " Here," continues May, after following in detail the actions of Wilkes, Crosby, and Oliver in the City, and the proceedings of the House in respect to the men who had so boldly defied it, " the prisoners received every mark of public attention and sympathy. Visited by the most distinguished leaders of the opposition, attended by deputations, flattered in addresses, complimented by the freedom of many cities, and overloaded with presents, their imprisonment instead of being a punishment, was a long-continued ovation. They failed to obtain their release under writs of *habeas corpus*, as the legality of their commitment could. not be impeached. But on the 8th of May, after six weeks' confinement, the prorogation of Parliament set them at liberty. Attended by a triumphal procession, they proceeded from the Tower to the Mansion House; and the people exulted at the liberation of their popular magistrates[2]."

Defeat of the House. A year later, when the sheriffs of the City of London, in an address to the Livery, boasted that the House of Commons had " tacitly acquiesced in the claim made by London citizens on behalf of the public at large that the constituents had a right to be informed of the proceedings of their servants in Parliament[3],"

---

[1] May, *Constitutional Hist.*, II. 40, 41.

[2] May, *Constitutional Hist.*, II. 48, 49.

[3] Trevelyan, *Fox*, 400.

the boast was amply justified; for the results of the conflict of the House with the City were decisive. The publication of debates was still declared to be a breach of privilege. But the offence was committed with impunity[1]. The conflict, begun in the days of the news-letter writers in 1694, was at an end; and from 1771, in practice if not in theory, the position of the House of Commons to the outside world in this respect has been what it is to-day.

For nearly a quarter of a century to come, no official or semi-official recognition was given to the reporters of newspapers. They had to crowd into the gallery with other strangers, and were liable to be told at any time by the sergeant-at-arms that taking notes was contrary to the orders of the House[2]. Under such disadvantages imperfections in reporting were to be expected. But by 1775 Horace Walpole, after telling one of his correspondents that "the House of Commons sat till past nine o'clock last night," excused himself from going into details, because "the newspapers are now tolerable journals[3]." By 1786 shorthand reporters were employed at Westminster[4]; and by 1803 the reporters had so well established the usage which gave them the exclusive occupation of the back bench in the strangers' gallery, that, although unrecognised by any formal order of the House, their right to this place was acknowledged by Speaker Abbot and the sergeant-at-arms, which for the reporters was equivalent to recognition by the House[5]. *Gradual Recognition of Reporters.*

Recognition by the House never came while the Commons met in the old Chapel of S. Stephen's. But in 1835, when, after the fire of 1834, the House met in a temporary chamber, a separate gallery was provided for the reporters. Even then their recognition by the House was informal; and not until 1845, when Parliament met for the first time in the new Palace at Westminster, were reporters recognised by the orders of the House; though this tardy recognition did not supersede the ancient rule that they could be excluded on the word of a single member. To-day their position is still technically the same as it was after the House had been worsted in its conflict with the City of London in 1771. "We are accustomed," writes Anson, "to be daily informed throughout the Parliamentary session of every *Present Position of Reporters.*

---

[1] May, ii. 49.   [2] May, ii. 50.
[3] Cunningham, *Letters of Horace Walpole*, vi. 182.
[4] Cf. Colchester, *Diary*, iii. 332.   [5] Colchester, *Diary*, i. 421.

detail of events in the House of Commons, and so we are apt
to forget two things.   The first is that these reports are made
on sufferance; for the House can at any moment exclude strangers,
and clear the reporters' gallery.   They are also published on
sufferance; for the House may at any time resolve that such
publication is a breach of privilege, and deal with it accordingly.
The second is that though the privileges of the House confer a
right to privacy of debate, they do not confer a corresponding
right to the publication of debate. * * * Within those walls he
(a member) may say what he pleases, and is protected by the
general privilege of the House.   But if he chooses to circulate
outside the House statements made within it, he does so at his
peril; and if they contain defamatory matter he will be liable
to proceedings for libel[1]."

A Parlia-
mentary
Fiction.

"We sit," said Sir Robert Inglis, in 1833, "under the fiction
that the public neither sees nor hears us[2]"; and as late as 1859
a similar dictum was differently expressed by Speaker Denison,
when a member complained of an incorrect report of his speech.
"The House," said the Speaker, "does not recognise the reports
of debates.   Therefore a correct or an incorrect report is out of
its cognisance[3]."

[1] Anson, pt. i. 153, 154.   [2] *Mirror of Parliament*, 1833, iv. 3400.
[3] Denison, *Notes from My Journals*, 31.

INDEX.

Abbot, Charles, Speaker, represents Oxford University, 102
  and contributions to Helston, 163
  and patron of Helston, 232
  as nominee of Duke of Leeds, 337
  held sinecure, 450
  his peerage, 453
  his speeches in committee, 463
  his speech at bar of House of Lords, 464
  motion of censure on his speech, 465
  his ordeal, 466
  and public opinion, 470
  and admission of reporters, 595
Abercrombie, Speaker, his Speakership, 479
  his party ties, 479
  his resignation, 480
  and appointment of chaplain, 500
Abingdon, 29, 98, 245, 293, 374
Abjuration, oath of, *see* Oath of abjuration
Absenteeism from House of Commons, end of, 253
Absentees from House of Commons, punishment of, 238
  Lord J. Russell's description of, 250
  complaint from Canterbury of, 252
  inquiry into punishment of, 428
Act of 1427, transferring election cases to assizes, 546
Act of 1444, fixing place of borough elections, 42
Act of 1512, extending privilege to utterances in Parliament, 568
Act of 1514–15, forbidding departure from Parliament, 156
Act of 1535–36, representation of Wales, 104
Act of 1543–44, representation of Wales, 105
Act of 1603, defining privilege, 569
Act of 1606 and Act of 1610, imposing Oaths of Allegiance and Abjuration, 130
Act of 1661, regulating petitions, 573
  enforced against Chartists, 574

Act of 1689, nominations to Cinque Ports, 547
Act of 1694, excise officers, 74
Act of 1695, excluding minors, 227
Act of 1695–96, county elections, 186
Act of 1700–1 (Settlement), clause in, excluding office-holders, 206
  clause never went into effect, 210
  clause abrogated, 210
Act of 1701, restricting privilege, 570
Act of 1705, excluding specific office-holders, 210
  re-enacted in 1707, 212
Act of 1710, property qualifications for members, 152
Act of 1710, postmasters, 74
Act of 1710–11, imposing property qualifications, 169
  its working, 170
  members unseated under, 171
  amended in 1760, 172
  amended in 1838, 176
  notorious evasions of, 177
  exclusions under, 177
  repealed, 1858, 178
Act of 1712, imposing first statutory election charges, 187
Act of 1738, restricting privilege, 571
Act of 1742 (place), 216
Act of 1745, throwing election charges on candidates, 188, 195
Act of 1764, affecting privilege, 571
Act of 1770, affecting privilege, 571
Act of 1781, Coventry, 192
Act of 1782, civil list, 214
Act of 1782, excluding contractors, 217, 219
  and joint stock companies, 219
Act of 1805, affecting privilege, 572
Act of 1809 against sale of seats, 346
Act of 1811, Westminster election charges, 195
Act of 1812, imposing disabilities on bankrupts, 572
Act of 1828, throwing charges in boroughs on candidates, 195
Act of 1829, disqualifying governors of East India Company, 220

Act of 1875, returning officers' charges, 202

Act of Supremacy of 1563, 127
  its provisions, 128
  opposition to it, 128

Acts excluding from House of Commons, 221
  number of men excluded under, 221
  effect of, 222

Acts levying taxation, originating in House of Lords, 549

Acts of Parliament, promulgation of, 584

Acts repealed in deference to public opinion, 275

Addington, Speaker, his formal excuses, 453
  his peerage, 453, 463
  his Speakership, 461
  his speeches in committee, 461
  his failure to control Pitt, 461
  he becomes minister, 461
  as ex-Speaker in House of Commons, 463
  and exclusion of women from House of Commons, 581

Addresses, loyal, 268, 269

Admiralty, places under, as spoils, 300

Agmondesham, 354, 382

Aldborough, 33, 96, 336, 358, 374, 519

Aliens, excluded from House of Commons, 235

Allegiance, oath of, *see* Oath of allegiance

American Revolution and Reform, 11, 218
  and gradual reform, 235
  its effect on English politics, 456

Amersham, *see* Agmondesham

Andover, 159, 375, 388

Anglesea, county of, 378

Anglo-Indians, and the House of Commons, 357, 521
  sit below the gangway, 509, 522
  their wealth, 521
  their prodigality in electioneering, 521
  support Government, 522
  peerages for, 524

Anne, and elections, 407

Annuities, votes in respect of, 22

Anson, and publication of Parliamentary proceedings, 596

Anti-Catholic Committee, thanks Speaker Abbot, 464

Appleby, 314, 316

Appropriation Act, preamble to, 554

Archdale, J., Quaker, 134
  his letter to the Speaker, 134

Aristocracy, in municipal politics, 80, 83
  and control of House of Commons, 310

Army, pressure on, in elections by George III, 412

Ashburton, 167, 537, 539

Ashton, Sir R., and taking of Communion, 132

Assizes, judges of, and controverted elections, 546

Association Pledge of 1696, 146

Athenry, 526

Athlone, 341

Attendance in House of Commons, no means of securing, 238
  efforts to enforce, in 1554, 239
  in Pensioner Parliament, 427
  no obligation on members for, 428

Aubrey, Sir John, buys a seat, 358

Aylesbury, 16, 87

Ayscough, Dr, and bargains for seats, 356

Bacon, Francis, nominated by Burleigh for Gatton, 376
  and court party in House of Commons, 380

Bagehot, his characterisation of the nomination system, 337, 363

Bagg, James, election manager in Devon and Cornwall, 386
  his care for his friends, 387
  his idea of the office of Speaker, 433

Baines, M. T., describes working of property qualification Acts, 176

Ballot, first Act sanctioning use of, 207
  used in House on election petitions, 537
  proposal to choose Speaker by, 538
  unpopular with Government, 538

Banbury, 29, 98, 161, 197, 211, 374, 399

Bandon, 234

Bankes, his amendment to Morpeth's motion regarding Speaker Abbot, 467

Barham, J. F., sells nomination for Stockbridge, 361

Baring, Mr, and bill to amend Place Acts, 253

Barnard, Sir John, achieves reputation as a debater, 525

Barnstaple, 67

Basingstoke, 6

Bath, 212, 336, 399, 415

Bath, Earl of, and surrender of charters, 395

Beaumaris, 111

Bedford, 66, 197, 213

Bedford, county of, 385

Bedford, Duke of, and developement of Covent Garden, 566

Bedwin, 35

Bell, Sir Robert, Speaker, rewarded by the Crown, 436

Bentinck, G. W. P., opposes repeal of property qualification Act, 178

Berkeley, Grantley, his brother as patron, 325
  and Ladies' Gallery, 580

Berkhampstead, stewardship of, 243

Berwick-on-Tweed, 373, 397

Beverley, 177, 247

Bewdley, 29, 66, 362, 522

Bexley, Lord, and Speaker's levies, 472
Bill, first entered on Journals, 529
  reading of *pro formâ*, 542
Bill of Rights, Society of, 593
Bill of Subsidies, and absentee members, 428
Birch, Col., proposes Seymour's re-election as Speaker, 437
Birmingham, 6, 81, 88, 198, 263
Bishop's Castle, 268, 331, 350
Bishops and electioneering, 296
Bishops, bill to prevent translation of, 297
Black Book, characterisation of lawyer members in, 518
Blackburne, J., 302
Blackfriars, Parliament meets at, 372, 423
Blackstone, and relations of members to constituents, 271
Blandford, Marquis of, objects to paying election charges, 188
  his reform bill of 1830, 361
Bletchingley, 243
Bodmin, 56, 198
Borlase, Dr, describes Cornish boroughs, 93
Borough areas, restriction of, 32
Borough control, disappearance of, 15
Borough franchises, variety of, 4, 5
  narrowing of, 7, 13
Borough managers, of treasury boroughs, 340
Borough masters, *see* borough patrons
Borough members, seating of, 502, 504
  distinguished from knights, 502
  fees paid by, 503
  personnel of, 512
Borough mongers, *see* borough patrons
Borough owners, in Parliament, 9
  official patronage for, 330
  proposal to buy out with peerages, 331
Borough patron, a, and his rewards, 324
  makes a bargain with Whig govern-ment, 326
  bargains for a peerage, 331
  his conditions with his member, 335
Borough patrons, their forerunners, 45
  letters to boroughs from, 46
  term comes in use, 47
  and control of corporation boroughs, 54
  and control of freeman boroughs, 76
  compensation for, 81
  and treasury patronage, 302
  in reign of James II, 309
  and Irish boroughs, 310
  orders to members returned by, 312
  getting free from, 313
  conditions insisted upon by, 318
  brothers as, 325
  usually supporters of Government, 326

Borough patrons (*continued*)
  their claims on official patronage, 329
  bargains of, 332
  motives of, 333
  and re-election of members, 335
  in opposition, and nominees, 348
  return relatives without conditions, 350
  family claims on, 352
Borough representation, lack of uni-formity in, 4
  reasons for the lack, 8
  a characterisation of, 15
Borough seat, a bargain for, 356
Boroughbridge, 96, 358, 374
Boroughs, as property, 9, 10
  classification of, 29
  members from English, 29
  number of, 29
  sale of, 97, 354
  electors in and patronage, 294, 305
  brokers in, 354
  leasing of, 354
  surrender of charters to Charles II, 394
Boroughs, burgage, number of, 30
  franchise in, 33, 39
  and election petitions, 34, 38
  residential qualification in, 35
  their friends in Parliament, 37
  women in, 39
  expensive of control, 41
Boroughs, contributory, Wales, and contests with shire towns, 109, 110, 111
Boroughs, corporation, number of, 30, 52
  representation of, 41
  with charters, 46
Boroughs, decayed, proclamation of James I concerning, 379
Boroughs, delinquent, punishment of, 15
  writs withheld from, 15
  Acts for punishment of, 16
Boroughs, freeman, number of, 30
  and control by corporations, 52, 70
  and patron control, 58
  franchise in, 58
  qualifications in, 63, 68
  their friends in Parliament, 67
  expensive of control, 77
  women in, 78
Boroughs, inhabitant householder, 29
Boroughs, potwalloper, franchise in, 31
Boroughs, scot and lot, 29
  number of, 30
  population of, 30
  residential qualification in, 31
  and corporation control, 53, 54
Boroughs, treasury, nominated members for, 340, 341
  managers for, 340
  in Ireland, 341
  and office-holders, 342

Boroughs, treasury (*continued*)
  re-election in, 343
  shifting around of members for, 343
  jobbers in, 344
  members for, support Government, 347
Boroughs, Welsh, franchise in, 105
  franchise based on payment of wages, 107
  changes in franchise in, 108
  controverted elections from, 108
  survey of history of, 117
Bosses, American, English prototypes of, 333
Bossiney, 75, 374, 523, 526
Boston, 47, 160
Boyer's *Political State*, 592
Bradford, 19
Bradlaugh, C., and Affirmation Act, 124
Bramber, 95, 186, 249, 370
Bramber, rape of, 16, 541
Brecon, 117
Brewer, and Tudor policy, 371
  and Parliament of 1529–36, 372
Bribery, of municipal corporations, 56
  after Reform Act, 57
  in freeman boroughs, 79
  becomes general, 154
  suppression of, 164
  used by William III in House of Commons, 406
  in time of George III, 409
Bribery of constituencies, early instances of, 155
  by freeing them of expense, 157
  and local patriotism, 162
  at present time, 164
Bridgwater, 32, 167, 198, 299, 408, 415
Bridgwater, Earl of, controls Flint, 116
Bridport, 47, 123
Bristol, 17, 18, 66, 71, 78, 155, 261, 267, 353, 399, 416, 519, 531
British Museum, Speakers as trustees of, 453, 474
Bromley, Wm., Speaker, 447
  in House as ex-Speaker, 447
Brougham, Lord, candidate for Yorkshire, 179
  and minors in House of Commons, 230
  his characterisation of Lonsdale, 317
  his characterisation of Pitt's peers, 328
Broughton, Bryan, 276
Browne, Sir Thomas, describes election in 1679, 186
Brudenell, Lord, compelled to resign seat, 322
Buckingham, 49, 373
Buckingham, county of, 266, 323
Buckingham, Duke of, controls elections from Cambridge University, 101
  electioneering manager for James I, 381

Buckingham, Duke of (*continued*)
  and dissolution of 1625, 383
  and Cornish elections of 1628, 386
  his innovations in electioneering, 390
Buckinghamshire, Duke of, as patron of Horner, 352
Bucknall, Sir Wm., named by Charles II as candidate at Liverpool, 395
Bulkley, family, control Beaumaris, 114
Burdett, Sir Francis, and reform, 87
  and contest over election expenses, 193
  describes his purchase of a seat, 361
Burgage, definition of, 4
  market value of, 7
Burgage boroughs, *see* boroughs, burgage
Burgages, appreciate in value, 33
  restriction of number of, 34
  not peculiar to Parliamentary boroughs, 34
Burgoyne, M.P. for Preston, 350
Burke, Edmund, his property qualification, 173
  and Civil List Act, 214
  and representation of Bristol, 261
  and the passing of instructions, 271
  leader in economy movement, 280
  returned for Wendover, 352
  returned for Bristol, 353
  complains of treatment by House of Lords, 563
  advocates publication of division lists, 587
Burleigh, Lord, his orders to sheriff concerning Gatton, 376
Burnet, G., and property qualification bills, 168
  and office-holders in Parliament, 207
  and James II's electioneering in counties, 404
  and abuse of privilege, 570
Bury, 523
Bury St Edmunds, 132, 265, 285, 351, 382, 400
Bussy, Sir John, Speaker, 1397–98, 369

Cabinet, government by, suspended by George III, 456
  and rights of House of Commons as to taxation, 554
Cade, Jack, and freedom of elections, 21, 369
Calais, 373, 392
Caledonian Canal, Speaker as commissioner of, 474
Callington, 375, 519
Calls of the House, 238
  in Pensioner Parliament, 427
  Sergeant-at-Arms and, 492
Calne, 198, 349
Cambridge, 61, 67, 70, 101, 198
Cambridge, county of, 407

Cambridge, University of, enfranchised, 99, 382
    under court control, 101
    represented by Pitt, 102
    number of electors, 103
    represented by a minor, 382
    Manners-Sutton as member for, 476, 478
Camelford, 92, 327, 335, 374
Camelford, Lord, in control of Old Sarum, 342
Campbell, Sir J., characterises freeman voters, 70
Candidates, origin of charges on, 22
    entertain freeholders, 22
    pledges demanded from, 271
Candles in House of Commons, 543
Canning, George, and Grampound, 87
    exchanges Liverpool for Harwich, 315
    his defence of Speaker Abbot, 468
    and petitions for reform, 575
Canning, Stratford, M.P. for Old Sarum, 312
    returned by his father-in-law, 351
Canterbury, 18, 155, 252
    and Speaker's chaplains, 499
Card, Griffith, news-letter writer, 590
Cardiff, 117
Cardiganshire, 186
Carlisle, 58, 64, 69, 74, 75, 76, 77, 160, 198, 267, 297, 424
Carlisle, Bishop of, and electioneering, 297
Carlow, 341
Carmarthen, 18
Caroline, Queen, and controverted elections, 408
Carrington, Lord, as patron of Horner, 352
Cashel, 341, 347, 523
Castle Rising, 314, 374
Castlereagh, Lord, and Grampound, 86
    and close boroughs in Ireland, 310
    and price of seats in England, 358
Catesby, Wm., Speaker, 1483, 434
Catholic Relief Act of 1829, 127, 140
Catholic Relief bill, Abbot's opposition to, 463
Catholics, Roman, James II's policy towards, 399
Cave, supervisor of franks, 287
Cavendish family and control of Derby, 66
Cecil, Gen. Sir Ed., 44, 46
Cecil, Lord, and Cambridge University, 100
Cecil, Sir Robert, 158
Ceiling of S. Stephen's Chapel, 426
Chair, Speaker's, and office bestowed by the Crown, 437
    as a perquisite, 472
    attitude of House towards, 482
    increasing deference towards, 485

Chairman of Ways and Means, origin of office of, 532
Chaplain, office of, 489
    appointment of, 497, 498
    first reference to, in Journals, 498
    payments to, 499
    recommendations for preferment for, 499, 500
    salary of, 500
    duty of, 500
Chapter House of Westminster Abbey, meeting-place of House of Commons, 424
Charities, municipal, used in electioneering, 73
Charles I, his efforts to keep men out of the House of Commons, 383
    his choice of sheriffs, 384
    his efforts to influence county elections, 385
    his non-success in elections of 1628, 388
    and election of 1640, 389
    his personal government, 390
    his instructions concerning elections, 390
Charles II, his first Parliament, 48, 50
    his second Parliament, 51
    and Nonconformists in boroughs, 393
    and writs of *quo warranto*, 393
    and attack on corporations, 394
    his personal interest in elections, 395
    his menial servants as M.P.'s, 395
    and re-election of Seymour as Speaker, 437
    and Commons' assertions of right to elect Speaker, 441
    his compromise over election of Speaker, 443
Charter, Maidstone loses, 375
Charters, borough, of Henry VI, 370
    of Henry VIII, 373
    of Edward VI, 373
    of Mary, 374
    of Elizabeth, 375
    Charles II grants the last, 391
    surrender of, 394
Chartists, their petition of 1848, 574
Chatham, Earl of, scourges Anglo-Indian corruption, 521
Cheney, Sir J., Speaker, 487
Cheshire, 187, 296, 373
Chester, 18, 285, 297, 373, 399
Chester, Mr, and expense of Gloucester election, 416
Chesterfield, Earl of, *see* Stanhope, P. D.
Chiltern Hundreds, Steward of, toast of, 320
Chiltern Hundreds, stewardship of, 242
    date of revival of, 243
    partisan use of, 244

Chiltern Hundreds (*continued*)
  abandonment of partisan use of, 249
  Irish equivalent of, 249
Chimneys in burgage boroughs, 35
Chippenham, 370
Chorister, vote in respect of office of, 23
Christchurch, 224, 343
Christian Club, and New Shoreham, 541
Church, effect of spoils system on, 307
Church of Ireland, clergy of, excluded from House of Commons, 127
Church of Rome, priests of, excluded, 127
Church of Scotland, ministers of, excluded, 126
Church preferments and offices, confer right to vote, 22
  treated as spoils, 295
  turned over to treasury, 298
Church rates and county franchise, 25
  in scot and lot boroughs, 31
Church, Scotch Episcopal, and prayers for royal family, 149
  Act for relief of, 150
Cinque Ports, barons of, in House of Commons, 502
  fees of barons of, 503
  nomination of members from, 547
Cirencester, 198, 375
Civil List Act, of 1782, 214
Civil Service, appointments in, obtained through M.P.'s, 293
  qualifications for, 303
  making of appointments in, 303
  number of places in, in 1854, 304
  reform of, in 1853, 308
Civil Service Commission, report of 1854–55, 304
Clancarty, Earl of, opposes repeal of property qualification Act, 178
Clarendon, Lord, and dissolution of 1625, 383
Clarges, Sir Thomas, and Charles II's rejection of Commons' Speaker, 440
Clarke, his account of work of regulators for James II, 402
  and James II's electioneering, 404
Clergy, become of the electorate, 3, 22
  excluded from House of Commons, 125
  Act of 1801 excluding, 126
Clerk assistant, 490
  first appointment of, 491
  at table in committee, 491
Clerk of the Crown, collects fees on return of writs, 154
  fees to, 503
Clerk of House of Commons, place of, 426
  under clerk of the Parliament, 489
  oath of, 489
  salary and emoluments of, 490
  appointments made by, 490

Clerk of House of Commons (*continued*)
  and Journals of House of Commons, 490
  duties of, 491
  and committee, 491
  dress of, 496
Clerks of the Peace as voters, 23
Clerks, under, collections for, from members, 503
Clifford, Mr, his quarrel with Andrew Marvell, 486
Clifton, Lord, and complaint of absenteeism from Canterbury, 253
Clitheroe, 83, 132, 397
Clive, Lord, bargains for a peerage, 331
  patron of Wedderburn, 350
Clotworthy, Sir John, 526
Cobbett, Wm., complains of lack of room in Chamber, 428
  takes Peel's place, 505
Cochrane, Lord, 193, 575
Cockburn, Lord, and public opinion in 18th century, 270
Cockermouth, 232, 336
Cockpit, meetings at, exclusion of opposition from, 509
Coke, Sir E., advice to Cambridge University, 100
  and minors in House of Commons, 224
  made sheriff by Charles I, 383
  elected to House of Commons, 384
  as Speaker, rewarded by Crown, 436
Colchester, 47, 64, 68, 76, 172, 372, 377
Colchester, Lord, *see* Abbot
Colonial Governments, and right of Lower Houses to tax, 557
Commissions of the peace, changes made in, to influence elections, 385
  revision of, by James II, 403
Committee, for remodelling corporations, 400
Committee, Foley speaks in, 446
  Harley speaks in, 446
  Hanmer speaks in, 447
  Abbot speaks in, 463
  Manners-Sutton speaks in, 475
  disadvantage of intervention of Speakers in, 475, 476
  modern Speakers and, 477
  last intervention of Speaker in, 480
  first bill referred to, 529
  of whole House, 531
  meeting-places of, 531
  instructions to, 534
Committee, private bill, scandals in organisation of, 535
  voting in, 535
Committee stage, 445
  Eliot urges advantages of, 445
  rights of Speaker at, 446
  Hooker's statement concerning, 530
  character of debate at, 532
Committees, chairman of, 446
  creation of permanent office of, 532

Committees, chairman of (*continued*)
  position of, 533
  emolument of, 533
  acts as Deputy-Speaker, 533
Committees of privilege and elections, hear election cases, 539
Commonwealth, franking originates under, 284
Communion, taking of, as a test, 130
  members suspended for not having taken, 133
Compton, Bishop of London, 297
Compton, Speaker, 447
  and George II, 447
  his formal excuses, 452
Conference, on money bill of 1671, 550
  on bill of 1678, 552
  precedure in, 557
  place of, 557
  Commons' rules for, 558
  failure of House of Commons at, 560
  decline of, 560
Conference, free, procedure at, 559
Congress, U.S., strangers in, 578
Conservatives, name first used, 478
Constituencies, bribery of, 7
  single member, 29
  never able to rid themselves of members, 250
  no complaints of neglect from, 251
  responsibility to, 256
  number of, 392
Contractors, and government contracts, 217
  excluded by Act of 1782, 217
  reasons for exclusion of, 218
  first bill aimed against, 219
  George III opposes exclusion of, 419
  sit below the gangway, 509
Controverted election cases, trial of, 7
  partisan determinations of, 12
  from counties and boroughs, 14
  at the Restoration, 48
Convention Parliament, reform expected from, 8
Convocation, members of, and House of Commons, 100, 125
Convocations and Prayer for Parliament, 500
Conway, secretary of state, tries to find a borough for his son, 388
Cooper, Wm., Chaplain, 498
Copley, Dame E., 224
Copley, Mrs, and nomination for Gatton, 377
Copley, Sir Thomas, 223
Copyholders, vote at Cricklade, 16
  a protest from, 27
Corbett, Thomas, 213
Corn Bill, amended in House of Lords, 555
Cornewall, Wolfran, Speaker, George III recommends for Speaker, 460
  his speech in committee, 460
  and exclusion of women, 581

Cornish boroughs, former importance of, 91
  notoriety of, 91
  clustering of, 92
  character of members from, 363
  transaction in, 414
Cornwall, county of, 266, 363, 374, 375, 376, 385, 389, 395
  Duchy of, 409
Coronation oath, 2
Corporation boroughs, *see* Boroughs, corporation
Corporations, municipal, elections by, 41
  right of election generally conceded, 43
  opposition to, 44
  assaults on, 48
  and contests with inhabitants, 52
  and indirect control, 52
  qualifications for members of, 53
  non-resident members of, 54
  and Reform Act, 55
  bribes to members of, 56
  loss of advantages after 1832, 57
  reform of, 57
  Charles II's interference with, 393
  attack on, renewed in 1687, 398
  remodelling of, by James II, 399
  number remodelled, 400
  example of remodelling of, 400
Corrupt Practices Act, 1883, 57, 165
Corruption in borough elections, punishment of, 15
  date of origin of, 77
Coryton, warned not to stand for Cornwall, 386
Cottoners, in House of Commons, 523
Council, His Majesty's, member of, proposes Speaker, 435
Counties, controverted election cases from, 14
Counties, cities and boroughs of, 17
  charters of, 17
  freeholders in, 18
Counties, Welsh, franchise in, 105
County Courts, elections take place at, 41
  promulgation of Acts of Parliament in, 585
County electoral districts in Act of 1885, 89
County franchise, regulated by statute, 20
  three changes in, 24
  residential qualification for, falls into desuetude, 24
  and payment of taxes, 24
  and Act of 1712, 25
Courtney, W. P., and Cornish boroughs, 363
Coventry, 18, 67, 69, 192, 258, 287, 369, 370, 399, 416, 424, 519
Coventry, Act of 1781, 69
Crewe, Speaker, his election in 1625, 438

Crewe Act of 1782, 74
  circumventions of, 75
Cricklade, 16, 34, 87, 198, 355, 357
Croker, J. W., describes election ball,
  56
    and Reform, 88
    and number of members returned
      by patrons, 310
    his entry into the House, 345
Cromwell, O., his reforms reversed, 48
    made freeman of Cambridge, 61
    his redistribution measure, 86
    recommends a Speaker, 437
Cromwell, Thomas, as election manager
  for Henry VIII, 371
    one reason for downfall of, 380
Crosby, Brass, Lord Mayor, 594
Crown, protection of by oaths, 145
    and elections, 367
    relations of, to the franchise, 390
    power of, to enfranchise falls into
      desuetude, 392
    and S. Stephen's Chapel, 424
    and Speaker's retention of cham-
      bers, 425
    and election of Speaker, 433
    nominates Speaker, 435
    sends orders to Speaker, 435
    rewards services of Speaker, 436
    influence in choice of Speaker, 443
    Speakers and office held at pleasure
      of, 450
    and representative system, 456
    Speaker as spokesman to, 486
    and Sergeant-at-Arms, 491
Crown control, and exclusion Act, 221
Crown lands, stewardships of, 243
Crown livings, treated as spoils, 295
    and borough management, 299
Crown Office and election expenses,
  184
Cunninghame, Gen., at issue with his
  patron, 321
Curwen, his bill to prevent sale of seats,
  463
Curwen, Samuel, his description of Old
  Sarum, 36
Cust, Speaker, his formal excuses, 452
    his Speakership, 458
    rebuked by Rigby, 458
Customs and Excise, places in, as spoils,
  294
    officers in, disfranchised, 300

Dalton, and residential qualification, 24
    and duties of sheriff, 185
Danby, Charles II's efforts to avoid
  impeachment of, 437
    at issue with Speaker Seymour, 439
Darlington, Lord, his rewards as a
  borough master, 327
Dartmouth, Earl of, and representation
  of Birmingham, 263
Debate, order of, 530
Decayed boroughs, 2, 5

Declaration of Indulgence, and Non-
  conformists, 400
Defoe, Daniel, and loyal addresses, 269
Delaney, Mrs, and franks, 286
Democracy, barrier between England
  and, 151
Denbigh, 110
Denbighshire, 297
Denison, Speaker, intervenes in com-
  mittee, 480
    on the office of Speaker, 487
    and Commons' right to tax, 556
    and reports of debates, 596
Denman, as nominated member, 338
Denman, Lord, opposes repeal of pro-
  perty qualification Act, 178
Deputy-Speaker, creation of office of, 533
    difficulties connected with office of,
      534
Derby, 66
Derbyshire, 295
Devon, county of, represented by a
  minor, 224
    and James Bagg, 386
    represented by Seymour, 437
Devonshire, Duke of, returns Denman,
  338
Devizes, 153, 164, 199, 463, 522
D'Ewes, compiles *Journals*, 529
    describes committee stage, 530
    and second reading stage, 531
    describes procedure in divisions,
      536
    describes reading of a bill *pro
      formâ*, 543
    on exclusion of strangers, 576
Dick, Quinton, member for a treasury
  borough, 347
Dissenters, excluded from corporations,
  55
    bills to exclude from House of
      Commons, 133
    George III fears to disoblige, 277
Division lists, as electioneering litera-
  ture, 587
    Burke advocates publication of, 587
    official publication of, 587
Divisions, procedure at, 535, 536
    in 1593, 536
    precedent for, 536
    new rules for, 582
Dodington, Bubb, in control of Wey-
  mouth and Melcombe, 94
    forbids his members to attend elec-
      tions, 251
    and church patronage, 299
    and George II, 408
Donegal, county of, 325
Dorchester, 226, 243
Dorset, county of, 385
Dorset, Duke of, complains of nominee
  not resigning seat, 321
Dover, 44, 78, 158, 541
Dowdeswell, his bill disfranchising civil
  servants, 74, 419

Dowers, votes in respect of, 22
Downpatrick, 345
Downton, 36, 97, 322
Downton, hundred of, 15, 175
Droitwich, 36, 97, 522
Drummond, George III's debt to, 417
Dublin, city of, and presentation of petitions, 574
Dublin, University of, enfranchised, 101
Dundalk, 341
Dunning, 280
Dunstanville, Lord, 56
Dunwich, 64, 71, 76, 97, 155
Durham, 6, 65, 269, 392
Durham Act of 1763, 65
Durham, county of, 105, 392, 425
Dyer, news-letter writer, at the bar, 589
    again in conflict with the House, 590

East Grinstead, 64, 73, 321, 344, 351
East Hendred, stewardship of manor of, 242
East India Company, 521
East Looe, 92, 163, 341, 375
East Retford, 16, 72, 88, 142
Eaton, Dorman B., and civil service, 292
Edgcumbe, Lord, his transactions in boroughs, 341, 356, 414
Edgcumbe, Sir Richard, court candidate for Cornwall, 385
Edinburgh, Speaker Abercrombie, member for, 479
    and privilege to present petitions, 575
Edward I, and control of elections, 367
Edward III, demands a subsidy, 256
    and Parliamentary elections, 368
Edward IV, eagerness for seats in reign of, 370
Edward VI, letters to sheriffs in reign of, 373
    boroughs enfranchised by, 373
    assigns S. Stephen's chapel to House of Commons, 425
Egmont, Lord, threatens Dodington's control, 299
Election, renunciation of, 241
Election expenses, thrown on candidates, 152, 181, 189
    originally small, 182
    in London and in constituencies, 184
    become heavy, 190
    in cities and boroughs, 191
    dispute about, at Coventry, 192
    contested by Burdett, 193
    in boroughs, thrown on candidates, 195
    bills to relieve candidates of, 195
    in 1833 in boroughs, 200
Election petitions, procedure on, 539
    heard at the bar, 539
    number of, 539

Electioneering, excise officers and post-masters and, 74
Electioneering literature, division lists distributed as, 587
Elections, controverted, manner of deciding, 539
    bill for hearing at the bar, 539
    heard by committees, 539
    and House of Lords, 545
Electoral abuses, turned to account by the Crown, 2
Electoral map, changes in, 89
    features of, 90
Electoral power, unequal distribution of, 85
    no redistribution of, before 1832, 86
Electoral system, changes in between 1604 and 1832, 3
Electors and elected, tie between, 237
Electors, restriction of number of, 8
Eliot, Edward, Earl of St Germains, as patron of Gibbon, 320
Eliot, Sir John, 46, 123
    warned not to stand for Cornwall, 386
    his estimate of the Speakership in 1625, 435
    his characterisation of excuses of Speakers-elect, 438
    urges advantages of committee stage, 445, 523
    expounds rules of House of Commons, 484
Elizabeth, enfranchises boroughs, 375
    her letter of direction to the sheriffs, 377
Ellenborough, and candidates' liability for election expenses, 194
Ellice, Edward, borough monger for the Whigs, 346
Enfranchisement, by Act of Parliament, 391
    by resolution of the House of Commons, 392
    petitions for, 392
Engrossment, 530
Enniskillen, 341
Ernley, Sir John, proposes Crown nominee for the Chair, 439
Escheatorships, of Irish provinces, used as Chiltern Hundreds, 249
Escourt, Sir Thomas, 241
Essex, county of, 260, 311, 385
Evelyn, laments incoming of the newly rich, 520
Evesham, 142, 382, 388
Excise duty in 1733, and instructions to M.P.'s, 267
Excise officers and elections, 74
Exclusion bill, agitation over, 393
Exeter, 18, 241
Ex-Speakers in the House, 447, 463

Faggot voter, 22
Falmouth, 92

Falmouth, Lord, sells nominations to treasury, 340, 414

Fanshawe, Lord, 138

Fenwick, at bar of the House of Commons, 495

Fifeshire, by-election for, 214

Finch, Chancellor, orders new election of Speaker, 439

Finch, Speaker, as link between the Crown and the House, 433
  the King's servant, 434
  Gardiner's estimate of his position, 434

Flint, 115

Flying Post, 591

Foley family, rise of, 522
  Parliamentary connections of, 522, 525

Foley, Paul, elected Speaker, 444
  his independence, 444
  speaks in committee, 446
  becomes Speaker, 522
  and Harley alliance, 525

Follett, Sir William, 79

Forty-shilling freeholder, *see* Freeholder, forty-shilling

Foster, Irish Speaker, 476

Fowey, 92, 322, 375

Fox, C. J., freeman of Cambridge, 71
  his property qualification, 173
  his election for Midhurst, 228
  refrains from voting until of age, 229
  characterises patrons' members, 311
  opposition candidate at Westminster, 417

Franchise, eighty-five avenues to, 23
  wide at Preston, 49
  original borough, 58

Franchises, local contests for wider, 10

Franking, principle underlying, 284
  for English members in Ireland, 284
  institution of, 284
  abuse of, 286
  advantages of, 288
  curtailment of privilege of, 288
  in Canada and United States, 290
  abolition of, 290

Franks, cost of, in 1717, 286
  demand for, 286, 289
  first, 287
  popular idea as to cost of, 288
  number of, in 1837, 290

Freedom, payments for, 62, 154
  refusals of, 72

Freehold, extension of meaning of, 21

Freeholder, forty-shilling, Act of 1430, 20
  applicable to Wales, 106

Freeholders, non-resident, polling of, 186
  act to prevent making of, 187

Freeholders, pressure on, by Charles I, 385

Freeholds, subdivisions of, 22

Freeman boroughs, *see* Boroughs, freeman

Freemen, and county franchise, 20
  and borough franchise, 58
  honorary, 58, 60, 63
  non-resident, 58, 60
  and trade guilds, 58
  rights and duties of, 59
  restricting number of, 60
  members made, 60
  patrons made, 62
  non-resident, brought to vote, 63
  making of honorary, 64
  bills aimed against making of, 66
  restriction of number of, 72
  intimidation of, 73
  value of vote of, 76
  House of Lords defends rights of, 79

French Revolution, delays reform, 12
  and effect on English political life, 456

Friends of the People, petition of, 310

Galleries in S. Stephen's, 429

Gallery, ladies', 426, 580
  ventilator as, 581

Gallery, peers', 563

Gallery, reporters', 595

Gallery, Speaker's, 563

Gallery, strangers', 577
  contests over clearing of, 578
  difficulty in clearing, 581
  women excluded from, 581
  reporters in, 595

Game of All Fours, 94

Gangway, benches before, 509
  and Anglo-Indians and army contractors, 509

Garaway, and Charles II's rejection of Common's Speaker, 440

Gardiner, S. R., his estimate of Speakership in reign of Charles I, 434

Gascoyne, Gen., and representation of Liverpool, 262

Gatton, 30, 64, 97, 223, 361, 370, 376, 377

Gazetteer and New Daily Advertiser, 593

Gentleman's Magazine, 592

George I, and elections, 407

George II, his interest in elections, 408
  his indifference to a general election, 408

George III, and bestowal of Chiltern Hundreds, 245
  procures loyal addresses, 270
  defers to public opinion, 277
  opinion of popularity, 279
  and disfranchisement of office-holders, 300
  his rule as to promotions in the peerage, 328
  his concern in elections, 409, 420

George III (*continued*)
nominates members for Cornish boroughs, 409
his care for members' interests, 410
his watchfulness of by-elections, 411
precipitates dissolution of 1774, 411
and Westminster election of 1774, 412
and Middlesex election of 1774, 413
and Windsor election of 1780, 415
makes electors at Windsor, 415
and election expenses, 416
and place bills, 419
and Grenville bill, 419, 540
and exclusion of contractors from House of Commons, 419
his attitude towards the representative system, 456
and Speaker Norton, 459
recommends Cornewall for Speaker, 459
his appreciation of Addington, 472
his attitude towards the newly-rich, 524
George IV, and elections, 420
occupies Speaker's chambers, 425
Gerrard, Sir T., excluded as a Papist, 132
Gibbon, Edward, gives offence to patron, 320
Gideon, Sir Sampson, 143, 192
Gladstone, W. E., eulogy of nomination system, 313
Glamorgan, county of, 385
Glanville, 241
Gloucester, 18, 66, 326, 330, 399
Gloucester, county of, 241, 325, 407, 416
Glover, E. A., imprisoned for swearing to fictitious qualification, 177
Glynn, Sergeant, 247
Goldsmid, and Jewish disabilities, 143
Gordon, Lord George, seat purchased for, 359
Government, procures loyal addresses, 270
not unmindful of public opinion, 273
and treasury boroughs, 340
Grampound, 16, 86, 356, 374, 375
Grand juries, and loyal addresses, 269, 396
Grange, Lord, 217
Grantham, 64, 238, 378, 396
Grattan, and Catholic Relief bill of 1813, 463
Great Bedwin, 38
Gregory, Wm., chosen Speaker, 443
Grenville Act, 12
Speaker Norton supports, 459
Speaker Cornewall testifies to success of, 460
provisions of, 540
Hatsell's eulogy of, 540
made perpetual, 542

Grenville Committees, their fairness, 14
service on, 261
creation of, 540
balloting for, 540
procedure in, 540
partisanship in, 541
slowness of procedure in, 541
expense of, 541
difficulty of securing service on, 542
Grenville, George, and resignation from House of Commons, 246
King's opposition to his bill, 419
Grenville, Lord, and Whig borough mongering, 346
Grenville, Speaker, and formal excuses, 453
his Speakership, 461
Grey Administration and Speaker Abbot, 477
Grey, Anchitell, takes notes in House of Commons, 588
Grey, Earl, defends property qualification Act, 178
defeated in Northumberland, 314
Grosvenor, Lord, and locum tenens for Shaftesbury, 232
Grimsby, 78, 79, 158
Guildford, 32, 73, 243
Guildhall, committees meet at, 531
Guilds, trade, in freeman boroughs, 59
honorary members of, 59
Guilford, Lord Keeper, and electioneering for James II, 397
Gymber, H., 122

Hackwell, 240
Halifax, Lord, and *quo warranto* proceedings, 394
Hampden, 47
Hampden, Richard, offers seat at Wendover to Government, 355
Hampshire, 249, 373, 385, 416
Hanbury, W., 277
Hanmer, Sir Thomas, Speaker, 447
speaks in committee, 447
in House as Ex-Speaker, 447
his formal excuses, 452
Hants, county of, *see* Hampshire
Harbord, Edward, contests Norwich, 191
and seat for Shaftesbury, 232
member for Yarmouth, 323
at issue with patron brother, 324
Hare, Bishop of Chichester, 296
Harley, Speaker, 446
Harwich, 177, 299, 315, 340, 344, 382
Haslemere, 34, 53
Hassard, John, 240
Hastings, 72, 157, 165, 171, 315, 340
Hatsell, on stewardships of Crown lands, 244
and Onslow's adherence to rules, 450
and defaulting members in custody, 492

Hatsell (*continued*)
    his eulogy of Grenville Act, 540
    and clearing of strangers' gallery, 578
Haverfordwest, 18
Hedon, 158
Helston, 92, 163, 232, 335, 337, 344
Henry IV, and county elections, 369
Henry VI, and elections to Parliament of 1459, 369
    and borough charters, 369
Henry VII, his control of House of Commons, 371
Henry VIII, his interest in elections, 371
    his household officers as M.P.'s, 372
    his interference in elections, 372
    his additions to House of Commons, 373
Herbert, James, 224
Heritable Jurisdictions, bill for abolition of, 555
Heron, Sir R., 86
    describes Speaker Abbot's speech, 463
Herries, Chancellor of the Exchequer, 525
Hertford, 62, 64, 78, 158, 199, 382
Hertford, county of, 385
Hervey, John, letters to Bury St Edmunds, 265, 285
Hervey, Lord, and instructions from boroughs, 267
    room for his son at Bury St Edmunds, 352
High Constables, commanded to bring in freeholders, 385
Higham Ferrers, 29, 98, 159, 374
Hill, Sir Roland, and franked mail, 290
Hindon, 15, 132
Hobby, Sir Edward, and secrecy of proceedings, 585
Hobhouse, and "His Majesty's Opposition," 510
Hoghton, Sir Henry, and relief of Dissenters, 277
Holland, Lord, 228
Holles, Denzil, and Speaker Finch, 123, 505
Holroyd, Maria, and franks, 287
Holt, 110, 115
Holy Orders, renunciation of, 127
Honiton, 31, 167, 172, 357
Honorary burgesses, in Welsh boroughs, 108
    at Holt, 110
    at Radnor, 110
Hooker, describes borough elections, 43
    describes House of Commons at S. Stephen's, 426
    member of English and Irish Houses of Commons, 526
    defines privilege, 569
    on exclusion of strangers, 576
    on secrecy of proceedings, 584

Hope, J., gives offence to patron, 320
Horner, Francis, his seat wanted, 352
Horrocks, family of, rise of, 523
Horrocks, John, M.P. for Preston, 524
Horsham, 139, 140
Horton, W., asks church preferment, 295
House of Commons, additions to, 3
    difficulty of securing attendance in, 238
    calls of, 238
    liberation from, 238
    loses hold on its members, 244
    secession from, 246
    bill to enable members to resign from, 248
    and procedure on local bills, 261
    appeals to Crown for repair of building, 424
    and dispute with Charles II over election of Speaker, 437
    asserts right to elect Speaker, 444
    party lines in, in eighteenth century, 454, 506
    disorder in, 484
    privileged places in, 506
    pairing in, 506
    personnel of, 511
    first Irish member of, 526
    and peers' interference in elections, 546
    standing order against such interference, 547
    claims right to originate taxation, 550
    declares its right to originate taxation, 553
    position of, in regard to taxation, 554
    right to grant supply recognised in speech from the throne, 554
    vigilance of, in guarding right to tax, 554
    and local rates, 556
    and procedure on bills, 557
    and bills affecting House of Lords, 562
    attendance of, in House of Lords, 562
    right of admittance to, 574
    intrusion of strangers into, 576
    and secrecy of proceedings, 584
    and transcripts of proceedings, 585
    orders printing of proceedings, 585
    orders publication of proceedings, 586
    its conflict with the newspapers, 593
House of Lords, shields delinquent boroughs, 15
    untouched by Reform Act, 151
    Irish Bishops excluded from, 152
    life peers admitted to, 152
    rejects bill for property qualification, 168

House of Lords (*continued*)
    and repeal of property qualification Act, 178
    and place bills of 1693 and 1694, 208
    and rejection of place bills, 216
    rejects bill to exclude contractors, 219
    used as shield for House of Commons, 277, 278
    place of meeting of, 423, 424
    and bill for hearing election petitions at bar, 539
    and controverted elections, 546
    bills levying taxation originating in, 555
    and procedure on bills, 557
    and messages from House of Commons, 561
    bills affecting, 562
    sanctions publication of proceedings, 587
House of Representatives U.S., and fiscal legislation, 556
Householder, inhabitant, and county franchise, 20
Howard, Col. Charles, describes debate on place bill of 1734, 215
Howell, J., accepts election for Richmond, 263
Hucks, Wm., promises patronage, 293
Hughes, Owen, mayor of Newborough, 313
Hull, *see* Kingston-upon-Hull
Hume, Joseph, qualifies Roebuck, 173
    purchases a seat, 360
    and salary for Chaplain, 500
    and Speaker's service of plate, 473
Hungerford, Sir Thomas, Speaker in 1377, 432
Hunt, his eulogy of Manners-Sutton, 476
Huntingdon, 45, 61, 318, 320, 372, 547
Huntingdon, county of, 233, 407
Hutchinson, Archibald, 171
Hyde, in chair of committee, 533
Hythe, 132

Ilchester, 97, 160, 314, 382
Ilchester, Lord, 228
Income tax, origin of, 461
    incidence of, 474
Incomes, men without, debarred from House of Commons, 151
Indemnity Acts for Dissenters, 134
Indenture, blank, from Flint, 116
Indentures, blank, James I forbids to seal, 380
Inglis, Sir Robert, 596
Ingram, Sir Arthur, letter to Wentworth, 384
Inns of Court and London season, 565
Instructions, from constituents, 263
    made use of by James II, 265
    in 1701, 266

Instructions (*continued*)
    inspired by court, 266
    and proposed excise, 267
    fall into desuetude, 268
    pass away, 271
Instructions to committees, 534
Inverness-shire, 359
Ipswich, 44, 52, 155, 199
Ireland, and Union, 86
Irish borough seats, sale of, in England, 341
Irish judges, excluded from House of Commons, 220
Irish Parliament, members of, and franking in England, 284
Irishmen in English House of Commons, 526
Islay, Earl of, 217

Jail, voting from, 70
James I, effort for reform, 2
    enfranchises universities, 99
    his proclamation on calling his first Parliament, 379
    his second proclamation, 381
    his personal interest in elections, 381
    his charters of enfranchisement, 382
James II, makes use of instructions to members, 265
    and the regulation of corporations, 396
    his personal part in elections, 396
    gives directions concerning candidates, 396
    his satisfaction with the election, 398
    dissolves Parliament, 398
    his electioneering tour, 399
    his plan of election in counties, 403
    charges against, in Act of Settlement, 405
James, Mr and election at Carlisle, 77
Jebb, and demand for pledges, 272
Jeffreys, Judge, and *quo warranto* proceedings, 393
    and remodelling of corporations, 400
Jenks, on character of legislation, 258
Jervoise, C. J., 249
Jews, constitutional position of, 140
    relief Act for, of 1753, 140
    and Parliament, 142
    naturalisation of, 144
    admission of, to Parliament, 144
Johnson, Sir Thomas, and representation of Liverpool, 262
Johnstone, Sir James, and Speaker's salary, 473
Joint Stock Companies and Contractors' Act, 219
Journals of the House of Commons, 10
    date of commencement of, 239, 528
    early entries in, 482
    first entry of bill, 529

Judges, excluded from House of Commons, 220
    as electioneering agents for James II, 403
Judiciary, offices in, confer right to vote, 23
Juries, grand, commanded to support James II's policy, 403

Kent, county of, 385
Kent, prepares designs for new Parliament House, 430
Keppel, Admiral, anti-court candidate at Windsor, 415
Kevenllesce, lordship of, 117
King, Locke, his bill to repeal property qualifications Acts, 178
King's Friends, in Parliament of 1614, 380
King's Lynn, 42, 61, 64, 153, 257, 314, 520
King's printers, in House of Commons, 218
Kingston-upon-Hull, 18, 51, 153, 264, 284, 398
Knaresborough, 186, 349, 351
Knighthoods, rewards of manufacturers, 524
Knights of the shire, carry writs to sheriff, 184
    place of election of, 185
    seating of, 502, 504
    distinctions of, 502
    fees paid by, 503
    privileges of, 503
    personnel of, 511

Lancashire, 260, 302
Lancaster, Chancellor of Duchy of, sequestered for undertaking, 380
Lancaster, Duke of, and elections of 1376, 368
Land tax, 18
    votes in respect of purchases of, 23
    certificates of payment of, as title to vote, 25
    publications of lists of, 26
    lists in use until 1832, 28
Langdale, Lord, conveys James II's orders to Hull, 398
Langdon, Walter, manages elections in Cornwall, 385
    ordered to the Tower, 387
Langton, Sir Thomas, 375
Lansdowne, Marquis of, returns Denman, 338
    patron of Macaulay, 349
Last Determinations Acts, 8
    House of Lords and, 9
    and value of boroughs, 10
    its effect in delaying reform, 10
    number of boroughs affected by, 13
    stops movement for reform, 48
    and enhanced value of seats, 356
Laud and the Prayer for Parliament, 501

Launceston, 72, 92, 200, 333, 418
Lawyers, as members for nomination boroughs, 376
    James I counsels exclusion of, 381, 513
    summoned from courts, 493, 516
    in House of Commons, 512
    objections to them, 512
    excluded by Act of 1372, 512
    claim pre-audience in court, 513
    clash between professional and Parliamentary business of, 514
    pamphlet against choice of, 514
    Pride's hostility to, 515
    Whitelocke's defence of, 515
    Prynne and, 516
    and term "gentlemen of the long robe," 516
    prizes for, in Parliamentary life, 517
    Trevelyan's characterisation of, 517
    characterisation of, in *Black Book*, 518
    in modern House of Commons, 518
    and attendance in House of Lords, 563
Leamington, 481
Leaseholders for life, as voters, 22
Lecky, Mr, and enforcement of place Acts, 214
Lee, Sir Thomas, and Charles II's rejection of Speaker, 440
Leedes, Sir John, excluded as a Papist, 132
Leeds, 19, 81, 86, 88, 176, 262
Leeds, Duke of, nominates Abbot for Helston, 337
Lefevre, Shaw, Speaker, his Speakership, 480
    impartiality of, 480
Legislation, based on petition, 258
    popular demands for, 281
Leicester, 267, 519
Leicester, county of, 396
Lenthall, chosen Speaker on recommendation of Cromwell, 437
    asked to sit by, at grand committee, 532
Letters, from members to constituents, 283
    of Andrew Marvell, 284
    of John Hervey, 285
    of Peter Shakerley, 285
Lewes, 47, 173, 199, 271
Liberals, nominate Abercrombie as Speaker, 479
Lichfield, 18, 68, 159, 373, 399
Lidford, castle of, Strode imprisoned in, 568
Lieutenants, Lord, commissioned to examine boroughs, 400
    as electioneering agents for James II, 403
    not willing to put questions for James II, 404

Lincoln, 18, 257, 394
Lincoln, county of, 385, 407
Lincoln's Inn Hall, committees meet at, 531
Linlithgow, 320
Liskeard, 92, 320
Litany read by clerk, 483, 490, 497
Liturgy for House of Commons, 497
Liverpool, 65, 71, 76, 132, 262, 287, 315, 395, 519, 526
Liverpool, Lord, 230
Llanidloes, 109
Llanvylling, 109
Lloyd, Bishop of Worcester, 296
Lobbies, division, date of, 535
Local bills, first charge on M.P.'s, 261
Local contests for wider franchises, 10
    checked by Last Determinations Act, 11
    at an end, 13
Locum tenens, in House of Commons for minors, 227
    instances of, 231, 232
London, city of, 17, 18, 29
    freemen in, 59
    Act of 1724, 69
    franchise in, 69
    number of freemen of, 71
    Rothschild elected for, 144
    petitions against property qualifications from, 167
    instructions from, 266
    demands pledges from candidates, 271
    attack on its charter, 393
    regulation of corporation of, 394
    George's III's interest in by-election in, 411
    expense of court contest for, 417
    places of members for, in House of Commons, 426, 504
    aldermen and Speaker Trevor, 448
    confers freedom on Speaker Onslow, 454
    represented by Thomas Norton, 497
    represented by merchants and traders, 519, 520
    and presentation of petitions, 574
    and contest over newspaper reporting, 594
London Gazette, 428
London Magazine, 592
Long Parliament and publication of votes and orders, 588
Lonsdale, Earl of, *see* Lowther, Sir James
Lonsdale, second Earl of, refuses Brougham as nominee, 317
    letter from a nominee of, 336
Lopes, Sir Manasseh, 143
Lord Steward, and administration of oaths, 128, 130
Lostwithiel, 341, 344
Louis XIV, 147

Lowther, Lord, requires a locum tenens, 232
Lowther, Sir James, and land tax lists, 26
    his colony at Haslemere, 34
    his "ninepins," 313
    his relations as a borough master with Pitt and Robinson, 316
    his squad of members, 317
    his rewards, 327
Lowther, Sir John, and minors in the House of Commons, 225
Ludgershall, 38, 330, 350, 359, 418
Ludlow, 49, 72, 399
Lushington, S. R., complaint of his absence from House of Commons, 253
Luttrell, N., and place bill of 1714, 215
Lyme Regis, 156, 168, 232, 240, 257
Lymington, 159, 333
Lyttleton, Speaker, 446

Macaulay, Lord, as a nominated member, 349
Mace, carried by Sergeant-at-Arms, 493
    first, 493
    of Commonwealth, 493
    of Charles II, 494
    place of, 494
Mackintosh, Sir James, as a nominated member, 348
Magazines, report Parliamentary proceedings, 591
Magistrates, exert pressure on freeholders, 385
Mahon, Lord, and contractors in House of Commons, 218
    candidate while a minor, 412
Maidstone, 373, 375, 392
Maitland, Professor, characterises municipal corporations, 55
    describes Oxford and Cambridge, 70
Malden, 66, 79, 370
Malmesbury, 302, 354
Malton, 241, 322
Manchester, 6, 19, 81, 88, 196, 262, 263
Manchester, Duke of, in control of Huntingdon, 233
Manchester, Earl of, votes at election for Huntingdon, 547
Manners-Sutton, Speaker, George IV occupies his chambers, 425
    speaks in committee, 475, 476
    his impartiality, 476
    his party connections, 477
    his re-election after the Reform Act, 478
    charges against, 478
    his re-election opposed in 1835, 479
Manucaptors, 5
Manufacturers, as members of the House, 522
    knighthoods as rewards for, 524
    and Cabinet rank, 525
Marlborough, 322

Marlborough, Duke of, in control of city of Oxford, 410
Marlow, 382
Martin, Richard, protests against minors in the House of Commons, 224
Marvell, Andrew, 51, 153
  asks instructions from Hull, 264
  his letters and franking, 284
  his quarrel with Mr Clifford, 486
  his letters, 588
Mary, enfranchises boroughs, 374
Masson, R., and election from Cambridge University, 101
Maunsell, Sir R., 240
May, Sir Erskine, and relations between members and patrons, 353
  and sale of boroughs, 360
  and Abbot's address to Prince Regent, 470
Mayors of corporation boroughs, 54
  laws excluding them from representing their boroughs, 123
  and election to House of Commons, 241
Melcombe Regis, 93, 161, 167, 251, 350
Mellish, W., 142
Members of House of Commons, number of, 15, 17, 392
  calls on, 165
  cannot waive election, 240
  long absent, 250
  do not go near constituencies, 251
  do as they please after election, 252
  become regular in attendance, 253
  feel responsible to constituents, 256
  address constituents on receipt of wages, 257
  extra Parliamentary duties of, 259
  report recusants, 260
  keep order in counties, 260
  and choice of sheriffs, 260
  assist in collection of poll tax, 260
  and local bills, 261
  receive instructions from constituents, 263
  pledges demanded from, 271
  never unmindful of public opinion, 273
  humour constituents, 279
  and impending elections, 280
  asked for franks, 286, 289
  number of, returned by patrons, 310
  code of patrons', 311
  prefer county constituencies, 312
  number of, in reign of Edward VI, 425
  in reign of Elizabeth, 426
  in reign of James I, 427
  in Pensioner Parliament, 427
  at the Unions, 428
  levies on, 490
  seating of, 502
  collections from, 502
  privilege of, 567

Members of House of Commons (*contd.*)
  admonished to keep secret proceedings, 584
  and private journals, 585
  print speeches, 585
  forbidden to take notes, 588
  forbidden to publish proceedings, 588
Members, nominated, classes of, 311
  and patrons' orders, 312
  uncertainty of tenure of, 315
  Lowther's squad of, 317
  conditions usual between patrons and, 318
  code of conduct of, 319, 335
  "noble" conduct of, 319
  give offence to patrons, 320
  compelled to resign seats, 322
  members of peers' families as, 323
  conduct expected from, 326
  and their patrons' interests, 334
  and official preferment, 334
  and humiliating dependence on patrons, 336
  opinions of patrons of the system, 338
  for treasury boroughs, 340
  choosing, 342
  for treasury boroughs, code of conduct of, 347
  with easy conditions, 348
  length of tenure of seats of, 351
  insecurity of tenure of, 351
  and relations with patrons, 353
  free from patron control, number of, 362
  few eminent, 363
Menial servants, Charles II's, in House of Commons, 395
Merchant Taylors' Hall, Peel's speech at, 525
Merchants as Members of the House of Commons, 519
Meres, Sir Thomas, Charles II's nominee for Speakership, 439
Merioneth, 105
Messages, carried by Masters in Chancery, 557
  between the two Houses, 560, 561
  rules for reception of, 561
Messenger from the Crown, 574
Methuen family, rise of, 522
Middle Temple Hall, committees meet at, 531
Middlesex, 207, 247, 320, 412, 413
Middlesex Journal, 593
Midhurst, 228, 418
Milbourne Port, 357
Mildmay, Sir E., 311
Mileage, allowances to members, 157
Militia, appointments in, used to vacate seats, 249
Mill, J. and Grampound, 88
Milton, Viscount, 230
Minehead, 6, 375

Minority, rights of, in House of Commons, 450

Minors, excluded from House of Commons, 223
  in House of Commons, 224, 226
  excluded by statute, 226
  objection to, in the House, 227
  cease to vote in the House, 228
  cease to enter the House, 231

Mohun, J., court candidate in Cornwall, 385
  comes into collision with House of Commons, 387
  created a peer, 387

Molesworth, Sir Wm., and fictitious property qualifications, 174

Monmouth, 29

Montagu, Lady Mary Wortley, and purchase of Cornish boroughs, 312, 354

Montagu, Lord, opposes Act of Supremacy, 128

Montague, and Speaker's salary, 473

Montgomery, 109, 115

Montgomery, county of, 260

Moravians, excluded from House of Commons, 134
  relieved of disabilities, 137

Mordaunt, Col., and sale of nomination at Malmesbury, 354

Moritz, describes House of Commons in 1780, 579

Morley, John, offers to withdraw from House of Commons, 254

Morpeth, 126, 172, 231, 335

Morpeth, Lord, his motion of censure on Speaker Abbot, 464, 469

Mortgagees, as voters, 22

Mortlake, election manager, 71

Mounson, Sir H., excluded from the House, 138

Mount-Charles, Lord, threatens to resign seat, 325

Mowbray, Sir John, and Shaw Lefevre's Speakership, 480

Mowtlow, H., first M.P. for Cambridge University, 100

Moyle, Sir Thomas, Speaker, 487

Municipal politics, and Parliamentary elections, 54
  aristocracy in, 80
  and party elections, 81
  and elections in Wales, 118

Municipal Reform Act of 1835, 70, 79

Nares, Sergeant, and representation of Oxford, 410

National Debt, Speaker as commissioner for reduction of, 474

Naturalisation Acts and admission to House of Commons, 236

Naturalisation of Jews, 143

Nauton, Sir R., M.P. for Cambridge University, 101

Navy, treasurer of, office held by Speakers, 437

Nesbitt, obtains control of Winchelsea, 343

New Shoreham, 16, 87, 541

Newark, 6, 16, 285, 392

Newborough, 111

Newcastle, Duke of, 139
  and excise agitation, 139
  aided by bishops, 296
  rebukes his members, 315
  patron of Pitt, 336
  sells seat to Burdett, 361
  and George III, 409

Newcastle-on-Tyne, 51

Newcastle-under-Lyme, 228, 268, 276, 397

Newly rich, the, in society and politics, 524

Newport, 92, 126, 160, 185, 251, 374, 388, 399

News-letters, 285
  superseded by newspapers, 455
  value of, 589
  in hands of Speaker, 590

Newspaper press, and Reform, 12
  and political life in 18th century, 252
  government seeks support from, 274

Newspapers, franking of, 286
  supersede news-letters, 289, 455, 590
  their reports of Parliament in 1813, 470
  orders against, 590
  first to offend, 591
  order of 1762 against reports in, 592
  contest of 1771 with, 592
  praised by Horace Walpole, 594

News-writers, and franks, 286
  in 1641, 585
  between 1660, and 1688, 588
  in the lobby, 589
  in conflict with the House, 589
  orders against, 589, 590

Newton, 97, 354, 375

Nicholson, Bishop of Carlisle, 297

Nomination system, at its height, 327, 409
  and reformers, 360
  and men of ability, 363

Nominations to seats, 4
  sale of, 354
  advertised for sale, 357
  sold without political conditions, 361

Nonconformists, and instructions to M.P.'s, 265
  and borough corporations, 392, 400
  and Declaration of Indulgence, 400

Non-residents, vote at county elections, 22
  become members, 157

Norfolk, county of, 24, 186, 314, 370, 374

Norfolk, Duke of, 139
North Briton, 593
North, Lord, and compensation to
  borough owners, 81
  and bestowal of Chiltern Hundreds,
    245
  uses House of Lords as shield to
    House of Commons, 277
  his opinion of popular M.P.'s, 279
  his letter to Lord Falmouth, 340
  his letter to Robinson, 341, 344
  George III's letters to, 410
  and transactions in Cornish
    boroughs, 414
  and George III's electioneering
    fund, 415
  his excuses to George III, 416
Northallerton, 243
Northampton, 31, 42, 48, 49, 65, 153,
  277
Northumberland, 314
Norton, Sir Fletcher, Speaker, and
  Dunning's resolution, 280
  his peerage, 453
  his partisanship, 458
  displeases George III, 459
  fails of re-election, 459
  and exclusion of women, 581
Norwich, 18, 69, 71, 75, 76, 82, 83, 191,
  268, 314
Norwich Act of 1730, 69
Nottingham, 18, 167, 339
Nottingham, county of, 368, 385, 407
Nowell, A., excluded from the House,
  125

Oath of Abjuration, imposed in 1610,
  130
  required of members, 137
  continued at Revolution, 138
  abrogation of, 148
Oath of Allegiance, imposed in 1610,
  130
  required of members, 137
  abrogation of, 138, 148
  imposed in Canada, 146
Oath of clerk of House of Commons,
  489
Oath of 1701, 147
  modifications of, on deaths of Pre-
    tenders, 148
Oath of 1866, 148
  of 1868, 148
Oath of Supremacy, its purpose, 128
  administration of, 129
  required of members, 137
  abrogation of, 138
Oaths, members excluded for not taking,
  138
  modification of, in 1858, and 1866,
    144
  for protection of the Crown, 145
  cost of administering to electors,
    190
  as to landed qualifications, 171

Obstruction, early, in House of Commons, 543
O'Connell, Daniel, and relief Act of
  1829, 140
  and nomination seats in Ireland, 310
Office-holders, objections to, in House
  of Commons, 204
  bills to exclude, 204
  resolution concerning, 205
  specific, excluded, 206, 210
  re-election after appointment, 211
  enforcement of Acts concerning, 211
  excluded from House, 211, 212
  disqualified from petitioning against
    return, 213
  number of, in George I's reign, 215
  number of, in 1742, 216
  number of, in Parliament, 221
  proposal to disfranchise, 300
Okehampton, 73, 336
Old Sarum, 35, 64, 97, 126, 312, 342,
  344, 351, 356
Oldfield, describes Welsh boroughs, 116
  as a borough broker, 358
Oldham, 428
Oliver, Alderman, 594
Onslow, Arthur, Speaker, approves plan
  for new Parliament House, 430
  resigns office of treasurer of navy,
    437, 449
  requested to aid in legislation, 448
  his Speakership, 448
  his ideals, 449
  his attitude towards administra-
    tions, 450
  omits formal excuses, 451
  his pension, 453, 471
  his farewell speech, 454
  his merits and rewards, 454
  his five chairs, 472
  and Speaker's place in Committee,
    532
  fears reporting of proceedings, 591
Onslow, Col. George, complains against
  newspapers, 593
Onslow family, and Speakership, 446
Onslow, Richard, Speaker, 446
  fails of re-election for Surrey, 446
Opposition benches, 508
"Opposition," "His Majesty's," 510
  used in colonial Parliaments, 510
Outsitters, 67, 68, 70, 77, 80
Oxford, 70, 82, 101, 161, 162, 167, 201,
  372, 373, 399, 410
Oxford, county of, 407
Oxford, Parliament of, loyal addresses
  on dissolution of, 269
Oxford, University of, enfranchised, 99,
  382
  represented by Peel, 102, 314
  represented by Abbot, 102
  canvassing by candidates, 103

Painted Chamber, place of conference,
  557

Pairing, 506
  resolution against, 506
Palmerston, Lord, as member for Newport, 251
    describes Whig borough mongering,
    346
Papists, efforts to discover in House of
  Commons, 131
  new writs in place of, 132
Parliament, places of meeting of, 423
  contact of, with country, 474
  opened by commission, 488
  session of, opened with sermon, 496
Parliament Houses, of England, Scotland and Ireland, 423
  destroyed by fire, 424
  petition for new, to George II, 429
  other petitions for new, 430
Parliament of Canada, resignation of
  members, 248
Parliament, Officers', 207
Parliament, Pensioner, 208
  minors in, 224
  Prynne's description of, 225
  difficulty of securing attendance of
    members in, 427
  mode of determining election peti-
    tions in, 538
  and right of Commons in taxation,
    556
  attendance of women during, 580
Parliament, Scotch, exclusion of Roman
  Catholics from, 140
Parliamentary papers, sale of, 587
  exempted from postage, 587
Party, divisions in George III's reign,
  456
  Tory, in control, 457
  growth of, 506
Party lines, in House of Commons, 506
  in chamber, 507
Paston, Sir John, anxious to be of the
  House, 370
Patronage, government and municipal,
  in elections, 74
  Chiltern Hundreds treated as, 245
  claimed by M.P.'s, 292
  treated as spoils, 294
  promises of, declared to be bribery,
    300
  members decline to ask for, 301
  scramble for, 302
  claim of borough owners on, 329
  use of Irish, 329
  use of American, 329
  shares in loans as, 330
Patronage secretary of the treasury,
  appointment and duties of, 302
  present position of, 303
Peace, Retrenchment and Reform, 282
Peebles, 313
Peel family, rise of, 523
Peel, Sir Robert, 79
  represents Oxford University, 102
  and property qualification Acts, 176

Peel, Sir Robert (*continued*)
  and election expenses, 196
  finds seat at Westbury, 314
  and seating of House of Commons,
    505
  the elder, 523
  member for Cashel, 523
  becomes home secretary, 525
  becomes prime minister, 525
  his speech at Merchant Taylors'
    Hall, 525
Peel, Speaker, his re-election to House
  of Commons opposed, 481
Peerage, additions to, due to borough
  mongering, 327
  privileges for commoners allied to,
    562
Peerages for bankers and Anglo-Indians,
  524
Peers, and interference in elections,
  546, 547
  number of members returned by,
    547
  feudal obligations of, and taxation,
    548
  and money bills, 548, 550
  contest claim of House of Commons
    to originate money bills, 550
  amend a money bill, 550
  again amend a money bill, 552
  and procedure at conference, 558
Peers, eldest sons of, excluded from
  House of Commons, 122
  admitted to House of Commons, 123
  privileges of, in House of Commons,
    505
  and privileges in conference, 558
  privileges of, in House of Lords,
    562
Peers, Irish, as members of House of
  Commons, 526
  and bargains for borough seats, 526
Peers, life, admitted to House of Lords,
  152
Pelham, and Onslow's Speakership, 450
Pembroke, county of, 260, 541
Penal laws, James II's questions con-
  cerning, 403
  answers to questions concerning,
    from counties, 404
Penrhyn, Lord, and election at Liver-
  pool, 76
Penryn, 196, 374
Pension list, rearrangement by George III
  at downfall of North, 418
Pensioners, included in place Acts, 212
  from Scotland, 214
  excluded by Act of 1714, 217
Pensions, grounds for granting, 214
Peploe, Bishop of Chester, 296
Perceval, Viscount, 276
Percy, Lord, and George Rose, 333
  and Westminster election, 412
Personal government, and Crown con-
  trol of elections, 367

Petersfield, 38

Petition from freeholders of Middlesex, 247

Petitions, legislation based on, 258, 528, 573

    bills take the place of, 528

    presentation of, to House of Commons, 573, 575

    orders of House of Commons concerning, 574

    speeches and debates on, 575

Petitions for enfranchisement, refused, 6

    from Universities, 99

Pews in church, votes in respect of, 22

Phelips, Speaker, rewarded by the Crown, 436

Pitt (Earl of Chatham), his letter to his patron, 336

Pitt, John, first holder of Chiltern Hundreds, 243

Pitt, William, his relation to Reform, 11

    represents Cambridge University, 102

    property qualification of, 173

    and ecclesiastical preferment, 298

    his relation to Sir J. Lowther, 317

    his creation of peers, 328

    a nomination placed at his disposal, 342

    and bill for Parliamentary reform, 420

    his taxation proposals, 461

    his quarrel with Tierney, 461

    and Speaker's salary, 473

Place Act of 1742, 216

Place Acts, interpretation of, 213

    number and provisions of, 217

    used to enable members to resign, 248

    and East India Governorships, 253

    and instructions to M.P.'s, 268

Place bill, of 1693, defeated, 208

    of 1694, vetoed, 208

    of 1700, 1704, and 1705, 209

    in Walpole's time, 215

    defeat of, in House of Lords, 216

Pledges demanded of candidates, 271

Plunket, his attack on Abbot, 466

Plunkett, Lord, and borough patrons in Ireland, 310

Plymouth, 49, 167, 370, 529

Plympton, 72, 265, 323, 386

Poll-clerks, authorised by law, 186

    paid by candidates, 189

Poll-tax, members assist in collection of, 260

Pontefract, 382

Poole, 18, 159, 162, 370

Poor law, manipulation of, 53

    bill originates in House of Lords, 555

Poor Man's Box, contributions to, 129, 502

Poor rate, relief from, as a disqualification, 50

Popham, Speaker, and speeches at first reading, 531

Popular interest in elections, awakening of, 44

Portland, Duke of, controls Cambridge, 71

    his letter describing use of Chiltern Hundreds, 250

Portsmouth, 51, 160, 399

Post, penny, establishment of, 290

Postage, Parliamentary papers exempt from, 587

Postmaster-general, complains of abuse of franking, 286

Postmasters and elections, 74

Post-office, places in, regarded as spoils, 294, 304

Potter, Chris., 172

Potwalloper, definition of, 31

Potwalloper boroughs, *see* Boroughs, potwalloper

Powle, and Charles II's rejection of Commons' Speaker, 440

    gives dinners as Speaker, 472

Powney, court candidate at Windsor, 415, 420

Praed, W. M., buys a seat, 361

Prayer for High Court of Parliament, 500

Prayers, first read in House of Commons, 129

    become customary, 497

    in London Common Council, 497

    daily reading of, 500

    at Ottawa, 500

Precepts, eagerness for, 6

    evasion of, 6

    sent to boroughs, 42

Preston, 31, 37, 49, 65, 277, 350, 373, 523, 524

Pretender, proclamation of, 147

    oath abjuring, 147

Pride, his hostility to lawyer members, 515

Prince of Wales, and nominations in Cornwall, 389

Prince Regent, Speaker Abbot's address to, 464

Printers, at bar of House of Commons, 593

    imprisoned in Tower, 594

Privilege, of members of House of Commons, 567

    reasons for, 568

    punishment for breach of, 568

    extended to speeches in Parliament, 568

    extensions of, 569

    defined by enactment, 569

    limited by Act of 1701, 570

    abuses of, 570

    limitations of, 571

    decline of, 572

    breach of, by newspapers, 591

    publication of debates, a breach of 595

Privilege (*continued*)
for members' speeches, 596
Privy Council, recommends candidates, 373
and members for Gatton, 376
seats of members of, in House of Commons, 426
members of, as commissioners for House of Commons, 488
and seating in House of Commons, 504, 505
Procedure, slight change in, 528
by bill, commencement of, 529
evidence concerning early, 529
in committee, 530
establishment of present-day, 530
in House and in committee, 531
nineteenth century changes in, 534
at divisions, 535
in election petitions, 539
innovations in, 542
summary of changes in, 544
on bills in the two Houses, 557
simplification of, 561
on petitions, 573
Prynne, and determination of election petitions, 12
and oath of Supremacy, 128
describes Pensioner Parliament, 225
and Parliamentary wages, 257
and lawyers in the House, 516
Public opinion, and attendance of members, 254
members never unmindful of, 273
Government seeks to influence, 273
and place bills, 274
and excise bills, 275
instances of deference to, 276
adverse to Irish demands, 278
on American war, 279
in large constituencies, 279
supports repressive legislation, 282
indifference of, until 1761, 455
on Abbot's speech, 470
Publication of proceedings, debate on, in 1681, 586
considered by committee in 1642, 588
declared breach of privilege in 1771, 595
Pulteney, his wager with Walpole, 507
opposes newspaper reporting, 591
Pye, Sir Robert, nominated for Westminster, 388

Quaker, a, elected to the House of Commons, 134
not allowed to take his seat, 135
Quakers, excluded from House of Commons, 134
and affirmations, 135
poll at elections, 136
relieved of disabilities, 136
Qualification, for knights of the shire, 122

Qualification (*continued*)
ability to pay election expenses as a, 203
Qualifications, landed, agitation for Act imposing, 166
petitions against, 167
creation of fictitious, 171
oath as to, 171
personal estate made equivalent to, 176
fees for procuring, 176
in counties, 179
no bar to adventurers, 180
fees for administering oath as to, 187
Qualifications, residential, for members, 122
in desuetude, 122
laws imposing, repealed, 122
Queenborough, 75, 225, 299, 319, 340, 347
Quo warranto proceedings, 393
Quorum, 542

Radicals, and Manners-Sutton's re-election for Speaker, 479
Radnor, 110, 115
Radnor, Earl of, stipulates that his members vote for reform, 322
his description of Downton, 36
Rawlinson, Sir W., offers to resign seat, 319, 347
Reading, 357
Recorders, as members for their boroughs, 513
Recusants, reported by members, 259
Rede, Thomas, 157
Redistribution Act of 1885, 15, 89
Reform, need of, admitted by Elizabeth and James I, 1
at the Commonwealth, 1
sporadic movements for, 10
origin of movement for, 11
movement becomes general, 11
demand for, during Commonwealth, 11
movement general, 12, 14
Reform Act of 1832, its preamble, 1
its effect, 4
its effect on borough franchises, 13
changes in borough representation by, 89
throws election expenses on candidates, 195
and Whig borough mongering, 346
schedule A of, 376, 382
Reform Act of 1867, and borough representation, 89
Reform Act of 1884, 15
Reform Acts and attendance of members, 253
Reform bill of 1831, proposal in, to reduce number of members, 250
Reform, Parliamentary and economic, movement for, 456

Registration of county voters, 25
Registration of county voters Act, of 1788, 26
    petitions for its repeal, 27
    cost of working, 27
    its repeal, 27
Rent charges, votes in respect of, 22
Reporters, gallery provided for, 595
    present position of, 595
Representation, distribution of, 17
Reresby, Sir John, describes remodelling of corporations, 400
    commanded by James II to stand for York, 401
    his account of remodelling of York, 402
Restrictions on choice of constituencies, period of fewest, 124
Retford, *see* East Retford
Return, Parliamentary, of electors registered and returning-officers' charges, 197
Returning-officers, duties of, 182, 185
Returning-officers' charges, paid by candidates, 153
    not statutory, 182
    increase in, 183
    attempt to limit, in 1679, 183
    first statutory imposition of, 187
    Act of 1745 concerning, 188
    in boroughs, 191
    no statute authorising, 193
    Act of 1875 concerning, 202
Revolution, and widening of franchise, 50
Revolution settlement, oaths securing, 145
Reynolds, Serjeant, his seat wanted, 351
Rice, Spring, and Grampound, 88
Richard II, and parliamentary elections, 368
    and the sheriffs, 368
    and committee of parliament, 369
Richmond, 38, 126, 263, 320, 350
Rigby, and resignation from House of Commons, 246
    his rebuke of Speaker Cust, 458
    never sat on government benches, 509
    complains of treatment at bar of Lords, 562
Robinson, J., his relation with Lowther, 317
    becomes a borough monger, 318
    and transaction in Lord Edgcumbe's boroughs, 341
    and elections of 1774, 413
    and transactions in Cornish boroughs, 414
    receives £20,000 from George III, 414
Rochester, 155, 411
Rodney, Lord, 279
Roe, Rev. Thomas, asks for preferment, 295

Roebuck, his property qualification, 173
Roll of members, no calling of, 238
Rolle, seizure of his goods, and privilege, 389
    member for Callington, 519
Roman Catholics, excluded from House of Commons, 127
    and declaration against transubstantiation, 138
    the first to sit in Parliament, 139
    in Scotland, 140
Romilly, Sir Samuel, and purchase of seats, 360
Romney, 314
Roscoe, H., and civil service patronage, 301
Rose, Geo., and official patronage, 333
Rothschild, Baron, 144
Rotten boroughs, from time of enfranchisement, 375
Rules of House of Commons, early, 482
    and deference to the Chair, 483, 485
    additions to, in reign of James I, 483
    need of, in reign of Elizabeth, 483
    in reign of Charles I, 484
    concerning phraseology, 485
Rushworth, appointed clerk assistant, 491
    not to take unauthorised notes, 588
Russell, Lord John, and Grampound, 86
    and Reform, 87
    and Act of 1832, 89
    and election expenses, 196
    elected when under age, 230
    as locum tenens for Huntingdonshire, 233
    as member for Bandon, 234
    his proposal to reduce number of members, 250
    and Manners-Sutton's political bias, 478
    opposes Manners-Sutton's re-election, 479
    his conception of the Speakership, 479
Russell, Sir F., 123
Ruthen, 110
Rutland, county of, 545
Rutland, Earl of, his control of Grantham, 64
    his control of Cambridge, 71
    manages elections for James II, 396
Rye, 60, 71, 76, 160, 167, 230, 263, 267, 340

Sacheverel and Charles II's rejection of Speaker, 439
Sackville, Lord, patron of Wraxall, 350
Sacrament, as test for members of House of Commons, 130
St Albans, 373

St Germains, 228, 361, 375
St Ives, 49, 93, 287, 374
S. Margaret's Church, 130, 131
St Mawe's, 92, 352, 375, 447
St Michael, 49, 93, 315, 322, 327, 360, 374
S. Stephen's, 33
S. Stephen's Chapel, place of meeting of Parliament, 424
    part of Royal palace, 424
    lent to Commons by Edward VI, 425
    in need of repairs, 426
    want of room in, 428
    provision of more seats in, 429
Salisbury, 399
Salt springs, burgesses of, 36
Saltash, 213, 374, 386
Sandwich, 45, 159, 299
Sandwich, Earl of, his idea of a desirable candidate, 318
    patron of Queenborough, 319
Sandys, Mr, introduces place bill, 215
Savile, and letters to Newark, 285
Sawbridge, his bill for shorter Parliaments, 419
Scarborough, secures wider franchise, 14
Scarlett (Lord Abinger) resigns seat at Malton, 322
Schoolmasters, their votes, 23
Scot and lot boroughs, *see* Boroughs, scot and lot
Scotch judges, excluded from House of Commons, 217, 220
Scotchman, a, as Speaker, 479
Scotchmen, as members of House of Commons, 525
    effort to make them ineligible, 526
Scotland, and Union, 86
    Roman Catholics in, 140
    religious restrictions in, 149
    and property qualifications Act of 1710, 169
    members from, and pensions, 214
Scott (Lord Eldon), as a nominated member, 349
Seagrave, Lord, his bargain with Whig government, 326
Seal, Great, messenger of, 22
Season, London, and Parliament, 565
Seating accommodation, 427
Seats, sale of borough, 354
    price of, 355
    purchased to elude creditors, 359
    purchased by reformers, 359
    Crown control and value of, 367
    sale of, in reign of George III, 409
Seats in demand, 5, 21, 42, 96
    in Pensioner Parliament, 51
    in reign of Elizabeth, 94
    in eighteenth century, 354
    after Union of 1800, 355, 358
    in reign of George III, 357

Seats, purchase of, by the year, 341
    assistance of treasury in, 342
    Act of 1809 against, 346
Second reading stage, 531
Select bodies, *see* Boroughs, corporation
Selwyn, George, and clergy in politics, 298
    his bargain with North for Ludgershall, 418
    his pension, 418
Septennial Act, and value of seats, 356
    passing of, 408
Sergeant-at-Arms, his office, 491
    his relation to Crown, 491
    deputy, 491
    his duties, 492
    custodian of the mace, 493
    dress of, 495
    tenure of, 495
    payment of, 495
    fees to, 503
    and exclusion of strangers, 577
Sergeants' Inn Hall, committees meet at, 531
Sermon, Parliament opened with, 496
Servants of members, and privilege, 567, 570
Seymour, Sir Edward, Speaker, rewarded by Crown, 437
    attempt to re-elect, 437
    omits customary excuses on election, 439
    refused confirmation by Charles II, 439
Seymour, Sir Francis, made sheriff by Charles I, 384
Shaftesbury, 232
Shaftesbury, Earl of, argument for reform by, 8
    argues for property qualifications, 166
    suggests making election expenses a public charge, 183
    and minors in House of Commons, 226
Shafton, 167
Shakerley, Peter, 285
Sheffield, 19, 81
Sheffield, Lord, 287, 288
Shelburne, Lord, and official patronage, 332
Sheridan, B., his property qualification, 173
Sheriffs, freemen vote at election of, 20
    irregularities on the part of, 42
    excluded from Parliament, 121
    laws excluding, 123
    Richard II's order to, 368
    letters to, in reign of Edward VI, 373
    letters to, in reign of Mary, 374
    letters to, in reign of Elizabeth, 377
    directions to, from James I, 379

Sheriffs (*continued*)
  pricking Charles I's opponents for, 383
  unable to enter House of Commons, 383
Sherlock, bishop of Bangor, 296
Shire towns, county courts held at, 41
  (Wales) and contributory boroughs, 109, 110, 111
Shoreham, *see* New Shoreham
Shorthand reporters, 595
Shrewsbury, 42, 73
  Parliament meets at, 369
  James II visits, 399
Smith, Evelyn Levett, chaplain, 499
Smith, John, Speaker, 446
Smoking in the House, 429
Snatch papers, 35
Somerset, county of, 568
Somerset, Lord Granville, and private bill committees, 535
Southampton, 18, 275, 389
Southampton, county of, 185
Southey, R., and property qualification, 175
Southwark, 31, 32, 132, 167
Speaker, his reprimand to Oxford, 162
  hostile to Edward III, 368
  requests permission of Crown to retain his chambers, 425
  sovereign resumes possession of his chambers, 425
  the first, 432
  manner of choosing, 433
  nominated by the Crown, 434
  method of electing in 1641, 435
  receives orders from the Crown, 435
  paid by the crown, 436
  pay and rewards of, 436
  formal excuses of, 438
  debate on Charles II's rejection of, 439
  Commons assert right to elect, 441, 444
  Crown influence in election of, 443
  evolution of non-partisan, 445
  rights of, at committee stage, 446
  requested to aid in legislation, 448
  and office held at pleasure of the Crown, 450
  and omission of formal excuses, 451
  pension and peerage for, 453
  trustee of British Museum, 453, 474
  fees of, 471
  payments to, 471
  perquisites of, 471
  social obligations of, 472
  dinners given by, 472
  remuneration of, 473
  forbidden to hold office under Crown, 473
  precedence of, 473
  offices held by, 474
  last intervention in committee of, 480

Speaker (*continued*)
  reads prayers, 482, 497
  deference paid to, 483
  his duty as regards debate, 483
  powers of, before Rebellion, 484
  authorised to reconcile quarrels, 486
  his relation to House of Commons, 487
  spokesman to the Crown, 487
  claims for House of Commons made by, 487
  appoints chaplain, 489
  and sergeant-at-arms, 492
  and admonitions, 495
  dress of, 496
  his place at committee stage, 532
  his relation to chairman of committees, 533
  prestige of, 534
Speakers, of party in majority, 457
  impress of, on House of Commons, 462
  and political clubs, 480
  and constituencies, 480
Speakership, two periods in history of, 433
  Gardiner's estimate of, in Charles I's reign, 434
  Eliot's estimate of, in 1625, 435
  Hooker's estimate of, 445
  still partisan, 448
  Onslow's impress on, 454
  halt in evolution of, 454
  non-partisan conception of, 461
  growing dignity of, 471, 474
  attainment of non-partisan, 478
  Peel's conception of, 479
  Shaw Lefevre and, 480
Speeches printed by order of the House, 585
Spoils system, demoralising effect of, 306
Stafford, 57, 522
Stafford, county of, 276
Stamford, 330, 396
Stanhope, P. D., in House of Commons as a minor, 228
Stannary court, in conflict with Richard Strode, 568
Staunton, Sir G. T., refused re-election at St Michael, 322
  as nominated member, 339
  his opinion of the purchase system, 339
  refused nomination for St Michael, 360
Stephens, Sir P., and admiralty patronage, 300
Steward, N., first member for Cambridge University, 100
Steyning, 14, 33, 38, 39, 95, 370
Stockbridge, 354, 361, 375, 380
Stockdale case, 587
Storer, Anthony, 173
  letter to his patron, 335

Strangers in House of Commons, 575
exclusion of, 576
intrusions of, 576
orders against, 577
admitted to floor of House of Commons, 579
orders against, unheeded, 579
excluded from converences, 579
withdraw during divisions, 582
Strode, Richard, in conflict with Stannary court, 568
Sudbury, 159
Suffield, 2nd Baron, his use of family borough, 324
Suffolk, county of, 373, 385, 407
Sunderland, Earl of, recommends candidates, 117
Supply bill, preamble to, 554
Supremacy, oath of, *see* Oath of supremacy
Surrey, county of, 243, 376, 417, 446
Surrey, Earl of, 139
Sussex, county of, 296
Sussex, Earl of, interferes in elections of 1554, 374
Swift, Jonathan, and property qualification Act, 170
Sydney, Lord, letter concerning franking, 283

Table of House of Commons, 491
Tamworth, 200, 375, 523
Taunton, 32, 98, 163, 415
Tavistock, 9, 123, 177, 230, 351
Tax, land, *see* Land tax
Taxation, rights of two Houses concerning, 545, 548
development of, 548
first contest between two Houses on, 548
Commons claim right to originate, 549
renewal of contest over, 552
Tellers, in divisions, 536
Temple Church, 130
Temple, Earl, qualifies Wilkes, 173
Tenants, pressure on, 21
Test Act, proposal to extend to House of Commons, 134
and Nonconformists in boroughs, 392
Test and Corporation Acts, 55
Tewkesbury, 161, 226, 382
Thetford, 158
Thompson, Thomas, 142
Thurlow, Lord Chancellor, and electioneering for George III, 415
Thurlow, Lord, patron of Scott (Lord Eldon), 350
Tierney, his quarrel with Pitt, 461
his attack on Abbot, 466, 469
Tiptoft, Sir John, Speaker, receives gifts from the king, 436
his excuses on election to the Chair, 438

Tiverton, 231, 382, 426, 526
Tomline, Bishop of Lincoln, 298
Tooke, Horne, elected for Old Sarum, 126
his proposal to buy out borough owners with peerages, 331
Torrington, 6
Torrington, Earl of, 224
Tory, not found in Journals, 506
Tralee, 341
Transubstantiation, declaration against, 137
Treasury bench, 507
Treasury notes, 509
Treby, George, memorandum of advice to, 265
Tregony, 92, 341, 344, 375
Trelawney, John, comes into conflict with House of Commons, 387
made a baronet, 388
Trevanion, Richard, manages election in Cornwall, 385
Trevelyan, Sir G. O., his characterisation of lawyer members, 517
Trevor, Sir J., Speaker in James II's Parliament, 443
dismissed from Chair, 444
offered money to assist legislation, 448
Triennial Act, 408
Truro, 49, 327
Trustees as voters, 22
Tupper, Sir Charles, and function of opposition, 510

Undertaker, first use of term in electioneering, 380
Undertaking, protest against, in 1614, 380
Universities, mode of election from, 102
qualifications, of members for, 103
members for, exempted from property qualifications Acts, 169
enfranchised by James I, 382

Vansittart, and treasury boroughs, 344
supports Speaker Abbot, 467
Ventilator as ladies' gallery, 581
Verney, Earl of, as patron of Burke, 352
Verney, Lady, describes ladies' gallery, 582
Vernon, describes use of ballot in House of Commons, 537
Vote houses, 35
Voters by virtue of offices, 23
Voters, non-resident, 22
Voyce, Edward, chaplain to House of Commons, 499

Wade, General, and place Acts, 212
Wages, last payment of, 51
claims for, 51
paid by University of Cambridge, 100.
paid to Welsh members, 105

Wages (*continued*)
　　payment of, and Welsh borough franchise, 106
　　candidates agree not to charge, 153
　　rate fixed by law, 155
　　forfeited by deserting Parliament, 156
　　members forego, 157
　　deprivation of, 238
　　and responsibility of members, 257
　　addresses on receipt of, 257
　　remission of, 257
Wages, certificates for, not demanded, 106, 109
Wages of knights of shire, assessments for, 20
　　serving without, 21
　　for Wales, 105
Wales, enfranchised, 86, 104
　　county representation of, 104
　　borough representation of, 104
　　corporation borough, in, 108
Walpole, Horace, his account of rejection of place bill by House of Lords, 216
　　his characterisation of Onslow, 451
Walpole, R., and excise, 267
　　his resignation, 268
　　and public opinion, 274
　　represents nomination boroughs, 314
　　his wager with Pulteney, 507
Walsingham, electioneering by, 377
Warburton, his bill amending property qualification Acts, 176
Ward, Plumer, 232
　　his letter to Earl of Lonsdale, 337
Wareham, 243, 338
Warrington, 199
Warwick, 47, 481
Warwick, county of, 263, 407
Wedderburn, gives offence to patron, 220
　　returned for Bishop's Castle, 350
Weights and Measures, standards of, conveyed by M.P.'s, 259
　　and Speaker of House of Commons, 259
Wellesley, Sir Arthur, and Croker's election for Downpatrick, 345
Wellfit, Dr, chaplain, 500
Wellington, Duke of, and reform, 89
　　letter from, concerning patronage, 292
Welshpoole, 109
Wendover, 171, 352, 355, 382, 527
Wentworth, Sir Thomas, made sheriff by Charles I, 383
Weobley, 35, 287, 350, 443
West Looe, 92, 125, 374
Westbury, 245, 314, 370
Westminster Abbey, members attend service in, 129
　　meeting place of Parliament, 423
　　sermon at, at opening of Session, 496

Westminster, city of, 31, 193, 200, 266, 272, 276, 279, 314, 373, 388, 412, 417, 420
　　bill concerning paving of, 548
　　the Parliament city, 566
　　attempt to suppress manufactures in, 567
Westminster election of 1807, bill of expenses for, 194
　　verdict concerning, 195
Westminster, governors of school and almshouse of, and chaplain, 498
Westminster Palace, keeping order near, 565
Westminster school, and House of Commons, 579
Westmorland, 276, 297, 317
Westmorland, Earls of, and control of Lyme Regis, 232
Weymouth, 93, 155, 160, 167, 199, 251, 299, 351, 360, 408
Wharton, Marquis of, and electioneering, 82
Wharton, proposes Crown nominee for Speaker, 444
Whig, not found in Journals, 506
Whigs, and borough mongering in 1806, 345
Whip, T. Cromwell as, 372
　　establishment of party, 509
Whips, issued in 1621, 509
　　in Pensioner Parliament, 509
Whitbread, his attack on Abbot, 466
　　withdraws his amendment, 469
Whitchurch, 39, 40, 399
White Chamber, meeting place of House of Lords, 424
Whitelocke, his defence of lawyer members, 515
Wigan, 159, 247
Wilberforce, M.P. for Yorkshire, 301
Wilkes, and movement for reform, 81
　　and property qualification, 173
　　and Chiltern Hundreds 247
　　instructions to M.P.'s concerning, 269
　　agitation concerning, 270
　　public opinion in favour of, 279
　　and Middlesex election of 1774, 413
　　and Speaker Cust, 458
　　and contest of 1771 with House of Commons, 593
William III, vetoes place bill, 208
　　and bribery in House of Commons, 406
　　chooses time for dissolution, 407
　　his election tour, 407
William IV, and compensation to borough owners, 81
　　and elections, 420
Williams, and attempted re-election of Speaker Seymour, 439
Williams, Lord Keeper, and management of elections, 382
Williams, Speaker, his independence, 443

Williamson, Sir Joseph, 158
    establishes *London Gazette*, 428
Wilson, D., 276
Wilts, county of, 522
Winchelsea, 76, 79, 183, 343
Winchester, 159, 185, 397
Windebank, Secretary, receives instruc-
    tions from Charles I, 390
Windsor, 200, 399, 408, 415, 420
Windsor, Lord, made freeman of Wor-
    cester, 62
Wirkesworth, 6
Women, and Parliamentary votes, 40
    and electioneering, 40
    transfer burgages, 40
    in freeman boroughs, 78
    as borough patrons, 97
    attend House of Commons, 580
    as lobbyists, 580
    attend election petition trials, 580
    excluded from gallery in 1778, 581
Wood, his bill to enable members to
    resign, 248
Woodfall, Mr, 593
Woodstock, 163, 184, 188, 199, 201
Wootton Bassett, 287
Worcester, 18, 62, 319, 399, 411
Worcester, county of, 385, 522
Wraxall, as nominated member, 350
Wren, Sir Christopher, reports on con-
    dition of S. Stephen's Chapel, 426
    and alterations of Chamber, 429
Writs, withheld from corrupt boroughs,
    15
    where sent, 17
    eagerness for, 21
    irregularities in connection with, 21
    sent by post, 21

Writs (*continued*)
    refusing new, 238
    attitude of House of Commons to-
        wards new, 240
    for new Parliament, burnt by James
        II, 405
    Speaker empowered to issue, 474
Wyatt's rebellion, 375
Wycombe, Chipping or High, 134, 351
Wylson, refuses charter of enfranchise-
    ment, 1
Wyndham, Sir W., and price of seats,
    355
Wyvill, and county associations for re-
    form, 281

Yarmouth, 323, 374
Yarmouth, Isle of Wight, 200, 249, 388
Yelverton, Christopher, Speaker, formal
    excuses of, 438
Yonge, Sir William, and relations of
    members to constituents, 271
    and letters from members to con-
        stituents, 282
York, city of, 18, 157, 401, 424, 426,
    504
York, county of, gains two members, 16,
    86
    and statutory election expenses, 187
    register of deeds of, excluded from
        House of Commons, 206
    Wilberforce's connection with, 301
    and pressure on freeholders, 385
Yorke, Philip, earl of Hardwicke, 173
Yorktown, effect on Parliament of, 418
Young, Dr, chaplain, 499, 580

Zouch, Lord, 44, 45